PELICAN BOOKS

THE NEW PELICAN GUIDE TO ENGLISH LITERATURE

2

THE AGE OF SHAKESPEARE

THE EDITOR

Boris Ford read English at Cambridge before the war. He then
spent six years in the Army Education Corps, being finally in
command of a residential School of Artistic Studies. On leaving
the Army, he joined the staff of the newly formed Bureau of
Current Affairs and graduated to be its Chief Editor and in the
end its Director. When the Bureau closed down at the end of
1951, he joined the Secretariat of the United Nations in New
York and Geneva. On returning to England in the autumn of
1953, he was appointed Secretary of a national inquiry into the
problem of providing a humane liberal education for people
undergoing technical and professional training.

Boris Ford then became Editor of the *Journal of Education*,
until it ceased publication in 1958, and also the first Head of
School Broadcasting with independent television. From 1958
he was Education Secretary at the Cambridge University Press,
and then in 1960 he became Professor of Education and Director
of the Institute of Education at Sheffield University. He moved
to the new University of Sussex in 1963 as Dean of Cultural and
Community Studies, and later became Chairman of Education.
Since 1973 he has been Professor of Education at the University
of Bristol. Boris Ford has been editor of *Universities Quarterly*
since 1955. He also edited *Young Writers, Young Readers*.

The Age of Shakespeare

VOLUME

2

OF THE NEW PELICAN GUIDE TO ENGLISH
LITERATURE

EDITED BY BORIS FORD

PENGUIN BOOKS

Penguin Books Ltd, Harmondsworth, Middlesex, England
Penguin Books, 625 Madison Avenue, New York, New York 10022, U.S.A.
Penguin Books Australia Ltd, Ringwood, Victoria, Australia
Penguin Books Canada Ltd, 2801 John Street, Markham, Ontario, Canada L3R 1B4
Penguin Books (N.Z.) Ltd, 182–190 Wairau Road, Auckland 10, New Zealand

First published in *The Pelican Guide to English Literature* 1955
Reprinted seventeen times
This revised and expanded edition published 1982

Made and printed in Great Britain by
Cox and Wyman, Reading
Filmset in 'Monophoto' Bembo by
Northumberland Press Ltd
Gateshead, Tyne and Wear

CONTENTS

CONTENTS

PART IV
Compiled by BRIAN VICKERS

GENERAL INTRODUCTION

The publication of this *New Pelican Guide to English Literature* in many volumes might seem an odd phenomenon at a time when, in the words of the novelist L. H. Myers, a 'deep-seated spiritual vulgarity . . . lies at the heart of our civilization', a time more typically characterized by the Headline and the Digest, by the Magazine and the Tabloid, by Pulp Literature and the Month's Masterpiece. Yet the continuing success of the *Guide* seems to confirm that literature – both yesterday's literature and today's – has a real and not merely a nominal existence among a large number of people; and its main aim has been to help validate as firmly as possible this feeling for a living literature and for the values it embodies.

The *Guide* is partly designed for the committed student of literature. But it has also been written for those many readers who accept with genuine respect what is known as 'our literary heritage', but for whom this often amounts, in memory, to an unattractive amalgam of set texts and school prizes; as a result they may have come to read only today's books – fiction and biography and travel. Though they are probably familiar with such names as Pope, George Eliot, Langland, Marvell, Yeats, Dr Johnson, Hopkins, the Brontës, they might hesitate to describe their work intimately or to fit them into any larger pattern of growth and achievement. If this account is a fair one, it seems probable that very many people would be glad of guidance that would help them respond to what is living and contemporary in literature, for, like the other arts, it has the power to enrich the imagination and to clarify thought and feeling.

The *Guide* does not set out to compete with the standard Histories of Literature, which inevitably tend to have a lofty, take-it-or-leave-it attitude about them. This is not a Bradshaw or a *Whitaker's Almanack* of English literature. Nor is it a digest or potted version, nor again a portrait gallery of the great. Works such as these already abound and there is no need to add to their number. What it sets out to offer, by contrast, is a guide to the history and traditions of English literature, a contour map of the literary scene. It attempts, that is, to draw up an ordered account of literature as a direct encouragement to people to read widely in an informed way, and with enjoyment. In this respect the *Guide* acknowledges a considerable debt to those twentieth-century writers and critics who have made a determined effort to elicit from literature what is of living value to us today: to establish a sense of literary tradition and to define the standards that this tradition embodies.

The *New Pelican Guide to English Literature* consists of nine volumes:

1, Part One. *Medieval Literature: Chaucer and the Alliterative Tradition* (with an anthology)
1, Part Two. *Medieval Literature: The European Inheritance* (with an anthology)
2. *The Age of Shakespeare*
3. *From Donne to Marvell*
4. *From Dryden to Johnson*
5. *From Blake to Byron*
6. *From Dickens to Hardy*
7. *From James to Eliot*
8. *The Present*

Each separate volume, with the exception of the last and the European volume, has been named after those writers who dominate or stand conveniently at either end of the period, and who also indicate between them the strength of the age in literature. Of course the boundaries between these separate volumes cannot be sharply drawn.

Though the *New Pelican Guide to English Literature* has been designed as a single work, in the sense that it attempts to provide a coherent and developing account of the tradition of English literature, each volume exists in its own right and sets out to provide the reader with four kinds of related material:

(i) *A survey of the social context of literature* in each period, providing an account of contemporary society at its points of contact with literature.

(ii) *A literary survey* of the period, describing the general characteristics of the period's literature in such a way as to enable the reader to trace its growth and to keep his or her bearings. The aim of this section is to answer such questions as 'What *kind* of literature was written in this period?', 'Which authors matter most?', 'Where does the strength of the period lie?'.

(iii) *Detailed studies* of some of the chief writers and works in the period. Coming after the two general surveys, the aim of this section is to convey a sense of what it means to read closely and with perception; and also to suggest how the literature of a given period is most profitably read, i.e. with what assumptions and with what kind of attention. This section also includes an account of whichever one of the other arts (here music) particularly flourished at the time, as perhaps throwing a helpful if indirect light on the literature itself.

(iv) *An appendix of essential facts for reference purposes*, such as authors' biographies (in miniature), bibliographies, books for further study, and so on.

Thus each volume of the *Guide* has been planned as a whole, and the contributors' approach to literature is based on broadly common assumptions; for it was essential that the *Guide* should have cohesion and should reveal some collaborative agreements (though inevitably, and quite rightly, it reveals disagreements as well). They agree on the need for rigorous standards and have felt it essential not to take reputations for granted, but rather to examine once again, and often in close detail, the strengths and weaknesses of our literary heritage.

As has been explained in the General Introduction above, this volume has been planned and written as an entity and this means that its individual parts and chapters are meant to be read in immediate relation to each other. It is for this reason that the literary survey (Part II) adopts the method, which might otherwise seem odd, of giving more attention or at least more space to minor authors than to major – more to Nashe than to Marlowe, for instance. The major authors receive more extended and detailed treatment in the essays allotted to them individually in Part III.

Moreover, the individual volumes of the *Guide* have also been planned in close relation to each other, and it is this that explains why Donne does not figure much in this volume, though on a strictly chronological interpretation, as well as on literary grounds, one would have expected him to appear as a major author. However, in a multi-volume *Guide* of this kind, divisions have to be made some-where; and it was inevitable that Donne should mainly figure as the first great poet of the post-Shakespearean volume, *From Donne to Marvell*.

All the quotations from Shakespeare in this volume have been taken from *William Shakespeare: The Complete Works* ed. Peter Alexander (London, 1951).

BORIS FORD

NOTES

Notes designated by an asterisk or glosses by a
letter are given at the foot of each
page. Numbered notes are given at
the end of each chapter.

PART I

THE SOCIAL SETTING
L. G. SALINGAR

The Nation and the Drama, 1558–1625

Europe in the sixteenth century was dominated by kings. In the Middle Ages, culture and to a large extent the forms of government had been moulded by the Church of Rome. But the Middle Ages in this sense came to an end in England with the Reformation of Henry VIII (1529–39); and, after a contentious interval, Elizabeth I made certain that the Church of England was to remain a national, Protestant institution, with the monarch for supreme governor. There was no complete break with the past, but the whole balance of political and religious life in England was altered, and consequently the balance of literature, art, and thought. The new literature of Elizabeth's reign (1558–1603) was centred on the Crown.

The Court of the Tudors, as of their predecessors, contained both the royal household and the chief organs of government. Since the military strength of feudalism had been liquidated, however, the royal Council and its subsidiaries could now take over far more direct control of the country's affairs than before. Parliament was to challenge the royal authority as early as the reign of James I (1603–25). But Elizabeth's power was almost unquestioned, thanks to the nation's desire for security at home, to the conditions of the struggle with Spain, and, not least, to her own remarkable ability.

Yet the Tudors could not have governed effectively (in the absence of a regular army, police, or bureaucracy) without the willing co-operation of the leading classes of society. The new monarchy needed a new kind of aristocracy. The material was there, partly in older families, partly in new men like Elizabeth's leading minister, William Cecil (Lord Burleigh) – men who had begun as merchants or lawyers or even yeomen, had acquired estates under the Tudors, and were wedded to their interests by the spoils of the monasteries. But something more was called for in administration and diplomacy than a gentleman who could manage a horse and go to law with his neighbours; it was a problem, in short, of advancing the scholars and educating the gentry. Cecil noted in 1559 that 'the wanton bringing up and ignorance of the nobility forces the Prince to advance new men that can serve'; and in his *Book named The Governor* (1531), Sir Thomas Elyot had already argued for a class of landed 'magistrates' not only willing and wealthy enough to serve the Crown, but qualified to do so by their education. As Elyot urged, moreover, an ideal instrument for a liberal training was at hand in the new type of classical scholarship which men like Erasmus and More had transplanted from Italy to Northern Europe during the previous generation. The Renaissance in England was thus bound up with the consolidation of the Tudor regime.

By Shakespeare's lifetime (1564–1616), a gentleman of any ambition needed some accomplishment in languages and literature. The new, humanist culture matured during Shakespeare's youth. It is reflected in the Roman and Mediterranean settings of the drama, and the character-studies of princes, wits, and gallants; or, again, in the immense new vocabulary of the poets, largely classical or foreign by derivation.

What makes the age outstanding in literary history, however, is its range of interests and vitality of language; and here other factors contributed besides the humanism of the Universities and the Court. One of these was the persistence of popular customs of speech and thought and entertainment rooted in the communal life of medieval towns and villages. To some extent the old traditions obstructed the new. But they also combined, inasmuch as the Tudors established a firm and broadly based national community; and by combining they invigorated the whole idiom of literature. The Elizabethan literary language, especially with professional writers like Shakespeare, is addressed to a mixed public, more trained in listening than in reading, and more accustomed to group life than to privacy. Elizabethan writing lacks the intimate conversation and psychology of the modern novel, but is supreme in expressing sensation and the outward, demonstrative aspects of feeling. It tends continually towards a superabundant eloquence, which arises both from popular sources and from the educational methods of the humanists.

These factors together largely explain why the drama was the chief form of Elizabethan art. Like music, the second national medium, drama was a communal art, admitting personal virtuosity. A tradition of entertainment in the form of festival or pageantry – communal celebration of communal events – accounts for many prominent features of Elizabethan plays. And the central theme of Elizabethan literature is the clash between individuals and the claims of social order.

Here a third social factor needs to be considered. Though most of Elizabeth's five million subjects were country-dwellers, their prosperity depended on foreign trade; and all the main events of the reign were connected with the rise of merchant capital – the long duel with Spain, ranging from Ireland to the Indies; the raids on Spanish treasure; the sudden expansion of English trade to touch all four of the known continents. Shakespeare's interest in the sea reflects the outlook of an increasingly mercantile society. Moreover, Shakespeare's lifetime has been described as the period of most rapid advance in mining and manufacture that England was to know until the late eighteenth century. 'The realm aboundeth in riches, as may be seen by the general excess of the people in purchasing, in buildings, in meat, drink, and feastings, and most notably in apparel.' This statement of 1579 implies new industries and technical knowledge, a rising standard of living for many, a thriving atmosphere in which the newly built theatres could prosper.

This rise of capitalism affected society in two contrasting ways. It strengthened the monarchy, especially against Catholicism; and by such means as the Puritan sermon, the printing-press, the commercial playhouse, it helped knit together a new national consciousness. The culture that reached maturity towards 1580 with Spenser and Sidney, the immediate forerunners of the great dramatists, amalgamated the varied elements of the nation's life more closely than the culture of any other generation since Chaucer.

On the other hand, capitalism, in a century of steeply rising prices, brought about radical changes in the composition of society. Spending habits of 'excess' upset the customary standards founded on old routines of farming the soil. And a new spirit of competition loosened the whole social hierarchy. After 1600 the popular elements in literature were submerged by those aristocratic and bourgeois ideals that the Elizabethans summed up together as 'civility'. And at the same time the rule of the Stuarts brought a division within the governing classes that ultimately led to the Civil War. In social life, in thought, and in literature the period about 1600 marks a turning-point in English history.

The Individual and the Order of Nature

The general movement of ideas in Shakespeare's time can best be understood by reference to the medieval background.[1] Higher education was still largely based on Aristotle, or on the work of St Thomas Aquinas in reconciling Aristotle with medieval Christianity. But scholasticism had been crumbling since the fifteenth century, if not earlier, and new tendencies broke the unity of its abstract reasoning. The new conditions favoured a pragmatic outlook and the ideal of self-development through action. But the sixteenth century was restless, in the atmosphere created by the new discoveries and the new wealth, by political upheavals and religious wars; and there was no fresh intellectual synthesis. The humanists looked to classical antiquity for a moral and intellectual revival, while the Protestant Reformers tried to find salvation exclusively in the Scriptures. Thus it was left to the following century to consolidate the advances in knowledge.

The Tudors inherited from the medieval world-view a coherent system of beliefs bearing on social order. In the traditional view, restated by Elyot, by Hooker (c. 1553-1600), and by many others, the Creation consisted of numberless but linked 'degrees' of being, from the four physical elements up to the pure intelligence of angels. The whole universe was governed by divine will; Nature was God's instrument, the social hierarchy a product of Nature. It followed for Tudor theorists that subordination and unity were the natural rules for families and corporations and, above all, for the state, a 'body politic' which should be subject to a single head. The state was concerned with men's souls as much as their goods. But at the same time, the order founded on Nature existed for man's benefit, and man as such was an integral part of it; in Donne's phrase (c. 1617), he was 'a little world made cunningly Of Elements, and an Angelic sprite'. His godlike qualities had been depraved by the Fall, and he was constantly visited by divine wrath – manifest, for example, in wars, plagues, even thunderstorms. Yet he could enjoy a civilized happiness, provided that he treated this world as preparation for the next, and kept his body subject to his soul. This was the main task of human reason, enjoined by Nature and Revelation alike.

The finest exposition of these ideas is the analysis of law in Hooker's *Laws of Ecclesiastical Polity* (1593–7). Law, for Hooker, is an all-embracing concept, at once the inherent tendency of things and a principle of regulation: 'that which doth assign unto each thing the kind, that which doth moderate the force and power, that which doth appoint the form and measure, of working, the same we term a Law'. Divine and natural and man-made laws are thus ranged in the same definition; and a famous passage on natural law shows how closely Hooker identifies its physical and its moral aspects (which the next century was to separate):

Now, if nature should intermit her course, and leave altogether though it were but for a while the observation of her own laws; ... if the frame of that heavenly arch erected over our heads should loosen and dissolve itself; ... if the moon should wander from her beaten way, the times and seasons of the year blend themselves by disordered and confused mixture, the winds breathe out their last gasp, the clouds yield no rain, the earth be defeated of heavenly influence, the fruits of the earth pine away as children at the withered breasts of their mother no longer able to yield them relief: what would become of man himself, whom these things now do all serve? See we not plainly that obedience of creatures unto the law of nature is the stay of the whole world?

Elsewhere, Hooker adds that the law of Nature is 'an infallible knowledge imprinted' in the mind; the need to maintain a regulated order, then, is dictated by man's place in the universe.

Such a passage has the age-old sanction behind it of men's dependence on the earth and on 'heavenly influence'. And the Renaissance gave new force to the notion of order in the stress it laid on such urban terms as 'civil' and 'civility'. These implied not only polish or good breeding, but the sobriety and mutual deference of men associated in well-governed cities and corporations.* A dialogue on *Civil and Uncivil Life* (1579), urging gentlemen to leave the country and

* cp. 'smooth civility' in *As You Like It* (II. vii. 96); or Bacon, *Essays: or Counsels Civil and Moral*. Vagabonds are said to be 'of no civil society or corporation' (c. 1599); again, 'a Citizen is a professor of civility' (1616; see Wright, *Middle-class Culture*, 132, 31). The *New English Dictionary* quotes 'civil war' and 'civil [i.e. Roman] lawyer' from fourteenth-century texts; but a [Roman] 'civic garland' is first mentioned in 1542 and most of the senses of 'civil' discussed above come after this date. 'To civilize' was first printed in 1601.

settle in town, indicates the direction of the current.[2] Renaissance theorists held that art was, or should be, a construction of human reason, continuing and completing the work of Nature; and so too with their views of organized society.

Yet there were contradictions in this scheme of ideas. The very effort of the Tudors to reshape the medieval order on a national footing placed it under increasing strain. Protestantism outran the wishes of Henry VIII and Elizabeth. The new monarchy itself stimulated unruly ambitions. And the desire was gradually forming to master Nature, not obey her.

Hooker's restatement of scholastic Reason in defence of the new Church settlement is itself a sign of these changes. In the early years of the Anglican compromise, advanced Protestants still hoped that Elizabeth might carry out more thoroughgoing reforms; and the revolt of the northern earls in 1569, the Papal excommunication of Elizabeth in 1570, and the Spanish-supported plots of the next twenty years, all helped to stimulate an intense political loyalty. Politically, at least, Puritans as well as Anglicans applauded the Church Homily of 1571: 'Such subjects as are disobedient or rebellious against their princes, disobey God and procure their own damnation'. But from 1570 Cartwright and others were demanding a Calvinist, or Presbyterian, reform of Church government, purified of ceremonies and of bishops and free from state control; while the 1580s saw a Presbyterian system in preparation – in the shape of religious discussion groups (or 'classes') – coupled with a determined effort at reform through Parliament. 'A sect of perilous consequence', Elizabeth called them in 1590, 'such as would have no kings but a presbytery.'[3]

The Puritans refused to recognize any authority in religion outside the Bible. In reply, Hooker argued that their agitation was dangerous socially; that Church and State were inseparable in ideal as well as fact; and that the Scriptures were not exhaustive, but left room for historical expedience and the law of Nature. The latter, he added, drew men together in 'civil society' for 'sociable life and fellowship', 'a life fit for the dignity of man'. This adumbration of the social contract remains nearer to Aquinas than to Hooker's admirer, Locke. Yet Hooker's line of argument converges with the reasoning of men like Bodin in France and Sir Thomas Smith in England, who were thinking of the state, not in religious terms but in terms of law and security. The next stage in the high debate of the time was the curt affirmation of James I – 'No bishop, no king' – and the disputes of the constitutional lawyers.

Moreover, while the Puritans attacked the state religion from one side and the Catholics from another, the 'pestilent policy' of Machiavelli seemed to cut away the ground from religious theories altogether. For most Elizabethans, Machiavelli was simply a monster, an advocate of murder and treachery, the cynical atheist who introduces Marlowe's *Jew of Malta* (c. 1589). But the storm of abuse against him in the last quarter of the century indicates uneasiness – 'we are all (in effect) become comedians in religion', said Ralegh – and there was enough in common between contemporary Europe and the Italy of 1513 to give point to the tone of grim irony in which *The Prince* had been written:

> I thought it better to follow the effectual truth of the matter, than the imagination thereof; ... for there is such a distance between how men do live and how men ought to live, that he who leaves that which is done, for that which ought to be done, learns sooner his ruin than his preservation.

While Machiavelli was abused in public, therefore, he was studied in private for his effectual truth. His realism influenced both Bacon and Ralegh, the two ablest political writers after Hooker. Though neither formulated a coherent philosophy of politics they were both of them students of the naked element of power, as well as legally minded Elizabethans.

By about 1600, then, the old order of ideas, theological and Aristotelian, was seriously weakened in its political aspects. Human motives were no longer to be judged in the old way. And this sense of doubt, or ambiguity, was reinforced meanwhile by the gathering stream of Renaissance opinion about the conduct of the individual. Statesmen, merchants, humanists, divines were all united in praise of the life of action (as opposed to contemplation). And many who loathed Machiavelli would have agreed with him at least to the extent of preferring the active, if pagan, virtues of ancient Greece and Rome to the 'idleness' of monasteries.

One sign of transition in personal morality was the gradual rehandling of the doctrines of the later Middle Ages on 'contempt of the world' –

What is it to trust on mutability,[a]
Sith[b] that in this world nothing may endure?

Certainly, events in the Reformation period taught the same harsh
lesson of 'mutability' as the medieval allegories of the Dance of Death
or of Fortune's wheel; so that Fortune's wheel is made prominent in
the *Life of Wolsey* by his servant Cavendish (1557), for example, and
again in the influential *Mirror for Magistrates*, a collection of versified
English biographies by Inns of Court men (including the future statesman, Thomas Sackville), which first appeared in 1559. But here a new
attitude appears. The catastrophes in the *Mirror* are now traced to sin
and to providence, rather than to Fortune; the writers examine historical causes and look for remedies, such as contentment with the
golden mean. They no longer contemn the world; in Elyot's tradition,
they want to fashion a responsible governing class. And this involves
conflicting views about Fortune, which the *Mirror* – many times
enlarged from 1563 to 1610 – projected into the poetry and drama
of Shakespeare's day. A similar evolution also shapes the popular
Morality plays following *Everyman* (*c.* 1470): instead of renouncing
the world, the soul struggles for worldly virtues; in place of the priest
comes the civil magistrate.

But the clearest note of the new morality was its positive summons
to fame, to public glory, to the ideal of the courtier devoted alike to
statecraft and poetry, to love and war. These humanist ideals came
partly from the classics, partly through Italy. Ascham's *Schoolmaster*
(published in 1570) and North's translation of Plutarch's *Lives of the
Noble Grecians and Romans* (1579) are examples of the first kind – two
formative books for Shakespeare's generation. Ascham (1515–68)
was a younger member of Elyot's group, at one time Elizabeth's
tutor. Despising 'all the barbarous nation of Schoolmen', he had
urged that Englishmen should gain 'praise unto themselves, and ...
profit to others' by joining action with learning, like Caesar; and he
composed his programme of classical studies in *The Schoolmaster* to
show how to educate 'a learned preacher or a Civil Gentleman'. And
North introduces his work in the same spirit:

---

a mutability was the term applied to changes of all kinds (cp. Spenser's *Mutability
Cantos*), but especially to changes due to Fortune, *b* since. (These lines – *c.* 1483? –
are attributed to Skelton, and are included in the *Mirror for Magistrates*.)

> There is no profane study better than Plutarch. All other learning is private, fitter for Universities than cities ... But this man, being excellent in wit, in learning and experience, hath chosen the special acts, of the best persons, of the famousest nations in the world.

A new scale of values is implicit in this veneration of heroic antiquity.

Men like Ascham and North were also Puritan in their sympathies. They overcame any contradiction in their outlook, however, by means of the idealism of Plato – enlisted in the humanist cause against the Schoolmen and their Aristotle since the time of Petrarch in the fourteenth century. The Italians had elevated Neoplatonism to a synthetic religion, which reached England through such books as Castiglione's *Courtier* (1528; Hoby's translation, 1561); and Ascham, who detested Italy, made an exception of Castiglione. From him the Elizabethans learned to admire a graceful versatility, a harmony of mind and body, the cultivation of the soul through courtly love. Neoplatonism fostered a worship of beauty, interpreted as geometrical proportion ('all things stand by proportion', writes Elyot's courtly nephew Puttenham, 'and ... without it nothing could stand to be good or beautiful'); while the Neoplatonist search for harmony in the universe – the music of the spheres – could influence astronomers such as Copernicus and Kepler.[4] The whole work of Spenser (*c.* 1552–99) and of Sidney (1554–86) was an exposition of Platonic, courtly, and yet Puritan ideals. One aspect of this movement of thought appears in the Petrarchan sonnets of the 1590s, with their thirst for personal and immortal fame; another, in Spenser's *Hymn of Heavenly Beauty* (1596), where he describes the fairest of Plato's heavens as those

> Which in their high protections do contain
> All mortal Princes, and imperial States;
> And fairer yet, whereas the royal Seats
> And heavenly Dominations are set,
> From whom all earthly governance is fet.

Courtly ambition could thus be reconciled with the notion of eternal order.

Nevertheless, the ideal of the active life still had difficulties to encounter – moral problems and the problem of Fortune. Machiavelli, and Bacon after him, tried to work out techniques for the individual to master Fortune (so that the Italian was regarded as the prophet of self-seeking courtiers and usurers). Others turned for aid here to the Roman Stoics – particularly to Seneca, stylist and dramatist as well as moral adviser. The Stoics, like the Puritans, tightened the subjective sense of individuality. They concentrated on the ideals of character in their classical teachers – ideals such as the indifference to Fortune's blows that Hamlet praises in Horatio, or the self-mastery and lofty public spirit of Brutus. And some writers, especially Chapman (c. 1559–1634), tried to link the austerity of the Stoic sage with an ardent Neoplatonism. In the drama, this line of thought completed the formation of the typical tragic hero; but at the same time the Stoicism of the Renaissance implied a further weakening of traditional values. Part religious and part secular, it emphasized contradictions between public and private values, between self-realization and self-control. One admirer of Seneca might recommend him to Henry IV of France as the proper study for commanders, raising them above human nature and enduing them with 'firm and absolute resolution against death and fortune'; another might reply that 'the true note of a Philosopher is to repose all his expectation upon himself alone'. Either Caesar or nothing – the tragic heroes of the Elizabethans are driven hard by these alternatives.

The growing interest in problems of personality also gave rise to a succession of Elizabethan handbooks on psychology, culminating in Burton's *Anatomy of Melancholy* (1621). The psychologists dealt with conflicts of mind and body. They pictured man as a little state, wherein the bodily fluids ('humours'[a]) could break out in disease and unruly passion if not temperately governed by the faculties of the soul, with its agents the vital spirits. So far they were conservative, treating their topic as a sub-department of theology. But they showed the bias of their time in their emphasis on abnormal psychology and their efforts to deal with it as a kind of spiritual mechanics. Their ultimate criterion might still be clear, but not its relation to experience. The fascination of these problems is evident from the 'humour' satires of the late 1590s and the many studies of melancholy and violent passion in the tragedies of the next decade, from *Hamlet* to *The Duchess of Malfi*.

[a] A *humour* could mean one of the four bodily fluids (blood, phlegm, melancholy, choler); a kink of temperament, due to excess of one of these; or a caprice; see further Herford and Simpson's edition of Jonson, i. 339–43; and Part II, p. 78 below.

The New Philosophy

Two factors that emerge from the Renaissance ferment are a challenge to Aristotle's authority and a desire for a more productive form of scientific learning. When Donne wrote of the astronomers in his *Anatomy of the World* (1611) that 'new Philosophy calls all in doubt', he was aware that the whole traditional picture of the universe was in question: ''Tis all in pieces, all coherence gone'. At the moment of Donne's poem, however, hardly anyone could foresee the decisive scientific advances of the next generation. There was no such clear-cut opposition of ideas over science, meanwhile, as held, in the field of ethics, over Machiavelli's 'effectual truth'. Yet the two lines of speculation were connected – in the minds of Marlowe, Ralegh, Bacon, for example – and together they contributed to the sense of unrest, even of crisis, in the literature of the opening seventeenth century.

The desire for scientific knowledge was stimulated from one side by the sublime confidence of Renaissance scholars in the capabilities of pure intellect:

> Our souls, whose faculties can comprehend
> The wondrous Architecture of the world,
> And measure every wand'ring planet's course,
> Still climbing after knowledge infinite,
> And always moving as the restless Spheres,
> Wills us to wear ourselves and never rest . . .

When Marlowe was writing these lines of *Tamburlaine* (c. 1587), the Copernican hypothesis was already under discussion in England; and besides the mathematical theorists of science, there were the numerous 'empirics' – medical men, navigators, land-surveyors, mining engineers, and a variety of charlatans – whose learning mingled, as in *Faustus*, with belief in astrology and alchemy, in magic and witchcraft. There were others, too, like the Cambridge don Gabriel Harvey, who wanted a general alliance between philosophy and experiment, to 'bestead the Commonwealth with many puissant engines and other commodious devices for war and peace'. Harvey was urging young wits in 1593 to leave poetry for studies of more 'effectual use', such as Hakluyt's *Principal Navigations* or 'natural magic'; and he therefore praises a number of empirics, including a shipwright, an instrument-maker, John Dee (the alchemist and geographer), and the astronomer and colonist Thomas Hariot, who was a friend of Ralegh and of Marlowe.[5] In similar vein, Ralegh later defended the natural magic of the alchemists and the Neoplatonists – 'not the brabblings of the Aristotelians, but that which bringeth to light the inmost virtues, and draweth out of nature's hidden bosom to human use'. During this period, England made direct contributions to experimental science with Gilbert's work on magnetism in 1600 and William Harvey's on the circulation of the blood in 1618.

On the other hand, it was a long step from enthusiasm, or even major discoveries, to a general perspective of scientific advance. In astronomy, there were technical as well as religious objections to accepting Copernicus until after 1609 (when the additional research of Kepler and Galileo became known); and even then there was no agreement among astronomers: 'The world', says Burton, 'is tossed in a blanket amongst them.' Another obstacle was belief in pseudo-sciences like alchemy, to which Neoplatonism lent support. And behind this lay the general difficulty due to Renaissance teaching – the expectation of rational certainty and completeness. This is the difficulty that besets the versatile curiosity of Ralegh in his philosophical writings (c. 1607–14). We are ignorant, he complains, 'how second [physical] causes should have any proportion with their effects'; and the little we do know 'time hath taught us, and not reason'. If Aristotle is wrong about the causes of motion, as he almost certainly is, then Nature has 'no other self-ability than a clock, after it is wound up by a man's hand'; but if so, what becomes of the traditional conception? 'There is a confused controversy about the very essence of Nature.' Ralegh falls back, therefore, from high intellectual ambition to a scepticism recalling that of Montaigne a generation earlier. He feels sure that God wills the human soul to examine His works and use them; but what the soul is, and how it comes by knowledge, are indecipherable.

In this situation, the great achievement of Francis Bacon (1561–1626) was to extricate science from its philosophical entanglements and to give it a method and a new lease of hope. *The Advancement of Learning* (1605) was a clearing of the ground, a magnificent survey of the whole range of Renaissance scholarship, from divinity to natural history; and he followed this by elaborating his system of linked experiments and of generalization founded upon experiment. In effect, Bacon thus solved the problems that were troubling Ralegh. But to do this, he found it necessary to reject some of the central doctrines of his age, and in particular what he called its 'adoration' of the human intellect. He classified the errors due to over-ambitious reasoning as the Idols of the mind; and the first group of these (the Idols of the Tribe), 'have their foundation in human nature itself . . . For . . . the human understanding is like a false mirror, which, receiving rays irregularly, distorts and discolours the nature of things by mingling its own nature with it' (*Novum Organum*, 1620). There is a fundamental contrast here with the attitude of the Elizabethan poets or of Hooker.

To some extent, then, the mental unrest of the Jacobeans was not due to fears about science but to disappointment. It sprang from doubt as to what were the profitable methods of inquiry. On the other hand, a feeling that 'second causes' were all that was likely to matter did seem to encourage an amoral individualism. When Donne complains that his world has lost coherence, it is not astronomy he blames but egotism: 'Prince, Subject, Father, Son, are things forgot'. From this point of view, the unrest connected with science was only a further symptom of the general transformation of values.

Gentlemen and Clowns

The Reformation period had eliminated the armed retainers and the monks, and had swollen the ranks of the landless poor. Otherwise, it could be said (subject to wide local variations) that Elizabethan country life kept in the main to the pattern left by feudalism: the same manorial organization, the same common-field system of farming. And the government, backed by public opinion, sought to preserve these arrangements by holding labourers to the land by force of law, and by protecting the yeomen and lesser tenant-farmers who supplied most of the nation's corn and much of its revenue and manpower. Moreover, the government continued to rely on the landowning classes for administration. But, partly for this very reason, it was unable to control the rapid development of capitalism in the countryside. By 1590 it was said that the shift of property since the

Reformation had 'made of yeomen and artificers gentlemen, and of gentlemen knights, and so forth upward, and of the poorest sort stark beggars'.[6]

The first half of Elizabeth's reign saw the consolidation of power by the new men like Burleigh and Leicester, the Herberts and the Sidneys, who had taken their place beside the remnant of the old feudality. As local magnates and as Crown servants, they formed the kind of aristocracy that Elyot had hoped for, leading a public life of liberality and splendour. A great household (such as Shakespeare depicts in *Twelfth Night* or *Lear*) might consist of several hundred persons – family, dependants, expert officials, and servants – to say nothing of the scores of guests and neighbours feasted in a gentleman's hall on festive occasions, or the beggars who waited for scraps at his gate. And a nobleman's retinue was correspondingly impressive – the Duke of Norfolk riding into London with 300 horsemen, or Lord Berkeley hunting with a daily attendance of 150, gentlemen and others, all wearing his livery and tawny coats. In terms of trade and employment, therefore, as well as social influence, the 'housekeeping' (or 'hospitality') of the landed gentry was of first-rate importance. The management of an estate and the discipline and 'decorum' of a household – minutely regulated by the conscientious – were vital factors in social life as a whole.

Thus the private lives of the gentry, great and small, merged with their public privileges and duties. As Lords-Lieutenant, they were responsible to the Privy Council for the defence and order of the shires. As justices of the peace, besides their criminal jurisdiction, they were charged with increasing administrative tasks – with keeping an eye on recusants, with helping in musters (as in *Henry IV*), with supervising the repair of highways, the regulation of markets, the quality of consumer goods, with fixing the rate of wages, and with repressing vagrancy. And in addition to these legal powers they held a vast network of social patronage which stretched from the Privy Councillors downwards. There were the 'Captains, Scholars, Poets, cast courtiers, and the like' who lived at a great man's table or otherwise shared his bounty; the gifts of Church livings, state offices, crown lands, wardships, and similar privileges, to be granted directly or through intercession at Court; the interventions in marriage-treaties and lawsuits; the protection afforded to servants and to companies of actors (otherwise punishable as vagrants); and, not least, the direct appointment of members of Parliament (a measure often welcome to constituencies as a means of furthering their interests). Thus, cutting across the religious issue, the political life of Elizabeth's reign, especially at the end, was dominated by factions or patronage-groups – forming a transitional stage of political organization between the Wars of the Roses and the party struggles of the eighteenth century.

The pull of this active, public life influenced Elizabethan culture profoundly. In the Universities, and hence in literature, it gave preeminence to the study of public speaking, which now formed the first aim of a general education for a gentleman, together with some knowledge of law, ethics, and history. Wolsey was said to have owed his rise to 'his filed tongue and ornate eloquence' in the council chamber; Sir Humphrey Gilbert placed logic and rhetoric high on the list of studies for his proposed academy for gentlemen about 1564; and Ben Jonson, advising a nobleman to educate his sons at school and not at home, takes it for granted that accomplishment in public life is the primary aim – 'Eloquence would be but a poor thing, if we should only converse with singulars; speak, but man and man together.'[7] It was therefore significant for the growth and outlook of a literary public in London that Harrison in the 1570s should come to praise the learning of the Court; and that the members of Parliament who had attended the legal Inns or the Universities should have increased from a third of the Commons in 1563 to nearly half in 1584, and more again subsequently. The rhetorical training of humanism and the ideal of ordered display were thus woven into the texture of common life. There were visible signs of the same movement in the lavish costume of the gentry, and, above all, as Harrison also noted, in their building of country houses, with newfangled chimneys and extensive panes of glass. Though their interest in painting did not amount to much (apart from miniatures), Elizabethans like Burleigh took great pains over their houses and gardens, giving detailed architectural instructions to the steward or the master mason, with the aid of Renaissance French or Flemish textbooks. So, too, with their pretentious family monuments. With regard to church buildings, there was spoliation rather than endowment; but schools and colleges benefited considerably.

The gentry were thus involved, however, in a huge and competitive scale of expenditure, whether due to state service, to 'hospitality', to legal adversity, or personal 'excess'. And in England, as elsewhere, the value of landed incomes was falling, in so far as they were derived from long-established rents and dues. Although a well-run estate was still basically self-providing, the quantity of purchased goods was mounting, and their price roughly doubled during Elizabeth's reign. Moreover, many gentlemen, like Lord Berkeley, were brought near to ruin by simple fecklessness. Most of Elizabeth's aristocracy were heavily in debt, therefore, mortgaging and selling off their estates; so that a sample investigation of over 2,500 manors has shown the transfer of a third of their properties from great landowners to smaller ones during the eighty years preceding the Civil War. The sale of lands by the nobility was particularly marked during the 1590s – a period of war-time depression, bad harvests, and sharply rising prices and taxation. An observer of 1600 saw 'great alterations almost every year' in noblemen's estates;[8] and financial desperation, hard on political failure, drove Essex and his companions to their foolhardy rising of 1601.

In these conditions, Elyot's ideal of a magistrate class, 'having of their own revenues certain', was less and less tenable. By way of remedy, the country gentleman could run his estate on commercial lines, enclose the commons for pasture to meet the huge demand for wool, and cut down his 'housekeeping'. He could invest in industry or privateering. He could marry money, and bring up his son as a lawyer or a merchant. Or he could profit from any influence he had at Court. Much could be gained from these measures (though not enough to restore the earlier balance of wealth). But most of them entailed social changes and grievances.

Increased rents and manorial fines, whether due to old landlords or to new purchasers eager for profit, and enclosures, which might depopulate a whole village, were two of the principal grievances of the age. There were hunger-riots in 1596, for example, notably against enclosing gentry in Oxfordshire, and in 1607 came a rising of 'Levellers' or 'Diggers' in the most enclosed region, the Midlands.[9] Mutual obligation between landlord and tenant was still regarded as the normal pattern of society; but in many cases, as these outbursts signified, it had lost any real hold.

Secondly, the cutting down of 'hospitality' in the country hit the whole circle of gentleman-servants and professional men who depended on patronage. Preachers declaimed against 'wealthy Gentlemen that turn towns into sheep-walks; sell Benefices for ready money; contrive hospitality into the narrow room of a poor lodging taken up in the City', and 'subvert the strength of the land by unreasonable renting the tenants' (1613);[10] while men of letters, from Nashe in the early 1590s to Tourneur and Webster twenty years later, were increasingly bitter against grandees whose waste or self-interest had poisoned their liberality. The unprovided younger sons of the gentry (such as Orlando in *As You Like It*), and the soldiers, scholars, and minor officials felt themselves to be the superfluous men of Jacobean society.

And thirdly, the whole national position of the gentry was affected. They lost prestige by settling in London for long periods in search of advancement – 'the younger sort to see and show vanity, and the elder to save the cost and charge of hospitality' (*c.* 1578); and the notion of honour was commercialized, especially by the sale of titles under the Stuarts. Moreover, the gentry themselves were now divided between those who were allied with the Court and those whose business interests aligned them with the Puritan-minded City; while the connection of the Jacobean Court with a number of ambitious financial speculators made this division at once more complex and more acute. Its beginnings had been evident in the struggle over courtiers' patents of monopoly in the Parliaments of 1597 and 1601; and the drama of the next decade was full of searching reflections on 'greatness' and the perversion of the order of Nature.

Besides the rise in prices that affected the gentry (and incidentally depressed the status of country parsons), a long-term cause of insecurity was the rise in population, which grew faster throughout the sixteenth century than the means of subsistence. These forces affected the mass of country folk, the tenant farmers and rural craftsmen who formed the majority, and the shepherds and labourers. A widening gap appeared between the well-to-do and the poor or destitute.

The rising price of foodstuffs and the heavy demand for wool brought advantage to those farmers, and especially to the yeoman class, whose initiative, luck, or spare capital enabled them to tide over a bad year and invest in a good one. (In Gloucestershire, according to the muster roll of 1608, there were 927 yeomen, besides 3,774 smaller farmers or 'husbandmen', 1,831 country labourers, and 430 gentlemen; in addition, the yeomen together employed 387 servants, the much larger husbandman class 437, and the gentlemen 750.)[11] Everywhere in Elizabeth's reign admirers and satirists noted the advance of the yeomen, buying lands from their neighbours and 'unthrifty gentlemen', branching out into industries such as coal, iron, clothing, and improving their homes as the gentlemen were rebuilding theirs. They now had three rooms or more instead of two, used glass in their windows (after the 1570s) like townsmen, and bought joiner-made furniture, sheets and feather-beds, as well as 'a fair garnish of pewter' for their cupboards. Many sent their sons to gentlemen's households or to grammar schools and the professions – this was the class that produced Shakespeare, Drayton, Chapman, William Harvey, and the eminent lawyer Selden – and the more ambitious rose to the ranks of the gentry themselves. It was said in Suffolk in 1618 that the yeomen were the only class thriving, thanks to 'continual underliving, saving, and the immunities from the costly charges of these unfaithful times'.

While some authors depicted the yeoman as grasping, others, from Greene in *Friar Bacon* (*c.* 1589) to Dekker in *The Witch of Edmonton* (1621), praised his solid hospitality, his diligence, and contentment. To be a good neighbour and 'keep good hospitality' were his recognized social virtues. But economy was vital, as the Suffolk writer implies. Any 'lavish expenses or unthrifty disposition' could be damaging to a man's character in a lawsuit if not ruinous financially; while the thrifty gained new dignities thanks to the growth of local government, such as the office of churchwarden or (as in *Much Ado*) of head constable. To these weighty arguments for thrift the Puritans added godliness.

Meanwhile Parliament was working out a stern policy towards the thriftless. The Privy Council might revive traditional measures of relief during the bad years of the 1590s, by pressing local authorities to distribute grain and gentlemen to return to their 'housekeeping' in the country, or might seek to renew the Acts against enclosures in the Parliament of 1597; but the Commons were demanding 'the extirpation of beggars'. The resulting Poor Laws of 1598 codified the legislation of the previous half-century.[12] Begging was forbidden.

Relief was to be provided for the helpless unemployed, and work for the able-bodied, by means of compulsory parish rates levied by the churchwardens; but 'rogues, vagabonds, and sturdy beggars' were to be flogged. Since 1572, the legal category of vagabonds had included labourers refusing to work at the fixed rates, fortune-tellers and petty chapmen (like Autolycus in *The Winter's Tale*), and actors not licensed by a baron of the realm – the inclusion of the actors being part of the general Tudor policy of censoring opinion and forestalling disorders.

This mounting pressure against idleness exerted by the market, the pulpit, and the law reacted in turn on the whole culture of the English countryside. A literature of roguery grew up, part hostile, part sympathetic. And the conflict of opinion about May-games and similar holiday pastimes had a deep effect on the drama during the last quarter of the century.

The May-games, morris dances, 'feasts of misrule' and similar 'disguisings' of the villages and country towns formed a lively and semi-independent culture connected with seasonal festivities.[13] As the Puritans saw, this culture was pagan by origin, though now largely ecclesiastical in colouring; and it was independent in the sense that craftsmen and peasants could sing, dance, and mime without waiting for professionals to show them how to do it. A strong local feeling supported these customs: in 1575, for instance, when Leicester was entertaining the queen with the 'Princely Pleasures' of Kenilworth, 'certain good-hearted men of Coventry' (led by a mason, Captain Cox) presented their annual Hock-tide play before Elizabeth, partly in the hope of saving it from their preachers – 'men very ... sweet in their sermons, but somewhat too sour in preaching away their pastime'.

As the mainstay of communal merry-making, these songs and dances were frequently renewed with ballads, wooing-songs, and the dances (or rudimentary comic operas) known as jigs. They provided a focus for local sentiment in voicing a grievance or ridiculing a bad neighbour; and many of the jigs especially were both farcical and libellous. A Yorkshire case of 1602, for example, turned on a libellous jig devised by a gentleman's household servant, 'that they might be merry at Christmas withal'; a May-game procession at Wells in 1607 libelled a group of prominent Puritans and employers; and the tenants of Kendal in 1621 voiced their resentment against their landlords by means of a local play. In many of these pastimes – morris dances, games of misrule, jigs – a leading role was taken by the Fool, with his grotesque antics and trappings. The character of the Fool thus came to typify the simple countryman, idle and roisterous in the eyes of his critics, but determined to hold his own against interfering Puritans, encroaching landlords, or the sharks and pickpurses of the city.

The primitive substance of folk-plays also gained accretions from more literate sources – from historical legend (as at Coventry), from legends of Robin Hood and St George. And many people (a relatively high and increasing proportion, including perhaps half the urban adults)[14] were able to read the broadside ballads sold by pedlars like Autolycus, with their miscellaneous learning, news items, and propaganda. The chance record of Captain's Cox's library gives an outstanding example of the reading matter dear to a leader of pastime, though frowned upon by Puritans and strict humanists like Ascham: Arthurian romances, ballads, jest books, almanacs, morality plays, and poetic satire, such as Skelton and *The Ship of Fools* – much of it reading familiar to Spenser and Shakespeare also. This kind of material mingled with home-made proverbs, riddles, and folk-lore.

Elizabethan journalism set out to cater for the country as well as for readers in London. A booklet of 1590, *The Cobbler of Canterbury*, a farcical medley of verse and prose, claiming to imitate Chaucer, illustrates this phase of Elizabethan taste. Towards gentlemen, the author feels obliged to apologize for his 'plain Dunstable' style (a proverbial expression for language without ornament); but he is also addressing 'clowns', and colloquial idiom is more in evidence than literary graces. The book is meant to be read aloud, like most Elizabethan fiction:

Here is a gallimaufry [*medley*] of all sorts, the Gentlemen may find *Salem* [*salt, wit*] to favour their ears with jests, and Clowns plain Dunstable doggerel to make them laugh, while [*until*] their buttons fly off. When the Farmer is set in his chair turning (in a winter's evening) the crab in the fire, here he may hear, how his son can read, and when he hath done, laugh while his belly aches. The old wives that wedded themselves to the profound histories of *Robin Hood, Clim of the Clough*, and worthy *Sir Isumbras* may here learn a tale to tell amongst their gossips. Thus have I sought to feed all men's fancies . . .

Thus the yeoman's son is a central figure in this provincial public; while Captain Cox had owned copies of all three of the 'histories' mentioned.

Moreover, literary traffic passed inwards to London as well as out. A significant newcomer to Elizabethan English was the word *clown*, with its paradoxically linked sense of 'rustic' or 'ignorant rustic' and 'stage buffoon' (*As You Like It* and *Hamlet* provide two of the earliest examples of the latter). The Puritan campaign against 'devilish pastimes', conducted in the name of morals, thrift, and 'civility', had opened seriously in the 1570s, so that May-games and stage-plays faced a common threat. This strengthened the ties between the actors and their country audiences; and in the 1580s, Tarlton and Kempe brought country jigs and sympathetic clown figures to the London stage. Tarlton, in particular (noted for his russet coat, the countryman's dress), was rustic Fool as well as jester. In this way country pastime became a vital factor in forming the comedies of Shakespeare and his predecessors.

But both the literary evidence and that of surviving folk-plays suggest that contact between stage and 'clown' was broadest towards 1600, and then tapered off. Meanwhile, Puritanism was gaining a stronger hold on the country towns. And London, with its 'civility', had reached the peak of its national influence.

Court and City

The literature of the 1590s, particularly the drama, owed its breadth of appeal to the position of national leadership achieved by the aristocracy. After 1600, however, the unity of national taste broke down as the Court and the middle classes moved apart.

The Court was the highway of patronage. And Court life affected literature directly, not only through the esoteric personal allegories dear to Sidney and his friends, but in songs like Campian's, where the national love of music reached mature expression, and in stately poems of ceremony like Spenser's 'Spousal Verse', *Prothalamion*, or Davies's *Orchestra, A Poem of Dancing* (1596). Above all, the Court influenced drama, as the supreme great household of the country.[15] The Queen's Master of the Revels employed musicians, actors, poets, and craftsmen; and play-acting was thus assimilated at yet another point to the general tradition of public festivity. In courtly revels, like those at Kenilworth, folk-pastime alternated with mythological pageantry in honour of Gloriana. Here courtiers themselves shared in the performance; and this custom had crystallized in the art of the masque, a spectacular variant of folk 'disguisings', forming the climax of entertainment at a banquet – part concert, part ballet, and part dramatized ceremonial leading to a general dance. The masques of James I (especially Jonson's) were the gala events of a Court season, at which ambassadors jockeyed for precedence; they brought fame to their designer, Inigo Jones – before he had shown his genius as an architect – by virtue of his transformation scenes and neo-classical landscapes. And from Lyly in the 1580s onwards, scenes of masques and revels on the stage commonly symbolize the life of the Court as an ideal or an institution.

The tone of such scenes, however, becomes increasingly critical. The sense of political unity was weakened by the costly but inglorious campaigns following the Armada victory, and again by the peace with Spain in 1604. The parliamentary outcry against monopolies during Elizabeth's last years broadened, after her death, into a continuous opposition, religious and now constitutional. And resistance to the prerogative powers of James I was bound up with opposition to the Court.

The depreciation of landed and official incomes towards the end of the century threw additional burdens on the patronage of the Crown. But the Crown, too, was now faced with acute difficulties of the same kind. From the 1590s, first Elizabeth and then James unloaded vast parcels of Crown lands to eager speculators, securing immediate returns at the expense of the future. Hence, a general congestion at Court, and an intensification of faction struggles (which the prospect of Elizabeth's death would in any case have made acute); increasing bribery (for which Bacon became the scapegoat in 1621); the engrossing of appointments by Burleigh and his son and successor, Robert Cecil; and the frantic attempts of Essex to oust their nominees with his, in Ireland, the Commons, the Council of the North, the royal household. The Queen's godson, Sir John Harington, comments on the suspicion and frustration at Court towards the end of her reign:[16]

I have spent my time, my fortune, and almost my honesty, to buy false hopes, false friends, and shallow praise; – and be it remembered that he who casteth up this reckoning of a courtly minion, will set up his sum like a fool at the end, for not being a knave at the beginning.

The downfall of Essex, the popular hero, seemed the end of an epoch.

With the same thronging of suitors for office, the Jacobean Court suffered from intemperate favouritism, resulting in wilder spending for reasons of prestige (though 'our wants grow worse and worse'), and an undercurrent of fear. James refers to the 'factions and deadly feuds which are the motives of great mischief in great families' in a pronouncement against duelling about 1610.[17] 'So dangerous are the times' that a nobleman guards his words in a letter mentioning a recent vendetta; 'men must learn not to speak of great ones', observes a confidential news-writer.

This was the immediate background to much of the opposition in Parliament. Although many patents of monopoly had been called in after 1601, James multiplied them again by scores; and these, with the sale of lands and titles, made a harvest-time for 'projectors' (one of whom wrote to another in 1607, proposing to 'join together faithfully to raise our fortunes by such casualties as this stirring age shall afford'). But the general reaction – as in Jonson's satires – was nearer to disgust. The most important monopoly, Alderman Cockayne's project for the export of dyed cloth, lavished bribes on Somerset and the Howards in 1613, only to lead three years later to a major crisis, with thousands of unemployed, and thence to the hostile Parliament of 1621. Already, in 1614, the courtiers had been denounced in the Commons as 'spaniels to the king, and wolves to the people'.

After 1600, then, the theatres were quick to satirize social climbers and projectors. But the towering egotists of *Lear* or *The White Devil* are grandees, not businessmen.

The agitation over monopolies is also significant from another point of view. It reveals a critical phase in the general development of English commerce and the gathering strength of new conceptions of individualism.

In theory, the structure of Elizabethan trade rested, like the rural economy, on medieval foundations. The aims of Burleigh had been to canalize foreign trade where it could be strategically useful; to safeguard internal order; and to preserve the hierarchy of occupations. This meant limiting competition, and protecting, or instituting, sectional and corporate privileges, at all economic levels, which might serve to maintain the existing balance of wealth. Thus, the Statute of Artificers in 1563 tried to confine apprenticeship in most handicrafts to the towns and, in the export trades, to the upper middle class. And a conspicuous example of 'well-ordered trade' was the great company of Merchant Adventurers, holding exclusive rights of traffic with Germany and the Low Countries, England's principal markets. Most of their apprentices were said in 1601 to come from the gentry or families of means. They traded as individuals, but subject to internal regulations governing in detail the places, times, and methods of trading, the quality of the cloth they exported, and even the conduct and living conditions of their factors abroad. Moreover, a system of 'stinting' restricted the quantities of cloth each member could handle on any of his ventures.

By upholding guilds and corporations, Burleigh and his successors intended to protect the small producers and traders who formed the majority. But their policy could not be stretched over the whole of an expanding economy; and where it was enforced, on the other hand, it tended to favour the wealthy capitalists in the privileged groups more than anyone else.

In the first place, there had been a great extension of capitalist enterprise outside the traditional framework. In the cloth trades, which had moved away from the towns, there were more middlemen and large employers (a few of them factory owners, like the hero of Deloney's novel, *Jack of Newbury*). In mining and manufacture, the rapid advances of Elizabeth's reign were due to large-scale undertakings, many of them the work of individual merchants and landowners. And the consequent demand for freer credit and a freer movement of capital led to the forming of chartered companies on a new, joint-stock basis – from the Russia Company of 1553 and the government-sponsored Mines Royal of 1564 to the East India Company of 1600 and the Virginia Company of 1606. (It was this company whose voyages suggested part of the setting to *The Tempest*.) The same need had contributed to the legalizing of usury in 1572.

But, secondly, the road to new investment was blocked by monopolies – by those of merchant companies as well as patents granted to courtiers. Tyneside coal, now a major industry, was virtually monopolized by the corporation of Newcastle Hostmen; and the bulk of the nation's foreign trade passed through London, while in cloth, by far the most important export, as much as a third of the London trade could be controlled by a handful of the Merchant Adventurers (twenty-six of them in 1606, for example). 'The mischief of Monopolies', one critic had declared (*c.* 1588), 'can never be avoided as long as there be any Corporations.'[18]

This critic made an exception in favour of the corporations of craftsmen; but here, too, the regulated economy was failing. Mastercraftsmen complained that 'the shopkeepers growing rich do make the workmen their underlings' (1619); journeymen were losing their hopes of becoming masters. In the handicrafts, as in agriculture, the poorer men were slipping into the status of wage-earners or toppling over the brink into unemployment and vagrancy. And, though wages rose, they still lagged behind the cost of living.

These problems came to a head during the depression, which lasted from 1586 to the end of the war. A confused struggle ensued, of groups and individuals each seeking to preserve or enlarge their own spheres of privilege. Journeymen demanded a strict application of the clauses limiting apprenticeship in the Statute of Artificers; craftsmen sought protective charters of incorporation (at least ten such groups were incorporated in London during the years 1604–6);[19] and – chiefly to the profit of courtiers and projectors – some of the industrial crafts went on to negotiate for patents of monopoly. On the other side, monopolies annoyed consumers by raising prices; they restricted the demand for wool; they shut out new merchants, especially in the outports; and in some trades they dispossessed the craftsmen already established. From these quarters, therefore, arose a general demand for freedom of trade.

These views found expression in Sir Edwin Sandys' Bill for Free Trade in 1604:

> All free subjects are born inheritable as to their land, as also to the free exercise of their industry ... Merchandise, being the chiefest and richest [of occupations], ... it is against the natural right and liberty of the subjects of England to restrain it into the hands of some few ...

This was to claim an unusually broad sanction for individual freedom; and others were now speaking with the same voice. In 1607, for example, one opinion defended enclosures with the novel argument that 'the good individual is the good general'; while a London pamphleteer of 1616 was prepared to go further still – 'A Citizen, however he may be noted for covetousness, and corruption in trading; yet under colour of private enriching himself, he laboureth for the common good'. Clearly, these arguments (including Sandys') were not disinterested. But they had behind them the authority of the great common lawyer, Coke; and, as Sandys claimed again after the depression due to Cockayne's project, the case for a free market touched the artisan as well as the trader: 'the poor man's inheritance is his hands', and 'to seek another inheritance is difficult'. In this sense, the new individualism sprang directly from the old assumption underlying a regulated trade – the assumption of inherited security.

In this sense, too, economic developments favoured the Puritans, with their emphasis on personal initiative and thrift. The Puritans have been considered the prime agents in creating a capitalist mentality. But their doctrines developed gradually from their setting; and a recent historian has described Elizabethan Puritanism as a movement of intellectuals who tried, unsuccessfully, to impose a theological (and essentially conservative) social outlook on the lawyers and businessmen with whom they found themselves conjoined. 'Usury', said a Puritan preacher in 1589, 'is a devil that all the disciples of Christ in England cannot cast out.'[20] Middle-class literature took on a distinctly Puritan colouring in the last quarter of the century; but in the same process the Puritan outlook itself became more utilitarian.

The most popular London preacher of the 1590s was the moderate Puritan William Perkins, whose Treatise of the Vocations (c. 1599) gives a representative statement. God has 'ordained the society of man with man, partly in the commonwealth, partly in the Church, and partly in the family'. Further, 'God giveth diversity of gifts inwardly, and distinction of order outwardly'; while personal callings are 'imposed on man by God, for the common good'. On these traditional grounds, Perkins condemns usury and ambition. But his main criticism is reserved for the 'idleness' of monks and beggars, of nobles and their serving-men. He deals at length with the problem confronting many Londoners in the middle classes, the problem of ensuring freedom of occupation: 'every man must choose a fit calling to walk in; that is, every calling must be fitted to the man, and every man be fitted to his calling'. And, above all, Perkins illustrates the Puritan tendency to link Christianity with industriousness: 'we must consider the main end of our lives, and that is, to serve God in serving of men in the works of our callings'. Even a menial occupation is worthy if diligently pursued.

The influence of this kind of outlook on the theatre has perhaps been underrated – partly because plays and sermons were rivals for public notice. Playwrights like Dekker and Heywood – and even the satirist Middleton – shared the moral attitude of Perkins, and wrote primarily for the London middle classes. The treatment of family relationships on the stage, from *Romeo and Juliet* to *Women Beware Women*, reflects middle-class opinion in the playwrights' emphasis on the sanctity of marriage, in their criticism of the tyranny of parents, and their plea for a moderate liberty in the choice of a wife or husband. Again, the middle-class desire for the rule of law and fear of a recrudescence of feudalism are leading motives in Shakespeare's history plays, and in the series of revenge tragedies, from Kyd onwards. And, with all his respect for 'degree, priority and place', Shakespeare gives more weight to personal merit and the loyalties founded on it than to bare prerogative or the 'idol ceremony'.

On the other hand, the Puritans were hostile towards the actors, and backed the London Council in their efforts to suppress them – so that the theatres came to be built outside the Council's jurisdiction (though remaining within the metropolitan area). The attack on plays was part of the general Puritan campaign for moral discipline, and especially the discipline of labour. Theatres led to riots and infection; they had, in fact, to be closed when deaths from plague in London exceeded thirty a week. Theatre-going profaned the Sabbath and damaged trade; above all, it was 'very hurtful in corruption of youth ... and also great wasting both of the time and thrift of many poor people'.[21] 'You will have nothing but the word of God' – runs a playgoer's retort (1580): 'you will permit us no recreation, but have men like Asses, who never rest but when they eat.'

The city where this conflict over play-acting was chiefly waged was now a great European capital. It was a major centre for credit and navigation. And, though less important in numbers than in wealth – perhaps one in twenty of Elizabeth's subjects – its population was increasing rapidly, with an additional influx during the legal term-times. Noblemen settled in the bishops' palaces along the Strand or crowded into lodgings; former ecclesiastical property was sub-let for tenements. Despite the government's efforts to stop new building and send the gentlemen home, the numbers – and the ground-rents – continued to rise. A new world of fashion arose, with its varied hangers-on: the 'gulls', or would-be gallants, airing themselves in ordinaries and playhouses, visiting the sights of the Tower and the new Royal Exchange, or mixing with the crowds on business at St Paul's; the mercers, fencing-instructors, hackney coachmen; the 'cony catchers' and other rogues depicted by the satirists. And mixing with these again were the alien immigrants and the craftsmen who had lost their custom in other towns; the growing numbers of watermen, sailors, porters; the vagabonds from the country. The contrasts of an age of rapid transition were concentrated in the surroundings of the new profession of letters.

The Profession of Letters

'Poetry in this latter Age', says Jonson, 'hath prov'd but a mean Mistress, to such as have wholly addicted themselves to her.' But those, he adds, 'who have but saluted her on the by' have been 'advanced in the way of their own professions'. Here Jonson appears to sum up the experience of his time: the status of the writer was honoured but insecure.

The first generation of Elizabethan writers – the courtiers like Sidney and the lesser men in their orbit like Spenser and Lyly – were professional writers only in the sense that literature for them was a secondary means of advancement. Their aim was that of *The Faerie Queene*, 'to fashion a gentleman ... in virtuous and gentle discipline'; their writing was intended for their friends, much of it only for circulation in manuscript. George Gascoigne (c. 1542–77) was one of the first of the Elizabethan gentry to turn to miscellaneous publication; but his main object, too, was to show the queen that his talents were worth employment.

The first wave of purely commercial writers came after 1580 with the University wits – Lodge and Peele from Oxford, Greene, Marlowe and Nashe from Cambridge – who popularized their learning for theatres and bookstalls. These men and their rivals made a distinctive social group; they were joined by Kyd, then by Shakespeare, by Jonson, and the host of others who hurried forward in the 1590s to make or supplement a living with their pens. Their plays and pamphlets straddled from the territory of Spenser to that of *The Cobbler of Canterbury* and the ballad-mongers. Somewhere between these men and the courtiers were ranked well-connected professional poets like Daniel and Drayton.

The earlier critics – Ascham, Puttenham, Sidney – are largely defensive in their attitude to the poet and his calling; they want to show that literature is an interest fit for gentlemen. But they are carried much further than this by their Renaissance faith in book-learning and its contribution to the active life. And Spenser asserted for his age the full humanist doctrine of the poet as independent public moralist and commemorator of heroic action. By the end of the century, therefore, Daniel, Jonson, or Chapman could speak of the public dignity of letters with unprecedented confidence. In Daniel's *Musophilus* (1599), for example, learning is at once a personal necessity and 'the State's soul'; eloquence is the active part of learning, poetry the summit of eloquence. Granted more and wiser patronage (so that the mass of competing talents may find their proper levels), English scholarship may go forward to unheard-of glories.

Admittedly, however, Daniel is contrasting the possible with the actual. Patronage was still the poet's main hope; failing a secure office, the patron could give encouragement and, not less needed, the protection of his name. There were dazzling patrons, like the Sidneys and Essex, from whom Daniel himself, Jonson, and others gained solid benefits and appreciation. But these were the great names; smaller fry might have to content themselves with an occasional gift, or bare thanks, in return for a florid (and unwanted) dedication. And the 1590s brought the same congestion for authors as for other suitors. From Spenser to the Cambridge writers of the *Parnassus* plays (1598–1601), scholars complain indignantly of the corruption surrounding appointments in Church and State, of the decay of patronage and 'hospitality'.

Printing was a meaner but no less hazardous form of support. The market was limited; the wealthier members of the Stationers' Company (the corporation of booksellers and printers who held exclusive rights of publication) were secure in their privileged position; some of the poorer ones were unscrupulous. And the author's position was the weaker, because the copyright in his manuscript was not his but the stationer's (or, in the case of a play, the actors'). Forty shillings was the average price for a pamphlet, selling at a few pence – (a play sold at sixpence, or half a day-labourer's wage; a ballad at a half-penny) – while, for more ambitious writing (apart from a few commissioned works of scholarship) an author might well feel like Drayton, when 'in Terms' with the booksellers over his masterpiece: 'They are a company of base Knaves, whom I both scorn and kick at.'

Insecurity, then, was one reason why many writers, like Drayton himself, turned to the theatre in the 1590s. Francis Meres, a faithful echo of literary opinion, declares in 1598 that English poets can make their language as illustrious as Latin, if only 'liberal patrons' are forthcoming –

or if our witty Comedians and stately Tragedians (the glorious and goodly representers of all fine wit, glorified phrase, and quaint action) be still supported and upheld, by which means for lack of Patrons (O ingrateful and damned age) our Poets are solely or chiefly maintained …[22]

Certainly, the demand was impressive, with two or sometimes five companies active in London, and one leading company at least employing a dozen writers – dividing and subdividing the work between them – to produce a play a fortnight. In the three years 1598–1600, Dekker alone contributed eight complete plays and parts of twenty-four others to Henslowe, the money-lender and financier of the Lord Admiral's men, at about £6 a play. This may have brought him £30 in a good year – more than a parson or a schoolmaster, perhaps, but not enough to keep Dekker or his fellows from urgent requests to Henslowe for additional loans. And Jonson was to grumble that his plays had only earned him £200 in twenty years – an amount he might have got by sticking to bricklaying. Shakespeare must have been the most prosperous of the dramatists; but then Shakespeare was also a principal actor and 'sharer' in the Lord Chamberlain's men, who were independent of any Henslowe.

On the other hand, there were genuine compensations. It was a taunt against the actor (and hence against the playwright, too) that 'his wages and dependence prove him to be the servant of the people'. But this also meant that the poet was relatively free of any patron or group of patrons; free, that is, to take his stand squarely as a humanist and critic of men and manners. The poets of the popular stage are also the representatives of humanism, from Marlowe to Shakespeare, Jonson, Chapman, and Webster.

But this phase of the relation between the writer and his public came to an end as national feeling divided under James I. The actors were both drawn and driven towards dependence on the Court; and in 1609, Shakespeare's company (now the King's men) began to concentrate on their 'private' theatre, the Blackfriars – too expensive for penny-paying groundlings – which soon became more important than their popular house, the Globe. The courtly and fashionable sections of the London public were thus separating from the rest; while Beaumont and Fletcher, the rising professional dramatists, were newcomers from the same social group as their audience at the Blackfriars. With Beaumont and Fletcher and their successors, the independent note of humanism faded from the drama; the dramatists now tended to identify themselves solely with the dominant Cavalier section of their public. The age of a national drama was over.

Bacon and Donne, in their different ways, continued the main traditions of Renaissance humanism. But in the social, as in the intellectual, history of literature, Bacon and Donne mark the beginnings of a new age.

NOTES

1. For reading lists, and for publishing details of books referred to in the notes to all my chapters in this *Guide*, see Part IV.

2. *Civil ... Life* – in *Inedited Tracts, illustrating ... Manners* (ed. W. C. H(azlitt), Roxburghe Library).

3. Scott Pearson, *Church and State*, 61; cf. M. M. Knappen, *Tudor Puritanism*, 187ff.; J. E. Neale, *Queen Elizabeth*, 308.

4. On Neoplatonism in the Renaissance, see Kristeller, *Renaissance Thought*, I and II; Garin, *Italian Humanism*.

5. Harvey (G. G. Smith, *Elizabethan Critical Essays*, II, 235, 260, 279). cp. Ralegh, *Works*, II, xlv, lvi, 24ff., 48ff.; 381df.; VIII, 548ff., 571ff.; G. Bullough, 'Bacon and the Defence of Learning', in *17th Century Studies Presented to Sir Herbert Grierson* (ed. D. Wilson); C. Hill, *Intellectual Origins of the English Revolution*, ch. ii.

6. R. H. Tawney, *The Agrarian Problem in the 16th Century*, 383. On the households of the gentry, see. W. Harrison, *Elizabethan England*, 84ff.; A. L. Rowse, *The England of Elizabeth*, 251ff.; L. C. Knights, *Drama and Society in the Age of Jonson*, 112–17; J. Smyth, *Lives of the Berkeleys* (1618; ed. Maclean), II, 264ff.; and Appendix II.

7. Jonson, *Discoveries* (ed. Harrison), 65; cp. Cavendish, *Life of Wolsey*, 13, 16; J. B. Mullinger, *The University of Cambridge*, II, 168, 214, 399, 401ff.; Neale, *Elizabethan House of Commons*, 301ff.: Harrison, *Elizabethan England*,

218, 248ff. See F. Caspari, *Humanism . . . in Tudor England*, ch. vi; J. H. Hexter, 'The Education of the Aristocracy', in *Reappraisals in History*.

8. T. Wilson, *The State of England*, A.D. *1600*, 22; cp. J. E. Neale, *The Elizabethan Political Scene*, 20–23. The period about 1590–1610 was a time of financial instability for many landowners, but the long-term economic trends have been much debated since R. H. Tawney's article 'The Rise of the Gentry' (1941); see Hexter, *Reappraisals*, ch. vi; articles in L. Stone, ed., *Social Change . . . in England 1540–1640*, 6–80; Stone, *Causes of the English Revolution*, 27–31, 72–5. Stone, *Crisis of the Aristocracy*, is detailed and extensive; for short surveys of the position of the nobility and gentry, see G. R. Elton, *England under the Tudors*, 255–9; G. Davies, *The Early Stuarts*, 264–8; J. Hurstfield, 'Social Structure', in *The New Cambridge Modern History*, III (ed. W. B. Wernham), 126–48; and H. Kamen, *The Iron Century*, 129–65.

9. Cheyney, *History of England*, II, 3–36; Lipson, *Economic History of England*, II, 401–4.

10. Quoted, L. B. Wright, *Middle-class Culture*, 290; cp. Wilson, *The State of England*, 23–4; J. Earle, *A Younger Brother* (*Microcosmography*, 1628); Smyth, *Lives of the Berkeleys*, II, 364, 411.

11. See A. J. and R. H. Tawney, in *The Economic History Review*, V, 1934.

12. Lipson, *Economic History*, III, 416ff. On the growth of population as a cause of poverty in the sixteenth century, see P. Williams, *The Tudor Regime*, 139–43, 175ff.; Kamen, *The Iron Century*. On migration to the towns and urban poverty, see also P. Clark and P. Slack, eds, *Crisis and Order in English Towns 1500–1700*; cf. P. Corfield, 'Urban Development', in *Trade, Government and Economy in Pre-Industrial England*, ed. D. C. Coleman and A. H. John, 214–47.

13. See Appendix XI. For extracts from *The Cobbler of Canterbury*, see *Tarlton's Jests* (ed. J. O. Halliwell); Captain Cox is described in *Robert Laneham's Letter* (ed. Furnivall); see Bradbrook, *Rise of the Common Player*, 143–61. On popular festivals and their influence on drama, see C. L. Barber, *Shakespeare's Festive Comedy* and R. Weimann, *Shakespeare and the Popular Tradition in the Theater*.

14. On literacy and schooling, see J. W. Adamson, in *The Library*, 1930; M. H. Curtis, 'Education and Apprenticeship', in *Shakespeare Survey*, XVII; L. Stone, 'The Educational Revolution in England, 1560–1640', in *Past and Present* 1966; J. Simon, *Education . . . in Tudor England*; cf. C. M. Cipolla, *Literacy*.

15. See Chambers, *The Elizabethan Stage*, I; Welsford, *The Court Masque*; M. Axton, *The Queen's Two Bodies*, and 'The Tudor Mask and Elizabethan Court Drama', in *English Drama* ed. M. Axton and R. William, 24–47; cf. P. Williams, *The Tudor Regime*, 293–310.

16. Harington, *Nugae Antiquae*, I, 168; cf. Sir R. Naunton, *Fragmenta Regalia*, 16; Sir W. Cornwallis, *Of . . . Factions* (1600; *Essays*), 24; Neale, *Elizabethan Political Scene*; id., *The Elizabethan House of Commons*, 233ff.

17. Quoted, F. T. Bowers, *Elizabethan Revenge Tragedy*, 23; cp. T. Birch, *Court and Times of James I*, I, 179, 213; see Stone, *Crisis of the Aristocracy*,

199–270; M. Prestwich, 'English Politics and Administration', in Alan G. R. Smith, ed., *The Reign of James VI and I*, 140–59; for a contrasting picture, D. Mathew, *The Jacobean Age*. On 'projectors', see Lipson, *Economic History*, III, 357; L. C. Knights, *Drama and Society*, 71ff.; R. Ashton, 'Conflicts of Concessionary Interest in Early Stuart England', in *Trade . . . in Pre-Industrial England*, ed. Coleman and John, 113–31.

18. *Tudor Economic Documents* (ed. Tawney and Power), III, 266; cp. B. E. Supple, *Commercial Crisis and Change in England, 1600–42*; C. Wilson, *England's Apprenticeship 1603–1763*, 36–107.

19. Lipson, *Economic History*, III, 331; cp. Unwin, *Industrial Organization*, chs v–vi. On the Bill for Free Trade, see Scott, *Joint-Stock Companies*, I, 119ff.; R. Ashton, *The City and the Court 1603–1643*, chs i–iii.

20. Knappen, *Tudor Puritanism*, 417–23; on the vexed question of Puritanism and capitalism, see also Tawney, *Religion and the Rise of Capitalism* (1937 ed.); C. Hill, 'Protestantism and the Rise of Catholicism' (in F. J. Fisher, ed., *Essays . . . in Honour of R. H. Tawney*, 15–39) and *Society and Puritanism*. On Perkins, see L. B. Wright, *Middle-class Culture*, 170–85.

21. E. K. Chambers, *Elizabethan Stage*, I, 236ff.; IV, 291; A. Harbage, *Shakespeare's Audience*, 69; cf. Salingar, Harrison and Cochrane, 'Les Comédiens et leur public', in *Dramaturgie et Société*, ed. J. Jacquot, 560–73.

22. Meres (G. G. Smith, *Elizabethan Critical Essays*, II, 313). See Chambers, *Elizabethan Stage*, II, 158–73; Henslowe, *Diary*; G. E. Bentley, *The Profession of the Dramatist*.

PART II

THE ELIZABETHAN LITERARY
RENAISSANCE
L. G. SALINGAR

Shakespeare and his Age

If Shakespeare's plays and poems are the monument of a remarkable genius, they are also the monument of a remarkable age. The greatness of Shakespeare's achievement was largely made possible by the work of his immediate predecessors: by Spenser and Sidney in the mastery of verse, for example; by Marlowe and the University wits in the theatrical management of character and situation. The literature of Shakespeare's generation, moreover, proved exceptionally wealthy in minds of the first order. After a long fallow period of dependence on Chaucer, and of timid innovation in a language that was changeable and uncertain,[1] there came a moment of mounting confidence in the power of human reason to interpret Man and Nature, in the value of literature as an instrument of reason, in the dignity of modern English as a literary medium. The thirty years or less of Shakespeare's career as actor and poet were also the culminating years of Spenser's essay in heroic idealism, the years of Jonson's superb satires, of the momentous speculations of Bacon in the philosophy of science, of a new subtlety of introspection in the poetry of Donne. When Sidney undertook his *Apology for Poetry* about 1583 – a few years before Shakespeare's coming to London – he could show very little in modern English to support his hopes for the future; but by 1613, when Shakespeare's last work was written, the literature of modern English was already rich in varied achievements, self-confident and mature.

Behind the new literature was the training in classical imitation of a long line of humanist scholars and translators, reaching back to the time of Erasmus at the beginning of the century. The first tangible sign of it for the Elizabethans was the poetry of Wyatt and Surrey, published after their deaths in Tottel's miscellany of 1557; and the lesson they drew from *Songs and Sonnets* was a conscious delight in the artifice of poetic form. 'Their conceits [*conceptions*] were lofty', says an advocate of the new courtly verse, 'their styles stately, their conveyance [*employment of figures of speech*] cleanly, their terms proper, their metre sweet and well proportioned, in all imitating very naturally and studiously their Master Francis Petrarcha' (G. Puttenham, *The Art of English Poesy*, 1589). Skilful handling of conventions, economy and force of language, and, above all, the development of a rhetorical plan in which metre, rhyme scheme, imagery, argument should all combine to frame the emotional theme and throw it into high relief – these were the aims of humanist poetry from Wyatt and Surrey onwards; and with these went their new verse models, such as Wyatt's Petrarchan sonnets and the blank verse of Surrey's translation of Virgil. Poetry was to be a concentrated exercise of the mind, of craftsmanship, and of learning.

Effective progress from *Songs and Sonnets* was delayed, however, until 1579 and the appearance of Spenser's *Shepherd's Calendar*, which was even more impressive as a technical triumph. Spenser showed how the pastoral convention could be adapted to a variety of subjects, moral, amatory, or heroic, in a diction consistently eloquent, recalling both Chaucer and Virgil; and he showed how the rules of 'decorum', or fitness of style to subject, could be applied, through variations in the diction and the metrical scheme. The half-decade of *The Shepherd's Calendar* was decisive. It brought the writings of Sidney and a new generation of poets at Court, and the success of Lyly's novel, *Euphues* (1578), a fashionable pattern book of manners and studied phrasing. And some ten years after the building of the first London playhouse in 1576, the new literature reached the popular stage, with a new group of professional writers – the University wits.

For all its emphasis on scholarship, humanism could flourish in the popular theatre because it was attached both to long-established traditions and to the powerful emergent sentiments of nationalism and individual self-consciousness. It was attached to the medieval tradition of moral teaching through allegory; poetry, as humanists like Sidney contended, combined the universal doctrines of philosophy with the telling examples of history. The heightened imitation of Nature in poetry was no submission to the snares of the world and the flesh, as some Puritans alleged, but the means of firing men to active virtue and 'civility'; even more, of revealing 'the highest point of man's wit', the creative spark of divinity in the human mind (*An Apology for Poetry*). Sidney's arguments here are widely representative; they join the imitation theory of the Aristotelians with the Platonists' belief in poetic rapture, the Protestant's urging the use of one's talents with the humanist's ardour for personal fame. Similarly, for the readers of *The Shepherd's Calendar*, there was representative force behind the claims of the poet's friend and spokesman 'E. K.', asserting with novel assurance the paradox that poetry is at once an art and no art:

> no art, but a divine gift and heavenly instinct not to be gotten by labour and learning, but adorned with both: and poured into the wit by a certain *enthousiasmos* and celestial inspiration ...   (*October*; E. K.'s 'Argument')

Decorum, then, is secondary to celestial inspiration; and, with this exalted language, Spenser claims public authority for the poet at the very point where his utterance is most deeply personal.

Poetry thus conceived is essentially declamation; it belongs to the theatre. Where a fifteenth-century love poet would linger with his melancholy, –

> In black mournyng is clothyd my corage,[a] –

Sidney, for example, is concerned with rhetoric, with resonant persuasion:

> I sought fit words to paint the blackest face of woe.

What is new in the later poet is not his feeling or his introspection but his manner of address, the concentrated interplay between emotion and rhetoric: '"Fool", said my Muse to me, "look in thy heart and write"' (*Astrophel and Stella*, Sonnet I). With Petrarch's sonnets and his passion for formal perfection, English poetry had also been invaded by the restless, self-dramatizing spirit of the forerunner of modern humanism; after Wyatt, even the tradition of writing for music had willingly given up to rhetoric some of its lightness and grace.

The underlying theme of a great part of Elizabethan literature is a conflict between this demonstrative individualism and the traditional sense of a moral order. In Marlowe's giants of self-assertion, 'Affect-

---

[a] heart, ardour.

ing thoughts co-equal with the clouds', this conflict is projected on to the stage.

Humanism alone, however, was not the source of vitality in Shakespeare's theatre. Its vitality was due to its broad contact with popular entertainment and popular thinking, quickened by the Reformation. Above all, it was a vitality of the spoken language; and here, too, the Reformation contributed immensely. From Tyndale to the Authorized Version, through more than ten separate efforts (1525–1611), the English language was sifted in its Anglo-Saxon and its Latin elements for fitness to render accurately the dignity of the Bible, and at the same time to 'be understood even of the very vulgar'. The language of the Authorized Version was a decisive achievement of English Reformation culture in its capacity to combine a homely, racy quality, close to everyday speech, with figurative subtlety and a sense of awe.

At the same time, literature gained, in consequence, a vastly sharper sense of the relative values of words and idioms, popular and learned, which was nowhere more active than in the theatre. The drama flourished as long as humanist-trained poets remained closely in touch with popular speech and popular traditions; and as popular influence grew weaker the drama declined. The interplay between humanism and popular taste during the first part of Shakespeare's career is therefore made the subject of the next two sections of the present survey; then the general style of poetry during the same period; then the development of tragedy during Shakespeare's later years; and, finally, the new tendencies in Jacobean prose.

The Background of Popular Taste

The theatre was the point of closest contact between humanism and popular taste. A number of plays were specially prepared for select audiences of 'the judicious' at the Court, the Universities, or the legal Inns. But the great majority were written for the commercial theatres, whose repertory the Court shared, and in which the judicious were outnumbered and often outweighed by 'the groundlings' who paid their penny for standing room. 'Your carman and tinker', Dekker wrote in 1609, 'claim as strong a voice in their suffrage, and sit to give judgement on the play's life and death, as well as the proudest Momus among the tribe of critics.'[2] If the tribe of critics at their best called out the force and subtlety of a classical training, it was the groundlings who saved the drama from academic stiffness and preserved its essential bias towards entertainment – towards a high-spirited entertainment which was also a criticism of life.

Except at the two extremes of closet tragedy and country jig, it would be difficult to separate the humanist from the popular layer of taste. So far as it can be distinguished, however, the taste of the groundlings shows a striking elasticity. Without abandoning their old favourites, they were ready to welcome new themes of classical inspiration – or even, as with Quince and Bottom, to act them. They welcomed Marlowe at once, in spite of his disdain for 'jigging veins of rhyming mother wits' (c. 1587), and long remained faithful to him; and they made Shakespeare, too, an immediate box-office success. Despite the Prince's coolness towards the popular excesses of clowning and rant, *Hamlet* itself (1601) provides an outstanding instance of the groundlings' quickness of response. Its success was prompt and lasting, not only with 'the wiser sort' at the Universities (1601), but with 'all', and especially in 'the vulgar's Element' (1604). This relation to the groundlings was vital to Shakespeare's work, both practically and artistically.

It was vital to the whole evolution of the drama. Literary playwrights borrowed freely from popular sources, from folk traditions as such, or from material already familiar through older plays, sermons, street ballads, or pamphlets. From the double tradition of Mysteries and Moralities came stock characters like the comic Vice and Herod the tyrant, threatening heaven and earth; scenes of vivid caricature and realistic comedy; and even the deep-seated tendency of Elizabethan dramatists to think of a play as a kind of animated sermon where the characters and situations are allegorical types. In its exhibitions of spectacular violence, its loose and episodic plotting, and its mingling of comedy with tragedy, the drama followed popular taste, not classical instruction; while the popular tradition of musical 'pastime' combined with humanist declamation to impart a form to it closer to opera than to the modern drama of naturalism.

Grammar schools and Universities had trained their students in rhetoric with the aid of Seneca, Terence, or modern Latin imitations; and, when Seneca's *Ten Tragedies* (1559–81) joined the broad stream of Elizabethan translations, the time was ripe for a neo-classical drama in English. But humanism in the theatre was obliged from the first to come to terms with popular custom; in effect, there was no other practical experience of how a play ought to be given. The first notable effort in comedy, the school play of *Ralph Roister Doister* (Nicholas Udall, *c.* 1552), shows one side of this formative process; with its songs, its mock dirge, and its countrified farce, it is near to the May-game or the Christmas Feast of Misrule. And even in Senecan tragedy there was a similar reorientation, beginning with *Gorboduc* by Sackville and Norton (presented by the lawyers of the Inner Temple for the Christmas revels of 1561), with its subject drawn from British legend and its dumb-shows of processions and miming. There was a period of awkward adjustment between learning and custom until the 1580s, when the drama approached the freedom of maturity with the University wits. But there was no diminution in comedy of the elements that were much later to separate off as comic opera and burlesque; nor, in tragedy, of the spectacular. 'Our public', said a German Latinist, 'cannot away with narratives [the medium for violence in strictly classical tragedy]; it will have everything go on before its eyes; ... how then can we follow the laws of ancient drama?' He might have been speaking for the English. A few academic tragedies on statecraft by Daniel, Fulke Greville, and others, drew closer than *Gorboduc* to the formal reserve of their Latin model; but the Senecan material of *Hamlet* and the major Jacobean tragedies had passed through the popular *Spanish Tragedy* of Kyd (*c.* 1589), with its clamorous ghost and its public and gory revenges.[3]

Among the University wits, Marlowe's work (*c.* 1587–93) stands apart, not only for his vastly superior force of imagination but for philosophical depth. Yet much of it had a ready appeal for the jig-loving groundlings. Even the seemingly disdainful prologue of his first play, *Tamburlaine*, offers them, in compensation, a new vesture of majesty for the blustering Herod of the mystery plays:

> From jigging veins of rhyming mother wits,
> And such conceits as clownage keeps in pay,
> We'll lead you to the stately tent of War,
> Where you shall hear the Scythian Tamburlaine
> Threat'ning the world with high astounding terms
> And scourging kingdoms with his conquering sword.
> View but his picture in this tragic glass,
> And then applaud his fortunes as you please.

The high astounding terms of the shepherd conqueror, coming at the peak of enthusiasm for the exploits of men like Drake, gave a decisive momentum to the dramatic speech of the next twenty years; and Marlowe, more than anyone else, gave shape to the new drama by finding the meeting-points between humanism and popular traditions. In *The Massacre of Paris*, this meant anti-Catholic hack-work; while his chronicle play, *Edward II*, is still an immature experiment. But *Doctor Faustus* is the first great tragedy of humanism; and the story of Faustus was taken from a popular pamphlet which was reproduced in ballad form as well. In its main plan, moreover, it retraces the allegorical struggle between Good and Evil of early Moralities such as *Nature* or *Mankind*, though with the highly important difference that the central figure is no longer Mankind but an individual hero; while its horseplay and comic devilry, like Greene's rival play, *Friar Bacon*, again belong to the Morality vein or to that of popular jest books. In the powerful *Jew of Malta*, similarly, the Senecan revenge theme and the presiding spirit of Machiavelli have suffered a sea-change, so that violence takes on a colouring of grotesque satire. This colouring comes, as T. S. Eliot has pointed out, from the popular tradition of farce, with its 'terribly serious, even savage comic humour', which passed on from Marlowe to Jonson, and 'spent its last breath in the decadent genius of Dickens'.[4]

Greene and Peele wrote, like Marlowe, for the public theatres, and gained personal fame, or notoriety, as literary bohemians. Their plays have the attraction of liveliness and fluency, and the interest of pioneer work in which some of the main threads of Shakespearean drama are deliberately woven together.

Greene (1558–92) was one of the first men of letters to make his profession the entertainment of a broad reading public, and most of his output belongs to the early history of the best-seller. He began writing in 1583, with romantic novels in the manner of Lyly's *Euphues*, and turned to the stage about four years later with imitations of Marlowe. His plays, however (*c.* 1587–91), were partly intended as conventional retorts to Marlowe's 'atheism'; one, *A Looking Glass for London*, written with Lodge (*c.* 1590), is a sensational biblical Morality, in the same vein as Greene's autobiographical pamphlets of 'repentance' and his 'cony-catching' exposures of the London underworld. The best of his plays, *Friar Bacon and Friar Bungay* and

James IV, are romantic medleys in which he seems to have been experimenting with the possibilities of variety in a double or multiple plot. There is only an accidental connection between Friar Bacon at Oxford and Margaret, the keeper's daughter at 'merry Fressingfield'; but Greene is enabled to vary the exchanges between one tale of magic and wonderment and another of romantic love. Moreover, both plots have in common that they display a powerful force, magic in one, love in the other, which leads from 'frolic' to the borders of tragedy, happily averted.[5] This method of construction, with a latent or symbolic parallel between two separate plots (which may also contrast with each other) became the common method of the Elizabethans. Its debt to the older Moralities is evident in *A Looking Glass for London*, which is virtually a series of diatribes against vice by the prophet Oseas, borne out by illustrative episodes on the two planes of court and tavern. At one point, for example, a tavern scene in which one drunken ruffian murders another for a wench is followed by a court scene in which an aspiring princess poisons one husband so as to marry a second; whereupon Oseas exclaims:

> Where whoredom reigns, there murder follows fast ...
> London, behold the cause of others' wrack.

A similar principle of construction is made explicit by Gloucester in *King Lear* (1605), where Shakespeare deliberately brings together two plots of different origin:

> This villain of mine comes under the prediction; there's son against father; the king falls from bias of nature; there's father against child.

(I. ii)

A similar principle, again, explains the otherwise puzzling sub-plot of the mad-house scenes in Middleton's fine tragedy, *The Changeling* (1622); in this sub-plot, the gentleman–changeling who pretends to idiocy for the sake of access to the wife of a keeper of madmen, and the wife herself, who virtuously repels him, both provide an implicit comment on Beatrice–Joanna, the heroine of the main plot, who forfeits her social dignity and her moral sanity through lust. The guiding principle for the Elizabethans was that of extending and diversifying a moral situation, and not, as often used to be argued, that of comic relief.

On the other hand, Greene recognizes the latter principle as well;

towards the end of *James IV*, for example, Bohan, the Presenter, announces:

> The rest is ruthful; yet, to beguile the time,
> 'Tis interlac'd with merriment and rhyme.
>
> (III. iii)

The printed play was advertised, misleadingly, as a *Scottish History ... Intermixed with a pleasant Comedy, presented by Oberon, King of Fairies*; and, for further variety, there are passages of antic dances and clowning in popular style, scenes of symbolic dumb-show in the manner of *Gorboduc*, discourses on the common weal, a hunting song, a wedding masque, and a battle scene with the English and Scottish armies marching 'with all their pomp, bravely' (i.e. with pageantry). Moreover, Bohan (who first emerges from a tomb) calls the main action his 'jig', and sends his two sons to join it as clowns while he is presenting it. Nevertheless, Greene makes some attempt to match variety of entertainment with a faint moral symbolism. 'Here I see good fond actions in thy jig', says Oberon, 'And means to paint the world's inconstant ways.' There is an attempt to suggest the varied skein of life as the interest shifts from the lascivious king, his ruthless sycophant Ateukin, or the saturnine Bohan to the two patterns of constancy, Ida and Dorothea; and Queen Dorothea links together the varied themes of the play, national and domestic, in her closing speech:

> Come, royal father, enter we my tent: –
> And, soldiers, feast it, frolic it, like friends: –
> My princes, bid this kind and courteous train
> Partake some favours of our late accord.
> Thus wars have end, and, after dreadful hate,
> Men learn at last to know their good estate.

The diverse elements of Shakespeare's romantic comedies are already foreshadowed in Greene, including the motif of a heroine disguising herself as a man; while one of Greene's popular novels and one of Lodge's furnish the main plots respectively of *The Winter's Tale* and *As You Like It*.

Less of a storyteller than Greene, Peele is more of a poet and more a man of the theatre. Three of his surviving plays (*c.* 1581–91) appeal, like Greene's, to the patriotic and moralizing sentiment of the middle classes – the journalist *Battle of Alcazar*, the historical medley *Edward I*, which was indebted to a ballad, and the more dignified biblical tragedy of *David and Bethsabe*. But Peele's work also illustrates, more broadly than Greene's, the range of national traditions which combined in the making of Shakespeare's theatre; and in particular it illustrates the opera-like quality of Elizabethan drama, the combined influence of courtly revels and folk pastime, which was later to culminate in the masques of Ben Jonson.

Peele's first original work, *The Arraignment of Paris* (1581–4), belongs to the same class of courtly entertainment as the 'Princely Pleasures' at Kenilworth (1575), or Lyly's 'Court Comedies' (*c.* 1584–90); like the latter, it was given before the Queen by the boys' company of the royal Chapel. It opens with the goddess Ate promising 'the tragedy of Troy'; but it quickly strays from narrative, tragic or otherwise, so as to frame a compliment to Elizabeth, based upon the pastoral mythology of Spenser. Mount Ida, the setting of sylvan gods and idyllic country festival, turns out also to be the home of the Maiden Queen herself; the rivalry of Juno, Pallas, and Venus for the Apple of Discord is varied by pastoral wooing episodes (sophisticated versions of country jigs); and both actions are brought to a happy conclusion by the appearance of Diana and her nymphs, Diana presenting the golden apple to the Queen in person. There are songs in Latin and Italian, and a formal oration by Paris; but this courtly and academic material is skilfully merged with reminiscences of folk tradition. In the first 'merry merry roundelay' between Paris and Oenone, for instance, Paris is 'The fairest shepherd on our green ... As fresh as bin the flowers in May' (I. ii); and Oenone's song of complaint (III. i) keeps the air of folk-song in spite of its classical allusions. The punishment of Thestylis for disdaining her shepherd Colin is frankly borrowed from country jigs:

Enter a foul crooked Churl, *with* Thestylis *a fair Lass, who woos him, and sings an old song called* The Wooing of Colman: *he crabbedly refuses her, and goes out of place: she tarries behind.*

The gods on Mount Ida 'Hold hands in a hornpipe, all gallant in glee' (I. i); and Diana's nymphs sing a country song for Vulcan and Bacchus:

> Some rounds or merry roundelays, we sing no other songs;
> Your melancholy notes not to our country mirth belongs ...
> *They sing* 'Hey down, down, down,' *&c.*

(IV. i)

The song and its preceding dialogue – the 'quirks' and 'frumps' [taunts] of the nymphs, especially at the cost of Vulcan the cuckold – recall the unsentimental tone of Elizabethan folk-song, which balances the extravagance of courtly pastoral. This enlivening tartness comes from the atmosphere of 'country sport' and public festivity; while country sport and classical mythology could be linked by their common reference to the predominance of Nature. Together, they symbolized a universal concord, cemented in the national concord of peasant and courtier in the worship of Gloriana.[6]

Peele, following his father, was also a designer of pageants. His two pageants for the London Lord Mayor's show (1585, 1591) made it a fashionably classical affair instead of a procession of folklore heroes, as it had been before. On the other hand, his later work returns to folk traditions. In Edward I there appears the old favourite of country pastimes and civic processions, a Robin Hood game (besides many ballads, two of the earliest printed plays (c. 1550) had been devoted to Robin Hood, one of them advertised as 'very proper to be played in May Games'; and he also figures in later stage productions, such as the anonymous George-a-Greene, the Pinner of Wakefield (c. 1590) and other plays). The liveliest of Peele's plays, moreover, The Old Wives' Tale (c. 1590), is closer to pure folk-story than any other Elizabethan play. As in The Arraignment of Paris, its songs are essential to the action.

The pastoral myth in courtly entertainments like Peele's was one expression of the sentiment of nationhood and political unity that was crystallizing under the Tudors; Spenser's romantic epic was another, universal in scope, with its allegories of heroic virtue, moral and political, converging on Prince Arthur and the Faerie Queen herself. But this sentiment was plainest in the many popular works on British history or pseudo-history appearing in the latter half of Elizabeth's reign. There were the patriotic chronicles of Holinshed (1577) and Stow (1580) in prose; the verse chronicles of Warner (1586) and the additions of 1587 to The Mirror for Magistrates; and works such as Hakluyt's Voyages and Navigations (1582–1600), or Stow's Survey of London (1598), making a similar appeal to national pride. And these gave rise to a long series of national chronicle plays, owing little or nothing to classical models, which took the place, in the popular theatre, of the obsolescent religious mysteries of the guilds. For a quarter of a century they embodied the strongest unifying sentiment in the London public; and during this period – from *The Famous Victories of Henry V* (*c.* 1586) to the early years of James I, when they began to disappear – it has been estimated that they accounted for more than a fifth of the plays written, sharing the popularity of 'the multiform romantic drama' with which they overlapped. Besides Marlowe, Greene and Peele, Shakespeare, Dekker, Heywood, Drayton, and many lesser men contributed to this vogue, at its height in the 1590s; it was particularly associated with Shakespeare, nine of whose plays were histories among the eighteen he produced in the first decade of his career (*c.* 1590–99).

The main themes behind Shakespeare's histories are the main themes of Tudor political thought – kingship, the sinfulness of rebellion against God's deputy on earth, the problems arising from royal misgovernment. Protestant absolutism was a central question in all the main public events of Shakespeare's youth, from the rising of the northern earls in 1569 and the subsequent Catholic plots against Elizabeth to the execution of Mary Queen of Scots in 1587 and the commercial–religious war against Spain. After 1588, moreover, despite the Armada victory, the nation became more heavily involved in warfare abroad than before; while the fear of civil war, backed by foreign intervention, grew more acute than ever. The succession to the throne remained unsettled; the court of the ageing Queen was divided by rivalries between the Essex and the Cecil factions. There was contemporary France to illuminate the danger; there was Roman history – as in Lodge's clumsy tragedy *The Wounds of Civil War* (*c.* 1588) and Shakespeare's *Titus Andronicus* (1594); more relevant still, there was English history itself. The precedent of reconstructing the past as a warning 'mirror' for the present had been established by the authors of *Gorboduc* and their associates in the original *Mirror for Magistrates*; it was followed both in Shakespeare's theatre and by Daniel (1595) and Drayton (1596) in their verse histories of baronial wars.

In other senses, moreover, the history plays of Shakespeare's time belonged to popular stage traditions. There were popular Moralities satirizing abuses, in which history was subordinate to general social ethics: the Armada battle in Wilson's *Three Lords of London* (1589), for instance, is reduced to a symbolic episode (a struggle for shields), while the legendary kings in *A Knack to Know a Knave* (1592) or

Nobody and Somebody (*c.* 1606) are merely vague ciphers for the magistrate in general. And even where history provides the real substance of the play, it follows this universalizing pattern. Thus, *The Famous Victories of Henry V*, the first history proper and the germ of Shakespeare's plays on Prince Hal, presents the Morality theme of a prodigal son reforming; and there are strong traces of the ruler as Mankind, torn between good and evil counsel, in the admirable *Woodstock* (*c.* 1592) and the *True Chronicle History of King Leir and his Three Daughters* (*c.* 1590), the anonymous predecessors of *Richard II* and of *Lear*. The transformation of the central allegorical figure from Mankind into the Prince (or the Commonwealth) was a common feature of Tudor and Stuart Moralities, from Skelton's *Magnificence* (*c.* 1517) to Middleton's *Game at Chess* (1624); and this, in turn, helped to form Shakespeare's histories almost as much as the chronicles of Hall and Holinshed.

Shakespeare also follows familiar patterns of stage technique. His *Richard III*, for example, stems from the Morality tradition of comic devilry, of deception frankly proclaimed to the audience: 'Thus, like the formal Vice, Iniquity, I moralize two meanings in one word' (*Richard III*, III. i). Again, Shakespeare follows Marlowe, untroubled by anachronism, in preparing this ambitious villain to 'set the murderous Machiavel to school' (*3 Henry VI*, III. ii); while the planning and tone of his first group of histories (*1–3 Henry VI* and *Richard III*; *c.* 1590–93) owe much to the Senecan tragedies of revenge. As a man of the theatre, Shakespeare gained in this way much what the Greek dramatists had gained from public knowledge of their myths; assured of familiarity with his general themes and imaginative assent, he could enlarge the more freely on his own interpretation.

On the other hand, only Shakespeare among the dramatists had continuous grasp of the deeper interests of sixteenth-century historians. In his four plays on the Wars of the Roses, the final advent of the Tudors has the force of a heaven-sent deliverance after the long chain of disasters due to weakness or ambition; and a similar chain of crime and retribution adds a cumulative power to his later group on the House of Lancaster (from *Richard II* and the two parts of *Henry IV* to the expiation of *Henry V*; 1595–9). In shaping, compressing, and altering the chronicles, Shakespeare gained the art of dramatic design; and in the same way he developed his remarkable insight into character, its continuity and its variation. His Richard III has more humanity and more comic gusto than, for example, Marlowe's Jew of Malta; his Richard II and Bolingbroke are more complex and solid figures than their counterparts in Marlowe's *Edward II*. And as he developed he treated the chronicles with greater freedom. In the last three, the Falstaff plays, historically minor characters have a powerful reality of their own; the English people are represented concretely, no longer by means of puppets; and the problems of statesmanship, of expediency, honour, and authority are examined more searchingly and from a broader point of view. These problems of the histories were still active in Shakespeare's mind when he turned from the pageantry of *Henry V* to the psychological probing of his first major tragedy, *Julius Caesar* (1599).

The common sentiment of the chronicle plays was their appeal to the Protestant nationalism of the middle classes. This sentiment makes an anti-papal champion of Shakespeare's King John (1596?), for example, and resounds in the closing lines of the play:

> Come the three corners of the world in arms
> And we shall shock them; naught shall make us rue,
> If England to itself do rest but true;

and to this sentiment Nashe had appealed (with *1 Henry VI* as his example) in defending the theatre against the Puritans. 'How would it have joyed brave *Talbot* (the terror of the French)', he exclaims, 'to . . . triumph again on the Stage, and have his bones new embalmed with the tears of ten thousand spectators at least (at several times) who . . . imagine they behold him fresh bleeding?' (*Pierce Penniless*, 1592). Similarly, Heywood meets the Puritans on their own ground by citing the educative influence of the stage on 'the unlearned' (*An Apology for Actors*, c. 1608; published 1612). Plays, he says,[7] 'have made the ignorant more apprehensive' and 'instructed such as cannot read in the discovery of all our English chronicles':

what man have you now of that weak capacity that cannot discourse of any notable thing recorded even from William the Conqueror, nay, from the landing of Brute [the legendary Trojan founder of Britain], until this day? . . .

And while the exhibition of 'notable things' is the substance, the purpose of histories is propaganda:

... because plays are writ with this aim, ... to teach their subjects obedience to their king, to show the people the untimely ends of such as have moved ... insurrections, to present them with the flourishing estate of such as live in obedience, exhorting them to allegiance, dehorting them from all traitorous and felonious stratagems.

This is the moral of such plays as the collaborative *Sir Thomas More* (*c.* 1596) – in which Shakespeare probably had a hand. It carried a direct appeal to middle-class sentiment; and with it went an increasing interest in the figure of the London merchant, his loyalty, his domestic virtues, and his commercial achievements. Dekker's *Shoemaker's Holiday* (1599) and Heywood's *Edward IV* (*c.* 1599) are examples of this tendency; while Heywood's plays on Elizabeth's reign concentrate on Sir Thomas Gresham erecting the Royal Exchange (*If You Know not Me, You Know Nobody*, Pt 2; 1605).

One offshoot of the chronicles was the 'true and home-born Tragedy' of recent domestic crime, as in the dignified *Arden of Feversham* (*c.* 1592) or *A Warning for Fair Women* (*c.* 1599), with its ballad-like ending; another was the journalist play of travel and adventure, preferably in a setting of Italians, Spaniards, or Moors. Both kinds were foreshadowed in the dramas of Peele.

Many 'true chronicles' were in fact romances, padded with balladry and addressed in a spirit of buoyant exhortation to the London tradesman, his wife, and his country cousin. Besides ballad warnings, where there was already a strong bourgeois colouring, the ballad theme of camaraderie between king and yeoman is repeated in such plays as *George-a-Greene* and *Edward IV*, and echoed in Shakespeare's Agincourt scenes. Another favoured subject, as in Greene's pseudo-histories, was a romantic marriage, usually bringing social advancement; while extravagant adventure plus extravagant flattery of the groundlings brought popularity to Heywood's early play, *The Four Prentices of London* (*c.* 1600). The prentices here are Godfrey of Bouillon and his brothers, sons of a mythically banished earl – 'all high born, Yet of the city-trades they have no scorn'; as it happens, they also conquer Jerusalem. Civil doctrine is not forgotten, however; two of the brothers become captains of a band of cut-throats, to whom (like Shakespeare's Valentine in *Two Gentlemen of Verona*) they promptly impart a town-bred respectability:

> We have reformed these villains since we came,
> And taught them manners and civility.

Another city playwright, Munday, performs a similar office for his yeomanly hero, *Robert, Earl of Huntingdon*, the *ci-devant* Robin Hood (1598). Few of these histories and pseudo-histories have any distinctive merit; their dramatic form was too fluid, and success at a merely sensational level too easy. Yet they played an important part in the evolution of the London theatre, if only by binding together the many and varied interests of a national public.

They also confirmed the general tendency of the popular stage towards episodic narratives, straggling over time and place and crowded with incident. Their emergence in the 1580s coincided with that of a group of actors strong enough to make themselves national personalities – the comedians Tarlton (who acted in *The Famous Victories of Henry V*) and Kempe, and the tragic actors Alleyn and Richard Burbage. And these actors' companies, employing the University wits, established the technical conventions of Elizabethan staging, which remained broadly similar from the building of the first playhouse in 1576 to the closing of the theatres in 1642. Although many details concerning the theatres are uncertain, the main features can be briefly summarized.[8]

Whether 'circular' (polygonal) in shape, like the Globe, or square, like the Fortune, a public playhouse resembled a compact amphitheatre, with an unroofed central 'yard' for the groundlings, surrounded by tiers of covered galleries and the taller structure of the actors' 'tiring-house'. The main stage was a large platform, shoulder high, jutting forward from the 'tiring-house' nearly thirty feet into the centre of the yard. As the platform, three parts surrounded, could not be curtained off, there was no possibility of picture-stage scenery; it was usually bare, leaving the imagined stage locality fluid and indeterminate, to be indicated, when necessary, by the actors themselves. Sometimes these indications are vague (as in *Edward II*, where a speaker, somewhere in London or near it, simply announces: 'Here comes the king and the nobles From the parliament'); sometimes they are more precise ('Well, this is the forest of Arden'); the overriding concern, however, is rapidity of action. In modern editions, this neutral, uninterrupted staging is generally obscured by scene-divisions and place headings; but when an Elizabethan dramatist wanted to convey the impression of a particular setting he could use his speeches for the purpose, as with Duncan's description of

Macbeth's castle. This appeal to the ear was seconded by music and 'noises off '.

Visual, spectacular appeal was by no means lacking, however. There were arras hangings – black for tragedy – at the back of the stage; and the stage manager was well supplied with large movable properties – bedsteads, arbours, mossy banks, 'trees', chariots, dragon outfits, even 'i Hell mouth'. Battles, executions, and bloodshed in general could be staged with spectacular if conventionalized realism; drownings, symbolically, with river-gods appearing to carry the victims away. Visual realism, then, took the form of an impressive token, as in medieval staging, not a consistent setting; thus, the tents of two opposing army commanders could be seen on the stage at once (*Richard III*, v. iii).

As there was no artificial lighting (except in the expensive 'private' theatres, which were roofed and candle-lit), effects such as darkness had to be suggested in the public theatres by means of tokens; but there was direct pictorial interest in the many scenes of fighting, dancing, and procession. Expensive and magnificent costumes were prominent here; they also served to designate nationality, social status, or character (as with Hamlet's black, or the homespun 'frieze' of the Duke in *Woodstock*, which is opposed to the fantastic panoply of Richard and his favourites). Disguise was a common convention in a theatre so highly conscious of apparel. Sometimes it merely kept the story running, as in the farcical *Look About You* (1600), where there are eight disguises by one character alone; but sometimes, in the tradition of the Moralities, it symbolized important dramatic changes, as with the transformation of Edgar into Poor Tom in *Lear*, or the black robe of the defeated Pompey in Chapman's tragedy: 'We now must suit our habits to our fortunes' (*Caesar and Pompey*, c. 1605).

But the greatest resource of the Elizabethan theatre was its unequalled adaptability. There were two doors at the back of the main stage, which probably had a width of forty-one feet in the Globe; by means of a curtain in front of one of the doors, a narrow space could be contrived where an actor might be 'discovered', as if in his study or tent. Above the doors was a partitioned gallery which held spectators but could also be used in part as an upper stage representing a bedroom or the battlements of a castle, and could be climbed or even assaulted from below (e.g. *1 Henry VI*, II. i). The stage musicians played 'above', either visible or curtained off, or else 'within' the tiring-house. This flexible structure was completed by two other features, reminiscent of the Middle Ages; above, a painted canopy known as 'the heavens', surmounted by a hut for properties and supported by two pillars rising from the platform stage; and, below the platform, the space of 'hell'. Both were pierced by trap-doors, so that a throne or a deity could be lowered, and a ghost, a devil or a magical tree could arise from below, with spectacular effect. With its several levels and places of entrance or 'discovery', the stage provided for varied movement and continuity of action.

Yet it remained an intimate theatre. Front stage, the actor stood next to the groundlings; rear stage, in the Globe, he was no more, apparently, than eighty-five feet away from the farthest spectator. There was thus no necessity to drop the old convention of direct address to the audience, in soliloquy or aside; it was a theatre for eloquence as much as for pageantry. If classical humanism was set aside in the matter of construction and the Unities, it triumphed in the actor's rhetoric. Even here, however, it was intimately connected with popular tradition and popular taste.

Humanism and Popular Taste – the 1590s

The decade of the 1590s was the flowering time of the English Renaissance. When Marlowe died in 1593, Shakespeare, with some half-dozen plays, was already the most prominent of living dramatists. The London theatres had a broadly representative public; by 1600 they had attracted Chapman, Jonson, and other successors to the University wits, who, with Shakespeare now at the height of his powers, were to make the glory of the English drama in the early years of the seventeenth century. There was a similar influx of new writers in poetry and journalism. England was at last possessed, said the Cambridge humanist Gabriel Harvey in the year of Marlowe's death, of 'Eloquence in speech and Civility in manners' – 'the goodliest graces of the most noble Commonwealths upon Earth'. And the triumph of Tudor humanism, long prepared and at last confirmed, had come at a moment when the heritage of the Middle Ages was still familiar and significant. In the public for literature and drama there was a varied community of interests, an imaginative interchange at every branch and level, as never before or since.

Except for Sackville, in the 1560s, and Gascoigne, in the 1570s, there had been at first few notable imitators of Wyatt or Surrey; Puritan suspicion of secular literature and the indifference of the gentry had been too discouraging. But the humanist triumph had been prepared by Wilson's *Art of Rhetoric* (1533) and Ascham's *Schoolmaster* (1570) – both Calvinist in temper; it was foreshadowed in the courtly injunctions of Puttenham's *Art of English Poesy* (written *c.* 1569–89; published 1589); it was well advanced in the years following *The Shepherd's Calendar* (1579); and by the 1590s it was fully accomplished, with the posthumous appearance of Sidney's *Arcadia* and his sonnets (1590–91) and Spenser's publication of *The Faerie Queene* (1590–96), which made manifest a new range of power for English poetry. In his synthesis of romantic knight-errantry, sophisticated allegory and ardent Protestant moralism around a core of patriotic myth, Spenser created a new imaginative realm answering to Elizabethan idealism, just as he rivalled the leading modern poets of Italy or France in the self-conscious artistry of his language and versification.

Sidney and Spenser found an immediate following in poetry of courtly neo-classical inspiration. Besides a host of minor sonnet sequences, there was the reflective wit of older poets at Court like Ralegh and younger ones like Davies; the heroic and amorous verse of Daniel and Drayton, among professional men of letters; Harington's Ariosto and Chapman's Homer. The decade was stimulated, moreover, by the sensuousness and energy of Marlowe's *Hero and Leander* (1593), which was completed as a philosophical poem by Chapman in 1598 and had already helped to form Shakespeare's popular *Venus and Adonis* and his *Rape of Lucrece* (1593–4), somewhat as Sidney's example helped to form his *Sonnets* (? 1595–1600). Yet a further development in the poetry of sense and intellect during this immensely versatile decade was the writing of Donne's songs and satires, by which the lyrical conventions of Spenser and the Petrarchans were radically transformed. Well might Harvey praise his friend Spenser and his contemporaries, then, for 'enriching and polishing their native Tongue, never so furnished or embellished as of late' (1592); or Daniel laud Sidney's memory and his example,

Now when so many pens (like Spears) are charg'd
To chase away this tyrant of the North;
Gross Barbarism ...
> (*Cleopatra*; dedication to the Countess
> of Pembroke, Sidney's sister, 1594)

Writers vied with one another in extolling England's 'golden', 'sugared', and 'passionate' eloquence, or in listing new English poets for comparison with the famous names of Italy and ancient Rome; and with Hooker's *Laws of Ecclesiastical Polity* (1593) and Bacon's *Essays* of 1597; the decade also brought new lustre to formal English prose.

The triumph of humanism, however, involved a profound conflict of cultural standards; for 'civility', especially in its Puritan setting, meant reducing the 'barbarous' influence of folk tradition and popular taste.[9] Popular entertainments and 'idle pastime' in general were the targets of moral condemnation by Puritans such as Northbrooke, Gosson, and Stubbes (1577–83), powerfully supported by the Council of London; and the humanists seconded the attack in the name of literary decorum. Sidney, in particular, objects to popular taste in comedy on both moral and aesthetic grounds; it contradicts classical decorum by 'mingling kings and clowns' and 'matching hornpipes and funerals' in a 'mongrel tragi-comedy'; and it is morally dangerous in preferring gross laughter to intellectual delight, in its 'scornful tickling' at 'mischances' and even at 'sinful things, which are rather execrable than ridiculous' (*An Apology for Poetry*, c. 1583). Puttenham, though no Puritan, has a similar attitude: he condemns Skelton, for example, as 'a rude railing rhymer', fit only for 'country fellows'; and he would seek to confine the language of poetry to 'the usual speech' of the educated in the London area only, since, in the provinces, 'the gentlemen, and also their learned clerks, do for the most part condescend' to the language of 'the common people' (*Art of English Poesy*). Again, Lodge (who became a Roman Catholic) attacks folk pastime indirectly when he embodies the spirit of 'Disordinate Joy' in a drunken buffoon, who 'hath all the feats of a Lord of Misrule' (at Christmas games) 'in the country'; 'his study is to coin bitter jests, or to show antic motions, or to sing bawdy songs and ballads' (*Wit's Misery*, 1596). And the playwrights themselves, Jonson especially, but Shakespeare, too, if Hamlet's views are his own, complain incessantly of the vogue of the country jig which Tarlton had introduced, and of the popularity of clowning and 'antics', defacing 'nature' on the stage.

Nevertheless, looking back on Shakespeare and even Jonson from the standpoint of the Restoration, Dryden could complain of both that 'their wit was not that of gentlemen; there was ever somewhat that was ill-bred and clownish in it, and which confessed the conversation of the authors'. If 'civility' prevailed, then, it was not without a struggle. And it was highly fortunate for literature that popular 'barbarism' proved so tenacious in the 1590s. It gave an unequalled racy vigour to common prose and the language of the stage; and it suggested some of the most fruitful themes of comedy and satire – and even, ultimately, of tragedy too.

Elizabethan literature is a literature of the spoken word. Just as oratory dominated the academic training of the humanist, so – in the age of the Reformation and popular controversy – the spoken literary forms of preaching and acting dominated the printed forms of journalism and fiction; while in poetry there was the related influence of song. Humanists like Puttenham were eager, moreover, to show that English, of its native resources, could be as 'copious, pithy, and significative' as any language of learning; and in view of the tremendous changes in sixteenth-century English, the only sure foundation for a standard literary language was in customary usage, in idiom and proverb. There was thus a constant two-way exchange between learned speech and popular, together producing the unique combination of racy tang and majestic stateliness that informs the language of Shakespeare or the Authorized Version.

An important aspect of this situation was the popular enjoyment of vigorous speech and the conscious artifice of eloquence.[10] This is evident, for example, from Harrison's remark about the beggars of his day (*The Description of Britain*, 1577):

how artificially they beg, what forcible speech, and how they select and choose out words of vehemence, whereby they do in manner conjure or adjure the goer-by to pity their cases.

It is evident, again, from Puttenham's amusement over old-fashioned mouth-fillers like 'remuneration', 'recapitulation', which 'smatch more the school of common players than of any delicate Poet' (*c.* 1585). But the same admiration for high astounding terms assured a welcome for *Tamburlaine* a year or two later; while the authors of the Marprelate tracts (1588–90) could count on stylistic parody as a popular weapon of ridicule against the bishops.

The popular hankering after 'inkhorn' language proves fatal to Dogberry and many another clown on the stage; but it was balanced by a genius for the homely and the concrete, and a pungent facility in nicknames and ridicule. Mockery was a popular art, rooted in folk pastime with its miming and dancing (as in the song of the nymphs in Peele's *Arraignment*), admiringly recorded of the heroes of jest books, and dramatized in the libellous farce jigs that delighted the London streets. Though much of it was gross or aimless, this popular 'railing' pervaded Elizabethan wit at every level, whether the wit was inspired by indignation or hatred, or simply enjoyed, as 'merriment', for its own sake. Even the puritanical Stubbes, for example, has recourse to caricature in his flourish against the enormities of feminine dress (*The Anatomy of Abuses*, 1583):

> But if *Aeolus* with his blasts, or *Neptune* with his storms chance to hit upon the crazy barque of their bruised ruffs, then they go flip-flap in the wind, like rags flying abroad, and lie upon their shoulders like the dish-clout of a slut.

The popular bent appears again, unexpectedly, in the courtly language of Puttenham; it is implicit in his conception of poetry as a means of direct emotional release, and still more in his treatment of words as physical objects, almost as creatures with a life of their own. He speaks, for example, of 'flowing words and slippery syllables'; and in his detailed analysis of classical figures of rhetoric he strives, like Wilson before him, to personify the terms themselves or to anglicize them with the aid of homely illustrations. Thus the figure *Zeugma* he names 'single supply' –

> because by one word we serve many clauses of one congruity, and may be likened to the man that serves many masters at once, but all of one country or kindred;

and another of his figures is still further dramatized, with its close linkage between word and gesture:

> when we give a mock with a scornful countenance as in some smiling sort looking aside or by drawing the lip awry, or shrinking up the nose; the Greeks called it *Micterismus*, we may term it a fleering frump, as he that said to one whose words he believed not, No doubt Sir of that . . .

Fleering frumps belong to the same Elizabethan family as Irony ('the Dry mock') or Sarcasm ('the Bitter taunt') – or the 'unsavoury similes' that Falstaff admires in Prince Hal. Journalists like Nashe, accordingly, will vaunt their talent for 'railing': 'Have I not an indifferent pretty vein in Spurgalling an Ass? If you knew how extemporal it were at this instant, and with what haste it is writ, you would say so' (*Pierce Penniless*, 1592). And even at its most polished (as with Beatrice and Benedick), Elizabethan wit has the violence of caricature, not the neat understatement of Dryden or Addison.

This popular tendency to ridicule and burlesque came to a head in the writings of Nashe (1567–1600?), who is the typical man of letters of the 1590s. Nashe first appeared as a University wit like Greene and Lodge, an admirer of Ascham, Lyly, Spenser, and Sidney; and throughout his career (1588–99) he maintained the pose of a humanist indignant at the follies of the age: 'my true vein', he claims, is 'to be *tragicus Orator*, and of all styles I most affect and strive to imitate *Aretine's*'. But there is a strong flavour of the popular jest book in most of his writing, whether controversy or fiction; and his effective contribution was to exploit the mock-heroic possibilities latent in popular forms of satire.

Three significant factors seem to have determined the bent of Nashe's style. One was the pressure of competing for the favours of a small and compact but heterogeneous public – a factor inherent in the new profession of letters. Another was the economic instability of the 1590s, affecting scholars in particular. And the third was the breach in religious opinion, marked by the success of the Marprelate tracts. By the 1590's therefore, 'civility' was no longer an ideal but a problem, while the synthesis of courtliness and Puritanism that Sidney had stood for was now in dispute. Nashe's reaction was to turn back to folk tradition for weapons of ridicule against all the new tendencies he disliked; and he soon developed as a 'young Juvenal' and 'biting Satirist', out-railing Marprelate in comic invective against 'unlearned sots' like the ballad-mongers and Stubbes, on the one hand (*Anatomy of Absurdity*, 1588); and, on the other hand, burlesquing the 'Eloquence and Civility' of Gabriel Harvey, who had both condemned the new journalism and defended the Puritans (1592–5). In addition, in *Pierce Penniless* Nashe struck a new attitude which Harvey dubbed his 'villany' – a satiric attitude combining the caustic mood of a disgruntled scholar and the mockery of the rustic Fool in folk-games or the Vice or clown of the popular stage.

Nashe, then, is another Skelton, with a vastly augmented vocabulary and a nicer sense of the incongruous. He has the double exuberance of the trained rhetorician and the popular mimic, and he excels in burlesquing formalities of language; at one point, for example, Marlovian blank verse ('the spacious volubility of a drumming decasyllabon'); at another the 'inkhornism' of Harvey – 'he never bids a man good morrow, but he makes a speech as long as a proclamation'. Harvey might retort with justice that Nashe's 'frisking pen' was schooled in the common playhouse on 'Tarlton's surmounting rhetoric'; but precisely this quality made it vigorous and representative. Nashe helped to stimulate three of the main developments in the literature of the 1590s – the rebirth of satire; the allied creation of 'humour' comedies at the end of the decade; and Shakespeare's treatment, in his comedies, of the themes of Folly and 'civility'.

The revival of satire in the 1590s accompanied the rise of professional literature.[11] 'Heavenly Spenser' himself alternates between eulogy and the satirist's indignation in his portrayal of the Court (*Colin Clout, c.* 1591); and, amid the general confusion of social standards, it seemed to be fated, as Marlowe said, that learning and poverty 'should always kiss'. Frustrated in his hopes of patronage, disgusted by the flourishing of social pretenders in City and Court alike, and more conscious than ever before both of the dignity and the insecurity of his calling, the man of letters turned to satire as a corrective of public morals through which he could also give vent to his personal discontent. Greene makes capital of his own indiscretions, as well as his acquaintance with the underworld, in his *Groat's-worth of wit, bought with a million of Repentance* (1592); and a comparable though much deeper subjective strain is the source of tragic pity in *Faustus*, where Marlowe exposes the raw nerves of the Elizabethan scholar-poet, equally dissatisfied in his servitude and his grandeur. In Davies's fashionable *Epigrams* (*c.* 1590) and the pamphlets of Nashe and Lodge, dissatisfaction gives rise to generalized satire; and the scholar-poet himself advances irritably to the foreground, surrounded by his friends and enemies – the wit and the would-be wit (or 'gull'), the melancholy gallant and the malcontent, the professional charlatan, the seedy adventurer, the travelled and Machiavellian sceptic, the usurer and the sycophant. A slightly younger group of wits model themselves directly on the conventions of Latin poetic satire, in harsh rhythms, scornful invective, and grotesque character-portraits (Donne, c. 1593–7; Hall, *Virgidemiae*,[a] 1598; Marston, *The Scourge of Villainy*, 1598); while the Cambridge trilogy of *Parnassus* plays (1598–1602) resumes the complaints of the scholar in search of patronage.

These satires were doubly significant of the growth of a professional spirit in literature, since they contained literary criticism as well as professional complaint; and even the courtly and temperate Daniel was touched by the prevailing unrest. With all its confidence in the future of English, his verse dialogue *Musophilus* (1599) shows him retreating from the optimism of a few years before. Learning, neglected by 'the great-seeming best of men', has lost its sanctity; religion is clouded by sects and opinion, while poetry has been vulgarized by 'Emulation, that proud nurse of wit'; and though Daniel, an Elizabethan Matthew Arnold, can yet affirm that poetry has a high calling of imaginative enlightenment, he turns aside from the present, with regretful stoicism, to write for himself, for posterity, and for the understanding few. Unlike Daniel, however, others were heated and probably libellous; so that the year of *Musophilus* saw a general ban imposed on the printing of satires, while the bishops, who had encouraged retorts to Martin Marprelate ten years previously, now called in for burning all copies of Nashe's and Harvey's pamphlets, with recent verse satires such as those of Marston and Hall.

Humanism in satire involved a change from the medieval outlook still current in Barclay's translation (1508) of *The Ship of Fools*, or even in Gascoigne's *Steel Glass* (1576) – a change from denunciation to irony, from the tone of the preacher to that of the wit. Yet, since they are attacking the social pretensions interwined with 'civility', the satirists of the 1590s follow Nashe in reverting to popular mockery and the theme of Folly. For the English contemporaries of *Don Quixote*, Folly was a theme of complex associations, ranging from folk-games to journalism, poetic satire, and the stage.[12] It recalled the duality of the simpleton, the duality of the public jester who is fondled and buffeted in turn, the duality of a universal human

---

[a] 'a harvest of rods' (on this Latin title, see Hall's *Poems*, ed. A. Davenport (1950), 159).

impulse. In the early Renaissance, Folly had been presented either as 'the eighth deadly sin' of Barclay and the Morality writers, or else, with Erasmus, as man's presiding genius, binding him in superstition and selfishness, but also spurring him to heroism, to love, and to poetry. And the later sixteenth century had sharpened these contrasts. The Puritans condemned the paganism of country sports, like the May-games, with their primitive leader, the Fool; while popular feeling reacted against 'civility' through the heroes of rogue stories and jest books, through farces and jigs.

This reaction reached the theatres in the 1580s, when Tarlton and Kempe replaced the Morality Vice with clown-commentators reminiscent of Piers Plowman, the typical countryman. One such clown, for example, – a distant forerunner to the role of Kent in *Lear* – is 'a plain man of the country' in the pseudo-chronicle play *A Knack to Know a Knave ... With Kempe's applauded Merriments of the Men of Gotham* (1592). His name is Honesty; and he is given the part of unmasking and punishing an up-to-date set of rogues. Hence, while Puritans might exclaim against the 'craft, mischief, deceits and filthiness' of popular entertainment, journalists like Chettle and Nashe could defend it as 'anatomizing ... all cunning drifts over-gilded with outward holiness', and could taunt its opponents with the threat of a stage-play containing 'a merriment of the Usurer and the Devil' (Nashe, *Pierce Penniless*). And meanwhile the stage clown was gaining sophistication from the wily servants of Latin comedy. 'Better a witty fool than a foolish wit', says Feste (*Twelfth Night*, 1600); much of the comedy of the 1590s is a variation on this antithesis, alternately contrasting and identifying the wit and the fool.

Here, again, Nashe's writings contained suggestive links between humanism and popular traditions. *Summer's Last Will and Testament* (1592) – the only surviving play wholly of his authorship – is a topical satire under the forms of revelry and burlesque. It pleads for the patronage of letters and defends the seasonal pastimes of the countryside as against the Puritan arguments for thrift; while, on the other hand, it deplores the wasteful extravagance of many courtiers. Nashe attempts to reconcile these contraries through a prolonged and lively allegorical debate, which balances Nature's excess in her seasons of scarcity against the excesses of her abundance. But he has been visited too long by the classical dream of heroic grandeur and ideal beauty to rest entirely content in this traditional reconciliation; and in 'Adieu, farewell earth's bliss', the famous dirge for Summer the dying king, he rises to a moment of tragic intensity, finely poised between the fear of death and the acceptance, between magnificence and decay. In the main, however, the tone of the 'show' is set by the jester, who is named Will Summers, with a punning reference to the famous court fool of Henry VIII. Will Summers presents and criticizes the rest of the play; turns the debates into intellectual switchback; breaks from allegory into topical jesting; and breaks from seriousness into absurdity and inconsequence. He thus provides at once a symbol of Folly and a mask of detachment for the author.

Literary clowning (or 'villany') was also the mode of Nashe's prose. In *Pierce Penniless, His Supplication to the Devil* (written just before the 'show'), the substance of the satire descends from the Moralities and *The Ship of Fools*; but Nashe himself, as Pierce, now adopts the manner of the Vices and servant clowns of popular comedy. 'Malcontent' in his poverty, Pierce turns to the Devil, the arch-patron of success, with a mock petition denouncing the parvenus and impostors of contemporary London as fresh incarnations of the Seven Deadly Sins. The petition is delivered, at the universal rendezvous, St Paul's, to a minor devil resembling Greene's 'cony-catchers' [*confidence tricksters*], 'a neat pedantical fellow, in form of a Citizen', with whom Pierce then holds discourse on the subject of demonology. Pungently topical, Nashe's pamphlet found several imitators, such as Lodge's *Wit's Misery* (1596) (a satire embedded in a theological tract); but to Harvey, at least, there was something 'mad-brained . . . or blasphemous, or monstrous' in Nashe's 'impudency' of tone. Not only was the older man offended in person; he was disgusted that 'a certain pragmatical secret, called Villany' should bring fame to new 'whipsters in the world' like Nashe; and he was scornfully indignant that 'one smart pamphlet of knavery' should be preferred to 'ten blundering volumes of the nine Muses' (*Pierce's Supererogation*, 1593). Nashe stuck to pamphlets of knavery, however; and Jack Wilton, the mischievous page and hero of his only novel, is another exponent of Villany. *The Unfortunate Traveller* (1594), where he relates his adventures, disavows any serious purpose; it begins as a jest book, continues as a mock chronicle, and concludes as an experiment in Italianate melodrama. Another variant of the literary clown appears in Nashe's *Lenten Stuff* (1599), his last pamphlet, a comic extravaganza in praise of Yarmouth and red herring, which includes a mock-heroic version of the tale of Hero and Leander.

Nashe's treatment of 'humours' in *Pierce Penniless* is characteristic of his methods in transforming allegory into farce. 'Humour' had previously signified irrational egotism ('a jealous humour', 'a covetous humour'); but fashionable usage had dignified the term. 'As 'tis generally received in these days', Jonson scathingly explains, 'it is a monster bred in a man by self-love and affectation, and fed by folly' (*Every Man in His Humour*, III i; 1598); later he added – 'a gentlemanlike monster, bred in the special gallantry of our time'. Nashe assails this gentlemanlike monster with caricature, with 'unsavoury similes', with exuberant and sophisticated mockery. In Pierce's Supplication against Pride, for example, there is the social upstart who 'scorneth learning':

All malcontent sits the greasy son of a Clothier, and complains (like a decayed Earl) of the ruin of ancient houses ... He will be humorous, forsooth, and have a brood of fashions by himself. Sometimes (because Love commonly wears the livery of Wit) he will be an *Inamorato Poeta*, and sonnet a whole quire of paper in praise of Lady *Swine-snout*, his yellow fac'd mistress, and wear a feather of her rainbeaten fan for a favour, like a forehorse ...

To this drooping student of gentility, Nashe also gives the features of the classical braggart and those of the pretended traveller, the 'dapper Jack', who has barely crossed the Channel, yet will 'wring his face about, as a man would stir a mustard pot, and talk English through the teeth ...' Nashe's mimicry is savage, because the self-willed 'humours' that appear simply follies on the surface reveal, beneath the surface, the Seven Deadly Sins. The Devil himself, Pierce is told, is held by the sceptics of the time to be only an allegory (like Dame Fortune), or else 'only a pestilent humour in a man, of pleasure, profit, or policy, that violently carries him away to vanity, villainy, or monstrous hypocrisy'. Pierce, too, seems not immune to this scepticism; so that his 'humorists' become the grotesque caricatures of the shifting and ambiguous values of his world. The 'counterfeit politician', whom Nashe consigns to the Ship of Fools, and the atheist scholar (of Ralegh's circle); the thriftless young heir at the Inns of Court, 'his Mother's Darling', who 'falls in a quarrelling humour

with his fortune, because she made him not King of the Indies';
Mistress Minx, the merchant's 'simpering wife' (who 'will eat no
cherries forsooth but when they are at twenty shillings a pound'),
and the 'curious Dames' who plaster themselves with paint and oint-
ment 'to enlarge their withered beauties' – they are all of them bogus
as well as sinfully proud. And finally, anticipating Jonson's *The
Alchemist*, there is the quack antiquarian and the equally 'fantastical
fool' who buys his rubbish: 'This is the disease of our newfangled
humorists, that they know not what to do with their wealth.'

In his social attitude, then, in his language and satiric methods,
Nashe's writing reveals the close and complex relationship between
the humanism of the 1590s and popular traditions. The 'humour'
comedies of Chapman, Jonson, and Marston at the end of the decade
show a further phase of the same relationship; they follow directly
from Nashe and the verse satirists.

Jonson's scorn of false civility was much more controlled than
Nashe's, more searching and inclusive, and more scholarly. But he
began by collaborating with Nashe in a satire of 1597 (now lost),
for which they were both in trouble; and his writing springs from the
same background. In his first important play, *Every Man in His
Humour* (first version, 1598), the central comic trio recall Nashe's
composite caricature of the Pride that 'scorneth learning'; and,
though Jonson refined his rhetorical technique, it is still closely allied
to popular Morality and farce. In *Every Man out of His Humour* (1599)
– virtually a critical manifesto – Jonson distinguishes the monomania
of genuine 'humour' from what is merely eccentricity. Henceforth
almost all his characters are blind instruments of a dominant passion,
avarice or vanity, envy or lust, or, above all, the speculative passion
for quick money and for social aggrandizement. They are depicted
with minute observation, with painstaking scholarship, with a superb
flexibility in the psychological development of the dramatic situation. Yet for Jonson, a humour character (as their names often show)
is still allegorical, a vehicle for moral judgement, not a rounded
portrait; not so much a man possessed by a quality as the quality
itself embodied in the man. 'He that will truly set down a man in a
figured story', writes Jonson's friend, the lawyer-poet John Hoskins,
'must first learn truly to set down an humour, a passion, a virtue, a
vice, and therein keeping decent proportion add but names and knit

together the accidents[a] and encounters' (1599). Hoskins here is praising Sidney's *Arcadia*; but the same approach to the construction of characters, in terms of allegory and rhetoric, was fundamental in the theatre as well, and particularly in satire. Commonly, a whole scene is constructed so as to exhibit a 'humorist' who caricatures himself by his behaviour, dress, and language; and Jonson excels in making such satire general. One of his gulls is advised, for example (again in Nashe's terms), to 'give over housekeeping in the country, and live altogether in the city amongst gallants . . .' (*Every Man out of His Humour*, I. i):

> You must endeavour to feed cleanly at your ordinary [tavern], sit melancholy, and pick your teeth when you cannot speak: and when you come to plays, be humorous, look with a good starch'd face, and ruffle your brow like a new boot, laugh at nothing but your own jests, or else as the noblemen laugh. That's a special grace you must observe . . .

Another method of Jonson's is to deploy his figures in combination, like the elegant Fastidious Brisk (ancestor to a long line of Restoration fops), who is used to mock one gull and tantalize another while his own absurdity is paraded with exquisite mimicry:

> FAST. 'Fore heavens, his humour arrides me exceedingly.
> CARLO BUFFONE. Arrides you!
> FAST. Ay, pleases me: a pox on't! I am so haunted at the court, and at my lodging, with your refined choice spirits, that it makes me clean of another garb, another sheaf, I know not how! I cannot frame me to your harsh vulgar phrase, 'tis against my genius . . .
>
> (*E.M.o.o.H.H.*, I. i)

These methods are supplemented with set character sketches by the wits, brief formal essays modelled on Theophrastus, like that of Carlo the buffoon on the embittered satirist Macilente:

> SOGLIARDO. Is he a scholar, or a soldier?
> CARLO. Both, both: a lean mongrel, he looks as if he were chop-fallen, with barking at other men's good fortunes: 'ware how you offend him; he carries oil and fire in his pen, will scald where it drops: his spirit is like powder, quick, violent; he'll blow a man up with a jest: I fear him worse than a rotten wall does the cannon; shake an hour after at the report. Away, come not near him.
>
> (I. i)

a *Accidents* (e.g. of time and place) as distinct from *substances*; the writer has Aristotle in mind. (*Directions for Speech and Style*, ed. H. H. Hudson (Princeton, 1935); xii, 41, 93.)

This speech serves the additional purpose of disclosing a dramatic antagonism; and Carlo has the essayist's terse mannerism of style. But his startling ejaculation of images from common life also owes something to Nashe's caricatures; while the portrait as a whole is a personification of Envy, traditionally – as in Langland – lean, quivering, and murderous. Jonson resorts to traditional allegory again in *Cynthia's Revels* (1600), where, in the closing masque, 'each of these Vices, being to appear before Cynthia [Elizabeth], would seem other than indeed they are; and therefore assumes the most neighbouring Virtues as their masking habit'. The conventions of courtly revels, with their fine-spun myths of gallantry such as Lyly's *Endymion* (1588), are thus inverted by means of a device familiar from the Moralities. The latter represent for Jonson the permanent groundwork of Nature beneath the flimsy if glittering surface of civility.

Though their plots are often taken from Latin or Italian sources, the construction of humour plays follows the same traditions. Jonson was eager to reform dramatic technique, and to move part way at least towards the classical position of Sidney by cutting out aimless clowning and the rambling construction of popular romance and farce. His great technical achievement was to unify a handful of separate actions, each exhibiting a distinct humour, so that they close together on a common catastrophe in the breathless ascending spirals of *Volpone* (1606) and *The Alchemist* (1610). In this sense, he is both neo-classical and realistic. The business of comedy, he says, is to 'shew an image of the times', an image of London. But, he adds, it is also to 'sport' with human follies (*Every Man in His Humour*, prologue to revised version, *c*. 1605); and photographic realism is foreign to his conception. His greatness lies in the way he used the possibilities of his own theatre. His scene-construction, for example, continues to reflect the popular desire for pageantry and multiple actions – as he indicates in *Every Man out of His Humour* (II. i) when his spokes-man explains why the fools have been brought on the stage in groups and not successively:

. . . is it not an object of more state to behold the scene full, and relieved with variety of speakers to the end, than to see a vast empty stage, and the actors come in by one, as if they were dropt down with a feather into the eye of the spectators?

Equally, his plots are so contrived that the realism of single episodes is adjusted to the developing of a rhetorical climax. It is not his purpose to administer moral correction to the humorists right away, explains the same spokesman; but it is not his purpose, either, simply to reflect life as it is:

> Why, therein his art appears most full of lustre, and approacheth nearest the life; especially when in the flame and height of their humours, they are laid flat, it fills the eye better, and with more contentment. How tedious a sight were it to behold a proud exalted tree lopt and cut down by degrees, when it might be fell'd in a moment! and to set the axe to it before it came to that pride and fulness were as not to have it grow.
>
> (IV. vi)

Jonson therefore keeps buffoonery for his climax, as the most telling means, provided it be made relevant, of flattening the humorists. In the first version of *Every Man in His Humour*, for example, Bobadill the counterfeit soldier ('in a large motley coat') and Mathew the counterfeit poet, with the ashes of his verses, are to mourn all day at the market cross, 'and at night both together sing some ballad of repentance very piteously' (v. i); in *Every Man out of His Humour*, Carlo Buffone the impudent jester has his mouth sealed with wax (v. iv; an incident said to be taken from real life); and Crispinus – or Marston – in *The Poetaster* (v. i; 1601) is compelled to vomit his indigestible vocabulary into a basin.

This latter episode belongs to the complicated and acrimonious 'War of the Theatres' (1599–1601), in which Jonson was tilting against Marston and Dekker; but symbolic punishments of this kind were general in satire – for instance, in Marston's pageant of the 'Ship of Fools' at the end of *The Fawn* (c. 1605). Humour satire remains closely attached, then, to the complex tradition of the Fool, as it had been modified by Nashe, with its background of farcical revelry and pastime. Burlesque and practical joking fill a large place in Chapman's comedies, such as *An Humorous Day's Mirth* (1597), or *May Day* (c. 1602), with its reminiscence of folk custom, or *All Fools* (1604); and the master-intriguers of the humour plays, who jerk the humorists into action like puppets, again recall Nashe's treatment of the Fool, or literary Villanist, as satiric mouthpiece. They are either scholar-wits with a background of academic revelry, like the young poet and the eccentric Justice in *Every Man in His Humour*, or else

compounds of jestbook rogue and Latin comic servant, like Jonson's
Brainworm in the same play or Marston's Cocledemoy in *The Dutch
Courtesan* (1604). The vigorous clowning of the humour plays – which
they share with Shakespeare's farces – is compatible with vigour and
agility of thought; but not with the polite restraint that governed the
classicism of the following century.

On the other hand, the strictly humanist intention behind them
should not be underrated. In their many discussions of poetry and the
ideal poet, they share some of the classical impulse behind Chapman's
translation of the *Iliad* (1598) and Daniel's *Musophilus* (1599). From
his study of Latin satirists, Marston turns immediately to the exalted
declamations on poetic rapture and poetic fantasy in his early
comedies and the first of his tragedies (1599–1601). And Jonson is
even more deliberate in his portraits of the true poet – partly, but not
wholly, justifications of himself – culminating in *The Poetaster*, which
is set, significantly, in Augustan Rome. The poet is vindicated in his
public role as the teacher of mankind, qualified by inspiration, by
learning, and by judgement; he is 'the interpreter and arbiter of
nature', says Jonson again, 'a teacher of things divine no less than
human, a master of manners' (*Volpone*; dedication to the Universities); and it is this, his magisterial office, that makes of him a satirist.
Moreover, though Jonson is less fascinated by the poet's rapture than
either Marston or Chapman, his poetic satirist, as a dramatic character,
comes from the heroic world of Plutarch and Seneca. He has the
stamp of tragedy, like Shakespeare's Brutus; a man apart, the complete man of the Stoic philosophers, unshaken by poverty or insult,
firm as a rock in his intellectual composure:

> Lo, here the man, celestial Delia,
> Who (like a circle bounded in itself)
> Contains as much as man in fulness may.
> Lo, here the man, who not of usual earth,
> But of that nobler and more precious mould
> Which Phoebus' self doth temper, is composed; . . .
> (*Cynthia's Revels*, v. iii)

Both Jonson and Marston are at pains, therefore, to separate the
genuine poetic satirist from the presumptuous fakes who surround
him. Macilente is contrasted with the parasitic buffoon, Horace with
the poetaster Crispinus and the libertine Ovid. There is thus a

notable shift of attitude from Nashe's Villany. The poet as hero is distinguished from the poet as Fool; and some at least of the links with popular tradition are snapped.

Along this line, then, the tendency of satire about 1600 was to move away from popular interests towards tragedy and the philosophical problems of humanism. Stoicism, for Jonson, not only marks the satirist: it is the public virtue of classical Rome in his tragedies of *Sejanus* (1603) and of *Catiline* (1611), where the stoical orator Cicero is the saviour of the Commonwealth. And the stoical man, again, is the protagonist of Chapman's tragedies, as with *Bussy D'Ambois* (1604) or the Cato of *Caesar and Pompey*. Yet in two important respects at least this development from satire towards tragedy was still coloured by popular tradition. The many-sided conception of Folly reacts adversely, for example, on some of the more ambitious stage satirists, captious representatives of 'civility' gone sour: Shakespeare's Jaques, eager, in his 'humorous sadness', for the freedom of motley, reveals himself a Fool in more senses than he intends (*As You Like It*, II. vii, IV. i; 1599); Jonson's Macilente is stained with the humour of envy; and the austere philosopher in Marston's *What You Will* (1601) is made futile and ridiculous. And secondly, even in tragedy the popular tradition of savage farce was still continuously active. A humour, as Nashe had seen, could be sinister as well as bogus, diabolic as well as grotesque; in its gross distortion of common humanity, the tragic and the comic were latent together. The plot of Jonson's *Sejanus* – the conspiracy and falling-out of two rogues in league against society – becomes the ground-plan of his major comedies; while Chapman's tempestuous *Bussy D'Ambois* follows closely, both in date and manner, on his most elaborate study of a humorous fantastic in *Monsieur D'Olive* (1604). And Jonson and Chapman had already been preceded by Shakespeare's *Hamlet* in exploring the affinities between the terrible and the absurd. It was deeply characteristic of Shakespeare's public that, despite classical precept to the contrary, their tragedy and their comedy should overlap and interfuse.

There are striking differences in this respect between the humour satires and the comedies of Shakespeare (which divided his interest with histories during his first ten years as a playwright). Shakespeare responds to more of life, and responds with more active sympathy.

He ranges more widely over land and sea; his people seem rounded, spontaneous personalities; and the mingling of farce and near-tragic romance, typical of his comic plots from *The Comedy of Errors* (1592) onwards, is essentially lyrical in effect, not satiric. Nevertheless, Shakespeare shares some of the main interests of the satirists. His comedies are preoccupied with defining and celebrating genuine 'civility', tangled in the web of pretension and injustice; and for Shakespeare, most of all, the problem is illuminated by the unconfinable light of Folly, flickering from dry mockery to the mysterious depths of the imagination.

Revels and pastime are prominent in Shakespeare's comedies as important links between the stage and the expression of 'civility' in actual life. *Love's Labour's Lost*, for example, is the comedy in which he first showed his scope (1595),[13] and here the main action – the wooing of the Princess of France and her three ladies by the King of Navarre and his three lords – is adapted consistently to the pattern of the masque in which it culminates:

> For revels, dances, masks and merry hours,
> Forerun fair Love, strewing her way with flowers
> (IV. iii)

The masque is followed by a comic variant, the village schoolmaster's pageant of the Nine Worthies, which unites the main and sub-plots together. Thus the scheme of the play forms a courtly entertainment; while its verbal arabesque of wit, its rhyming and sonnets, and the dance-like patterning of its dialogue suggest the influence of courtly writers like Lyly. But beneath this lies another, more complex pattern, where Shakespeare anticipates *Cynthia's Revels*, and may in turn have been indebted to *Summer's Last Will* and to Nashe – a versatile topical burlesque on punctilio and pedantry, on the high ambitions of scholarship and the ceremonial of courtly love:

> Folly in fools bears not so strong a note
> As foolery in the wise, when wit doth dote.
> (V. ii)

The ladies and the 'villanist' Lord Biron are the chief agents of this satire, which counterbalances the masque with references to seasonal country pastimes. When, for example, the lords make their rash vow

– soon to be broken – to pursue fame through three years of academic seclusion from women, Biron reminds the others darkly that 'The spring is near, when green geese*a* are a-breeding' (I. i. 97): the scene where their common lapse is involuntarily disclosed is 'All hid, all hid; an old infant play' (IV. iii): and their confident plan of wooing under the disguise of their masque is 'dashed' 'like a Christmas comedy' (V. ii). These references are extended in broader imagery of the seasons, representing the fitness of things, as in *Summer's Last Will:*

> At Christmas I no more desire a rose
> Than wish a snow in May's new-fangled shows;
> But like of each thing that in season grows;
>
> (I. i.)

and similarly the play ends with a song of debate between winter and spring. This contrast of the seasons has already been deepened in a series of moral and emotional contrasts, which lead to the love-service imposed on the crestfallen wits (V. ii) – to 'jest a twelvemonth in hospital' before they can be accepted.

The wits are made Fools, for 'justice always whirls in equal measure' (IV. iii). When love forces Biron to drop his sophisticated jesting, in addition to his unwilling vow of austerity, he renounces the 'spruce' garb of the courtier – 'Taffeta phrases, silken terms precise, Three-pil'd hyperboles' – in favour of 'russet yeas and honest kersey noes', the costume of Tarlton and country clowns (V. ii). And the most pregnant comment on the play's humours is given to the clown Costard (who recalls the Fools of country jigs in his rivalry in love with Don Armado, the 'refined traveller of Spain'). When Nathaniel the curate stumbles in his part during the pageant of the Nine Worthies, as the wits had stumbled in their masque, Costard steps forward with kindly village shrewdness:

> There, an't shall please you: a foolish mild man; an honest man, look you, and soon dashed! He is a marvellous neighbour, in sooth, and a very good bowler; but, for Alisander, – alas! you see how 'tis, – a little o'erparted.
>
> (V. ii)

This image of the actor 'o'erparted' in his mighty role remained profoundly suggestive for Shakespeare, not only in the comedy of Bot-

a alluding (1) to rash inexperience, (2) to 'light wenches', and (3) to Green Goose Fair, a Whitsun festivity.

tom that followed, but in the tragic portrayal, at his full maturity, of Lear and Macbeth.

Although Shakespeare's characters are more sharply individualized after *Love's Labour's Lost*, he continues to dwell upon the symbolism of revelry and of Folly. The varied comic themes of *A Midsummer Night's Dream* (possibly first prepared as a wedding-play, 1595–6) are unified by Theseus when he expounds the nature of poetic fantasy:

> The lunatic, the lover, and the poet
> Are of imagination all compact . . .
>
> (v. i)

Hence Titania's infatuation with Bottom is no digression, but the symbolic centre of the comedy. Again, the folly of Dogberry in *Much Ado* (1598) unconsciously exposes the deceptions and self-deceptions of the serious actors, who are conducted through scenes of masquerade and 'infant play' after the fashion of *Love's Labour's Lost*. Almost the whole range of Folly as counterpart to 'civility' appears in *As You Like It* (1599), with Jaques, Touchstone, Corin, and the pastoral lovers. And in *Twelfth Night* (1600), last and finest of the romantic comedies, symbol and reality are combined. 'Would you have a love-song, or a song of good life?'; the main theme, of varied attitudes towards love, is profoundly coloured by the secondary theme of revelry as the direct subject of moral conflict. Feste the clown touches the comedy at every point, even in its melancholy. In *Romeo and Juliet* (1595) comedy and love-story had been kept distinct; in *Twelfth Night* they are intermingled.

Moreover, the figures in Shakespeare's comedies who seem most inspired with a life of their own are still closely attached to stage conventions. His vivacious heroines are attuned to the custom of acting women's parts by boys. And the most living and complex of his men's parts in comedy are still shaped by the multiform tradition of Vice, Jester and Fool – Biron, Benedick, Jaques, for example: Petruchio in *The Taming of the Shrew* (1594) at one end of the scale; Shylock (1596), despite his almost tragic intensity, at the other. In the unique Falstaff (1597–8), long the most popular of Shakespeare's characters, there are two conflicting sides of the symbolism of Folly; he is at once the satirical Villanist and 'that trunk of humours, . . . that reverend vice, that gray iniquity' from the Morality plays. And conversely, Feste, gay and melancholy, is the most completely humanized of Elizabethan clowns.

The stage tradition of Folly is essential even to *Hamlet* (1601), where Shakespeare seems to reveal himself more deeply and more urgently than in anything he had written before. Hamlet's 'madness' may have come from Belleforest (*Histoires Tragiques*, 1570), or the lost Hamlet tragedy by Kyd (*c.* 1589). But it neither resembles the craftily feigned madness of Belleforest's Hamlet nor the frenzy leading to vengeance of Kyd's Hieronymo in *The Spanish Tragedy*, to which Shakespeare was indebted for the machinery of his plot. Its importance is chiefly psychological; in dramatic form, it comes from the conventions of satire. The world of the play is a corrupted world of Renaissance civility; and Hamlet, the stage figure, is as much a humanist who has turned to satire as an avenging son frustrated by melancholia. His friendship with Horatio shows his leaning towards the stoicism of the day; and the mood and topic of his formal speeches are those of contemporary satirists (of Marston, for example), from the invective against woman's frailty in his first soliloquy to his baiting of Osric's humour at the end. His disgust with the world is more savage, but no more effective, than Jaques'; and when his meeting with the Ghost betrays his terrible inadequacy, he too can only determine to 'put an antic disposition on'. In his dealings with the court he becomes very largely the Fool of popular tradition, with his snatches of ballad and proverb, his dark riddling wisdom, his mockery and irresponsibility, his sudden violent mischief. But while Folly in the comedies shows civility and practical reason inverted, in *Hamlet* they are agonizingly broken into fragments. The supreme 'antic' is Death itself (IV. iii, v. i), the skull of Yorick the jester in the graveyard scene. One by one, in the tradition of the Dance of Death, Hamlet reduces the murderer, the politician, the courtier, the land-purchasing lawyer, the court lady, even Alexander himself, to the same ignoble ending as the clown:

... Now get you to my lady's chamber, and tell her, let her paint an inch thick, to this favour she must come; make her laugh at that.

This is the final biting mockery of traditional satire against the disguises of civility. And, while it is tragically poignant as well as grotesque, the pathos is related chiefly to the memory of Yorick the jester, of whom Hamlet has been speaking with unusual tenderness and affection.

In *Hamlet*, however, the conventions of the theatre are turned to a new use. Shakespeare now dwells on contrasts in the midst of likeness, strangeness in familiarity, using the external roles and symbols of the theatre to suggest the inner life of his people in their uniqueness and complexity. Thus Hamlet, in his first dialogue, stresses the differences between his inward sorrow and other 'customary suits' and 'shows of grief', such as the black cloak he is wearing (I. ii). His contact with the Player, again (II. ii), serves to silhouette his own painful inability to command his feelings to customary purpose and to 'drown the stage with tears'; and when for a moment, by Ophelia's grave (V. i), he does attain the towering rant of the avenging hero – 'This is I,/Hamlet the Dane' – then the effect is, designedly, a tragical discord. The theme of Folly, in particular, is thus adapted to new ends. One of Marston's heroes, situated like Hamlet, envies the Fool in conventional terms for his 'patent of immunities, . . . not capable of passion' (*Antonio's Revenge*, IV. i: 1600). Hamlet, on the contrary, is anything but impassive; his fooling only stresses his isolation; and the effect is largely as Ophelia perceives it (III. i), 'Like sweet bells, jangled out of tune, and harsh'. There is a profoundly suggestive disparity, or dualism, between the man and his mask. So, too, with the madness of Ophelia herself (IV. v): her stage business with the flowers and the indecorum of her songs convey by contrast the heartbreak that has driven a girl of courtly breeding back to her memories of childhood and the naïve grossness she has learned from her country-bred maids. And yet the conventional values in her part are retained at the same time. The disorder in her songs symbolizes the disorder in her world; their impersonal simplicity, on the other hand, makes a poignant contrast with the oppressive atmosphere of the Danish court.

Hamlet, then, marks a turning-point in the drama. It gives a new intensity to the traditions of melodrama and satire, relates them more intimately to the problems of the humanist, and keeps the stage custom of animated courtly revelling as an ironic background for tragedy. Above all, it reaches a new dimension in the art of the theatre, in its exploration of personal consciousness. It shows a consciousness strained to breaking; but there is still the sense of normality in life, and continuity, that Shakespeare could express on the stage in terms of popular tradition.

Rhetoric and Poetry

Elizabethan poetry is neither 'classical' nor 'romantic'. It lacks the restraint and economy, the mental repose of the finest classical art; but equally, it joins 'labour and learning' to 'enthusiasm' – in Spenser's terms – in a manner that divides it from the Romantics. Following the main tradition of antiquity and the Middle Ages, it is addressed to Reason as a universal moral guide. It is composed on the assumption, barely questioned until the nineteenth century, that the function of poetry is to teach by delighting – to 'interpret nature' and to influence men's actions. Poetry, says Puttenham, is 'more eloquent and rhetorical' than prose because, with its music and imagery, it 'sooner inveigleth the judgment of man'; and for Jonson, writing in his private commonplace-book, it is 'a dulcet, and gentle Philosophy, which leads on, and guides us by the hand to Action, with a ravishing delight, and incredible Sweetness' (*Discoveries*, c. 1620–35). Such a conception gives high place to the senses and the emotions; but an equal one, at least, to the training in formal logic which the poet and his readers shared throughout their education. The Elizabethan poet is continually reasoning, persuading, demonstrating analogies and logical connections; even his imagery and his rhythm are marshalled into argument. He is 'the nearest borderer upon the Orator'; and 'the duty and office of Rhetoric', according, for example, to Bacon, 'is to apply Reason to Imagination for the better moving of the will' (*The Advancement of Learning*, 1605). Rhetoric was one of the few branches of contemporary learning that the great Chancellor found not deficient.

This attitude to literature, part classical, part medieval, was shaped by the principles of 'decorum'. Decorum meant consistency and fitness of style, every detail in a composition being suited to its purpose, occasion, audience, its material, characters, and formal conventions. It might also carry with it the Neoplatonic taste for symmetrical 'proportion' transmitted from the Italy of Raphael by such books as Castiglione's *Courtier*. But in general, 'seemliness' of structure and language had a far wider bearing. Puttenham, for example, would trace it to the 'just correspondency' implanted by Nature between the human mind and appetites and the sensible world (*Art*, III. xxiii); while Hoskins makes even plainer the ideal relationship between Nature and the arts of speech (*Directions for ... Style*, 1599):

The order of God's creatures in themselves is not only admirable and glorious, but eloquent; then he that could apprehend the consequence of things, in their truth, and utter his apprehensions as truly, were a right orator.

To observe decorum, then, was to follow Nature; while the very act of doing so 'artificially' demonstrated the rational nature of man. It might be hazardous to press the latter argument too boldly, as Polixenes finds in *The Winter's Tale* (IV. iv); nevertheless, confidence in the root attachment between Art and Nature was vital to the Renaissance poet.

Rhetoric not only governs the larger and graver kinds of Elizabethan poetry, such as philosophical poems, or heroic narratives, or satires; it also governs pastoral (which becomes a variant of allegory), familiar verse letters, and even elegies and lyrics. Donne was by no means the only poet to philosophize in love. Where a modern reader, accustomed to romanticism, might expect to find the appearance of spontaneous feeling alone, he finds instead some of the favoured devices that were grouped together under the heading of Amplification – making the most of one's theme – the best means, according to Wilson's *Art of Rhetoric*, for 'apt moving of affections'. Amplification includes 'vehemency of words', 'heaping of words and sentences [*proverbs, aphorisms*] together', hyperbole, antithesis, and a number of other figures.[14] Its prominence in theory and practice is significant of the temper of Elizabethan verse, always concerned with 'raising the mind', as Campian puts it (1602), 'to a more high and lofty conceit'. But this must be done 'aptly', by the aid of reasoning, not by mere agitation or intensity of feeling. Imagery should be public, not introspective. The logic of the matter is described again by Hoskins, when he explains that 'to amplify and illustrate are two the chiefest ornaments of eloquence'. These ornaments are functional; they 'gain of men's minds two the chiefest advantages, admiration [*astonishment*] and belief':

For how can you commend a thing more acceptably to our attention than by telling us it is extraordinary and by showing us it is evident? There is no looking at a comet if it be either little or obscure, and we love and look on the sun above all stars for these two excellencies, his greatness, his clearness; such in speech is amplification and illustration . . .

To require a rational structure for emotions seems almost as foreign to modern habits of thought as to link the evident with the extraordinary; yet this rhetorical approach led to many of the splendours of Elizabethan poetry, if also to its many excesses.

Sidney's *Astrophel and Stella* (written *c.* 1580) was hailed as the mirror of passionate melancholy (Nashe, *Preface*, 1591), and its publication released a flood of Petrarchan sonnet sequences. It runs through the whole gamut of the self-dramatizing lover, with his ecstasies of hope and despair, of reproach and entreaty, of 'living deaths, dear wounds, fair storms, and freezing fires'; and Sidney's drama, like Petrarch's, is intensified by the conflict between earthly love and the poet's religion. But, again as in Petrarch, personal feeling leads directly to the humanist problem of Art and eloquence. Sidney may reject the surface tricks of rhetoric for the heartfelt 'forcibleness' of passion:

> . . . in Stella's face I read
> What Love and Beauty be, then all my deed
> But copying is, what in her Nature writes.
> (Sonnet III: 'Let dainty wits cry
> on the Sisters nine')

But this chiefly means that Stella is the Platonic Idea of goodness, which all true Art is bound to reflect; while, even on a lower plane, mere verbal trickery is insufficiently persuasive. His own outcries to Stella are models of Amplification. For example, Sonnet LXIV, opposing love to active wisdom, is an argument in a debate; and Hoskins, who took most of his quotations from Sidney's *Arcadia*, could have used the octet for Amplification by means of 'division', and the sestet for amplifying both by 'progression' and by comparison of contraries, 'the most flourishing way of comparison';

> No more, my dear, no more these counsels try;
> O give my passions leave to run their race;
> Let Fortune lay on me her worst disgrace;
> Let folk o'ercharged with brain against me cry;
> Let clouds bedim my face, break in mine eye;
> Let me no steps but of lost labour trace;
> Let all the earth with scorn recount my case –

But do not will me from my love to fly.
I do not envy Aristotle's wit,
Nor do aspire to Caesar's bleeding fame,
Nor aught do care though some above me sit,
Nor hope nor wish another course to frame,
But that which once may win thy cruel heart:
Thou art my wit and thou my virtue art.

Far from clogging it, the forensic turn of the sonnet, adroitly be-littling the opposing case, gives it urgency and a delightful poise. And Sidney's language is strictly in decorum, with its clearness and energy, and its compact 'illustrations' of learning and government.

In rhythmical movement, too, Sidney's poetry is typical of the age. Rhyme and metre are made conspicuously regular, partly in reaction against the clumsiness of the preceding decades, but chiefly for the sake of emphasis. Elizabethan experiments with sonnets and stanza forms were designed to produce flowing rhetorical units, varied in course and length according to the argument, but leading (as with Sidney's eighth and last lines in his sonnet) to what Daniel calls 'the apt planting the sentence where it may best stand to hit' and 'the certain close of delight with the full body of a just period well carried'. Daniel's *Defence of Rhyme* (c. 1603) makes general decorum the criterion of versification; 'is it not more pleasing to Nature', he asks, '. . . to have these closes, rather than not know where to end, or how far to go, especially seeing our passions are often without measure?'

To impose a form on measureless passions was almost a moral duty for Sidney's generation. *Astrophel and Stella* exalts passion, but only by demonstrating its agreement with civility – 'Thou art my wit and thou my virtue art'. So, too, the first books of his *Arcadia* confirm that love leads to active virtue; while his critical *Apology* does the like for literature. Admittedly, he contends, the secular poet may flatter the senses, making 'the too much loved earth more lovely'; but even in this he affords an ethical demonstration:

with no small argument to the incredulous of that first accursed fall of Adam, since our erected wit maketh us know what perfection is, and yet our infected will keepeth us from reaching unto it.

This Neoplatonic line of thought promises release from emotional conflicts to Sidney, as also to the far deeper and more impressionable genius of Spenser; and it reconciles the myths of paganism to

Calvinist orthodoxy. It both rarefies the poet's senses and holds him coolly, with all his exaltedness, in the sphere of courtly wit. Sidney's famous sonnet to the moon, for instance (XXXI), couples that mournful luminary with himself by a sudden spring of dialectic, not by sensuous reverie. And in *The Nightingale*, again, he listens more to the stately cadence of his lines than to the 'anguish' of the bird, 'a thorn her song-book making'. The nightingale is an emblem of Nature, sorrow and music; and poor Philomel, bewailing her rape, receives a cool scholastic consolation, 'Since wanting is more woe than too much having'. 'Thine earth now springs, mine fadeth'; the situation thus serves to amplify the poet's 'craving', while at the same time it re-embodies his belief in order. Silhouetted against Nature, his darkness strengthens the surrounding light. There remains the genuine, irreducible disturbance of passion; indeed, the whole taste of his time for Amplification is a sign of unrest. But for Sidney, as for Puttenham, 'it is a piece of joy to be able to lament with ease', 'to play the Physician' in verse, causing 'one dolour to expel another'.

There is abundant sensuousness in Elizabethan verse, especially in mythological fantasies, such as *Hero and Leander* and *Venus and Adonis*; it came, as Sidney acknowledged, from one of the strongest impulses of the Renaissance. Yet Elizabethan descriptions are not exclusively luscious, or ornate, or fanciful. They have the positive quality of rhetoric, a firm intellectual structure modulating the imagery and the rhythm. A representative example of this kind of writing is the description of nightfall in the poem that Keats admired, Drayton's *Endimion and Phoebe* (1595). Phoebe (or Cynthia) has returned to the heavens, having wooed the shepherd Endimion, seemingly in vain, under the disguise of a nymph; while Endimion, now alone on Mount Latmus, has begun to find himself in love. This description (l. 327ff.) prepares for the moment when his longing becomes intense:

> Now black-brow'd Night plac'd in her chair of Jet,
> Sat wrapt in clouds within her Cabinet,
> And with her dusky mantle over-spread
> The path the Sunny Palfreys us'd to tread;
> And *Cynthia* sitting in her Crystal chair,
> In all her pomp now rid*[a]* along her Sphere,

a rode (an archaism in the manner of Spenser).

The honeyed dew descended in soft showers,
Drizzled in Pearl upon the tender flowers;
And *Zephyr* husht, and with a whispering gale,
Seemed to hearken to the Nightingale,
Which in the thorny brakes with her sweet song,
Unto the silent Night bewrayed her wrong.

If the scene here is by no means humbly accurate, neither is it officiously ornamental. The gentle transition of contrasts, from dusk to 'pomp', from the lavish sweetness of the couplet about the dew to the solemn introduction of the song of the nightingale, leads skilfully from Nature to the emotional changes about to follow in Endimion. Moreover, the images of Night's Cabinet and the moon contribute to Drayton's Neoplatonic allegory of the soul's awakening through love to knowledge and wisdom; so, too, with his deliberate appeal to the senses. As Drayton saw, this aspect of his myth became too cumbersome for him; on the other hand, mythological description of scenery was wholly congenial – it is the normal method, for example, of his vast *Poly-Olbion* (1612–22), where he surveys the topography and antiquities of England county by county. It was wholly to the taste of the age. Nature mythologized was endowed with a meaning and purpose; and descriptions were encrusted, as here, with urban images of jewels and pageantry, symbolizing the agreement of Nature with a courtly, civilized order.

Like Shakespeare, a year his junior, Drayton came of Warwickshire yeoman stock (1563–1631); he was thoroughly representative. He relates in a verse letter *Of Poets* (1627) how in boyhood he was fired by the new poetic ambition of the time; and this ambition he fulfilled in every kind of poem, from love-song to topography – in chronicles and biblical verse, in drama, journalism, satire; and especially in Spenserian pastoral, from his first imitations (1593) to the graceful burlesque of fairy-tale in *Nymphidia* (1627), and his last work, *The Muses' Elizium* (1630) – an idyll of Art in the midst of Nature. He broke new ground in his *Heroical Epistles* (1597–9), love-letters inspired by English history and by Ovid, which had something of the appeal for their day that romantic novels were to gain in the age of Scott; he brought dignity and vigour to a declining popular strain in his *Ballad of Agincourt* (1606–19); and his sonnets to *Idea* (1593–1619) unite convention and self-revelation with much more than usual independence. A man of many literary friendships, he praised as freely and judiciously as he borrowed; and he revised assiduously. His *Odes*, the most lasting of his innovations (1606–19), proclaim that poetry can exalt every clime, every verse form, and every kind of subject; and though this faith in his vocation (upheld against disappointments), was hardly the stuff of original genius, the verse it produced was continually masculine and delightful.

The basis of Drayton's confidence was the common basis of humanist learning, scientific as well as literary; belief in the rationality of Nature, its 'just correspondency' with the ordering and inquiring mind. And much of the best verse shaping the transition from the age of Spenser to that of Milton is directly concerned with this assumption, and strongly coloured by philosophical interests. Moral philosophy is the theme, for example, of the later verse of Daniel (*c.* 1563–1619), Sidney's direct successor in poetic style and outlook, and of Sidney's friend, the statesman Fulke Greville (1554–1623), Calvinist and questioning stoic. Chapman (*c.* 1559–1634) typifies the Renaissance in his philosophical ardour and gravity, his massy and intricate workmanship; while the reflective verse of Jonson (1572–1637), elegant as well as weighty, remoulds Elizabethan rhetoric into the neatness and economy of the seventeenth century. This change of style had also been anticipated in the impassioned lucidity and the sharp logic of Ralegh (*c.* 1552–1618) and in the courtly wit of the lawyer, Sir John Davies (1569–1626). In *Orchestra* (1596), Davies is wholly Elizabethan, celebrating court revels as symbols of the harmony of the universe; but there are many signs of transition in *Nosce Teipsum* [*Know Thyself*] (1599), where he contends for the immortality of the soul against the sceptics and epicureans who would fuse it with the body. Its doctrine and arrangement are more than half scholastic; it already belongs to the seventeenth century, on the other hand, in its intimate, dispassionate tone. Davies' tone, his contained emotional fire, and his close, energetic reasoning, leaping from outer world to inner, prefigure the 'metaphysical' wit of the next generation. And Donne (1572–1631), first and greatest of metaphysical poets, belongs to the same phase of poetic development. He makes the Elizabethan lyric more dialectical and more intimate; and he shares the poetic interests of both Chapman and Davies.

But this group of philosophical poems, while continuing the

rhetorical tradition of humanism, also marks a growing mood of uncertainty and unrest. *Nosce Teipsum*, for example, questions the value of science and learning:

> We seek to know the moving of each sphere,
>   And the strange cause of the ebbs and floods of Nile;
> But of that clock within our breasts we bear
>   The subtle motions we forget the while.
>
> We that acquaint ourselves with every zone
>   And pass both tropics, and behold the poles,
> When we come home, are to ourselves unknown,
>   And unacquainted still with our own souls.

Affliction has taught him, Davies says, that the soul 'hath power to know all things, Yet is she blind and ignorant in all'; supreme in the scale of Nature, Man is yet constantly 'mockt' through his senses. It is interesting to contrast this attitude with the detachment of Pope in a similar context (*Essay on Man*, II. 1–18; 1732); the Augustan is much more habituated to the process of doubt. For Pope, the restless, heaven-scanning ambition of human reason is the sign of absurdity; for the Elizabethan, on the contrary, the guarantee of greatness. To look for a wholly intelligible universe and not to find it is thus a source of bitter tension for him. In this recoil from the high expectations of earlier humanism, Davies' poem is related to the movement of satire in the 1590s and the widespread intellectual interest in the subject of melancholy;[15] and it is significant that it appeared at the same moment as *Musophilus, Every Man out of His Humour*, and *As You Like It*. The resemblance is still closer, moreover, between Davies' summary view of Man as 'a proud, and yet a wretched thing' and the disenchanted humanism of Hamlet. The tension in late Renaissance poetry, the sense of contradictions within the order of Nature, issues at full in the great tragedies of the next decade.

Jacobean Tragedy

The main achievement of Elizabeth's age in poetry was to find a style of measured grandiloquence that answered to the Renaissance ideals of civility and the active life. The rhetoric of the Jacobeans is more accomplished, more supple and condensed, with 'words perpetually juxtaposed in new and sudden combinations'; in Eliot's pregnant phrase, 'the intellect was immediately at the tips of the senses'.[16]

There is unbroken development from the 1590s, and the world of the Renaissance is depicted more intimately and more completely. But the temper of the years after 1600 is also more critical, searching, and analytic. The crowded subtlety of the Jacobeans denotes a quicker sense of the ambiguities of humanism, its uncertainties and contradictions. In seeing their civilization as a whole, they grow deeply aware of its disharmonies and its impermanence.

The crisis of the early seventeenth century was a far-reaching conflict of values – between the religious traditions of the Middle Ages and the secular bias of the Renaissance, between values relating to the social order and values centred on the individual.[17] It came to a head, largely through economic causes, about the turn of the century; the social system of the Tudor aristocracy, poised between local patronage and 'greatness' at Court, was undermined by the spreading influence of capitalism and distorted by rising expenses. The aimless and fatal revolt of the Earl of Essex in 1601 not only signified the end of a generation, it was an extreme symptom of a deep-seated malaise. As land followed money to the businessman, the lawyer, or the speculator, 'greatness' decomposed in a scramble for wealth and privilege. But while grandees at Court chased after patents of monopoly or City heiresses, or squandered estates in competitive display, there was acute distress for their dependants – 'gentlemen spent in their fortunes . . . and fit for all alterations' like the Gunpowder Plotters of 1605 – and for workmen and tenants like the 'Levellers' of the Midlands who rioted against enclosures in 1607 (the year of *Coriolanus*), protesting against 'tyrants' who would 'grind our flesh upon the whetstone of poverty'. A general corruption of social values seemed to have set in, a universal egotism confirming the dark legend of Machiavelli. 'We are much beholden to Machiavel and others', Bacon remarks dryly, 'that write what men do and not what they ought to do' (1605); and for Ralegh, contemplating *The History of the World* from the sombre vantage-point of the Tower (1614), it is axiomatic that 'riches and glory', 'Machiavel's two marks to shoot at', are the universal aims. 'To hold the times we have, we hold all things lawful . . . The heavens are high, far off, and unsearchable.' Futile, then, to upbraid the blindness of Fortune; 'one, whose virtue and courage forbiddeth him to be a dissembler, shall evermore hang on the wheel'. Amid the guesswork of the Sciences – 'There is a confused controversy about the very essence of nature' – Nature seemed reduced to 'second causes' (mundane as opposed to divine); while the image of the Renaissance hero, resolute, magnanimous, and self-sufficient, dissolved into mirage or monster.

The dramatists responded with intensified satire. While the wave of chronicles and romances subsided, the players (it was noted in 1605) 'do not forbear to represent upon their stage the whole course of the present time, not sparing either King, state, or religion, in so great absurdity, and with such liberty, that any would be afraid to hear them'.[18] Jonson's Volpone, for example (1606), is the concentrated essence of financial speculation, a legacy-hunter preying upon his kind. He is introduced with his servant in a style of ironic amplification surpassing Marlowe's *Jew of Malta*:

> VOLPONE.　　...Yet I glory
> More in the cunning purchase of my wealth
> Than in the glad possession, since I gain
> No common way; I use no trade, no venture;
> I wound no earth with plough-shares, fat no beasts
> To feed the shambles; have no mills for iron,
> Oil, corn, or men, to grind them into powder;
> I blow no subtle glass, expose no ships
> To threat'nings of the furrow-faced sea;
> I turn no moneys in the public bank,
> Nor usure private.
> MOSCA.　　　No, sir, nor devour
> Soft prodigals. You shall have some will swallow
> A melting heir as glibly as your Dutch
> Will pills of butter, and ne'er purge for it; ...
> You loathe the widow's or the orphan's tears
> Should wash your pavements, or their piteous cries
> Ring in your roofs, and beat the air for vengeance ...

Language evoking Venice and ancient Rome is subtly and then sharply modified into an image of contemporary London – where, with audacious topicality, Jonson later sets *The Alchemist* (1610) and *The Devil is an Ass* (1616). Volpone and his successors incarnate a whole world whose 'soul' is 'riches', a whole society animated by greed and credulous 'self-love', from Abel Drugger, the humble tobacconist, to the gigantic Sir Epicure Mammon, or 'the great projector', Meercraft, with connections in Court and City. So, too, there is continual satire on greed and hypocrisy (though much less profound), in Middleton's lively but cynical comedies of intrigue, which fix upon London and the battle of wits between tradesmen and gentry: 'They're busy 'bout our wives, we 'bout their lands' (e.g. *Michaelmas Term, A Trick to Catch the Old One, A Chaste Maid in Cheapside; c.* 1602–13). The satirists attack sexual relations, as well as social, with ridicule or disgust; their picture is that of Shakespeare's Ulysses (*Troilus, I. iii; 1601*), where 'degree is suffocate' –

> And appetite, an universal wolf,
> So doubly seconded with will and power,
> Must make perforce an universal prey
> And last eat up himself . . .

Measure for Measure and its predecessor, *All's Well*, belong to the same period (1603–4), with their unromantic analysis of sex and degree.

The highest expression of this crisis in humanism is the sequence of Shakespeare's great tragedies, from *Hamlet* to *Timon* (1601–8). Here the positive values of the Renaissance – in self-awareness, freedom of mind and body, the dignity of active living in an ordered civilization – are seized in vivid detail and far-ranging perspective. And their prelude, *Julius Caesar* (1599), is the first mature tribute to Rome on the Renaissance stage, the first convincing version of Plutarch's *Lives* ('our breviary', as Montaigne had called them).[19] But the starting-point of the tragedies, their source of development, is Shakespeare's many-sided perception of conflict within humanism. This is already apparent in *Julius Caesar*, with the cleavage between society and individual greatness; it deepens in *Hamlet*, in the prince's weariness with life to the pitch of physical revulsion; it fills the vast canvas of *Antony and Cleopatra* (1607) with tension between senses and will. And the contemporary aspects of this conflict are prominent in such figures as the bastard Edmund in *Lear* (1605), self-dedicated to a Nature of brute instinct and mechanical force: 'Let me, if not by birth, have lands by wit' (I. ii). At this point, however, tragedy converges with the satire of humours, so that the popular heritage of the 1590s affects tragedy more deeply, if less directly, than before. Edmund, and D'Amville in Tourneur's *Atheist's Tragedy* (*c.* 1611), are Machiavellians of the stamp of Volpone, and the vein of satiric irony and invective in *Hamlet* continues through most of its successors; while the Senecan plays of Marston, Tourneur, and Webster are loud with the bitterness voiced by Ralegh, in the acid, defiant mockery of their poverty-haunted scholars and dispossessed gentry. After Shakespeare and Jonson, Tourneur's *Revenger's Tragedy* (1606) is the drama most fully typical of the period; and here the Senecan, pseudo-Italian horrors of the plot are absorbed into grotesque satire and moral allegory.

This mixture of styles in tragedy indicates the strength of the medieval ideas still influencing the Jacobeans. Essentially, tragedy, like humour satire, was regarded as a variant of the Morality play. Hamlet voices the popular view when he touches on the ethical purpose of holding the mirror up to nature (III. ii), or speaks of tragedies prompting guilty spectators to confess their crimes (II. ii); so does Heywood, when he claims that tragedies show 'the fatal and abortive ends of such as commit notorious murders, . . . aggravated and acted with all the art that may be to terrify men from the like abhorred practices' – adding that classical and foreign subjects are 'so intended' as to praise or reprove the qualities of 'our countrymen' (*Apology for Actors, c.* 1608).[20] And the classics were received in the light of a similar (though non-theatrical) medieval idea, by which tragedy was the story of a fall from high estate; an idea preserved in the many editions of *The Mirror for Magistrates* (1569–1610). It showed the turn of Fortune's wheel. Thus even for Sidney, tragedy presents 'tyrannical humours' and 'teacheth the uncertainty of this world'. Daniel, anxious to shield his *Philotas* ('in the ancient form') from close application to Essex, cites ambition and 'the frailty of greatness' as 'the perpetual subjects of . . . Tragedies' (1605); and Heywood, for the popular stage, mentions the fall of Pompey as a warning 'that no man trust in his own strength'. Most Elizabethan plots reflect this attitude to tragedy, from Marlow's *Edward II: with the tragical fall of proud Mortimer* to *Sejanus: his Fall*, or Chapman's *Byron* plays (1608), or *Macbeth*; it also shapes significant details, like the proud boast that Shakespeare gives to Caesar the moment before he is assassinated. How this attitude could blend with the irony of satire is shown, for example, by *The Revenger's Tragedy*, in the words of the old but lecherous Duke, preening himself before an imaginary fresh conquest:

> How sweet can a duke breathe! Age has no fault.
> Pleasure should meet in a perfumed mist . . .
>
> (III. iv)

He is about to be poisoned.

The medieval bias was strong in tragedy even for those writers who, like Sidney and Daniel, were specially interested in classical theory and form. Since Seneca's declamations were more familiar than the Greeks, the chief mark of tragedy was held to be its 'passionate and weighty' eloquence. Sidney follows Aristotle in assigning specific emotions to tragedy, but changes Aristotle's terror and pity into 'admiration [*wonder*] and commiseration', sentiments stirred by rhetoric. And practising dramatists follow the same line, while regretting the loss of 'the sententious Chorus' (Webster, *The White Devil*, 1612). Thus, Jonson speaks of 'truth of argument, dignity of persons, gravity and height of elocution, fulness and frequency of sentence' as the substance of tragedy (*Sejanus*); Chapman, of 'elegant and sententious excitation to virtue' (*Revenge of Bussy D'Ambois*; *c.* 1610). The two chief elements, then, are moral instruction and amplification; and these are precisely what is implied by contemporary references to acting, on the one hand, and, on the other, by the broad conventions of dramatic structure. Thus, Hamlet instructs the Players in gesture and delivery (branches of rhetoric), and stresses the importance of decorum in the midst of amplification: 'in the very torrent, tempest, and ... whirlwind of passion, you must acquire and beget a temperance that may give it smoothness' (III. ii); while Webster identifies *An Excellent Actor* (perhaps Burbage) with a 'grave orator' who displays Nature as she is, 'neither on stilts nor crutches', and 'fortifies moral precepts with examples' (in Overbury's *Characters*, 1615). There are maxims and set speeches everywhere, persuasion, narration, deliberation, outcry; while the horrors of the action and similarly the choice of exalted or remote protagonists are meant, in part at least, to 'aggravate' or amplify the moral theme. The characters are both tyrants, and high examples of Everyman.

Although this traditional and academic scheme only touches externals, it indicates the lines on which the dramatists were thinking. Modern studies of the Elizabethans bringing out the importance of poetic imagery in the plays have shown how it was applied in practice. The repetition of poetic symbols and the general handling of language mould the imaginative structure as much as action and character. Imagery connected with storms or shipwreck, with music, with jewellery (to list some examples), takes a part in the action throughout Shakespeare's writing; there are cumulative metaphors of disease in *Hamlet*, comparisons between men and beasts in *Lear*, references to blood and to sleep in *Macbeth*, to 'the world' in *Antony*. As Wilson Knight has shown, a Shakespeare play is a closely knit stage poem, unified in 'personification, atmospheric suggestion, and direct poetic-symbolism' – 'an expanded metaphor, . . . projected into forms roughly correspondent with actuality, . . . according to the demands of its own nature'.[21] A highly complex and sensitive organism such as this has little resemblance to the simple outline of the Morality plays or the formal structure of poetic allegory. Nevertheless, Shakespeare's construction is still based, in important features, on the tradition of which the Moralities were part; and to this they owe their opportunity of appealing with universal and yet immediate significance. At the centre of his tragedies are the familiar metaphors of man as a 'little kingdom' and the state as a 'body politic', both reflecting in little the whole plan of Nature. In *Othello*, domestic passions stand out, in *Coriolanus*, political; but both aspects of life are always treated together; while beyond them 'the heavens themselves' participate to 'blaze forth the death of princes'. Thus, instead of limiting his cast, Shakespeare enlarges it so as to extend the tragic conflict continuously from the hero's mind towards the outer limits of the cosmos. And while his crowds of minor figures disclose the 'form and pressure' of society in realistic fashion, they also embody moral relationships, linked with the mind of the hero (much as in allegories like *Magnificence*) by being personified in household servants or in counsellors – the porter, the doctors, even Banquo in *Macbeth*, for example, or Kent, the steward Oswald, the Fool in *Lear*. Shakespeare's attachment in this to popular tradition, his sense of the hero as Everyman, is particularly evident where he dwells on 'the frailty of greatness', or looks at the prince through the eyes of the clown, as a would-be Alexander 'a little o'erparted'. In his Roman plays he follows Plutarch realistically, though with increasing freedom of technique; but in *Lear* and *Macbeth* he boldly merges history into an allegory of Nature – at once the base of civil order and the chaos surrounding it, the wild heath where the king in madness meets the mad vagabond and sees that 'unaccommodated man is no more but such a poor, bare, forked animal as thou art'.

To a great extent, then, Shakespeare's treatment of the problems of humanism in his tragedies reproduces, in form and conception, the medieval outlook persisting through the century of the Tudors. But at the same time, the very fullness of this achievement, the vivid sense of humanity's uniqueness that burns through *Lear* and *Macbeth*, detaches them from the past and exposes the incompleteness of the traditional map of Nature. In this aspect of the tragedies, indeed, lies a main source of their tension; and here again Shakespeare speaks for his age. While, for example, the asceticism of the Middle Ages is deeply ingrained in the dramatists as well as the Puritans, so, too, tensely opposed to it are the Roman worship of greatness and the intimately subjective consciousness of humanist and Reformer. And no medieval restraint could bound in the 'aspiring' curiosity of a Marlowe. Thus the frailty of human pride and reason seems more poignant to the Elizabethans, more calamitous, than to Chaucer or the writer of *Everyman*. But return to the Middle Ages was neither possible nor desired; and the crucial feature of Jacobean tragedy is not disillusionment with the Renaissance but the affirmation of no return, however strained or perplexed. Its restlessness and its splendour come from the same origins.

The emotional restlessness of the age is most apparent in its concentration upon death as a subject for the theatre. The thought of death was a gathering point for their fears and ambitions, a theme where every writer could be eloquent and moving, particularly with the example of Seneca before him. Even a mediocre playwright like Chettle could be pathetic and sententious (*Hoffman*, 1602):

> ... the King and Captain are in this alike,
> None hath free hold of life, but they are still,
> When death heaven's steward comes, tenants at will.
> I lay me down, and rest in Thee my trust,
> If I wake never more, till all flesh rise
> I sleep a happy sleep, sin in me dies;

while Romeo laments Juliet with the passionate outcry of the sonneteers:

> ... O my Love, my wife,
> Death that hath suck'd the honey of thy breath,
> Hath had no power yet upon thy beauty:
> Thou art not conquer'd, beauty's ensign yet
> Is crimson in thy lips and in thy cheeks,
> And death's pale flag is not advanced there ...

But the sentiments of religion, of Petrarch, of the *danse macabre*, all tend to gravitate towards stoical defiance. In this posture dies Chettle's avenging hero-villain; and Romeo, too, as he drinks the poison:

> Come bitter conduct, some unsavoury guide,
> Thou desperate pilot, now at once run on
> The dashing rocks thy sea-sick weary bark;
> Here's to my love. O true apothecary;
> Thy drugs are quick. Thus with a kiss I die.

The note of weariness and desperation here is seldom absent from tragedy after 1600. Much of it is directly due to Seneca and his feigned elevation, as Bacon calls it (1605), of affecting, with the frailty of a man, the security of a god. Except as a cloak for satire, none of the Jacobeans are at rest with Seneca's natural religion – 'out upon him', cries one of Marston's characters, 'he writ of Temperance and Fortitude, yet lived like a voluptuous Epicure, and died like an effeminate coward' (*The Malcontent*, III i; 1604) – but Senecanism held the attraction of making good rhetoric out of conflicting emotions. Thus Chapman will use the bravado of Bussy D'Ambois to strike out a fine Senecan image, one of the sudden glories of the Jacobean stage:

> Here like a Roman Statue I will stand
> Till death hath made me marble; oh, my fame,
> Live in despite of murder; take thy wings ...
> Fly, where the evening from th' Iberian vales
> Takes on her swarthy shoulders Hecate,
> Crown'd with a grove of oaks: fly where men feel
> The cunning axletree: and those that suffer
> Beneath the chariot of the snowy Bear:
> And tell them all that D'Ambois now is hasting
> To the eternal dwellers; ...
>
> (v. i; 1604)

And then, a few speeches later, he will amplify the moral of fallen pride:

> O frail condition of strength, valour, virtue,
> In me, like warning fire upon the top
> Of some steep beacon, on a steeper hill,
> Made to express it ...

Yet this inconsistency, in the only dramatist serious about the philosophy of stoicism, points to the emotional interest of the theme. In the tragedy of Bussy, Chapman is concerned with the social problem whether 'nature hath no end In her great works, responsive to their worths'; and in the dying orations of the hero, and again of Byron (who speaks of 'the endless exile of dead men'), he evokes a sense of vast loneliness not only for the hero but for mankind in general, homeless in the midst of Nature. The stoical defiance of death on the stage brought to a head the inner tensions of the Renaissance.

It is one of the qualities of Shakespeare's greatness, therefore, that – after *Julius Caesar* – he can use the Senecan gestures of the theatre purely as a sign of emotion in his characters.[22] He expresses the terror of his age (the physical terror of Claudio in *Measure for Measure*, or the death-in-life of Macbeth), and he expresses the grandeur of defiance. But his attitude to death is more balanced than his contemporaries' because his sense of life is keener and more inclusive. He imagines more, and more coherently.

Cleopatra's paean for dead Antony illustrates Shakespeare's manner at the height of his career, and the development of his technique. Death in his tragedies commonly brings with it an enhanced perception of life; and here the many images of the play – of the period – relating love and greatness with 'the world' are concentrated together with an effect of masterful sensuous vitality. The speech is linked with the Senecan theme of the hero deified; but on both sides, as it were, it out-reaches other dramatists, amplifying the heroic image with tremendous power and yet maintaining a unique sense of proportion. Cleopatra has 'dreamt there was an Emperor Antony':

> His legs bestrid the ocean: his rear'd arm
> Crested the world: his voice was propertied
> As all the tuned spheres, and that to friends;
> But when he meant to quail and shake the orb,
> He was as rattling thunder. For his bounty,
> There was no winter in't; an autumn 'twas
> That grew the more by reaping: his delights
> Were dolphin-like; they show'd his back above
> The element they lived in: in his livery
> Walk'd crowns and crownets; realms and islands were
> As plates dropp'd from his pocket.
>
> (v. ii)

Beyond the profusion of images of Nature and royalty, the most striking feature of this speech (as of the play) is the way that all its

images and the physical senses of the speaker seem to be working together. Shakespeare writes elsewhere of the 'quick forge and
working-house' of thought; Cleopatra does not think about Antony,
still less express a sentiment about him: she forges and creates him.
The first line and a half, for example, have gained enormously in
vigour and compression since the writing, only a few years earlier, of:

> Why, man, he doth bestride the narrow world
> Like a Colossus.

Here, not only is the giant in motion, but two metaphors combine
together in place of a single simile – Antony as Colossus and as
heraldic device; and by this compression he seems at once to dominate the world, to symbolize its glory, and to protect it. And the
solidity of the images, with the hurried yet strongly articulated
movement of sound, makes the speech doubly expressive for the stage:

> ... his delights
> Were dolphin-like; they showed his back above
> The element they lived in: in his livery ...

As the sound ecstatically doubles upon itself, Cleopatra finishes with
a note of superlative colloquial ease:

> Walk'd crowns and crownets; realms and islands were
> As plates[a] dropped from his pocket.

Yet this godlike image belongs to a 'dream'; and the unreality of
dream is faintly but sufficiently present, as well as its vividness. It can
be felt in the first lines, as Antony's reared arm is suddenly trans-
shaped by the heraldic metaphor of 'crested'; or in the supernatural-
ness of a bounty with 'no winter in't'; or again in the prodigal
casualness, the odd quality of folk-tale, in the last two lines. The
deification of Antony is thus set in perspective – especially as the
audience have seen and heard of his weaknesses from the outset: 'The
triple pillar of the world transform'd Into a strumpet's fool' (i. i) –
and so, too, is the ecstasy of Cleopatra herself. Before expounding her
dream, she has received Dolabella, the envoy from conquering
Caesar, with her old regal indifference, but with more than a hint of
her gipsy temper as well:

a i.e. silver coins.

You laugh when boys or women tell their dreams;
Is't not your trick?

After the dream, she returns to earth for a moment, then soars again;
but this time with a difference:

> CLEOPATRA. Think you there was, or might be, such a man
>   As this I dreamt of?
> DOLABELLA.   Gentle madam, no.
> CLEOPATRA. You lie, up to the hearing of the gods.
>   But, if there be, or ever were, one such,
>   It's past the size of dreaming: nature wants stuff
>   To vie strange forms with fancy; yet, to imagine
>   An Antony, were nature's piece 'gainst fancy,
>   Condemning shadows quite.

Cleopatra's spring of theatrical cunning in this speech leaves the wonder of her vision untouched, but alters the way it is received by the audience. And as she thinks of it as an imaginative creation, in effect a work of art, it recedes to the normal plane of the tragedy, at which the audience participates in sympathy with the lovers, and yet views them critically from without. This dual insight, detaching but not diminishing, is continuously renewed; here it is guided for the audience by Dolabella, struggling to get his word in before the dream is told, and then incredulous but sympathetic.

The consummate art of this dialogue marks a long process of development. The whole structure of Elizabethan rhetoric has been changed. The regular emphatic verse of Sidney, Marlowe, or Kyd has been reshaped into something more fluid and colloquial, while the high-pitched but stiff decorum of early rhetoric has yielded to more deliberate elevation at one extreme and sudden intimacies of tone at the other. And stage convention as such has come to be used as a mediating lens between audience and character, serving a new kind of insight into human relationships. Most of Shakespeare's early speeches are purely rhetorical or operatic in method, like Romeo's lament for Juliet, amplifying the speaker's emotion so as to carry the audience with it. But Shakespeare has been fascinated from the outset – in *Richard III*, for instance – by contrasts between acting and feeling, between the ceremony, the formal eloquence, of the stage and the sentient or calculating personality behind it; and he comes to treat rhetoric designedly as an art by which natural feeling can be distorted as well as amplified. In the sharp realism of *Julius Caesar*, he masters this new theatrical technique, as when the two aspects of Antony are distinguished in the Forum scene – 'I am no orator, as Brutus is' – and with *Hamlet* this technique becomes an integral part of his tragedies, continually developing. The characters, as they see themselves and as others are to see them, are made and remade by the turns of the language, exalting and qualifying, weaving a dense tissue not only within the play but between the actors and the audience.

No other poet of the Renaissance was so deeply fascinated by the connections between art and nature. In his last group of plays, the tragi-comedies beginning with *Pericles* and *Cymbeline* (1608–9) and ending in *Henry VIII* and *The Two Noble Kinsmen* (written jointly with Fletcher, *c.* 1612), Shakespeare is still experimenting. The violent struggles of the tragedies have given way to reconciliations and a poised sense of wonder; and here, in *The Winter's Tale* and *The Tempest* (1610–11), Shakespeare brings to a triumphant issue his study of the interplay between normal experience and the artificial conventions of the stage in language, action, and spectacle. Other playwrights after 1600 could anatomize the heart, and knew how to modulate the grand manner; and Jonson, at least, could form a poetic world from his reading and observation in the bustling capital; but only Shakespeare could consistently project himself to the inner minds of his people as distinct individuals, and yet retain a total vision of his world of the theatre and the outer world it represented.

The full variety of interests in Shakespeare's public can only be appreciated if one turns from stoicism and satire to works with a middle-class background, to forerunners of the drama of sentiment and the domestic problem play such as Heywood's *A Woman Killed with Kindness* (1603) and Dekker's *Honest Whore* (1604); or to Middleton's supreme achievement in tragic realism, *Women Beware Women* and *The Changeling* (*c.* 1621–2). Shakespeare's many-sided triumph in the art of the theatre depended on the many-sided interest of his public. But by 1609, when his company began performing in the aristocratic Blackfriars theatre rather than the popular Globe, the effective unity of the public was beginning to break. As the conflicts of the age flowed into politics, middle-class opinion grew harder against the playhouse, now virtually a Court appendage. Dekker and Heywood were still writing for the popular stage as late as 1630; and Middleton's anti-Spanish morality, *A Game at Chess* (1624), had the widest immediate appeal since the opening of the theatres. But it was also the last expression of the sentiment of national unity; while literature in general had already moved away from its contact with folk traditions in the 1590s. The division of public taste and feeling was already evident, before Shakespeare's retirement, in the tragedies of Webster; it was emphasized by the fashionable success of Beaumont and Fletcher. The reign of Fletcher in the drama (*c.* 1608–25) brought its greatness to an end. There were new developments in the comedy of manners; and among the tragic playwrights who followed Fletcher, Massinger could declaim with eloquent correctness and Ford with a tremulous excitement of the nerves; but the decay of tragedy was complete long before the Puritans closed the theatres in 1642. No one could appeal to groundlings and judicious together, or revive the full-bodied rhetoric of Jonson and Shakespeare.

Jacobean Prose

The changes in the theatre under the Stuarts were linked with two major developments outside it. One was the consolidation of 'the town' with its standards of 'politeness' – drawing Fletcher and Shirley (1626–42) towards a comedy of manners; the other, confirmed by the authority of Bacon, was the advance of scientific thought. As the composition of the public altered, the centre of gravity in literature shifted, from the rhetoric of drama towards discussion and information, towards the evolution of modern prose.

A more positive demand grew up for writings of utility addressed to 'the plain man'. In religious works and sermons (which included nearly half the output of the press), 'the plain man' chose direct practical guidance rather than the subtleties of an Andrewes or a Donne. In popular journalism, where Dekker's plague pamphlets (1603–30) showed a sobering of tone since Nashe's day, the demand for utility also produced in 1621 the first regular English newspapers (the weekly 'corantos' of foreign war items ridiculed by Jonson in *The Staple of News*), and led on to the heyday of pamphleteering in the era of the Commonwealth and Defoe. But courtly romances languished meanwhile, as old favourites were read again, or new brought in from France: 'in stead of Song and Music', says a typical adviser on the breeding of gentlewomen (1631), 'let them learn

Cookery and Laundry. And in stead of reading Sir Philip Sidney's *Arcadia*, let them read the grounds of good huswifery. I like not a female Poetess at any hand'.[23] This depreciation of fiction was by no means confined to Puritans.

In scholarship, too, the heroic ambitions of the Renaissance have begun to change their course. Bacon's vast undertaking, to survey and reform the whole field of exact knowledge (*c.* 1603–23); Ralegh's attempted *History of the World*; the variegated lore of Burton's *Anatomy of Melancholy* (1621); or, in verse, Drayton's *Poly-Olbion*: these are reminders that the age of specialists is still far away. Nevertheless, Bacon's limitations in experimental science were already evident to Harvey, the investigator of the circulation of the blood; and Camden, Selden, and Bacon himself – in *Henry VII* (1622) – were establishing more rigorous methods in historical research. The attitude of poets was also changing. 'Verses are wholly reduced to chambers,' Drayton complained in 1612 – glancing perhaps at Donne – 'and nothing esteemed in this lunatic age but what is kept in cabinets, and must only pass by transcription'; while the sonnets published in the 1590s were replaced by prose collections of essays or 'characters', witty instead of passionate and urban rather than courtly. From the moment of *Hamlet* onwards, the judicious had been interested in self-observation and detached analysis.

This development in prose was stimulated by Bacon's *Essays* of 1597 (enlarged in 1612 and 1625). Bacon, however, was writing 'Counsels, Civil and Moral', practical maxims like those of *Advice to His Son* by the Earl of Northumberland and by Ralegh, but more intent than either on the problems of courtiership; and if his main concern was man, it was man as a political animal or an object of experiment – best observed, like natural substances, in a state of 'vexation':

> A man's nature is best perceived in privateness, for there is no affectation; in passion, for that putteth a man out of his precepts; and in a new case or experiment, for there custom leaveth him ... A man's nature runs either to herbs or to weeds; therefore let him seasonably water the one, and destroy the other.

In his tightly formed aphorisms, Bacon owes less to the essays of Montaigne (1580–88) than to Seneca's letters and a methodical common-place book: less again, in his impersonal concentration on the active will.

The aphorism was Bacon's cure for the 'first distemper of learning, when men study words and not matter', the chosen instrument of his thought even in its maturest statement, the *Novum Organum*[a] (1620). 'No man', said Jonson, 'ever spoke more neatly, more pressly, or suffered less emptiness, less idleness in what he uttered.' And since others, too, the historians for example, were seeking a 'plain English', 'rather respecting matter than words', Bacon's example was decisive. The luxuriant images of the Elizabethans were clipped for perspicuity; while, instead of their copiousness, in the cadences of North or Sidney, Hooker's Ciceronian fullness, or Nashe's 'frisking' versatility, the new ideal (in Burton's phrase) was 'neat, polite and terse' – an ideal to be acknowledged even when meandering by 'the froth of human wit, and excrements of curiosity' in Burton's own 'extemporanean style ... writ with as small deliberation as I do ordinarily speak'. A legal manner of exposition is the model, again, for Henry Peacham, writing on conduct and elegance (*The Compleat Gentleman*, 1622); significantly, he would decry the

ampullous [*inflated*] and Scenical pomp, with empty furniture of phrase, wherewith the Stage, and our petty Poetic Pamphlets sound so big, which like a net in the water, though it feeleth weighty, yet it yieldeth nothing.

The influence of Bacon is already noticeable here, forming Elizabethan English into the medium of philosophers.[24]

Bacon's achievement marks the turning-point of the Renaissance. His agile curiosity could range from interpreting fables in *The Wisdom of the Ancients* (1609) to projecting the Utopia of New Atlantis (*c.* 1626); and though he looked to Latin for durability, *The Advancement of Learning* (1605) is a monument of vigorous English, incisive, orderly, and majestic. Yet his influence was inseparable from his singleness of purpose – even his fables unfolding science, and his Utopia, technology – so that his limitations were impressed on literature together with his strength. Thus *The Advancement of Learning* presents the Renaissance view of poetry more arrestingly than Sidney or any other Elizabethan critic; but also, both by tone and statement, it sharpens the latent conflict between active reason and the imagination:

a i.e. New Logic (to replace Aristotle).

The use of this Feigned History [*poetry*] hath been to give some shadow of satisfaction to the kind of man in those points wherein the nature of things doth deny it; the world being in proportion inferior to the soul ... So as it appeareth that poesy serveth and conferreth to magnanimity, morality, and to delectation. And therefore it was ever thought to have some participation of divineness, because it doth raise and erect the mind, by submitting the shews of things to the desires of the mind; whereas reason doth buckle and bow the mind unto the nature of things.

'Feigned History' indicates Bacon's severance between the words of poetry and its matter, though even so he is uneasy ('it is not good to stay too long in the theatre'). But the last sentence, contrasting poetry with reason, carries the full weight of his mind – both in its psychological penetration and its tone of utilitarian disapproval; and this contrast, together with his broader, and primary, distinction between the mind of man and the nature of things, was reinforced in the next decades by the physical and mathematical sciences. No room seemed left for Nature to vie with fancy; and poetry was to reduce itself, for later neo-classicism, to a clear, neat, and decorative reflection of the external world. The problem of the relations between science and poetry had already been interposed between Bacon, Donne, or Jonson and the succeeding generation of Milton, Marvell and Hobbes.

Besides the prose of utility, however, there was also the prose of leisure. The broadening psychological interests of the Jacobeans are suggested by the list of words that Florio thinks new in his translations of Montaigne (1603) – such as *conscientious*, *amusing*, *effort*, and *emotion*; while *entrain*, *comport*, or *facilitate* suggest at once the refinements of leisure and the abstractions of science. And these interests, quickened perhaps by Shakespeare as well as Montaigne, are already evident in Sir William Cornwallis (1579–1614) – a friend of Donne, and by date (1600–1601) the second of English essayists. Even when he treats Baconian subjects, such as *The Instruments of a States-man*, Cornwallis can write:

I like nothing better in *Montaigne* than his desire of knowing *Brutus'* private actions, wishing more to know what he did in Tent than in battle; for there being himself, not over-awed by respect and company, he spreads himself open, and in this corner gives a discerning eye a more liberal view than when it stands upon the allowance of the general sight of men.

Cornwallis follows Montaigne, again, in using his essays 'as a Painter's boy a board, that is trying to bring his hand and his fancy acquainted';

much as Burton plucks the reader into his labyrinth of melancholy with the assurance that 'Thou thyself art the subject of my discourse'. The character-writers, meanwhile, direct a discerning eye upon colleges and taverns. Especially in Overbury's widely read volume, which Webster, Dekker, Donne, and others added to (1614–22), the character-writers sharpen the earlier 'humour' sketches with Baconian terseness and self-conscious wit. But they share, too, something of Montaigne's urbanity; and the best collection, Earle's *Microcosmographie* (1628), has sharpness and urbanity together. His Pot-Poet, or ballad-monger, for example, 'is the dregs of wit, yet mingled with good drink may have some relish':

His frequentest works go out in single sheets, and are chanted from market to market to a vile tune and a worse throat; whilst the poor country wench melts like her butter to hear them; and these are the stories of some men of Tyburn, or a strange monster out of Germany; or, sitting in a bawdy-house, he writes God's judgements …

Earle is still Elizabethan, clearly; but his tone is cooler, and his technique of recording observation more precise. In the same period the letters of Donne and Sir Henry Wotton, or even the news-reporter John Chamberlain, show a further maturing in detached observation of minds and personalities; while Greville's discursive essay on Sidney points forward to the great development of biography in the time of Charles I.

In Jacobean prose, then, as in the poetry of metaphysical wit, the guiding interests of modern literature have begun to define themselves against their medieval and Renaissance setting. With Bacon, it establishes the modern language of analysis, abstract or practical; with the essayists on character, it provides an essential link between the older traditions of allegory and humours and the beginnings of the modern novel in the eighteenth century.

NOTES

1. See Appendix VIII. For literary opinions about the language, see G. G. Smith, *Elizabethan Critical Essays*, I, lv–lx, 203–7; II, 149–53, 285–94; cp. E. J. Sweeting, *Early Tudor Criticism*; R. F. Jones, *The Triumph of the English Language*; and pp. 227–44 below.

2. Dekker, *The Gull's Hornbook*, ch. vi; cp. A. Harbage, *Shakespeare's Audience*; B. Beckerman, *Shakespeare at the Globe*, 20–23; A. Gurr, *The Shakespearean Stage*, ch. 6; Part I, n.13, above.

3. See J. W. Cuncliffe, *Early English Classical Tragedies*; W. Clemen, *English Tragedy before Shakespeare*; G. K. Hunter, 'Seneca and the Elizabethans', in *Shakespeare Survey*, XX; F. P. Wilson, *English Drama 1485–1585*, chs v–vi; cp. D. Bevington, *From 'Mankind' to Marlowe*; G. Wickham, *Shakespeare's Dramatic Heritage*; L. Salingar, *Shakespeare and the Traditions of Comedy*; R. Weimann, *Shakespeare and the Popular Tradition*; E. Jones, *The Origins of Shakespeare*.

4. T. S. Eliot, *Selected Essays*, 123.

5. M. C. Bradbrook, *Themes and Conventions of Elizabethan Tragedy*, 29–49; W. Empson, *Some Versions of Pastoral*, 27ff.; cp. R. Levin, *The Multiple Plot in English Renaissance Drama*.

6. cp. C. R. Baskervill, *The Elizabethan Jig*, and E. Welsford, *The Court Masque*.

7. Heywood, *Apology for Actors*, 21, 52. On history plays, see I. Ribner, *The English History Play* and Appendix, 'Shakespeare', below; cp. M. Axton, *The Queen's Two Bodies*. On the public interest in history, see L. B. Wright, *Middle-class Culture*, 297ff., 603ff., and A. L. Rowse, *The England of Elizabeth*, 31ff.; cp. H. S. Bennett, *English Books and Readers 1558 to 1603*, 214–20. (The lesser-known plays mentioned in this survey without authors' names are anonymous; cp. Appendix.)

8. On the actors see Heywood, *Apology for Actors*, 43; Webster (?), 'An Excellent Actor' (in Overbury's *Characters*, 1615; see Chambers, *Elizabethan Stage* IV, 252, 257). On methods of acting, see B. Beckerman, *Shakespeare at the Globe*; A. Gurr, *The Shakespearean Stage*, and pp. 245–59, below; D. Seltzer, in *A New Companion to Shakespeare Studies*, 35–54 and Appendix X. On the structure of the theatres, see also Appendix X, and the summary of recent research by R. Hosley in C. Leech and T. W. Craik, eds, *The Revels History of Drama in English*, III, 119–235. On stage uses of music, see F. W. Sternfield, in *A New Companion to Shakespeare Studies*, 157–67, and J. Jacquot, 'Le Repertoire des compagnies d'enfants', in *Dramaturgie et Société*, ed. Jacquot, 749–57.

9. On puritanism, see J. D. Wilson (*Cambridge History of English Literature* VI). On 'civility': G. G. Smith, *Elizabethan Critical Essays*, I, 4–5, 26–33, 199; II, 9, 62, 84–8, 142ff., 248–9, 266; Baskervill, *The Elizabethan Jig*, 94, 111. cp. Part I above.

10. See Appendix VII, and Appendix, 'Nashe'. J. D. Wilson, *Life in Shakespeare's England*, and M. Roberts, *Elizabethan Prose*, are relevant anthologies.

11. See O. J. Cambell, *Comicall Satyre*, 1–81; J. B. Leishman, *The Three Parnassus Plays*, 41ff.; J. Peter, *Complaint and Satire*; M. Bradbrook on 'Spenser's Pursuit of Fame', in *Elizabethan Poetry*, ed. J. R. Brown and B. Harris, 91–109.

12. See Erasmus, *In Praise of Folly*; cp. Part I, n.13, above.

13. cp. H. Granville-Barker, *Prefaces to Shakespeare, 1st Series*; C. L. Barber, *Shakespeare's Festive Comedy*, ch. v; R. L. Colie, *Shakespeare's 'Living Art'*, ch. i.

14. See T. Wilson, *Art of Rhetoric*, 114ff., 156; cp. Part I, n.7, above; for studies of poetry and rhetoric, Brown and Harris, eds., *Elizabethan Poetry*; M. Alpers, ed., *Elizabethan Poetry: Modern Essays in Criticism*; and Appendices VII and IX.

15. cf. Bullough, 7 (Part I, n.5, above); L. C. Knights, *Drama and Society*, 315–32.

16. Eliot, *Selected Essays*, 209–10, 272–4; cp. James Smith, 'On Metaphysical Poetry', in *Scrutiny*, II (1933).

17. See F. P. Wilson, *Elizabethan and Jacobean*; P. Cruttwell, *The Shakespearean Moment*; R. Ornstein, *The Moral Vision of Jacobean Tragedy*; J. W. Lever, *The Tragedy of State*. cp. Ralegh, *Works*, II, xxxi, 40–42; Part I, notes 5, 16 and 18 above.

18. E. K. Chambers, *Elizabethan Stage*, I, 325–8; but see R. W. Chambers, *Man's Unconquerable Mind*, 256ff.

19. cp. H. Craig, *The Enchanted Glass*, 212, 252; M. W. MacCallum, *Shakespeare's Roman Plays*. On 'Nature', see Part I above; also Willey, *The Seventeenth-Century Background*; L. G. Salingar, '*The Revenger's Tragedy*', in *Scrutiny*, VI (1938); T. Spencer, *Shakespeare and the Nature of Man*; J. F. Danby, *Shakespeare's Doctrine of Nature*.

20. Heywood, *Apology for Actors*, 43, cp. W. Farnham, *Medieval Heritage of Elizabethan Tragedy*.

21. G. Wilson-Knight, *The Wheel of Fire*, 16; cp. L. C. Knights on *Macbeth* (*Explorations*); M. C. Bradbrook, *Elizabethan Stage Conditions*; and K. Muir, 384ff., in this volume.

22. T. S. Eliot, *Selected Essays*, 129–31; F. R. Leavis, *The Common Pursuit*.

23. L. B. Wright, *Middle-class Culture*, 111, 228, 375; D. Bush, *English Literature in the Earlier Seventeenth Century*, 40, 294; Lord Ernle, *The Light Reading of our Ancestors*, ch. x.

24. See A. C. Baugh, ed., *Literary History of England*, 590ff.; F. P. Wilson, *Elizabethan and Jacobean*; Bush (see n.23 above) 181ff.; B. W. Vickers, *Francis Bacon and Renaissance Prose*; S. E. Fish, ed., *Seventeenth-Century Prose: Modern Essays in Criticism*.

PART III

SPENSER AND *THE FAERIE QUEENE*

W. W. ROBSON

For many Elizabethan readers Edmund Spenser (?1552–99) was 'our principal poet', 'divine Master Spenser', 'the prince of poets in his time'. Since those days he has always been ranked with the great English poets, and so far as I know his place among them has never been formally challenged; there has been no 'dislodgment' of Spenser, no 'Spenser controversy'. Scholarly study of him has certainly been abundant, especially in the twentieth century. Yet it is difficult to feel that his work is really alive today. It seems to be unpopular with university students, and it is being gradually dropped from school syllabuses.

In part this decline of interest in Spenser may be connected with the growing neglect of English Renaissance literature as a whole, apart from the drama. The sixteenth-century part of Elizabeth I's reign – that is to say, most of it – is a blank period to more and more students. But there may be other reasons for it, more specifically related to Spenser's own peculiarities. His poems tend to be long, and his main work, *The Faerie Queene*, is enormously long. It is the longest good poem in English, longer than *Jerusalem Delivered*, and *Paradise Lost* put together. Perhaps English-speaking readers do not really care for any long poem, however much they are told to admire it. Modern poets like Pound or Auden have tried to revive the long poem. But they are not essentially narrative poets. The modern reader tends to go to the novel for fictitious narrative, and for disquisition and sustained reflection he goes to the prose treatise or essay. From poetry we want something more tense and concentrated.

Less voluminous poets of that time may have a more direct appeal to us. In poems like 'The Lie' and 'The Passionate Man's Pilgrimage' Spenser's friend and patron Sir Walter Ralegh (?1552–1618) speaks to us with greater immediacy. In the best of the Tudor Court poetry we hear a familiar and forceful voice. In comparison, the impact of

Spenser is vague and blurred. And the Tudor Court poets are in continuity with those better-known Stuart Court poets who inhabit a different mental world which, rightly or wrongly, has seemed to modern readers more like our own.

What troubles some readers is that 'Edmund Spenser' hardly exists for them as a human being. The modes and conventions he uses keep his own character and individuality at a distance. Whether in pastoral costume or not, he seems always to write in a sort of literary code, which is most difficult to penetrate. He is only an implied author, not a real historical person. With other writers – Milton, Kipling, D. H. Lawrence – we have the sense of a strong personality behind the work. We can feel this even in historically remote poets like Catullus, of whose life nothing is known. This personality may be liked or disliked, but it is always *there*, something to bump up against. With Spenser there is nothing.

It would seem that as a man Spenser made little or no impression on his contemporaries. To them he was 'the new poet', 'Immerito', 'Colin Clout', almost anonymous. Anecdotes about him are few and unrevealing. There are personal references in his work, but they are incidental, and mixed with fiction. We never learn the inner facts. The most important event in Spenser's public career was his appointment, through the patronage of the Earl of Leicester, Elizabeth's close friend and adviser, to a post in Ireland. But we do not learn from Spenser whether he saw this as a splendid opportunity or as exile. There is little sense of a changing individual in his work. His poems are difficult to date on internal grounds. The differences among them are differences of poetic kind and style, not of 'periods', phases of development.

But perhaps the heart of the Spenser problem is that modern readers, even those who still read poetry, simply find him tedious. He is certainly voluminous, and he might be more admired if he had written less. He is also temperamentally diffuse. He does not seem to have had the instinct for concentration which some other poets have had.

> I hate the heaven, because it doth withhold
> Me from my love, and eke my love fro me;
> I hate the earth, because it is the mold
> Of fleshy slime and fraile mortalitie;

I hate the fire, because to nought it flyes,
I hate the Ayre, because sighes of it be,
I hate the Sea, because it teares supplyes.

I hate the day, because it lendeth light
To see all things, and not my love to see;
I hate the darknesse and the drery night,
Because they breed sad balefulnesse in me;
I hate all times, because all times do flye
So fast away, and may not stayed be,
But as a speedie post that passeth by.

Daphnaida

And so Spenser goes on weaving his verbal patterns, day/night, man/
woman, life/death, past/future, hate/love. His stanza forms may be
simple, as here or in *Four Hymns*, or complicated, as in the
Epithalamion, but they are never hurried, always graceful. Each stanza
must be complete in itself: Spenser thinks in stanzas, not in single lines.
It is significant that the word 'Spenserian' has passed into the language
to describe the beautiful stanza he invented for *The Faerie Queene*.
In lines like these (*F. Q.* II. xii. 71) we see what English poetry
gained from Spenser's love of pattern-making. As W. L. Renwick
says in his book (1925), they represent a brilliant transference into
words of the effects of polyphonic music: the entry of the different
voices can be heard.

The joyous birdes shrouded in chearefull shade,
Their notes unto the voyce attempred sweet;
Th'Angelicall soft trembling voyces made
To th'instruments divine respondence meet:
The silver sounding instruments did meet
With the base murmur of the waters fall:
The waters fall with difference discreet,
Now soft, now loud, unto the wind did call:
The gentle warbling wind low answerèd to all.

Spenser's deliberateness, his refusal to crowd his thoughts, the slow
and gradual development of his rhythms, can yield marvellous results
in *The Faerie Queene*. But the question has to be raised whether much
else of his is worth reading, except for historical reasons. The leading
Spenserian of our time, C. S. Lewis, remarked that while Virgil
would still be thought a great poet without the *Aeneid*, or Milton
without *Paradise Lost*, or Goethe without *Faust*, Spenser without *The*

Faerie Queene would probably have been forgotten. And in recent times Spenser scholarship and criticism have concentrated on it almost exclusively. In the Penguin English Poets series Spenser is represented only by *The Faerie Queene* (edited 1978 by Roche and O'Donnell). This isolation of Spenser's chief poem from all his others may be based on sound judgement but it does tend to make *The Faerie Queene* seem even more a bizarre curiosity than it is already. And while it may be admitted that much in the minor poems does not greatly appeal to us, there are elements in them that are more interesting and poetically alive than some things in *The Faerie Queene*. (Readers may be reminded of the similar situation in Pound criticism, with its overwhelming emphasis on the *Cantos*.) And even the reader who cares only about *The Faerie Queene* will find plenty of material in Spenser's other work to help him understand the author's characteristic thought and temper of mind.

The most famous of these other works is *The Shepherd's Calender* (1579), often compared with the *Lyrical Ballads* of Wordsworth and Coleridge as heralding a poetic revival. But it is likely to affect many readers as it affected the young Stephen Potter, coming to it with happy anticipation of pristine pleasure from 'the poet's poet'. His disappointment was complete.

> Instead of breath-taking images, there was smooth poetistical language. Instead of apprehensions of nature (making me see something as if for the first time) there was talk of *oaten stop*, and the shepherds' *fleecy care*. Instead of naiveté and idealism, confident force (my conception, then, of what a young poet's poetry was likely to possess) there was careful imitation, use of classics chosen from models for which I still had a schoolboy antipathy.
>
> (*The Muse in Chains*, 1937)

Potter's reaction is understandable. He had not yet enough literary experience to realize that the 'poetic diction' he found so objectionable would not have had, for Spenser and his friends, the hackneyed, unfresh quality which it came to have in the eighteenth century; it had still something of the excitement of a new discovery. But though historical extenuations are possible, the *Calender* has been traditionally much overrated. The pastoral convention is dead for most of us, and it has been plausibly argued that Spenser's use of it is not happy: he gives us neither the sense of real country life, such as we find in the work of Homer or John Clare, nor a completely idyllic world, such as Michael Drayton portrays in his later poetry. The experiments in language and metre have some historical interest, but they represent on the whole a dead end for Spenser and for English poetry generally. The attempt to combine the neo-Chaucerian (evident in the rugged metre and archaic spelling) with the neo-classical produces an incongruous effect, and criticism of the 'old rustic' language goes back as far as Sidney's *Apology for Poetry*. But there are fine things in the *Calender*. The song on Elizabeth in 'April' shows Spenser as already a remarkable 'word-musician'; and these lines from 'December' have the freshness of real experience in them, for all the 'pastoral' costume:

> Whilome in youth, when flowrd my joy full spring,
> Like Swallow swift I wandred here and there:
> For heat of heedless lust*ᵃ* me so did sting,
> That I of doubted danger had no feare.
>   I went the wastefull woodes and forest wyde
>   Withouten dread of Wolves to bene espyed.
>
> I wont to raunge amydde the mazie thickette,
> And gather nuttes to make me Christmas game;
> And joyed ofte to chace the Trembling Pricket*ᵇ*,
> Or hunt the hartless*ᶜ* hare, till shee were tame.
>   What wreaked I of wintry ages waste,
>   Tho deemed I, my spring wold ever laste.
>
> How often have I scaled the craggie Oke,
> All to dislodge the Raven of her neste:
> How have I wearied with many a stroke
> The stately Walnut tree, the while the rest
>   Under the tree fell all for nuts at strife:
>   For ylike to me was libertee and lyfe.

Much more immediate pleasure can be got from other poems of Spenser. There is strong plain writing in *Mother Hubberds Tale* (1591), a beast-fable in heroic couplets (it is in fact a group of stories). Here Spenser is the heir of the comic Chaucer, and his verse-manner looks forward to Dryden's satires. In *The Ruins of Time* there is some moving elegiac writing, as the poet commemorates the deaths of Sidney, Leicester and Walsingham. It is notable that the lines which seem to reveal the strongest feeling are not on Sidney, but on his uncle Leicester, to most of us a less attractive figure:

a pleasure, *b* young buck, *c* timid.

He now is dead, and all with him is dead,
Save what in heavens storehouse be uplaid:
His hope is faild, and come to pass his dread,
And evil men, now dead, his deeds upbraid:
Spite bites the dead, that living never baid[a].
He now is gone, the whiles the Foxe is crept
Into the hole, the which the Badger swept.

These bitter lines were to stick in the mind of Yeats (see 'The Municipal Gallery Revisited'). There is real observation behind them: the fox is a dirty feeder, the badger clean and neat. This earthy simplicity is characteristic of Spenser. Quite different is the sunny poem, the miniature epic *Muiopotmos; or the Fate of the Butterflie* – in its graceful charm suggesting a temporary release from puritan ethics and piety:

What more felicitie can fall to creature
Than to enjoy delight with liberty . . .

The full extent of Spenser's powers as a lyric poet is shown in a volume of 1595, containing the sonnet sequence *Amoretti*, together with *Epithalamion*. It seems clear that he meant this volume to be read as the poetic record of his courtship of and marriage to his second wife, Elizabeth Boyle. The sonnets themselves are too much in one key, and do not consistently rise above the level of average Elizabethan sonneteering. Spenser does not bring to this verse-form the force and originality of the English masters of the sonnet, Shakespeare, Milton, Wordsworth, Rossetti, Hopkins and Auden. It is the *Epithalamion* that is unique and unsurpassable, conveying something of the exultation to be felt in poems like Smart's *Song to David* or Hopkins's *The Wreck of the Deutschland*: the joy of a technical accomplishment which is at the same time an emotional satisfaction. The structure of this marriage ode is based on the progression of a summer day, from dawn to nightfall. Modern scholarship has discovered an elaborate astrological and numerological symbolism in the poem. But whether or not the secrets of Spenser's art can be discovered in this way, no lover of English poetry can miss the musical pattern of the stanzas and the interweaving of Christian and pagan motifs, the association of sensuousness and spirituality. In this

a barked.

exalting of marriage the 'Renaissance' and the 'puritan' elements of Spenser's temperament are at one.

> Now al is done; bring home the bride againe,
> Bring home the triumph of our victory,
> Bring home with you the glory of her gaine,
> With joyance bring her and with jollity.
> Never had man more joyfull day than this,
> Whom heaven would heape with blis.
> Make feast therefore now all this live long day,
> This day for ever to me holy is,
> Poure out the wine without restraint or stay,
> Poure not by cups, but by the belly full,
> Poure out to all that wull*,
> And sprinkle all the postes and walls with wine,
> That they may sweat, and drunken be withall.
> Crowne ye God Bacchus with a coronall,
> And Hymen also crowne with wreathes of vine,
> And let the Graces daunce unto the rest;
> For they can doe it beste:
> The whiles the maydens to their carroll sing,
> To which the woods shall answer and theyr eccho ring.

Prothalamion (1596), written for the weddings of the two daughters of the Earl of Worcester, is on a smaller scale and does not have so much emotional unity. But its refrain ('Sweet Themmes, runne softly till I end my song') is one of the few lines of Spenser that are well known, perhaps because of T. S. Eliot's use of it in *The Waste Land*.

To know the marriage odes is to know Spenser as a poet of celebration. In other poems he is the poet of complaint and elegy, of pastoral and satire. But it was to be in epic and romance – a peculiar mixture of them – that he was to achieve his most lasting fame, with *The Faerie Queene*. It is clear that this was his life work, and all his other poems were, in some sense, interruptions of it. But its status now appears ambiguous. One of the few things that can be said with confidence about *The Faerie Queene* is that it is enigmatic, problematic, protean.

To see *The Faerie Queene* as part of English poetic history is to realize what different things it has meant to different poets. It was extolled during Spenser's lifetime, though there are signs that his contemporaries really preferred *The Shepherd's Calender*, and for long

a will.

Spenser was more esteemed as a pastoral than as an epic poet. And the seventeenth-century 'Spenserians' are not the liveliest poets of that time. Already in Cowley and Milton there are signs of the divided, divergent response to *The Faerie Queene* which is the central problem of Spenser criticism. Cowley as a boy was delighted by it, 'the stories of the Knights and Giants, and Monsters', and for many readers this level of response is the only true one. For Milton, on the other hand, the poet was 'our sage and serious Spenser', 'a better teacher than Scotus or Aquinas'. Spenser's first critic, Sir Kenelm Digby (1603–1665), did something to bring these two aspects of *The Faerie Queene* together. But on the whole it was Spenser's fantasy, and his curious style, plain and forceful yet flavoured with archaism, that appealed to later poets. In the eighteenth century Spenser's poem contributed substantially to the romantic medievalism of the time. And its influence is plain in the work of the poets of the late eighteenth and early nineteenth century. Wordsworth admired Spenser as a teacher and moralist, and he felt the beauty of Spenser's poetry keenly. Keats and Shelley use the Spenserian stanza, and Keats especially was drawn to Spenser's erotic world, as we see in *The Eve of St Agnes*. Byron imitates Spenser's style in *Childe Harold's Pilgrimage*, and uses his stanza; but Byron's temperament was too unlike Spenser's for him to keep up the imitation for very long, and the slow-moving Spenserian stanza was not so suited to him as the *ottava rima* he adopted in *Don Juan*. Tennyson in *The Lotos-Eaters* was better able to make a more positive use of Spenser, the Spenser of the Despair episode and the house of Morpheus. But after Tennyson and the Pre-Raphaelites the presence of Spenser, as part of the English poetic consciousness, seems less palpable. The last major modern poet to show much interest in him was Yeats (the others, if they were interested in sixteenth-century poetry at all, have preferred other poets, such as Skelton or Wyatt). And Yeats's essay makes it clear that he was bored and repelled by much in Spenser; his final verdict is not enthusiastic. Apart from isolated figures like C. M. Doughty there seems to be no twentieth-century poet for whom Spenser has counted for much.

The history of scholarly study and interpretation of *The Faerie Queene* is quite different. It began early in the eighteenth century with writers like Upton and Hughes, who are still well worth reading, though Upon was committed to the hopeless opinion that

The Faerie Queene has a single 'story' (that of Prince Arthur), with beginning, middle and end. Eighteenth-century criticism was much concerned with questions about the form of Spenser's poem: what kind of poem is it? Many modern ideas, such as those expounded by Rosemond Tuve in *Allegorical Imagery* (1966) about its 'interlaced' narratives, are anticipated in commentators of that time who maintained that *The Faerie Queene* is to be understood (and enjoyed) as an example of 'Gothic', not 'classical', form. The romantic movement brought something of a reaction against Spenser commentators. Hazlitt advised readers not to bother with the allegory and moral significance but to enjoy *The Faerie Queene* as a glorious verbal symphony. What it was 'about' was not of any great consequence. The likeness to great Renaissance paintings which Spenser had never seen was expounded in extensive detail by Leigh Hunt, who called Spenser England's greatest painter. It was the colour work, not the themes, of this particular Old Master that interested Hunt. The 'escapist' view was carried further by James Russell Lowell, who found the didactic element in *The Faerie Queene* irrelevant or distasteful. But he was opposed firmly by the Irish critic Edward Dowden. And there were other critics who took Spenser's allegory seriously. Ruskin in *The Stones of Venice* supplied a point-by-point interpretation of Book I of *The Faerie Queene* which anticipates much modern work of this kind. The topical, or historical, allegory has of course always been a matter for controversy. The great American scholar Greenlaw played it down, as did C. S. Lewis, the most influential of modern Spenserians; but it has been revived in recent times by Frank Kermode, with special emphasis on Books I and V.

The Variorum edition of 1949 can be seen as a landmark in traditional Spenser scholarship. Up till then the critics, though increasingly scholarly, had been within the 'genteel', men-of-letters tradition. After the Second World War there appeared the modern academic specialist and the new development of 'Renaissance studies'. Spenser was now to be 'read' as Panofsky or Edgar Wind taught us to 'read' Renaissance paintings. Iconography, rhetoric and other technical studies of language, astrology and numerology, and other recondite aspects of Renaissance thought, were brought to bear. The emblembooks, the shows and heraldry of the age were studied, as well as the inner politics and cultural life of the world Spenser knew. And the interconnections of symbolism, ambiguity and world-play within the poem were more and more studied; all this, it must be remembered, at a time when Freudian dream-interpretation and all its ramifications had spread into literary criticism, and the widely held view that speculation about a poet's intentions is irrelevant seemed to license the utmost extravagances of subjective interpretation. Today the reader in search of guidance to Spenser's work is caught between some experts using freedom of association ever more and more widely, and others demanding a heavier and heavier burden of esoteric knowledge.

All this is understandable. *The Faerie Queene* was said by the poet, in his prefatory letter to Ralegh, to contain an allegory, or 'dark conceit', and it has long been a rich mine for symbol-seekers, allusion-spotters, and source-hunters. As with Dante's *Divine Comedy*, the crossword-puzzle appeal is strong. But the question does arise: what is the purpose of all this activity? In an age which has produced *The Road to Xanadu* and *Finnegans Wake*, it may be that intellectual complications are enjoyed for their own sake. In the meantime, however, the question why Spenser matters, why his poem rather than, say, Phineas Fletcher's *The Purple Island* (1633), is the pretext for all this, goes unanswered. The Spenserian scholars do occasionally venture into evaluation. They admit faults, or judge one book of *The Faerie Queene* inferior to another. But the whole enterprise of *The Faerie Queene* goes unquestioned, as does its status relative to works which are admitted to be less problematically 'great'. How does it compare in value and significance with the plays of Shakespeare? or even with one of Shakespeare's major plays?

The stock answer to such evaluative questions has been that the poem must be understood before it can be judged. But the quest for a 'correct' understanding of *The Faerie Queene*, even with the full resources of modern scholarship, seems illusory. Studies multiply, often repetitive; one scholar may differ from another, but no interpretation gets eliminated; more and more are added. And as this is a world without a common reader, there is no common-sense check on these interpretations, no public opinion that need be attended to. It is not a healthy state of affairs for a supposedly 'classic' poet.

There has, however, been one hopeful development, as far as the general reader of poetry is concerned. Up to the 1940s Spenser scholars tended to be either indifferent to modern poetry and criticism, or actually hostile to it. Since then there have been good books by scholars like Nelson (1963), Alpers (1967), and Sale (1968), who are in sympathy with modern taste as well as aware of the many historical and exegetic problems which Spenser presents.

It should be clear, then, that in our time the status of *The Faerie Queene* is problematic, and an innocent, 'told to the children' account of it is not only insulting, but impossible. Until the old question 'What kind of poem is it?' is answered, we cannot read the poem; and the question is not easy to answer. Any assertions about the poem must therefore remain provisional and tentative.

But it might be asked why we should not simply go to the poet himself for an account of his intentions. There is the letter to Ralegh to be consulted. However, this document itself requires so much interpretation that it is no use simply passing it on to new readers as a helpful introduction to the poem. It is full of words and phrases that are themselves highly problematic and the interpretation of which is controversial. And it describes only what may have been the poet's plan at the time of writing it: a twelve-book poem (with, perhaps, another twelve-book poem as its sequel) which we do not possess. What we have appears to be two fragments of that design, Books I, II and III, published together in 1590, and Books IV, V and VI, published together in 1596. (There is also the mysterious fragment known as the Mutability Cantos, published posthumously in 1609, which appears to be part of another Book, not extant.) The letter to Ralegh is prefixed to the first of these fragments. But it does not, on the face of it, fit even that part of the poem very well. The sketch of Book I is correct, but the sketch of Book II is not. Scholars have tried to reconcile the poem as we have it with the letter to Ralegh, but this is difficult to do. It would be wrong to say that the letter is not of great interest and historical value. But the problems of the poem as it actually exists, empirically, still remain.

What is reasonably uncontroversial is Spenser's choice of basic form for his narrative: the romance of knight-errantry. The Italian chivalrous epics of Boiardo and Ariosto are also based on this material, and Spenser's debt to the Italian poets is obvious. But he also draws directly on the traditions of this kind of romance as it came down to them. It has often been remarked that he creates a world of his own, Fairyland, even more remote from real history or geography than the world of the Italians. These are 'the brave days of old', exempt, as Coleridge said, from any particular space and time: an enchanted forest, a land of knights and fair ladies, castles and bowers and temples, vile witches, cunning enchantresses, sorcerers ('He to his studie goes'), demons and goddesses, ogres and monsters, nymphs and satyrs.

Why Spenser chose to write about knights and their adventures is not completely clear. Apart from references to his old-world romanticism and antiquarian, backward-looking disposition, the only explanation that used to be given was his ambition to emulate or to 'overgo' Ariosto, whose *Madness of Roland* (1532) had long delighted Renaissance readers and puzzled Renaissance critics. But it now seems reasonable to connect *The Faerie Queene* with the Elizabethan passion for tourneys in which nobles took part for royal entertainment, and the deliberate idealization of life and times under an imaginary 'Arthurian' chivalry which is mixed up with contemporary politics and ideology.

The Madness of Roland, of all famous poems, is the one most obviously like *The Faerie Queene*. And Spenser clearly knew Ariosto's poem intimately, and adapts or imitates much of its contents. But he is very different. It was for long a critical commonplace that the English poet was grave, even humourless, that he took seriously incidents and reflections which in the Italian poet were ironical. It was regretted that the other great sixteenth-century Italian poet, Tasso, came too late with his *Jerusalem Delivered* (1581, 1583) to influence Spenser greatly, though Spenser was able to draw on him, with exquisite results, for the beautiful song in the Bower of Bliss (II. xii. 75). Tasso was as devout and serious a child of the Catholic Counter-Reformation as Spenser was of the Protestant Reformation, and no doubt they have much in common. But why was Spenser attracted to Ariosto? Is it not possible that he understood Ariosto perfectly well, but used him for his own purposes and in his own way? The really great difference between Spenser and Ariosto is that we very soon come to know the implied author as we never know Spenser. One of the charms of Ariosto's extravaganza is that we are always aware of his presence beside us. Spenser is enigmatic: he has reverted to the manner of the old, anonymous storytellers. Even in the moralizing proems and explicit comments on the action there is no 'Spenser voice'. Or rather, there are many 'Spenser voices'.

The next unchallengeable observation about *The Faerie Queene* is that though the world of the poem is obviously an imaginary world, a dream-landscape, there is considerable realism of presentation within its confines. Fairyland may contain angels, goblins, giants, but it is full of observations of humanity and nature, detailed and always visualized. This peculiar realism of *The Faerie Queene* is perhaps the only respect in which it resembles a novel. Here is Britomart suspicious of her lover's good faith:

> One while she blam'd her selfe; another whyle
> She him condemn'd, as trustlesse and untrew;
> And then, her griefe with errour to beguile,
> She fayn'd to count the time againe anew,
> As if before she had not counted trew,
> For houres but dayes; for weekes, that passed were,
> She told but months, to make them seeme more few;
> Yet when she reckned them, still drawing neare,
> Each hour did seem a month, and every month a yeare.
>
> (V. vi. 5)

But if in some ways the characters of *The Faerie Queene* may be said to inhabit an ordinary world, it is the ordinary world of romance, in which strange adventures, misunderstandings, magic, taboos respected and violated, are routine. In this respect it is very unlike the 'classical–realist' novel. Metamorphosis, shape-shifting, dream-like projections of states of mind and soul, which in the realistic novel have an awkward status, flourish in *The Faerie Queene*. At no point is the distinction between characters and their 'inner world' a distinct one. It is a piquant irony that Spenser, who has been relegated by some literary historians to an antiquarian backwater even in his own time, should turn out to have much in common with some ultra-modern writers who have undermined the classic realism, the three-dimensional 'illusionism', of the traditional novel. But for the most part, and for most people, English literature has remained a literature of characters as the realistic novelist understands them; and this may in part account for the uncertain position of Spenser's work.

Finally, there can be no doubt that *The Faerie Queene* is not offered merely as a series of romantic tales. It has another dimension of meaning, for which the poet himself uses the word 'allegory'. Innumerable books and articles have been written about this aspect of the matter: what he, and Renaissance poets and critics and readers generally, understood by allegory, the different types and modes of it, different 'depths' at different places, the emblematic details which are lost on the reader who merely reads the poem as he finds it, without benefit of Natalis Comes or all the other mythographers Spenser may or may not have drawn on. That much in the poem points to other levels than the literal is obvious. It is full of symbolic names, some transparent, like Sansloy and Sansfoy and Sansjoy, or Mammon, or Despair, some more opaque but none the less meaningful, like Archimago. The actual words of the poem, the odd spellings, constantly reflect Spenser's conviction that, at the linguistic level no less than the level of images, nothing is merely accidental or arbitrary. Contrary to the ideas of a modern thinker like Saussure, he sees nothing that is only contingent in the etymology and phonology of words as he understood them. Hence no paraphrase of an episode in *The Faerie Queene* can bring out its meaning, unless attention is paid to its puns and wordplay.

Nevertheless Hazlitt was not wholly wrong in advising us not to bother with the allegory: 'it will not bite us'. It must be understood that all interesting and significant works of art have more than one meaning, that they all contain elements which function in complex ways. The British film-maker Lindsay Anderson has said that no film-maker likes being asked what his work 'means'. What does *Gulliver's Travels* mean? What do *The Arabian Nights* mean? Is *Dick Whittington* 'real'? It may be guessed that Spenser, in his own way, wanted to fend off such questions. But the tone of Tudor high culture was ethical and didactic. We may think of the austere religious practices of even a worldly statesman like Lord Burghley, who seems to have been displeased by something non-moral, some element of eroticism he found in *The Faerie Queene*. Faced with 'mighty peers' and critics who demanded explicit ethical teaching from poetry, Spenser had no choice but to use the critical idiom of his day and talk about 'allegory', and Aristotle's twelve private moral virtues, and 'fashioning' a virtuous gentleman. Not that his avowed didactic aims should be dismissed as hypocritical, merely a sop to 'puritan' readers while the 'Renaissance' readers enjoyed his gallery of beautiful nudes, or goddesses in deshabille. If Spenser aspired to emulate Ariosto, he also wanted to be an English Virgil. And Virgil, like all great poets, was credited with numerous allegorical meanings, moral and religious. He held up images of good to be cherished, of evil to be reprobated. Spenser does this in the temptation of Mammon (II. vii), one of the trials to which the hero of Book II, the representative of Temperance, is subjected. The incident echoes the descent of Aeneas, led by the Sibyl, to the world of shades (*Aeneid* VI). As they enter, they are surrounded by shadowy figures – Grief, Care, Disease, Old Age – which we associate with the thought of death. Spenser makes the scene a correlative for the evil of Money-lust.

> Before the dore sat selfe-consuming Care,
> Day and night keeping wary watch and ward,
> For feare lest Force or Fraud should unaware
> Breake in, and spoil the treasure there in gard;
> Ne would he suffer Sleepe once thither-ward
> Approch, albe his drowsy den were next;
> For next to Death is sleepe to be compared;
> Therefore his house is unto his annext;
> Here Sleep, there Richesse, and Hell-gate them both betwixt.

Besides the classical allusion, Spenser in this episode dwells on the teaching of the Bible: 'How hardly shall they that have riches enter into the kingdom of heaven!' And the triple temptation of Guyon, which follows, alludes to Biblical temptations: Adam and Eve in the Garden of Eden, Jesus in the wilderness. The ethical allegory in such incidents has to be recognized, and taken seriously.

But it is important also to recognize that these classical, 'moral' episodes, like the romantic tales, represent only what Spenser *started with*. His poem is full of enigmas, and it seems clear that there is an element in his work of the deliberately enigmatic. At one time interest in this centred on the topical allegory, the significances that may have been there for court readers, if not for Spencer's printed-book public. All we can be certain of here is what Spenser vouches for in the letter to Ralegh, that Gloriana is Queen Elizabeth, who is also alluded to as 'Belphoebe'. It can be regarded as reasonably certain that the episode of Timias and Belphoebe refers to Ralegh's relations with the Queen. And that Duessa refers, in Book V, to Mary Queen of Scots may be taken as highly probable, since the identification was made so early (King James VI protested, or affected to protest, at the insult to his mother). But Duessa in Book I seems to be the Church of Rome, rather than a particular individual. And in general the historical allusions of the poem are fugitive. The longest stretch of topical allegory is in the last five cantos of Book V, almost a sustained commentary on foreign affairs and events in Ireland. But that these allusions are so obvious suggests that the search for other topical references is misguided.

To look for one main meaning in the poem is to fall into a sort of critical monism. Its character is to be protean. It is unlike all other famous Western poems in having no clear 'profile'. No brief account can suggest what it is about. In sources, allusions, mythology it is eclectic. Everything that goes through the Spenserian looking-glass is transformed, mutated. We can guess, however, that the main characters are human beings, not personified abstractions, or cardinal virtues. They encounter allegorical beings; they can even *become* them, as the jealous Malbecco 'becomes' Jealousy at the end of that blackly farcical story (III. ix, x). But the essential subject-matter is the inner life, the psychological landscapes, of men and women.

The presentation and tone vary in different Books. Books I and II have a similar pattern: the knight hero on his quest in company with a super-ego or conscience figure. The problems are perhaps too explicitly religious and ethical to be attractive to modern readers. Book I is the story of Redcrosse, a combination of the legend of St George with a sustained use of imagery drawn from the Book of Revelation. This is the book of Holiness, and the tone appropriately is one of high gravity, though the stories are of romantic enchantments: some of the deeper meanings in the Book depend upon both Redcrosse and Una mistaking an evil replica, the work of magic, for the beloved. Book II is more concerned with psychological than theological problems: the knight of Temperance is tempted by violence and lust. The lengthy and bloody fighting in this Book suggests that it is largely a study in the repressed sadism of the chilly hero. The things that 'happen' to him are the fantasies that are appropriate to such a personality. The great closing canto, culminating in the destruction of the bower of Acrasia, Spenser's version of Homer's Circe – the canto is an *Odyssey* in miniature – seems best read in such a way, rather than as an expression of Spenser's personal prurience. The violence with which Guyon destroys the Bower of Bliss seems to be a substitute for the climax of sexual enjoyment which is forbidden to him.

It is a pity that these Books are perhaps the best known. They contain some fine things, but they do not represent the whole of Spenser. Books III and IV have a less clear-cut quality. They are free from the anti-Catholic propaganda of Book I, the black-and-white moral tones of Book II. Here we are in a many-coloured world, voluptuous yet enchanted, surrealistic. The structure of these Books is much less apparent than that of the earlier ones. But many of the episodes turn on the qualities of contrasting women: the warrior Britomart, the tormented Amoret, the timid, fleeing Florimell, the lecherous Hellenore. Britomart is by general agreement Spenser's best 'character'; and however anti-feminist may have been his official doctrines, it is clear that, like his unfortunate Artegall, he is drawn to warrior women. In Book V the tone changes again, to the world of the 'iron man' Talus, Artegall's torturer and executioner, and his mission of 'justice', and we have a glimpse of the hard side of Spenser that we see in his prose dialogue on the state of Ireland. But Book VI offers yet another metamorphosis. Here we are in the world of Sidney's *Arcadia*, pastoral brought to life, so much more than in *The Shepherd's Calender*, by the admixture of chivalrous romance. Shakespeare seems to have drawn on this attractive Book in his *Winter's Tale*. The finest thing in the whole Book, and perhaps in the poem, is the passage in which we are shown a vision of the naked Graces dancing to the music of Colin Clout – the poet himself. It has been thought that by introducing himself in this way Spenser was saying farewell to his readers.

To convey the quality of so miscellaneous a work is not possible in a short space, let alone to attempt to judge it. But perhaps the essential question is this. Spenser's best modern critics agree on his 'undramatic' quality. We might take the story of Phedon (II. iv) as an example. It is a Hero and Claudio story, of deceit and murder and jealousy as cruel as the grave. It is crisply and vividly told. But when it is told Guyon simply remarks:

> Squire, sore have ye beene diseasd;
> But all your hurts may soone through temperance be easd,

as if temperance were a patent medicine; while the Palmer moralizes. The effect is to make the tragic events seem *not to have happened*: the story becomes a mere cautionary tale, an *exemplum*. What did Spenser intend here? It is hard to say. Why should he have taken the 'drama' out of his own work? In the end the effect on us is to produce a feeling of detachment: this is tapestry, not flesh and blood. The question is whether this 'undramatic' quality does not entail the omission of other potentialities that have usually been held to be essential to great imaginative writing in any kind. Perhaps the conclusion must be drawn that Spenser's achievement in *The Faerie Queene* appeals to a very *special* taste, and does not convey at once that conviction that we are reading a great work which comes before 'understanding' and analysis. All that can be added to qualify this is that in every age, despite all the changes of taste since the 1590s, there have been a few readers who have felt the fascination of this problematic, enigmatic work, taken up its challenge to normal modes of perception, and come to terms with its elusive art.

SIDNEY'S *ARCADIA* AND *ASTROPHEL AND STELLA*

J. C. A. RATHMELL

Since T. S. Eliot dismissed the *Arcadia* some fifty years ago as 'a moment of dullness' there has been a gradual but marked rise in Sidney's literary stock.[1] This has been due in large part to an increasing recognition of the fact that, so far from being a work of gratuitously elaborate artifice, the *Arcadia* embodies a genuine attempt to grapple imaginatively (and often humorously) with problems that were close to the author's heart and conscience. Sidney himself (1554–86), in accordance with prevailing literary etiquette, deprecated his eight-hundred-page book as 'a trifle, and triflingly handled'. But the preposterousness of such modesty is half-acknowledged in his venturing to hope – almost in the same breath – that it would be 'made much of', for all its defects. In the sixty or seventy years following his death at the age of thirty-one in 1586 the *Arcadia* did in fact firmly establish itself as a classic of its kind, and during that period more than a dozen editions were published. In 1660 a representative seventeenth-century reader William Higden, author of the *Institution of a Gentleman*, reminded his grandson that in his youth it had been considered 'a defect in a gentleman not to be versed in Sir Philip Sidney'.[2] Even Milton, who notoriously rebuked Charles I for taking solace in such an 'amatorious' book on the eve of his execution, admitted that as a secular work the *Arcadia* was 'full of worth and wit', and referred admiringly to a number of passages from it in his commonplace book.[3]

In speaking of Sidney's 'wit' Milton had in mind, no doubt, the quality of his intelligence rather than his sense of humour, but Sidney's works are indeed far from solemn. The *Arcadia*, like his sonnet sequence *Astrophel and Stella*, is characterized by the frequent appearance of a sly and subtle wit that is always threatening to call in question, albeit affectionately, the heroic and romantic values it ostensibly celebrates. Although only printed posthumously, the two works, it is now generally recognized, were written more or less concurrently in the early 1580s and grow out of similar emotional experience. The *Arcadia* is of course a much larger scale undertaking and Sidney may still have been at work revising it as late as 1585, the year before he died; but in its emotional springs, it clearly draws – like his poems – on the experience and sensibility of a young courtier harassed by a sense of his obligations and of the high expectations that were pinned upon him.

Although he could claim, with characteristically restrained pride, that his mind was 'none of the basest', Sidney was keenly aware of the difficulty of living up to the golden opinions that from an early age he attracted. Groomed for high office and despatched on a Grand Tour to make important contacts with the leading Protestant princes of Europe, Sidney was never allowed to forget what was expected of him as nephew of the Earl of Leicester and son of a respected Elizabethan statesman. Sidney's modern reputation as the epitome of the many-talented Renaissance courtier derives, of course, mainly from the lavish poetic tributes he elicited at the time of his premature death and from Fulke Greville's highly eulogistic *Life* of his former friend written some twenty-five years later; but even in his own lifetime Sidney clearly felt embarrassed by the unreasonably high hopes that were entertained of him. Both his poems and his surviving letters testify to an oppressive awareness of that 'friendly foe, Great expectation', and a nagging sense that he had never quite come up to the mark stayed with him to the end. As early as 1577 Sir Francis Walsingham had said of him that 'the gentleman hath given no small arguments of great hope'; and, ironically, even in the year of his death nine years later he was still being referred to as 'a gentleman of great hope, and exceeding expectation'. There is surely a powerful personal animus behind Sidney's characterization of 'o'er shooting expectation' as 'the most cruel adversary of all honourable doings'.[4]

The veteran diplomat Hubert Languet was only one of several close associates who took it upon themselves to nudge Sidney with needling reminders of his responsibilities:

To offend me is of little consequence; [Languet writes in a typical letter] but reflect how grievously you would be sinning against your excellent father, who has placed all his hopes in you, and who now being in the flower of life expects to see the full harvest of those virtues which your character promises so largely to produce.[5]

Outwardly Sidney attempted to preserve the demeanour of an apt pupil but it would have been surprising if he had not occasionally mutely rebelled against such admonitions, as he does for instance in Sonnet XXI:

> Your words, my friend (right healthful caustics) blame
> My young mind marr'd, whom Love doth windlass so,
> That mine own writings like bad servants show
> My wits, quick in vain thoughts, in virtue lame ...

As Sidney insouciantly confesses in a number of his poems (such as the delightful Sonnet XXX with its comically weary references to affairs in Turkey and Poland), his mind at this time was not fully engaged by his public duties. It would be fruitless to press too hard the biographical relevance to his poetry of his relationship with the capricious Penelope Devereux (later Lady Rich, and subsequently the wife of three more husbands) but there can be little doubt that Sidney was both mortifyingly and impenitently aware that his infatuation with her did him little credit. Much of the attraction (and complexity) of his verse derives from the honesty with which he attempts to come to terms with his confused feelings. Some of the most convincing of his poems (such as Sonnet XIV) acknowledge with engaging candour an awareness of his imprudence and a simultaneous helplessness to remedy the situation:

> Alas have I not pain enough, my friend,
> Upon whose breast a fiercer gripe doth tire
> Than did on him who first stale down the fire
> While Love on me doth all his quiver spend,
>
> But with your rhubarb words you must contend,
> To grieve me worse, in saying that desire
> Doth plunge my well-form'd soul even in the mire
> Of sinful thoughts, which do in ruin end?

A large proportion of the *Astrophel and Stella* poems are characterized by this kind of rather wan, self-deprecating humour. Sonnet LXXII, like many others, teasingly reflects a determination (that never quite amounts to a firm resolve) to subjugate his unruly passions:

> Desire, though thou my old companion art,
> And oft so clings to my pure love, that I
> One from the other scarcely can descry,

> While each doth blow the fire of my heart;
> Now from thy fellowship I needs must part . . .

Here as elsewhere the humour and authenticity of these lines lies in Sidney's tacit admission that he is moved more by a sense of the irksome obligation to give up his erring ways than by any very positive enthusiasm to pursue a more virtuous course; and that reluctance is eloquently reflected in the halting movement of the passage and the syntactical suspensions that intervene as the poet nerves himself to make his decision.

Sidney's verse is not, of course, radically innovatory either in form or language, and neither the sonnets nor the *Arcadia* are free from mawkish sentiment and over-elaboration: what is immediately discernible, however, is his critical awareness of these elements in his work and his readiness to subject them to a good-humoured scrutiny. Self-mockery, sophistry, bantering raillery and an often disconcertingly dry and caustic wit are crucial components of Sidney's style, and it is their alliance with other quite contrary elements – vulnerability, sensibility, and a lingering attachment to the old high ways of romance and chivalry – that combine to make his writing so distinctive, and so winning.

A characteristic feature of Sidney's subtle and subdued sense of humour, and one that immediately distinguishes it from the more aggressively masculine wit of later poets such as Donne, is its almost invariable association with a rueful consciousness of his own in-adequacies and self-deceptions. Sidney retains a remarkable capacity to be undeceived by his own sophistries. A recurring theme of his sonnets, as we have seen, lies in the conflict between his sense of the responsible conduct demanded of him by his office and birth and a half poignant, half hapless awareness of his inability to suppress or check his recalcitrant desires. Similarly much of the comedy (and moral complexity) of the *Arcadia* derives from a sharply ironic sense of the gap between man's life as it is and as it should be. The predicaments and harassments experienced by Astrophel have in fact a good deal in common with those undergone by the princely heroes of the *Arcadia*. Conventionally enough the *Arcadia* ends happily, but only after Pyrocles and Musidorus have been brought to a chastening and discomfiting sense of how easily and how prematurely they have allowed themselves to believe in their own glittering public reputations. It is in fact a central tenet of Sidney's philosophy that no man is free from that 'secret assurance of his own worthiness, which although it be never so well-clothed in modesty always lives in the worthiest minds' (p. 794).[6]

Despite its immense length, the basic plot of the *Arcadia* is simple enough. In its bare outline it is neither more nor less ridiculous than the kind of plots which form the basis of Shakespeare's romantic comedies. Pyrocles and Musidorus, having miraculously survived a shipwreck and found their way to Arcadia, learn that King Basilius in order to avoid the fulfilment of an alarming oracular prophecy has retired with his family to a forest retreat. In order to gain access to the king's beautiful daughters, Pamela and Philoclea, the two young princes make the fatal mistake of resorting to subterfuge, Musidorus assuming the disguise of a shepherd, Pyrocles (more intriguingly) that of a maidservant. Sidney fully exploits the dramatic potential of the latter's absurd situation (which of course involves a comic reversal of the conventional romance device by which, as in *Twelfth Night* or *As You Like It*, a woman dresses as a man) and, indeed, the main complexities of the ensuing narrative grow out of the deceptions and confusions that arise directly from it. It is notable, however, that Sidney is careful to insist on the true absurdity of Pyrocles' female disguise only when his sexual desire gets the better of him (as, for instance, when in his maidservant role he accompanies the princesses on a bathing expedition), and even on these occasions the humour is not so much prurient as teasingly playful.

In so far as the young princes are treated critically by Sidney it is not of course because they have allowed themselves to fall in love but because of the deceptions to which they resort in order to pursue their desires. Although by and large honourable in their intentions, neither are free from 'fond desire' and ultimately they must pay the penalty for their indiscretions. The trials to which they have to submit are not arbitrary: they are subtly related to their failures of judgement at crucial junctures. In fact none of the central characters entirely escape censure and the way in which high and low characters alike seek to evade the consequences of their actions and are all the more surely defeated in their purposes provides one of the most insistently recurring motifs of the *Arcadia*, and, incidentally, ample evidence of Sidney's exceptional constructive skill.

Pyrocles and Philoclea, for instance, are vividly depicted as experiencing the 'contradictions growing in those minds, which neither absolutely climb the rock of virtue, nor freely sank into the sea of vanity'. Philoclea, the younger and more trusting of the two princesses, is confused and embarrassed by the strength of her feeling for her apparent maidservant. On a superficial reading the princess may seem to be conventionally pure and innocent in all her dealings but Sidney clearly signals a warning when he refers to her 'unmeasurable liking' of the maid, her 'exceeding delight' in her company and her nervous fear 'to be alone with whom alone she desired to be'. Philoclea, it is intimated, is invaded by 'whole squadrons of longings' that she cannot easily control or indeed fully comprehend. Her confusion is only compounded by her observation of the puzzling fact that her mother (who has been quicker to pierce Pyrocles' disguise than her inexperienced daughter) evidently loves the maid 'as well, at least as furiously' as herself. Sidney's whole treatment of this relationship is surprisingly complex and sophisticated in its appreciation of the conflict between conscious and unconscious impulses.

Then dreams by night began to bring more unto her, than she durst wish by day, whereout waking did make her know herself the better by the image of those fancies.

One of the most striking features of the *Arcadia* is the uninsistent way in which Sidney points a moral; judgements frequently remain implicit and comedy is commonly the vehicle employed to embody them. Sidney is remarkably free from the tiresomely explicit didacticism so commonly encountered in Elizabethan fiction. One of the climactic episodes of the book concerns the way in which Pyrocles extricates himself from the potentially compromising situation that results directly from his donning of female disguise. Wading an increasingly precarious course 'betwixt constancy and courtesy' and embarrassed by the passionate advances of both Basilius and Gynaecia, Pyrocles finds to his cost that 'deceit cannot otherwise be maintained but by deceit'. Accordingly he buys himself time and frees himself temporarily of their unwanted attentions by independently promising to each of them a midnight rendezvous, hoping in the meantime to flee the country with their daughter.

The infatuations of Basilius and Gynaecia are treated quite distinctly. The king (still under the delusion that Pyrocles is a woman) is comically absurd in his ungoverned lust and flatters himself that he 'was old enough to know that women are not wont to appoint secret night meetings for the purchasing of land'. Queen Gynaecia, on the other hand, is knowingly in the grip of an uncontrollable passion and 'was not ignorant of her fault'. In a brilliantly managed scene the king and queen, having found their separate ways to the secret rendezvous, make rapturous love to each other in the enclosing darkness. By an extraordinary turn of events Basilius is made in effect to commit adultery with his own wife and Sidney misses no opportunity for pointing up the ironies of the situation.

Earlier the king had taken great umbrage at the suggestion that he was not his wife's master ('What, said he, shall my wife become my mistress? Think you not that thus much time hath taught me to rule her?'). But now as he wastes no time in 'laying his lovingest hold' on the woman he assumes to be his daughter's servant, Gynaecia in a quite unintended sense becomes his mistress and hearing her enraptured husband marvel on the 'difference betwixt women' is obliged to accept in bemused silence his unusually passionate attentions. As dawn breaks and the mistakes of the night are humiliatingly clarified, it is perhaps a token of her own confusion and misgivings that the rebuke she addresses to her husband is couched in surprisingly temperate terms: 'Well, well my Lord, said she, it shall well become you so to govern yourself as you may be fit to direct me, than to be judged of me . . .' (p. 727). It is of course part of the irony of the situation that Gynaecia is hardly the person to remind her husband of the necessity for self-government and when by a further turn of the plot Basilius is seemingly poisoned by the love-potion the queen had prepared for Pyrocles she is brought to a fuller recognition of her misdeeds. Gynaecia's contrition, as Sidney presents it, is heartfelt.

But it is not only the king and queen who are thus humbled, and an important aspect of Sidney's moral and dramatic purpose is missed if we fail to see that he deliberately juxtaposes this thread of the story with that concerning the way in which the young lovers' plans come unstuck. The passage describing Pyrocles' mounting desire as he prepared to abduct Philoclea is clearly meant to recall Basilius' eagerness as he awaited his assignation, and to hint to the reader at the thin line which separates the conduct of the supposedly honourable prince from that of the erring king. Aroused by the sight of Philoclea lying 'upon the top of her bed, having her beauties eclipsed with nothing but with a fair smock', Pyrocles is in danger of 'quite forgetting himself'. Like Basilius, however, he suffers an unexpected setback and when, in the course of a lover's quarrel, Philoclea bitterly inquires if he has some 'third sex' left to transform himself into to 'inveigle my simplicity', he is forced into humiliating awareness that he is something less than the virtuous and valorous hero he is reputed to be. He is as much convinced of his own noble intentions as Philoclea of her 'simplicity' and both are equally self-deceived.

Much has been made of the fact that in an earlier draft of his romance[7] (only discovered at the beginning of this century and now known, for convenience, as the *Old Arcadia*) Pyrocles and Philoclea were allowed to make love at this point and that the revised version involves some pusillanimous whitewashing on Sidney's part. But it is of course a highly appropriate irony that despite (and partly because of) all his cunning stratagems Pyrocles should be denied the fulfilment of his physical desires at this juncture and that he should instead fall asleep alongside Philoclea out of sheer mental exhaustion. It is an equally apposite irony that attaches to his being discovered in this compromising posture the following morning by the clownish Dametas. Folly, in the moral universe of the *Arcadia*, repeatedly reveals 'that which far greater cunning had sought to conceal'. Pyrocles cuts a wretched figure at this stage and it is a token of his state of mind that his bitterest accusation of himself is not so much that he has seriously compromised Philoclea's reputation (though that of course concerns him) but that he had not taken more care to lock all the doors, hardly the worthy consideration of a noble prince, but very much the kind of thing that might occur to the ignominiously discomfited and very ordinary person that Pyrocles has by this time been reduced to.

A full account of the *Arcadia* would entail a more detailed consideration than is possible here of the capture (in an antecedent chapter) of the princesses by the villainous Queen Cecropia and of the sufferings they are made to endure as prisoners in her castle. This dark and protracted episode (pp. 443–595) is certainly graver and more sombre in tone than anything else in Sidney's work, but it is difficult for the modern reader not to feel that it is somewhat overdone and that Cecropia is too much (and too simply) an evil fairy-tale witch. Predictably enough the princesses successfully withstand the siege to their virtue and in so doing exhibit notable qualities of constancy and endurance. Presumably Sidney, in revising the less complex *Old Arcadia*, felt the need here to switch the focus of attention from the princes to the princesses and to counterbalance the comic and ironic aspects of the narrative with a weighty central episode of indisputably serious and moral tenor, but if so he did not sufficiently take into account the difficulties involved in harmoniously integrating it with what follows.

Possibly Sidney would have modified the concluding sections of the romance had he lived, but this can only be speculation. As it is there is a hiatus in the narrative and an awkward gearshift in tone as the focus of interest returns to the predicament of the princes as they are ironically frustrated in their attempts to make off with their loved ones. No doubt Sidney intended his readers to detect an irony in the fact that the princesses, having shown such admirable dignity and resolve in withstanding the evil temptations of Cecropia and her son, should so readily acquiesce in the plans of their lovers to abduct them. Certainly both pairs of lovers, however much they may plead the force of love to excuse their actions, are guilty at least of errors of judgement and must face the consequences. Accordingly the fifth and final book of the *Arcadia* is devoted to the trial of the princes and their eventual acquittal. Something of the high seriousness that characterizes the imprisonment episode also attaches to this concluding part of the romance, but here Sidney's narrative mastery (and his sense of irony) is very much more in evidence. In a brilliant and thoroughly dramatic denouement the reader is presented with yet another illustration of the old truth that 'all is lip-wisdom that wants [lacks] experience'.

In the absence of Basilius who is assumed dead, Euarchus is asked to act as judge in the case concerning the two princes (Musidorus, like Pyrocles, has been apprehended as he tries to flee the country with Pamela). The princes have assumed false names 'to cover the shame of their royal parentage' and to keep 'the evil news from their careful kinsfolk'. They are not aware that their judge is none other than Musidorus' father and it is the same 'strange and secret working of justice' (Sidney suggests) that prevents Euarchus in turn from realizing that he is sitting in judgement on his own son and nephew. He considers the case carefully and announces that laws 'fold us within assured bounds: which once broken man's nature infinitely rangeth'. It is useless for the princes to plead in mitigation that they had intended to marry the princesses. Such marriage, the judge magisterially observes, 'might be fit for them, but very unfit were it to the state, to allow a pattern of such procurations of marriage'. He has therefore no alternative but to condemn the princes to death.

We must pause here. This judgement has commonly been interpreted as reflecting Sidney's own stern Puritan morality finally asserting itself. Indeed when Euarchus belatedly recognizes that he has condemned to death his own son and nephew he insists that his ruling must stand for he has 'weighed the matter ... with most unpartiall and farthest reach of reason'. It should be clear, however, that Sidney does not endorse the extremely severe justice meted out by Euarchus. He has already hinted at the overconfidence in their judgement that characterizes even 'the worthiest minds' and the popular dismay at the outcome of the trial reflects the general view that Euarchus, for all his wisdom, has in this instance pursued 'too precise a course of justice'. His assurance in the wisdom of his verdict has no more validity than any other character's confidence in his own wisdom.

The trial scene, involving as it does the humbling of both the judged and the judge, plays an important role in the overall moral design of the *Arcadia*. Earlier Sidney had observed (in connection with the capture of Pyrocles) that 'the almighty wisdom' delights in showing the world 'that by unlikeliest means greatest matters may come to conclusion; that human reason may be the more humbled, and more willingly give place to divine providence'. That kind of homiletic intrusion is very rare in the *Arcadia* but it clearly has a bearing on the contrived sequence of events that allow the romance to conclude on a conventional happy note. Basilius unexpectedly revives from his drugged sleep and Euarchus surrenders his office to the legitimate ruler. Basilius, conscious of his own great fault, reprieves the princes, is reconciled to his wife, and the *Arcadia* ends with the prospect of happy marriage festivities for the two pairs of lovers.

The ending of the *Arcadia*, like the last scenes of Shakespeare's romantic comedies, is blatantly contrived and the manipulation of the plot is positively flaunted. At the last we are purposely allowed a glimpse of the puppet-strings as if to remind us that it is only in the charmed world of fairy-tale romance that such happiness can be achieved. Basilius, for instance, publicly desires his wife's pardon and kissing her:

left her to receive the most honourable fame of any Princess throughout the world, all men thinking (saving only Pyrocles and Philoclea, who never betrayed her) that she was the perfect mirror of all wifely love. Which though in that point undeserved, she did in the remnant of her life duly purchase, with observing all duty and faith to the example and glory of Greece ...

(p. 847)

The laconic blandness of 'though in that point undeserved' is sufficient to subvert any confident assurance in 'the most honourable fame' that Gynaecia will receive in her latter years. Nevertheless, the whole tenor of these last pages is, as in Shakespearean romance, towards an atmosphere of forgiveness and reconciliation. The reader's sympathies remain with Pyrocles and Musidorus, despite their errors, and he has shared too fully in the fortunes of the two pairs of young lovers to endorse any narrow judgement on the frailties of 'wormish mankind'. Sidney is not a doctrinaire Calvinist insisting on man's innate depravity (as some interpreters of the trial scene would suggest); nor does he subscribe to any glib Renaissance doctrines regarding the nobility of man's reason. Sidney adheres to a sane middle course: men have to live with their imperfections, recognizing their own weaknesses and forgiving them in others. He shares with Erasmus, the author of *The Praise of Folly*, the view that 'to err, mistake, and know nothing truly ... is the common condition of us all'; though, characteristically, he never requires his readers to contemplate this truth about the human condition too solemnly. For all his Protestant upbringing Sidney is no narrow moralist and a good measure of his primary allegiances remains with the heroic world of romance that he so affectionately portrays and criticizes here. If

Sidney is at heart too much the Renaissance courtier to ridicule more comprehensively the chivalric and martial postures of romance (as later satirists were to do), it is precisely this fact and Sidney's recognition of his divided loyalties that provides the *Arcadia* with its rich complexity and delicacy of texture.

NOTES

1. T. S. Eliot, *The Use of Poetry and the Use of Criticism* (London, 1932), 51.

2. *Harleian Miscellany* (London, 1812) IX, 592.

3. Don M. Wolfe (ed.), *Complete Prose Works of Milton* (New Haven, 1957), I, 371–2, 463–4.

4. See A. C. Hamilton, *Sir Philip Sidney: A Study of his Life and Works* (Cambridge, 1977), 18–20.

5. S. A. Pears (ed.), *The Correspondence of Sir Philip Sidney and Hubert Languet* (1845), 2.

6. Sir Philip Sidney, *Arcadia*, ed. Maurice Evans (Harmondsworth, 1977). Page references throughout are to this edition.

7. See, for a discussion of the revisions to this text, Sir Philip Sidney, *The Countess of Pembroke's Arcadia* (*the Old Arcadia*), ed. Jean Robertson (Oxford, 1973), lii–lxiii.

TWO ELIZABETHAN POETS:
DANIEL AND RALEGH
PETER URE

Sir Walter Ralegh's personality was a puzzle to his contemporaries. A sombre strain, perhaps the greed for personal glory, vitiates it; 'a tall, handsome, and bold man . . . but damnable proud' says Aubrey. To become a favourite of Elizabeth and a victim of James, to help found a new Empire and to have his opinions examined by a government suspicious of his orthodoxy, to patronize savants and Spenser, and finally to be condemned for high treason (1603) and write *The History of the World* (1614) in the Tower of London – such things are not done and suffered, save by exceptional men, even in the age of Shakespeare.[1] That last drama in Guiana (winter, 1617–18), with his son dead in the mountains, his faithful lieutenant shot and poniarded in his cabin, and the scaffold awaiting him at home, was Ralegh's most awful failure. Why did such a man write poetry? And what has he in common with Samuel Daniel, a quiet, schoolmasterish sort of man? – friend, it is true, and tutor of the great, concerned in a minor way with 'theatre-business, management of men', but, so far as we can tell, aptly characterized by Thomas Fuller's vignette: 'As the Tortoise burieth himself all the winter in the ground, so Mr Daniel would lie hid at his Garden-house in Oldstreet, nigh London, for some months together – the more retiredly to enjoy the company of the Muses – and then would appear in public to converse with his friends.'

Ralegh wrote poetry partly because he belonged to the tradition of Spenser's 'gentleman or noble person', the Renaissance courtier and man of action, of the kind most finely exemplified in Sir Philip Sidney. Castiglione in his famous book *The Courtier* – a work translated by Hoby in 1561 and widely read in Ralegh's England – puts the matter shortly:

Let [the courtier] much exercise himself in Poets, and no less in Orators and Historiographers, and also in writing both rime and prose, and especially in this our vulgar tongue. For beside the contentation [*enjoyment*] that he shall receive thereby himself, he shall by this means never want pleasant entertainments with women which ordinarily love such matters ... at the least wise he shall receive so much profit, that by that exercise he shall be able to give his judgement upon other men's doings [i.e. writings].

Daniel, although he was, unlike Ralegh, a professional writer, would doubtless have agreed; and, from his point of view as a detached observer, he must have found much to admire and wonder at in the mystery of Ralegh's adventurous undoing. In one of the *Delia* sonnets he asks:

> For who gets wealth that puts not from the shore?
>   Danger hath honour, great designs their fame,
>   Glory doth follow, courage goes before.
>   And though th' event oft answers not the same,
> Suffice that high attempts have never shame.
>   The mean-observer, whom base Safety keeps,
>   Lives without honour, dies without a name,
>   And in eternal darkness ever sleeps.[2]

And Ralegh himself, meditating on the falls of great men in his *History of the World*, quoted some sombre lines, very pertinent to his own condition, from Daniel's *Philotas* (1605), a play about an ambitious favourite who falls foul of the servants of an envious monarch. Daniel was indeed almost the only contemporary English poet honoured by quotation in Ralegh's vast book.[3]

But it is not these mutual interests that make Daniel (1562–1619) and Ralegh (*c.* 1552–1618) worth considering together in the same essay; nor yet do the great differences between the two men's lives oblige us to keep their poems apart. What their work really has in common is the tradition of Sidney's *Apology for Poetry* and of Renaissance poetic generally, which does not view poetry primarily as a means of 'self-expression', of releasing and relieving the personality in Byron's fashion. Sidney declared that the speaking picture of poesy illuminates and shadows forth, not the chance melancholy and passion of the moments, but 'many infallible grounds of Wisdom'. Though we may think that he settles too easily, or neglects, the delicate problem of the relation of a poet's innermost experience to what he writes, and although it must be true that the awful excitements of Ralegh's nature and the quiet satisfactions of Daniel's do affect their poetic work in various and indecipherable ways, it is none the less a mistake to read the poetry of either Ralegh or Daniel simply as though it provided footnotes to their personal histories, miraculously preserved records of the joys and griefs of historical characters. Sidney believed that the poet was more efficient than the philosopher at the shadowing forth of wisdom; another analogy between philosopher and poet still holds: both may feel that their work ought to be read as meaningful statements about a chosen subject. Elizabethan poets use their rhetoric, ornament, forms, and metre not simply to register the 'passionate fragmentary man', but to point inwards at meanings, often of quite an abstract kind, which show that emotion has become a thing to be reflected upon rather than to be communicated to a sympathetic reader in all its fresh disorder.

In what follows, then, I turn away from Guiana and the Tower as well as from 'Oldstreet nigh London'. In the next section I discuss the two poets' evaluative handling of emotion, and in the after section I draw attention to the way they shape each poem purposively with a care for conscious design and logical control. These, of course, are not the only features of Elizabethan poetry which require emphasis, nor are they necessarily always found together (although both happen to be exemplified in Ralegh and Daniel); but they are very important. Of the differences between the two poets, of the fact that Ralegh is nearer to Donne, and Daniel to Spenser, I have said nothing. This is because it seems more urgent to imply, through these minor representatives of the tradition of Elizabethan poetry, that Spenser and Donne do both belong to that tradition, and that, though Donne may have widely modified it, he must not be falsely separated from it.

In choosing poems for analysis, I have been guided by this desire to see Ralegh and Daniel in relation as sharers of a common phase in the history of poetry. Two things make this attempt difficult. Daniel's work is much the greater in bulk and the more various in form. He printed his first poems in 1592, and went on writing verse, lyrical, epistolary, narrative, and dramatic, up to at least 1614. Of Ralegh's poems, only about thirty which can certainly be attributed to him have survived, and we do not know when most of these were written, although they seem to belong mainly to the period 1576 to 1603. (Ralegh unfortunately followed that other recommendation of Castiglione to 'keep his poems close, lest he make other men to laugh at him' – because of their imperfections, not because writing poetry was considered effeminate; and while some of his work appeared in anthologies during his lifetime, his courtier-like discretion is responsible for much uncertainty in the canon.) I have tried to overcome these difficulties by taking my illustrations mainly from Daniel's sonnet sequence *Delia*. For, although an Elizabethen reader would justly expect to find in a sonnet sentiments and techniques very different from those used in a piece of furious anti-Court rhetoric like Ralegh's 'The Lie' or in a grand and lapidary epitaph like his poem on Sidney, it is none the less more appropriate to juxtapose Daniel's sonnets, rather than his epic or his epistles, with Ralegh's lyrics and pastorals.

In reading Daniel's earliest collection, the fifty sonnets called *Delia* (first authorized edition 1592), it is plain that what Calvin described as 'labyrinthine man' is not yet a subject for his pen. *Delia* does not show us a Daniel concerned to record the moments or the impacts of passion, or the variable quickenings of thought in the mind. Thought and passion have already been raised to that level where they are controlled by a steady awareness of the rhetorical functions of poetry to praise or persuade. The sonnets evaluate experience and even, quite often, invite us to 'glide through an abstract process' in a way which T. E. Hulme would have much disliked. A good example is Sonnet XXXVIII (in A. C. Sprague's reprint of the edition of 1592):

> Fair and lovely maid, look from the shore,
> See thy *Leander* striving in these waves;
> Poor soul fore-spent, whose force can do no more.
> Now send forth hopes, for now calm pity saves.
>   And waft him to thee with those lovely eyes,
>   A happy convoy to a holy land.
> Now show thy power, and where thy virtue lies;
> To save thine own, stretch out the fairest hand.
>   Stretch out the fairest hand a pledge of peace,
> That hand that darts so right, and never misses:
> I'll not revenge old wrongs, my wrath shall cease;
> For that which gave me wounds, I'll give it kisses,
>   Once let the Ocean of my cares find shore,
>   That thou be pleas'd, and I may sigh no more.

In this beautiful poem, the continued metaphor of Hero and Leander steers the reader away from physical sensations and sensuous impressions. It is not these that are being evoked, but those generalized features which the situation of Hero and Leander has in common with that of the poet and Delia, namely the peril of the lover and the mistress's ability to save him if she is willing. Attention is not directed to the flesh and blood of the old story, Leander plunging in the real and chilly waves, crying 'O Hero! Hero!'. Even the movement of the verse itself seems to avoid any suggestion of physical striving. In 'Poor soul fore-spent, whose force can do no more', the poet is contemplating his own pain as though from some distance away; the waves are those of care engendered by Delia's former cruelty; the hand which wounds him and is stretched forth is a hand only in the carefully delimited signification represented by *hand* when we say 'Stretch forth your hand', meaning 'Make the symbolic gesture of kindness, not the cruel one of rejection (which the hand can also make)' or (a further abstraction) 'be merciful'. We look towards abstract qualities and towards ways of describing behaviour, *kindness, cruelty*, not towards the physical object, four fingers and a thumb. The poem would be badly misread, and the reader inexpert in grasping the way this metaphorical language guides us towards qualities and concepts, if the 'gliding through an abstract process' were conscientiously avoided because poetry is not supposed to deal in such matters. If we insist on visualizing the struggle, the wounds, the hand, the lovely eyes making gestures of waftage, and the kiss implanted on the darting fingers, we make a little chaos of the poem. The function of the figurative language is essentially that of ordering experience at a level where the poet can confidently rely on us to perceive the dialectical points he is making with the aid of figure.

Similarly, within the fairly simple logical structure of no. ix, we will not catch the poet in the act of venting grief: the reader is not eavesdropping on some scene of private disorder, but attending to an argument and listening to the poet adding up a sum. This is grief 'fetter'd in verse' and therefore 'tamed', in Donne's phrase. Daniel adds each valuable number to the next and arrives at a conclusive total, summing his experience, always with the persuasive purpose, the forwarding of the tiny logical argument, in his intention:

> If this be love, to draw a weary breath,
> Paint on floods, till the shore, cry to th' air;
> With downward looks, still reading on the earth

The sad memorials of my love's despair:
　　If this be love, to war against my soul,
Lie down to wail, rise up to sigh and grieve me;
The never-resting stone of care to roll,
Still to complain my griefs, and none relieve me:
　　If this be love, to clothe me with dark thoughts,
Haunting untrodden paths to wail apart;
My pleasures, horror; music, tragic notes;
Tears in my eyes, and sorrows at my heart:
　　If this be love, to live a living death –
　　O then love I, and draw this weary breath.

Here again, 'painting the floods', 'tilling the shore', and 'crying to the air' suggests consideration not of the physical action,[a] but of that quality which such activities, if performed, would have in common with the poet's state – *futility*, the performance of some task utterly vain in its very nature, for the water cannot retain the colours, nor the shore blossom, nor the air reply: such is his relation to the fickle, barren, and unresponsive Delia. Although no conscious effort at conceptualization is needed, we can grasp all that the poet is saying only by gliding through an abstract process. So with the buried classical allusion (to Sisyphus) in line 7: it immediately directs us to that part of Sisyphus's story which is relevant – that, as a punishment in Hell, he eternally rolls a stone which ever tumbles back. But a still higher degree of abstraction is needed – punishment without hope of relief, futile absorption in a task itself immensely burdensome, are the common elements. The hint at Sisyphus is important because it defines, far more precisely and economically than non-figurative language can do, these elements in the poet's misery, but to define is not to give us physical sensations. 'Sisyphus' sharpens the mental instruments with which we perceive analogies, so that we read such a line with a quickness of apprehension that makes a conscious process of 'working-out' as unnecessary in practice as attempts to reduce it to visualization would be wrong-headed. That, after all, is one of the great blessings of what Matthew Arnold called 'the language of figure and feeling'.

Ralegh's pastoral poem of some five hundred lines, *The 11th: and*

---

a The phrases are perhaps proverbs and have a generalizing force. Dr Johnson told Boswell that it would be indeed *limning the water* to form friendships and then allow them to be broken by a trifling quarrel.

Last Book of the Ocean to Scinthia, was probably composed on one of the occasions, between 1589 and 1595, when Ralegh was out of favour at Elizabeth's Court, and may be part of a larger poem now lost.[4] In it Ralegh, under the guise of the Shepherd Ocean ('Water' was his punning nickname at Court) makes an indirect appeal to his royal mistress for restoration to favour; he defines his miserable state, recalls past happiness, praises beauty and laments cruelty, and ends by affirming that his love is of so absolute a kind that no disdain can alter it. The poem is comparable to the *Delia* sonnets because here too the poet defines and evaluates feeling and manipulates it to serve the formal ends of praise and persuasion. In the following fine passage, for example, Ralegh is defining, with the aid of several similitudes, the condition of forceless, mechanical activity, of posthumous existence, in which the abandoned lover feels himself to be:

> But as a body violently slain
> retaineth warmth although the spirit be gone,
> and by a power in nature moves again
> till it be laid below the fatal stone;
>
> Or as the earth even in cold winter days,
> left for a time by her life-giving sun,
> doth by the power remaining of his rays
> produce some green, though not as it hath done;
>
> Or as a wheel, forc'd by the falling stream,
> although the course be turn'd some other way,
> doth for a time go round upon the beam
> till wanting strength to move, it stands at stay;
>
> So my forsaken heart, my withered mind . . .
>
> (73–85)

Here the figures of the slain body, the earth, and the water-wheel are quite disparate and incoherent if they are read as an attempt to create a sensuous counterpart of the lover's emotion. Instead, each figure helps to define and illuminate more brilliantly the fairly complex *notion* that the lover once operated with full spiritual energy, 'powered' or 'driven' by the force of the lady's favour; now that the favour is withdrawn activity still continues, but only as a residue, a reflex, a mechanical movement that must shortly slow down for ever.

To say that the mistress animates the lover as the sun warms the earth, as the spirit enlivens the body, as the stream turns the wheel, is an ample and enriching way of describing various aspects of the relationship and pointing at qualities; but Ralegh also succeeds in conveying the 'after' as well as the 'before' of the situation, so that his figures have a dimension in time.

So, again, when Ralegh reaches his Definition of Love towards the end of the poem, he piles similitude upon similitude in order to convey his idea in its 'minutely appropriate words', not to ornament bare statements with encrusting figures. The concept, developed in the next stanza, of love as the 'essence' of the lover's mind may well remind us of Donne's perplexing the mind of the fair sex with 'nice speculations in philosophy'. But there is no need to associate such writing exclusively with the metaphysical poets: Sidney himself, perhaps the greatest of all Elizabethan poets after Spenser, and certainly the master of both Ralegh and Daniel, made frequent use of the 'angel's sophistry' of a learned God of Love (see *Astrophel and Stella*, lxi).

Daniel's *The Complaint of Rosamond* (1592) is a late example of the form widely popularized by *The Mirror for Magistrates*, wherein Daniel brings up the 'whining ghost' of Rosamond Clifford, the mistress of Henry II, 'to tell how old misfortunes had her tossed' (as Joseph Hall, hostile to this kind of poetry, sneeringly put it). Here the form itself invites moralization upon passions that have long been recognized by consciousness:

> Then write (quoth she) the ruin of my youth,
> Report the down-fall of my slipp'ry state.
> Of all my life reveal the simple truth,
> To teach to others what I learnt too late.
> Exemplify my frailty . . .
>
> (64–8)

There is nothing purely decorative about the writing in this poem. Daniel is not concerned simply to give us a lively impression of Rosamond's beauty and personal tragedy, but to define them both in the light of such concepts as dishonour and the corruption of courts; he moralizes his song by obliging his reader at every step to draw distinctions between innocence and shame. To this purpose both historical narrative and characterization are subordinated. For Daniel labours, in Marston's phrase, to enlarge everything as a poet rather than to tie himself to relate anything as a historian. Even the mythological tales, engraved on a casket which the king gives to Rosamond, quite disobey any canons of plausibility in character and are chosen and described, in a lively and glittering set-piece, because they reinforce the moral significance of the narrative; what royal philanderer would wish to remind his victim of Neptune's rapes or Jove's fantastic jealousy? So, when Rosamund compares herself to a grounded vessel, or to a comet whose blush amazes the Court, or to Atalanta who stoops for a golden ball and loses the race, the imagery subserves Daniel's purpose of directing attention not to a subtle verbal counterpart of Rosamond's feelings but to that level of abstraction whereon we may understand how 'Disgrace darkt honor'.

I have tried to illustrate the general principle that these poets are not afraid of handling emotion at a stage where an abstract process is both necessary and appropriate – necessary where their use of imagery to point meaning is concerned, and appropriate where moral discriminations are being encouraged. Both this principle and a second one of comparable importance are exemplified in another sonnet of Daniel's (*Delia*, XXIX):

> O why doth Delia credit so her glass,
> Gazing her beauty deign'd her by the skies,
> And doth not rather look on him, alas!
> Whose state best shows the force of murthering eyes?
> The broken tops of lofty trees declare
> The fury of a mercy-wanting storm;
> And of what force your wounding graces are,
> Upon my self you best may find the form.
> Then leave your glass, and gaze your self on me,
> That mirror shows what power is in your face;
> To view your form too much may danger bee,
> Narcissus chang'd t' a flower in such a case.
> And you are chang'd, but not t' a Hiacint;
> I fear your eye hath turn'd your heart to flint.

Coherence of development, conscious design, and logical control are amongst the characteristics of this sonnet. Its purpose is not only to praise Delia's beauty but to seem to persuade her to a course of action by presenting her with cogent arguments in its favour. Why does Delia gaze upon her glass? Let her rather look upon her lover, whose condition, unlike the mirror, accurately reflects her beauty's true nature: its destructiveness. The 'Alas' of lamentation and the epithet 'murthering' prelude the second stage of the argument; the image of the tree broken in the storm tells Delia more about her beauty than she will ever learn from the glass: in nature, it is without mercy like the 'mercy-wanting' storm; in its effects, it is destructive, breaking the lover as the storm breaks the trees. But there is a second reason why she should turn from the glass: let her beware the fate of Narcissus who, gazing at his own image, was strangely metamorphosed. With a witty virtuosity which is an indication of the very high degree of conscious purposiveness in this poem, Daniel rejects one element in the Narcissus metaphor as being inappropriate to the present case ('chang'd, but not t' a Hiacint'), but retains a second – Delia, like Narcissus, has certainly suffered a metamorphosis through too prolonged study of her own image. The idea of *change* vital to the similitude is taken up but adjusted, so that it applies to a metamorphosis (the gazer's eye turning her own heart to flint) radically different from the other and one which ties into a clinching argument the previous case for the 'murthering' and 'mercy-wanting' character of Delia's self-contemplative beauty. Firmness of control and the coherence resulting from the forwarding of a logical argument to persuade have already been seen in the other *Delia* sonnets which I have quoted; in 'O why doth Delia credit so her glass' a certain daring in the wit and what is, for Daniel, an exceptional complexity in the argument serve to make conscious design and logical control more plainly seen.

Amongst Ralegh's poems there are several that make their point with similar cogency. *A Poesie to Prove Affection is not Love* (before 1602, number XVII in A. M. C. Latham's edition of 1951) suggests in its title that it must be judged by the efficiency with which it proves its distinction between what Ralegh variously calls 'Conceipt', 'Affection', and 'Desire' on the one hand and 'perfect love', a genuine 'passion of the mind' on the other. There are many possible varieties of logical structure; this poem is not constructed in the same manner as the *Delia* sonnet XXIX. Ralegh divides up his subject and bases his proof on three initial propositions of a sentencious kind: about Conceipt ('Conceipt begotten by the eyes Is quickly born, and quickly dies'), about Affection ('Affection follows Fortune's wheels'), and about Desire ('Desire himself runs out of breath And getting, doth but gain his death'). His business is to elucidate and develop each one of these so that the poem moves in a dialectical order. Development and elucidation is managed by the use of similitudes (in the first and fourth stanzas here quoted) which direct our attention to common elements that help to define Conceipt and Desire, and by personification, not for the sake of its quaintness or beauty only, but because to present Affection and Desire in terms of behaviour is a clear and cogent way of defining their nature and so of amplifying the proposition:

> For as the seeds in spring time sown,
> Die in the ground ere they be grown,
> Such is conceipt, whose rooting fails,
> As child that in the cradle quails,
> Or else within the mother's womb,
> Hath his beginning, and his tomb.

> Affection follows Fortune's wheels;
> And soon is shaken from her heels;
> For following beauty or estate,
> Her liking still is turn'd to hate.
> For all affections have their change,
> And fancy only loves to range.

> Desire himself runs out of breath,
> And getting, doth but gain his death.
> Desire, nor reason hath, nor rest,
> And blind doth seldom choose the best,
> Desire attain'd is not desire,
> But as the cinders of the fire.

> As ships in ports desir'd are drown'd,
> As fruit once ripe, then falls to ground,
> As flies that seek for flames, are brought
> To cinders by the flames they sought:
> So fond Desire when it attains –
> The life expires, the woe remains.

A final stanza clinches the proof with a contemptuous dismissal of other poets' attempts to equate Affection (Desire) with Love – 'As if wild beasts and men did seek, To like, to love, to choose alike!' A similarly controlled argument will be found in other poems by

Ralegh, such as *The Excuse* (IX), *The Nymph's Reply to the Shepherd* (XVI), and *The Advice* (XV).

We have seen that expectations of formal control and of a purposefully evaluative handling of emotion may justly be brought to the reading of Ralegh's and Daniel's poetry. It is worth while to examine what is perhaps the most admired of Ralegh's poems with these and other elements in mind. This is 'The Passionate Man's Pilgrimage: supposed to be written by one at the point of death' ('Give me my Scallop shell of quiet...', XXX in the Latham edition); it may well have been composed in November–December 1603, when Ralegh was expecting death on the scaffold.[5]

'A man awaits his end Dreading and hoping all', wrote Yeats. In Ralegh's poem, the passionate man's dread and hope have already been transformed into two not uncommon ideas, which have, however, to be stated as figures: (1) The soul is like a pilgrim, (2) Heaven is like a court of justice. These are the very bases of the poem; beyond them is nothing and they cannot be further reduced. A search for 'sincerity' which tries to look beneath them for untransmuted feeling is likely to be baffled. It is worth noting, too, that these basic ideas are themselves figures, and, except as figures, cannot come to life at all. Ralegh's method is to build his poem upon them, continuing each metaphor and making each additional detail contribute to our grasp of them, after the manner of the allegorist. Structurally, then, the poem consists of two continued metaphors which are brought to a close in a final prayer (47–58) whose two pleas, to Christ to act as the sinner's advocate and to God to make the soul fit for the pilgrimage, link the prayer to the allegories (the pilgrim's journey and the heavenly court of justice) that have preceded it.

'Poetry is of all religions: and popery is a very poetical one', commented Thomas Warton. In his first stanza Ralegh, though no papist, boldly wrests the traditional attributes of the pilgrim – shell, staff, scrip, flask, and gown – to continue and enlarge the metaphor of the pilgrim-soul. The pilgrim is rhetorically 'divided' and each attribute is coupled to an abstract – quiet, faith, joy, salvation, glory. These point inward, not at the seen pilgrim in all his particularity, but at the unseen meaning of his attributes, now transformed to emblems. The next two stanzas send the pilgrim soul forth through a strange postmortem vale of soul-making. The meeting with other souls after death and the refreshment in that state with the waters of immortality suggest a fusion of Christian with Platonic ideas: Ralegh crosses the conception of the pilgrimage of man's soul in this life (found in the medieval sermon, in Spenser, George Herbert, and Henry More, and culminating in Bunyan) with the idea of the soul's purification in another life. The image of the thirsty soul has, of course, Biblical analogies; and what may strike us as the occasional floridity of the language ('silver mountains', 'Nectar fountains', 'milken hill') has a few parallels in immediately contemporary devotional poetry (in Southwell, and in Sir John Davies's account in *Nosce Teipsum* of the soul drinking nectar in the presence of God), but more nearly anticipates the manner of their successors (for example, Crashaw's paraphrase of Psalm xxiii). The saints drawing sweetness from the wells with crystal buckets suggests that Ralegh is thinking on the same lines as the makers of contemporary emblem-books.

In the fourth stanza the soul reaches the courts of heaven which glitter with jewels.[6] Once there, it proceeds to the hall where the trial is to take place. Although there may be medieval and homiletic analogies to this description, here is no apocalyptic Last Judgement with Christ as the Judge, such as we find in religious art of the thirteenth and fourteenth centuries, in *The Pricke of Conscience* or the miracle cycles; instead, Christ is imagined not as the Judge but as an advocate pleading before the court. The wit with which the metaphor is continued lies in the contrast between this upright lawyer and the corrupt accusers of earthly courts: all the figures (the jury of sins, the verdict, the 'pleading' Christ as 'King's Attorney') point inwards at the metaphor 'Heaven is like a court of justice', but again it is not the seen court that is indicated but the idea 'In Heaven there is true justice, not found on earth'. The persuasive coherence of the scheme of judicial trappings, as in the case of the pilgrim's attributes, directs attention not towards their concreteness as things but towards their emblematic function: each detail brings out the inner meaning of the whole comparison.

A great poem such as this needs longer discussion, for it contains confusions as well as clarities.[7] But perhaps it is most remarkable for what M. Janele, in discussing Southwell, has named 'spiritual optimism'. The process of purification and judgement quite lacks the grimness that informs Purgatory and Apocalypse as well as the Platonic after-life as described by Er at the end of *The Republic*. There is little trace of the determined emphasis on sin which prevails in the contemporary devotional poetry of Greville, Constable, or Donne. The dying Elizabethan was enjoined to think upon his hardly eradicable taint of sin and repent it in many exercises before he was allowed to hope for heaven.[8] If Ralegh really wrote the poem in the Tower in 1603, he must have done so very near indeed to the day when the reprieve arrived to postpone the end.

A good deal of Daniel's later work belongs to what W. B. C. Watkins has called 'poetry's lost provinces', and deserves recovery. There is no space to speak here of his *Musophilus* (1599) or his *Poetical Epistles* (1604), although they show a continued capacity to use figurative language to enforce doctrine and moral discriminations. He also wrote eight books of *The Civil Wars between the Two Houses of Lancaster and York* (1595–1609), and it may have been this poem that induced Jonson to call Daniel 'no poet' and Drayton to describe him as 'too much historian in verse'. None the less, even in this work Daniel is continually 'beautifying [his history] for further teaching and more delighting', pointing continually at his 'universal Doctrine' (the danger of civil war), re-shaping reigns to bring out this pattern, and elevating his subject with epic figures. It was perhaps his Dedicatory Epistle (1609) that riled Jonson, for in that he seems to value historical accuracy more than the 'enlarging every thing as a poet', and is shamefaced about 'poetical licence'. His part in the contemporary 'transition to prose', pointed out by Thomas Gray in a severe essay, is signalized by his announcement in the Epistle of his last project, the prose *History of England* (1617). Daniel was moving with the Baconian times and could no longer follow Sidney in his contempt for the historian's 'bare *Was*'. But our theme may be more fittingly concluded with a reminder that even that feeblest of Elizabethan devotional poets, Henry Lok, writing in 1597, could repeat as a commonplace that poetry's virtue consists in its 'contriving significatively in few words much matter'. It is in that word *significatively* that there lies the force of the great tradition of poetry that reaches from Spenser to Donne.

NOTES

1. Ralegh's 'atheism' and scepticism have been much speculated upon, because the subject has connections with Shakespeare and the so-called 'School of Night', which is supposed to have been a group of poets, scientists, and noblemen including Ralegh, Marlowe, Chapman and the famous astronomer Thomas Hariot, who took 'Night' as their symbol for a deep knowledge hid from the vulgar, and were interested in heterodox ideas that may have aroused suspicion amongst officials and the ignorant. Some believe that Shakespeare's *Love's Labour's Lost* contains an attack on it and that Chapman's first poem, *The Shadow of Night* (1594), is in part a 'manifesto' of the school. (For discussion, see, for example, *The School of Night* (1936), by M. C. Bradbrook; *A Study of Love's Labour's Lost* (1936), by F. A. Yates; *Ralegh and Marlowe* (1941), by E. G. Clark; *Christopher Marlowe* (1946), by P. Kocher; in 'Chapman's Shadow of Night: an Interpretation', *Studies in Philology* XXXVIII (1941), Roy W. Battenhouse shows that it is not *essential* to read the poem as having any bearing on the 'School'). The extant evidence for such a group is shaky (see E. A. Strathman, *Sir Walter Ralegh: a Study in Elizabethan Skepticism,* New York 1951, 262–71). Ralegh was certainly suspected, however, of encouraging atheistical and heretical notions down at his Dorset estate at Sherborne, but nothing thought worth further action emerged from an inquiry conducted by a government ecclesiastical commission in March 1594 at Cerne Abbas. (The evidence taken before the commission, which provides a very fascinating sidelight on the Elizabethan age, is conveniently reprinted as Appendix III in G. B. Harrison's edition of the anonymous poem *Willobie his Avisa, 1594*, Bodley Head Quartos, 1926.) Aubrey (*Brief Lives*, ed. Powell, 1949, 329) says that Ralegh's reputation was blackened with the charge of 'atheism', but adds, 'but he was a bold man, and would venture at discourse which was unpleasant to church-men'. Strathmann's important *Study* shows that nothing in Ralegh's extant writings confirms this reputation for 'atheism', even under the wide-ranging Elizabethan applications of the word. (See further C. A. Patrides' Introduction to his edition of selections from Ralegh's *History of the World*, 1971.)

2. Ralegh also meditated on the emptiness of ambition, on great men and fame, and on the queer problem of the 'man of action' in *The History of the World* (see especially the Preface; Book II, xiii. 7 and Book IV, ii. 3).

3. *The History of the World*, Book IV, ii. 17. Ralegh quotes *Philotas*, III, ii. 1110f. (ed. Michel, 1949, 131).

4. The problems of the character and date of this poem have been most recently discussed by A. M. Buchan, 'Ralegh's Cynthia – Fact or Legend?', in *Modern Language Quarterly*, i (1940).

5. The poem is accessible in many collections; I have, therefore, not thought it necessary to quote largely from it here. Note, however, that the *Oxford Book of English Verse* presents an outrageously mutilated version.

6. See Revelation xxi. 17–21 and the Red Cross knight's vision of the

heavenly Jerusalem in *The Faerie Queene*, I, x. 55: there is a purifying well in Spenser's eleventh canto which may also have been suggestive to Ralegh.

7. For a poem by Ralegh which seems to lack the high degree of coherence in the allegorical scheme found in 'The Passionate Man's Pilgrimage' see the first three stanzas of 'Nature that wash'd her hands in milk' (no. XX).

8. See Beach Langston, 'Essex and the Art of Dying', in *Huntington Library Quarterly*, xiii (1949–50).

WORDS AND MUSIC
IN ELIZABETHAN ENGLAND
WILFRED MELLERS

The Elizabethan and Jacobean age is one of the greatest epochs in the history of European music; and the finest things in it were created in a relatively brief period stretching from about 1600 to 1615. This period corresponds exactly with the highest point of contemporary culture in poetry and the drama; and while such parallels must not be driven too hard, one can see some relationship between the position of Byrd (1543–1623) in our musical history and that of Shakespeare in the evolution of our literature. Shakespeare's greatness cannot be separated from the mature and profound reconciliation he effected between ideas of order inherited from the Middle Ages and the humanist's intensifying concern with the individual consciousness. Similarly Byrd's greatness cannot be separated from his acceptance of a linear and polyphonic technique which is derived from the Middle Ages, but is reinterpreted in more harmonic, emotionally introspective terms. We can trace a comparable relationship between the two greatest literary and musical personalities of the later Jacobean age – Ben Jonson and Orlando Gibbons (1583–1625). Just as Jonson's acute understanding of the forces which conditioned the development of civilization in his day led him to an elegiac view of the world, so Gibbons' awareness of the most 'modern' developments in musical technique was consistent with a valedictory turn of mind. He is almost the last of the great age; and his music is most forward-looking in its implications when it appears to be most archaic in technique. The supreme achievements in music as in literature appear at the end of an epoch, in time to profit from the riches of a religious inheritance, while recreating that inheritance in the light of experience that was to lead to its destruction.

The range of Elizabethan and Jacobean musical activity was wide. At one extreme we have folk-song and dance – the un-notated art of the unlettered and formally uneducated. At the other extreme we have ecclesiastical polyphony★ for voices. In between these two extremes come secular polyphony for voices (the madrigal); polyphony and dance music for stringed instruments; music for keyboard instruments of various kinds; and the ayre for solo voice with lute. These various media and conventions involved different types of musical experience directed towards different types of audience. Yet the strength of Elizabethan musical culture consists in the fact that these different audiences were not mutually exclusive. Ecclesiastical polyphony could be as complicated and profound as folk-song was direct and simple; yet folk-songs could be used by learned composers in their motets and masses without any feeling of self-consciousness. The learned composer accepted folk-songs as *his* music, not as the property of a special class called 'the people'. On the other hand, the 'people' could not avoid hearing the subtle ecclesiastical polyphony in church. Similarly the madrigal, which became largely a middle-class entertainment, derives from liturgical polyphony but treats the style in a more lively and more immediately accessible form; while at a still cruder level come the round and tavern catch. These may be a rudimentary kind of polyphony compared with a Byrd Mass; yet they imply familiarity, even among artisans, with contrapuntal practice. Shakespeare is not romanticizing when he makes rustics sing in parts.

In the same way keyboard music ranges from simple arrangements of folk-songs and popular dances of the town (comparable with the 'sheet' arrangements of dance tunes today) to complicated and sophisticated compositions for which folk-tune or dance rhythm provide no more than an initial impetus. Bull's variations on the melody *Walsingham* are a highly elaborate example of 'art' music which could be performed only by the exceptional virtuoso, and are, moreover, one of the most profound emotional experiences in the whole range of keyboard music. Yet the fact that the piece is built on a melody which was then popular currency meant that it was not entirely inaccessible even to people who could not appreciate its finer points. Like Shakespearian tragedy, it appealed at a number of different levels; at the worst one could hum the wonderful melody through the maze of polyphonic and figurative embroidery.

The solo ayres with lute accompaniment illustrate the same point;

★ Music conceived in 'many voices', each part being of equal importance.

for these were sophisticated art songs which often attained the popularity of a modern best-seller. Sometimes they were composed songs which acquired the character of urban folk melodies, as for instance Dowland's *Fine Knacks for Ladies*.* At other times, as with the most famous of all examples, Dowland's *Lachrymae* ('Flow my tears'), they were subtle organisms which called for a highly developed rhythmic sense for their full appreciation. Yet there is abundant evidence – particularly in the contemporary drama – that this most poignant melody was immensely popular in all classes. It was a household word, a catch-phrase, as much as the crudest popular jingle today.

During the Elizabethan and Jacobean period we can observe a gradual tendency for the more 'progressive' techniques and media to oust the old. Especially during the later Jacobean age we find a tremendous creative impetus in the field of keyboard music; for keyboard techniques lend themselves readily to experiments in dissonance and brilliant figuration, and these were appropriate to the new, more secular and emotional approach to music. For a similar reason string polyphony survived when vocal polyphony was in decline; and a modified, more sensuous version of the fantasy for viols† became the most representative style of the Caroline court. None the less, it remains true that, up to the close of the great age (round about 1620), the human voice was the dominant influence on musical styles. One imagines that even Gibbons – with Bull (1563–1628) the greatest of English keyboard composers – would have agreed with Byrd, the leading master of the previous generation, when he said that 'there is not any music of Instruments whatsoever, comparable to that which is made of the voices of Men, when the voices are good, and the same well sorted and ordered. The better the voice is, the meeter it is to honour and serve God therewith; and the voice of Man is chiefly to be employed to that end.'

Inevitably a creative musical culture which puts the main stress on the human voice must imply an intimate connection between words and music. We talk nowadays as though the relationship between

---

* See Note on Recordings, p. 194.

† Family of bowed string instruments preceding the violins. The quality of the tone and the nature of the bowing made the violins especially suitable for the performance of polyphonic music. They were tuned in fourths on a principle comparable with that of the lute.

these two modes of expression constituted a problem; even as though there were a natural antipathy between them which composer and poet must overcome as best they may. Yet the separation of the two arts is comparatively recent, and the link between them would seem to be rooted deep in human nature. In folk-art, music can hardly be separated from either words or physical movement. Cecil Sharp tells us that the singers from whom he collected melodies had great difficulty in remembering a tune if they could not also recall the words; and although no exhaustive study of the subject has as yet been made, it seems certain both that the rhythmical subtleties of ballad poetry are conditioned by music and that recurrent formulas in tunes grow out of verbal clichés and metrical conventions in the verses.

Such interrelation between musical and literary techniques is, in the ballads and other folk-songs, largely intuitive and unself-conscious. The most sophisticated artists of the Middle Ages, the troubadours, prove the same point, however. They were poets who were their own composers, or composers who were their own poets; they regarded each activity as equally significant. 'A verse without music is a mill without water.' Thus one cannot speak of a troubadour tune 'fitting' the text. The music grows out of the words, and the words are an illustration of the melody; often it is difficult to know which came first. Even the liturgical tradition of the Middle Ages – plain-chant – is a musical convention which began as a lyrical heightening of speech.

Most composers in the Middle Ages were also literary men or clerics – and often astronomers, mathematicians, and diplomats as well. The separation of music from poetry was a part of the growth of professionalism in both arts. In some ways it would seem to represent a decline in cultural vitality; for the relation of music to language is itself direct evidence of music's relation to life. It is not an accident that the cultivation of music for music's sake in the later nineteenth century coincided with a phase in which the main emphasis was put on 'pure' instrumental music.

In Shakespeare's day there was an increasing tendency for the professional musician and the professional man of letters to become distinct. None the less, by Shakespeare's time the process was not far advanced, and there were many people who deplored the tendency in no uncertain terms. Almost all the musical theorists made the union of words and music a cardinal feature of their creed. It is interesting that the theorists, like so many of the greatest composers, were consciously elegiac in approach. With Gibbons and Dowland (1563–1626), they took the line that 'more geese than swans now live, more fools than wise'; they fought to preserve the traditions in which they had been nurtured. Again we see how the richness of this musical culture depends on the fact that it is the consummation of centuries of growth, and at the same time, almost reluctantly, the beginning of something new.

The theorists put great insistence on music's expressive function; and its expressive value was to them inseparable from a just rapport between the conventions of the music and the meaning of the words. Byrd, in one of his prefaces, remarked to his patron that the text which he had been called upon to set was so admirable that he had only to go around for a while saying the words over to himself and there, 'in some inexplicable way', were the melodic lines, fully developed and 'framed to the life of the words'. Of course, however potent an impulse words may give to music, the composer will not create music as good as Byrd's unless he has a measure of Byrd's genius. Yet Byrd's pronouncement is indicative of a general habit of mind among his contemporaries. They all thought it was not only music's function but its duty to reveal the meaning of the words. They wished for no better incentive to creation.

An extreme theoretical statement of the case is made by Thomas Morley, in his *Plain and Easy Introduction to Practical Music* of 1597. He advises students to:

dispose your music according to the nature of the words which you are therein to express, as whatsoever matter it be which you have in hand, such a kind of music must you frame to it ... For it will be a great absurdity to use a sad harmony to a merry matter, or a merry harmony to a sad lamentable or tragical ditty. You must then when you would express any word signifying hardness, cruelty, bitterness or other suchlike, make the harmony like unto it, that is, somewhat harsh and hard but yet so that it offend not. Likewise when any of your words shall express complaint, dolor, repentance, tears, sighs and suchlike, let your harmony be sad and doleful.

The light music hath of late been more deeply dived into, so that there is no vanity in it which hath not been followed to the full ... If therefore you will compose in this kind, you must profess yourself with an amorous humour (for in no composition shall ye prove admirable except you put on and possess yourself wholly with that vein wherein you compose) so that you must in your music be wavering like the Wind, sometime wanton, sometime drooping, sometime grave and staid, otherwhile effeminate, and the more variety you show the better shall you please.

Also if the subject be light, you must cause your music to go in motions, which carry with them a Celerity or quickness of time, as minims crotchets and quavers; if it be Lamentable, the notes must go in slow and heavy motions, as semibreves, breves and suchlike, and of all of this ye shall find example everywhere in the works of the good musicians. Moreover, you must have a care that when your matter signifieth ascending, high heaven and suchlike, you make your music ascend; and by contrary where your ditty speaketh of descending lowness, depth, hell and others such, you must make your music descend ... Lastly you must not make a full close till the full sense of the words be perfect; so that keeping these rules you shall have a perfect agreement, and as it were Harmonical Consent between the matter and the music, and likewise you shall be perfectly understood of your Auditor what you sing, which is one of the highest degrees of Praise, which a musician in dittying can attain unto or wish for.

Such a conception of music's illustrative and expressive purpose as is here outlined by Morley was not an invention of Elizabethan times. It had appeared in the vivid nature music of the fourteenth-century Florentines; and more systematically in the church music of the fifteenth-century Flemish school. Here it had paralleled the Renaissance delight in the observation of natural phenomena, as reflected in the realistic etchings of Dürer. Some of these naturalistic formulas were, indeed, visual rather than aural; for instance, the use of black notes to symbolize darkness. More commonly, however, the expressive word served merely to suggest an appropriate musical convention. Thus references to eternity involved long-sustained notes, references to heaven and hell provoked high and low notes respectively, while angels floated in ascending-scale passages.

In the work of a Flemish master such as Ockeghem (c. 1420–95) this musical literalism is allegorical rather than dramatic; though very occasionally a textual reference to the anguish of the Crucifixion may prompt him to a dramatically tense dissonance.* In the later Renais-

* The boundary line between consonance and dissonance has varied at different times in musical history, and is conventional rather than scientific. But as a general principle one may say that consonances are combinations of notes whose vibration rates bear a simple relation to one another (such as the octave – 2 : 1 or the fifth 3 : 2), whereas dissonances are combinations of notes whose vibration rates bear a complex relation to one another (such as the seventh – 15 : 8). Or more simply that consonances are intervals which involve a low degree of tension, dissonances intervals which involve a high degree of tension.

sance we find that the composers encourage the dramatic implications of musical expression at the expense of the purely symbolic ones. Byrd, in his liturgical music, does not attempt to illustrate musically each detail of the text; yet his treatment of the mass is dramatic when compared with that of Fayrfax (d. 1521). He is, for instance, eager to exploit the theatrically effective contrast between the '*sepultus est*' and the '*et resurrexit*'. Similarly, in his motet *Exsurge Domine* the gradually increasing leap through which the theme rises is prompted by the text, and is the source of the music's overwhelming dramatic climax when the melody finally shoots up through the forbidden interval of the minor ninth. In church music, of course, such devices must not be allowed to disturb the devotional atmosphere. In the secular madrigal, however, they can come into their own. Indeed, expressive considerations may dictate the relative proportion of polyphonic and homophonic sections and the entire structure of the piece.

Sometimes the madrigals acquire through these methods an almost programmatic character. Some examples in the work of Thomas Weelkes (c. 1575–1623) even approach an operatic treatment, for the various voices represent different persons in the story. His 'Three Virgin Nymphs' are represented by three sopranos who are aggressively interrupted in their demure measure by the bass, representing 'rude Silvanus'. He attacks one of them in an energetic quaver movement, while the others interject harmonically pathetic 'ay me's'. Similarly in the well-known *As Vesta was from Latmos Hill descending*, Weelkes gives the phrase 'two by two' to two voices, adding a third for 'three by three', and so on.

More important than these implicitly theatrical elements was the general influence that expression had on melody, rhythm, and harmony. Much of the expressive treatment of melody is a survival from the allegorical methods of the fifteenth century. Thus references to descent or falling will be accompanied by drooping intervals or descending scales. This interpretive technique becomes, however, less purely illustrative and physical, more *emotionally* descriptive; big leaps may suggest not only violent physical movement but also emotional strain. The technique of the 'melisma' or the writing of several rapid notes on a single syllable is also much more prevalent in the madrigal than it is in church music. The conventional entangling in nets of golden wire is always an excuse for such lyrical vocalise; so, often, are the flames of desire, and also tears and laughter. The Elizabethans preserved a delicate balance between the natural syllabic declamation of a text and the musical interest of the lyrical arabesque; the latter is always justified by literary content.

A similar balance between literary and musical elements can be observed in the madrigalian treatment of rhythm. The metre of the dance is often strongly marked in madrigals; not only the many specific references to dancing but almost any mention of joy or merriment in the text suffices to set the composer off in a lilting triple measure. Yet this metrical homophony* is reconcilable with traditional polyphony and with the rhythmic independence of each part. Often the bar-line has no accentual significance. Each melodic line follows its own rhythm, in accordance with the natural inflection of the words as they would be spoken; the metre, which governs the harmony of the whole concourse of voices, is only latent. This dual rhythmic conception is comparable with that of mature Shakespearian blank verse, which depends upon an equilibrium between the spoken inflection of the words and a metre that is merely implicit. When the Elizabethan composers employ elaborately contradictory rhythms in the various parts, there is nearly always an expressive reason for it; we may mention Farnaby's (c. 1560–1600) treatment of the words, 'In fury down he flang her', in *Daphne on the Rainbow*.

But it is in their use of the tensions of dissonant harmony to reinforce verbal pathos that the English madrigalians were most audacious. Weelkes was particularly fond of the acute effect of the false relation, a device whereby the major and minor third were sounded simultaneously in the same chord. This formula had originally been evolved from the movement of melodic parts; yet there is no doubt that the composers, especially in the Jacobean period, came increasingly to exploit it for its harmonic effect; they almost always used it in association with the idea of pain and anguish, on words such as 'bitter' and 'sting'. Chromaticisms were used in similar contexts and for the same reason – they substituted a violent harmonic tension for the serene stability of the vocal modes, or a clearly defined tonality. Weelkes' great chromatic madrigal *O Care thou wilt despatch*

---

* Music in which the main interest is centred in a single line, usually the top, the other parts being of an accompanying nature. (See note on polyphony, p. 166 above.)

me becomes almost operatic in effect.★ One can imagine the care-laden words declaimed rhetorically by a solo voice, while the accompanying dissonances are played on instruments. Even in a diatonic texture most abstruse dissonances may be created by the technique of suspensions, whereby one or more notes from one concord are held on while the other parts proceed to the next. The 'suspended' notes are then dissonances, which are only belatedly resolved. The composer Ward (d. *c.* 1641) is especially fond of the intense effect created by these double and even triple suspensions. He always associates them with textual references to pain or melancholy or an ecstatic sweetness.

At this stage it will perhaps be as well if we offer some more specific comment on the relation between words and music in a single madrigal. We will take as our example not one of the more extravagant and exceptional cases of 'expressionism' such as can be found in the work of Weelkes or Ward, but one of the ripest examples of the work of John Wilbye (1574–1638), who is probably the greatest English madrigalist. In Wilbye's *Draw on sweet night* most of the expressive techniques we have mentioned occur, though without excessive emphasis.

Ostensibly the madrigal is polyphonic in style. Its contrapuntal† craftsmanship is certainly magnificent and not excelled by any liturgical composer of the earlier generation. Yet the emotional power of the music depends largely on harmonic effects which are associated with our modern major and minor tonality rather than with the modal system. The opening paints a wonderful picture of the tranquillity of evening, the melodies moving smoothly by step. Tension comes into the music, however, when the verse refers to sleep as 'best friend unto those cares that do arise from painful melancholy'. A sus-

★ *Chromaticism, modes, major* and *minor tonality* – the modal scales established by the Medieval Church are indicated by playing the white notes on the piano. That on C is the Ionian, on D the Dorian, on E the Phrygian, on F the Lydian, on G the Mixolydian, on A the Aeolian, on B the Locrian. They differ from the major and minor scales of the eighteenth century in that most of them have a whole tone between the seventh and eighth notes instead of a semitone, and in their more varied distribution of tones and semitones. They were also conceived in just intonation (in accordance with the natural series of overtones), whereas major and minor scales are artificially modified or 'tempered' for harmonic reasons. The chromatic scale is that which proceeds entirely by semitones.

† Strictly speaking, the various devices of imitation, etc., used to give order to polyphony. Thus all counterpoint is polyphony, but not all polyphony is counterpoint.

DRAW ON SWEET NIGHT

John Wilbye

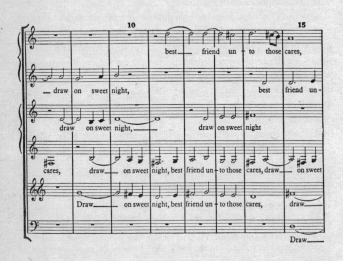

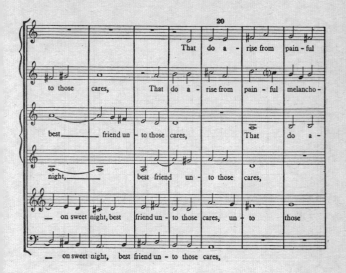

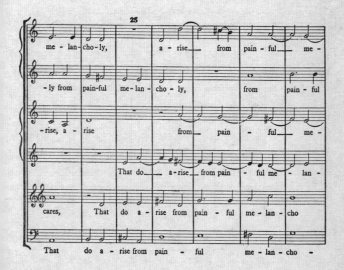

45

con-se-crate it whol - ly, That

-crate it whol - ly, That un - to thee to thee

thee I con - se - crate it whol - ly, That un - to thee I con - se - crate it wholly,

con - secrate it whol - ly, That

I con - se-crate it wholly, That un - to thee I con - se - crate it whol-

-crate it whol - ly, That un - to thee, to thee

50

un - to thee I con - secrate it whol - ly: Sweet night draw on &c.

I con-se-crate it whol - ly: Sweet

That un - to thee I con-se-crate it wholly: Sweet night draw on

un - to thee to thee I con-se-crate it wholly:

-ly, it whol - ly: Sweet night draw on

I con - se-crate it whol - ly.

tained pedal note on A produces an acute clash between A and G sharp on the words 'those cares' (bar 16); while 'painful melancholy' is expressed through a procession of triple suspensions, creating seventh and ninth chords★ which are at once sensuously rich and painful. At the words 'My life so ill through want of comfort fares' (bar 32) there is an abrupt change from major to minor; at the words 'unto thee I consecrate it wholly' (bar 40) the religious metaphor suggests a modulation to the serene relative major (F)†, the words being set fugally to a noble phrase rising up a fourth and then falling down the scale in a dotted rhythm – a traditional convention of liturgical polyphony. A similar dramatic contrast between major and minor occurs on the words 'my griefs when they be told'.

The rest of the madrigal can be analysed by the reader on the same principles, paying special attention to the lyrical roulade evoked, towards the close, by the word 'enfold', and to the delicate equilibrium between verbal and metrical rhythm which is achieved in the setting of the final phrase, 'I then shall have best time for my complaining'. Here the cross accents of the triple rhythm in the individual parts are sufficient to convey a suppressed querulousness, without destroying the dusk-like tranquillity of the underlying duple rhythm in the harmony of the close. In music such as this, the demands of the Renaissance for an art that should be directly emotional and expressive are satisfied without damage to the inherent musicality of the convention.

We have spoken of the manner in which the musician's sensitivity to words conditioned his style in the writing of madrigals; we have not specifically mentioned the way in which the poet's sensitivity to music conditioned the kind of verse he wrote. Madrigalian verse is, in general, on the Spenserian model. Suave and mellifluous, it aims to express a general mood rather than particular and personal experience. Contrasts of mood are desirable, for they imply contrasts of musical style; for instance, the lover's lament may be interspersed with passages recalling past happiness, which will employ a lilting dance measure. The stanzaic forms may be varied and preferably not strophic since, as we have seen, the Elizabethan conception of musical

★ The chords are D, F sharp, A and C natural; and A, C sharp, E, G, and B.

† Major and minor keys, having the same key signature, are said to be relative to one another.

rhythm was not rigidly metrical. Frequent repetition of phrases is advisable, or the words will not be intelligible in the maze of poly-phony. Short antithetical verbal phrases are suitable, because they suggest a sequential treatment in music; often isolated words ('and tears ... and sighs ... and groans ...') are imitatively treated in sequence.* Refrains are obviously appropriate. Some refrains, especially cheery ones, are conventionally treated in contrapuntal style; others, such as lamenting 'ay me's', are usually treated harmoni-cally.

Significant as was the implicit operatic tendency in the madrigal, and intimate as was the madrigalists' union of music and words, it is in the solo ayre with lute that we find the most advanced experiments towards a theatrical style. The leading theorist among the writers of ayres was Thomas Campian (1567–1620), who was equally celebrated as poet and composer; and while he protested against the type of musical literalism advocated by Morley, it is clear that he did not object to the principle, but only to a slavish and unimaginative inter-pretation of it. There was some justification for his saying:

but there are some, who appear the more deep, and singular in their Judgment, will admit no music but where the nature of every word is precisely exprest in the Note, like the old exploded Action in the Comedies, where if they did pronounce *Memini*, they would point to the hinder part of their heads, if *Video*, put their finger in their eye. But such childish observing of words is altogether ridiculous, and we ought to maintain as well in notes as in action a manly Carriage, gracing no word, but that which is Eminent, and Emphatical.

But when we look at his own practical and theoretical work we see that its purpose was to insist on a union of words and music which was in some ways still more intimate than that found in the madrigal. He stressed the solo ayre with lute accompaniment precisely because in pieces for a solo voice music and sweet poetry could agree without the absurdities sometimes occasioned in the madrigal by contrapuntal treatment.

Campian's work as theorist and as poet-composer thus parallels that of the Pléiade group associated with Ronsard in sixteenth-century France, and that of the Italian experimenters who worked for Count Bardi in the early years of the seventeenth century. All were making a plea for simplicity and naturalness of diction. They

* The repetition of a musical phrase at a different pitch.

wrote for a solo voice with a chordal instrumental accompaniment because in this form the meaning of the words, and their human significance, would be immediately comprehensible. All of them imagined, in conformity with the spirit of the humanist movement, that in thus making music the overflow of poetry they were reviving the musical principles of classical antiquity. Campian, like the French artists before him, went so far as to try to systematize the setting of words by a literal equation of long and short syllables with long and short notes. Yet though his theory may seem pedantic, his practice is another matter. Basically he followed traditional notions of the relation between music and words. He resembled the French in that he wanted the musical rhythm to derive directly from the inflection of the text as spoken, since music was '*la sœur puisnée de la poésie*'; he resembled the Italians in that he wanted the lyricism of the musical line to be convincing in itself.

In both Italy and France these experiments in the mating of words and music combined with the progressive elements which we have referred to in the madrigal to create opera, in which the human drama implicit in the madrigal took outward shape on a stage. Monteverdi significantly remarked that his Arianna moved people so profoundly simply because she was a woman, his Orfeo because he was a man. In England this operatic consummation of humanism did not take place. The closest approach to it was in the collaboration of Ben Jonson, Alfonso Ferrabosco the younger (c. 1575–1628), and Inigo Jones in the production of masques. The elements of a music drama were present in the masque, but they remained undeveloped. The reason for this may have been that the court culture in England was more deeply impregnated with popular elements than it was in France or Italy. All the dramatic energy of Jacobean society went into the creation of poetic drama, an art which is at once aristocratic and popular. While being rhetorical, stylized, and non-realistic, it is not as rigidly formal as the almost ritualistic conventions of court opera. At least it may be argued that if there had been as vigorous a poetic drama in Italy as there was in England during the early years of the seventeenth century, the opera might have taken longer to come to fruition. In France the evolution of the court opera is closely linked with that of the equally ritualistic heroic tragedy; but England produced nothing comparable with the classical French drama, unless one counts

Jonson's two tragedies as experiments in that direction. They had no direct successors.

Nonetheless, there are aspects of Campian's practice which look towards the theatrical future. His textbook, *A New Way of making four parts in Counterpoint*, published in 1618, shows a definite breach with the polyphonic tradition. He recommends the construction of chords in four parts with the foundation in the bass, formalized by a regular metre, in much the way that was practised in the eighteenth century. It is not surprising that the book was reissued in 1655, and went through many editions during the Restoration. When Campian says:

> Base is the foundation of the other three parts in music ... Of all things that belong to the making up of a musician the most necessary and useful for him is the true knowledge of the Key, or Mode, or Tone, for all signify the same thing, with the closes belonging unto it, for there is no tune can have any grace or Sweetness, unless it be bounded within a proper Key, without running into strange Keys which have no affinity with the Air of the song,

he is expressing a radical departure from the sixteenth-century view of tonality; but his prescription was sedulously followed by the Restoration adventurers in the operatic field.

The failure of the Jacobeans to create an operatic convention does not mean that the music which they composed for solo voice is deficient in passion. It sometimes achieves a dramatic vehemence of almost Shakespearian intensity, though it makes its effect through musical and literary, rather than through explicitly theatrical, means. The poems which the composers set seldom have the personal and introspective energy of the lyrics of Donne; yet we should not be deceived into thinking that because the words are stylized they are therefore insincere. The music that grows out of these words may well be, in the work of a Dowland or a Daniel, as powerful and personal, in terms of its own language, as the poetry of Donne is in literary terms. The poems, like madrigalian verse, are deliberately generalized rather than specific, because music is of its very nature a generalizing art. Many of the conventions in Elizabethan lyric poetry which seem to us frigid and unconvincing were hardly intended to be self-subsistent. In the ayre, even more than in the madrigal, the words serve merely to evoke an appropriate musical response; the literary convention is completed only in the musical convention, the music being an essential part of the expressive significance of the words. In this the Elizabethans were the direct successors of the troubadours and of a late medieval poet-composer such as Guillaume de Machaut (*c.* 1300–1377). English Chaucerian scholars are never tired of pointing out how inferior Machaut's poetry is to that which Chaucer made out of it. What they ignore is that Machaut's ballades were not meant to be read out loud, let alone read in the study. They become complete works of art – and remarkably poignant and passionate works they are – only when they are sung by solo voices with an accompaniment of instrumental polyphony. The poetic stylization is conditioned by music, and vice versa.

Since Campian was equally talented as poet and composer, and was the most conscious experimenter in the possibilities of music for a solo voice, we should perhaps start with him when inquiring into the manner in which this union of words and music worked. We shall not find in his music the heights and depths of a Dowland or a Daniel; but we shall obtain from it an idea of the general principles by which Elizabethan composers tackled the setting of a text. We will therefore first analyse a song by Campian, and then consider a few examples which will illustrate the supreme development of the style in the work of Dowland.

Unlike the madrigal, the ayre was normall strophic, the same melody serving for several verses of the poem. We do not know, of course, precisely how a man such as Campian set about the task of writing an ayre; but it seems likely that he may have written the first verse of his poem and then composed the music for it – unless, indeed, the melody grew almost simultaneously with the words. This music must reflect the meaning of the text; so that thus far the music has been moulded by the poem. It is probable, however, that the poem will be incomplete in one stanza, and any further stanzas the poet writes must now fit the conventions of the already existing music. If in the first verse the music is conditioned by the poetry, in the second verse the poetry must be conditioned by the music.

On the following pages is the song *Author of Light*. Though it has not the introspective intensity of the greatest songs of Dowland, it is, in point of fact, extremely fine.

The words are of a religious nature; and the opening apostrophe to the divinity is set to the noble interval of the falling fifth – the most stable of all interval relationships after the octave – accompanied by a rising bass line to suggest the flooding of light, and its revivifying effect. 'My dying sprite' is expressed by a drooping phrase, syncopated★ across the bar-line to create a little catch in the breath, and with a tremulous semiquaver melisma, underlined by a harsh dissonance in the lute part. The reference to redemption in the next line suggests a clear diatonic phrase, built on a firmly rising fourth, in the relative major (B flat) instead of the initial G minor; whereas 'all confounding night' is set again to a strained syncopation and a confounding melisma. 'Lord light me to my blessed way' is in hopefully rising thirds, which are contradicted by the blindness of 'worldly vain desires', most subtly suggested by a cross rhythm in the voice part which really does make the melody 'wander astray'. 'Sun and moon' significantly recalls the opening address to the Author of light: we may note that the moon is lower than the sun and the underlights below the stars. The leaping sixth and the cross rhythm of 'but all their glorious beams' convey the poet's rising excitement. The mists and darkness are set chromatically, because chromaticism destroys tonal stability and the natural order; but the passage begins low and rises, because it is an ascent from the uncertainty of the mists to the certainty of God's love. The major triad† at the end is thus, though conventional, also symbolic.

Having created this music, flowering so inevitably from the text, Campian then writes another stanza which fits the music. Instead of 'Author of light' we have, for the noble fifth, 'Fountain of Health'. For the syncopation, melisma, and dissonance we have 'deep wounds' instead of 'dying sprite'. 'Sweet showers of pity' take the place of redemption; and 'uncleanness' that of 'confounding night'. The 'faint and fading heart' serves the same musical purpose as the blindly wandering eyes. 'Sin and death, hell and tempting fiends', though convenient dualisms, are not allegorically appropriate to the phrase built on the falling fifth. On the other hand, the assuagement of 'sharp pains and grief' is perfect for the chromatic ascent of the last line.

This, then, is a devotional song which preserves contact with the

---

★ Syncopation is the displacement of the accent from what would normally be a strong beat to a weak. The conception applies only to the metrical aspects of musical rhythm, and so is not always relevant to sixteenth-century technique.

† The common chord of three notes – the keynote, the third, and the fifth.

AUTHOR OF LIGHT

Thomas Campian

Voice

1. Au – thor of light, re-vive my dy – ing sprite:
2. Foun – tain of health, my soul's deep wounds re-cure:

Lute

Re – deem it from the snares of all
Sweet show'rs of pi – ty rain, wash my

con-founding night. Lord, light me to thy bless – ed
un-cleanness pure. One drop of thy de-sir – ed

way, For blind for blind with world-ly vain de-sires I wan-der
grace The faint the faint and fa-ding heart can raise and in joy's

as a-stray. Sun and moon, stars and un-der lights I
bo-som place. Sin and death, hell and temp-ting fiends may

see, But all their glo-rious beams are mists and
range, But God his own will guard, and their sharp

dark-ness being com-pared to thee.
pains and grief in time as-suage.

old liturgical tradition; yet it gives a much more comprehensive treatment of the technique of musical illustration that had been explored in the work of fifteenth-century masters such as Ockeghem. Musical allegory becomes emotional realism. If this realism appears to be still somewhat naïvely systematic, we shall see that the same technique achieves artistic maturity in the work of Dowland.

The first example is *Shall I sue?* It is an unpretentious song, of a very lyrical character. The melody is remarkable, however, not only for its memorability, which gives it an almost popular flavour, but also for the subtlety of its organization; and this richly satisfying musical structure is inseparable from the composer's sensitivity to his text. As in the Campian piece, the poem is set in a simple strophic form, built around the literary idea of heavenly joy and earthly love.

Short phrases grouped in sequence suggest the suing and seeking. The opening phrase is inverted and then augmented in time value, and aspires yearningly up the scale till it reaches a climax on the words 'heavenly joy'; it is then balanced by the short subsiding phrase for 'earthly love'. The second half of the stanza musically mirrors the first; only this time the sigh ascends to the clouds on a high G instead of F. The sense of release as the phrase droops down to the tonic★ becomes the more affecting. One should note, too, how the final climax is anticipated by the increase in animation created by the cross rhythm, reflecting the words 'or a wounded eye'.

The tune is so beautiful and sounds so lyrically inevitable that one might not suspect that its musical contour is so intimately linked with the text. Having arrived at the melody, moreover, Dowland does not think it necessary to adapt the words to it as literally as does Campian in our previous example. In his second stanza there is nothing to parallel the crucial contrast between heaven and earth in the first; there is no poetic reason why the melody should take the form of that soaring ascent and declining resolution, though of course there is every musical reason why it should. The contradictory rhythm of the 'wounded eye' is, however, complemented by a reference to 'worth so base'. In this stanza the melody stands magnificently on its own feet; it is only in minor details that an attempt is made to accommodate the text to it.

★ The keynote, or the note on which the scale starts and ends.

SHALL I SUE

John Dowland

Rather quick

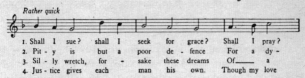

1. Shall I sue? shall I seek for grace? Shall I pray?
2. Pit - y is but a poor de - fence For a dy -
3. Sil - ly wretch, for - sake these dreams Of a
4. Jus - tice gives each man his own. Though my love

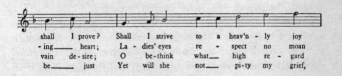

shall I prove? Shall I strive to a heav'n - ly joy
- ing____ heart; La - dies' eyes re - spect no moan
vain de - sire; O be-think what____ high re - gard
be____ just Yet will she not____ pi - ty my grief,

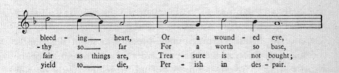

With an earth - ly love? Shall I think that a
In a mean de - sert. She is too wor -
Ho - ly hopes re - quire. Fa - vour is as
There-fore die I must. Sil - ly heart, then____

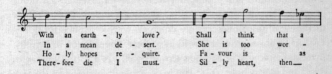

bleed - ing____ heart, Or a wound - ed eye,
- thy so____ far For a worth so base,
fair as things are, Trea - sure is not bought;
yield to____ die, Per - ish in des - pair.

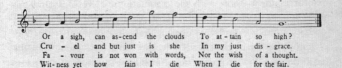

Or a sigh, can as-cend the clouds To at - tain so high?
Cru - el and but just is she In my just dis - grace.
Fa - vour is not won with words, Nor the wish of a thought.
Wit - ness yet how fain I die When I die for the fair.

The third stanza, on the other hand, verbally mirrors the musical structure, 'high regard' taking the place of 'heavenly joy'. The last stanza has nothing to correspond with the celestial yearning of the tune, though it refers to death in both the declining final phrases. The cross rhythm is most effectively applied to the words 'perish in despair'.

Our second example is more complicated. The song *In Darkness let me Dwell* was contributed to a collection made by Dowland's son Robert, and published under the title of *A Musical Banquet* in 1610. It is one of Dowland's last works and can establish considerable claims to being the greatest song in the English language.

Shall I sue? is a strophic song, and the rhythm, though flexible, has a metrical basis. In *In Darkness* the rhythm flows from the words, and the sense of metre and the bar-line dissolves; at the same time, the melody is entirely convincing as a lyrical structure in its own right. The lute part is much more elaborate than in the earlier songs; while being more polyphonic in style, it is also more tensely harmonic in effect. An instrumental prologue sets the mood, out of which the voice almost imperceptibly emerges, with its wonderful, long-sustained phrase, pitched low in its register, lingering on its penultimate suspension – 'in darkness let me dwell', as if half in love with death and melancholy. Dissonant major sevenths underline the words 'sorrow', and the anguished chord of the augmented fifth* occurs repeatedly and sighfully in the lute part; on the words 'shall weep still' it is reinforced by a sobbing melisma in the voice part. The reference to 'hellish jarring sounds' produces a slight but sinister chromatic intrusion in the lute part and a feverish repetition of the word 'jarring'. This effect is more potently developed in the panting sequential repetitions of 'let me living die', in which the lute reinforces the passion with close imitations. Here Dowland approaches the declamatory effects of Monteverdi and the Italian operatic composers without imparing the lyrical continuity of his line.

This rising excitement leads into the climacteric phrase on 'till death do come'. This phrase starts on the highest note of the piece and falls nobly through two fourths, the second of which, however,

---

* The chord formed by 'augmenting' the fifth of the triad by a semitone – e.g. D, F sharp, B flat.

IN DARKNESS LET ME DWELL

John Dowland

In____ dark - ness let me dwell,

The ground, the ground shall sor-row, sor - row be.

The roof des-pair to bar all, all cheer-ful light from me.

The walls of mar - ble black that mois-tened, that mois - tened still shall

weep—still shall weep, My mu-sic, my mu - sic

hell - ish, hell - ish ∧ jar-ring sounds, jarring, jarring sounds, to—

ban - ish, ban-ish friend - ly sleep. Thus wed - ded

to my woes and bed - ded to my tomb—

O let me, liv-ing, die, O let me, liv-ing, let me

liv - ing, liv-ing, die, Till death, till death do come,

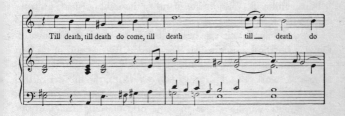

Till death, till death do come, till death till death do

come, In dark-ness let me dwell.

preserves the music's concentrated intensity by being diminished (C natural to G sharp). The passion subsides through a brief episode for the lute, and the song concludes with a whispered repetition of the opening phrase, verbal and musical. Its penultimate note is sustained still longer and more lovingly than in the first instance over the acute dissonance of the major seventh.

There could be no second stanza to this song. Dowland has left the strophic method far behind; the enormous melody grows and expands, and returns to its source. It is obvious that the words in themselves are not of much significance. They exist for their musical implications, and Dowland does not hesitate to repeat the operative 'expressive' words when the musical sense demands it. The conventional melancholy of the words is no more than a formula; yet it releases an intensity of passion that is highly personal. This music is a fitting complement both to the self-analytical love poetry of Donne, especially in its tragic, elegiac mood as in the *Nocturnall upon St Lucies Day*, and to the introspective melancholy of Hamlet. It belongs to a transitional epoch, for it profits equally from the old polyphonic tradition, the harmonic experiments of the madrigalists, and the declamatory explorations of the Italian opera composers. It bears within its consummate maturity the riches of past, present, and future.

The only ayres that can be put beside the great lute songs of Dowland – those published in *The Musical Banquet* and in his last big, significantly titled volume, *A Pilgrimes Solace* – are the few large-scale works of John Daniel (c. 1565–1630), the brother of the poet. His sequence called *Funeral Tears*, written in 1606 and published in a modern edition under the title of *Chromatic Tunes*, rivals Dowland's work both in inherent musical power and as a supremely successful setting of the English language. Here again the dolour is of an intensely introspective character; and here, too, the poem is designed mainly to serve as an impetus to music:

> Can doleful notes to measur'd accents set
> Express unmeasur'd griefs which time forget?
> No, let chromatic tunes, harsh without ground,
> Be sullen music for a tuneless heart.

> Chromatic tunes most like my passions sound,
> As if combined to bear their falling part.
> Uncertain certain turns, of thoughts forecast,
> Bring back the same, then die and dying last.

These words are divided to make three related songs. In the first we may note the setting of the words 'Express unmeasur'd griefs which time forget', where the voice's passion breaks in descending syncopations; in the second we can observe the astonishing harmonic treatment of the 'chromatic tunes'; and in the third the fevered repetition of the phrase 'then die and dying last', in contorted, conflicting rhythms.

The perfect union of words and music, typical of the work of Dowland and Daniel, disappears with their generation. In the music of the Caroline court the two elements of song metre and verbal rhythm become differentiated into formal aria and narrative recitative. Purcell (1659–95) achieved a magnificent new declamation of the English language, a recitative heightened to lyrical intensity; but his song forms are not inevitably derived from verbal rhythm, as Dowland's are. In the eighteenth century the influence of Handel (1685–1759) destroys the old reciprocity. This is not merely because Handel was imperfectly sensitive to the English language, but also because he wanted to create a kind of music which depended on a broad harmonic effect rather than on rhythmic subtlety. During the nineteenth century the lack of any vital relation between musical rhythm and the English language was one of the most depressing effects, and even a contributory cause, of the decline of an English tradition. In our own day the efforts of men such as Holst and Vaughan Williams, Rubbra, Tippett, and Britten, to give our tradition a fresh start cannot be separated from their renewed approach to the problem of words and music.

A NOTE ON RECORDINGS (1981)

A very wide selection of recordings of Elizabethan and Jacobean music is now available. Particularly recommended are:

William Byrd, the complete Masses performed by The Deller Consort: Harmonia Mundi 211–13

English Virginal music played by Colin Tilney: Argo ZRG 675

The Complete Works of John Dowland performed by the Consort of Musicke: Harmonia Mundi DSLO 551–6

ELIZABETHAN FICTION
IAN WATT

The Elizabethan public for fiction was very different from that for fiction now. It was much smaller: most of the population were illiterate or nearly so; and among the literate the number of those who read books to any extent was limited by many factors. For one thing the much longer hours of work left less leisure for reading; for another, the price of books was much higher in relation to wages. A single printed sheet containing a ballad with a woodcut illustration cost a halfpenny or a penny, and the cheapest pamphlet cost sixpence – about one tenth of the average weekly wage of only about five shillings. If a penny was available for amusement, it was likely to be spent, not on reading matter, but on things that seemed to provide better value for money – a quart of small beer perhaps, or a place in the theatre pit to see a play by Shakespeare or Marlowe.

Nonetheless, although the reading public was numbered in tens of thousands rather than millions, it was larger and more varied than it had ever been before, especially in London.[1] But – again in significant contrast to the situation today – the majority of this public tended to read books that we should call serious rather than light. The daily newspaper,[2] the magazine, and the popular novel were unknown; and there was also a strong feeling on the part of many readers that what light reading there was – ballads, jest books, chivalric and pastoral romances, miscellaneous collections of poems and short stories – was immoral or at best a waste of time. The divine art of printing, these readers thought, had been bestowed for more useful purposes; and so the 'best-sellers' of the Elizabethan period were either serious and improving works such as Bibles, prayer-books, religious tracts, Latin grammars, or practical but ephemeral works such as almanacs.[3]

Even the lighter reading of the Elizabethans was much more concerned with moral and literary education than its modern equivalent. From Spenser, Lyly, and Sidney to Munday, Greene, and Deloney, most writers of fiction tried to combine instruction with pleasure, to teach proper ways of talking and behaving as well as to provide entertainment. Nor must we forget that nearly all the works of the period which we still read today would then have been classed by most educated people as 'light reading', if they had understood the term. For example, poetry, which is today classed as 'non-fiction' by librarians and as 'heavy' by most readers, was then considered to be 'fiction', because, as opposed to history and philosophy, it was 'invented'; and the poetic medium was regarded as inherently more pleasure-giving than prose.[4]

This contrast brings us to our final general comparison between Elizabethan and modern fiction. Even the word 'reading' suggests similarities which are misleading. Most Elizabethan writing then received – as it still requires and rewards – reading aloud, or at the very least pronouncing the words internally or sub-vocally. The modern habit of fast silent reading, combined with the development of matter which can be easily and swiftly absorbed by the eye alone, is perhaps the greatest obstacle between our literary pleasures and those of the Elizabethans; the linguistic and rhetorical style of their most casual and popular prose works requires the same kind of alertness to the pattern of sound and meaning which we now tend to reserve for poetry.

So much for the general context in which our subject must be placed. We can now briefly consider some of the characteristic features of Elizabethan fiction as they appear in some of its most representative works.[5]

The two most admired and influential works of Elizabethan fiction, Lyly's *Euphues: The Anatomy of Wit* (1578) and Sidney's *Arcadia* (published 1590), were composed for the gentlemen and ladies of the Court, who found in them their ideal of perfection in style and manners. John Lyly's *Euphues*, and its successor, *Euphues and his England*, are really dialogues about proper conduct, especially in matters of love.[6] There is, however, space to consider only one of the great courtly novels of the period, and so it is probably better to concentrate on the *Arcadia*, which has certainly a greater variety of literary interest, and is arguably the finest achievement of Elizabethan fiction.

Sir Philip Sidney (1554–86) wrote the *Arcadia* primarily for the entertainment of his sister, the famous Countess of Pembroke. The essential plot is a simple and familiar one. Two young princes, Musidorus and his cousin Pyrocles, go through a series of perilous, incredible, and very confusing adventures before they are eventually united in marriage to their original loves, Pamela and Philoclea, the beautiful daughters of Basilius, king of Arcadia. The great length of the book depends upon elements which, though not in themselves original, are combined in a way that is wholly characteristic of Sidney and his period.

The careful elaboration of the plot and much else are modelled on the *Aethiopica* of Heliodorus, a long Greek romance of the third century A.D. which was much admired by many Renaissance writers. Many of the narrative elements in Heliodorus, the heroic and incredible exploits, and the complications of magic and witchcraft, found their most popular form in the Spanish romances of chivalry, of which *Amadis of Gaul* and *Palmerin* were the most famous in England; Sidney thought that the first of them, *Amadis*, 'moved [men's] hearts to the exercise of courtesy, liberality, and especially courage'. Sidney's country setting comes from a Renaissance revival of an even more ancient literary tradition. Arcadia, a mountainous sheep-raising part of Greece, had given its name to the idealized rural world described by Theocritus, and later by Virgil in his pastoral poems, the *Eclogues*. Their themes had been revived in Italy, especially by Jacopo Sannazaro in his series of verse dialogues connected by prose narrative, called *Arcadia* (1504). Later, the setting and manner of pastoral had been combined with the narrative elements of the chivalric romance by Jorge de Montemayor in his *Diana Enamorada* (1559–60), a popular Spanish story about a beautiful shepherdess.[7]

To this amalgam of classical, Italian, and Spanish elements, Sidney added his own fervent moral zeal and his highly polished poetic style. He is deeply in earnest to show the reader how virtue can be achieved and how vice is both ugly in itself and fatal in its consequences. This is not to say that the moral purpose of the *Arcadia* is very convincingly embodied in Sidney's characters or their actions.

To understand why involves the vast range of differences between Sidney's literary tradition, that of the romance, and those which are implicit in the modern novel.

Sidney was the great critical theorist of the ideas that underline romance. He thought of all creative writing, including, of course, the *Arcadia*, as poetry; 'It is not riming and versing that maketh a poet', he wrote in the *Apology for Poetry* (1580). Poetry was not a mere literary technique but a great vocation, whose aim was to transfigure ordinary experience in the light of Sidney's Platonic and Christian view of perfection. The philosopher can give 'precept', and the historian can record 'example'; but only the poet can give in his fictitious example 'a perfect picture ... of whatever the philosopher saith should be done'. Sidney did not conceive of any such literary form as the novel in which apparently real people in real settings behave in the way they normally do. For him, the poet disdained 'to be tied to any such subjection ... as the natural rule of things'; the writer had the higher duty of 'making things either better than Nature bringeth forth, or quite anew, formes such as never were in Nature'.

The novel in general implicitly accepts a roughly naturalistic point of view, at least as its starting point; the characters, emotions, and settings all have ordinary experience as their implied criterion, a criterion accepted by the author and expected by the reader. Sidney had quite different criteria, and they are reflected in his idealization of character, action, and setting.

Some characters in the *Arcadia*, especially the vicious ones, such as Cecropia, are at times convincingly drawn. But any plot which depends heavily upon multiple mistaken identities, oracles, and love potions, tends to undermine the psychological reality of the characters.[8] And so in the *Arcadia*, as in most Elizabethan romances, the plot tends to be apart from, if not in violation of, psychological realism. Much the same can be said of the Elizabethan delight in rhetoric. They believed that, in the intrinsic beauties of his language, an author should offer his readers models of excellence for imitation. When these flowers of style are applied to the description of events, Sidney seems, as far as the modern reader is concerned, to undermine the reality of the action. Here, for instance, is Basilius trying to escape: 'Each coffer or cupboard he met, one saluted his shinnes, another his elbowes, sometimes ready in revenge to strike them againe with his face.' Where inanimate obstacles ironically 'salute', our attention is focused, not on the plight of the hero, but on the skill with which the metaphor is sustained. Actual behaviour is obviously not Sidney's main objective; and no more is actual emotion when Musidorus exclaims: 'But alas to what a sea of miseries my plentiful tongue doth lead me!'. The reader's attention goes, not to the feeling, but to the words; but for Sidney and his audience this was as it should be, as we can tell from the fact that the two passages just quoted figure as examples of two types of metaphor, those 'of the senses' and 'of hyperbole', in a contemporary textbook of eloquence, *The Arcadian Rhetorike* (1588), by Abraham Fraunce. It is so called because, in an interesting testimony to the pre-eminence accorded Sidney's masterpiece by his contemporaries, its English illustrations are largely drawn from the *Arcadia*.

One final quotation will serve as an example, both of the assured elegance of Sidney's pastoralism, and of how the idealized beauty of the setting militates against any sense of the reality of the environment.

The banks of either river seemed arms of the loving earth that fain would embrace, and the river a wanton nymph which still [*always*] would slip from it; either side of the bank being fringed with beautiful trees, which resisted the sun's darts from overmuch piercing the natural coldness of the river. There was among the rest a goodly cypress, who, boughing her fair head over the water, it seemed she looked into it, and dressed her green locks by that running river.

The *Arcadia* is a great work, although its virtues are very remote from our ideas of the novel;* that these virtues reflect the highest literary aspirations of the Elizabethans can be seen in the terms which a historian of the next generation, Peter Heylyn, chose to praise it:

A book which beside its excellent language, rare contrivances, and delectable studies, hath in it all the strains of Poesy, comprehendeth the universal art of speaking, and to them that can discerne and will observe, notable rules for demeanour both private and publike. [*Microcosmus*, 1620]

The narrative traditions established by Lyly and Sidney were

* Mr Rathmell offers a more detailed analysis of *Arcadia* in his chapter on Sidney on pp. 137–48.

continued by Robert Greene (1560–92) and Thomas Lodge (?1558–
1625). They were among the growing number of professional authors
that wrote primarily for the printing press,[9] and they wrote shorter
works in which the story was a good deal more important. This
must have helped to give their works a wider audience, which
included the tradesman as well as the courtier; nevertheless, the code
of gentility and the literary style are very similar to those of their
predecessors.

Greene's attention to literary style is made clear by his Dedication
of *Menaphon: Camilla's Alarum to Sleeping Euphues* (1589), later called
Greene's Arcadia. The dedication is to 'The Gentlemen Readers'.
Greene begs that they will 'thinke the metaphors are well meant,
and that I did it for your pleasure, whereunto I ever aimed my
thoughts', and that they should not take his work so lightly that
they do not 'take a little pains to prie into my imagination'. The
somewhat mechanical euphuistic elaboration of style is certainly the
most striking feature of Greene's pastoral romances, of which the
best are probably *Pandosto, The Triumph of Time* (1588), which gave
Shakespeare the plot of *The Winter's Tale*, and *Tully's Love* (1589),
a romance in which Cicero saves the young lovers with a speech
to the Roman Senate!

Greene was, above all, prolific. Although no one of his works
was as celebrated as *Euphues* or the *Arcadia*, he was certainly the
best-seller among Elizabethan writers of prose fiction – over a
hundred editions of his works appeared before 1640. Thomas Lodge's
fame depends upon the perfection of two pastoral romances:
Rosalynde: Euphues Golden Legacy (1596), which gave us the plot
of *As You Like It*, and is probably the most charming of Elizabethan
romances; the other, *A Margarite from America* (1596), is equally
readable and has a wider emotional range. Lodge's mastery of the
pastoral romance is illustrated by a passage in which the chaste
heroine, Margarite, encounters a lion in the forest:

Fawnia [her attendant] that first spied him was soon surprised, and rent
in pieces (in that she had tasted too much of fleshly love) before she feared.
Margarite that saw the massacre, sate still attending her own tragedy, for
nothing was more welcome to her than death, having lost her friend, nor
nothing more expected: but see the generositie and virtue of the beast, instead
of renting her limbes he scented her garments, in the place of tearing her

piecemeale, he laid his head gentlie in her lap, licking her milk-white hand, and showing all signes of humilitie instead of inhumanitie.

In the world of Lodge's fiction what a lion would actually do is much less important than the traditional belief, culled from the medieval bestiaries, that a lion, being royal, naturally reveres eminent virtue, and, conversely, punishes incontinence. What matters is not the literal credibility of the episode, but the rightness of the moral and the rhetorical aptness of the language; these reach their climax in the elegant alliance of sound and meaning in the concluding phrase about the lion's emblematic 'humilitie instead of inhumanitie'.

The incredible adventures of pastoral romance are to be found at a lower literary level in the Spanish romances of chivalry. Translations from Greek, Latin, Italian, French, and Spanish supplied a very large part of the reading matter for the Elizabethan public, and the proportion was particularly high in prose fiction. The Spanish romances were translated, adapted, and imitated mainly by hacks of little education or literary skill – men such as Anthony Munday, a 'dismal draper of misplaced literary ambitions', who translated *Amadis of Gaul* (1590), and three parts of the *Palmerin* cycle. There was also the more original Emanuel Ford, whose *Parismus*, *The Renound Prince of Bohemia* (1598), *Ornatus and Artesia* (1607), and *Montelyon, Knight of the Oracle*, remained popular until the eighteenth century. The firm hold of the chivalric romances on the imagination of tradesmen and apprentices was mocked by the aristocratic Beaumont in his comedy, *The Knight of the Burning Pestle* (1608). The public appetite for these endless, repetitive and often inane adventures serves as a corrective to any notion that the Elizabethan period was one of universally high literary standards; but the English versions of the chivalric romances also show that English middle-class readers demanded a high standard of morality (not always to be found in the Spanish originals), and of patriotic fervour. This demand was exploited by two somewhat later hacks, Henry Roberts, and especially Richard Johnson, author of the famous *Seven Champions of Christendom* (1596), *Tom a Lincoln* (1599), and *Tom Thumbe* (1621).[10]

So much for the staple novels of the time. At best eloquent, charming but unreal, at worst boring but not vicious, they must be approached on their own terms. To see them primarily as unsuccessful realistic novels was for long the general tendency among literary historians, and traces of it are still found in Margaret Schlauch's *Antecedents of the English Novel, 1400–1600*, which remains the most lively and informative survey of its subject. This approach inevitably tends to favour those works or passages which are largely concerned with realistic description; and by this criterion there are some other miscellaneous forms of Elizabethan fiction which rate more highly than the romances.

Stories of 'real life' – usually 'low life' – are found in at least four separate types of Elizabethan writing.[11] First, there were auto-biographical pamphlets, usually sensational and exaggerated repent-ances – notably those of Greene and Nashe – which contain some of our most vivid pictures of the seamy side of daily life in Elizabethan England. Second, there were also popular compilations of short stories mainly based on the Italian erotic *novella*, such as William Painter's *The Palace of Pleasure* (1566–7).[12] Third, there was another kind of compilation of ostensibly real stories, the jest books, collec-tions of anecdotes similar to the medieval fabliaux. These two kinds of compilation were the nearest Elizabethan equivalent of our maga-zines; neither was influenced by the prevailing idealization of the romances, and they consequently provided something of a tradition for the writing of realistic narrative, as Nashe and Deloney show.

The fourth realistic tradition is that of 'roguery'. Roguery belongs in part to the picaresque novel, the adventures of unscrupulous *picaros* – rogues – of which the most famous example was the Spanish *Lazarillo de Tormes* (1553, translated 1576). A related native genre was begun in England by John Awdeley, a printer, in his *Fraternitie of Vagabonds* (1561), and Thomas Harman, a J.P. for Kent, in his *Caveat for Common Cursitors, vulgarly called Vagabonds* (1567) – both of these handbooks describing the types and methods of criminals, enlivened by character sketches and illustrative incidents. Robert Greene wrote four very readable booklets of the same type 'for the general benefit of all Gentlemen, Apprentices, Country Farmers and Yeomen'. Called the 'Cony-Catching Pamphlets', they detail with great liveliness the innumerable tricks practised by rogues on the 'rabbits' in the game of London life.

None of these four realistic forms had anything like a unified plot. The picaresque novel was a loose stringing together of comic or satirical adventures on a biographical thread; and in the jest books all kinds of anecdotes and brief stories were, for the most part erroneously, attributed to a single figure, as in *Scoggin's Jests* (1566), *Skelton's Merry Tales* (1567), and *Tarlton's Jests* (?1592).[13] There was, in general, the same lack of coherence or development as regards the psychology of the characters and the moral implications of their actions.

Thomas Nashe's *The Unfortunate Traveller, or the Life of Jack Wilton* (1594) combines elements of all four of these kinds of writing. It is purportedly an autobiographical confession which ends with repentance; but the narrative offers an extreme illustration of the contradictions between plot and character. The tale begins like a jest book, but goes on to adapt the realistic Italian *novella* to an unprecedentedly realistic and at times macabre intensity.[14] Before falling back into the tradition of roguery, Jack Wilton, Nashe's anti-hero, changes his character according to the nature of the incident which is being narrated. We see him first as a page-boy rogue, then he becomes a cultivated traveller, and later a hero of the starkest melodrama and intrigue, before he finally reforms and marries. It is the incidents themselves, and above all the brilliance of the prose in which they are narrated, rather than the character of the hero, which are Nashe's main concern: he fashions jewels of realism, but they do not match and they are not strung together in a consistent narrative and psychological thread.[15]

There are two partial exceptions to these generalizations about the absence of unified, realistic narrative and convincingly real characters in Elizabethan fiction. Except for its high literary quality, George Gascoigne's *A Hundred Sundrie Flowres* (1573) is a typical miscellany of lyrical poetry, plays, and stories, mainly translations; but it contains a long short story, 'The Adventures of Master F. J.', which is the most authentic-sounding study of an *amour* to be written in English until the eighteenth century. It was probably autobiographical. The intrigues of a noble household, as well as their pastimes and conversation, are described in a wholly naturalistic manner, if we except the poems which punctuate Gascoigne's narrative as they do nearly all the fiction of the period. But Gascoigne's story seems to be something of an accident; there was nothing in the literary tradition to make him think that his direct presentation of an episode in his own life was a worthwhile enterprise; and he later rewrote the story in a much more conventional way.[16]

The other exception is Thomas Deloney. He was a 'ballading silkweaver of Norwich', who succeeded Elderton as the chief composer of topical broadside ballads. However, the topicality on which the sale of ballads depended led him into indiscretions, and he sought safety by turning to writing prose narratives, notably *Jack of Newbury* (1597), *The Gentle Craft*, i.e. shoemaking (1597–8), and *Thomas of Reading* (1600). Although his stories are set in the earlier part of the sixteenth century, the heroic period of the independent artisan, they give us our most living (and almost only) picture of daily life for the Elizabethan middle and lower classes, specifically clothiers and shoemakers. The plots are simple – roughly chronological accounts of the fortunes of the semi-legendary success-ful tradesmen who are Deloney's heroes; the incidents are strung together in a way very like that of the jest books. But Deloney's subjects allow ample scope for realistic detail, and his scenes and dialogues always ring true. This, together with the vigour and direct-ness of his style, makes his fiction the most immediately accessible and rewarding until that of Defoe, whom Deloney in many ways resembles.

Deloney, however, is not the precursor of a new tradition; he is at the end of an old one,[17] one which partakes in the verbal vigour and complexity of a culture in which Shakespeare, too, was popular entertainment. This can be suggested by two quotations. Here is Jack of Newbury, the virtuous apprentice about to marry his employer, a rich widow, being rallied by the beer-swilling wild youths of the town:

Nay (quoth another) I'll lay my life, that as the Salamander cannot live without fire, so Jack cannot live without the smell of his Dame's smock.
And I marvel (quoth Jack) that you being of the nature of the herring (which so soon as he is taken out of the sea, presently dies) can live so long with your nose out of the pot.

When a ballad-monger could depict the life of the street corner in such racy yet elaborate terms, the language of Shakespeare was not likely to be found as difficult as it sometimes is today; nor, apparently, did it seem inappropriate for a self-made man to turn out as pointed and compressed a maxim as Jack of Newbury's reproof to his wife for having stinted the victuals of their employees: 'Empty platters make greedy stomachs, and where scarcity is kept, hunger is nourished.'

Elizabethan prose fiction, we may conclude, is unmistakably the literature of a people that produced the Elizabethan drama. Their culture was too oral, too symbolic, and too traditional to entertain the idea of that mainly representational prose genre – the novel; but if we approach their fiction as something quite different, in the spirit which has been suggested here, it is very rewarding for its own sake, as well as for the light it sheds on the age of Shakespeare.[18]

NOTES

1. See Henry Stanley Bennett, *English Books and Readers, 1475–1557, 1558–1603* (Cambridge, 1965); *1603–1640* (Cambridge, 1970).

2. For a study of the methods of printed distribution of news, see M. A. Shaaber, *Some Forerunners of the Newspaper in England, 1476–1622* (Philadelphia, 1929). Topical ballads, occasional pamphlets and single-sheet broadsides were the commonest method, at least until towards the end of the reign of James I.

3. See Marjorie Plant, 'The Demand for Books', in *The English Book Trade* (London, 1974), 35–51.

4. The miscellanies of poetry, ranging in kind from *Tottel's Miscellany* (1557), which contained the poems of Wyatt and Surrey, to Clement Robinson's *A Handful of Pleasant Delights* (1584), which contained such ballads as 'Greensleeves', were a characteristic Elizabethan form of publication.

5. Two substantial general studies of Elizabethan prose fiction are: Margaret Schlauch, *Antecedents of the English Novel, 1400–1600* (London, 1963), 'a quest for precursors of modern novels', and Walter R. Davies, *Idea and Art in Elizabethan Prose Fiction* (Princeton, 1969), in which the author treats Elizabethan fiction from a more modern critical point of view. There is also a useful and fairly up-to-date bibliography, Sterg O'Dell's *A Chronological List of Prose Fiction in English, 1475–1640* (Cambridge, Mass., 1954). One of the several anthologies deserves special mention: *Elizabethan Prose Fiction*, ed. Merritt Lawlis (New York, 1967) contains a good selection of works (Gascoigne, Lyly, Rich, Greene, Lodge, Nashe, Deloney) with head-notes and footnotes, together with an introduction and biographical sketches of the authors. A more general perspective on the tradition of Greek romance is given in Arthur Heiserman, *The Novel Before the Novel: Essays and Discussions About the Beginnings of Prose Fiction in the West* (Chicago and London, 1977).

6. The sequel is less episodic, and Joseph W. Houppert argues that it 'reads more like a novel' (*John Lyly* (Boston, 1975), 22, 41).

7. A. C. Hamilton argues that in combining the two traditions for prose fiction Sidney created a substantially new literary form ('Sidney's *Arcadia* as Prose Fiction: Its Relation to its Sources', in *English Literary Renaissance*, 2 (1972), 29–60).

8. For a defence of the way Sidney interwove his actions, see Walter R. Davis, 'Narrative Methods in Sidney's *Old Arcadia*', in *Studies in English Literature, 1500–1900*, 18 (1978), 13–33.

9. See Edwin Haviland Miller, *The Professional Writer in Elizabethan England: A Study of Nondramatic Literature* (Cambridge, Mass., 1959).

10. For an account of these two last, see Louis B. Wright, *Middle-Class Culture in Elizabethan England* (Chapel Hill, 1935), 375–417, a fine large-scale historical survey of its subject. See also Dale B. J. Randall, *The Golden Tapestry: A Critical Survey of Non-Chivalric Spanish Fiction in English Translation, 1543–1657* (Durham, N. C., 1963).

11. Works of travel might perhaps be added to the list, as a popular and still very readable form of Elizabethan writing.

12. One of the most attractive works of this type is Barnabe Riche's *Riche his Farewell to Militarie Profession* (1581). It contains the story 'Of Apolonius and Silla', in a form that offers an interesting contrast to *Twelfth Night*, which was based on it.

13. One recent collection is P. M. Zall's *A Hundred Merry Tales and Other English Jestbooks of the 15th and 16th Centuries* (Lincoln, Nebraska, 1963).

14. See especially the lively and instructive introduction by John Berryman whose wayward brilliance matches his topic (*The Unfortunate Traveller ... Newly edited, with an Introduction by John Berryman* (New York, 1960)).

15. This, at least, is the conclusion of the most recent full-length study, G. R. Hibbard's *Thomas Nashe* (London, 1962).

16. See Charles T. Prouty's *George Gascoigne: Elizabethan Courtier, Soldier and Poet* (New York, 1942). Since then, Gascoigne has attracted much critical attention and been given credit for a great deal of conscious literary artistry, as in Gregory Waters' article, 'G. T.'s "Worthles Enterprise": A Study of the Narrator in Gascoigne's "The Adventures of Master F. J.", in *Journal of Narrative Technique* 7 (1977). See also Robert P. Adams' influential 'Gascoigne's *Master F. J. as Original Fiction*', in *PMLA* LXXIII (1958), 315–26, and Richard A. Lanham's 'Narrative Structure in Gascoigne's *F. J.*', in *Studies in Short Fiction* IV (1966), 42–50.

17. In his *Apology for the Middle Class: The Dramatic Novels of Thomas Deloney* (Bloomington, 1961), Merritt E. Lawlis sees Deloney as the only writer of dramatic novels in English before Fielding; he does not, however, argue that Deloney was a precursor of later realistic fiction.

18. I am indebted to Robyn Housley, Steven Mullaney, and Jack Prostko for help in the revision of this essay.

PRINTING IN ENGLAND FROM CAXTON TO MILTON

D. F. MCKENZIE

William Caxton was a man of two worlds. For thirty years he lived abroad as a Merchant Adventurer and diplomat, representing the interests of English traders in the Low Countries and serving also for a time as Governor of the English Nation at Bruges. It was there, in 1473–4, that he printed in his own translation the *Recuyell of the Histories of Troy*, the first book in English to be produced from movable types. And then, for the last fifteen years of his life, he worked as editor, translator, printer, publisher and bookseller at Westminster. A dated Indulgence makes it clear that he was in business there as a printer sometime before 13 December 1476.

In a simple way his divided life helps to direct our understanding of Caxton's achievement. What gave it unity was his impulse to translate. Like several European printers of his time he published first in the vernacular. He and his Bruges associate Colard Mansion collated texts, made translations, and then introduced, edited, printed and published them in that rich blend of scholarship, craftsmanship and commerce which we know better from the next century. The works he first chose, or turned to at his patrons' direction, were naturally enough in French, their content historical, chivalric and moral; but with few exceptions their language when printed was 'our Englissh and maternal tongue'. Caxton quickly added to his continental editions texts of Lydgate's poems *Churl and Bird* and *Horse, Sheep and Goose*. He printed Chaucer's *Parliament of Fowls*, *Anelida and Arcite*, his translation of Boethius and, in two quite distinct editions, *The Canterbury Tales*. Higden's *Polychronicon*, Gower's *Confessio Amantis*, and pre-eminently Malory's *Morte D'Arthur* were further important additions to the corpus of English literature which he made more widely and cheaply accessible by printing, and established more firmly for his own time and ours as national classics. His loyalties, therefore, and a patriotism sharpened by absence, were political, literary and linguistic. His press served Yorkist and Tudor royalty and they repaid him with patronage. His commendatory prologues and epilogues are critical manifestos which celebrate the redeeming power of print over author, work and language. His zest for translation, 'a noble and meritorious dede' as he called it, drove him towards a definition of English to which the printed word, more than anything else, would give an enduring authority.

Caxton only once testifies outright to what might now be called the impact of print, but he goes straight to the point, contrasting the sequential writing out of multiple copies by hand ('my penne is worn, myn hande wery and not stedfast, myn eyen dimmed with overmoche lokyng on the whit paper') and the printing of an edition in which all copies are begun together, completed together, distributed and to some extent read together ('to th'ende that every man may have them attones. For all the books of this storye ... thus enpryntid as ye here see were begonne in oon day and also fynysshid in oon day'). The technology of print (an impressive conjunction of type-mould, paper, ink and press) had its proper dynamic in the fertile fluidity of type, the re-use implicit in its form. Since its destiny was to be active, not merely within one book as section by section was finished and the same types redeployed, but in a whole progeny of others, it was by its very nature generative in a way that scribal tools were not.

So too with the form of the book itself and its medium, paper. The vellum codex had displaced the scroll in the early Christian era (papyrus survived better if rolled, the codex packed and travelled better than a roll); but the inherent virtues of this evolution were fully realized only when printers adopted the codex as their standard book form and made it ubiquitous. It kept the accretive, sequential order of the scroll and therefore remained hospitable to the time-bound forms of narrative or the logical progression of an argument. But since it could now be opened at any point its form also gave instant access to any part of the text. Freedom from physically constrained sequential reading in turn permitted quick referencing (aided by pagination and indexing), fresh combinations and permutations within the text, and tangential uses of parts of it. That propensity of the book to create as it records became significantly active through printing. The substitution of paper for vellum made the book cheaper, more compendious and yet less bulky. Standard letter forms had the same effect by compressing the text in the very act of making it more uniformly legible.

The idea of an edition – a significant number of copies released together – had its own potency. Although Caxton repeatedly addressed both his 'redars and herers', a printed edition extended a specific audience into an abstract readership more or less unified in time but not in place. This new power of communal address beyond the range of the spoken word gave force in turn to conservative and reformative ideals (in Caxton's case 'the comyn wele' before 'singuler prouffyte'). By the same token the simultaneous distribution of copies greatly increased the speed with which ideas were circulated and therefore bred more immediate and topically volatile reactions. In time this ability to generate a widespread communal response through printing made censorship both more urgent and, since an edition once dispersed takes on the elusive particularity of any one copy from it, harder to effect.

An edition made texts common in another way. Whereas multiple manuscript copies might differ extensively one from another, all copies of any printed edition were virtually the same. The 'work' in print therefore assumed an identity regardless of time, place or readership. When manuscripts did differ, their collation and correction to provide a sound text for printing served an emergent awareness of authorial intention in vernacular, classical and, at a higher level, biblical texts. So, when Caxton reprinted *The Canterbury Tales* in 1483, he chose a different, and as he thought better, manuscript as his copy, 'Whyche book I have dylygently oversen and duly examynd to th'ende that it be made accordyng unto his owen makyng'. The ready proliferation and wide dissemination of identical texts gave a peculiar and influential authority to their linguistic forms, especially in the vernacular. Caxton noted the historical fact that 'our langage now used varyeth ferre from that whiche was used and spoken whan I was borne' and the geographical one that the 'comyn Englysshe that is spoken in one shyre varyeth from another'. He quite seriously wished to speak to 'the condycions and maners of the comyn people whiche without enformacion and lernyng ben rude and not manerd'; and in his judgement, as he wrote, 'the comyn terms that be dayli used ben lyghter to be understonde than the olde and auncyent Englysshe' or, from the standpoint of West-minster, its regional varieties. But the economic imperative of quitting a whole edition (instead of a single manuscript) reinforced the educational one of disseminating knowledge in a common and stable language.

The economics of printing and bookselling virtually ensured that the effects would be socially pervasive. The edition itself was an inherently expansive unit simply because the cost per copy fell as the number printed rose. To secure a regular living, however, a printer had to diversify his sources of income and draw on all at once. The most obvious way of doing so, again expansive, was to spread his risks by defining several markets by age, sex or profession, and to print a range of titles for each. So Caxton declared his Cicero 'not requysyte ne eke convenyent for every rude and symple man ... but for noble, wyse and grete lordes, gentilmen and marchauntes'. And enough of Caxton's popular work survives to reveal that he set the pattern for printers of serving their societies at almost every level, in order to secure their own economic stability. Reprints destined for markets already tested, stock work for schools, ephemera for city, church and court, and personal or institutional patronage (whether by direct subsidy or guaranteed sales), all offered continuity of work and more immediate returns. Almost as important for economic survival was a certain variety in the material and workaday realities a printer had to manage: types, format, length, edition quantities. The more varied his work, and to that extent the more socially diverse its ends, the more efficiently could he organize its printing.

For as long as the functions of printing and publishing were united in one shop, author, artisan and entrepreneur were also closely linked and the printing house itself was the focus of many disciplines. Its practices were internally collaborative and externally competitive and in both ways this worked to establish a body of past knowledge and accelerate the growth of new. As tools for learning, and under competitive market pressures, books rapidly acquired an extensive set of conventions with which to display their content to best effect (title pages; chapter, paragraph and verse divisions; colour, decoration and illustration; standard number forms; distinctions in size and style of type; headings, side- and foot-notes; braces; column and tabular setting; indexes; paper size and quality). The *Morte D'Arthur* was, as Caxton said, 'by me devyded into xxi bookes, chapytred and enprynted'. Woodcut figures, 'without whiche it may not lightly be understande', appeared in the *Mirror of the World* (1481) and, among several books thereafter, in his reprints of *The Canterbury Tales* and *Game of Chess*. A book in the hand was a stimulus to self-instruction and thereby bred a desire for more books. As personal collections and institutional libraries (many created by charities for the greater public good), they became systems and thereby a resource for the comparative and syncretic work which was itself born of the proliferation of titles.

Italian humanism flowered too late for Caxton to know its force, but the printers who made it a European movement used the same seed-beds of editing, printing and marketing. His preference for the vernacular had powerful issue ultimately in the Reformation. His love of his own literature and his esteem for its makers were expressed with vigour and a full understanding of his role as printer to define, promote and preserve. Chaucer's 'wysedom and subtyll understondyng' lived on in his printed works: 'alle ye that shal in thys booke rede or heere wyll of your charyte ... remembre the sowle of the sayd Gefferey Chaucer'. Converse with the past, present and future, a principle dear to the humanists, was at the heart of Caxton's enterprise as England's first printer.

In the forty years following Caxton's death the London trade was dominated by two foreign-born printers, Wynkyn de Worde and Richard Pynson. This did not mean an immediate infusion of humanist ideas, let alone their adoption as a leading motive for printing. Even their forms came slowly: Pynson introduced roman type in 1509, de Worde a few words of Greek, cut in wood, in 1517 and italic type only in 1528. Put simply, the importance of de Worde and Pynson lies in having created the general English market. In doing so, they socialized the book, established the typical conditions of trade as commercially and culturally promiscuous, and relocated its centre by moving from Westminster to Fleet Street. Prices settled to roughly two sheets a penny, edition quantities to between 750 and 1,000 copies. De Worde's productivity was prodigious (some 700 editions at least), with an emphasis – alongside the staple religious works – on elementary school texts, Latin grammars, liturgies, and cheap popular manuals in formats to fit the hand. Pynson catered for the same needs but with more typographic style, quality and perhaps literary awareness. Pynson's special interest in law books, however, and from 1508 his role as King's Printer, foreshadow the growth of restrictive practices. These would consolidate the position of London printers, encourage the enterprise of native-born craftsmen, protect the market from un-controlled foreign competition, and, by royal grants of privilege, help to safeguard a printer's investment from piracy at home. So in 1523 it was ordered that aliens' apprentices must be English and that no printer should employ more than two foreign journeymen; in 1529 aliens were prohibited from setting up any new press; in 1534, as a protection for local binders, the importing of bound books was forbidden and, to establish London control of the wholesale trade, aliens were forced to market their books through native-born stationers. Since before 1534 most humanist literature had been printed abroad and imported, it was only after that date that English printers had any commercial incentive to compete for the same market in England.

Such protective measures certainly favoured the long-term eco-nomic interests of the domestic trade, but they must also be seen as a means of defining and controlling it. A system of censorship to stop the spread of heresy and a prohibition on translations from scripture had been in effect since 1407. By the 1520s, however, book-sellers began to find themselves in serious trouble with the church authorities. Lutheran books were one cause, the Bible in English another. Book burnings were ordered by Wolsey in 1521 and 1524. A proclamation of 1529 lists prohibited books, another of 1530 establishes the first licensing system under secular authority for books 'concernynge holy scripture'. Tyndale's *New Testament* (printed abroad, 1525–6) quickly made its way into England only to be suppressed wherever it was found. The fall and death of Wolsey and the break with Rome opened up an easier if still uncertain passage for the dispersal of Coverdale's translation of the complete Bible (1535). A revised version of the Tyndale and Coverdale translations was attributed to a fictitious Thomas Matthew, approved by the King and printed by Richard Grafton under royal privilege in 1537.

A further revision, known as *The Great Bible* and printed partly in Paris and partly in London, followed in 1539. It too was protected by privilege and its market doubly assured by a royal injunction which ordered that a copy be placed in all churches for anyone to read. At last, in the words of John Foxe, 'the blessed wisdom and omnipotent power of the Lord began to work for his church not with sword and target to subdue his exalted adversary, but with printing, writing and reading, to convince darkness by light, error by truth, ignorance by learning'. In more mundane terms, one of printing's most valuable properties was, under licence, at last on the market.

The printed English Bible was the ultimate growth of Caxton's devotion to the vernacular, but its position was still far from secure; indeed, the translation of any learned text into English and its general dispersal by printing was often attacked as a danger. To make the law common by taking it out of Law Latin and Norman French, or to reduce physic to a matter of self-treatment by describing it in plain English, was some threat to professional practitioners. When it permitted a layman to bypass a priest it was perilous to the profession as well as the spirit. As a 'popysh pryest' told Piers Plowman in a dialogue of about 1530, if 'hobbes and his rusticals be suffred to be thus busy in readyngs of Englysh heresy and to dyspute after this maner wyth us which are sperytual men, we shal be fayne to learne some other occupacion'.

The most powerful voice of reaction was that of Stephen Gardiner, Bishop of Winchester under Henry VIII and Mary Tudor's Lord Chancellor. After Cromwell's execution in 1540 he had the authority to effect his wishes. He is reported by Foxe as one who 'wrangleth much against players, printers, preachers' and unlike most printers he had no faith in the future of English to do other than deform the truth: 'As for the English tonge, it selfe hath not continued in one forme of understanding CC yeares; and without Gods work and speciall miracle it shall hardely containe religion long, when it cannot last it selfe.' In 1542 it was forbidden to read *The Great Bible* in churches. The following year an Act 'for the advancement of true religion' proscribed Tyndale's translations, ordered the obliteration of notes and marginal commentaries and prohibited the reading of the Bible in English to ordinary men and women.

Although noble women and gentlewomen might read it in private, only noblemen, gentlemen and merchants might read it to their families. Gardiner's power lapsed with the accession of Edward VI but in Mary's reign he again suppressed the English Bible. Indirectly his action led to the composite translation by Protestant exiles of *The Geneva Bible* (1560), with its instructive engravings and maps, arguments, marginal notes, and title-page woodcut of Time raising Truth from her grave.

For all Caxton's concern to give Chaucer his due as the true maker, it was to be some two hundred years before the trade would be forced to acknowledge an author's rights in all copies of his work and so to sustain, in equity, a professional authorship. It soon became very clear, however, that a printer's (and occasionally an editor–translator's) investment in a book could be seriously jeopardized if others were free to reprint it. The granting of royal privileges to prevent unauthorized reprinting for a specified time seems to have begun about 1512 (with Linacre's *Progymnasmata*), but inevitably such privileges soon acquired a double function: they were valuable to the holders but only good conduct would secure them. It is no surprise therefore that a proclamation of 1538 refers both to licensing (which, in approving a work, confers the commercially valuable right to print it) and to privilege (which protects that right). More precisely, the proclamation requires the regular pre-publication licensing of all printing 'for expellinge and avoydinge the occasion of errours and seditiouse opinions', forbids the importing of English books printed abroad, and demands that the production of books printed *Cum privilegio regali* be clearly shown to be limited to the holder of the privilege by the addition of the words *ad imprimendum solum* ('for sole, or exclusive, printing'). Patents were granted soon after for complete classes of books, their value thereby increasing automatically with any growth in the market, and the rights to print common law books, ABCs and catechisms, chronicles, dictionaries, bibles and testaments in various formats, psalters, primers, almanacs, Latin grammars, music books and ruled paper, works in Latin, Greek and Hebrew, were sold off to individual printers and booksellers. By virtue of their patents, many of these men became important members of the trade; because they were dependent on those patents, they could be relied upon to police them. It is likely that by about 1540 or not long after, London printers also came to see the merits of introducing their own informal system for the registration of copies as a commonly agreed self-regulating practice. Such registration was subject only to internal sanctions but, as it does today, the resulting system of commercial copyright simply reinforced other controls on the printed word. It is a further sign of the counter-movement of protection, licensing and privilege which followed the first radically expansive period of printing in England.

It is a measure of the printing trade's general conformity with government policy (of restrictive trade practices, that is, with pro-Catholic containment of printing) that the Stationers' Company of London finally received its charter from Mary Tudor in 1557. Concessions were granted to Oxford and Cambridge, otherwise printing was effectually confined to London (because it was restricted to freemen of the Company or those with royal privileges) and controlled by an oligarchy of patentees happy enough in their own interests to regulate the conduct of other members. Since the Master and Wardens were given nation-wide powers of search, seizure and imprisonment to suppress seditious and heretical books, they could exercise these powers equally well against commercial piracy. Elizabeth's *Injunctions* of 1559 to prevent the printing of anything 'hereticall, seditious, or unseemly for Christian eares' confirmed the necessity of pre-publication licensing of all new books (including pamphlets, plays, ballads and reprints of works on religion and government). The same concerns were vigorously restated in a Star Chamber decree of 1586 in order to control the expression of both extreme Puritan and Roman Catholic thought. This not only confirmed the Company's powers of search and seizure and ordered pre-publication licensing by the Archbishop of Canterbury or the Bishop of London, but it also set legal limits to the growth of printing by moving to control the number of printers, presses and apprentices, and made the entry of copies (in addition to licensing) obligatory. Such constraints were not unwelcome to the more powerful members of the trade as they advanced the aims of the charter by further limiting competition, by validating the principle of commercial copyright, and by explicitly sanctioning its enforcement.

The actions which Gardiner had taken against the Bible in English reflected a deep distrust not merely of printing but of the word itself as an educative force. They were in fact part of an extended debate over the Catholic preference for priestly mediation and instruction by images (laymen's books, which speak directly to the mind) and the Protestant belief in the superiority of the word (since any visual image, by reducing a concept to material forms, must falsify it). The Catholic view assumed older conditions of mass illiteracy, the Protestant one the growth of a new and universal readership through printing. The Protestant view was of course to prevail for at least the next four hundred years but in its English victory over popery, episcopacy and kingship it was also fundamentally opposed to, and broke up and swept away, the kinetic icons of Shakespeare's theatre.

Opposition to the translation of works other than the Bible was soon overcome, and since translation was an easy way of expanding the market for learned works printers did much to promote it. John Rastell, lawyer, playwright, brother-in-law of Thomas More and the first substantial English-born printer to follow Caxton, published an English version of the *Abridgement of the Statutes* (1527). In it he noted that 'the unyversall people in this realm had greate plesure and gave themself greatly to the redyng of the vulgare Englyssh tonge', but he went on to claim the civic value of such a work in which every man 'by the knowledge wherof and by the dylygente observyng of the same maye the better do hys dewte to hys prynce and soveraynge and also lyve in tranquylyte and peace wyth his neyboure'. Another printer, Robert Redman, introducing his edition of Magna Carta and other statutes (1534), acknowledged that 'though percase it shal not satysffye the learned, yet shall it be a good helpe for the unlerned', and it was Redman who first printed in English a Primer which accorded throughout with the use of Salisbury (1535).

After religion and the law, most translations were not of the great classical or learned humanist works but of texts with a practical bias and broad appeal. Since foreign work in English was bound to sell better than an English work in Latin, it was inevitable that those who wrote new books on technical subjects should feel compelled to do so directly in English. In this way an author's wish to reach and inform a wider readership coincided with his printer's concern to capture a larger market. Andrew Borde's *Breviary of Health*

(1552) was published that 'simple and unlerned men ... may have some knowledge to ease them in theyr diseases and infirmities'. Thomas Gale echoes that remark a decade later in *Certain Works of Chirurgery* (1563): 'I goe about to make everiebody cunning in the arte of medicine.' So too the rules of logic and rhetoric were given an English dress in Thomas Wilson's *Rule of Reason* (1551) and *Art of Rhetoric* (1553); and in compliment to the work of Ramus, first translated into English in 1574, Abraham Fraunce applied the method in his *Lawyers Logic* (1588) as it was one whereby 'every cobbler can cogge a syllogisme, everye carter cracke of propositions'.

The vulgarization of knowledge was the primary social achievement of the sixteenth-century London book trade. Encyclopaedias, herbals, recipe books, ballads and pamphlets on trials and executions, works on husbandry, distillation, popular medicine, arithmetic, geometry, geography, navigation and judicial astronomy: such books have a modest enough role in literary or intellectual history, but together with ephemera, sermons, scriptural commentaries, and works produced under patent, they were the staple products of the trade. Its motives in producing them were often genuinely educative as well as commercial and its dedication to the popular market had one profound effect: it created a general public numerous and literate enough to be influenced by the radical press. In the next century that press would overthrow the edifice of protection and censorship and establish a freedom for the printed word ahead of all other countries.

Notwithstanding that populist bias, the spirit of Caxton was not wholly stifled. Many early printers combined, as he had done, the roles of author, editor and printer, actively applying their learning in writing and editing. There is plenty of evidence that some printers at least earned the trust of distinguished scholars. Moreover, in serving scholarship, many printers showed a degree of editorial sophistication that is not generally recognized. Obvious aids to the reader, capitalized on by the Geneva Bible, were illustrations, marginal notes, glossaries and indexes. When translating Herodian's *History of the Roman Emperors* (*c.* 1555) Nicholas Smyth added arguments to each book and, in alphabetical order, annotations on 'wordes, Histories, Fables, sytuacions of places, and descriptions of Countreyes, servynge to the more easye understandynge of the present Hystorye'. Tottel's edition of *The Great Charter* (1556) claims to have divided and numbered the chapters truly, ordered and quoted the alphabetical table justly, and correctly numbered the leaves 'with mani other helps'. In Sir John Harington's advertisement to the reader prefacing his translation of Ariosto's *Orlando Furioso* (1591), he notes the several functions of the marginal notes; his 'exact and necessarie table' locates people, places and things, and his method of indexing creates narrative summaries for each of the principal characters. Even more significantly, he shows how the poem may be read in any of at least three ways for its narrative (straight through, selectively, pictorially) and in each of four ways for its import (as moral, history, allegory, allusion). Ramist texts deliberately used all the devices of linear display, indenting, italics, numbering and bracketed dichotomies. Engraved title pages were used increasingly as emblematic arches giving entry to the world of the book within. Collected works, especially posthumous ones with frontispiece portraits, even came close to equating a book with the body of its author: it contained at one level his 'relics', at another his creative spirit 'as in a phial'. Montaigne made much play with the idea; so did Jonson in respect of his *Works* (1616) and in directing the readers of Shakespeare's folio (1623) to 'looke, Not on his Picture, but his Booke'.

Jonson's perception was unusual and it was rare for an English literary text to receive the respectful care given to 'serious' writers. Chaucer, who was part of English book-trade history and who belonged to the tradition of spoken epic still alive when printing was born, was an honoured exception. Thomas Speght could boast in 1602 that he had 'reformed the whole worke, whereby Chaucer for the most part is restored to his owne Antiquitie', but his was the last collected edition for many years. E.K's glosses to *The Shepherd's Calendar* (1579), let alone Harington's elaborate apparatus for Ariosto, find no parallel in *The Faerie Queene* (1590–96). Heminge and Condell seem to have started to edit Shakespeare with the best of intentions, but their spirits obviously quailed before the scale of the task and the lack of adequate editorial and typographical conventions within which to perform it for the drama. English printers were capable of fine work – Pynson's splendid Sarum Missal of 1500, John Day's edition of Cunningham's *Cosmographical Glass* (1559), Henry Denham's three-volume *Monuments of Matrons* (1582) and Walton's *Biblia Sacra Polyglotta* (1653–7) as printed by Thomas Roycroft may serve to make the point. But the trade's real interest lay elsewhere. Despite Caxton's example, it did little to generate and propagate adequately a national literature, and the major literary monuments of Shakespeare's age – its dramatic texts – were on the whole only fortuitously preserved.

In any society subject to political and religious censorship, fictions and Caxton's 'cotydyan witnesse', history, assume a quite central function in commenting directly on the present. For 150 years the book trade employed the obliquities of chronicle history and translations from classical historians. Renaissance dramatists were freer: they could create new fictions in tune with the times, or they could bring pertinent historical incidents to vigorous life on stage. Of the two, history, whether narrative or dramatic, was the more dangerous for it was traditionally expected to instruct the present. Sir John Hayward in his *Lives of the III Norman Kings of England* (1613) drew the distinction:

> Men might safely write of others in manner of a tale, but in manner of a history safely they could not: because, albeit they should write of men long since dead, and whose posteritie is worne cleane out; yet some alive, finding themselves foule in those vices, which they see observed, reproved, condemned in others, their guiltinesse maketh them apt to conceive, that whatsoever the words are, the finger pointeth only at them.

Not to have made such applications of course would have undermined the purposes of historian and poet alike. 'Every good subject according to the levell of his witte,' wrote Thomas Wilson introducing his translation of Demosthenes (1570), 'should compare the time past with the time present, and even when he heareth Athens, or the Athenians, to remember Englande and Englishmen.'

Although the classical dramatists (Seneca and some Terence apart) were left untranslated for a long time, the lessons of history were quickly unveiled: Sallust's 'ryght fruytful historie' of *Jugurtha* in 1520 and his *Catiline* in 1557, Caesar in 1530, Xenophon in 1532 and 1552, Thucydides in 1550, Quintus Curtius in 1553, Pliny in 1566, Plutarch in Thomas North's translation in 1579, and pre-eminently, in 1591 and 1598, Tacitus.

Before news books became common in the 1620s, the only forums for discussion of current events were the pulpit and the playhouse.

The role of the pulpit in offering political and social comment is neatly illustrated in the politically sensitive play of Sir Thomas More (c. 1593):

LINCOLN.   You knowe the Spittle Sermons being the next weeke, I have drawne a [bill] of our wrongs, and the straungers insolencies.
GEORGE.   Which he means the preachers shall there openly publishe in the Pulpit.

The stage was the secular forum for public debate and the writers who used it were in an important sense the news reporters of their day. Their professional duty was, as Jonson put it, to

> Speake of the intents,
> The counsells, actions, orders and events
> Of state, and censure them.

Jonson was no democrat but one who moved with some confidence at court among scholars, and with his fellow actors, writers and their mongrel public, dignified his role as Renaissance poet: 'he which can faine a *Common-wealth* (which is the *Poet*) can governe it with *Counsels*, strengthen it with *Lawes*, correct it with *Iudgements*, informe it with *Religion*, and Morals'. The poet, that is, was philosopher, divine and statesman rolled into one; but essentially he was an interpreter placed midway between prince and people, and the playhouse was his element. '*A Prince* without Letters, is a Pilot without eyes,' he wrote, but the people too needed counsellors, for without the dramatic poet's powers of observation, analysis and re-creation, the flux of events would make no sense to them and society would stumble through novelty to confusion and error. It was a role which demanded a professional integrity toughened by learning and a clear sense of social morality; and because any serious analysis must reveal the deeper forces at work beneath the surface, mere reportage was contemptibly shallow compared with the subtleties of fiction. At the highest levels, the poetry of courtliness had at last been displaced, at least in Jonson's mind, by a poetry of real moral substance and political responsibility; and at another level again the popular drama, seriously conceived but with all the pleasurable aids appropriate to it, had its matching function for the people at large – at large at least in the metropolis.

What must now be noted is the professional disjunction and

increasing rivalry of playwrights and printers. As the economics of theatre required the confinement of a group of people to one place, rather than a wide and scattered audience, the theatre companies were naturally at odds with printers who wished to transform plays into books. Important though the spoken words were, it was the moving images of performance, not the words themselves, which gave the theatre its social focus, commanded the physical presence of an audience, and unified it. Printers welcomed a good turnover of ephemera, but the ephemerality of theatre was the very heart of its mystery. Theatre had its dangers and Peter Quince warned that acting extempore might well be 'enough to hang us all'. Nevertheless when topicality proved irrepressible, the players could, by improvising and adapting to the occasion, as well as by selective playing from their repertory (like Hamlet, they knew 'the severall graces of historie and how to apt their places'), benefit from the immediate contact with their audience and an elusiveness from censorship unparalleled by print.

So Middleton's *Game at Chess* drew audiences in their thousands in 1624 before it was closed. But Jonson had already seen that theatre and the central role of dramatic poetry as he had defined it were under serious threat from the expanding news-book trade. *The Staple of News*, performed in 1626 but probably started in 1621–2, is his perceptive analysis of an immense social change which was to be fully evidenced only in the 1640s. He saw the booksellers dangling the bait of novelty, of 'the times *Newes*, (a weekly cheat to draw mony)'. By 1623 a syndicate of booksellers (Butter, Bourne, Downes, Sheffard, Archer and Newbery) had in fact formed a Staple of news with a share capital, one can infer from Jonson, of about £1,400. To note such a development and make its implications clear to the public was, in Jonson's view, real news and it was his job as dramatist to report it:

[It] could not be fitter reprehended, then in raising this ridiculous *Office* of the *Staple*, wherin the age may see her own folly, or hunger and thirst after publish'd pamphlets of *Newes*, set out every Saturday, but made all at home, & no syllable of truth in them: then which there cannot be a greater disease in nature, or a fouler scorne put out upon the times ... If you have the truth, rest quiet, and consider that

Ficta, voluptatis causa, sint proxima veris.

Jonson still affirms that the truest poetry is the most feigning, but even he was about to give it all away in despair of an intelligent and sympathetic hearing from his audiences. The hostile reception of his *New Inn* three years later prompted the Ode ('To himself' – the most select of auditors) in which he castigated his public as unfit for anything but acorns, husks, draff to drink and swill. They were ripe for the news-men who, with their unsifted reports, vulgarity of language, partisan interests and patently commercial motives, were tearing the body of poetic truth apart and offering the dispersed relics as commodities for a new kind of consumer:

> Baites, Sir, for the people!
> And they will bite like fishes.

It is not wholly a paradox that Jonson turned to the learned press to salvage his work. He deeply respected scholars like Camden, Saville and Selden who wrote for it, and in editing his plays for print he sought with intelligent deliberation that continuity of life which only printing could bestow. The paradox is that, like Heminge and Condell in addressing 'The great Variety of Readers. From the most able to him that can but spell', he came to rest his hopes in the merely literate: 'If thou canst but spell, and joyne my sense, there is more hope of thee, then of a hundred fastitidious *impertinents*.' But the merely literate were to settle for newspapers. The shift from an oral culture to a literate one is to be dated, not from the invention of printing but from its effective creation of such a readership. In England that meant the 1640s.

The Staple of News is a superbly integrated attack on the prostitution of money, truth and learning, a powerful indictment of what Jonson saw as a disastrous economic and cultural conspiracy, and it is singularly percipient in seeing an organized publications network run for profit as the phenomenon of a new mass medium with comprehensive political and educational consequences. These consequences, however, included the virtual death of theatre as a vital organ of public information and debate and the relegation of poetry to the minority culture of an elitist press. The future belonged to journalism; making sense of it – restoring the body of truth – was up to the individual reader.

Brilliant as Jonson's contemporary analysis is he was unable to discern the true roots of the news books, or to understand the historical role of printing in creating a literate public, and he could not accept the crucial political importance and cultural vulgarity (in a market economy) of general but low-level literacy. The origins of printing were impeccably orthodox, but its phenomenal growth in the sixteenth century was stimulated by a radical non-conformity as the press was used to promote the Reformation and later, in non-Catholic countries such as England, to launch the Counter-Reformation. Against the dominant tendency of the trade in London to secure its economic basis by creating a neutral popular market, one has to place the zealous adoption of printing to fight the establishment. Before Elizabeth's reign Catholic and Protestant alike might suddenly find themselves the anti-establishment group, the minority press, committed to printing abroad or surreptitiously at home, and at risk of their very lives secretly dispersing their books. Under Elizabeth, the Catholic press abroad was relentless in its production of books for the English market, and by the 1580s the domestic Puritan press was beginning to trouble the authorities as well. Martin Marprelate's attacks on the Bishops, printed largely by Robert Waldegrave, John Hodgkins and Thomas Orwin in 1588–9, sounded a note which echoed through to the 1640s. The printing of such 'schismaticall and seditious books' was a great temptation to the poorer printers whose livelihood had been put at risk by the monopolists in control of the trade. For this reason there was often a clear connection between radical groups trying to promote their schismatic and seditious causes, despite the censorship, and those within the trade who opposed the patentees' control of the bulk of profitable printing. The piratical printer John Wolfe makes the point in a telling analogy: 'Luther was but one man, and reformed all the world for religion, and I am that one man, that must and will reforme the government in this trade.' In the early seventeenth century, the Stationers' Company itself bought up many of the privileges, forming English, Irish and Latin Stocks, ostensibly to apportion work fairly among its members and help the poor. But because of the disproportionate way in which shares were held and the parsimony with which the profitable printing was doled out, the discontented members of the trade were unmollified. Such a move towards joint stock ventures also reflects a shift in the balance of power within the Company, a move away from printers, whose role since Caxton had included publishing and retailing, and towards the booksellers. Several reasons might be given. Official controls on the number of presses limited the number of jobs available to young printers; bookselling was not confined to London; some patents passed, by reversion, to men who were not printers; and, perhaps most important of all, the booksellers as middle men closest to the market increasingly assumed an entrepreneurial role as investors in copies and employers of a depressed group of trade printers.

By the 1630s reasonably widespread literacy, an increasingly vocal radical Puritan movement, a tired censorship, and a disaffected body of printers (and binders) presented a set of problems which the Star Chamber tried ineffectually to stamp out by a further decree in 1637. But there was no containment of the pamphlet press. News books returned in 1638. When the Court of Star Chamber and Court of High Commission were abolished in 1641, all licensing provisions lapsed. The following year all public plays, being 'Spectacles of Pleasure, too commonly expressing lascivious Mirth and Levity', were ordered to cease. For the same year the number of pamphlets preserved in the Thomason collection in the British Library soars to a record figure of 1,966. There could be no doubt that the actors' popular function as the abstracts and brief chronicles of the time was over. Printing had claimed the poet – in the role of the pamphleteer.

The Stationers' Company moved quickly to have restrictions restored, pleading a need for fresh authority to clamp down on unruly printing but more covertly concerned to protect its privileges. An Order of the Lords and Commons of June 1643 for 'suppressing the great late abuses and frequent disorders in Printing many false, Scandalous, Seditious, Libellous and unlicensed Pamphlets, to the great defamation of Religion and Government' also gave the Stationers the power they needed to search for and seize books which infringed other men's copyrights. Milton, a little late and under pressure himself from the Lords, responded with *Areopagitica* in November 1644. His franchise is that of the learned and Protestant, but he writes of licensing as an insult to all:

Nor is it to the common people lesse then a reproach; for if we be so jealous over them as that we dare not trust them with an English pamphlet, what doe we but censure them for a giddy, vitious, and ungrounded people, in such a sick and weak estate of faith and discretion, as to be able to take nothing down but through the pipe of a licenser?

In those words he seals the compact between press and people. Printing in England had been backward compared with the splendid achievements in scholarship and book-making by continental printers, but its service of Milton's 'common people', albeit from mixed motives of principle and profit, found its fruition in a political idea of profound importance to western society.

The principles underlying Milton's case for freedom of the press (the printed word) had of course already received vital expression in the drama as a pervasive concern for freedom of speech (the spoken word), as even a cursory reading of *Julius Caesar* or *Sejanus*, *Coriolanus* or *Catiline* would show. But Milton's timing was perfect. He caught a moment of transition when the press as we know it was emergent if still undefined, a moment when the principles of modern parliamentary democracy were being forged if not yet tempered. To Milton it was given to say then, as none before him might, that 'the liberty to know, to utter, and to argue freely according to conscience' could be effectual in promoting good government only if men had 'the liberty of unlicensed *printing*'. Milton's views were brutally rebuffed by the severity of succeeding Orders and he himself was destined to spend his final years under the yoke of Roger L'Estrange. But neither the renewed vigour of the censorship in its dying phase nor the fitful resurrection of politics in the Restoration theatre could stay the deeper forces of change. The lapse of the Licensing Act in 1695, the creation of author copyright in 1709, the continued growth in literacy and successive extensions of the franchise, have in retrospect fully confirmed the modernity, the now naturally understood rightness, of Milton's subject, printing, and his form, the prose pamphlet. For 300 years the press has been thought of as the primary forum and its freedom the defining mark of an open democracy. By 1644 it had begun to create a parliament without walls, and *Areopagitica* was the first eloquent voice to be heard in it.

Milton's imagery is organic. Books, he says, are 'borne to the

World' and their 'potencie of life' is 'as active as that soule was whose progeny they are'. He understood perfectly and exploited skilfully the complementary political role of the popular press, in a way that Jonson did not, but both poets poured their 'pretious life-blood' into a 'good Book' that might be 'imbalm'd and treasur'd up on purpose to a life beyond life'. Caxton had, more simply, asked his readers to 'remember the sowle of the sayd Gefferey Chaucer' for he too knew its power, through print, to be an agent of change.

NOTE

The generality of the above account would make detailed annotation cumbersome. I am much indebted, however, to several books which must be listed here:

Elizabeth Eisenstein's *The Printing Press as an Agent of Change*, 2 vols (Cambridge, 1978) is the most recent general survey of the impact of printing in Europe during the later fifteenth and early sixteenth centuries, but it says little about the trade in England. N. F. Blake's *Caxton and his World* (London, 1969) and *Caxton: England's First Publisher* (London, 1976) are most useful for their detail, as are his editions of Caxton's own writings and selections from books printed by him: *Selections from William Caxton* (Oxford, 1973) and *Caxton's own Prose* (London, 1973) – see also George D. Painter's *William Caxton: A Quincentenary Biography of England's First Printer* (London, 1976). Any survey of the trade in the period would be impossible without recourse to *A Short-title Catalogue of Books Printed in England, Scotland, and Ireland and of English Books Printed Abroad, 1475–1640*, first compiled by A. W. Pollard and G. R. Redgrave (London, 1926). A revised edition is in progress of which Vol. II was published in 1976. Especially valuable for their use of contemporary references to all aspects of the book trade over the same years are H. S. Bennett's three books (see Appendix, p. 530). Louis B. Wright's *Middle-class Culture in Elizabethan England* (London, 1934, reprinted 1958) remains the best account of the staple products of the book trade in the reign of Elizabeth. Other studies essential to an understanding of the role of printers in England before the mid-seventeenth century are: F. S. Siebert's *Freedom of the Press in England 1476–1776* (Urbana, 1952); Cyprian Blagden's *The Stationers' Company* (London, 1960); Leona Rostenberg's *The Minority Press and The English Crown: A Study in Repression, 1558–1625* (Nieuwkoop, 1970); D. B. Woodfield's *Surreptitious Printing in England 1550–1640* (New York, 1973); and Joseph Frank, *The Beginnings of the English Newspaper 1620–1660* (Cambridge, Mass., 1961).

Caxton in Focus: The Beginning of Printing in England (London, 1982), by Lotte Hellinga, offers a thorough revision of the chronology of Caxton's printing and should also be consulted.

THE ENGLISH LANGUAGE
IN THE AGE OF SHAKESPEARE
CHARLES BARBER

In 1564, when Shakespeare was born, the English language[1] was spoken by about four million people in England and southern Scotland; the remaining parts of the British Isles were still predominantly Celtic-speaking. Outside Britain the language was hardly known and was held in little esteem. Even in England the prestige of English was low, though this was something that changed during Shakespeare's lifetime. English was often compared unfavourably with French, Italian, and Spanish, and above all with classical Latin and Greek. Compared to these languages, it was said to be deficient in vocabulary, and to be 'barbarous' (usually meaning 'unexpressive, lacking in eloquence').[2]

Latin, the international language of western Christendom, was still the language of education in grammar schools and universities, and was a serious rival to English, especially for works of science and scholarship. Learned works on astronomy, physics, medicine, logic, rhetoric and history were commonly written in Latin. This tradition died slowly; as late as 1689 Newton's great work on the laws of motion was published in Latin.

In the sixteenth century, however, there was a movement in favour of the use of English in such works. There were various reasons for this: a wider reading public, with the spread of literacy and the introduction of printing; strong nationalist feeling; and the influence of Protestant reformers, who wanted their works to reach the uneducated, and who sometimes distrusted Latin as a 'papist' language. The process of de-Latinization began with the making of translations of standard Latin works; next came English imitations of these, often heavily dependent on their sources; and finally there were fully original English works. This process is seen in many branches of science and of the liberal arts. It is also seen in the development of academic drama in England: performances of classical plays in Latin in schools and universities were followed by translations (especially of Terence and of Seneca) and by English plays in imitation of these.

The replacement of Latin by English was not unchallenged by traditionalists. Physicians in particular seem to have been fiercely hostile to the publication of medical books in English, but in all fields there were scholars who believed that the retention of Latin was essential. The controversy that went on can be deduced from translators' prefaces, which frequently defend translation and answer what were obviously current objections to it.

There were various arguments against the use of English. Learning would decay, because there would be no incentive to learn classical languages. It was dangerous to let knowledge fall into the hands of the vulgar. English was unsuitable for scholarly works because it lacked the necessary technical vocabulary. English was a 'rude' or 'barbarous' language, lacking expressiveness. It was unstable and changing, unlike classical Greek and Latin, which were 'fixed'. It was not commonly understood outside Britain, whereas Latin was an international language.

The supporters of English had counter-arguments. It was useful to have works of scholarship in English, so that time and effort did not need to be wasted in learning languages. Those who wished to keep learning away from ordinary people had sinister motives (especially papist ones). Greek and Latin had themselves once been mother tongues; and the Romans had written their science and philosophy in Latin, not in Greek. Deficiencies in the vocabulary of English could be remedied by borrowing or coining new words. Producing substantial works in English would enrich the language, which would then cease to be barbarous.

In the course of Elizabeth I's reign, a change took place in people's attitudes to the language. The earlier view was that English, however useful, was a rude and ineloquent language. By the end of the century, however, it was commonly and confidently asserted that English was a rich and eloquent language, to be compared favourably even with Greek and Latin. Richard Foster Jones[3] finds that the change took place quite suddenly between 1575 and 1580. Before 1575, most people are saying that English is a barbarous language; after 1580, everybody is saying what a copious and eloquent language it is. The change is no doubt connected with general social and cultural changes in the period, such as the rising self-confidence and patriotism of the late Elizabethan age. There were, however, more specific causes too. Jones argues that four main things were believed to make a language eloquent: (1) the language had to be the key to much learning and literature. Poetry in particular was thought to confer eloquence, and the writings of Sidney, Lyly, and Spenser probably played a part in convincing Englishmen around 1580 that their language was now eloquent; (2) to be eloquent, a language needed a rich vocabulary. The expansion of the lexicon in Elizabeth's reign helped to make English eloquent, and one of its qualities often singled out for praise was copiousness. Words borrowed from Greek and Latin were thought to be particularly expressive; (3) a language was made eloquent by being adorned with the devices of classical rhetoric. Rhetoric was a major subject in the Elizabethan grammar schools, and it was precisely in the later sixteenth century that its methods were carried over in a big way from Latin to English literature. The Figures were especially influential, and were used extensively by late-Elizabethan poets; (4) the fourth quality contributing to eloquence was regulation. Classical Greek and Latin were 'fixed' or 'ruled': grammar, vocabulary and acceptable usage were clearly defined and laid down in authoritative works (grammars, dictionaries). English, by contrast, was unregulated. The first grammars and dictionaries of English did not appear until around 1600, and even spelling was not standardized. English, therefore, managed to become eloquent even though it lacked one of the four major criteria.

Today we cannot subscribe to Elizabethan criteria for eloquence, but we must surely agree that the literature of Shakespeare's age is embodied in a language of unsurpassed vitality and richness. If we had to choose any period of twenty-five years as the most creative in English history, we should probably take the period from 1587 to 1612. In drama, that period encompasses the works of Shakespeare and of Marlowe, and the best work of Jonson; in non-dramatic poetry, the work of Spenser and much of that of Donne; in prose, the splendour of the King James Bible of 1611. Moreover, it is not only the major literary works that evince this vitality and richness: similar qualities can be found in the minor authors – prose-writers such as Nashe, part-time and amateur poets such as Ralegh. Indeed, vitality and inventiveness of language are not confined to works of literature, but are found in the general prose of the age – in philosophy, in sermons, in works of political and religious controversy, in books of travel and exploration, in technical and specialist handbooks. Even the hack-writers of the period can surprise us with a vivid and original turn of phrase. This widespread vitality in the use of language must surely have rested on a similar liveliness in the everyday speech of the age.

Unfortunately, we have little direct evidence about Elizabethan speech: there are few documents which claim to be transcriptions of speech, and even the ones which do exist may have had their language touched up by the transcribers. The indirect evidence, however, points to an everyday spoken language of unusual vigour and imaginativeness. It can be no accident that the greatest literary works of the age are found in the drama, which (however much influenced by rhetorical training) purports to offer us the language of people actually speaking. Particularly striking in the drama is the speech of 'ordinary' characters, people without pretensions to style or education, such as Shakespeare's gardeners, carriers, serving-men, tapsters, plebeians, inn-keepers, common soldiers. Even when Shakespeare is making fun of such people (as with Mistress Quickly), they usually speak with a remarkable vigour, concreteness, and inventiveness. We know that drama is not a transcription of real speech, that dramatists select and condense and refine; but even so we must believe that the speech of these characters reflects qualities of the ordinary spoken language of the time, and that the great literature of the age is rooted in a creative and imaginative use of language in ordinary everyday speech. It would indeed be rash to assert that the state of the spoken language was the *cause* of the creativity of the age: it is notable, for example, that the period 1587–1612 is also a very great age of English music; but the state of the spoken language must at any rate have been a *necessary condition* for the creation of the literary masterpieces of the age.

Just as today, there were regional and social varieties of English: the speech of a Londoner differed from that of a Northerner or a West Countryman; and, within a single region, the speech of a nobleman differed from that of a peasant or a citizen. To some extent, these differences are concealed by the existence of a standard literary language, which had arisen at the end of the Middle Ages. More accurately, there were two standard literary languages, one centred on London, and one on the Scottish lowlands; but even in the sixteenth century the Scots literary language was being deeply influenced by the southern language, and in the course of the seventeenth century it effectively disappeared.

The standard literary language in England offered considerable variety of choice to its user, more than in later ages. It was above all the grammarians and lexicographers and schoolmasters of the eighteenth century, with their passion for regulation and propriety, who narrowed the choices available; on the grounds of 'reason' or classical precedent they rejected such things as double negatives and split infinitives, and many of their prescriptions are influential even today. In Shakespeare's day there was more freedom of choice: often a writer could choose from two constructions where now there is only one; he felt free to coin new words, and to develop the meanings of existing ones; the whole linguistic situation encouraged an adventurous and creative attitude to language.

The same variety of choice existed in the spoken language, and there was also considerable variety of pronunciation. There was indeed a style of pronunciation with high prestige, that of the court, and we can perhaps regard this as a Standard English pronunciation. Nevertheless, some people of high rank and of education spoke with regional accents: there was no single Received Pronunciation for members of the English upper classes, as there was to be later. Even in the speech of an individual, the same word might have variant pronunciations, and poets in particular seize on such variants to suit their rhyme or metre.

Between about 1550 and 1650, the vocabulary of English expanded enormously.[4] One common way in which new words were introduced was by borrowing from Latin. The translator or popularizer, needing an English technical term, found it natural to adapt the Latin word he already knew. It was particularly natural because English already contained many French words, of transparently Latin origin, which had been borrowed in the Middle Ages, and these provided a model for the borrower. Indeed, Elizabethans borrowing words from Latin often gave them a form influenced by these earlier French loans: such are *invisibility* (1561) and *invitation* (1598), with the French-influenced endings *–ity* and *–ation* (compare the Latin nominative endings *-itas* and *-atio*). Many of the Latin loans are from specialized fields of discourse, especially science, medicine, religion and the liberal arts; but a substantial number belong to the general vocabulary, such as *relevant* (1560), *relegation* (1586), *invidious* (1606).

The only other language from which large numbers of words were borrowed was French, though French loans were much less numerous than Latin ones. Many of them belong to the general vocabulary, like *docility* (1560) and *prejudge* (1561). The specialized fields of discourse represented are especially biology (mainly anatomy) and the military, with such words as *parietal* (1597) and *bayonet* (1611). There are also words to do with religion, heraldry, commerce, and social life, but surprisingly few from the arts. No other language was an important immediate source of loan-words. Technical terms of rhetoric and logic often go back to Greek, but most of them entered the language via Latin. Many of the words going back to Italian, similarly, came into English via French. There were some direct loans from Italian, Spanish and Dutch, but their numbers were very small.

It was loan-words which struck contemporaries, but in fact many more words were created by various methods of word-formation than were borrowed from other languages. The commonest of all methods of word-formation was the coining of words by means of living prefixes and suffixes. In many cases the elements from which such words were formed had originally been loans, but they had since become naturalized in English. The adjective *comfortable* had been borrowed from the French in the fourteenth century; in 1592 the adjective *uncomfortable* was formed from it by means of the native prefix *un-*. Similarly, almost any adjective borrowed from abroad will eventually have an adverb formed from it, using the native suffix *-ly*, as with *immature* (1548), *immaturely* (1620).

There were many productive suffixes. The very common ones include *-ness* and *-er* for forming nouns, *-ed* and *-y* for adjectives, *-ly* for adverbs and *-ize* for verbs. Examples are *delightfulness* (1579), *gormandizer* (1589), *latticed* (1565), *briny* (1612), *commandingly* (1603) and *memorize* (1591).

There were numerous active prefixes, some of which are illustrated in the coinages *bedim* (1583), *counterstroke* (1596), *disabuse* (1611), *entrust* (1602), *foreshorten* (1606), *interlink* (1587), *re-lay* ('lay again', 1590) and *undergrowth* (1600). By far the commonest prefix, however, was *un-*, which was used freely with words of foreign origin as well as with native ones, and with nouns, adjectives, verbs, adverbs, and participles. Enormous numbers of such coinages are recorded in the *Oxford English Dictionary*, and they occur in works of all types – poetry and prose, philosophy and theology, romance and drama. Many of the first-recorded uses occur in well-known works of literature, Sidney's *Arcadia* (1586) offering a particularly large number. Shakespeare, however, takes the prize: the *O.E.D.* attributes to him the first use of no less than 164 words beginning with *un-*. Even when we allow for the fact that some of these words may have occurred in earlier works, but been missed by the *O.E.D.*, this figure is astonishing. They occur throughout Shakespeare's career, and at least one coinage occurs in every single play, and in the major poems. They include occurrences in famous phrases, such as Lear's '*unaccommodated* man', the Ghost's '*Unhouseled, disappointed, unaneled*', Hamlet's '*Unhand* me, gentlemen', Cleopatra's characterization of Caesar as 'ass *Unpolicied*', Ophelia's 'fair and *unpolluted* flesh', Macbeth's address to the Ghost of Banquo as '*unreal* mockery', Lady Macbeth's invocation to the powers of darkness to *unsex* her, Lear's 'So young, and so *untender*', and Hamlet's view of the world as 'an *unweeded* garden'. Some of the coinages have remained nonce-usages, hardly used since; such are Prince Hal's punning 'thou art not colted, thou art *uncolted*', and Macduff's thought that he may sheathe his sword *undeeded*. Many others, however, are now quite common words, so that it comes as a surprise to find that Shakespeare invented them; they include *undress* (*Taming of the Shrew*), *uneducated* (*Love's Labour's Lost*), *unfix* (*Henry IV 2*), *unhelpful* (*Henry VI 2*), *unmusical* (*Coriolanus*), *unrivalled* (*Two Gentlemen of Verona*), and *unsolicited* (*Titus Andronicus*). Such coinages were obviously made very easily, and it is probable that many of them had occurred in speech before they were recorded in texts.

Less common than affixation, but still a considerable source of new words, was the process of compounding, by which two existing words are combined to produce a new one. The majority of new compounds were nouns, and many were everyday practical words, to do with such things as agriculture, the mechanical arts, seamanship, plant-names, and names for people (especially opprobrious ones). Examples are *bawdy-basket* ('hawker of indecent literature', 1567),

Frenchwoman (1593), *heaving-net* (1584), *lung-flower* (1597), *off-corn* ('the corn thrown out in winnowing', 1573), *pinchfart* ('miser', 1592), *sheep-brand* (1586) and *spoonwort* (1578). Less everyday compounds are often produced by the poets, as when Shakespeare invents the expressions *pinch-spotted* ('discoloured with pinch-marks', *Tempest* IV. i), and *toad-spotted* ('marked with infamy, as a toad is with spots', *King Lear* v. iii) and the famous *world-without-end hour* (Sonnet LVII). In both compounding and affixation, the poet's creativeness is a heightening of the creative process already going on in the speech community.

One final common method of word-formation was conversion (or zero-morpheme derivation). This is the process whereby one word is formed from another without any change of form. For example, Shakespeare takes the noun *uncle* (a thirteenth-century loan from French) and converts it into a verb: 'Grace me no grace, nor *uncle* me no uncle' (*Richard II*). In the opening speech of *Henry IV. 1*, similarly, he converts the noun *channel* (another Middle English loan) into a verb ('No more shall trenching war *channel* her fields'). The formation of verbs from nouns was the commonest type of conversion in the period, but it was also reasonably common to form nouns from adjectives, and nouns from verbs, as when the noun *brisk* ('a gallant, fop', 1621) was formed from the adjective, and the noun *scratch* (1586) was formed from the verb.

The flood of new words in the period, whether by borrowing or by word-formation, sets problems for the reader of the literature, since it is often difficult to assess the stylistic value of a word. It is disconcerting to discover that the verb *to contemplate*, which is commonplace enough to us, is not recorded in the *O.E.D.* until 1592, and so presumably came to readers in the 1590s with all the shock of novelty. Shakespeare, similarly, is the first recorded user of such ordinary words as *invitation* and *laughable*; but he is also the first recorded user of words now quite unknown, such as *invised* ('unseen') and *offenceful*. On the other hand, some words which to us are obscure or archaic were everyday words to his audience.

The expansion of the vocabulary did not take place without comment and controversy. It was the flood of loan-words, especially from Latin, that attracted attention, and there was a strong Purist movement which was opposed to them. An example of an Elizabethan Purist is Ralph Lever, who in 1573 published a textbook of logic, called *The Art of Reason, rightly termed Witcraft*. In the *Forespeache* ('preface') to the work, Lever argues that new technical terms should be made by forming compounds from existing English monosyllabic words, not by borrowing from Greek or Latin. His main argument is comprehensibility: the meaning of such a compound is self-evident, whereas, to the unlatined layman, classical loan-words are obscure. Examples of his own coinages are *witcraft* ('logic'), *endsay* ('conclusion'), *naysay* ('negation'), *saywhat* ('definition'), and *yeasay* ('affirmation'). These coinages, however, did not catch on.

Others opposed to loan-words argued that the vocabulary should be enriched by the revival of archaisms, or by the use of words from regional dialects. Edmund Spenser was the most celebrated user of archaisms in the period, but he was part of a movement, not the founder of it. Chaucer was a fashionable poet in Elizabethan court circles, and the cultivation of archaisms is found in much poetry before Spenser. A justification of archaisms is found in the preface to Spenser's *Shepherd's Calender* (1579), written by 'E.K.' (probably Edward Kirke). Kirke's only substantial argument is that archaisms, which often survive in the speech of countryfolk, are appropriate to the rustic characters of pastoral; but this plainly does not constitute a *general* justification for their use. Apart from this, Kirke merely appeals to the authority of the ancients, to concepts of naturalness and purity, and to patriotic feeling. He depends a good deal on loaded metaphors, as when he says that English, through the introduction of loan-words, has been 'patched up with pieces and rags of other languages' and is now 'a gallimaufrey or hodge-podge of all other speeches'. The prestige of Spenser encouraged the use of archaisms and dialect-words in poetry, and right through the seventeenth century there is a line of Spenserian imitators, who often lifted words and even whole phrases from his poetry. Spenser himself, however, used dialect-words and archaisms as only one element in a complex diction, which included recent classical loans, literary French loans of the kind introduced by Caxton, and coinages of his own (including pseudo-rusticisms and pseudo-archaisms).

The arguments in favour of loan-words can often be found, as we have seen, in prefaces to translations. All languages have enriched themselves by borrowing: the copiousness of French is due to its borrowings from Latin; Latin itself had borrowed words from Greek. In any case, there are already so many loan-words in English that it is impossible for us to express ourselves without using them. Many of the older loans are now ordinary current words in the language, and the more recent loans will in time be accepted in the same way. The problem of comprehension can be overcome by explaining the meaning of a new word when we introduce it.

Some of the attacks on loan-words were for their extravagance or pedantry. Some Latin loans were adopted to fill a gap in the vocabulary, but many were adopted because they were thought to be especially expressive, and superior to existing native synonyms. Richard Mulcaster, the eminent headmaster, refers in his *First Part of the Elementary* (1582) to the words which the English language borrows daily from foreign tongues 'either of pure necessity in new matters, or of mere bravery, to garnish itself withal'. In other words, some loans are adopted because they are needed ('of pure necessity'), and others from sheer ostentation ('mere bravery') so that the language can decorate ('garnish') itself. It was the introduction of words for magniloquence that sometimes led to affectation and obscurity, and in the pamphlet warfare of the 1590s writers often attack one another for their use of 'inkhorn terms'. Such attacks are seldom concerned with general principles: they usually confine themselves to ridiculing the alleged excesses and absurdities of opponents. In the plays of both Shakespeare and Jonson there is ridicule of the lunatic fringe, as in the Holofernes scenes of *Love's Labour's Lost*, but both dramatists are uninhibited in introducing new words themselves, either by borrowing or by word-formation.

Elizabethans sometimes had a choice of constructions or of grammatical forms where today there is no choice. In *The Tempest*, Ferdinand refers to Miranda as 'The mistress *which* I serve'; he could equally well have said *whom*. Today, the relative pronoun *who* is used to refer to persons, and *which* to refer to non-persons, but this regulation of usage took place only in the course of the seventeenth century. In the comparative and superlative of the adjective, Elizabethans could equally well say *sweeter* and *more sweet*, *famousest* and *most famous*. Moreover, it was perfectly acceptable to use double comparatives and superlatives, as when Shakespeare writes 'more rawer breath' (*Hamlet*) and 'the most unkindest cut of all' (*Julius Caesar*).

Similarly, it was possible to use double or multiple negation, as in 'I cannot go no further' (*As You Like It*) and 'nor never none Shall mistress be of it, save I alone' (*Twelfth Night*). The negatives do not cancel one another out, but on the contrary make the negation more emphatic.

Every reader of Elizabethan literature knows that many words have changed in meaning since that time, and understands the need to consult annotated editions or the *O.E.D.* But some grammatical features of Elizabethan English have a similar significance for meaning, and need to be understood by the modern reader. This is notably the case with the second-person pronouns, where Elizabethans had a choice between *you* and *thou*, a choice which can be especially significant in the drama.[5] I shall use *You* and *Thou* (with upper-case initial) to refer to entire related groups of forms: so *You* means one or more of *you, ye, your, yourself, yourselves,* and *yours*; and similarly with *Thou*.

In the plural, *You* was compulsory; it has never been possible to use *Thou* as a plural. In the singular, however, there was a choice between *You* and *Thou*. Among the polite classes, *You* was the normal, neutral form by Shakespeare's time, while *Thou* was the form which carried special implications, either social or emotional. So *Thou* could be used to a social inferior, to a child, to an animal; but its use was not compulsory, and in many scenes in the drama a master addressing a servant fluctuates between *You* and *Thou*, sometimes being more condescending, sometimes more peremptory. The inferior or the child, however, was obliged to reply with *You*, for to use *Thou* to somebody of greatly superior station was insulting. Among upper-class intimates, the use of *Thou* signalled intimacy or affection, while *You* was more neutral; here again speakers often fluctuate, according to the warmth or coolness of their feelings. To use *Thou* to a stranger, however, was insulting, as when in *Twelfth Night* (III. ii) Sir Toby advises Sir Andrew to insult Cesario in his challenge by calling him *Thou*. The artisan classes, however, normally used *Thou* to one another, even if not intimates, but were obliged to use *You* to a member of a higher social class. Contrary to what might be expected, God was always addressed as *Thou*; and under the influence of this (or perhaps under Latin influence) it was also normal to use *Thou* in addressing a pagan god or goddess, an abstraction, or an inanimate object. So in *King Lear* Edmund addresses the goddess

Nature as *Thou*; and in Jonson's *Volpone* Volpone addresses his gold as *Thou*.

It may be thought strange that there are two different emotional uses of *Thou*, one intimate and affectionate, the other hostile and insulting. The hostile *Thou* can in fact be used between intimates, as well as the affectionate *Thou*, but the context usually shows clearly which is intended. This can be seen in Jonson's *Volpone* (1607), in the exchanges between Corvino and Celia. Celia, a young and submissive wife, invariably addresses Corvino as *You*. He often addresses her as *You*, but tends to switch to the hostile *Thou* when he is angry with her (especially when he threatens her with physical violence), and to the affectionate *Thou* when he is trying to wheedle her. In the scene where he takes her to Volpone's bedroom we find, within a dozen lines of each other, 'I will drag thee hence, home, by the hair' (angry) and 'Pray thee sweet ... thou shalt have jewels, gowns, attires' (cajoling).

It may help the modern reader to think of the use of *Thou* as being rather like the present-day use of the Christian name in addressing a person ('George', 'Mary'), while *You* resembles the present-day address by title ('Mr Smith', 'Miss Jones'). Remember, however, that this does not apply to plural usages.

Inevitably, there are some cases where the present-day language has grammatical choices unavailable to the Elizabethans. One of these counter-examples is the choice between *its* and *his*. In the early part of Shakespeare's career there was no such choice, for the form *its* did not exist. The historical possessive form of *it* was *his*, and this is what Shakespeare most often uses, as in 'How far that little candle throws *his* beams' (*Merchant of Venice*), and 'But value dwells not in particular will, It holds *his* estimate and dignity ...' (*Troilus and Cressida*). It is important to realize that such uses of *his* do not imply personification. The first example of *its* recorded by the *O.E.D.* occurs in 1598. There are a few examples of *its* in Shakespeare, but none are found in texts earlier than the First Folio of 1623. It does not occur at all in the King James Bible of 1611.

Some Elizabethan grammatical choices have stylistic implications. In the verb-system, there were alternative forms for the third-person singular of the present tense, as in *he sings* or *singeth*, *he has* or *hath*. The -*(e)s* ending, originally northern, had spread into the standard southern language during the sixteenth century, and by Shakespeare's time was the normal form in speech. The *-(e)th* ending continued to be used in writing, however, and is quite frequent up to the middle of the seventeenth century. In general, *-(e)s* was the mark of a more colloquial style (and is extremely common in the drama, especially in prose scenes), while *-(e)th* was more formal and solemn. Some verbs, however, resisted the spread of the *-(e)s* ending more strongly than others. The forms *hath*, *doth*, and *saith* persist strongly: in many Shakespeare scenes, the *-(e)s* ending is used regularly, except for the forms *hath* and *doth*. In the first scene of *Hamlet*, the forms *has* and *does* occur once each, while *hath* occurs six times and *doth* three. There are seventeen other third-person singular endings in the scene, and all but one are *-(e)s* – *burns*, *comes*, *goes*, etc. The sole exception is the following:

> The bird of dawning *singeth* all night long.

Partly the form *singeth* is chosen for metrical reasons, but it is also to be noticed that it occurs in a particularly solemn and awestruck passage about the mysterious things that occur at Christmas, and this is surely no accident.

Other forms in which the *-(e)th* ending was particularly persistent were ones like *passeth*, *accuseth*, *chargeth*. These are verbs in which the change of ending does not change the number of syllables in the word, the *-(e)s* ending in such cases being pronounced as a syllable. The persistent *-(e)th* forms are not a positive indication of a formal style, as other *-(e)th* forms are. On the other hand, forms like *has* and *passes* are positive marks of a colloquial style, and are common (for example) in the early comedies of Thomas Middleton.

There were also alternative forms for the present-tense plural of verbs. The usual form had no ending, as today: *they go, we walk*. As rarer variants, however, we also find the endings *-(e)th*, *-(e)n*, and *-(e)s*, which were originally regional (southern, midland and northern respectively). By Shakespeare's time, the *-(e)n* ending (*they deemen, sayn*, etc.) had fallen out of use in the standard language, and when it occurs in literature it is an archaism or rusticism. It is found in the poetry of Spenser and his imitators, but is extremely rare in Shakespeare. There are a couple of examples in the Chorus passages of *Pericles*; the Chorus is the fourteenth-century poet Gower, who speaks in an archaic kind of language. There is also an example in *A Midsummer Night's Dream*:

> And then the whole quire hold their hips and loff,
> And *waxen* in their mirth, and neeze, and swear ...
>
> (II. i)

The speaker is Robin Goodfellow, and *waxen* is part of his rustic style of speech, seen also in *loff* and *neeze*.

The -*(e)th* plural is found occasionally, especially in *hath* and *doth*, as in 'thy wounds *doth* bleed at many vents' (*Troilus and Cressida*). The -*(e)s* plural is quite common in Shakespeare, as in 'My old bones *aches*' (*The Tempest*). These endings do not seem to have had any special stylistic significance, but it must be recognized that they were still acceptable usages, and not grammatical errors.

The Elizabethans also had a choice in the use of the auxiliary *do*. Chaucer did not use auxiliary *do*; he used constructions of the type 'I know not', 'Know you not?', 'Know you?'. Today, the use of auxiliary *do* is regulated: if there is no other auxiliary present, we are obliged to insert it in negatives ('I do not know') and in most types of question ('Do you know?'), but must omit it from affirmative statements ('I know'), unless we wish to obtain sentence-emphasis by stressing the auxiliary ('I DO know'). In Elizabethan English, by contrast, the use of *do* was optional: if there was no other auxiliary present, *do* could be inserted or omitted at will, in all types of sentence. When it was inserted in affirmative statements, it was not usually stressed: the sentence 'I do know him' was simply a stylistic variant of 'I know him', and the word *do* was completely unstressed. By Shakespeare's time, the use of *do* had begun to move towards its present regulation: between the Elizabethan age and the end of the seventeenth century it became more and more common to omit *do* from ordinary affirmative statements, and to insert it in negatives and questions; the process was completed in the early eighteenth century. During this slow process of regulation, the insertion or omission of *do* had some stylistic significance: the regulated usage was a mark of a more colloquial style, the unregulated usage the mark of a more formal or literary style.

Many individual words have changed in stress-pattern since Shakespeare's time, as any attentive reader of the poetry knows. In some cases, moreover, alternative stressings were available. The noun *envy* was stressed on the first syllable, as today, but the verb was usually stressed on the second, and rhymed with *fly*. In the following lines from *Coriolanus* it seems natural to give the verb this usual second-syllable stress:

> For that he has –
> As much as in him lies – from time to time
> *Envied* against the people.
>
> (III. iii)

Sometimes, however, the verb was stressed on the first syllable, as today, and in the same scene from *Coriolanus* there is an example that seems to demand this accentuation:

> But as I say, such as become a soldier
> Rather than *envy* you.

Many words had an alternative form with one more stress than today. This was especially the case with words of three or more syllables, such as *argument, ignorance, immediately, majesty, pilgrimage, temperate*, all of which could have an additional stress on the final syllable. Moreover, when the final syllable was stressed, it had a full vowel, so that these six words were exact rhymes to *went, advance, fly, sky, age*, and *date*. On the other hand, if the rhythm of the line required it, the poet could give such words their present-day stress-pattern.

In some cases, words of this type had an additional syllable when they had the additional stress. The words where this happened were ones which had a short /i/ vowel directly before the vowel of the extra stressed syllable; if the stress was lost, the /i/ vowel disappeared. So the word *imagination* could have six syllables, *i-ma-gi-na-si-on*, with stresses on the second, fourth, and sixth. But if the stress on the final syllable was lost, the word had only five syllables, as today. Poets could select either form: in *A Midsummer Night's Dream* we find the lines

> And as imagination bodies forth
> The forms of things unknown . . .

and then three lines later

> Such tricks hath strong imagination.

In the first example, *imagination* is stressed as today, but the second example requires the form with an extra syllable and an extra stress.

Because of changes in pronunciation, many Elizabethan puns are no longer self-evident, and many words which then rhymed no longer do so.[6] Conversely, the unwary reader may detect rhymes and puns which in fact did not exist for the original reader or audience.

One difference in the vowel-system of the language was that Elizabethan English had two long vowels where we have only one. The words *meet* and *meat* were pronounced differently, the former being approximately as today, while the second had a long vowel of about the same quality as that in French *faire* or German *fährt*. Both vowels were different from that of *mate*, which was rather like the long vowel heard today in London speech in such words as *bad*. Fortunately, even the non-specialist reader can usually tell which words had the *meet*-vowel and which had the *meat*-vowel, simply by looking at the present-day spelling. The *meet*-vowel occurred in words now spelt with *ee* or *ie*, such as *see, queen, siege, thief*; it also occurred in words like *me* and *be* when they were stressed. The *meat*-vowel occurred in words now spelt with *ea*, or *ei*, or *e-consonant-vowel*, such as *sea, quean, seize, conceit, mete, complete*. Consider the following lines from Donne's poem 'The Flea':

> It suck'd me first, and now sucks thee,
> And in this flea, our two bloods mingled be.

In Donne's time there was an exact rhyme between *thee* and *be*, which had the *meet*-vowel. On the other hand, there was no internal rhyme in the second line between *flea* and *be*, for *flea* (as its spelling suggests) had the *meat*-vowel.

In the consonant-system, the biggest change since Elizabethan times has been the loss of the / r / consonant before other consonants and in final position. In Shakespeare's time, the / r / was pronounced in such words as *barn* and *father*. Here again, the retention of *r* in the spelling is an indication of the earlier pronunciation. The existence of this / r / means that some words which today rhyme, or on which puns can be made, did not behave in this way in Elizabethan English. So *sought* did not rhyme with *port*, or *pass* with *farce*. And an Elizabethan audience, hearing the word *board*, would not have detected a pun on the word *bawd*; for the / r / in *board* was just as much a consonant to them as any other, and the two words were just as different from each other as, say, *sand* and *sad*, or *killed* and *kid*.

Many words had alternative pronunciations, and poets did not confine themselves to one pronunciation, but selected the form to suit their rhyme. In Sonnet IV, Shakespeare rhymes *gone* with *alone*; this was an exact rhyme, depending on the original form of *gone* with a long vowel. But in Sonnet V, he rhymes *gone* with *on*; this too was an exact rhyme, depending on the newer pronunciation of *gone* with a shortened vowel; indeed, the original edition of 1609 spells it *gon*. The shortening of long vowels in words of one syllable was a common process in the sixteenth and seventeenth centuries, but it was sporadic, so that usually there were two pronunciations in circulation, one with a long vowel and one with a short; since then, one or other has usually been standardized. Once again, the spelling is a good clue to the earlier pronunciation. Such words as *bread*, *breath*, *dead* and *sweat* had the same long vowel as *meat*; and words like *blood*, *flood*, *foot* and *look* had the same long vowel as *food* and *moon*.

Again, in Sonnet VII Shakespeare rhymes *are* with *car*, but in Sonnet XIII he rhymes it with *prepare*. The rhyme with *prepare* depends on the old pronunciation of *are* in stressed position; the rhyme with *car* depends on the pronunciation of *are* which had arisen in unstressed positions. Since then, the old stressed pronunciation has fallen out of use. There are other such cases of rhymes depending on old stressed forms now lost: *have* could rhyme with *cave*, *shall* with *ball*, *is* with *miss*, *was* with *pass*. In the case of *was* and *pass*, the vowels have subsequently been changed, in *was* through the influence of the / w / and in *pass* through the influence of the following consonant; in Shakespeare's time, *pass* was pronounced approximately as in Northern English today, and the old stressed form of *was* rhymed with it exactly.

There are various other reasons for variability of pronunciation in Elizabethan English, notably the circulation of regional and social variants, on which some rhymes depend. It is not true, of course, that all rhymes in the poetry were exact. The vast majority of them, however, certainly were. As has been seen, present-day spelling is often a clue to earlier pronunciations; it is certainly not a fool-proof guide, but it does frequently give good indications about earlier identities and differences.

NOTES

1. To avoid the clumsiness of 'Elizabethan–Jacobean', I shall refer to the language in Shakespeare's time as 'Elizabethan English'. Accounts of Elizabethan English will be found in the standard histories of the language, such as A. C. Baugh and T. Cable, *A History of the English Language*, 3rd edn (London, 1978). An account of the language between 1500 and 1700, with considerable emphasis on Elizabethan English, is provided by C. Barber, *Early Modern English* (London, 1976). Shakespeare's language is studied by G. L. Brook, *The Language of Shakespeare* (London, 1976).

2. The standard work on attitudes to the language in the sixteenth and seventeenth centuries is R. F. Jones, *The Triumph of the English Language* (Stanford, 1953). A small anthology of primary material is provided by W. F. Bolton, *The English Language: Essays by English and American Men of Letters 1490–1839* (Cambridge, 1966).

3. Jones, *The Triumph of the English Language*, 168–213.

4. On the general history of the English vocabulary, see J. A. Sheard, *The Words We Use* (London, 1970). On loan-words in English, see M. S. Serjeantson, *A History of Foreign Words in English* (London, 1935). A simple and straightforward account of methods of word-formation in the post-medieval period is given by V. Adams, *An Introduction to Modern English Word-Formation* (London, 1974). The major work of reference for the history of any English word is *The Oxford English Dictionary*, ed. J. A. H. Murray and others, 13 volumes (Oxford, 1933); all dates given in this chapter for the first recorded occurrences of English words are taken from this work.

5. There have been a number of studies of the use of *you* and *thou* in Elizabethan drama. See particularly A. McIntosh, '*As You Like It*: a Grammatical Clue to Character', in *Review of English Literature*, IV, 2 (1963); A. McIntosh and C. F. Williamson, '*King Lear* Act 1 Scene i. Two Stylistic Notes', in *The Review of English Studies*, N.S. XIV (1963); J. Mulholland, '*Thou* and *You* in Shakespeare', in *English Studies*, XLVIII (1967); C. Barber, '*You* and *Thou* in Shakespeare's *Richard III*', in *Leeds Studies in English*, N.S. XII (1981).

6. The standard work on the pronunciation of Elizabethan English is E. J. Dobson, *English Pronunciation 1500–1700*, 2 vols, 2nd edn (Oxford, 1968). This, however, is a work for the specialist, and the lay reader should rather consult the relevant sections of the works listed in n. 1 above.

THE ELIZABETHAN STAGE AND ACTING

ANDREW GURR

'An act hath three branches', says Hamlet's gravedigger. It is 'to act, to do, to perform'. *Hamlet* is a play built on, among other things, the word 'action' in the two main alternative senses it had in Elizabethan times, doing and play-acting, pretending to do. 'The name of action' applied equally to performing mighty deeds and to play-acting. In the middle of the play Hamlet admits to the ghost that, 'lapsed in time and passion', he has 'let go by/Th' important acting' of the ghost's command. Passion, the passive response, has supplanted action, the performance, and as a result Hamlet's 'acting' has been a pretence, no more than 'actions that a man might *play*', as he says with prophetic irony in his first scene. To perform, to act or to do are terms which apply equally to the reality of doing and to the pretence of it on stage. Elizabethans were deeply sensitive to the alternative meanings.

From one point of view the important consideration was to differentiate between the two meanings. 'Playing' was the standard Elizabethan term for acting. An actor was a player, his business the game of playing. It was certainly not a serious business. The theatre was not life. At its most serious it was a game which did not claim to be more than 'tragedy played in jest/By counterfeiting actors', players whose 'action' was an unserious travesty of the real thing. The assumption that the Elizabethan stage and its players could show nothing but games, more or less casual entertainment, was universal amongst the acting companies and the impresarios who backed them. Elizabethan theatre was a commercial enterprise, and its commercial health depended on the giving of pleasure, not instruction.

On the whole the reverse was true of the playwrights. They preferred to adopt the idea found in St Paul and the classical writers, that the stage was an instructive mirror for life, and that, as Hamlet himself puts it, the purpose of playing ... both at the first and now, was and is, to hold as 'twere the mirror up to nature, to show virtue her own feature, scorn her own image, and the very age and body of the time his form and pressure.

(III. ii)

Hamlet of course is a fine one to talk about 'acting' as an image of the times. His author saw the interrelationship of life and stage in terms far more complex than that.

Shakespeare was on both sides of the fence, playwright on the one hand, and player and shareholder in the company which owned his plays on the other. The complexity of acting, doing and performing on stage in *Hamlet* fairly represents both sides of his position, acting out a pretence for the 'distracted multitude'[1] which at the same time as it is a pretence of action is also the reality itself. 'What would *he* do', says Hamlet of the player who has just left with tears in his eyes after reciting the rugged Pyrrhus speech, 'Had he the motive and the cue for passion/That I have?' Hamlet's own passion is real in comparison with the feigned passion of the player. Later his action will also seem real compared with the players in the Mousetrap scene. And yet he too is a player awaiting his cue for passioning. No playwrights have ever taken quite such deliberate enjoyment in confusing the relationship between what is illusion and what reality as the playwrights of Elizabethan drama. And no body of plays does so more instructively. This counterpoise between pleasure and instruction, illusion and reality, 'action' and action, is central to an understanding of Shakespearean drama.

Nonetheless, the counterpoise was firmly embedded in a theatrical milieu wholly committed to the illusory or 'playing' end of the spectrum of acting, doing and performing. The playing companies controlled the entire enterprise of staging plays. They paid the playwrights and owned the plays absolutely, and their first objective was always money. It was the first age of professional theatre in England, and what it professed to be able to 'do' developed radically between 1576, when the first specially-designed playhouses were built, and 1642 when they were closed; but most of the developments were dictated by money. The first real playhouses were valuable largely because the players could charge admission at the door instead of sending gatherers hat in hand through the crowd to collect what they could, as they had to when performing in market-places. The playhouses were built for the sake of the auditorium, not the stage. When the second generation of amphitheatre playhouses was built between 1594 and 1604 the only change we can identify in their design relates to the system of charging different prices for different parts of the auditorium. Similarly the preference which appeared amongst the leading companies after 1608 for indoor halls rather than amphitheatres was not unrelated to the higher revenue they brought in. Money was the consideration which determined the nature and the whole set of priorities of the Elizabethan players. These priorities were inevitably also a basic influence on the writers who gave the players their raw material.

Play scripts, the great bulk of what has survived from Shakespeare's theatre, were only raw material for the stage. Playing companies did what they liked with what they bought from the poets. Even Shakespeare, a shareholder in his company and a performer in his own plays, made little or no attempt to prevent his fellow players from staging them in their own way. He wrote a stage direction for the council scene in *Hamlet* which carefully set the prince apart and out of his proper place, at the tail of the great procession of king and court.

Flourish, Enter Claudius, King of Denmark, Gertrude the Queen, Councilors, Polonius and his son Laertes, Hamlet, cum aliis.[2]

The transcription or prompt-book which the players used for their stage presentation restores Hamlet to the place his rank would normally have put him in:

Enter Claudius King of Denmarke, Gertrude the Queene, Hamlet, Polonius, Laertes, and his sister Ophelia, Lords Attendant.[3]

The evidence from these printed versions is not conclusive proof that the players did fudge Shakespeare's visual point about Hamlet being out of step with the rest of the court, but there is plenty of other evidence that they galloped through the plays without too much care for the finer details, either visual or verbal.

The repertory system alone would have damped any pretension to finesse. Even at its most stable and prosperous an acting company would expect to perform a different play every afternoon of the working week. In the prosperous years 1594–7 the rival company to Shakespeare's, the only other company allowed to perform in London at this time, staged between thirty and forty plays a year, of which between fourteen and twenty-one were new. The most popular play of all in their repertory, the first part of Marlowe's *Tamburlaine*, was staged at most fourteen times in one year, in a yearly total of as many as 250 performances.[4] While they were playing their six different plays each week the players would have a couple of new ones in rehearsal. Each new play made the transfer from playwright's script to stage in between two and four weeks. Obviously the leading players had to have prodigious memories. Rehearsals can have allowed little scope for the finer points of staging, and stock performances, stock responses and stereotyped characterization must have been every player's main standby.

The circumstances of performance were also hostile to any impulse to develop the finer arts of staging. Performances of plays which today simply cannot be pushed through in less than three hours took barely two on the Elizabethan stage, even including the jigs or music which began and rounded off each performance. *Bartholomew Fair*, which at 4,200 lines is matched for length only by *Hamlet* (the average was between 2,400 and 3,000 lines), was said by its author to take 'the space of two houres and an halfe, and somewhat more'. There were no intervals, of course – beer, bread, nuts and apples were hawked through the audience while the play was going on – and there was no scenery to be changed, but even without any such pauses the speed with which the players delivered their hastily-memorized lines was remarkable. It says a lot for the listening capacity of the audiences. Of course there were no armchairs in which the spectators could relax. In the open amphitheatres most of the audience were kept standing around the stage platform throughout the performance, and even the wealthier patrons in the galleries had only bare benches. Standing in a yard open to the sky, feet embedded in mud or at best on wet straw, jostled by beer-drinking neighbours, one can understand the sarcasm in the voice of the playwrights who called the audience 'understanding men'. A continuous flow of speech, preferably compelling and noisy enough to command the full attention of a foot-shuffling crowd of bystanders, was the first requirement of the Elizabethan playing company.

There is an obvious paradox here: how could playwriting of such supreme sophistication have been produced in such a hostile environment? It may well be that the example of Shakespeare drew his contemporaries and successors to heights in language and theatrical subtlety otherwise inconceivable, but Shakespeare was preceded by Marlowe and accompanied by Jonson, both of whom created their plays largely uninfluenced by Shakespeare. All three found in the last years of the sixteenth century conditions for the theatre which were congenial and stimulating to them. The quality of the Elizabethan drama as we read it today owes nothing to the commercial incentives of the time and everything to the dramatic opportunities grasped by Marlowe, Shakespeare and Jonson.

One partial answer to the paradox of Elizabethan playwriting must lie in its novelty. Writing for regular London audiences in custom-built theatres with famous players was new, and the possibilities raised were boundless. Poets had never before enjoyed such direct contact with their audiences. The new drama moreover combined the qualities of lyric poetry with narrative form, and the two together allowed the poets to manipulate audience response as never before. More than this, though, we as modern audiences of the Elizabethan drama should register our differences from the original audiences, and perhaps concede in them an ability to respond which we have lost and which might have gone a long way to minimize the crudity of the original performances. We do know that Elizabethan performances were relatively unsubtle. We cannot be at all sure that audience response was equally crude.

Modern audiences, relaxed in their armchairs in the dark, lack the constant alertness of an audience on its feet. Elizabethans were as accustomed to listening as we are to reading, and were better trained to appreciate complex rhetorical structuring and all the verbal tropes of which complex puns or quibbles are only a small element. Audiences must have enjoyed a speed of response which today belongs more with a quick-fire cabaret act or Marx Brothers wisecracking. Elizabethan players themselves were unlikely to have had much training in formal oratory, which was in the syllabus only of the higher forms in the grammar schools and at university, but the playwrights knew their rhetorical figures and so did much of the audience. 'Action' on the Elizabethan stage had a set of conventions which we have lost. The loss goes some way to explain why we have to take our Shakespeare on stage so much more slowly than did the Elizabethans.

During the sixty-six years of professional London theatre up to 1642 there was a flow of change which makes it peculiarly difficult to draw a simple picture of its main characteristics. The middle decade of the period, however, from *Hamlet* in 1600 to about 1610, was in some degree its heyday, and might be used as a kind of datum point to which the changes can be related. That decade for instance saw Shakespeare's own company adding to its 'popular' theatre, accommodating up to three thousand spectators, with the acquisition of a 'private' theatre seating only about six hundred but charging six times the admission price and aiming more at the wealthier sections of London's population.[5] To say that before 1600 playing was designed for the market-place and after 1610 it aimed at the court would be an overstatement. But the kinds of playhouse built before 1600 and those built after 1610 do suggest some such change in priorities, and the change is worth keeping in mind when we look at what the players set up for themselves in their struggle to make money out of the playing game.

There were two types of playhouse available to Elizabethan players: large, open amphitheatres and indoor halls. For most of the central decade, up to 1609, Shakespeare's company chiefly used the former, the type which was predominant in the earlier part of the period, and it is therefore appropriate to consider it first. Shakespeare's open playhouse, the Globe, was built in 1599 from the timbers of the very first playhouse, the Theatre, erected in Shoreditch in the suburbs to the north of the City of London in 1576. It was essentially an auditorium modelled on the structures built to entertain people with bear-baiting and bull-baiting. The bull-rings had a central arena or 'yard' surrounded by three ranks of galleries. For playing, the yard had a platform extending from the galleries on one side into the middle, and the cheapest position in the audience was a standing-place in the yard around the stage itself. This cost one penny. Another penny or more was needed for access to the galleries, and the best places in the galleries, the 'lords' rooms' adjacent to the stage platform, cost sixpence (old currency: 2½p in modern terms). The part of the galleries from which the stage projected was called the 'tiring-house' or dressing-room, which at stage level had two or more doors for players to enter by. Sometimes the gallery over the stage, variously called the balcony or 'tarras', was used for playing to supplement the stage platform – where Juliet addressed Romeo, for instance – and the curtains or hangings which hung across the tiring-house doors were sometimes used to reveal or 'discover' a static display, a study, cell or tomb. But players on the balcony were always accessories to the players on the platform, and players 'discovered' behind the hangings always came forward on to the platform to speak. The crowd in the yard were never far from the action.

Two playhouses were built in Shoreditch just outside the City of London, in Middlesex, in 1576 and 1577; others appeared later in Southwark on the Surrey bank of the Thames opposite the City, close to the main baiting-house. The governors of the City of London were hostile to playing, and it was more discreet to keep the playing-places beyond their jurisdiction, in the suburbs along with the baiting-houses and brothels. Some of the larger inns inside the City which had spacious courtyards with surrounding galleries were also used for playing, but in 1600 all playing at inns was prohibited, and so the City venues were effectively closed. In 1600 and 1604 two inns were converted into full-time playhouses, but both were outside the walls. By this time there were six open amphitheatres available to the playing companies, but only three companies licensed to perform in London. Consequently only three of the six, Shakespeare's Globe in Southwark, its chief rival the Fortune in Golding Lane, and one of the converted inns, the Red Bull in Clerkenwell, were regularly used for playing. All three led prosperous lives until all the playhouses were closed in 1642.[6]

The open amphitheatres were known as 'public' playhouses, to distinguish them from the 'private houses', or indoor halls. There was an element of class distinction in the two terms. The public playhouses catered for the same crowds which gathered in their thousands to watch bulls and bears being baited by dogs. The indoor halls were kin to the great halls of private houses where the aristocracy entertained their household guests with shows and plays. Moreover the first professional 'private' playhouses were used not by the common players, the adults who performed in amphitheatres and market-places, but by the boy choristers of St Paul's and the Chapel Royal at Windsor. In reality the distinction between public and private playhouses was largely a matter of snobbery. Companies of adult players performed in private halls as eagerly as they played in town halls or market-places. They probably used the large rooms of London inns when the weather made outdoor venues undesirable. Even before the City inns were closed to them, in 1596, the owner and builder of the first London public playhouse, James Burbage, bought a hall and set it up as a private playhouse for his adult players. On this occasion, in fact, snobbery did rule. The proposed playhouse was in the Blackfriars precinct, west of St Paul's, where the wealthy lived, and the local residents managed to block Burbage's attempt to set up his players – Shakespeare's company – there. Burbage died about that time, and in 1599 his sons, short of cash because they were building the Globe, made what they could of their inheritance by leasing their new playhouse to a boy company, which attracted less protest than the adult players. Thereafter the boys performed once or twice weekly in the Blackfriars playhouse for eight years, until they became unprofitable and the Burbages retrieved their indoor playhouse for the use of their own adult company. Thus in 1609 Shakespeare's company returned to the pattern of performing which the City governors had stopped in the 1590s, of playing either at an indoor hall in the City or in their public amphitheatre in the suburbs, as the season dictated. They soon fell into a pattern in which they used the Blackfriars private playhouse inside the City walls for the eight months of the English winter, and moved to the Globe across the river for the four summer months when the aristocracy was out of town and the Inns of Court lawyers were on vacation.

When James succeeded Elizabeth in 1603 he extended the protection which the Court had always given the leading companies of players against the City, and acknowledged the pre-eminence of Shakespeare's company by granting it the use of his own name. The rival company at the Fortune became the Queen's Men and the third company which settled at the Red Bull became the Prince's Men. This kind of support obviously helped the King's Men when they took over the Blackfriars playhouse in 1609 and started performing in it daily. From this time until the closure their pre-eminence was never seriously challenged.

The fact that after 1609 the King's Men became more closely identified with the Blackfriars indoor playhouse than with the public Globe probably reflects a general shift in the social status of plays and playing. Certainly after the construction of the Red Bull, which became known as a 'citizen' playhouse along with the Fortune, in 1604, the only new playhouses were the smaller indoor halls. The boy company which left Blackfriars in 1608 moved for a time to a hall in Whitefriars. The musician Phillip Rosseter was stopped from opening another, Porter's Hall, in Blackfriars in 1615. The player Christopher Beeston did succeed in opening one for his adult company in Drury Lane in 1617, a building he called the Phoenix but which was commonly known as the Cockpit. Another, Salisbury Court, opened in Whitefriars in 1629, and William Davenant was stopped from launching an ambitious new indoor project shortly before the closure.

There were many differences between the amphitheatres and the halls, by far the most significant of which was the disposition of the auditorium. Where in the amphitheatres the poorest stood closest to the stage and the wealthier sat behind them in the galleries, in the halls the cheapest places were in the upper galleries, and the 'pit' around the stage had benches which cost three times as much. The more you paid in the indoor playhouses, the closer you could be to the stage. The boxes flanking the stage were even more costly than the pit, while the more exhibitionistic of gallants in the audience could hire a stool and sit on the stage itself. The indoor playhouses of the early seventeenth century were the first commercial theatres to have a seating and pricing system similar to modern theatres, where the stalls are more expensive than the gallery, or circle, where the circle is more expensive than the upper gallery or balcony, and where the boxes adjacent to the stage are the most expensive of all. The lords' rooms of the public amphitheatres in Shakespeare's day were roughly equivalent to the boxes of the indoor theatres, but otherwise the disposition of the audience was reversed, and the mass audience paying the minimum price dominated the auditorium.

The King's Men regularly transferred the plays in their repertory between the public Globe and the private Blackfriars playhouse, and in the 1620s and 1630s plays were also transferred between the private

Cockpit and the public Red Bull. The social status of the audiences at the two kinds of venue may have differed, but not necessarily their taste in plays. Much more significantly from our point of view, the needs of the players for staging their productions did not vary either. The stage platforms of the indoor playhouses were much smaller than those of the Globe or Fortune, perhaps twenty feet in width compared with the forty feet of the public playhouses. Candles were used to light the halls while the public playhouses had the sky. Cannons were fired in the public venues, and devils never ran around the stage without fireworks spouting from their mouths and their backsides, whereas the indoor venues dared shoot off nothing louder than a pistol. The public playhouses used trumpets where the halls played recorders. The indoor stages were dangerously small for the battles with swords and the fencing bouts popular in the public play-houses. But the plays of Shakespeare, Beaumont and Fletcher, and Massinger were interchangeable between the Globe and Blackfriars, and the players could perform with equal facility either in their regular venues or at Court or in the house of any gentleman capable of paying their price. Staging plays was a portable activity for the Shakespearean player.

Plays were staged with no scenery of the kind we are familiar with today. The nature of theatrical illusion for the Elizabethan player was not based on the literal-minded realism which insists on a two-dimensional picture as backdrop to the action, or which sets mice scratching behind the wainscoting, as Stanislavsky did for the original Moscow production of *The Three Sisters*. Mice would not have got much of a hearing in the noise and rush of the Elizabethan stage. The players were on a platform, a thrust stage, not behind a proscenium arch in a picture frame, and their realism was a feature of what they did, their 'action', not what their audience saw. Duels would certainly be realistic, and stage blood was a commonplace. A scene in *The Battle of Alcazar* (1589) which requires three characters to be executed and disembowelled on stage has a direction at the appropriate point in the manuscript for the stage-keeper to provide '3 violls of blood & a sheeps gather'. A 'gather' contained liver, heart and lungs, and the three phials of blood presumably coloured each disembowelled victim as the appropriate piece of offal was flou-rished. The stage direction in *The Tempest* I. i, '*Enter Mariners wet*', suggests a rather less lurid form of realism. But on the other hand they might use symbolism such as the 'robe for to goo invisibell'[7] which appears in a 1597 inventory of stage properties, or the drowning on stage in the Red Bull's *Two Noble Ladies* of 1619–23, which is portrayed by a pair of 'Tritons' who enter and drag the victims off while blowing trumpets. The Shakespearean stage was capable of spectacular shows, especially in processions, which like a parade of fashion models served to display the company's stock of costumes to best advantage. 'Discoveries' too were the kind of set-piece designed to dazzle the eye. The company which performed *Faustus* in London in the 1590s had a 'Hell mought' or hell's mouth, and 'The sittie of Rome', presumably a painted cloth or hanging. Other and more portable properties included 'i bores heads & Serberosse iii heads', 'i dragon in fostes' (presumably a special kind of devil for *Faustus*), 'i lyone, ii lyone heads' and 'Nepun forcke & garland'. There was also a variety of swords and shields, a chime of bells and a solitary sackbut to supplement the martial trumpets and the drums which accompanied military scenes and the jigs of the company clown.[8] Visual and musical effects were usually a symbolic flourish on the omnipresent verbal effects.[9]

The staging of plays was mobile, in that scenes did not usually create a sense of a specific locality. In the years preceding the central decade plays ran continuously without interval or any pause between acts and scenes. This continuous flow meant that there was little time, and in most cases little need, to establish a sense of locality. For bedroom scenes a four-poster bed would be trundled out from the tiring-house. For banqueting scenes a table and benches would appear. A canopied throne or 'state' on a dais would be carried out for scenes at Court. Occasionally tents might be set up, or special devices carried on like a tree for Tantalus, or set-pieces 'discovered', like the hellmouth for Dr Faustus. Flaming torches might accompany the players entering for a night scene. Otherwise it was a matter of the words signalling the context. The fifteen or more scenes marked by editors in Act IV of *Antony and Cleopatra* would not have been recognizable on the Elizabethan stage. The custom of registering a new scene when all the characters leave and a new group walk on began only in the eighteenth century. There were no sets to change. In Shakespeare's day any property, being portable, could be whisked away when it was no longer needed, and the play could roar on unchecked.

There was one change in this tradition of non-stop action during the central decade. The boy companies which performed at the Blackfriars and at St Paul's, being an offshoot of the chorister boys, had voices trained for singing as well as speaking, and their managers usually had been trained as musicians. Consequently the private playhouses were in a position to provide a far more elaborate musical accompaniment to their performances than the adult companies. Where the adult players provided occasional noises 'within', i.e. trumpets and drums sounding in the tiring-house, the boy players kept a consort of string and wind instruments to play 'above', in a room on the balcony above the stage. And the boys used their musicians not only to provide an overture before the performance but for an *entr'acte* or interact break as well. The playwrights who wrote plays for the boy companies between 1600 and 1608 constructed their plays in five acts, on the expectation that an interval for music was necessary between each act. In Beaumont's *Knight of the Burning Pestle*, written for the Blackfriars boy company in 1607 as a burlesque on citizen tastes in plays, each interact is marked, successively, 'Boy *danceth. Musicke*', '*Musicke*', '*Musicke.* Boy *daunceth*', and at the end of Act IV the apprentice-hero enters to recite a Maylord speech presumably with a dance accompaniment, as an alternative form of interact designed to suit the citizen taste.

Music was the private playhouse equivalent of the jigs and knockabout farces with which the public playhouse companies began and ended their afternoon's entertainment. It was of course a more practicable proposition in the smaller indoor venues where all the audience were seated and the closed hall cut off any extraneous noises from the outside world. The act breaks also gave time for the candles to be trimmed. When the adult company took over from the boys at Blackfriars in 1609 they appear to have taken over the musicians as well, because from this point on through the seventeenth century the practice of act-breaks remained the norm for the playwrights who wrote for the private stages. The Blackfriars musicians developed a considerable reputation, and the concerts preceding the play came to last as long as an hour. The availability of music clearly had its effect on the plays written for Shakespeare's company after

1608. Mood music for instance became an occasional accompaniment to the staging. *The Duchess of Malfi*, first performed at Blackfriars in 1614, has a song by madmen '*to a dismal kind of music*', and in the same scene a dance by '8 Madmen, *with music answerable thereunto*'. There is a similar use of 'Solemn music' twice in *Cymbeline*, in *The Winter's Tale*, *The Tempest*, *Henry VIII* and *Two Noble Kinsmen* – all the plays Shakespeare had a hand in from 1609 onwards.

What happened when Shakespeare's company performed a play written for the Blackfriars at the Globe we do not know. Presumably the music went to the open-air playhouse with the play, since the only positive record we have of a performance of *Cymbeline* is at the Globe in 1611. Whether the act-breaks and interact concerts were maintained for the 'understanders' is doubtful. The prologue to Davenant's *News from Plymouth*, performed at the Globe in the summer of 1635, contrasts what the Globe audience expected with what the Blackfriars offered:

> This house, and season, does more promise shows,
> Dancing, and buckler fights, than art, or wit.

Wit-play at the Blackfriars, sword-play at the Globe. Shirley in his prologue to *The Doubtful Heir* (1640) apologizes sarcastically to the Globe audience for offering them a Blackfriars play:

> No shows, no dance, and what you most delight in,
> Grave understanders, here's no target fighting.

But by the 1630s there was a clear and emphatic distinction between the citizen plays of the Fortune and Red Bull, which were still offering *Faustus* and its devils with their firecrackers, and the witty or romantic plays written for the more courtly tastes of the private playhouses. By the 1630s the King's Men, owning both kinds of playhouse, seem to have provided both kinds of fare.

How far Elizabethan 'action' was akin to what we should think of as realistic is a question for which there is no simple answer. Elizabethan playwrights all had a strong sense that what they offered on stage was an illusion, a game or 'play'. The nature of Elizabethan staging made it impossible to sustain the illusion of reality in the way that the visual realism of cinema and television make possible today. The realistic theatre of Ibsen and Chekhov, which preceded the development of cinematic realism in this century, is almost antithetical to what Shakespeare and his contemporaries thought of as good theatre. The illusory nature of stage realism, and the extent to which everyone was sharing in a deception, could never be forgotten. The two periods in which the boy companies were a fashionable success, from 1576 to 1590 and from 1599 to 1608, suggest that it was not even necessary for audiences to see adult characters played by adults. Even in the adult companies the women's parts were played by boys. There was a shift towards the kind of characterization, both in playwriting and in playacting, which we would consider psychologically plausible, 'convincing' in the sense that the audience is enabled to forget for the moment that the character is only an actor and not a real person. But it never travelled the distance which modern cinema audiences are expected to go in 'identifying' with characters and consistently taking the illusion to be reality.

The Elizabethan players, generally speaking, began as masters either of clownage and extempore or of fustian verse-speaking. The famous players of the 1580s were the clowns, who danced jigs, sang ballads extempore on subjects the audience threw them, and played the farcical or knockabout roles when the play came on. In the 1590s Marlowe's great speech-makers, Tamburlaine, Faustus and Barabas, took over from the clowns, and brought fame and fortune to Edward Alleyn, who played them throughout the 1590s, and whose family nickname was 'the fustian king'.[10] The chief and possibly the only development in acting beyond this fashion was provided by Shakespeare's company. This development was signalled by Marston, a keen maker of new words, who invented the term 'personation' in 1599 to describe what we would call the actor's impersonation of the character he plays.[11] As the playwrights wrote plays containing more individualized personalities, so the players developed the new art of 'personation'. When Hamlet in 1600 derided the Player's fustian speech about rugged Pyrrhus, he was tacitly asserting his own non-fustian personality.

Even as he asserts his own reality compared with the Player, though, Hamlet admits that he too is a player. The speaker of the rugged Pyrrhus speech lacks 'the motive and the *cue* for passion/That

I have'. Hamlet has a much better theatrical 'cue' for passioning, to 'do' in the sense of gesturing and speaking his grief, but complains that he 'can *say* nothing'. Since he claims that he can say nothing in the course of a lengthy soliloquy to the audience, his role as actor in a play who is failing to 'act' in his position as revenger of his father's murder is nicely underlined. The contrast in styles between the Player's trope-laden speech and Hamlet's more loosely structured musing simultaneously asserts Hamlet's own realism and puts it in its true theatrical context, affirming the central pun on the play (and in the play) about 'action'. Hamlet is performing an act. Shakespeare is playing with reality. The Elizabethan stage illusion was marvellous partly because it would not forget that it was an illusion.

NOTES

1. Claudius says of Hamlet, 'He's loved of the distracted multitude/Who like not in their judgement but their eyes.' I suspect another 'play' with theatrical illusion here.

2. Second quarto (1605), I. ii.

3. First folio (1623), I. ii.

4. See R. A. Foakes and R. T. Rickert, eds, *Henslowe's Diary* (Cambridge, 1961), 21–37.

5. See Andrew Gurr, *The Shakespearean Stage 1574–1642* (2nd edn Cambridge, 1980), 114, 196.

6. The best modern account of the Elizabethan playhouses is Glynne Wickham, *Early English Stages 1300–1600* (London, 1959–   ) Vol. II, 1 and 2. Most of the available evidence about the Elizabethan stage and staging is collected in E. K. Chambers, *The Elizabethan Stage* (4 vols, Oxford, 1923) and G. E. Bentley, *The Jacobean and Caroline Stage* (7 vols, Oxford, 1941–68).

7. *Henslowe's Diary*, 325.

8. *Henslowe's Diary*, 319–20.

9. Shakespeare's company at the Globe in 1604 spoke of the 'not received custome of musicke in our Theater', though in later years at the Blackfriars they had a consort of musicians who frequently gave concerts lasting as long as an hour before the play was performed. See *The Shakespearean Stage*, 135–6.

10. M. C. Bradbrook, *The Rise of the Common Player* (London, 1962), 196.

11. See Andrew Gurr, 'Elizabethan Action' in *Studies in Philology*, LXIII (1966), 152–4.

THE PLAYS OF CHRISTOPHER MARLOWE

J. C. MAXWELL

We know more about Marlowe (1564–93) than about most Elizabethan and Jacobean dramatists, and even where we have no firm
knowledge, such accounts as we do have are often fascinating and
provoke speculation. For this reason, a good deal is said in most
studies of him about 'the man and his ideas'. As I have nothing to
add on these subjects and am sceptical about a good deal that has
been written on them, I propose to say very little about anything
that does not directly emerge from the plays. Marlowe was evidently
a man who made enemies, and it may be suspected that he rather
liked doing so. So we are likely to get a distorted picture of him
if we try to piece an account together from the mostly hostile gossip
of the day. But it is only fair to say that some of the most careful
students of his work[1] are much less agnostic than I am about the
possibility of knowing what Marlowe really thought.

As the first major Elizabethan dramatist, Marlowe has achieved
the doubtful distinction of being regarded as a 'pioneer', alongside
interesting minor dramatists such as Lyly and Kyd, and downright
bad ones such as Greene.

Marlowe's first publicly produced play, the two-part *Tamburlaine
the Great* (1587–8), already raises in the acutest form the question
of his attitude towards his creations. No one can ever have doubted
that Marlowe displays in a high degree the imaginative sympathy
with his hero which is required for successful dramatic presentation,
but beyond that most critics have felt impelled to raise the question:
'Is Marlowe for or against Tamburlaine?' More exactly, romantic
critics have tended to take it for granted that he embodies his own
aspirations in his hero; reaction against this began by claiming a

greater degree of objectivity for him, but finished by suggesting to us a Marlowe equally committed on the other side, the dramatic apologist of traditional ethics against the titanism depicted in the figure of Tamburlaine. It seems possible that Marlowe may have been more detached than has been admitted on either side.

The two parts of the play must have been written in rapid succession, but the Prologue to *Part II* indicates that it was composed because of the success of *Part I*, so that we must assume *Part I* to be in its original intention self-contained. That is to say, what Marlowe wrote in the first instance was a play of conquest, not a play of conquest followed by death. This is enough to put us on our guard against too close an assimilation of *Tamburlaine* to the morality pattern. Moreover, *Part I* has a dramatic and not merely a pageant structure: it is given shape and direction by the theme of love for Zenocrate as a force modifying Tamburlaine's ambition and resulting in a temporary pause in his career of conquest: 'Tamburlaine takes truce with all the world'.[2] Yet a truce is not a peace, and the conclusion, probably intentionally, at least leaves the way open for a sequel.

Part I is full of bloodshed, treachery, and ambition of a kind which was as unequivocally condemned by sixteenth-century as by twentieth-century moral orthodoxy. How has Marlowe contrived to give to different critics at different times the impression now of glorifying, now of condemning his hero's behaviour? It is important that the play does not open with Tamburlaine at all but with the weak, petulant, and effeminate Persian King Mycetes. It is questionable whether Marlowe has any wholehearted admiration for titanic ambition, but it is clear that he has a thorough contempt for weakness, especially when it does not admit to itself that it is weakness. Throughout Marlowe's work it is easier to see what he rejects than what he identifies himself with; perhaps (if speculative biography may be permitted for a moment) he did not himself know what values he really believed in. There is often more precise characterization in his contemptible figures than in his more majestic and impressive ones: Faustus is his greatest creation, because in him both elements are combined. Mycetes seems to be maliciously drawn from the inside. Whereas Tamburlaine is ruthless, he is morbidly cruel:

261

I long to see thee back return from thence,
That I may view these milk-white steeds of mine
All loaden with the heads of killed men,
And from their knees even to their hoofs below
Besmear'd with blood that makes a dainty show.

(I. i)

This opening scene is a brilliant presentation of a corrupt world that does not know its own mind, and into it Tamburlaine comes with something of the air of an archetypal Noble Savage. The evidence for Marlowe's direct study of Machiavelli seems to me inadequate,[3] but there is a Machiavellian clarity of political insight into the conditions in which a conqueror of this kind may be expected to arise. Tamburlaine, if not idealized, at least gains from us right away the admiration due to a man who knows what he wants and the road to it. Moreover, the amount of rant put in Tamburlaine's mouth ha been exaggerated by critics, including those who have thought that Marlowe admired him and it. The staple of the play, as Marlowe himself says, is 'high astounding terms', but if anyone uses absurdly inflated language it is Tamburlaine's opponents. His own claims for himself may often be overwhelming, but the rhythm of the lines and the development of the sentences is controlled and cool. This may be demonstrated from one of his most arrogant claims:

I hold the Fates bound fast in iron chains,
And with my hand turn Fortune's wheel about,
And sooner shall the sun fall from his sphere
Than Tamburlaine be slain or overcome.

(I. ii)

This is impressive partly because of the contrast between what is asserted and the measured, almost scientific, run of the verse. Throughout the play there is this sense of control, oddly at variance with the violence of the plot. Yet that plot itself is not overcrowded with action; indeed, the more common modern criticism is that the play is declamatory rather than dramatic. It certainly appeals to a taste which it is hard to recapture imaginatively, but one thing at least that its original admirers must have believed in is the genuine *power* of the word. Tamburlaine's speeches, in keeping with Elizabethan views on rhetoric, are seen as genuinely persuasive, or moving, and the highspots of his career, chosen to illustrate his progress, are ones in which a wholly articulate struggle of wills can be presented.

Marlowe's *Part II* tells something very different, and is a remarkable example of his power of varying his work even where he is committed to a fairly rigid framework. This part seems pretty clearly not involved in the original plan, though the writing of it need not have reversed a firm determination to leave *Part I* on its own. Marlowe has not left himself many of the most striking events of Tamburlaine's recorded career to deal with, and he has to meet a popular demand for something that will appeal to the admirers of the first part. This being so, it is surprising that he should manage to do something genuinely new and individual in *Part II*. It is probably not as good a play as *Part I*, but it is a work with its own central idea. M. M. Mahood[4] describes *Tamburlaine* as 'the only drama I know in which the *death* of the hero constitutes the tragedy', and I think one must admit the independence of the two parts to the extent of applying this description to *Part II* alone. Marlowe's aloofness comes out particularly clearly here. It is death simply as death – not as significant of anything beyond itself – that we are more and more plainly confronted with. Thoroughgoing moralizing treatments of the play are no more convincing than the older notion that Marlowe idealizes Tamburlaine and treats his attitude as nobly defiant – a 'free man's worship' in advance of its time. He does not give us anything so melodramatic as a punishment of Tamburlaine for his defiance of Mahomet.[5] Tamburlaine himself is gradually brought to recognize the unadorned fact which he expresses in the simplest possible juxtaposition: 'For Tamburlaine, the scourge of God, must die'. In a way, his presumption is punished, but it is the bare facts of the situation that punish it. The steps towards this, the increased thwarting of Tamburlaine's will, with the turning-point in his failure to save Zenocrate – 'All this raging cannot make her live', says Theridamas: no one would have ventured to speak so to Tamburlaine in *Part I* – have been traced by M. M. Mahood and more fully by Helen Gardner,[6] who points out that this play is in some ways more Shakespearian than the rest of Marlowe in its departure from a straightforward linear structure, and its substitution of the method 'in which episodes and sub-plots are linked to the main plot by ideas'. *Tamburlaine, Part II* is no *Henry IV, Part II*, but the process of devising a sequel brings Marlowe closer to Shakespeare than in his more thoroughly characteristic dramas.

The Jew of Malta (1588–9?) has been a happy hunting-ground for speculations on the revision of Marlowe's text after his death. It was not published (as far as we know) before 1633, and then it came out with Prologues by Thomas Heywood, spoken at revivals shortly before publication. But Heywood makes no claim to have altered the text, and attempts to detect his hand in it are not convincing. Objections to the play as we have it are largely the result of building up a picture of the sort of play critics would like Marlowe to have written; naturally they are disappointed when they find he did not follow their prescriptions. The usual complaint is that the play first presents Barabas as a lofty Marlovian hero, and then completely falls to pieces in the middle, with only a partial recovery in the last act. It is true that impressive set-speeches are confined to the beginning of the play, but it is hard to see these early scenes as pointing forward to anything substantially different from what we actually have. The guiding thread must always have been the overthrow of the rich Jew early in the play, followed by his cunning machinations and apparent triumph, in which, however, he overreaches himself and is overthrown by even more cunning villains than himself. He is, in the end, not enough of a hypocrite to come out on top in this world in which the thorough-going 'politician' can proclaim in the last lines of the play:

> So, march away; and let due praise be given
> Neither to Fate nor Fortune, but to Heaven.

We may not particularly like the intrigue and low comedy of the central scenes – though some of it is a good deal better than is usually admitted – but they are not out of key in this harsh, sardonic play.

The 'world' of the play is the important thing. As M. M. Mahood points out, it is limited, constricted. The scene, in contrast to that of Tamburlaine, is 'an island in the land-locked Mediterranean'. Barabas's ambitions are satisfied by infinite riches in a little room. When (II. iii. 175–202) he claims a wider scope for his activities, the natural interpretation is that he is inventing in order to impress his Turkish slave and encourage him to any villainy that may be required of him. The Barabas of the early scenes is indeed a more 'romantic' figure than anyone else in the play, but there is irony in such a presentation of him right from the start. For all the wealth which streams in to him from all over the world, Barabas's position is a very vulnerable one. 'Give us a peaceful rule; make Christians kings', he says (I. i. 132), but in fact the 'rule' obtained by his wealth depends on the reluctant toleration of the Christian rulers of Malta, and an arbitrary act of confiscation on their part is all that is required to ruin him, apart from the opportunity he seizes of stowing away some of his gold and jewels, which contributes to the next part of the plot. The kind of undignified weapons with which Barabas later fights are the only ones available for him.

I have already mentioned the way in which the Christians eventually outdo Barabas in Machiavellian 'policy'. It is of some importance for the structure of the play to decide how explicit Marlowe is in presenting this aspect of his theme. It seems to me as unconcealed here as in *Tamburlaine, Part II*. At most, there is a pretence, intended to be transparent even to a relatively naïve audience, of treating the Christians a little more indulgently. And of course in this world of plot and counter-plot there can be no pity for the victim, Barabas, in the cauldron he had prepared for Calymath. The Prologue spoken by Machiavel sets the tone. Machiavellian 'policy' is expounded at length, and then we are promised:

> ... the tragedy of a Jew
> Who smiles to see how full his bags are cramm'd,
> Which money was not got without my means.

We are not told in so many words that Barabas will be by no means the only Machiavellian in the play, but we have no difficulty in recognizing the Christians also as such when the plan for confiscating Jewish property is set forth. And particular emphasis is given – in Barabas's words, it is true, but he merely comments on what is obvious – to the contrast between profession and practice, most forcibly in these lines:

> For I can see no fruits in all their faith
> But malice, falsehood and excessive pride,
> Which methinks fits not their profession,
>> (I. i)

with its glance at New Testament passages on the fruits of the spirit, 'love, joy, peace, long-suffering, gentleness, goodness, faith, meekness, temperance'.

How should a play of this temper be described? That it is a 'tragedy' in the original edition need mean no more than that it ends with the death of the principal character, and reluctance to give it a different classification has weakened of recent years. T. S. Eliot's description of it as 'farce' and his stress on its 'savage comic humour' were regarded as paradox for some time after the original appearance of his essay in 1918.[7] Now they are accepted with slight variants of phrasing by such scholars as P. H. Kocher and M. M. Mahood. The danger of such descriptions is that Marlowe will be thought of as doing something particularly subtle and esoteric, so that doubts will arise whether he can really have hoped to get it across to an audience. But in fact the tone of the *Jew* is quite a natural result of the treatment of a melodramatic story with an attitude of ironic detachment. That is not the only sort of comedy it contains. Act IV, scene i, in which Barabas plays the two greedy friars off against each other, is sheer comedy, but of a kind which could be accommodated within the framework of a more normal Elizabethan tragedy. It is rather like Act III, scenes ii–iii, of *The Revenger's Tragedy*, the plot for the saving of the youngest brother, which goes wrong. But the rest of *The Revenger's Tragedy*, too, requires a treatment different from what we normally give to tragedy: perhaps the *Jew* could be described as a *Revenger's Tragedy* without the positive moral framework implied in that play. It has some of the deliberate exclusions of a comedy of humour, and it was a piece of sound insight on Mr Eliot's part to cite Ben Jonson's *Volpone* as its most notable successor.

Doctor Faustus is the greatest but the most controversial of Marlowe's plays. Many of its differences from his other works arise from the theme, more traditional and yet more sharply individualized than those of the other plays. Marlowe is here dramatizing a narrative which, however lacking in tragic dignity, was already complete in itself and had a manifest moral purport in his source, the English version of the German *Faust-Book* (earliest surviving edition 1592). I doubt whether any arguments from Marlowe's handling of his material give much help in deciding whether it was written before *The Jew of Malta* or after *Edward II*, or between the two, and external evidence is not enough to permit of a definite verdict.[8]

How much of the play as we have it comes from Marlowe, and how much of what he originally wrote is lost? The evidence is complex and needs the most delicate handling. Here I can only say dogmatically, but without claiming for the view either high probability or general agreement, that it seems to me justifiable to draw on both the main body of the play and the farcical prose scenes as a guide to Marlowe's conception of the story, even if he may have had a collaborator. The Bruno sub-plot, on the other hand, I believe to be out of key with the rest of the play, and to be by another author, even if, as Greg and others hold, it belongs to a collaborative version from Marlowe's own lifetime and not to later additions. I doubt whether in the process of transmission much of Marlowe's text has been lost to us.

The overt meaning of the play has given offence to some of those who are convinced that the accounts of Marlowe's anti-Christian views are to be taken very seriously, and also that Marlowe was determined to give expression to those views in his plays. I do not know what Marlowe's religious beliefs were when he wrote this play, but there is nothing in it which could not have been written by a convinced Christian: he does not twist the traditional story for anti-traditional ends. If doubts about his own attitude are aroused at all, it is because of the probing, ironical analysis he applies to his hero. There is never any danger of an excess of sympathy for the unorthodox aspirations of Faustus, but it could be argued that a believer might have been expected to treat the case with a less thoroughly objective detachment. Marlowe, it might be said, realizes the dramatic potentialities of the Christian 'myth' of damnation more as an observer than one who feels himself involved. But this would very likely be to underrate Marlowe's artistic powers. In any event, the need to work within a sharply defined scheme of ideas has been entirely beneficial to Marlowe.

One of Marlowe's principal tasks is to combine the sense of inevitability, of a transaction that exists as a whole from the very start, with a genuine tension from the point of view of his central character. The placing of the main action of a play within a framework is a device that enjoyed some popularity in early English tragedy. In Kyd's *Spanish Tragedy*, the whole of the main action is supposed to be completed or at least predetermined by the time the play opens, and, formally, Revenge simply displays to the Ghost of Andrea a sequence of events whose upshot he knows already, and the two are jointly described as a Chorus. Kyd's purpose does not require him to say whether this is preternatural foreknowledge on the part of Revenge, or whether what he shows is a re-enactment of past events rather than the events themselves. Whichever it is, the effect of artistic distancing is achieved. In *Faustus*, we have a completely anonymous Chorus, and a main action definitely set in the past, though in the opening chorus there is an effective fluctuation between present and past tenses. Most of the introductory sketch is in the present, taken up again in the last line:

> And this the man that in his study sits.

But at the most ominous part it lapses into the past:

> His waxen wings did mount above his reach,
> And melting, heavens conspir'd his overthrow.

With the audience in this ambiguous position, prepared to watch a developing action which is yet only a re-enactment of something complete, effects of compression and foreshortening can be accepted without difficulty. Faustus's whole intellectual career is presented in terms of a soliloquy placed at a crucial point of that career. The progress through the arts and sciences can thus be compressed into a few lines. Yet this is not a piece of purely stylized dramatic technique. We are in one sense seeing at a glance years of Faustus's intellectual life, but we are also at a definite point of time, and the introduction of the rather mysterious figures Valdes and Cornelius helps to fix this effect. The play's treatment of the theme of sin is in a way allegorical – or at least exemplary – and thus timeless; yet the very complications and technicalities of sixteenth-century witch-craft help to locate the action and prevent it from being too abstract. Valdes and Cornelius (not present in the *Faust-Book*) are sharply individualized though shabby figures, 'no deeply versed magicians welcoming a promising beginner', writes Greg,[9] 'but merely the devil's decoys luring Faustus along the road to destruction'.

In the first scene with Mephistophilis, the same combination of the specific and the broadly speculative is to be found, and most of the main characteristics of Marlowe's art can be studied in it. Faustus's self-dramatization can be seen from the opening lines; the proper setting has been achieved, and Faustus, as already in the first scene, uses his own name almost mesmerically as a sort of incantation – he is later to admit, 'the god thou servest is thine own appetite'. He also uses it as a means of screwing up his courage: 'then fear not, Faustus, to be resolute'. This word 'resolute', already impressed on Faustus by Valdes, echoes through the play, with its ironical claim to virtue on behalf of what is really weakness. The appearance of the spirit he has invoked affords an opportunity to show his aplomb by an anti-clerical joke. After the invocation, Mephistophilis first appears through the trap-door in the shape of a dragon.[10] Faustus exclaims:

> I charge thee to return and change thy shape,
> Thou art too ugly to attend on me.
> Go, and return an old Franciscan friar,
> That holy shape becomes a devil best.

When the dragon obeys his order and departs, Faustus continues:

> I see there's virtue in my heavenly words.
> Who would not be proficient in this art?
> How pliant is this Mephistophilis,
> Full of obedience and humility!
> Such is the force of magic and my spells.

Much of the play is concentrated in these few lines: Faustus's rather nervously showy jesting, his conviction or would-be conviction that it is he, by virtue of his spells, who is the real master, and his unwillingness to face the real nature of what he is doing ('heavenly words'). 'Ugly', too, is a key-word of the play: for true horror of evil, Faustus substitutes a squeamish distaste for its outward manifestations. On two later occasions the word is tellingly used on the occasion of one of Faustus's gestures towards repentance: Mephistophilis is dismissed with 'Ay, go, accursed spirit to ugly hell'. But it only takes the show of the Seven Deadly Sins to make him accept Mephistophilis's assurance that 'in hell is all manner of delight', and to reply in one of the most ironic lines of the play: 'Oh, might I see hell and return again safe, how happy were I then'. The desire for the pleasures of the morally uncommitted spectator, which was part of what traditional thought had meant by 'curiosity', is throughout strong in Faustus.[11] Last and most telling of all is the outburst at the very end of the play: 'Ugly hell, gape not! Come not, Lucifer'.

The opening dialogue with Mephistophilis is a comment on the speech we have just examined. Mephistophilis is so sure of his victim that he does not even need to encourage him in his delusions:

> FAUSTUS. Did not my conjuring speeches raise thee? Speak.
> MEPHISTOPHILIS. That was the cause, but yet *per accidens*:
>   For when we hear one rack the name of God,
>   Abjure the scriptures and his saviour Christ,
>   We fly in hope to get his glorious soul.

He can tell the truth, sure that it will not really be believed. It could be said that this is primitive dramatic technique, exposition for the benefit of the audience, but the more we read the play the less willing we shall be to find it primitive. Faustus's criminal blindness rises to:

> This word 'damnation' terrifies not me,
> For I confound hell in Elysium:
> My ghost be with the old philosophers.

The last line may be simply a piece of paganism, but our suspicions are aroused when we notice its identity with a saying attributed to the Arabic philosopher Averroes, expressing his hostility to Christianity.[12] Since Averroes was chiefly celebrated for his denial of individual immortality, the line links up with:

> Thinkst thou that Faustus is so fond to imagine
> That after this life there is any pain?
>
> (II. i)

And with the final wish, by this time despairing, of:

> O soul, be chang'd to little water-drops
> And fall into the ocean, ne'er be found.
>
> (v. ii)

So deeply embedded in the play is traditional and contemporary lore.

Equally pathetic in its blindness to reality is Faustus's assumption of the air of one potentate sending an ambassador to another:

Go bear these tidings to great Lucifer:
Seeing Faustus hath incurr'd eternal death
By desperate thoughts against Jove's deity,
Say he surrenders up to him his soul
So he will spare him four and twenty years,
Letting him live in all voluptuousness,
Having thee ever to attend on me,
To give me whatsoever I shall ask,
To tell me whatsoever I demand,
To slay mine enemies and aid my friends
And always be obedient to my will.

The lofty language is unable to conceal the complete one-sidedness of the bargain, and there is pathetic evasion in the pagan 'Jove' and in the Titan-pose of the whole line. 'Desperate' has a peculiar irony. Throughout the play, and more and more strongly as it proceeds, the notion of despair in the strict theological sense – conviction that one is inevitably damned – comes to the fore.[13] Here we have 'desperate' used in a less precise and more self-dramatizing way, as we talk of a desperate character meaning one who is 'extremely reckless or violent, ready to run any risk or go to any length' (*O.E.D.*). The progress of the play is just a deepening and intensifying of Faustus's conception of what 'desperate thoughts' are. The emphasis on 'all voluptuousness' and the line 'to slay mine enemies and aid my friends' brings home to us that Faustus's is no lofty and disinterested search for knowledge in itself.

In the first lines of his next speech Faustus again displays his irresponsible levity:

Had I as many souls as there be stars
I'd give them all for Mephistophilis.

The simile brings out the conception of a soul as a possession on a par with other possessions. We may remember this when we come to the prose of the last meeting with the scholars, strangely moving in its simplicity:

FAUSTUS. Ah, gentlemen, I gave them my soul for my cunning.
SCHOLAR. God forbid!
FAUSTUS. God forbade it indeed, but Faustus hath done it.

(v. ii)

I have dwelt on this scene (and even so have left unnoticed its most famous lines, Mephistophilis's denial that he is out of hell) in order to show its extraordinary concentration and grim irony. Similar methods could be applied to the other great scenes of the play, but here one or two more general comments will have to suffice.

Whether or not all the central part of the play is by Marlowe, there can be little doubt that most of what it contains is in accord with his conception of the situation. It was no part of his purpose to show Faustus's reward even in this world as imposing or dignified. There is more of a contrast than in the *Faust-Book* between what the translator of that work called Faustus's 'merry conceits' and the central tragic theme, just because the prose story makes so little of that theme. But the same genius that shows itself in the great scenes in tragic intensification is manifested, though less strikingly, in the selection exercised on the miscellaneous buffoonery. It has to remain buffoonery – that is what Faustus has committed himself to – but it is no longer wholly sprawling or aimless. A good example of Marlowe's power of bringing some order out of chaos is the way in which the high-life and low-life sides of Faustus's thaumaturgy come together with the irruption of the clowns into the presence of the Duke and Duchess of Vanholt. This drives home the point that Faustus's activities are all of a piece, though he can still make the best of a sorry business by commending the clowns to his hosts as 'good subject for a merriment'.

At one point Marlowe has not been satisfied with selecting from the 'merry conceits' of his source, leaving their triviality unconcealed. Perhaps the most famous lines of the play are those with which Faustus greets the second appearance of Helen, in response to his request to Mephistophilis:

> One thing, good servant, let me crave of thee
> To glut the longing of my heart's desire;
> That I may have unto my paramour
> That heavenly Helen which I saw of late.
>
> (v. i)

Here the corresponding passage in the *Faust-Book* (ch. 55) is of the most prosaic kind. But Marlowe's heightening does not mean romantic idealization. On the contrary, the play's irony is never deeper than here.

> Sweet Helen, make me immortal with a kiss,

exclaims Faustus, in the very act of finally sacrificing his true immortality. In the next line:

> Her lips suck forth my soul: see where it flies!

the age-old conceit of the soul on the lips, breathed out in a kiss,
gains a new and sombre meaning, and the mythological parallels
which he then goes on to cite – Semele and Arethusa – are apt
comments on the fate of those who aspire beyond the human condition. Marlowe is not taking a holiday from his main theme in
evocative poetry, and the scene is skilfully placed immediately before
the final appearance of the virtuous Old Man, who endures bodily
torments for the sake of true immortality, thus preparing for the
final scene. That scene has never lacked admirers, and there is no
need to add to the discussions of it, but it is worth while to see it
as the climax of a subtle and psychologically profound study, not
as an impressive fragment.

Marlowe can no longer be looked on as a pioneer in the English
history play.[14] The old belief that made him one depended on the
theory that the 'bad' Quarto and Octavo versions of (respectively)
2 and 3 *Henry VI* were earlier drafts of the plays as printed in the
Shakespeare Folio, and that Marlowe had an important share in them.
It is now generally agreed that the Folio prints the original texts,
that echoes of Marlowe in the corrupt versions are due to errors of
memory on the part of the compilers of those versions, who were
familiar with Marlowe's plays, and that *Edward II* follows rather than
precedes the *Henry VI* plays. When we look at *Edward II* with a
fresh eye, it is, indeed, hard to see how the old view was accepted.
The historical process, which captured Shakespeare's imagination
right from the outset of his career, has little interest for Marlowe.
He shows some skill in selecting from the chronicle material, but
the task is evidently burdensome to him. The problem of the king
and his 'favourites', which is primarily a political one for Shakespeare,
assumes a disproportionate and independent psychological interest
for Marlowe. We may feel in *Richard II* that Bushy, Bagot, and
Green, the 'caterpillars of the commonwealth', are rather too
shadowy and unindividualized figures, but they are in their right
place in relation to the whole scheme of the play. Marlowe's Gaveston,

on the other hand, is too dominant for the coherence of the play to survive his departure from the scene, and the forces he stands for have to be unconvincingly split up. For the theme of the favourite, Marlowe is reduced to a feeble duplication of what has gone before, with the younger Spenser for Gaveston, while the dynamic and ambitious element is transferred to the Machiavellian Mortimer, aided by Queen Isabella, whose character is ruthlessly transformed for the purpose. Marlowe is not content simply to chronicle, like the authors of the more unintelligent and pointlessly episodic history plays, such as Peele's *Edward I*. But he has not found a single unifying theme or a single appropriate tone. The play's very half-heartedness saves it from some of the criticisms to which *Tamburlaine*, *The Jew of Malta*, and *Faustus* are exposed at the hands of those who do not really like characteristic Marlowe. But it is lifeless in itself and does not open the way for later development. That Shakespeare could take something from it for *Richard II* is a tribute more to his genius for creative adaptation than to its intrinsic suggestive power. This does not mean that it is not far better than almost all non-Shakespearean history plays of the time, but that is only because they are very bad indeed.

The contrast with *Faustus* comes out most strongly in the final scenes of the two plays. That of *Edward II* is undeniably impressive in itself, but the effect is almost entirely one of isolated pathos, and Edward becomes more impressive the more his individuality falls into the background. The tone is set by Matrevis's introductory comment:

> Gurney, I wonder the king dies not,
> Being in a vault up to the knees in water,
> To which the channels of the castle run,
> From whence a damp continually ariseth
> That were enough to poison any man,
> Much more a king brought up so tenderly.
>
> (v. v)

Edward himself takes up the theme:

> And there in mire and puddle have I stood
> This ten days' space; and lest that I should sleep,
> One plays continually upon a drum.
> They give me bread and water, being a king;

So that, for want of sleep and sustenance,
My mind's distempered and my body's numb'd,
And whether I have limbs or no I know not.

(v. v)

'Much more a king', 'being a king' – the harsh contrast between the station in life and the indignities heaped on its occupant, that is what gives these lines their force, and Marlowe certainly achieves a harshness of statement that is new in his verse, and perhaps in English dramatic poetry. The Edward we have known is so much in the background that the effect is, if anything, weakened by the more famous and evocative lines which follow the passage last quoted:

Tell Isabel the Queen I look'd not thus
When for her sake I ran at tilt in France,
And there unhors'd the duke of Cleremont.

In *Faustus*, by contrast, there is no irrelevant picturesqueness at the end. Everything in Faustus's final monologue is intimately related to the whole of the drama, and the more Faustus is himself, the more is he Everyman as well.

Marlowe's career, then, ends in a question-mark. We cannot even be sure whether his last play was *Faustus* or the relatively lifeless and derivative *Edward II*, and even the greater play does not evidently point forward to any definable line of development.

NOTES

1. Notably P. H. Kocher, *Christopher Marlowe* (University of N. Carolina Press, 1946).

2. See G. I. Duthie, 'The Dramatic Structure of Marlowe's *Tamburlaine the Great*, Parts I and II', in *English Studies, 1948*, ed. F. P. Wilson.

3. In favour of Marlowe's knowledge, see R. Battenhouse, *Marlowe's Tamburlaine* (Vanderbilt University Press, 1941); for a non-proven verdict, see Kocher, n. 1 above. For disagreement with some of what I say on *Tamburlaine*, see Peet, 'The Rhetoric of *Tamburlaine*', E.L.H., xxvi (1959), 137–55.

4. M. M. Mahood, *Poetry and Humanism* (1951), ch. 3: probably the best essay-length study.

5. As Battenhouse thinks: see n. 3 above.

6. *Modern Language Review*, XXXVII (1942), 18–24.

7. Reprinted in *Selected Essays*.

8. Sir Walter W. Greg in his great edition argues strongly for a late date (1592–3). Dr H. Jenkins, in an important review of that edition (*Modern*

Language Review, XLVI, 1951, 86), gives good reasons for treating the question as still open.

9. W. W. Greg, 'The Damnation of Faustus', in *Modern Language Review*, XLI (1946), 99.

10. This explanation for the intrusive word *dragon* in the invocation is that of L. Kirschbaum, *Review of English Studies*, XVIII (1942), 312–15. I think it is convincing, supported as it is by the title-page woodcut in the 1616 edition, reproduced in Boas's (Methuen) edition from the 1624 reprint.

11. I have discussed this in 'The Sin of Faustus', in *The Wind and the Rain* IV (1947), 49–52.

12. I deal with this more fully in *Notes and Queries* CXCIV (1949), 334–5.

13. See H. Gardner, 'Milton's "Satan" and the Theme of Damnation in Elizabethan Tragedy', in *English Studies, 1948*, ed. F. P. Wilson, esp. p. 50.

14. See the discussion of this question in F. P. Wilson, *Marlowe and the Early Shakespeare* (1953).

SHAKESPEARE: THE YOUNG DRAMATIST
AND THE POET
DEREK TRAVERSI

A contemporary observer, viewing the state of the English stage in 1593, the year of Christopher Marlowe's early death, and comparing him with the emerging figure of William Shakespeare, might well have concluded that Marlowe was the more impressive and powerful figure. He would, however, have been mistaken in his estimate of the final status of these two great writers. Shakespeare, whose earliest work might well have seemed less striking in its individuality than the products of Marlowe's meteoric genius, developed more slowly but, as time would show, on a wider front. Showing from the first a consistent and, for his time, unique interest in the implications of the dramatic illusion, he began by experimenting in various styles and kinds of play, largely creating his own forms in the process of writing. From first to last each play of Shakespeare's represents not only a development from what has gone before, but a new beginning, a fresh attack on problems involved in the very decision to write a particular kind of play. These creative experiments were carried out on a variety of material and developed with a refusal to be confined by limiting categories of *genre*, which answer to his uniquely self-conscious conception of his art.

The plays with which Shakespeare embarked upon his career fall about equally into two categories: 'history plays' and 'comedies'. The three plays on the reign of *Henry VI* (1591–2), which may be the earliest works attributed to him, can be seen as attempts to discover what a 'history play' built upon certain coherent and dramatically viable ideas, as distinct from an episodic pageant, might be. These lead into the more accomplished play, *Richard III* (1593), in which the villainous royal hunchback whose presence dominates the action is perhaps the first of Shakespeare's tragic figures to emerge from the conventions of contemporary melodrama with a genuine force of personality. His opening definition of his own character is expressed with a linguistic resource that is already typical:

> I, that am not shap'd for sportive tricks,
> Nor made to court an amorous looking-glass –
> I – that am rudely stamp'd, and want love's majesty
> To strut before a wanton ambling nymph –
> I, that am curtail'd of this fair proportion,
> Cheated of feature by dissembling nature,
> Deform'd, unfinish'd, sent before my time
> Into this breathing world, scarce half made up,
> And that so lamely and unfashionable
> That dogs bark at me as I halt by them –
> Why, I, in this weak piping time of peace,
> Have no delight to pass away the time,
> Unless to spy my shadow in the sun
> And descant on mine own deformity.
> And therefore, since I cannot prove a lover
> To entertain these fair well-spoken days,
> I am determined to prove a villain
> And hate the idle pleasures of these days.
>
> (I. i)

Although a certain stilted quality survives in the movement of the verse (there is a sense, common in Elizabethan stage villains and heroes, of the speaker playing up to a dramatically acceptable picture of himself), the general effect is remarkably concise and pointed. Richard's state of mind is conveyed primarily through a series of sharp visual touches – the vision of himself as 'strutting' ludicrously before a 'wanton ambling nymph', as being 'barked at' by the dogs as he passes before them, 'spying' his misshapen shadow in the sun – and through the sustained contrast, implying contempt and repudiation, between the 'sportive tricks' and exigencies of 'these fair well-spoken days' and his own situation 'deform'd', 'unfinish'd', 'scarce half made up', 'lame' and 'unfashionable'. In this way, by making envy the vehicle for a criticism felt not to be altogether unjustified, the speaker is humanized, transformed from the abstract incarnation of a traditional vice exploited for melodramatic effect into something like a person.

The character, moreover, is developed in strict relationship to an action which at once conditions and reflects it. Richard is presented as a man constrained by his awareness of being excluded from the forms and fictions of polite society to make the pursuit of power his exclusive and obsessive aim. In following it he shows a combination of intense passion and ironic clear-sightedness which causes him to stand out from the world of shallow, time-serving politicians and helpless moralists in which he moves; but in the very act of attaining the 'golden crown' which he has made his goal, the cost of success is also revealed as he reflects, before his final overthrow, on the inevitability of his isolated doom. Already in the last of the *Henry VI* plays he has been made to say, in the act of striking down the helpless king,

> I have no brother, I am like no brother;
> And this word 'love', which greybeards call divine,
> Be resident in men like one another,
> And not in me! *I am myself alone.*
>
> (Part 3, v. vi)

And now, confronted in his dream on the eve of his final battle with the ghosts of his victims, he confirms his understanding of his situation: 'Richard loves Richard: that is, I am I'. The outcome of a life-long dedication to the egoist's desire for power is seen to be the impossibility of self-evasion, escape from what at the last emerges, with dreadful clarity, as the limits of the isolated self. The realization, with all its implications for an art that defines character through the interaction of converging points of view, is one that will be taken up in various and infinitely more complex forms in the great tragedies to come.

Still at this early stage in his career we find Shakespeare engaged, in another series of plays, in exploring the possibilities of the comic convention, shaping it into an instrument for expressing the finished statements about life – and more especially about 'love' and marriage as central aspects of it – that he was already, beneath the obvious desire to entertain, concerned to make. The experiments in the form represented by *The Comedy of Errors* (1592), *The Taming of the Shrew* (1593), and *The Two Gentlemen of Verona* (1594), led to *Love's Labour's Lost* (*c.* 1595), at once the most formal and the most impressive of these early comedies. As it opens the King of Navarre and his companions declare their intention of withdrawing from normal society to maintain themselves, in artificial seclusion, 'Still and contemplative in living art'. The impact upon this self-absorbed intellectual fantasy of reality, in the form of the Princess of France and her companions, soon reveals the inadequacy of the positions so confidently taken up. Costard, the most human and engaging of Shakespeare's early clowns, is there to remind us, in the face of so much flattering self-deception, that it is 'the simplicity of man to harken after the flesh'. Very soon the 'academicians' find themselves forsworn, subjected to the passion they have vowed to renounce and busily engaged in seeking comfort for their wounded self-esteem in the assurance that each of them is not alone in having deserted his ideals. Berowne, the detached and self-indulgent courtier, is able to caricature the excesses of romantic literary love even as he goes on to admit his surrender in the rueful phrase: 'As true we are as flesh and blood can be'. From this position it is natural for him to conclude that 'the true Promethean fire' lies not where he and his companions have vainly sought it, but in the affirmation of love as a principal source of life, of enhanced vitality. More directly than any other work of Shakespeare's, this is a play about *language*, its corruption and misuse, and about the false and self-deceiving attitudes to which such misuse leads. The artifice of the expression, which its very mode imposes, serves indeed to limit the validity of Berowne's 'Platonic' flights, placing them as products of ingenuity and sophistication; but the conclusion he reaches –

> Let us once lose our oaths to find ourselves,
> Or else we lose ourselves to keep our oaths.
>
> (IV. iii)

is serious enough to bear what is, in effect, a principal moral of the entire comedy.

The conclusion of the play is an elaborate drawing together of the separate threads of the action. Navarre and his companions, reversing their original attitudes, court the Princess and her companions in disguise and are wittily spurned, whilst those who accompany them in lower ways of life are in turn exposed for their more simple pretensions in the burlesque pageant of the Nine Worthies. With the various threads thus brought together, the last stage of the comedy raises the entire action to a different level by announcing the death of the Princess's father, the King of France. Under the shadow of this reminder of mortality, Berowne further confesses the nature, as he has now come to see it, of love as a valid and enriching emotion. The Princess, however, speaking in the new mood introduced by her father's surrender to 'the sudden hand of death', refuses to enter too easily into the 'world without end' bargain of marriage which is now offered her and her companions. Significantly, this is Shakespeare's only comedy which does *not* conclude with a fulfilling and harmonizing pattern of marriages. Navarre is directed to contemplation and Berowne receives from his Rosaline the obligation to set his wit in competition with the realities of death and suffering so that only what can stand this test may survive in his new state. Finally the songs of Spring and Winter set the entire comedy in the context of the pattern conferred upon life by the revolving seasons. The cuckoo and the owl, birth and death respectively, give their last words to a comedy which already conveys, beneath its surface polish and elaborate contrivance, no small measure of the Shakespearean intuition of life.

The majority of Shakespeare's poems are likely to have been written at about this stage in his career. The narrative poems *Venus and Adonis* (1593) and *The Rape of Lucrece* (1594) are, in the main, literary exercises in conventional forms, the writing of which no doubt helped him to assimilate the classical – mainly Ovidian – influences derived from his schooling and to give them a distinctively English bent. The Sonnets are a different matter. Published for the first time as a sequence late in the poet's career, in 1609, they have been variously dated, often to fit in with highly subjective interpretations of unknown facts in his life. Critical opinion seems, for the most part, to favour a relatively early dating for most of the poems: a conclusion to which we may give a measure of assent without excluding the probability that they do not correspond entirely to any single inspiration or reflect, beneath their variety of theme and treatment, any one stage in Shakespeare's development.[1]

A purely literary approach confirms this impression. Not all the poems are in any sense equal in interest. Some of them read like literary exercises, addressed either to a patron of letters who is also addressed as a friend or, in the case of many of the later numbers, to an imaginary and conventional mistress. Convention, however, need not in these poems necessarily be thought of in a limiting or depreciative sense. The opening sequence (I–XVIII), for example, in which a friend is urged to marry and promised immortality in verse, is likely to strike a modern reader as offering unpromising, or simply bizarre, material for poetry; but in urging the person addressed to accept the necessity of commitment, of the creative giving of self as a necessary condition of being truly alive –

> Profitless usurer, why dost thou use
> So great a sum of sums, yet canst not live?
> For having traffic with thyself alone,
> Thou of thyself thy sweet self dost deceive . . .
>
> (IV)

and by relating this imperative to the poet's urge to find fulfilment, affirmation of value, in his own creative action, Shakespeare is addressing himself to themes which will occupy a central position in some of his greater comedies.

All the poems, conventional or otherwise, show in varying degree signs of the way in which the sonnet form, by the very strictness of its formal limits, imposes upon language a distinctive economy and intensity; and the best of them develop these qualities to a degree which makes them, within their strictly observed limits, comparable to much in the mature plays. The presence of the characteristic Shakespearean immediacy can be felt in such lines as

> Against my love shall be as I am now,
> With Time's injurious hand *crush'd* and *o'erworn* . . .
>
> (LXIII)

and the famous

> Lilies that fester smell far worse than weeds.
>
> (XCIV)

In the first instance the impression of the passage of time is conveyed with a fresh vividness that produces a pairing of words in cumulative and dynamic effect that is one of Shakespeare's favourite ways of intensifying the emotional content of his poetry; in the second, which marks the conclusion of a poem which holds contrary judgements – virtue and vice, self-control and self-repression – in a state of constantly shifting suspense, the striking unexpectedness of 'fester' cuts sharply across the familiar associations of 'lilies' in a manner that recalls – to go no further – Angelo's tense, clipped utterances at critical moments in *Measure for Measure*.[2] This same keen economy of language, when set for wider dramatic purposes against the prevailing structure of the blank verse period, soon produced corresponding modifications in the field of stress. Taken together, these two factors – verbal immediacy and the moulding of stress to the movement of living emotion – account in great measure for the unique impression produced by Shakespeare's mature poetry. These tendencies in verse and rhythm were accompanied in the sonnets by the exploration of fresh themes. The most important of these are concerned with the relationship of individual experience (and especially the personal ties of love and friendship) with time. In places, the poems express a conviction of the permanence and unique validity of emotion in its different forms, and especially as expressed in time-defying verse; and then their attitude is that stated in one of the most familiar of all the sonnets:

> Love's not Time's fool, though rosy lips and cheeks
> Within his bending sickle's compass come ...
>
> (CXVI)

Splendidly as this conviction is expressed, however, there is about this sonnet, particularly in its closing lines, a suggestion of the rhetorical, of an effort to carry conviction by mere weight of affirmation:

> If this be error, and upon me prov'd,
> I never writ, nor no man ever lov'd.

The concluding couplet reads with an odd sense of weakness after the powerful development which has preceded it. The 'bending sickle's compass' is, in terms of linguistic and rhythmic vigour, superbly real in comparison with the lame, unsupported assertion in which the poem is supposed to culminate. The poet seems to say, in effect, that the experience with which he is dealing *must* have a timeless validity, because to accept the contrary would be to convert the experience itself into something tragically meaningless. It is precisely this situation, this sense of emotional conviction balanced by rational doubt, that Shakespeare dramatized in *Troilus and Cressida*.

Under such circumstances, it is not surprising that, in other moods, a contrary attitude prevails. Such is the case in the opening lines of the equally famous Sonnet CXXIX:

Th' expense of spirit in a waste of shame
Is lust in action.

Under the pressure of mutability 'love' becomes 'lust'; it changes from the most intense and affirmative of human experiences to an expenditure of 'spirit', because some of our deepest aspirations are involved, but it is destined to sterility and to lose itself in 'a waste of shame'. This sonnet and the one quoted above can, in fact, be considered together. Both are reactions to the facts implied in human subjection to time. Love, and friendship which is a reflection of it, are a reaction against the process of temporal decay, an attempt to grasp through accepted experience an intuition of value; but, precisely because they are born in time, they are destined to impermanence. What is rooted in time, time itself destroys. Since love and friendship, though so desirable, are to be vain, the poet's vision of them becomes at times vicious and repellent; their very value, failing to maintain itself by unsupported force of affirmation, only makes them, by an extreme paradox, more potent to corrupt: 'Lilies that fester smell far worse than weeds'.

It was perhaps not an accident that the writing (as we may believe) of many of the Sonnets in which these themes are developed coincides with the first unquestioned masterpieces of Shakespeare's dramatic career. Within a very brief period of time, certainly not more than two years, he produced his first considerable tragedy, *Romeo and Juliet* (1595), a comedy of startling brilliance, *A Midsummer Night's Dream* (1596), and, as if this were not enough, a historical drama, *Richard II* (1596), which gave the chronicle type of play a new dimension and laid the foundation for a series of still greater plays to follow.

Romeo and Juliet has a number of clear points of contact with the Sonnets. These are apparent in the style of the play which at certain points incorporates actual sonnets into the dramatic structure[3] and makes at all times considerable use of sonnet imagery; the theme too turns upon the relation of love to time and adverse circumstance. As the lovers declare their dedication in terms which combine lyrical intensity with conscious literary artifice – the kind of writing which produced many of Romeo's speeches in the famous balcony scene[4] – we are made aware of an intricate compound of conflicting circumstances. Because their youthful love neglects all realities except those which its own affirmation involves, it will end in death; but because it is also a true emotion, because its intensity answers, when all has been said, to an intuition of *value*, of life and generosity – in Juliet's words,

> My bounty is as boundless as the sea,
> My love as deep; the more I give to thee,
> The more I have, for both are infinite . . .
> (II. ii)

it will be able to achieve, even in the doom which overtakes it, a measure of triumph over external circumstance.

This precarious love is seen throughout against the pressure exercised by a world which consistently fails to understand it and which, in the effort to impose its judgements, achieves in the end only its own and the lovers' ruin. It is important to note that much in this tragedy, especially in the first part, shows certain affinities with comedy.[5] This is most obviously true of the interventions of the Nurse, whose speeches of advice and consolation to Juliet[6] catch the wayward rhythms of a meandering, reminiscent utterance in verse just constructed enough to carry us with it in its onward motion. The behaviour of the Capulet and Montague elders is at times comic to the point of farce, and the bickering between their servants so presented as to underline the futility of the motives which separate them. This persistent comic strain, indeed, answers to the very conception of the play. Up to the turning-point (III. i) represented by the unforeseen death of Mercutio, for which Romeo's well-meant intervention is unwittingly responsible, it might be possible to foresee a reconciling conclusion for this action, of the kind which Friar Lawrence is concerned to bring about; the love of the young couple could have served, under different circumstances, to bring about the healing of the feud which for so long and so irrationally divided their elders. This 'alternative' play, of course, is never written, and Romeo's banishment after the revenge wrought upon Tybalt makes it impossible; but the possibility has existed and is sufficiently present to colour our response to the tragic development.

Throughout the play the declared intentions of the characters are consistently thwarted by circumstances which escape their control. Capulet and his wife are determined to force Juliet into what they regard as an appropriate marriage with the Count Paris; but their facile good purposes serve only to hasten disaster, as – in the end – do the well-intentioned devices of Friar Lawrence, who has a truer, if still theoretical understanding of life, but whose age debars him from sympathizing with the urgency of the lovers' feelings. As he is moved to declare when faced with the final outcome of his contrivings,

> A greater power than we can contradict
> Hath thwarted our intents.
>
> (v. iii)

Against this ominous background Romeo and Juliet achieve the brief consummation of their love. It is a consummation at once intense, contradictory, and poised over fear: fear, above all, for the future, whilst life is plucked in breathless haste from the insubstantial present. The nightingale sings, for Juliet, in 'the fearful hollow' of her lover's ear, and Romeo, though exultant in the moment of achievement, can only precariously maintain his happiness. Life is, for him, with Juliet, and absence from her means death: so that when she clings to what she knows to be illusion – 'thou needst not be gone' – he is ready to deny reality in the name of his love: 'I'll say yon grey is not the morning's eye'. Even, however, as he asserts the illusion on which his life rests, she returns to common reality – 'It is the lark that sings so out of tune' – and foresees that they must separate. Truth, then, stands most delicately balanced against illusion: to decide which is which, and to what end they are interwoven, is the crux of this tragedy.

The second play of this period, *A Midsummer Night's Dream*, could be seen as a comic counterpoise to the 'romantic' tragedy. Within the framework of a rational and social attitude to marriage, expressed in the opening scene through Theseus and Hippolyta, it transports two pairs of youthful lovers – Lysander and Hermia, Demetrius and Helena – from 'daylight' life in Athens to the night-time world of the woods, where the irrational but potent impulses which love normally covers are released and their capacity to master these tested. The woods are the scene of jealous rivalry between Oberon and Titania, respectively king and queen of the fairy world: and the spell which Oberon casts on Titania, obliging her to 'dote' on the 'translated' figure of Bottom with his ass's head, is a central symbol of the irrationality and potential destructiveness which form part of the reality of love.

With Titania alienated from her true self, the love of the human pairs is turned into misapprehension and hatred until, having followed their fanciful purposes to a sorry end, they are ready to express themselves as thoroughly chastened. Their delivery depends on that of Titania, whom Oberon is at length ready to release from 'this hateful imperfection' of her eyes. He declares that everything that he has caused to happen in the woods shall be remembered only as 'the fierce vexation of a dream' once the dreamers have been re-called to their true selves, awakening from the following of desire in the night of error to the light of day and the truth of reason.

On the heels of these declarations Titania awakes and Theseus and Hippolyta enter as the sound of hunting horns greets the morning. The stress is now on harmony, the bringing together of 'discord' into music, the uniting of the sounds of nature to those of sociability in 'one mutual cry'. Lysander and Demetrius confess that their recent behaviour has reflected an unreasonable fury, whilst even Bottom, in the act of standing confirmed as an object of ridicule, asserts the 'vision' which he too has been afforded:

I have had a most rare vision. I have had a dream, past the wit of man to say what dream it was. Man is but an ass if he go about to expound this dream. Methought I was – there is no man can tell what. Methought I was, and methought I had, but man is but a patch'd fool if he will offer to say what methought I had. The eye of man hath not heard, the ear of man hath not seen, man's hand is not able to taste, his tongue to conceive, nor his heart to report, what my dream was.

(IV. i)

The substance of his dream lies, like that of every man, on the margin of his perception, and it is beyond his ability to recreate it in the poverty of words. It turns out to be nothing less than an echo, comically confused but none the less compounded of an elusive reality, of St Paul's vision of love as a transforming presence in human life.[7] Love is seen to be at once a folly and to carry within itself, obscured indeed and even subject to absurdity, but none the less real, a glimpse of the divine element in human life. At this point the ridiculous and the sublime meet at the heart of the comic vision.

In the conclusion the various elements of the action are drawn together in a social and civilizing vision. The marriage union is presented as life-giving, joining body and soul, reason and feeling, imagination and fancy in its essential 'truth'. Theseus, indeed, as the representative of 'cool reason', remains to the last distrustful of what he sees as the excesses of 'The lunatic, the lover, and the poet', with the tendency, common to all three, to impose their own imaginative vision upon the real:

> in the night, imagining some fear,
> How easy is a bush suppos'd a bear?
>
> (v. i)

His scepticism, however, is countered, if not annulled, by Hippolyta's answering assertion of the creative harmony which the entire action has so powerfully propounded:

> . . . all the story of the night told over,
> And all their minds transfigured so together,
> More witnesseth than fancy's images,
> And grows to something of great constancy,
> But howsoever strange and admirable.
>
> (v. i)

Against this vision Theseus, as he looks forward to the entry of Bottom and his companions with the Pyramus play, can still speak of 'the anguish of a torturing hour'. In easement of this 'anguish' the lovers are to witness another action in which romantic love is exposed to ridicule, and in relation to which their reactions to what they see – their charity, or lack of it – will throw light upon what kind of men and women they are. As Theseus says, defending in the name of rule the good faith which will render acceptable even the absurdity of these self-appointed actors:

> never anything can be amiss
> When simpleness and duty tender it.
>
> (v. i)

The lesson is once again that prompted by the pageant of the Nine Worthies in *Love's Labour's Lost*:[8] the lesson which those of simple heart offer in loyalty and which the arrogant and the sophisticated ignore at their peril.

The third play written by Shakespeare at this time, *Richard II*, is highly elaborate and formal in style and conception. The formality and the elaboration correspond to an acute and highly personal reading of history. In the play's very selective treatment of its theme we can detect a concern to distinguish fiction from truth, or – to put the matter in another way – to show the downfall of a traditional conception of royalty and its replacement by a political force at once more competent, more truly self-aware, and more precariously built on the foundations of its own desire for power.

The contrast between the two orders is firmly conveyed in terms of character. Richard is presented as a tragic sentimentalist, though one capable from time to time of rousing himself moodily and danger-ously to resentful action:[9] one who habitually uses his moments of misfortune to elaborate his woes, even – actor-like – to take a kind of perverse pleasure in giving expression to his unhappy state. As the new order represented by his rival Bolingbroke establishes itself, the spectacle of the downfall of an anointed but unworthy king merges into that of a human being hunted and betrayed. By the end of the play Richard has penetrated in his isolated prison to a desolate perception of his situation:

> Sometimes am I king;
> Then treasons make me wish myself a beggar,
> And so I am. Then crushing penury
> Persuades me I was better when a king;
> Then I am king'd again; and by and by
> Think that I am unking'd by Bolingbroke,
> And straight am nothing. But whate'er I be,
> Nor I, nor any man that but man is,
> With nothing shall be pleas'd till he be eas'd
> With being nothing.
>
> (v. v)

The intricate balancing of phrases ('am I': 'I am'; 'king': 'unking'd') is designed to lead up to Richard's final confrontation with that awareness of 'nothing' which he sees as built into the human condition. It will be his fate to succumb, almost immediately, to this reality, Bolingbroke's to strive to evade it in the pursuit of power: and at the last, as he is now and only now ready to recognize, the two paths meet in a common submission to illusion.

The achievement represented by the three great plays just con-sidered was followed by two pieces curiously tentative in quality. The first of these, *King John* (*c.* 1596), is one of Shakespeare's most uneven efforts. The dramatic structure of the play seems oddly primitive and much of the writing is either over-rhetorical or simply excessively contrived; but in Philip Faulconbridge, the Bastard, Shakespeare has found a character who stands out in a world in which rival factions, although always ready to assert the highest motives, are in fact moved by self-interest and political calculation. In what may be the play's most memorable utterance, the Bastard gives vivid expression to his sense of an England at war with itself and adrift from its moral bearings:

> I am amaz'd, methinks, and lose my way
> Among the thorns and dangers of this world.
> How easy dost thou take all England up!
> From forth this morsel of dead royalty
> The life, the right, and truth of all this realm
> Is fled to heaven, and England now is left
> To tug and scamble and to part by the teeth
> The unowed interest of proud swelling state.
> Now for the bare-pick'd bone of majesty
> Doth dogged war bristle his angry crest
> And snarleth in the gentle eyes of peace;
> Now powers from home and discontents at home
> Meet in one line, and vast confusion waits,
> As doth a raven on a sick-fall'n beast,
> The imminent decay of wrested pomp.
> Now happy he whose cloak and cincture can
> Hold out this tempest.

> (IV. iii)

His attitude is one that we are invited at once to share and to feel as a problem. On the one hand, the Bastard emerges as honest judge and bluff commentator in a play which he dominates by his level-headed, finally amoral impartiality; on the other, the very detachment which he so confidently asserts and which sometimes allies him to Richard III in his moments of ironic perception will turn, in the long run, into the problem of the man of intelligence and drive whose rational motives are entirely limited to the political. In the later historical plays, and eventually in the character of Edmund in *King Lear*, it will become apparent that the virtues represented by Faulconbridge are seen, by a fundamental paradox, to be founded upon his limitations and so to raise to a high degree what we may call the problem of political behaviour in its relation to moral issues.

The other play of this period, *The Merchant of Venice* (1596/7), is by contrast one of Shakespeare's best-known pieces. It strikes us as being in certain respects a little tentative, not altogether assimilated to a single dominating conception. The contrast between Belmont and the Rialto, 'romantic' love and the pursuit of wealth through merchant enterprise is perhaps incompletely worked out, and the allegory of the caskets through which Bassanio wins Portia can hardly bear the load of moral significance imposed upon it. Above all, the disturbing presence of Shylock threatens to load the comedy with a sombre sense of reality that leaves it, by contrast, and in his absence, curiously deprived of conviction.

It is essential, of course, to avoid any temptation to sentimentalize Shylock in the light of later attitudes. The melodramatic villain, the heartless usurer, and the enemy of Christianity all belong to the conception, and an Elizabethan audience would have found nothing unseemly in the downfall of all three. Shylock is finally condemned by the warped attitudes which lead him to reject life when it is offered to him – by Portia in her famous plea for 'mercy' in the trial scene – upon the only terms on which, according to this comedy, it is available; but the rejection itself takes possession of our minds as a dark and twisted strain that threatens to affect our attitude to the play as a whole. So much is conveyed by Shylock's incisive utterance at his moments of strongest emotion, as in his response to Antonio's embarrassed request for a loan:

> Well, then, it now appears you need my help;
> Go to, then: you come to me, and you say
> 'Shylock, we would have moneys'. You say so –
> You that did void your rheum upon my beard
> And foot me as you spurn a stranger cur
> Over your threshold; moneys is your suit.
> What should I say to you? Should I not say
> 'Hath a dog money?' Is it possible
> A cur can lend three thousand ducats?' Or
> Shall I bend low and, in a bondman's key,
> With bated breath and whisp'ring humbleness,
> Say this:
> 'Fair sir, you spit on me on Wednesday last,
> You spurn'd me such a day; another time
> You call'd me dog; and for these courtesies
> I'll lend you thus much moneys?'

(I. iii)

The flow of the rhythm, with its repetition of key-words ('moneys', 'dog', 'cur'), its calculated pauses, its breaks in the movement of the verse after the accumulation of indignant irony (the short 'Say this', following the broad sweep of 'bated breath and whisp'ring humbleness') all show writing no longer dominated, as even in Marlowe's stronger, simpler effects, by the rigid pattern of sound, but reaching out in the movement of thought and emotion to convey the true impulses of the speaker. We respond here to the unmistakable accents of a reality absent from the 'romantic' scenes of the play, as we do again when Shylock defends the right to 'revenge' which he says he has learnt from Christian example (III. i. 51–64). To 'better instruction' in this way is not to evade the charge of 'villainy' which remains firmly fixed; but we are free to believe that Shakespeare, having originally conceived his character to fit into the plan of his comedy, allowed his imagination to run freely in developing it, even at the risk of threatening the unity of his conception.

The following-up of *Richard II* with the trilogy on English history which bears the successive titles of *Henry IV* Parts 1 and 2 (1597–8) and *Henry V* (1599) brings us to one of the peaks of Shakespeare's achievement during the first half of his career. The broad conception of the series rests upon current interpretations of the events described, and in particular upon the dramatist's reading of the sixteenth-century chronicles of Hall (1548) and Holinshed (1577). The interest of the plays, however, lies less in the traditional conceptions which they embody than in their implications in terms of human behaviour. Already in *Richard II* we have been shown a contrast between a king lawfully enthroned but politically irresponsible and a born politician who achieves his ends through rebellion culminating in a murder which has some of the aspects of sacrilege. In the next two plays, which cover the reign of Bolingbroke as Henry IV, the new king calls his followers to unite in a crusade which is intended both to calm the political passions which he himself exploited to reach the throne and to provide a foundation for the national unity which he now desires. The fact remains that Henry's overthrow and murder of Richard fatally engender the very strife which he aims at ending. The reign which opened with a call to a crusade ends, in Part II, after years of weariness and disillusionment, in a room called 'Jerusalem', which is fated to be his nearest approach to the Holy Land; and in between it has seen little but rebellion, plot and counterplot, and battles where victory serves only to sow the seed for further domestic strife.

Once this conception has been grasped the process of Hal's 'conversion', which Shakespeare found in his sources and which no doubt contributed in no small measure to the popularity of the story can be seen in its true light. In a very important sense there is in Hal's progress no true 'conversion' at all. From the first, he is awaiting the opportune moment for his self-revelation. So much is plainly stated in his opening soliloquy and remains a principal key to his behaviour:

> So, when this loose behaviour I throw off
> *And pay the debt I never promised,*
> By how much better than my word I am,
> By so much shall I falsify men's hopes;
> And, like bright metal on a sullen ground,
> My reformation, glitt'ring o'er my fault,
> *Shall show more goodly and attract more eyes*
> Than that which hath no foil to set it off.
> I'll so offend to make offence a skill,
> Redeeming time when men think least I will.
>
> (Part I, I. ii)

Success in the political vocation, which Hal is conscious of not having sought, ('the debt I never promised') involves readiness to 'redeem time', to declare his choices at the opportune moment and with a mind to their public effect. From this point of view Falstaff and his companions are no more than living examples of the 'misrule' which his father's action has, against his intentions, promoted but which he has never properly understood. The future Henry V *will* understand it, because he has gone so far as to live with it and to experience it in his own person. He has done this in part, no doubt, to seek relief from a reality that has presented itself to him as a constraining imposition; but when the time comes for his tavern associates to be discarded, that necessary decision will come easily to a man who has from the first declared his intention of turning away from them as soon as he has extracted from his contact with them the knowledge he requires of men as they are, and – further – as soon as this rejection will appear at its full value in the public eye.

The stages of Hal's public 'redemption' are roughly speaking two, corresponding to the two plays into which the *Henry IV* action is divided.[10] As a result of his conflict with Harry Percy, a new and

politically practical virtue asserts itself victoriously over an inadequate, dated conception of aristocratic 'honour'. Percy's 'honour',
presented in him as a sincere attribute, is verbal in content, unable
to offer an alternative to the political manoeuvrings which it repudiates but which have nevertheless undermined the traditional
loyalties to which the leaders of the rebel faction, even as they follow
the claims of self-interest, make their appeal.

Set against this background, the Prince's declaration to his father,
made in the course of a scene which stands as a turning-point for the
entire action, resounds in its grim concentration of purpose as nothing
less than the birth of a new order:

> I will redeem all this on Percy's head,
> And, in the closing of some glorious day
> Be bold to tell you *that I am your son*,
> When I will wear a garment all of blood,
> And stain my favours in a bloody mask,
> Which washed away, *shall scour my shame with it*,
> And that shall be the day, whene'er it lights,
> That this same child of honour and renown,
> This gallant Hotspur, this all-praised knight,
> And *your unthought-of Harry* chance to meet.
> For every honour sitting on his helm,
> Would they were multitudes, and on my head
> My shames redoubled! For the time will come
> That I shall make this northern youth exchange
> His glorious deeds for my indignities.
> Percy is but my factor, good my lord,
> To engross up glorious deeds on my behalf;
> And I will call him to so strict account,
> That he shall render every glory up,
> Yea, even the slightest worship of his time,
> Or I will tear the reckoning from his heart.

> (III. ii)

The concentrated ferocity of the speech reflects Hal's response to his
father's bitter denunciation of him as an instrument devised by God
'out of my blood' to 'breed revengement and a scourge for me'. The
resentment is characteristically channelled into a declaration of
practical resolve. By contrast with Percy's flights of rhetoric, Hal's
conception of chivalry will be self-reliant and workaday, conceived in
strict relation to the sober and necessary ends he has proposed to himself. At Shrewsbury a dying tradition, shorn by the impact of new

circumstances of the values which originally justified it, meets a fresh conception of 'virtue',[11] founded on a less prejudiced estimate of the true nature of man as a political being, and inevitably succumbs. But beneath the triumph of the new conception, justified and necessary as it is, there lies a sense of relativity, of inescapable hollowness.

This sense, indeed, is projected for Hal in *Henry IV* Part 2 in a more intimately personal order. Having asserted himself as a modern prince in the exercise of the chivalrous virtues, the Prince needs to overcome himself, to attain the impersonality which his great office requires of him; and this is implied, against an increasingly sombre background of social realities, in his final reconciliation with the Lord Chief Justice:

> There is my hand.
> You shall be as a father to my youth;
> My voice shall sound as you do prompt mine ear;
> And I will stoop and humble my intents
> To your well-practis'd wise directions . . .
>   The tide of blood in me
> Hath proudly flow'd in vanity till now.
> Now doth it turn and ebb back to the sea,
> Where it shall mingle with the state of floods,
> And flow henceforth in formal majesty.
>
>   (v. ii)

After this alone, Hal – ostensibly at peace with himself, confirmed in the exalted selflessness of his vocation – is ready to be crowned.

From this exposition of the development of Hal it emerges that the king can only be understood in relation to the realm over which he exercises his indispensable authority. In *Henry IV* Part 1 this presentation of a reality which expands notably beyond the world of the Court and its 'political' concerns is primarily comic in intention, and concentrated upon the figure of Falstaff in his relationship to the Prince. Through this relationship, Hal is brought into contact with a character who lives by the imaginative transformation of reality, by ignoring 'time' and the necessity which so imposes itself upon the Prince, to 'redeem' it. The result is, in Falstaff, a living picture of disorder, which at the same time implies, without contradicting that reality, a valid comic commentary upon the surrounding action. His function up to the battle of Shrewsbury is evidently in some sense a critical one, involving a judgement, relevant if in no sense final, upon the verbal concept of 'honour' which can be so speciously evoked by generals and politicians to persuade lesser men to die for causes not finally their own. To the somewhat sanctimonious observation of the Prince that he 'owes God a death', his reply is decisive:

'Tis not due yet; I would be loath to pay him before his day. What need I be so forward with him that calls not on me? Well, 'tis no matter; honour pricks me on. Yea, but how if honour prick me off when I come on? How then? Can honour set to a leg? No. . . . Or take away the grief of a wound? No. . . . What is honour? A word. What is in that word? Honour. What is that honour? Air . . . Who hath it? he that died o' Wednesday.

(v. i)

The retort should not, of course, be taken out of its context, or endowed with a validity beyond its scope. When Falstaff refuses to accept the claims of 'honour' as the princes and politicians put them before him, it is not enough to say that he is being cynical. Neither of the contending parties at Shrewsbury is in a position to command the unquestioning allegiance with which, in the idiom of these plays, 'honour' is always linked. Henry, as king, is genuinely anxious to unite England under his rule; but, unable to accept the consequences of his own past, he is driven instead into the self-consuming vanity of civil war. On this conflict, and on the façade of 'honour' which can so speciously cover personal selfishness, Falstaff provides a relevant comment when, over the dead body of Walter Blunt, he advances the claims of life: 'I like not such grinning honour as Sir Walter hath. *Give me life*; which, if I can save, so; if not, honour comes unlooked for, and there's an end.'

The Falstaff of Part 2 is, by comparison a very different figure, grown notably in age and obvious decay as though in anticipation of his necessary rejection by the Prince. 'Do not bid me remember mine end', he begs Doll Tearsheet in the course of an exchange which is at once grotesque and deeply moving, and the plea is typical of a new and more explicitly moralizing spirit in the play itself. His closest acquaintance is now Justice Shallow, and the topic which binds them together is the memory of past youth, conceived partly in irony and partly in pathos:

SHALLOW. I was once of Clement's Inn, where I think they will talk of mad Shallow yet.
SILENCE. You were call'd 'lusty Shallow' then, cousin.

SHALLOW. By the mass, I was call'd anything; and I would have done anything indeed too, and roundly too ... Jesu, Jesu, the mad days that I have
spent! and to see how many of my old acquaintances are dead!

SILENCE. We shall all follow, cousin.

SHALLOW. Certain, 'tis certain; very sure, very sure. Death, as the Psalmist
saith, is certain to all; all shall die.

(III. ii)

Death is certain. The Falstaff of Part 2 is reminded at every turn of this
truth, which in the previous play he had so effectively evaded. Time
has caught up with him, as it has with nearly all the political agents in
this play. His age stresses at such moments as these a sense of death
which is shared, as one element in a complex effect, by the very order
which has seen Henry IV's rise to power. The picture of an England
in disorder, the background of the Prince's growth in political
competence, expands from court and tavern, already conceived in
parallel fashion, to include Gloucestershire, the local foundations of
life in a rural society; and the sense of age and decay which
accompanies this presentation is a necessary background to Hal's
assumption of the vocation which circumstances have imposed upon
him and which requires his rejection of Falstaff as a necessary condition.

The terms of that rejection, when it comes, are at once dignified,
appropriately regal, and strangely inhuman. Falstaff, with his tavern
associates, has come to be present at Hal's coronation and in the hope
of receiving the means to discharge his long-standing debt to
Shallow. He approaches the newly-crowned king with a mixture of
true feeling and outrageous appeal to sentiment: 'God save thee, my
sweet boy! ... My king! My Jove! I speak to thee, my heart', and
receives the stern, controlled expression of Henry's firm resolution:

> I know thee not, old man. Fall to thy prayers.
> How ill white hairs become a fool and jester!
> I have long dreamt of such a kind of man,
> So surfeit-well'd, so old, and so profane;
> But, being awaked, I do despise my dream.
> Make less thy body hence, and more thy grace;
> Leave gormandizing; know the grave doth gape
> For thee thrice wider than for other men –
> Reply not to me with a fool-born jest;
> Presume not that I am the thing I was,
> For God doth know, so shall the world perceive,

That I have turned away my former self;
So will I those that kept me company.

(v. v)

At this point, once more, we must not simplify the issues. Henry has made the choice which his birth and his vocation have imposed upon him and, in making it, has accepted the necessary cost, which – as we may feel – amounts to a certain rejection of common humanity. The cost is implied in the dismissal of past friendship ('I know thee not, old man'), in the tight-lipped implication of disgust conveyed by his 'leave gormandizing', and in the studied gesture to the gallery which accompanies his declared assumption of a new life:

For God doth know, *so shall the world perceive*,
That I have turned away my former self;

awareness of it affects our perception of the encounter and dissuades us from any one-sided or easy evaluation of its effect. It colours our understanding of Henry V's victorious progress in the last play of the series, in which Falstaff is remembered, significantly, in the moving account of his death (II. iii) and in which we are told of him by the Hostess that 'The king has killed his heart'. (II. i. 84)

To recognize this aspect of Henry's story must not lead us to the belief that Shakespeare intended to convict his hero of hypocrisy. The virtues which enabled him, on the eve of Agincourt, to unite his followers in the true fellowship of a 'band of brothers' are of no mean order, and are not made less so by their dedication to the public, the political sphere. The fact remains that the public vocation of the king, upon the exercise of which depends order within the realm and success in its foreign wars, demands from him an impersonality which borders on the inhuman. When Henry V, during his debate with Williams and Bates on the eve of battle (IV. i.), discusses most searchingly the implications of his power, he approaches closely the spirit in which the great tragedies were conceived:

... the king is but a man as I am; the violet smells to him as it doth to me; ... all his senses have but human conditions: his ceremonies laid by, in his naked-ness he appears but a man; and though his affections are higher mounted than ours, yet when they stoop they stoop with the like wing.

(IV. i)

The universality of the argument, in the true tragic fashion, transcends the royal situation. Men, differentiated by a 'ceremony' ultimately vain, are united in their common weakness, and the most notable feature of human behaviour seems to the speaker to be its helplessness before the universal stooping of the affections. In this respect, at least, the king is one with his men; and, just because he is so like them, because his senses too 'have but human conditions', there is something precarious and disproportionate in his absolute claim upon the allegiance of his followers. In the double link which, at the heart of an England which these plays have depicted in the widening scope of its varied social relationships, binds Falstaff to Hal as necessary sacrifice and vivid protest opposed to tried virtue and firm competence, we find ourselves in a mood that already anticipates the great tragedies.

NOTES

1. This point of view was well argued by L. C. Knights in an essay on Shakespeare's Sonnets in *Explorations* (1946).

2. cp. *Measure for Measure*, II. ii. 163–72.

3. The opening Prologue and the Chorus to Act II are both sonnets, and Romeo and Juliet, at their first meeting, address one another in sonnet form. See I. v. 93–106.

4. See, e.g., II. ii. 2–21.

5. For a study of the play from this point of view, see Susan B. Snyder's recent book, *The Comic Matrix of Shakespeare's Tragedies* (Princeton, 1979), 56–70.

6. For a good example of the Nurse's use of blank verse see I. iii. 16–48.

7. I Corinthians ii, 9.

8. *Love's Labour's Lost*, v. ii. 520–704.

9. cp. his reaction to the illness of his uncle John of Gaunt at I. iv. 54–64.

10. Whether the two plays were originally conceived as a two-part unit, or whether the second represents an afterthought, is a problem that has been much discussed and never definitively resolved.

11. I use the word in the Machiavellian sense of *virtù*, which implies self-awareness and a clear perception of ends in view and the willing of the means necessary to attain them.

SHAKESPEARE: THE MIDDLE PLAYS

J. C. MAXWELL

Every period of Shakespeare's work is likely, on close examination, to impress us by its diversity, but this is particularly true of the period dealt with in the present chapter. The earlier years had been dominated by the sequence of history plays, and the comedies of those years form a group through which some continuity of development can be traced. The 'tragic' period, too, however reluctant we may be to draw biographical inferences from it, is a chronological fact in so far as Shakespeare seems to have written nothing but tragedies between *Measure for Measure* and his share in *Pericles* (1607?), and the final romances or tragi-comedies have more in common with each other than any of them have with earlier plays. But for the years 1599–1603 we have, according to the accepted chronology, the oddly assorted group: *Julius Caesar, As You Like It, Hamlet, Troilus and Cressida, Twelfth Night*, and *Measure for Measure*, along with, possibly, *All's Well That Ends Well*, which is suspected of combining work of different periods, and *The Merry Wives of Windsor*, which may be earlier and in any case is of no great moment. *Othello*, too, though it has usually been dated later, must belong to these years, since it is echoed in the 'bad' Quarto of *Hamlet* (1603).

The beginning of this period coincides with an important event in Shakespeare's career as a man of the theatre. The Globe playhouse was opened in 1599, and it has been thought probable that *Julius Caesar* was the first Shakespeare play to be presented there, and that the 'All the world's a stage' speech in *As You Like It* (wholly traditional though it is in content) had a special topicality in view of the Globe's motto: *Totus mundus agit histrionem*. Both these plays look back as well as forward. The word 'transitional' is particularly apt for *Julius Caesar* as a link between the English histories and the tragedies to follow, and *As You Like It*, while recognizably the successor of the earlier comedies, has a higher satirical content than anything that precedes it.

The major plays that follow offer enough problems, both individually and as a group. *Troilus and Cressida* and *Measure for Measure* have long been classed (along with *All's Well*) as 'problem plays', or as 'bitter' or 'dark' comedies. Recently, the affinities between *Hamlet* and *Troilus and Cressida* have been emphasized, and, though in rather a different sense, *Hamlet* has always been a central Shakespearean problem. As for *Twelfth Night*, critics have tended to evade consideration of its place in Shakespeare's development by dealing with it (reasonably enough from the point of view of a classification independent of chronology) along with such earlier comedies as *The Merchant of Venice*, *Much Ado About Nothing*, and *As You Like It*. Yet it has at least one thing in common with *Troilus and Cressida* which differentiates it from earlier plays – a strong affinity with the comedies of Ben Jonson.

It seems safe to say – so long as it is realized that 'technique' is not for Shakespeare an end in itself – that during these years more than at any other time Shakespeare was deeply concerned with technical experiment and innovation. If none of the plays is entirely satisfying in comparison with the greater ones to come, or even with some that had preceded them, it may be less because of any spiritual crisis in Shakespeare's personal life than because of a tendency for virtuosity to outrun mastery over experience. Even in the least 'difficult' of these plays, *Twelfth Night*, which is justly praised as a masterpiece of stage-craft and is perhaps the most popular of Shakespeare's comedies, there is a certain lack of warmth, a sense that the poet is not creating from the deepest springs of his experience. And the other 'well-made play' with which this period closes, *Othello*, also has limitations. The discussions which follow are not proportionate in length to the relative importance of the plays. Rather than give a cursory survey of the whole period, I have preferred to go into some detail where it seemed possible to make fresh suggestions.

I defer to the traditional order of treatment to the extent of taking first *As You Like It* and *Twelfth Night*, although the latter is probably later than *Hamlet* and not much before *Troilus and Cressida*. There is no doubt that both are most naturally considered in relation to the comedies that precede them, and in reading *Twelfth Night* in particular we are not surprised that Shakespeare should have experimented no further with comedy of this kind. It has the limited perfection that marks the end of a process of development. It is through-and-through dramatic; there is no unresolved residue to lead Shakespeare on to an attempt to embody more adequately what he has to say.

As You Like It is less obviously a unified play than *Twelfth Night*, though it is pure comedy, in contrast to the tragicomedy of *The Merchant of Venice* and *Much Ado About Nothing*. It is customary to sentimentalize it as a carefree idyll, to lay stress on such trifling details as the supposed loyalty of Touchstone to his mistress (which Shakespeare takes no more interest in, once he has used it to get him into the forest) and in general to draw heavily on Shakespeare's notoriously ample reserves of 'ripe humanity'. But the play deserves more careful critical attention than this.

It is a play which it is well worth while to compare with its main narrative source, Thomas Lodge's *Rosalynde* (1590). This is an attractive if rather diffuse narrative, whose success (within its limitations) depends upon staking everything on unity of tone; it is the euphuistic pastoral from start to finish. Shakespeare does not greatly modify the main plot, though he concentrates it. What he adds is not narrative complication but comments from varying points of view. The result is that the play is as far as it could be from Lodge's single-mindedness. After the first act, it is substantially a series of relatively isolated scenes which provide a means of bringing together contrasting attitudes towards the life of the forest. But through them runs the narrative thread from Lodge: the theme of Orlando's wooing of the disguised Rosalind. This theme not only provides continuity, it is also the occasion for the most subtle version of the ironic treatment of pastoral convention with particular reference to love.

It is essential that the love between Rosalind and Orlando should be entirely genuine. There may be a touch of irony in Shakespeare's offhand acceptance of the love-at-first-sight convention in Act I, but once the stage is set there is never any doubt that the plot is destined to conform to the pattern of romantic love. The strength of the play lies in this: that it is into the heart of this love-making that Shakespeare is able to introduce, without cynicism, his most exquisitely balanced piece of irony, at once sympathetic and detached:

ORLANDO. Then in mine own person I die.
ROSALIND. No, faith, die by attorney. The poor world is almost six thousand

years old, and in all this time there was not any man died in his own person, *videlicet*, in a love-cause. Troilus had his brains dash'd out with a Grecian club; yet he did what he could to die before, and he is one of the patterns of love. Leander, he would have liv'd many a fair year, though Hero had turn'd nun, if it had not been for a hot midsummer night; for, good youth, he went but forth to wash him in the Hellespont, and being taken with the cramp was drown'd, and the foolish chroniclers of that age found it was 'Hero of Sestos'. But these are all lies: men have died from time to time, and worms have eaten them, but not for love.

(IV. i)

Shakespeare has led up to this by similar criticism applied to more obvious aberrations than Orlando's, as in III. v with its languishing swain and scornful shepherdess, and here too Rosalind has had the last word: 'down on your knees, And thank heaven, fasting, for a good man's love'; but it is where the underlying feeling is most serious that the wit is most vigorous.

Rosalind is not the only commentator in the play, and its nature will become clearer if we consider her relation to the others. Both Jaques and Touchstone are added to the narrative source, and both are onlookers rather than participants. The sententiousness of Jaques is a butt for all the other characters – when we first see him (II. vii) he is blissfully unaware that the fool he met in the forest has been fooling *him* – and Orlando, even in the throes of his love-melancholy, has been able to put him in his place (III. ii. 270–314). But it is Rosalind who gives the crispest exposition of his absurdity (IV. i. 1–31) in a passage which aptly leads up to the greater subtlety of her mockery of Orlando.

Touchstone* is a more complex figure. He is sometimes allowed to be the mouthpiece of a satiric intention, as in his low-life parody of pastoral love in II. iv. But even here his range is limited; he is, says Rosalind, 'wiser than he is ware of'. While he can fool Jaques, he is easily foiled in his attempt to confuse the rustic simplicity of Corin in III. ii; this seems to me the obvious point of that encounter, which has prompted the most extraordinarily solemn interpretations, crediting Touchstone now with penetrating critical insight, now with nihilistic gloom.[1] As the play proceeds, Touchstone is less and less able to

---

* He ought not, strictly, to appear under this name in the Dramatis Personae. *Touchstone* is an assumed name like *Ganymede* and *Aliena*; see the Folio's initial stage direction in II. iv.

convey the author's comment on the action, and he is finally restricted to providing in his marriage with Audrey a sort of hymeneal anti-masque and to playing the professional fool at tedious length – if anything in Shakespeare is dead, it is surely the satire on duelling etiquette in v. iv. We end with Rosalind in undisputed control of her own destiny and that of the other characters. There is not even a suggestion that the usurping Duke's melodramatic conversion is more than a device to wind up the play: it needs a Jaques to take it seriously. And the epilogue belongs to Rosalind with as full right as that of *Twelfth Night* to Feste.

The influence of Ben Jonson's early comedies[2] (in one of which, *Every Man In His Humour*, Shakespeare is recorded as having acted) is pervasive in *Twelfth Night*, but does not obtrude itself as something alien. That part of the play in which it is prominent – the story of Malvolio's gulling by Sir Toby and his associates – has been described as 'the comic underplot', but *Twelfth Night* is remarkable for the absence of a clear division into main action and sub-plot, and such a description is of use only as a corrective to romantic attempts to centre the whole play on Malvolio, who is no more sentimentalized by Shakespeare than is Shylock. There is not the contrast that is usual, especially in the plays of Shakespeare's early maturity, between a more and a less sophisticated society, each relatively self-contained, with cross-references and comments on the main action from the world of the subordinate action. There is, rather, a single society, with subtle internal gradations. This makes possible a delicately comic treatment of the love of Orsino and the self-conscious retirement of Olivia. Shakespeare does not want to satirize heavily the element of affectation in either. Hence our sense of the ridiculous is directed primarily towards Malvolio, whose sickness of self-love (I. v. 96) Olivia is well able to diagnose even before it is fully displayed in the plot against him. Olivia might tend to seem silly – the theme of infatuation for a girl in disguise calls for careful handling – if she were not so obviously sensible by contrast with Malvolio. In the more isolated 'world' of Belmont, Shakespeare would not have ventured to expose Portia to any comparable risk of ridicule. He goes even further towards presenting Orsino in a comic light, and here there is added difficulty that Orsino must be available for a sudden transference of affection at the end of the play; but Shakes-

peare prevents undue attention to this element of the story by inter-
posing the farcical climax to the gulling of Malvolio.

The comparison with Jonson may be dwelt on once more. With
the possible exception of Malvolio, *Twelfth Night* does not contain
any of the great 'characters' of Shakespeare. Now, even if we are
on our guard against the excesses of nineteenth-century 'character-
criticism', we have to admit as a matter of history that Falstaff,
Hamlet, and many other Shakespearian characters have imposed
themselves on the imagination of readers with a certain independence
of the plays in which they figure. While allusions to Jonson's plays in
the seventeenth century were considerably more frequent than those
to Shakespeare's, certain individual characters, especially Falstaff,
were far more often referred to than any of Jonson's.[3] Here, then,
is a Jonsonian trait in *Twelfth Night*, and the resemblance can be
illustrated also by reference to one of the best-known critical judgements on the two writers. 'Whereas in Shakespeare', says T. S. Eliot,[4]
'the effect is due to the way in which the characters *act upon* one
another, in Jonson it is given by the way in which the characters
fit in with each other.' The contrast is not an absolute one, but in
this respect too Shakespeare is closer to Jonson in *Twelfth Night* than
elsewhere.

Julius Caesar is a play which well deserves study for its own sake,
though its place in Shakespeare's development as a tragic dramatist
has often, reasonably enough, been the centre of interest. Shakespeare
has evidently carried over to a different subject some of the methods
used in the English history plays. He is, however, freed from certain
limitations. Especially in the first history plays, though even there
he remodels his historical material, he has to work within an annalistic
framework; and up to the end of the series the king's reign remains
the unit of construction. In *Julius Caesar* there is no restriction of
this kind. He can take the momentous event as the centre of his play,
and the peculiarities of construction in *Julius Caesar* arise largely from
the fact that it is the Shakespeare play which takes its unity most
notably from a single event: the death of Caesar, the central secular
event in world history. This is the simplest way of describing how
the play hangs together: it has been elaborated by critics who have
remarked that the 'spirit of Caesar' is more powerful than the living

Caesar had been, and Shakespeare himself makes this point: 'O Julius Caesar, thou art mighty yet!' It seems wiser to stop short of invoking such an abstraction as 'Caesarism'; Shakespeare shows conspicuous discretion in not raising in our minds the question of what Caesar's rule would really have been like. What matters for the play is people's hopes and fears about it, and the brutality and incompetence of the triumvirs' rule which takes its place.

So much for the relation of the play to the English history plays. The other element in it which has been discussed in relation to Shakespeare's development is the figure of Brutus. The notion of Brutus as an embryo Hamlet has been specially popular.[5] The comparison is legitimate so long as it does not seek to establish an exclusive line of development; more than *Hamlet* is foreshadowed by *Julius Caesar* as a whole, and Wilson Knight[6] has done a service by pointing out how much of Macbeth, too, can be seen in Brutus. But one Shakespearean theme which becomes predominant in *Hamlet* certainly makes its first notable appearance in the presentation of Brutus in *Julius Caesar*: the notion of a disparity between the man and what he does. This notion still seems somewhat intrusive: the play is not built around it as *Hamlet* is. The result is (to exaggerate a little) that where Hamlet is a mystery Brutus is a puzzle. Two factors contribute to make this so. The first is that, as I have said, Shakespeare is attempting something new. The second is that, as has often been pointed out, he is committed to presenting a doctrinaire intellectual, whose doctrine (classical republicanism) is one with which he has no spontaneous imaginative sympathy. Yet he is surprisingly successful in making something positive out of his limitations. The best example is Brutus's soliloquy in II. i. Coleridge's difficulties with this were the difficulties of a true critic; Shakespeare seems here to be whittling away the whole meaning of theoretic republicanism, and it is not an adequate answer to point to the monarchical assumptions of Shakespeare's day. Brutus in this soliloquy is and is not a republican, and the obscurities in the speech, though in part the result of Shakespeare's lack of sympathy with the ideas involved, also convey 'the instinct of a man over the threshold of whose awareness a terrible doubt perpetually threatens to lap'.[7]

Enough has been said about the links between *Julius Caesar* and some of Shakespeare's earlier and later work. Among its qualities considered as an independent play, I shall single out only one – its moral and political realism. When Shakespeare wrote, there was already a large body of interpretations of the fall of Caesar, both in drama and elsewhere, and there was by no means a single orthodox view. But there was a tradition of partisan interpretation, whether on the republican or the monarchical side. Shakespeare shows his preference for a more humanized treatment by taking Plutarch as his starting-point rather than any of the sixteenth-century dramatic versions. He does show the influence of the latter as well, but the bombastic elements in Caesar himself which have given offence, and have raised doubts as to Shakespeare's intentions, are markedly toned down from earlier Senecan dramas in Latin, and from that curious anonymous play – academic but with strong affinities to Marlowe – *Caesar's Revenge* (c. 1592–6). But in the latter the whole play is bombastic in tone. Shakespeare has modified the traditional stage Caesar, but he has modified the staple of the play's language far more, so that Caesar himself stands out. The exact purpose of this treatment is open to dispute, but what seems clear is that Caesar speaks as he does because of some realistic and psychological intention on Shakespeare's part, perhaps, as Stewart suggests, to convey 'the impression of one physically fretted to decay, and opposing to the first falterings of the mind an increasingly rigid and absolute assertion of the Caesar idea'.[8]

Here, then, there is psychological realism. Equally pronounced is the moral realism with which the conspiracy is viewed. Whatever may be the ideological veneer, murder remains murder. There are greater and more complex things in Shakespeare, but there is nothing which better displays clarity and sanity of moral vision than Act III of *Julius Caesar*, with Brutus's high-minded sacrificial attitude towards murder displayed without comment and condemning itself simply by expressing itself:

> Stoop, Romans, stoop,
> And let us bathe our hands in Caesar's blood
> Up to the elbows, and besmear our swords;
> Then walk we forth even to the market-place,
> And waving our red weapons o'er our heads,
> Let's all cry, 'Peace, freedom, and liberty'.
>
> (III. i)

Pope was shocked by this from Brutus, and transferred it to Casca. But Shakespeare knew better. And after self-revelation, the working-out of the consequences in action: Antony's servant comes with a message; Antony himself echoes and parodies the assassins' horrible self-exaltation – 'whilst your purpled hands do reek and smoke ... The choice and master spirits of this age'. But they are so infatuated that they cannot see themselves aright in the mirror held up to them, and we realize that their fate is sealed.

Many of the 'problems' connected with *Hamlet* have been such as to distract attention from the play itself. The existence of three independent texts, the earliest of which differs greatly from the other two, and the evidence for a still earlier play on the subject, have contributed to this. Fortunately, opinion has now come to rest at a point between absolute scepticism and excessive credulity. It is generally agreed that behind Shakespeare's play lies a play of the late 1580s, very likely by Thomas Kyd. But few would claim to be able to reconstruct that play even in outline, and there is very little in the earliest printed text, the 'Bad Quarto' of 1603, that cannot be explained as an attempt to reconstruct from memory the full Shakespearean play as we have it in the two 'good' editions (Second Quarto and Folio), a play probably written in or about 1600. These findings of recent scholarship have the value for the critic that good scholarship customarily has: to send him back to the play, and set him to work on his proper task, the imaginative interpretation of what he has in front of him and not of something else which may be conjectured to have once existed. The futility of much that has been written about *Hamlet* can be appreciated by imagining the sort of 'explanations' of difficulties in *King Lear* that might have been devised if *The True Chronicle History of King Leir* had not survived but had been known to have existed.

To say this is not to advocate taking *Hamlet* out of its historical and literary setting. It is more important that it is a 'revenge tragedy', with affinities to Kyd's surviving *Spanish Tragedy*, than that it may well be indebted to a play by Kyd on this very subject. There is even a sense, very well brought out by Professor Lawlor,[9] in which *Hamlet* is the *only* revenge tragedy of its period. It is the only play in which a real tragic conflict arises directly out of the imposition of the task of revenge upon its hero. In other plays dealing with the subject the ethics of revenge are raised directly as an issue bearing on the hero's conduct, and he makes his decision either for or (as in Tourneur's *Atheist's Tragedy*) against revenge. In such plays we have a combination of melodrama and thesis play. (This is not true, in spite of its title, of the *Revenger's Tragedy*, which stands apart from the main tradition in various ways.) But in *Hamlet*, just because the central moral question about revenge is not overtly raised, and is, indeed, kept from the full recognition of the hero, it can be built into the central fabric of the play, so that we have, in Professor Lawlor's words, 'a man commanded to do what he has no assurance is right . . . a situation of pure tragedy'.

Such a description gives precision to what has often been said about Hamlet from varying points of view: that he stands between two worlds, belonging fully to neither. If we are not careful, an account of this kind will dissolve both the prince and the play into mere symbols in a broadly sketched philosophy of history. Yet that sense of incongruity between central figure and background remains, and this is best attributed not to Hamlet's weakness, not to his inability to make up his mind, not to the recalcitrance of an inherited plot, not to Shakespeare's failure to find an 'objective correlative' for his experience, but to the decision to leave the framework of a revenge play standing, while raising the moral problem of revenge only by implication, and by that very fact giving it a more universal significance than it had had before on the English stage.

The incongruity I have referred to is felt very specially in the contrast between action and soliloquy. The action of the whole play is notably varied and spectacular. Dr Johnson recorded this with characteristic force: 'The incidents are so numerous that the argument of the play would make a long tale . . . New characters appear from time to time in continual succession, exhibiting various forms of life and particular modes of conversation.' And Shakespeare had been before him in the description of his own play:

> So shall you hear
> Of carnal, bloody, and unnatural acts,
> Of accidental judgments, casual slaughters;

> Of deaths put on by cunning and forc'd cause,
> And, in this upshot, purposes mistook
> Fall'n on th' inventors' heads.
>
> (v. ii)

Nor would a summary of Hamlet's own acts during the play make him seem out of place in it. It is in the soliloquies that we find practically all the evidence for the view of Hamlet as one who delays to act. The climax of this difficulty comes in Hamlet's dialogue with the ghost in the bedchamber scene. Hamlet asks:

> Do you not come your tardy son to chide,
> That, laps'd in time and passion, lets go by
> Th' important acting of your dread command?

And the ghost falls in with Hamlet's own view of himself:

> ... this visitation
> Is but to whet thy almost blunted purpose.
>
> (III. iv)

Analysis in the study may think out ingenious explanations of this dialogue, but the plain fact remains: Hamlet's purpose is said to be 'amost blunted' at a time when he has less than a hundred lines earlier performed the decisive action of stabbing the man he takes to be Claudius. (From some accounts of the scene, one would think, on discovering that the body was that of Polonius, Hamlet ought to have said to Gertrude: 'Excuse me, I must now go and kill the right man.') The double vision of Hamlet's behaviour is thus no oversight on Shakespeare's part: it is built into the fabric of the whole play.

The remainder of the space that can be spared for *Hamlet* I devote to a single problem of dramatic technique. The opening scene is deservedly a classic for stage-craft and creation of atmosphere. But it may be asked why it should be there at all. Is there not a risk of anticlimax in the next ghost scene once the theme of mystery has been so thoroughly exploited in this first one? The scene is, at any rate, typical of Shakespeare in two ways: it illustrates his technique of anticipation and his use of the false scent. He often paves the way for the full exploitation of a theme by introducing it in a less elaborate fashion at an earlier stage. As for the 'false scent', it may sound more appropriate to detective story than to poetic drama (and critics of *Hamlet* have not always kept the two things at a proper distance), but it has a very genuine function in this play. The suggestion of a danger threatening from outside is made at some length:

> ... tell me he that knows,
> Why this same strict and most observant watch
> So nightly toils the subject of the land?
>
> (I. i)

And the answer describes in considerable detail the political relations between Denmark and Norway, and the conclusion is drawn:

> Well may it sort that this portentous figure
> Comes armed through our watch, so like the king
> That was and is the question of these wars.
>
> (I. i)

If we start thus with a false but plausible diagnosis, we are the better able to realize the difficulties that a more searching investigation will involve. And right through, *Hamlet* is a play one of whose main themes is the bringing to light of what is hidden.

It is not perhaps so clear why Shakespeare sacrifices the effect of making the ghost's meeting with Hamlet coincide with his first appearance. One obvious thing he gains is an effective contrast between the first scene and the superficial brilliance of the second; we have the sense that behind all this the ghost and all he stands for is waiting. But is it necessary for this that Hamlet should not yet have met the ghost? Yes, if we are to have the soliloquy in I. ii, whose purpose is to show us the impact on Hamlet of the known, external facts: and the full effect of that soliloquy depends on the combination of ignorance on Hamlet's part with vague knowledge on that of the audience. As far as Hamlet knows, no action that will have any influence on what happens is possible for him – not even the substitute offered by words ('break, my heart, for I must hold my tongue'). Yet the audience at one and the same time partakes in this sense of impotence and anticipates the new factor that the news brought by Horatio and the others is just about to introduce. The new sense of direction and purpose that this brings is summed up in the final words of the scene:

> ... would the night were come!
> Till then sit still, my soul: foul deeds will rise,
> Though all the earth o'erwhelm them, to men's eyes.

This 'sitting still', in purposeful anticipation, is a very different thing from the state symbolized in the 'unweeded garden' of the soliloquy, that does nothing but grow to seed.

Part of the effectiveness of presenting the ghost and Hamlet separately in the first two scenes lies in the sense conveyed that each is groping out towards the other. Neither figure is complete in itself, and the play will make sense only when they are brought into contact. In fact, the imperfections of the contact, when it does come, are largely responsible for the complications of the central parts of the play. But further exploration must be here left to the reader.

Troilus and Cressida is probably the most isolated of the plays discussed here, though it is linked to *Hamlet* by its imagery and to *Twelfth Night* by its affinities with Jonsonian comedy.[10] It is pretty clear that the play was not written for Shakespeare's usual audience of the public theatre, and a number of legal references, and the general tone of the play with its combination of ratiocination and specially obtrusive bawdry, favour the suggestion that it was designed for an Inns of Court audience – the nearest thing that Elizabethan England could offer to an undergraduate audience of today.

Shakespeare takes advantage of the fact that he is addressing a sophisticated audience, to whom the central characters in this story are familiar, even proverbial, figures. He even calls attention to the familiarity, with ironic effect, at one of the crucial points of the action. Troilus has proclaimed his undying faithfulness, and Cressida replies, concluding with the wish that, if she is false, the accepted comparison for all 'false maids in love' may be 'as false as Cressid'. Pandarus then sums up: 'if ever you prove false one to another, ... let all pitiful goers-between be call'd to the world's end after my name; call them all Pandars; let all constant men be Troiluses, all false women Cressids, and all brokers-between Pandars! say, Amen' (III. ii. 206–12). The purpose of calling attention to the traditional roles which await the three is sufficiently urgent to override the logical contradiction between 'false *one to another*' and 'all *constant*' men'.

Shakespeare, then, has taken a traditional story, more medieval than classical in its associations – for the English reader, the three main characters are to all intents and purposes the creation of Chaucer – and made of it a play with affinities to Jonson's 'comical satire'. What can be said about the mood and purport of the play? Stagnation and inconclusiveness are perhaps the characteristics that strike us most forcibly. On the public (or military-political) side, when action does get going at the end of the play, it is purposeless violence. Hector for the second time in the play (the first has been his acquiescence in the refusal to surrender Helen) acts against his own better judgement, against the voice of reason and justice, ironically embodied on each occasion in the mad Cassandra, and goes to his death. Troilus, having lost all that makes life mean anything to him, ceases to be the model chivalrous warrior described by Ulysses, and becomes, as Hector calls him, a 'savage', and the action of the play ends with his unbalanced and (as we know) fruitless 'hope and revenge'. Is there, then, cynicism and nihilism at the heart of the play? There is no need to think so, although the society depicted in it is more radically diseased than that in any other play of Shakespeare, and more than in the comparable plays of Jonson, where the assumption is that the cure for what is amiss is in principle simple, though not necessarily easy to put into practice. But this is also the play which furnishes the fullest, and most often quoted, version in Shakespeare of the Elizabethan doctrine of social and cosmic order, the speech of Ulysses in I. iii. 75–137. It is equally important that that speech should be there and that it should be ineffectual. The doctrine stands, whether it can be put into practice or not, yet perhaps Shakespeare would not have given it such explicit and lengthy expression if he had not wanted to mark the contrast between what Ulysses here says and what he can actually do in the situation with which he is faced. He can only propose to exloit, in the public interest, the evil and disruptive individualism of Ajax and Achilles:

> Two curs shall tame each other: pride alone
> Must tarre the mastiffs on, as 'twere their bone.
>
> (I. iii)

If on the Greek side we have sound principles among the leaders, but a fatal gap between principles and application, the Trojan case is equally clear: open violation of 'these moral laws Of nature and of nations' – a technical phrase that would be full of meaning to Shakespeare's original audience. Nothing could be more misguided than the attempt to see the Greeks and the Trojans as the representatives of rival 'values' – 'intellect' and 'intuition' – with Shakespeare conveying his preference for 'intuition'. Certain positive qualities are, it is implied, more conspicuous on the Trojan side: the Trojans are more 'sprightly' than 'the dull and factious nobles of the Greeks', and the verse of the Greek council scene assumes a lighter, less constricted movement when Aeneas enters to propose an end to 'this dull and long-continued truce'. But the notion of a supra-rational intuition has no place in the thought of Shakespeare or of his age, for which the time-honoured antithesis of reason and passion is adequate, and in terms of that the condemnation of both sides is clear. The public world of the play is one in which action in defiance of moral standards proceeds unchecked, but the standards are plain for all to see, and they are the same for all: reasonable but not therefore coldly and restrictively intellectual. This view of the world of the play does not belong entirely to the medieval 'degradation' of the Troy story. Almost all that we find in Shakespeare had already been seen in Homer by Horace:

> seditione, dolis, scelere atque libidine et ira
> Iliacos intra muros peccatur et extra.
> *(Epistles*, i. ii. 15–16)★

Nor are other structural elements in the play without classical warrant. Achilles is indeed degraded, but the broad contrast between Ulysses on the one hand and Ajax and Achilles on the other – between intelligence and brute force – goes back to that most popular of Elizabethan classics, Ovid's *Metamorphoses*, where the contest between Ulysses and Ajax for the arms of Achilles is conceived precisely in these terms.

What relation does the story of Troilus and Cressida bear to the whole Greek and Trojan setting? Clearly, love and war are associated in a very intimate way. Troilus himself expresses this at the beginning of the play:

> Why should I war without the walls of Troy,
> That find such cruel battle here within?
> (I. i)

★ 'By faction, by deceits, by crime, by lust, and by anger, they offend within and without the walls of Ilium' (translation, Lonsdale and Lee).

where there is an effective double-meaning in 'within' – taking the two lines together, the obvious meaning is 'within Troy', but line 3 also conveys a suggestion of conflict within Troilus himself, and it is this idea that is carried further in what follows:

> But I am weaker than a woman's tear,
> Tamer than sleep, fonder than ignorance,
> Less valiant than the virgin in the night,
> And skilless as unpractis'd infancy.
>
> (I. i)

We are never allowed to forget the parallelism between love and war, and in this play, in spite of its impassioned set-speeches, we are never far from the innuendoes to which this parallelism gives rise. It is certainly present in the reference to the virgin's lack of valour, which suggests such comments as that of Marlowe in *Hero and Leander*: 'In such wars women use but half their strength'; indeed, the tone of Shakespeare's treatment of love in this play frequently recalls the mock-seriousness of Marlowe's poem. The hero of each is ironically presented as a mixture of naïveté and sophistication, and the detachment achieved in *Hero and Leander* by the tone of the narrator is embodied by Shakespeare in the commentary of Pandarus.

In this respect the first scene sets the tone of the play. There is a sharp contrast between Troilus's high-flown verse and Pandarus's prose comments. But Troilus is perfectly willing to move from the one plane to the other, and to enter into the spirit of Pandarus's bantering: 'He that will have a cake out of the wheat must needs tarry the grinding'. Thus, right at the beginning we have, in connection with love, the imagery drawn from food which Caroline Spurgeon[11] notes as linking this play with *Hamlet*. What is specially typical of *Troilus and Cressida* is the explicitness of such imagery, not only in the banter of this opening scene but also in Troilus's most impassioned utterances. When he exclaims:

> Th' imaginary relish is so sweet
> That it enchants my sense. What will it be
> When that the wat'ry palate tastes indeed
> Love's thrice-repured nectar?
>
> (III. ii)

it is difficult to find his love quite so 'idealistic' as Miss Spurgeon would have it. Not that Shakespeare is ever prudish or 'Platonic' about love, and metaphors from taste are thoroughly traditional, but in this play there is an oscillation between the overstrained and the obtrusively physical (especially in this matter of food images) which helps to build up for us a Troilus intensely vulnerable in his mixture of sensuality and romanticism. (To observe this reminds us how complex are the interrelations between Shakespeare's plays: for in spite of the great dissimilarities between the two plays in structure, Troilus is perhaps closer to Othello than to any other Shakespearean hero.[12])

Love and war, love and food – those comparisons permeate the play, and no attempt is made to conceal their conventional nature. One other reiterated and explicit use of a particular kind of comparison is worth following in some detail, because it is capable of very different colourings according to its context. In his early plays, Shakespeare often exploits the romantic associations of the activities of the merchant in his love-poetry:

> I am no pilot; yet wert thou as far
> As that vast shore wash'd with the furthest sea,
> I would adventure for such merchandise.
> (*Romeo and Juliet*, II. ii)

What happens to comparisons of this kind in *Troilus and Cressida*, where they are very frequent? The merchant is first introduced by Troilus as part of an elaborate comparison in which Pandarus is involved:

> Her bed is India; there she lies, a pearl;
> Between our Ilium and where she resides
> Let it be call'd the wild and wand'ring flood;
> Ourself the merchant, and this sailing Pandar
> Our doubtful hope, our convoy and our bark.
> (I. i)

Pandarus is not here the merchant, but throughout the play there are frequent references to his function, culminating in the phrase 'traders in the flesh' in the Epilogue, which is often, I believe wrongly, suspected of being non-Shakespearean. As a result, descriptions of love in terms of merchandise in this play tend to have unfavourable overtones, and to link up with the other trains of imagery already mentioned. Thus Troilus, arguing that Helen should not be given up:

> We turn not back the silks upon the merchant
> When we have soil'd them, nor the remainder viands
> We do not throw in unrespective sieve[a]
> Because we now are full.
>
> (II. ii)

Against this background Troilus's attempt later in the speech to use the old romantic language has an unsound ring:

> Why, she is a pearl,
> Whose price hath launch'd above a thousand ships,
> And turn'd crown'd kings to merchants.
>
> (II. ii)

The central event of the play, too, that which precipitates the whole catastrophe, is the exchange of Cressida for Antenor, and it is at the point where that exchange is being negotiated that we have the most vehement denunciation of Helen, in which the themes of exchange (with comparison between war and merchandise), sexual repulsion, and food are intricately interwoven (IV. i. 51–78; the passage is so closely knit that no extract from it is adequate to illustrate the technique).

In this discussion the genuine intensity of the love-poetry has fallen somewhat into the background. This has been intentional, because it has never gone unrecognized, whereas the degree to which Shakespeare qualifies our response to it has often been underestimated. That the love of Troilus, for all the youthful ardour which sometimes tempts us to think of Shakespeare as entirely carried away by it, essentially belongs to the shallow and corrupt world of Troy, is shown also by the arrangement of scenes. Throughout the play, Shakespeare's method is a sharp juxtaposition of contrasting and apparently disjointed scenes, and nowhere is this technique more forcibly used than in III. i–ii. Taken in isolation, III. i is one of the most tedious pieces of bawdry in Shakespeare, but in its context it is extremely effective. It presents us with Helen and Paris, who must surely represent the norm of sophisticated love-intrigue at Troy. In its intensity Troilus's love is very different, but he cannot escape from this world of Courtly Love in decay, of which Shakespeare is as

---

a 'Refuse-bucket' (if the text is sound; Quarto and Folio differ, and the word intended may be an old spelling of 'sewer').

unsparing an analyst as Spenser. One wonders whether in III. ii. 78–9, 'O! let my lady apprehend no fear: in all Cupid's pageant there is presented no monster', there is an ironic reference to the pageant of Cupid in the *Faerie Queene* (III. xii. 25), of which Troilus's assertion would be pitifully false. The last lines of this stanza:

> ... faint *Infirmitie*
> Vile *Povertie*, and lastly *Death* with infamie,

describe the traditional end of Cressida, which is also the end of Spenser's Hellenore in his brilliant satirical transposition of the story of Helen into Courtly Love terms (*Faerie Queene*, III. x), and it is tempting to see in the kissing of Cressida 'in general' on her arrival in the Greek camp a recollection of Spenser's Hellenore among the Satyrs:

> But every *Satyre* first did give a busse
> To *Hellenore*: so busses did abound.
>
> (III. x. 46)

Among the other themes of this rich and complex play, one deserves at least a passing reference. The intrigue in the Greek camp, and especially the scene between Ulysses and Achilles (III. iii), is made the vehicle for a remarkable analysis of the absurd and suicidal pride and self-sufficiency which is at the heart of the Greeks' failure. Nowhere in Shakespeare do we have so many pregnant compounds beginning with 'self-', and the theme is summed up with incomparable vividness in Ulysses' description of Achilles as one who:

> ... speaks not to himself but with a pride
> That quarrels at self-breath.
>
> (II. iii)

The significance of this theme was not missed by one of the profoundest students of Shakespeare (and a particular admirer of this play), John Keats, who echoes it several times in his famous letter on the poetical character (27 October 1818), and quotes a relatively unobtrusive instance of it, 'a thing per se and stands alone' (based on I. ii. 16–17) in his account of 'the wordsworthian or egotistical sublime'.

The theme of this play has often been conjectured to have been an uncongenial one for Shakespeare. How far it is a success is not to be hastily decided, but the investigation of a number of prominent themes has brought to light more signs of a perhaps over-exuberant virtuosity than of repulsion or of spiritual disquiet on the poet's own part. And those who imagine that its handling of a classical theme and its peculiarities of construction are such as to put it outside the orbit of 'neo-classical' sympathy may be reminded that Dr Johnson found it 'more correctly written than most of Shakespeare's compositions' and the characters 'preserved with great exactness'.

Troilus and Cressida is admittedly a play with many technical peculiarities, and it is not surprising that it should have been found difficult. With *Measure for Measure*, on the other hand, we have what is on the face of it a comedy of a more familiar kind. Disaster is warded off, and the tables turned on the villain, by the resource of the heroine; and the whole story ends with disclosure followed by reconciliation and forgiveness. Yet the play has been found 'bitter' and 'cynical', and inferences to its author's supposed state of mind drawn on the strength of this.

There is, of course, much more in the play than my summary indicates, and much in which the imagination of the tragic dramatist is visible, notably the presentation of Angelo. But it is not primarily this that has caused dissatisfaction with Shakespeare's handling of his material. The objection has been to the forgiveness of Angelo, though no doubt the question arises in critics' minds largely because of the force with which he has been portrayed. There are also a number of subordinate objections which may be taken first.

The very nature of the Mariana sub-plot of the 'substituted bride' has given offence. It is a relevant answer to point to the popularity of this as a folk-story theme, but the main question is the use Shakespeare makes of it. Its traditional character makes it at least improbable that Shakespeare, in introducing it, should have given a twist to it involving condemnation of both Isabella and the Duke. The manner (and even the fact) of Isabella's refusal to yield to Angelo in order to save her brother has also been criticized; in particular the terms in which she sums up the situation:

> Then, Isabel, live chaste, and, brother, die:
> More than our brother is our chastity.
>
> (II. iv)

On this, one comment may be added to the discussion by R. W. Chambers.[13] In the whole speech, of which the couplet quoted is a highly stylized summing-up, Isabella is expressing her belief that Claudio's indignation when he hears of Angelo's proposal will help him to meet death bravely. This is not just a high-flown fancy of the inexperienced Isabella: it is an assumption normal for the world of this kind of play. One of the wonderful things about Shakespeare's art is that Claudio does not play his expected heroic-romantic part, but by his passionate outburst of fear and hope provokes Isabella's equally passionate and equally anguished rejoinder – which incidentally does succeed in restoring Claudio's morale.

The objections so far mentioned are subordinate to the main difficulty about the play. *Measure for Measure* presents us with a more daring combination of realistic and symbolic techniques[14] than any other play of Shakespeare, and it is not easy for the present-day reader or spectator to adjust himself to the transitions so as to get the whole play in focus. From this point of view it will be best to concentrate not on the persons in the play who are most interesting as 'characters', but on the Duke.

He is perhaps the best example in Shakespeare of the type of character which is baffling to a reader who expects naturalistic characterization to be paramount in a play. But he is almost as unsatisfactory to one in search of overt symbolism or allegory. The Duke directs the action from behind the scenes, but he is at the same time involved in the detail of the intrigue, and becomes a figure of low comedy in his interchanges with Lucio. There is some excuse for treating the portraiture as not necessarily realistic, but at any rate belonging to the type of comedy that combines a low-life with a romantic interest. To counteract this, it is scarcely enough to point to situations and phrases in the play which imply a providential role for the Duke, such as Angelo's exclamation:

> I perceive your Grace, like pow'r divine
> Hath look'd upon my passes.

> (v. i)

Has Shakespeare any recognizable method of bridging the gap between the two methods of presentation? For one thing, the realism itself is largely of a kind presented so as to illustrate the problems of a corrupt society. The Duke, in his disguise as a Friar, remarks:

> My business in this state
> Made me a looker-on here in Vienna,
> Where I have seen corruption boil and bubble
> Till it o'er-run the stews.
>
> (v. i)

The whole treatment approximates to the parable, the technique of which involves a much less sharp contrast between literal sense and interpretation than does the allegory proper. The advance of parable at the expense of allegory is a development of the sixteenth and seventeenth centuries,[15] and here Shakespeare's approach is substantially modern rather than medieval; but he retains the capacity for assimilating into drama the more abstractly symbolic elements as well. Hence we do not need to make too precise the way in which the marriage between the Duke and Isabella is to be taken. It can be called romantic or even fairy-tale, and it would be anomalous for the heroine of a romantic comedy to remain unmarried at the end of the play. But the technique has moved far enough in the symbolic direction for us to apprehend as part of the total effect the idea of a holy union between Justice and Mercy.

Do such considerations as these meet all the difficulties that are liable to be raised by the behaviour of the 'old fantastical duke of dark corners' (IV. iii. 167–8)? Probably not entirely. Over and above possible dislocation of the text, especially in the fourth act, Shakespeare's purpose seems to involve conveying a sense of the sheer unaccountability and oddity of the way things happen. The critics who regarded the play as a savage attack on the governance of the universe were clearly standing it on its head, but they were right in so far as they saw that the world depicted did not display a neat 'poetic justice'. The Duke, at one of his most 'providential' moments, explains why he will not tell Isabella that her brother is alive:

> I will keep her ignorant of her good,
> To make her heavenly comforts of despair,
> When it is least expected.
>
> (IV. iii)

This quotation is illuminating in more ways than one. It is true that this decision of the Duke is necessary for the *coup de théâtre* of the last act. But it must also embody a conviction that life is, or can be, like this. The story Shakespeare has chosen to tell, however odd and melodramatic in detail, and however much indebted to old folk themes, reflects the same blend of the intelligible with the sheerly unaccountable which human life on a Christian interpretation has for Shakespeare.

Othello, if a less complex fabric than the great tragedies which follow it, *Lear* and *Macbeth*, is an assured success of a high order. In choosing a few topics to develop, I am ignoring much that is of very great interest, such as the tight-knit construction of the play (and especially its use of ironic anticipation), and the question of the degree of realism, or naturalism, with which Othello himself is presented. But since the play is one with a very well-defined centre, the temptation-scene of Act III, scene iii, I prefer to concentrate on that, and on the Othello–Iago contrast which achieves its greatest dramatic force there.

This contrast affords perhaps the most striking example of Shakespeare's use of modes of speech to convey a whole attitude to life.[16] The absence of any ground common to Othello and Iago is particularly noticeable in their speech, and makes us feel each to be something less than a complete human being. There is a certain element of symbolism in the play, whether or not we care to go as far as J. I. M. Stewart[17] who put it thus: 'Othello *is* the human soul as it strives to be and Iago *is* that which corrodes or subverts it from within.' The 'Othello-figure on the stage' is 'Othello's ego-idea ... the "noble" Othello imaginatively disengaged, though far from immune, from the lower Othello, the Othello who has been externalized in Iago.'

The sort of phrase we remember from Othello is well illustrated from the first speech of any length that we hear from him:

> But that I love the gentle Desdemona,
> I would not my unhoused free condition
> Put into circumscription and confine
> For the sea's worth.
>
> (I. ii)

The quality of the verse, flowing yet possessed of 'solidity and precision of picturesque phrase or image',[18] the heightened repetition ('circumscription and confine') which yet stops short of bombastic tautology, and the use of metaphor drawn from the sea, considered in all its majesty, to convey internal experience – all are of the essence of Othello. This language is particularly striking when we have become accustomed, as we have in the first scene, to Iago's idiom. His speech, too, is characterized by images, but when he talks, for example, of the sea, it is to present a clear-cut intellectualized analogy: 'I . . . must be be-lee'd and calm'd By debitor and creditor', and his images tend to occur not, like Othello's, in heightened passages, but in carefully patterned, persuasive, euphuistic prose: 'Our bodies are our gardens, to the which our wills are gardeners' etc. The first words he addresses to Othello are characteristic in their antithetic and detached style:

> Though in the trade of war I have slain men,
> Yet do I hold it very stuff o' th' conscience
> To do no contriv'd murder.
>
> (I. ii)

Not only have we heard Iago first, but we have heard him specifically directing his criticism against Othello. This means that the other way of looking at Othello's situation has already been presented through the eyes, and in the diametrically opposed language, of Iago in the first scene. All that can be said against Othello and his love for Desdemona has been put in the grossest terms by Iago, and Othello refutes it as much by being what his language shows him to be as by any particular things he says. Possible criticisms of Othello are counteracted by being associated with the discredited Iago, yet at the same time the Othello who completely ignores them is somehow incomplete. Iago is a figure of vivid lifelikeness and individuality, but he is concentrated on a single function. He embodies not just jealousy but every kind of sexual suspiciousness and suggestiveness, everything connected with the undermining of an ideal of life. A dramatic handling which is symbolic in this wide sense makes Othello a work of an entirely different order from the sensational story from which Shakespeare adapted his plot.

The temptation scene (III. iii) may now be considered, and here I want to concentrate on one point: the way in which Othello is manoeuvred into a position where his fate is certain. The central speech (III. iii. 176–92) is a long one, and only two crucial passages can be quoted:

> ... to be once in doubt
> Is once to be resolv'd,

and

> I'll see before I doubt; when I doubt, prove;
> And on the proof, there is no more but this,
> Away at once with love or jealousy!

Othello's demand here is logically absurd: a single 'crucial experiment' cannot demonstrate Desdemona to be faithful in the same way as it could demonstrate her to be unfaithful; yet that is what Othello has been manoeuvred into demanding. Iago's success has lain in eliciting the demand for ocular proof, which is to re-establish the assurance Othello had previously had, not as a result of weighing up evidence but by an act of faith. Once Othello's mind is turned in this direction, Iago can consolidate his position by infecting Othello with his own gross visualizing lust; he can do so in part by insisting on what Othello will *not* be able to see (III. iii. 395–409), and he also has in reserve the one tangible and visible token, the handkerchief. It is not introduced until all the ground has been prepared for its transformation. In the world to which the love of Othello and Desdemona belongs, it is a token of unquestioning faith. In the world into which Iago has initiated Othello, it becomes merely divorce-court evidence.

The reflection in language of the transformation in Othello deserves close study. That Othello begins to talk like Iago has often been observed, and one example will be helpful: the comparison between Iago's speech at III. iii. 165–70 and Othello's at III. iii. 339–44. Othello now sees through Iago's eyes, yet there is still the contrast between Iago's generalizing approach and Othello's agonized personal application: 'What sense had I? ... I found not Cassio's kisses on her lips'. Othello – and it is what saves him from irreparable degradation – cannot *organize* his experience on this level on which Iago moves naturally; for him, it means that 'chaos is come again'; reconstruction must be in terms of an ideal, even if it is a distorted ideal as in the final scene, to which we must now turn.

Here we again have in language the magniloquent and remote Othello of the early scenes. How are we to interpret his ceremonial and sacrificial attitude towards the murder? He has been seen as 'rationalizing' his impulse to revenge, and broadly speaking this may be accepted. The question is how Shakespeare would have regarded the process we call rationalization. We think of it in terms of unconscious and unacknowledged desires, but Shakespeare's frame of reference is much more objective and pictorial. Temptation, dramatically rendered as an assault from without, has turned Othello's whole being in the wrong direction. After the first shock he has reorganized his world, but he has built it on falsehood. It is on Othello's mistaking of white for black that our attention is directed, and it is all the more poignant because it is the old Othello we hear again. There is something more tragic than the modern 'romantic idealist' in the blasphemous adaptation of the Biblical 'whom the Lord loveth he chasteneth' in:

> ... this sorrow's heavenly,
> It strikes where it doth love.
> (v. ii)

It is 'the Truth' embodied in Desdemona more than the psychological 'truth about himself' that Othello turns his back on. And this means that when he is undeceived there is a re-conversion in a literal (though not specifically religious) sense. The ceremonial in which the clarified vision is displayed is splendidly effective. Yet a certain limitation in the vision of the play is perhaps indicated by this superbly orchestrated ending: the only one in the mature plays where, in a Christian setting, suicide is presented without implied criticism. For Shakespeare to say all that he has to say as nearly completely as a dramatist can, we must wait for the great tragedies that follow.

NOTES

1. For the first of these interpretations, see John Palmer, *Comic Characters of Shakespeare* (1947), 37, and R. G. Moulton, *Shakespeare as a Dramatic Artist* (3rd edn., 1893), 309; for the second, see James Smith, *Scrutiny*, IX, 20–22.

2. See O. J. Campbell, *Shakespeare's Satire* (1943) and P. Mueschke and J.

Fleisher, 'Jonsonian Elements in the Comic Underplot of *Twelfth Night*' in *P.M.L.A.*, XLVIII (1933), 722–40.

3. G. E. Bentley, *Shakespeare and Jonson* (1945).

4. *Selected Essays* (1932), 153.

5. The most judicial general survey in which this notion finds a place is that of H. Granville-Barker, 'From *Henry V* to *Hamlet*', in *Proceedings of the British Academy* XI (1924–5).

6. 'Brutus and Macbeth' in *The Wheel of Fire* (4th edn, 1949).

7. J. I. M. Stewart, *Character and Motive in Shakespeare* (1949), 52.

8. Stewart, *Character and Motive in Shakespeare*, 53.

9. 'The Tragic Conflict in *Hamlet*', in *Review of English Studies*, N.S.I. (1950), 97–113.

10. See O. J. Campbell, *Comicall Satyre and Shakespeare's 'Troilus and Cressida'* (1938).

11. *Shakespeare's Imagery* (1935), 320–24.

12. See W. B. C. Watkins's *Shakespeare and Spenser* (1950), ch. 2.

13. *Man's Unconquerable Mind* (1939), ch. 9.

14. On this whole subject see Watkins, *Shakespeare and Spenser*, ch. 3.

15. There is an interesting discussion of this by R. L. Ramsay, 'Morality Themes in Milton's Poetry', in *Studies in Philology*, XV (1918), 123–58.

16. I draw heavily on W. Clemen's admirable discussion in *The Development of Shakespeare's Imagery* (1951).

17. Stewart, *Character and Motive in Shakespeare*, 97–110, which gives references for other interpretations.

18. G. Wilson Knight, *The Wheel of Fire* (1949), 97.

SHAKESPEARE: *KING LEAR*
AND THE GREAT TRAGEDIES

L. C. KNIGHTS

In a little poem called 'Poets and their Bibliographies', Tennyson remarked of his favourite Latin writers that they should be glad they lived

> Before the Love of Letters, overdone,
> Had swampt the sacred poets with themselves.

A similar sentiment had inspired Pope and was to inspire Yeats, and anyone who sets out to write an introduction to Shakespeare's tragedies must feel the force of it. What seems to be wanted is something personal and appreciative, something more than information about external facts. Yet apart from 'facts' (approximate dates, sources, stage conditions, and so on[1]), there is nothing that can be simply handed over to the inquirer. Shakespeare's plays, and above all the great tragedies, offer an experience that can only be lived into and understood to the best of our individual powers, and our understanding changes as we change; there are no answers that the beginner can, as it were, look up at the end of the book. If one persists in feeling that there is a place for critical writing about Shakespeare, and even for a critical introduction to Shakespeare, it is only on condition that such writing shall combine apparently opposite qualities. Without a claim to personal enjoyment and some personal understanding on the part of the writer, there is no point in saying anything at all. But underlying the offered appreciation – unless it is to be merely propaganda for some new view – there must be an implicit appeal to the reader to take nothing on trust but to go and see for himself.

It is an obvious fact that the appreciation of Shakespeare, the kind of thing men have got from Shakespeare, has varied enormously at different periods.* Of course no single mode of appreciation was ever

---

* See Kenneth Muir's essay in this volume entitled 'Changing Interpretations of Shakespeare'.

completely dominant; and between critics sharing a roughly similar manner of approach there have been great differences of critical intelligence, of degree of exposure to the plays, so that the good critic of any one phase remains valuable long after that phase has passed. But from time to time major shifts of attention occur, and not the least significant and fruitful of these was the one that took place in, roughly, the second quarter of this century, which scholars and critics of very different kinds helped to bring about. Conceptions of the nature and function of poetic drama were radically revised; the essential structure of the plays was sought in the poetry rather than in the more easily extractable elements of 'plot' and 'character'; and our whole conception of Shakespeare's relation to his work, of the kind of thing he was trying to do as an artist whilst simultaneously satisfying the demands of the Elizabethan theatre – this conception underwent a revolutionary change. The 'new' Shakespeare of that period was much less impersonal than the old. Whereas in the older view Shakespeare was the god-like creator of a peopled world, projecting – it is true– his own spirit into the inhabitants, but remaining essentially the analyst of their passions, he was now felt as much more immediately engaged in the action he puts before us. If the verse now moved well into the centre of the picture, this was because linguistic vitality was felt as the chief clue to the urgent personal themes that not only shape the poetic-dramatic structure of each play but form the figure in the carpet of the canon as a whole.

We may take as an example Macbeth's 'aside' when he has been greeted as Thane of Cawdor:

> This supernatural soliciting
> Cannot be ill; cannot be good. If ill,
> Why hath it given me earnest of success,
> Commencing in a truth? I am thane of Cawdor.
> If good, why do I yield to that suggestion
> Whose horrid image doth unfix my hair
> And make my seated heart knock at my ribs
> Against the use of nature? Present fears
> Are less than horrible imaginings.
> My thought, whose murder yet is but fantastical,
> Shakes so my single state of man
> That function is smother'd in surmise,
> And nothing is but what is not.

(I. iii)

This is temptation, presented with concrete force. Even if we attend only to the revelation of Macbeth's spiritual state, our recognition of the body – the very feel – of the experience is a response to the poetry, to such things as the sickening see-saw rhythm ('Cannot be ill; cannot be good ...'), changing to the rhythm of the pounding heart, the overriding of grammar ('My thought, whose murder yet is but fantastical'), as thought is revealed in the very process of formation, and so on. But the poetry makes further claims, and if we attend to them we find that the words do not only point inward to the presumed state of Macbeth's mind but, as it were, outward to the play as a whole. The equivocal nature of temptation, the commerce with phantoms consequent upon false choice, the resulting sense of unreality ('nothing is but what is not'), which has yet such power to 'smother' vital function, the unnaturalness of evil ('against the use of nature'), and the relation between disintegration in the individual ('my single state of man') and disorder in the larger social organism – all these are major themes of the play which are mirrored in the speech under consideration. They emerge as themes because they are what the poetry – reinforced by action and symbolism – again and again insists on. And the interrelations we are forced to make take us outside the speeches of the protagonists to the poetry of the play as a whole. That 'smother'd', for example, takes us forward not only to Lady Macbeth's 'blanket of the dark' but to such things as Ross's choric comment after the murder of Duncan:

> ... By th' clock 'tis day,
> And yet dark night strangles the travelling lamp.
> Is't night's predominance, or the day's shame,
> That darkness does the face of earth entomb,
> When living light should kiss it?
>
> (II. iv)

It is in an explicit recognition of the dense verbal texture of the greater plays that one of the main services of mid twentieth-century Shakespeare criticism lies. Yet there are misunderstandings to be guarded against. It would, for example, be a mistake to regard the meaning of a play as residing exclusively or even predominantly in the imagery. Recurrent imagery certainly plays a large part in shaping the meanings with which we are concerned; but a too insistent concentration on imagery, let alone a mechanical classification of images, can only defeat its own purpose. What we attend to is not only the imagery but all the organic components of the living verse; and the verse in turn works in conjunction with the dramatic action and our sense of what the different persons of the drama stand for as each play develops. The greater Shakespeare plays thus demand an unusual activity of attention, forcing the reader to respond with the whole of his active imagination. It is only when the mind of the reader is thoroughly 'roused and awakened'[2] that meanings from below the level of 'plot' and 'character' crystallize out and form themselves into a living structure.[3] If that structure of meaning seems especially closely connected with recurring and interrelated imagery, that is not because possible associations and recurrences are puzzled out by the intellect, but because the mind at a certain pitch of activity and responsiveness combines the power of focusing lucidly on what is before it with an awareness of before and after, sensing the whole in the part, and with a triumphant energy relating part to part in a living whole. But it is only in relation to that larger all-embracing meaning – determined by the 'plain sense' of what is said, and by its overtones, by the dramatic situation and the progress of the action, by symbols and by the interplay of different attitudes embodied in the different persons of the drama – it is only in relation to this total meaning that the imagery, or any other component that may be momentarily isolated, takes on its full significance. We only hear Shakespeare's deeper meanings when we listen with the whole of ourselves.

There have recently been two major shifts in the critical approach to the tragedies, as indeed to Shakespeare's plays in general. There has been a renewed emphasis on Shakespeare as a man of the theatre, and on the plays as designed for public performance – visible action and spectacle as well as audible poetry. This is one way of emphasizing our absorbed engagement with an action where the flow and recoil of our sympathies is perhaps more direct than it is in silent reading. Of course any performance in which producers and actors have concentrated on what the play seems to demand from them (not on what a lively producer can do with it!) requires a lot of fairly intense reading. But in so far as my essay seems to disregard the theatrical qualities of the plays, it is a blemish which the reader can correct not only by going to the theatre but by reading with his dramatic imagination alert, considering the relation between the swiftly succeeding scenes, the timing of entrances, the possible grouping of the characters, and so on. *King Lear*, for example, is full of directions for significant physical action ('Give me thy hand', 'Poor Tom shall lead thee', 'No, Sir, you must not kneel' . . .). And in *Coriolanus*, although the sheer excitement of men in conflict in the central scenes can probably only be brought out in performance, the reader has no difficulty in imagining the effect of the unbending Volumnia kneeling to her son, or of the significant pause before Coriolanus replies to her final plea (v. iii).

In the second place, there has been an increasing readiness, not perhaps simply 'to return to Bradley', but to see the plays in terms of the motives, attitudes and developing relationships of the principal characters – in short, of their psychological make-up, in so far as this is revealed to us. I have sometimes used the word 'themes' to point to what seem to me the organizing principles that inform particular plays, and it has been rightly pointed out that 'themes' can be just as much an abstraction from a complex whole as can 'character'. But there is no need to set up rival critical factions: *no* critical idiom can do full justice to Shakespeare's complexity and variety.

It is generally accepted that *King Lear* and *Macbeth* belong to the years 1605–6, and *Antony and Cleopatra* and *Coriolanus* to 1606–7. The complete technical mastery of these plays thus has behind it some fifteen years' experience in the writing of poetic drama, years in which Shakespeare had learnt to master every difficulty and to take advantage of every opportunity offered by his stage; to perfect also a verse 'so rammed with life' that it could be at the same time dramatically effective, compressed, fluid, subtle, and exact – an almost transparent medium for the experience it defines; or so we should say if it were not through the 'medium' itself that the experience was simultaneously brought to consciousness *and* defined.[4] But the great tragedies are of course the result of much more than technical mastery; they mark the climax of a profound experience of life and a profound questioning of it. It need hardly be said that almost all the plays preceding the great tragedies have their own independent value; but it is impossible to read them through as a sequence without becoming aware of a coherent, though complex, *development*, in which the attempt to define and assert certain values is inseparable from a growing awareness of all that is most deeply disturbing in human life. A consciousness of change and death, of a world subjected to time and appearance, of an inextricable mingling of elements in energies and passions that are at once the necessary condition of achievement and, apparently, self-destructive, is deeply embedded in plays as different as *Henry IV*, *Hamlet*, *Troilus and Cressida*, and *Measure for Measure*.

The fact that *King Lear* was written so soon after *Othello* (1603) is a reminder of how misleading the phrase 'Shakespearean Tragedy' can be. Each play is 'a new beginning', a fresh 'raid on the inarticulate', for although there is development there is no repetition. Even from the narrowly technical point of view there are marked differences of manner and approach between the tragedies, corresponding to equally marked differences of intention. Thus *Othello*, although a poetic drama of which the success is determined by specifically poetic effects of language and symbolism, comes closer than any of the other tragedies to what is commonly understood by 'revelation of character', and its focus is on individual and, we might say, domestic qualities. *Lear*, on the other hand, though presenting the fate of particular individuals, is clearly 'universal', and its dramatic technique is determined by the need to present certain permanent aspects of the human situation, with a maximum of imaginative realization and a minimum regard for the conventions of naturalism.[5] In the scenes on the heath, for example, although we retain our sense of the dramatic identity of each person speaking, there is also the sense of being caught up in a great and almost impersonal poem in which we hear certain *voices* that echo and counterpoint each other; and all that they say is part of the tormented consciousness of Lear; and the consciousness of Lear is part of the consciousness of human kind. There is the same density of effect throughout. One character echoes another: the blinding of Gloucester parallels the cruelty done to Lear; Gloucester loses his eyes, and Lear's mind is darkened; Gloucester learns to 'see better' (as Kent had bidden Lear) in his blindness, and Lear reaches the recognition of his supreme need through madness. But there is not only this mutual reinforcement *within* the play: there is constantly the felt presence of a range of experience far wider than could be attributed to any of the persons regarded simply as persons. This is achieved partly by the use of simple but effective symbols – the bare heath, the hovel, the nakedness of Poor Tom ('unaccommodated man'), the 'cliff' from which Gloucester thinks to cast himself down;[6] partly by the use made of certain organizing ideas such as the Elizabethan conception of a necessary interrelation between man ('the little world of man'), the social body, and the cosmos; but above all by the poetry. The poetry of *Lear* is not only vivid, close packed, and wide ranging, involving in the immediate action a world of experience,[7] it has a peculiar resonance that would leave us in no doubt of the universalizing effect. It is what we hear when the blind Gloucester declares:

> I have no way, and therefore want no eyes;
> I stumbled when I saw,

or when Lear, crossed by Goneril, exclaims, 'Who is it that can tell me who I am?' and the Fool replies, 'Lear's shadow'.

S. L. Goldberg's *An Essay on 'King Lear'* begins:

Anyone who sets out to say what he makes of *King Lear* is soon likely to start wondering at his rashness. The further he goes, the less easy he finds it even to keep his critical balance. More perhaps than any other work ... it impels us finally to 'speak what we feel, not what we ought to say'. To 'obey' it is to answer with nothing less. And yet it also makes us feel that whatever we do speak, or could speak, is inadequate to everything else we are brought to feel – even, in some obscure way, a betrayal of it.[8]

It is difficult to write a short introduction to any of Shakespeare's tragedies, and this is especially true of *King Lear* with its compression, complexity, and vast scope of possible meanings. In one sense it is a family tragedy – or, rather, two inter-locked family tragedies – unusual only inasmuch as it reveals the explosive passions locked in the atomic structure. 'Dear, dear,' exclaims a character in Ivy Compton-Burnett's *Parents and Children*, 'the miniature world of a family! All the emotions of mankind seem to find a place in it.' The Lear and Gloucester families, even without the presence of a mother, exhibit an enormous range of familial emotions and attitudes, reaching from earliest childhood into adult life: authoritarian demands, rebellious submission, rivalries, the need for love and attempts to force it or to avoid it,[9] and so on. But the very intensity of the emotions, and their results in action, force us to explore as far as we can the psychological and 'philosophic' reaches of the play. This does indeed compel the kind of imaginative thought that leads towards an inclusive view of life. But if we *start* with a predisposition towards inclusive generality (whether derived from previous readings or from some critical work) we inevitably miss the basic action of the play in all its multifarious detail, shaped though it is by a master-plotter. It is that, and its direct appeal to our imagination, from which individual exploration must start. All the critic can do is to risk simplification: to state clearly the main 'meaning' for one reader, at one stage of his life, so that others are prompted to face their own immediate (not unpondered) responses, and then to go on from there to wherever the play takes them. In the book already referred to Goldberg comments on an essay of mine: 'In *King Lear*, the process of discovery matters more ... than Knights's account seems to allow; and it matters just because it is always open, problematic, and therefore profoundly disturbing.' That is something for the reader to keep in mind in reading the following paragraphs.

Lear, at the opening of the play, is the embodiment of perverse self-will. Surrounded by obsequious flattery ('they told me I was everything'), he knows neither himself nor the nature of things. It is his human self-will that is stressed, and we need not fuss very much about the apparent absurdity of his public test of his daughters' affections in the division of the kingdom. It is a symbol of something not uncommon – the attempt to manipulate affection which can only freely be given:

> Which of you shall we say doth love us most?
> That we our largest bounty may extend
> Where nature doth with merit challenge.
>
> (I. i)

To a demand of this kind the only honest reply is Cordelia's 'Nothing'. Now one result of perverse demands is a distorted view of the actual, and one way of discovering that our own lanthorn gives no light is, as Swift put it, by running our head into a lamp-post – something that is unquestionably *there*. Because Lear is perverse he is deceived by appearances, and because he allows himself to be deceived by appearances he sets in motion a sequence of events that finally brings him face to face with an actuality that can be neither denied nor disguised.

The subsequent action of the play is designed not only to force the

hidden conflict in Lear into consciousness, and, with the fullest possible knowledge of the relevant facts, to compel a choice, but to force
each one of us to confront directly the question put by Lear as Everyman, 'Who is it that can tell me who I am?' One answer to that
question is embodied in the group of characters who are most
directly opposed to Lear. Edmund, Goneril, and Regan take their
stand on the unrestrained self-seeking of natural impulse. The two
daughters, by their actions, by what they say, and by the imagery of
beasts of prey so consistently associated with them,[10] represent a
ferocious animality. Their indifference to all claims but those of their
own egotism is made explicit by Edmund, who brings into the play
conceptions of Nature and human nature, radically opposed to the
traditional conceptions, that were beginning to emerge in the consciousness of the age.[11] For Edmund man is *merely* a part of the morally
indifferent world of nature, and his business is simply to assert himself with all the force and cunning at his command: 'Thou, Nature,
art my goddess'; 'All with me's meet that I can fashion fit'. It is into
the world of indifferent natural forces, so glibly invoked by Edmund,
that Lear is precipitated by a perversity of self-will that clung to the
forms of human affection whilst denying the reality.

The storm scenes, and the scenes immediately following, represent
a two-fold process of discovery – of the 'nature' without and within.
No summary can attempt to do them justice, and perhaps the best
way of indicating what goes on in them is to revert to what has been
said of Shakespeare's superb and daring technique. The effect is analogous to that of a symphony in which themes are given out, developed, varied and combined. And since one of the characters goes
mad, one is an assumed madman, and one is a Fool, there is a freedom without precedent in the history of the drama – a freedom only
limited by the controlling purpose of the play – to press into service
all that is relevant to the full development of the main themes. The
storm itself is vividly presented in all its power to harm;[12] but this is
far from being the only way in which the action of Nature is brought
home to us. Part of the dramatic function of Edgar is to reinforce the
message of the storm. Disguised as one of the lowest creatures to be
found in rural England in the sixteenth century (and therefore, for
the purpose of the play, *becoming* one), a wandering madman and
beggar:

... the basest and most poorest shape
That ever penury in contempt of man
Brought near to beast,

(II. ii)

he brings with him continual reminders of rural life at its
most exposed and precarious – 'the winds and persecution of the sky',
'low farms, Poor pelting villages, sheep-cotes and mills'. When Lear
with Kent and the Fool surprises him in the hovel, he at once strikes
the note of the *familiar* indifference of Nature – familiar, that is, to
those who live close to nature, though not to those who, like
Edmund, invoke an abstraction that suits their bent. His talk is of cold
and fire, of whirlpool and quagmire, of natural calamity and disease.
Man may make for himself a self-flattering picture of the world, but
this is the reality. 'You talk of Nature,' Shakespeare seems to say,
'well, take a good look at her.' 'Still through the hawthorn blows the
cold wind.'

Shakespeare uses similar methods in the revelation of the world
within. A long catalogue of sins – ranging from the adulteration of
beer to usury, slander, perjury, and murder – could be collected from
the exchanges of Lear, Edgar, and the Fool, and as they accumulate
they give a sorry enough picture of man in his meanness. But the
recurring themes are lust and cruelty. Lust and cruelty are demonstrated in the action of the play; they are harped on in Edgar's 'mad'
talk, they are the horrible realities that Lear discovers beneath appearances. In the great speech beginning:

Thou rascal beadle, hold thy bloody hand!
Why dost thou lash that whore?

(IV. vi)

lust and sadism are – with superb insight – identified. The world of
appearances is based on artificial and unreal distinctions – 'Robes and
furred gowns hide all'. Strip them off and you find what Lear found
in the storm:

Is man no more than this? Consider him well. Thou ow'st the worm no silk,
the beast no hide, the sheep no wool, the cat no perfume. Ha! here's three on's
are sophisticated! Thou art the thing itself: unaccommodated man is no more
but such a poor, bare, forked animal as thou art. Off, off, you lendings! Come,
unbutton here.

(III. iv)

The 'thou' of that speech, the 'thing itself', is – we have just heard – 'one that slept in the contriving of lust and waked to do it ... false of heart, light of ear, bloody of hand; hog in sloth, fox in stealth, wolf in greediness, dog in madness, lion in prey'. This, we may say, is the Edmund philosophy, though presented with a violence of realization quite foreign to the Edmund of the play. Lechery? says Lear in his madness when finally broken by the storm, the world of nature is completely lustful. let us admit it. Anything else is mere pretence. 'To't luxury pell-mell! for I lack soldiers'.

Lear's expression of revulsion and disgust is, I suppose, one of the profoundest expressions of pessimism in all literature. If it is not the final word in the play, it is certainly not because Shakespeare has shrunk from any of the issues. Pessimism is sometimes regarded as a tough and realistic attitude. Shakespeare's *total* view of human life in this play has a toughness and actuality that make most pessimism look like sentimentality. It is because the play has brought us to this vision of horror – seen without disguise of palliation – that the way is open for the final insights. In the successive stripping away of the layers of appearance, what remains to discover is the most fundamental reality of all. In the play it takes the form of the love and forgiveness of Cordelia. But that love has to be earned in the way in which all things most worth having are earned – by the full admission of a need, the achievement of honesty and humility, the painful shedding of all that is recognized as incompatible with the highest good, by, in short, making oneself able to receive whatever it may be. *How* Lear feels – the attitudes with which he confronts experience – is as important as *what* he feels, for the final 'seeing' is inseparable from what he has come to be. There is of course no straight line of progress: there are developments, eddies, and recessions, as the tumultuous feelings whirl into sight now one, now another aspect of what lies beneath the surface. Lear's attitudes and emotions include ferocious cruelty, a desire to punish, self-pity, revulsion and disgust. But because the hard crust of his will is broken by the two-fold storm, new feelings and new insights have a chance to enter.

> Poor naked wretches, wheresoe'er you are,
> That bide the pelting of this pitiless storm,
> How shall your houseless heads and unfed sides,
> Your loop'd and window'd raggedness, defend you

From seasons such as these? O, I have ta'en
Too little care of this! Take physic, pomp;
Expose thyself to feel what wretches feel,
That thou mayst shake the superflux to them,
And show the heavens more just.

(III. iv)

This is pity, not self-pity; and condemnation of others momentarily gives way to self-condemnation. It is *after* this that Lear endures the 'physic' of his vision of unaccommodated man. When we last see him in his madness (IV. vi) he is obsessed by the idea of universal corruption, but he no longer thinks of himself as set over against the sinners whom he condemns; the very idea of legal justice is a mockery ('Change places, and, handy-dandy, which is the justice, which is the thief?'); and it is his own hand that 'smells of mortality'. We have indeed already been told of him:

A sovereign shame so elbows him; his own unkindness,
That stripp'd her from his benediction, turn'd her
To foreign casualties, gave her dear rights
To his dog-hearted daughters – these things sting
His mind so venomously that burning shame
Detains him from Cordelia.

(IV. iii)

This suggests purgatory rather than hell: the shame is 'burning', but it is also 'sovereign' or remedial.

The way is thus prepared for the meeting with Cordelia, which takes up all the positive movements of the play and stamps them with the seal of a reality that is even more deeply grounded in the nature of things than the formidable selfishness Lear has discovered beneath conventional appearances. Lear's final discovery is of his need for Cordelia's love. Cordelia, though rarely appearing in the play, is very much a positive presence. She is the daughter 'who redeems nature from the general curse that twain have brought her to'. Representing the opposite pole to the 'law of nature' to which Goneril and Regan abandon themselves:

... it seem'd she was a queen
Over her passion, who, most rebel-like,
Sought to be king o'er her –

(IV. iii)

she can yet be aptly described in terms of natural imagery:

> You have seen
> Sunshine and rain at once: her smiles and tears
> Were like a better way.
>
> (IV. iii)

It is because she is fully human – though there are also potent suggestions of divine grace – that she is 'natural' in a different sense from that intended in Edmund's philosophy. It is her sense of the bounty of nature (of 'our sustaining corn' as well as of the 'rank fumiter and furrow weeds') that lies behind her invocation:

> All blest secrets,
> All you unpublish'd virtues of the earth,
> Spring with my tears; be aidant and remediate,
> In the good man's distress.
>
> (IV. iv)

In that 'spring' there is an identification of human nature and the wider Nature from which it is born. But it is because of her love and pity ('the good man' is the erring Lear) that she can invoke so wholeheartedly the 'unpublish'd virtues of the earth'. Her tenderness is rooted in the same strength that enabled her to reject Lear's misconceived demands ('Corporeal friends', said Blake, 'may be spiritual enemies'). Her love is of a kind that, confronted with a real demand, does not bargain or make conditions; it is now, at last, freely given, and it represents an absolute of human experience that can stand against the full shock of disillusion. When Lear, dressed in 'fresh clothes' and to the accompaniment of music (the symbolism is important), is awakened in her presence, there follows one of the most tender and moving scenes in the whole of Shakespeare:

> COR.   O, look upon me, sir,
> And hold your hands in benediction o'er me.
> No, sir, you must not kneel.
> LEAR.   Pray, do not mock me:
> I am a very foolish fond old man,
> Fourscore and upward, not an hour more nor less;
> And, to deal plainly,
> I fear I am not in my perfect mind.
> Methinks I should know you, and know this man;
> Yet I am doubtful; for I am mainly ignorant
> What place this is; and all the skill I have

Remembers not these garments; nor I know not
Where I did lodge last night. Do not laugh at me;
For, as I am a man, I think this lady
To be my child Cordelia.

COR.   And so I am, I am.

LEAR. Be your tears wet? Yes, faith. I pray weep not;
If you have poison for me I will drink it.
I know you do not love me; for your sisters
Have, as I do remember, done me wrong:
You have some cause, they have not.

COR. No cause, no cause.

LEAR. Am I in France?

KENT.   In your own kingdom, sir.

                                        (IV. vii)

There remains the last act, in which by the definite withdrawal of
Albany from the forces opposed to Lear, the killing of Edmund by
Edgar in single combat, and the mutual treachery of Goneril and
Regan, the way is apparently cleared for an ending far different from
that represented by the stark stage-direction: 'Enter Lear with Cordelia dead in his arms'. The scene of Lear's final anguish is so painful
that criticism hesitates to fumble with it. ('I was many years ago so
shocked by Cordelia's death, that I know not whether I ever endured
to read again the last scenes of the play till I undertook to revise them
as an editor', Dr Johnson.) Yet it may be said that there are at least
two reasons why no other ending would have been imaginatively
right. We do not only look at a masterpiece, we enter into it and live
with it. Our suffering then, and our acceptance of suffering, no less
than Lear's, is an intrinsic part of what the play is; for as with Lear
and Gloucester our capacity to see is dependent upon our capacity to
feel. Now what our seeing has been directed towards is nothing less
than *what man is*, or is capable of being. The imaginative discovery
that is the play's essence has thus involved the sharpest possible juxtaposition of rival conceptions of 'Nature', even though these conceptions are, for the most part, implicit and embodied rather than
explicitly proclaimed. In the Edmund-Goneril-Regan group the
philosophy of natural impulse and egotism has been revealed as self-
consuming, its claim to represent strength as a self-bred delusion.
What Lear touches in Cordelia, on the other hand, is, we are made to
feel, the reality, and the values revealed so surely there are established

in the face of the worst that can be known of man or Nature. The hesitant, unemphatic lines with which the play ends,

> The weight of this sad time we must obey;
> Speak what we feel, not what we ought to say.
> The oldest hath borne most: we that are young
> Shall never see so much, nor live so long,

as though words cannot encompass all that the characters, and we with them, have lived through, are warning enough against facile summary. But it is still possible to say of *King Lear* that to keep nothing in reserve, to slur over no possible cruelty or misfortune, was the only way of ensuring that the positive values discovered and established in the play should keep their triumphant hold on our imagination, should assert that unconditional rightness, which, in any full and responsive reading, we are bound to attribute to them.

King Lear is the great central masterpiece to which the earlier plays lead and on which the later tragedies depend. Of course there are new developments, but these would have been impossible without the insights gained in that cataclysmic morality play. The plays before *Lear* stand firmly in their own right, but behind some of the most significant of them – and not only those in which there is an overt perplexity, such as *Troilus and Cressida* and *Hamlet* – there is an insistent and unresolved questioning. Is there any escape from appearance and illusion? Why do both the public world and the world of intense subjective experience seem somehow flawed and unsatisfactory? What is the status of human values in a world dominated by time and death? On what, in the world as we know it, can man take his stand? In *Lear* Shakespeare discovered an answer to these questions, not in terms of copy-book maxims but in terms of intense living experience. The resulting freedom from inner tensions is seen alike in the assured judgement and in the magnificent vitality of *Macbeth*, *Antony and Cleopatra*, and *Coriolanus*.[13]

Macbeth defines a particular kind of evil – the evil that results from a lust for power. The defining, as in all the tragedies, is in strictly poetic and dramatic terms. It is certainly not an abstract formulation, but lies rather in the drawing out of the necessary consequences and implications of that lust both in the external and the spiritual worlds. Its meaning therefore is revealed in the expansion and unfolding of what lies within the initial evil *in terms of direct human experience*. The logic is not formal but experiential, and demands from us, if we are to test its validity and feel its force, a fullness of imaginative response and a closeness of realization, in which both sensation and feeling become modes of understanding. Only when intellect, emotion, and a kind of direct sensory awareness work together can we enter fully into that exploratory and defining process.

In none of the tragedies is there anything superfluous, but it is perhaps *Macbeth* that gives the keenest impression of economy.[14] The action moves directly and quickly to the crisis, and from the crisis to the full working out of plot and theme. The pattern is far easier to grasp than that of *Lear*. The main theme of the reversal of values is given out simply and clearly in the first scene – 'Fair is foul, and foul is fair'; and with it are associated premonitions of the conflict, disorder, and moral darkness into which Macbeth will plunge himself. Well before the end of the first act we are in possession not only of the positive values against which the Macbeth evil will be defined, but of the related aspects of that evil, which is simultaneously felt as a strained and unnatural perversion of the will, an obfuscation of the clear light of reason, a principle of disorder (both in the 'single state of man' and in his wider social relations), and a pursuit of illusions. All these impressions, which as the play proceeds assume the status of organizing ideas, are produced by the interaction of all the resources of poetic drama – action, contrast, statement, implication, imagery, and allusion. Thus the sense of the *unnaturalness* of evil is evoked not only by repeated explicit references ('nature's mischief', 'nature seems dead', ''Tis unnatural, even like the deed that's done', and so on), but by the expression of unnatural sentiments and an unnatural violence of tone in such things as Lady Macbeth's invocation of the 'spirits' who will 'unsex' her, and her affirmation that she would murder the babe at her breast if she had sworn to do it. So, too, the theme of the false appearances inseparable from evil, of deceit recoiling on the deceiver, is not only the subject of explicit comment –

> And be these juggling fiends no more believed,
> That palter with us in a double sense;
>
> (v. vii)

it is embodied in the action, so that Macbeth's despairing recognition of mere 'mouth honour' among his remaining followers (v. iii. 27) echoes ironically his wife's advice to 'look like the innocent flower, but be the serpent under it' (I. v. 65–6), and the hypocritical play of the welcoming of Duncan; and it is reinforced – or indeed is one with – the evoked sense of equivocation and evasiveness associated with the witches, and the cloud of uncertainty that settles on Scotland during Macbeth's despotism. It is fitting that the final movement of the reversal that takes place in the last act should open with the command of Malcolm to the camouflaged soldiers, 'Your leavy screens throw down, and show like those you are.' But commentary of this kind, which may perhaps indicate the kind of thing that is going on everywhere in *Macbeth*, can only bring out the limits of expository criticism. You cannot isolate a single significant passage of the poetry without finding that the whole of the play is involved in its elucidation. And although we talk of themes as a way of indicating the play's main structural lines, those themes only have their being within the living poetry from which we have extracted them. Wherever the poetry enters deeply into our minds with a sense of special significance, we find that it is not only powerful in itself but that it is enriched by what has gone before, just as it will enrich what follows.

An example is the scene of Duncan's entry into Macbeth's castle (I. vi). It is set for full dramatic contrast between Lady Macbeth's invocation of the powers of darkness ('The raven himself is hoarse, that croaks the fatal entrance ...') and Macbeth's final resolution; and Duncan's courtesy underlines the irony. But the contrast is not confined to the situation. The evocation of a sweet fresh air, the pleased contemplation of the birds that build and breed, affect us first as sensory contrasts ('Come thick night'); but, in this corresponding to the images of darkness and disorder, they are inseparable from the values they embody and define. What we are dealing with is a natural and wholesome *order*, of which the equivalent in the human sphere is to be found in those mutualities of loyalty, trust, and liking that Macbeth proposes to violate. And it is an order inseparable from the life that it fosters. The opening lines of the scene, in short, are not only obviously beautiful in themselves, they are an image of life delighting in life. It is in terms of destructive and self-destructive energies that Macbeth's power-lust is defined, and it is from the 'life' images of the play, which range from the temple-haunting martlets to Macduff's 'babes', his 'pretty ones', and include all the scattered references to man's natural goods – sleep and food and fellowship – that we take our bearings in the analysis of evil.

In the great soliloquy of I. vii, Macbeth tries to provide himself with prudential reasons for not committing murder:

> But in these cases
> We still have judgement here, that we but teach
> Bloody instructions, which being taught return
> To plague th' inventor.

But the attempt at a cool calculation of consequences (already at odds with the nervous rhythm and the taut muscular force of the imagery of the opening lines) almost immediately gives way to an appalling vision of judgement:

> Besides, this Duncan
> Hath borne his faculties so meek, hath been
> So clear in his great office, that his virtues
> Will plead like angels trumpet-tongued against
> The deep damnation of his taking-off.

Those lines have of course behind them the traditional conception of the Day of Judgement, and it is nothing less than the nature of 'judgement' that the play reveals. Just as 'blessedness is not the reward of virtue, but virtue itself',[15] so the deep damnation of this play is revealed in the intrinsic qualities of an evil deliberately willed and persisted in. As the play proceeds the ironies multiply. Fear and disorder erupt into the specious security and apparent order that temporarily succeed the murder of Duncan.* 'Things bad begun' attempt to 'make themselves strong by ill' (III. ii. 56), yet each further step is as 'tedious' (Macbeth's word – III. iv. 138) and self-frustrating as the last. And the concomitant of the outer disorder and inner disintegration (with both of which Macbeth identifies himself in the great invocation of chaos in IV. i) is a deepening sense of the loss of significance. The aimed-at satisfactions are, in the nature of things, unreal;[16] and

---

* This is symbolized by the banquet scene (III. iv), where the formal ceremony of the opening ('You know your own degrees, sit down: at first and last, The hearty welcome') contrasts with the 'admir'd disorder' of the close. Macbeth's inner chaos is similarly reflected later in the uncoordinated violence of his 'royal preparation' for the battle, on which the Doctor dryly comments (V. iii. 57–8).

the closing scenes place in sharp proximity a moving evocation of natural fulfilment and a consciousness that can think only in terms of a meaningless temporal succession:

> And that which should accompany old age,
> As honour, love, obedience, troops of friends,
> I must not look to have; but, in their stead,
> Curses not loud but deep, mouth-honour, breath,
> Which the poor heart would fain deny, and dare not.
>
> (v. iii)

> Life's but a walking shadow, a poor player,
> That struts and frets his hour upon the stage,
> And then is heard no more; it is a tale
> Told by an idiot, full of sound and fury,
> Signifying nothing.
>
> (v. v)

Both these complementary recognitions have behind them the weight of an experience that the play has fully articulated.

Antony and Cleopatra is a tragedy of a very different kind from *Macbeth*. In *Macbeth* we are never in any doubt of our moral bearings. *Antony and Cleopatra*, on the other hand, embodies different and apparently irreconcilable evaluations of the central experience. There is the view, with which the play opens, of those who stand outside the charmed circle of 'Egypt':

> Take but good note, and you shall see in him
> The triple pillar of the world transform'd
> Into a strumpet's fool.
>
> (I. i)

This attitude is strongly represented in the play; there are repeated references to 'lascivious wassails', 'the amorous surfeiter', 'salt Cleopatra', 'the adulterous Antony' who 'gives his potent regiment to a trull', and so on. The 'Roman' world of war and government – the realm of political 'necessity' (III. vi. 83) rather than of spontaneous human feelings – is of course itself presented critically; but although the way we take the Roman comments is partly determined by our sense of the persons making them, they do correspond to something of which we are directly aware in the Egyptian scenes. We do not need any Roman prompting to be aware of something cloying in the sexual insistence (in the opening of I. ii, for example), and of something practised in (to borrow phrase from North) the 'flickering enticements of Cleopatra unto Antonius'.[17]

On the other hand, what Shakespeare infused into the love story as he found it in Plutarch was an immense energy, a sense of life so heightened that it can claim to represent an absolute value:

> Eternity was in our lips and eyes,
> Bliss in our brows' bent, none our parts so poor
> But was a race of heaven.

> (I. iii)

This energy communicates itself to all that comes within the field of force that radiates from the lovers, and within which their relationship is defined. In Enobarbus' description of the first meeting of Antony and Cleopatra (II. ii. 190ff.) the energy counteracts the suggestion of a deliberate sensuousness; the inanimate is felt as animate; and the passage, although a set piece, modulates easily into a racy buoyancy:

> The city cast
> Her people out upon her; and Antony,
> Enthroned i' the market-place, did sit alone,
> Whistling to the air; which, but for vacancy,
> Had gone to gaze on Cleopatra too,
> And made a gap in nature.

Wilson Knight rightly insists on 'the impregnating atmosphere of wealth, power, military strength and material magnificence', the cosmic imagery, and 'the continual suggestion of earth's fruitfulness', in terms of which Antony and Cleopatra are presented to us; and the suggestions of scope and grandeur are blended with continual reminders of what is common to humanity. It is the richness and energy of the poetry in which all this is conveyed that, more than any explicit comment, defines for us the vitality of the theme.

Shakespeare, in short, evokes the passion of the lovers with the greatest possible intensity, and invests it with the maximum of positive significance. But, more realist than some of his critics, he makes it impossible for us not to question the nature and conditions of that very energy that the lovers release in each other. The sequence of scenes between Actium and the final defeat of Antony opens, as Granville-Barker remarked, with a suggestion of dry and brittle comedy. In an apparent abeyance of feeling the lovers are more or less pushed into each other's arms by their respective followers: and there is an inert resignation in the reconciliation that follows. Feeling does not well up in Antony until he discovers Caesar's messenger kissing Cleopatra's hand. It is a perverse violence of cruelty – 'Whip him, fellow, Till, like a boy, you see him cringe his face' – that goads him into a semblance of energy; and it is in the backwash of this emotion that Cleopatra can humour him until she is, as it were, again present to him. Shakespeare, however, leaves us in no doubt about the overwrought nature of Antony's feelings: the very look of him is given us by Enobarbus – 'Now he'll outstare the lightning'.

Antony, here, is galvanized into feeling; there is no true access of life and energy. And the significance of this is that we know that what we have to do with is an emphatic variation of a familiar pattern. Looking back, we can recall how often this love has seemed to thrive on emotional stimulants. They were necessary for much the same reasons as the feasts and wine. For the continued references to feasting – and it is not only Caesar and his dry Romans who emphasize the Alexandrian consumption of food and drink – are not simply a means of intensifying the imagery of tasting and savouring that is a constant accompaniment of the love theme; they serve to bring out the element of repetition and monotony in a passion which, centring on itself, is self-consuming, leading ultimately to what Antony himself, in a most pregnant phrase, names as 'the heart of loss'. Indeed, the speech in which this phrase occurs (IV. xii. 9–30) is one of the pivotal things in the play. In its evocation of an appalled sense of insubstantiality it ranks with Macbeth's, 'My thought, whose murder yet is but fantastical ...' With this difference: that whereas Macbeth is, as it were, reaching forward to a region 'where nothing is but what is not', Antony is driven to recognize the element of unreality and enchantment in what he had thought was solid and enduring. The speech has a superb sensuous reality that is simultaneously felt as discandying or melting, until the curious flicker of the double vision – both intensified and explained by the recurrent theme of 'Egyptian' magic and gypsy-like double-dealing – is resolved in the naked vision:

> Betray'd I am.
> O this false soul of Egypt! this grave charm –
> Whose eye beck'd forth my wars and call'd them home,

Whose bosom was my crownet, my chief end –
Like a right gypsy hath at fast and loose
Beguil'd me to the very heart of loss.

Cleopatra's lament over the dying Antony, her evocation of his greatness and bounty, have perhaps weighed too heavily in the impression that many people have taken from the play as a whole. That these things are great poetry goes without saying. But the almost unbearable pathos of the last scenes is for what has *not* in fact been realized.[18]

> CLEOPATRA.   For his bounty,
>   There was no winter in't; an autumn 'twas
>   That grew the more by reaping: his delights
>   Were dolphin-like; they show'd his back above
>   The element they lived in: in his livery
>   Walk'd crowns and crownets; realms and islands were
>   As plates dropp'd from his pocket.
> DOLABELLA.   Cleopatra –
> CLEOPATRA. Think you there was or might be such a man
>   As this I dreamt of?
> DOLABELLA.   Gentle madam, no.
> CLEOPATRA. You lie, up to the hearing of the gods.
>   But if there be nor ever were one such,
>   It's past the size of dreaming. Nature wants stuff
>   To vie strange forms with fancy; yet t' imagine
>   An Antony were nature's piece 'gainst fancy,
>   Condemning shadows quite.
>
>   (v. ii)

The figure that Cleopatra evokes may not be fancy – the poetry invests it with a substantial reality; but it is not the Antony that the play has given us; it is something disengaged from, or glimpsed through, that Antony. Nor should the power and beauty of Cleopatra's last great speech obscure the continued presence of something self-deceiving and unreal. She may speak of the baby at her breast that sucks the nurse asleep; but it is not, after all, a baby – new life; it is simply death.

It is, of course, one of the signs of a great writer that he can *afford* to evoke sympathy or even admiration for qualities that his work is far from endorsing. In *Antony and Cleopatra* the sense of potentiality in life's untutored energies is pushed to its limit, and

Shakespeare gives the maximum weight to an experience that is finally 'placed'. It is perhaps this that makes the tragedy so sombre in its realism, so little comforting to the romantic imagination. For Shakespeare has chosen as his tragic theme the impulse that man perhaps most readily associates with a heightened sense of life and fulfilment. There has not been space to explore the range and depth of the poetry in which the theme of vitality twinned with frustration, of force that entangles itself with strength, is expressed; but it is, of course, the range and depth of the poetry that make Antony and Cleopatra into universal figures. At the superb close, Cleopatra — both 'empress' and 'lass unparalleled' — is an incarnation of sexual passion, of those primeval energies that insistently demand fulfilment in their own terms, and, by insisting on their own terms ('Thy beck might from the bidding of the gods Command me'), thwart the fulfilment that they seek. But a whole-hearted response to the play recognizes both sides of the paradox, the tremendous vitality as well as the inherent loss and limitation. The mere moralist can tell us as little about *The Tragedy of Antony and Cleopatra* as he can about *Anna Karenina*.

Shakespeare's earlier plays on political issues, from *Henry VI* onwards, had shown an increasing realism, a developing concern for the actuality — the specific human substance — of situations commonly seen in abstract and general terms. *Coriolanus*, in this respect, is the consummation of Shakespeare's political wisdom. But if *Coriolanus* thus links with a large group of earlier plays, it could only have been written after *King Lear* and *Macbeth*. There is now an assured grasp of those positive values that alone give significance to conflict; the play is a tragedy, not a satire. And the verse, close packed and flexible,* has that power of compressed definition that we associate with the plays of Shakespeare's maturity, so that the immediate action is felt as the focus of a vision of life that is searching and profound.

Caius Marcius dominates the action of the play to which he gives his name, but the protagonist is Rome, the city.[19] It is a city divided against itself, and the first scene presents the conflict in lively, dramatic terms. It also contains Menenius' fable of the belly, which is

---

* To bring out the vitality of the verse, compare the accounts of crowd behaviour in *Julius Caesar*, I. i. 42–52, and *Coriolanus*, II. i. 201–17.

a reminder of the ideal of mutuality in a healthy social organism – but which certainly does not answer the specific complaints of the citizens ('What authority surfeits on would relieve us'). Menenius himself habitually thinks in terms of a distinction between 'Rome' and 'her rats'; and although there is no idealization of 'the people' – who are a mixed assortment of individuals – the courtesy of the patrician class among themselves is more than once placed in effective contrast to their rudeness to the plebeians. A semblance of unity is restored by the granting of tribunes to the plebs and by the approach of external danger. The battle scenes show us the real bravery of Caius Marcius, as well as the less admirable characteristics of some of the commoners; they also make us vividly aware of the *simplifying* effect of war; but with the return of peace internal strain promptly reasserts itself. Coriolanus' behaviour in seeking the consulship brings the conflict to a head.

It is impossible in short space to do justice to the dramatic and poetic force of the third act which culminates in Coriolanus' banishment, but three points may be mentioned. The first is that in such things as Coriolanus' speech at III. i. 139–60, we are vividly aware of the social conflict as a conflict of vital energies that have become inextricably tangled in a process of mutual thwarting and stultification:

> ... purpose so barr'd, it follows
> Nothing is done to purpose.

Secondly, a large part of the meaning is conveyed by a sharp intensification of the imagery of disease; what each side wants is health or 'integrity', but each can think only in terms of surgery, of 'plucking out' a tongue (III. i. 154–5), or 'cutting away' a diseased limb (III. i. 292). And in the third place, when we relate this superb act to the play as a whole, it is impossible not to connect the 'disease' of the body politic with the lop-sided development, the defective humanity, of the central figure.

The fact that our sense of Coriolanus is created largely by poetic means[20] should not hinder us from seeing in the play a subtle 'psychological' probing of the springs of conduct, or a rich 'sociological' interest. When, in the first scene of the play, Coriolanus' prowess is mentioned, we are told, 'He did it to please his mother, and to be partly proud' (I. i. 37–8). Almost immediately after the first public appearance of the hero, we are given a domestic scene in which our attention is directed to the mother, and the mother as a representative of a class (the very tones of 'polite' conversation are caught in the Lady Valeria). Volumnia, the Roman matron, is a perfect embodiment of what has been called 'the taboo on tenderness'.[21] The culture of which she is a representative stresses those 'masculine' qualities that range from genuine physical courage to hardness and insensitiveness in the face of life: her laconic comment on young Marcius's 'mammocking' of the butterfly is worth several pages of analysis. Now in the great central scenes the patrician 'honour' to which she so frequently appeals is subjected to a radical scrutiny. Act III, scene ii, shows the patricians in council after Coriolanus' first reverse; the question is whether he shall submit himself to the people, and Volumnia urges a politic submission:

> . . . now it lies you on to speak
> To th' people, not by your own instruction,
> Nor by th' matter which your heart prompts you,
> But with such words that are but roted in
> Your tongue, though but bastards and syllables
> Of no allowance to your bosom's truth.
> Now, this no more dishonours you at all
> Than to take in a town with gentle words,
> Which else would put you to your fortune and
> The hazard of much blood.
> I would dissemble with my nature where
> My fortunes and my friends at stake requir'd
> I should do so in honour.
>
> (III. ii)

It is to the spirit of this that Coriolanus finally responds:

> Pray be content.
> Mother, I am going to the market-place;
> Chide me no more. I'll mountebank their loves,
> Cog their hearts from them, and come home belov'd
> Of all the trades in Rome.
>
> (III. ii)

I do not remember seeing it remarked in any commentary on the play that the 'honour' in question, being divorced from the 'bosom's truth', is of a very dubious quality, and that Coriolanus, in agreeing to this persuasion, shows a wanton disregard for the values that form the moral basis of any decent society, just as they are at the heart of personal relationships:

> I'll mountebank their loves,
> Cog their hearts from them ...

Coriolanus has none of the apocalyptic quality of *Macbeth*. It is not a world where the sun refuses to rise or horses eat each other; it is a world where petty justices 'wear out a good wholesome forenoon in hearing a cause between an orange-wife and a fosset-seller', where people 'buy and sell with groats', and 'tradesmen sing in their shops' – a familiar world; yet the evil at the heart of the state – though not, as in *Macbeth*, deliberately willed – is just as firmly stated as in the earlier tragedy. In cutting himself off from a responsive relationship to his society (as he had in fact already done before his banishment) Coriolanus' stature as a human person is correspondingly diminished:[22]

> – I go alone,
> Like to a lonely dragon, that his fen
> Makes fear'd and talk'd of more than seen.
> (IV. i)

And in the concluding acts there are constant reminders of the unnatural reversal of values in social life that springs from a *personal* failure to achieve integration and relationship. Thus the 'comic' talk of the serving-men about the superiority of war to peace (peace 'makes men hate one another' – 'Reason: because they then less need one another') merely transposes into another key Volumnia's denial of values essential to life. The logic of that denial, which her son accepts, is worked out to its end, and the imagery of falling and burning buildings in the latter part of the play is the public counterpart to the angry isolation and self-destruction of one who, being a man, can only find his true life in society:

> I'll never
> Be such a gosling to obey instinct, but stand
> As if a man were author of himself
> And knew no other kin.
> (V. iii)

In the face of his mother's dignified and moving appeal to spare the city, Coriolanus finds that he has to 'obey instinct', and there is tragic dignity in his reply to Volumnia:

> O, mother, mother!
> What have you done? Behold, the heavens do ope,
> The gods look down, and this unnatural scene
> They laugh at. O my mother, mother! O!
> You have won a happy victory to Rome;
> But for your son – believe it, O, believe it!
> Most dangerously you have with him prevail'd,
> If not most mortal to him, But let it come.
>
> (v. iii)

But there is also tragic irony; it is to his mother that he yields – the mother who has made him what he is. He returns to Antium, 'No more infected with my country's love Than when I parted thence', still unable to know, to recognize, 'the other kin', who would include even the plebeians, with their 'pardons, being asked, as free As words to little purpose'. At the height of the civil commotion, we may recall, Cominius had attempted to intervene:

> Let me speak.
> I have been consul, and can show for Rome
> Her enemies' marks upon me. I do love
> My country's good with a respect more tender,
> More holy and profound, than mine own life,
> My dear wife's estimate, her womb's increase
> And treasure of my loins.
>
> (III. iii)

There is suggested the reconciling conception of the state as an extension of the organic bonds of the family, a conception analogous to the ideal of creative mutuality hinted at by Menenius' fable of the belly. But a whole-hearted response to that ideal demands some personal integration and maturity, and Coriolanus, as Wyndham Lewis has remarked,[23] remains to the end the 'boy' that Aufidius taunts him with being.

The fundamental insight that this play embodies is that political and social forms cannot be separated from, are in fact judged by, the human and moral qualities that shape them, and the human and moral qualities that they foster. That is Shakespeare's answer to Renaissance and modern 'realism' that would resolve political questions solely to questions of power.

We may end by pausing to consider how it is that Shakespeare's tragedies, although stories of wrong, disaster, and defeat, so notably enrich our sense of life's possibilities. It is partly, of course, that the sheer vitality of the creating mind calls forth a corresponding vitality – Coleridge's '*activity* of attention'[24] – on the part of the reader or spectator. And as we have seen especially in *King Lear*, 'tragedy' it-self can elicit a firm and grounded sense of positive values. In *Macbeth, Antony and Cleopatra*, and *Coriolanus*, however, qualities making for wholeness and essential life, in short, for good, are glimpsed *through* the perversion or entanglement of energies and passions deeply rooted in human nature. In the latest plays, without discarding or ignoring the experience of the tragic period, Shake-speare puts in the forefront of his drama 'the possible other case',[25] and directly bodies forth experiences in which not only does good triumph, but the energies of 'nature' themselves contribute to the sense of life and renewal.

NOTES

1. See the books listed in Part IV, Appendix.

2. The phrase is from Coleridge, *Biographia Literaria*, ch. XV, which con-tains some of the most suggestive Shakespeare criticism in the language.

3. See G. Wilson Knight, *The Wheel of Fire*, 'On the Principles of Shake-speare Interpretation'. Of course Shakespeare shows an acute awareness of *persons*; but the revelation of 'personality' varies from play to play, and with-in each play, and is subordinated to the controlling vision and the more in-clusive statement that each play is *as a whole*. Arthur Sewell's *Character and Society in Shakespeare*, which appeared after this chapter was written, is an illuminating discussion of the meaning of 'character' in Shakespeare.

4. For some suggestive analysis, see F. R. Leavis, *Education and the Uni-versity*, 76–82, 121–5. For the *exploratory* quality of the verse see the same writer's 'Tragedy and the "Medium" ' in *The Common Pursuit*.

5. See Theodore Spencer, *Shakespeare and the Nature of Man*, 135–52 – pages to which I am considerably indebted.

6. For the significance of the macabre comedy of this scene (IV. vi), see G. Wilson Knight, *The Wheel of Fire*, 170–72. The abyss into which Gloucester peers with his sightless eyes, and into which he thinks to cast himself, may be regarded also as an image of the abyss of the mind that opens before Lear in the same scene.

7. 'But Shakespeare ... always by metaphors and figures involves in the thing considered a universe of past and possible experiences' – Coleridge, *Miscellaneous Criticism*, ed. T. M. Raysor, 96.

8. Marvin Rosenberg well expresses a similar sense of the play's multi-plicity of meanings in *The Masks of King Lear*, 328. In this book, in tracing the theatrical history of the play and the main shifts of critical opinion, Rosen-

berg brings out the enormous variety of responses that are possible, even – or perhaps especially – when we keep, as he does, in close contact with the text.

9. On this see Stanley Cavell, 'The Avoidance of Love: a Reading of *King Lear*', in his *Must We Mean What We Say?*

10. See A. C. Bradley, *Shakespearean Tragedy*, 266–8. Bradley's Lectures on *Lear* in this volume should certainly be read by the student of the play.

11. See J. F. Danby, *Shakespeare's Doctrine of Nature: a Study of King Lear* and R. C. Bald's essay, '"Thou, Nature, art my Goddess": Edmund and Renaissance Free Thought', in the volume *J. Q. Adams Memorial Studies* (Folger Library). Danby's book is not only relevant for 'background', it is a valuable critical study of the play.

12. As Granville-Barker pointed out, Lear *acts* the storm. See his 'King Lear' in *Prefaces to Shakespeare*, First Series.

13. There is no way of proving that *King Lear* precedes *Macbeth*. E. K. Chambers is inclined to assign *Lear* to 1605 and *Macbeth* to early in 1606 (*William Shakespeare*, Vol. I, 463ff. and 471ff.). *Timon of Athens*, though not one of the great tragedies, almost certainly belongs to the same phase. Much of the verse is flexible and forceful, and although the play makes use of something like a 'Morality' technique, it centres on a figure who is certainly not conceived in the fixed terms of a Morality Play. Scholars disagree about the date. Chambers puts the play in 1608, between *Coriolanus* and *Pericles* (*William Shakespeare*, Vol. I, 480–84), but the arguments for a late date are not conclusive. Act IV contains a number of interesting verbal parallels to *King Lear* (though Timon's invective serves an entirely different dramatic purpose from that of Lear), and the theme of the necessary close relationship between what an individual intrinsically is and what he conceives the outside world to be would seem to refer the play to the period when Shakespeare was especially preoccupied with the question of 'being' and 'seeing' (the period, say, from *Troilus and Cressida* to *King Lear*). But there is no way of determining exactly either the date of composition or the extent to which the Folio text represents Shakespeare's final intentions: internal evidence suggests that the play was abandoned before completion. The main interest of *Timon of Athens*, as we have it, is in the psychological relation between an excessive 'generosity' (prodigality) and an excessive disillusion (cynicism); and there are indications that Shakespeare intended to suggest the further relation between individual failure and corruption in society. See the essay by J. C. Maxwell in *Scrutiny*, XV, No. 3, and L. C. Knights, '*Timon of Athens*', in '*Hamlet*' and Other *Shakespearean Essays*.

14. Editors have argued that the original play has been both cut down and added to (see J. Dover Wilson's Introduction in the New Cambridge Series). I can see no reason for assuming that something is missing except, possibly, in I. ii. And it is possible that the Hecate scenes and the songs (III. v, and IV. i. 39–43) were added by 'another hand'. The problem is discussed by Kenneth Muir in his Arden edition of the play.

15. Spinoza, *Ethics*, Part V, Prop. XLII (Everyman edition, 223–4).

16. In *Shakespeare's Philosophical Patterns*, W. C. Curry shows the connection between Shakespeare's thought in *Macbeth* and the traditional Catholic doctrine of the illusory and negative quality of evil.

17. The *Lives* of Plutarch, in North's translation, that are the main source of Shakespeare's Roman plays, are included in *Narrative and Dramatic Sources of Shakespeare*, ed. G. Bullough, Vol. 5.

18. See pp. 106–8 of Salingar's Literary Survey, above; also 'The Shakespearean Dialectic: an Aspect of *Antony and Cleopatra*', by J. F. Danby, in *Scrutiny*, XVI, No. 3. In '"Nature's Piece 'gainst fancy": The Divided Catastrophe in *Antony and Cleopatra*' (Bedford College Inaugural Lecture, London, 1973), Anne Barton says that the 'second catastrophe' – Cleopatra's death, contrasted with Antony's – 'imposes a new angle of vision', and 'demonstrates how the ending of this story transfigured its earlier, more suspect stages'. This brilliant lecture, so different from the account given above, should be read.

19. Wilson Knight, in his essay on *Coriolanus* in *The Imperial Theme*, shows how city life is constantly present to us in imagery and allusion.

20. See D. A. Traversi's essay on *Coriolanus* in *Scrutiny*, VI, 1937–8.

21. See Ian D. Suttie, *The Origins of Love and Hate*, ch. VI, and D. W. Harding, *The Impulse to Dominate*, ch. XIV. See also Harding's 'Women's fantasy of Manhood: a Shakespearean Theme' (Shakespeare Quarterly, XX, 3, 1969): 'The ultimate view of the man as victim of the woman's ideal of manhood is given in *Coriolanus*.'

22. See the article by F. N. Lees, 'Coriolanus, Aristotle and Bacon', in the *Review of English Studies*, New Series, Vol. I, No. 2.

23. See Wyndham Lewis, *The Lion and the Fox*, 202–3, and Part VII, ch. II.

24. *Biographia Literaria*, ch. XV.

25. What Henry James says of irony (Preface to *The Lesson of the Master*, x) – it 'implies and projects the possible other case, the case rich and edifying where the actuality is pretentious and vain' – can be applied also, though with a difference, to tragedy.

SHAKESPEARE: THE LAST PLAYS
DEREK TRAVERSI

Though *Antony and Cleopatra* – with *Coriolanus* – is the last of Shakespeare's great tragedies, it does not represent the last stage in the dramatist's development. It was followed by a series of plays, written apparently between 1608 and 1612 (*Pericles, Cymbeline, The Winter's Tale* and *The Tempest*), which represent an effort to give artistic form to a new symbolic conception. At the heart of each of these plays lies an organic relationship between breakdown and reconstruction, the division created in the most intimate human bonds (and more especially in the unity of the family) by the action of time and passion and the final healing of these divisions. Near the opening of each play – even in *Cymbeline*, where the treatment of this central theme is partially obscured – a father loses his offspring through the excess of his own passion-driven folly or through his involvement in a corrupt world. The main action is devoted to the suffering and remorse which follow from this estrangement, and at the end of the play the lost child (a daughter whose name has clear symbolic associations: Marina in *Pericles*, Perdita in *The Winter's Tale*, Miranda in *The Tempest*) is restored to her father's blessing and becomes an instrument of reconciliation. In these plots the harmonizing theme first attempted in *King Lear*, and there broken by the prevailing tragic development, produces a symbolic conception of drama completely removed from realism and scarcely paralleled in English literature.

The first experiment in the new form, *Pericles, Prince of Tyre*, is perhaps best regarded as the work of an inferior author in which Shakespeare detected the presence of a significant symbolic pattern and to which he contributed, at moments of special interest, the expression of his own highly personal conceptions.[1] If this be a true account – and there are moments when the separation of the primitive foundations from the distinctively Shakespearean passages is admittedly difficult to maintain[2] – we can regard Pericles, when the play opens, as embarked upon a pilgrimage in search of true happiness. Driven by the discovery of hidden evil to abandon his first dream of felicity to be gained by marriage to the daughter of Antiochus, he is exposed to a variety of experiences which can be interpreted as representing various stages in moral growth. The anger of the tyrant, aroused by the discovery of his incestuous secret, obliges him to leave his kingdom, exposing him first to penury and then to a storm which, as in so many of Shakespeare's later plays, reflects the hero's subjection to tragedy. In the storm, and through the action of three Fishermen, he recovers the armour bequeathed to him by his father, an incident (II. i) itself capable of bearing a symbolic interpretation; and, once more clothed in the armour as his defence, he wins in tournament the hand of Thaisa, daughter of Simonides of Pentapolis.

The rest of the tragedy brings us, beyond all reasonable doubt, into contact with Shakespeare's first attempt to develop the theme of symbolic reconciliation which prevails in his last plays. With Pericles exposed to a storm at sea which he ascribes to the will of the 'gods', and with the death, on board ship and in childbirth, of his wife, the true sense of the action becomes apparent. Thaisa, dying through exposure to the elements, bequeaths her husband on her death-bed a living continuation of herself ('this piece of your dead queen'), and Pericles hails the event in words in which stress and calm, tragedy and the following peace, are blended:

> Now, mild may be thy life!
> For a more blusterous birth had never babe;
> Quiet and gentle thy conditions! for
> Thou art the rudeliest welcome to this world
> That ever was prince's* child. Happy what follows!
> Thou hast as chiding a nativity
> As fire, air, water, earth, and heaven, can make
> To herald thee from the womb.

> (III. i)

The balance of contrasted images here is an indication of the point reached at this stage in the symbolic pattern. Pericles prays that the 'mildness' of his daughter's life may compensate for the unprecedented 'blusterous' conditions of her birth, the future hope of a 'quiet and gentle' environment for the 'rudeliest' welcome to the world

---

* Princess? The Quarto's 'princes' could stand for either.

which she has undergone at the moment of her begetting. Behind the more superficial aspects of this prayer for peace lies the characteristic Shakespearean intuition of subsistent continuity, the sense that birth and death, tempest and the following calm, are related aspects of a single process to which the elements themselves – 'fire', 'air', 'water', and even 'earth and heaven' – are, in their universal presence, witnesses.

The rest of *Pericles* develops in highly individual poetic terms the conception thus introduced into the action. The new-born child grows into Pericles' daughter Marina, who is left by her father with Cleon, governor of Tarsus, and exposed through the jealousy of Cleon's wife Dionyza to tragedy in the brothel scenes (IV. ii, v, vi) which – though generally inferior in sentiment and execution[3] – clearly belong to the developing pattern. Thaisa, meanwhile, whom her husband thinks is dead, is cast ashore at Ephesus and restored to life by the beneficent wisdom of Cerimon 'to make the world twice rich' (III. ii. 102). The time to restore her to her husband, however, has not yet come. Before this can be, Pericles has to complete a long period of exposure to sorrow until Marina is ready to play her part as the instrument of reconciliation; the 'resurrection' of Thaisa needs to be balanced by the moral rebirth of Pericles, itself brought about by the recovery of the 'bond'[4] which unites him to the child of his own blood. When the time is at last ripe, the restoration of harmony is conveyed step by step through a subtle blend of dramatic action and poetic imagery. Pericles appears on board ship, curtained from the sight of onlookers and so cut off, in a sense, from a world which he has decided to abandon. Marina, still unaware that she is in her father's presence, goes in to him to exercise her healing gifts and, quickened by a sense whose true meaning is still hidden from him, he breaks into renewed speech and finally salutes her in terms that carry a step further the spirit of poetic symbolism in which all this part of the play is steeped:

> I am great with woe, and shall deliver weeping.
> My dearest wife was like this maid, and such a one
> My daughter might have been. My queen's square brows;
> Her stature to an inch; as wand-like straight;
> As silver-voic'd; her eyes as jewel-like,
> And cas'd as richly; in pace another Juno;

Who starves the ears she feeds, and makes them hungry,
The more she gives them speech.

(v. i)

Pericles' opening words, balanced between contrary emotions, indicate that the physical birth in the tempest is opening into its counterpart in the spiritual order. What is in process of being born under the
revival of poignant past memories, is expressed as a new vision of
humanity restored to a stature almost divine. In the healing figure
of Marina are reborn the 'square brows' of Thaisa, her perfect carriage, her 'silver voice' and 'jewel-like' eyes, and, above all, the 'pace'
of Juno, the queen of the gods; and to round off the transforming
splendour of the description, her utterance is such that it gives
sustenance without surfeit (she 'starves the ears she feeds'[5]) and, as it
nourishes her hearers, makes them 'hungry' for further speech.

The conclusion of the play is a rounding-off, in the light of this
reborn splendour and in terms of imagery superbly rich and tender,
of the dramatic situation. Pericles, having persuaded himself that the
girl before him is indeed 'flesh and blood', asks her to explain the
significance of her name; she replies with the revelation, full of
meaning in its double associations of past suffering and providential
preservation, that she was 'born at sea'. From this discovery to the
declaration of her mother's death is but a step: a step which leads in
turn to the overflow of Pericles' pent-up emotions and, at last, to the
explicit statement of the central symbol:

> O, come hither,
> Thou that beget'st him that did thee beget;
> Thou that wast born at sea, buried at Tarsus,
> And found at sea again!

(v. i)

Pericles, a second time 'begotten' through the saving action of his
daughter, now puts on 'fresh garments'[6] and calls for the music that
is, here as in all these final plays, the expression of harmony restored.
Thus clad, and after his sorrow has been, like Lear's, soothed in sleep,
he makes his way to the temple at Ephesus to be restored to the
wife whom he had lost. The restoration takes place to the echo of
the two basic conceptions of the play: that of the organic relationship that unites birth and death, both related to their origin in exposure to the elements —

Did you not name a tempest,
A birth and death? –

(v. iii)

and that of the sacred continuity of the family, recreated in the sea
and now restored in the flesh to be given its full redeeming sanction:

Look who kneels here! Flesh of thy flesh, Thaisa;
Thy burden at the sea, and call'd Marina,
For she was yielded there.

(v. iii)

With filial love once more responding, by kneeling, to paternal blessing, the family unity, temporarily shattered by tempest and the action
of time, is restored in deepened understanding and enriched by
spiritual splendour.

The second play of this period, *Cymbeline*, though without the disconcerting crudities of the early scenes of *Pericles*, is in some ways a
less interesting piece. More closely connected with the fashionable
dramatic convention of the moment, which called for sentiment and
a glorification of the simple life, it none the less shows Shakespeare
attempting to use these conventions for his own purposes. The theme
of loss and reconciliation, though less clearly defined than in *Pericles*,
is present in the new fable. Cymbeline loses his children, Guiderius
and Arviragus, whose place at Court falls to the uncouth and brutish
Cloten through the machinations of his twice-married queen. They
are exposed for long years to the simplicities, crude but noble, of the
primitive life under the charge of the banished Belarius, and finally
return to their father's embrace. Thus restored to civilized life, they
bring with them the virtues of barbaric honesty which are henceforth
to be integrated into the order of true courtliness.

That order is introduced into the play, and related in turn to the
master-theme of loss and gain, through yet another story of division
and exposure to trial, that of Imogen, Cymbeline's daughter by a
former queen, and Posthumus. The clash of loyalties occasioned by
Imogen's forced betrothal to Cloten is given a definite universality of
context in the opening scene of the play:

our bloods
No more obey the heavens than our courtiers
Still seem as does the king.

(I. i)

Against the background of concord which relates the observance of courtly 'degree' to the operation of the 'heavens', the arbitrary act of the monarch, occasioned by the blindness of the passion that binds him to his second wife, produces in his subjects an underlying sense of disquiet. First indicated indirectly in 'seem', it is openly expressed a little later in the First Gentleman's assertion that

> not a courtier,
> Although they wear their faces to the bent
> Of the king's looks, hath a heart that is not
> Glad at the thing they scowl at.
>
> (I. i)

The linguistic quality of this passage, with its suggestion in 'wear their faces'[7] of the masking of true sentiment and the conflict of natural feeling and duty implied in the contrast between 'glad' and 'scowl', indicates the prevailing state of moral dislocation. The return to normality through the integration of natural simplicity and true courtly virtue, and the subordination of both to a higher loyalty, is the true theme of *Cymbeline*.

In accordance with this general plan, Imogen's repudiation of the uncouth pretensions of Cloten implies her choice of a superior conception of humanity, at once supremely natural and truly civilized. This conception inspires the opening description of Posthumus, whom the king formerly endowed with

> all the learnings of his time
> Could make him the receiver of; which he took,
> As we do air, fast as 'twas minist'red,
> And in's spring became a harvest, liv'd in court –
> Which rare it is to do – most prais'd, most lov'd,
> A sample to the youngest; to th' more mature
> A glass that feated them; and to the graver
> A child that guided dotards.
>
> (I. i)

The virtues thus celebrated in Posthumus are those of true courtliness, fostered by a 'learning' imbibed as naturally as air and proceeding, in the normal course of youthful development, to its spontaneous 'harvest'. In a world in which true virtue is indeed rare, he has become an example to all ages and conditions, a mirror of the finer human qualities which Imogen, in loving him, has appreciated at their proper worth.

The 'rarity' of this example is emphasized by the success which attends the intrigues of the 'Italianate' courtier Iachimo. To the latter, apparently dispassionate but in reality enslaved to his own sensuality, true virtue is inconceivable. In his attack upon Imogen the overflow of physical imagery, product of

> The cloyed will –
> That satiate yet unsatisfied desire, that tub
> Both fill'd and running,
>
> (I. vi)

is at once intense and deeply repellent. This is a speaker to whose cynical intelligence passion seems sterile, even disgusting, but to whom no conception of value is conceivable as a check to the senseless operations of desire. It is his resentment against the physical embodiment of such a conception in Imogen that causes him to intrigue against her chastity, by proposing a wager – rashly accepted by Posthumus – in which the material value of a jewel which 'may be sold or given' is equated to a love which is 'only the gift of the gods'. Around the clash of contrary attitudes which this incident implies, the moral and material 'values' with which the play is concerned are finely interwoven. Posthumus is ready to expose his belief in his mistress' virtue to trial in terms of tangible worth and Iachimo uses his readiness to insinuate that the two conceptions of value, the moral and the material, are in fact identical, that the one is only to be conceived in terms of the other. To Posthumus' sweeping assertion that his jewel and the object of his love stand alike in his estimation – 'I praised her as I rated her. So do I my stone' – Iachimo's answer, inspired by his rooted relativity, is as far as it goes indisputable: 'I have not seen the most precious diamond that is, nor you the lady'. The weakness implied in Posthumus' rash attitudes bears fruit in the ease with which Iachimo persuades him to repudiate his love. Imogen repels, easily enough, his direct assault, but is powerless to meet the guile by which he steals from her in sleep the 'proof' of his conquest; and as a result of her defencelessness she is faced, not only with the passionate resentment of her father, but with the anger of her disillusioned lover.

At this point the story of the two lovers meets that of the lost sons of Cymbeline in a common exposure to 'nature'. They, in their discussion with their foster-father (III. iii), balance a realization of the advantages of the simple life against a sense of its limitations: on the one hand,

> Haply this life is best,
> If quiet life be best;

on the other, Ariviragus acknowledges himself to be 'beastly' and feels his limitations as a prison:

> Our cage
> We make a choir, as doth the prison'd bird,
> And sing our bondage freely.
>
> (III. iii)

Simplicity has limitations of its own, freedom under conditions of primitive life involves the 'bondage' of the higher, specifically civilized faculties. These will only be awakened in Cymbeline's sons when they are restored to free loyalty and to a proper relationship with the father they have lost.

The theme thus indicated is scarcely consistently developed in the play. It seems clear, however, that the 'death' of Imogen is part of the symbolism of the conception. It implies a certain liberation, fittingly expressed in the dirge over her 'dead' body:

> Fear no more the frown o' th' great;
> Thou art past the tyrant's stroke . . .
>
> (IV. ii)

and to it corresponds the captivity of Posthumus and the tone of his meditations in prison:

> Most welcome, bondage! for thou art a way,
> I think, to liberty.
>
> (V. iv)

Both, in their spirit of tempered acceptance, are proper preludes to the battle in which Posthumus and the sons of Cymbeline alike find their proper place fighting against the foreign invader in the orbit of patriotism and in devotion, respectively, to their king and father. The long passage (v. iii. 3–51) describing the ebb and flow of the battle and the victory finally achieved in 'a narrow lane' by 'an old man, and two boys' renders the whole episode significant beyond its surface meaning. It is also one of the finest examples of the free, charged complexity of Shakespeare's latest verse.

The play ends, in one of those deliberately extended scenes of reversal and recognition integral to Shakespeare's conception of comedy, on the familiar note of reconciliation. Posthumus is restored to Imogen, and Cymbeline to his 'lost' sons. The British, having won in battle their freedom from the imposed payment of tribute, recognize by free choice their natural part in the larger 'Roman' order of civility. To the Soothsayer's declaration of the relevance of supernatural purpose –

> The fingers of the pow'rs above do tune
> The harmony of this peace ...
>
> (v. v)

Cymbeline, restored to true self-knowledge and to his position as royal embodiment of unity, replies with a gesture of forgiveness and a final offering of thanks:

> Laud we the gods,
> And let our crooked smokes climb to their nostrils
> From our bles'd altars.
>
> (v. v)

In this vision of consecration to a unifying purpose, the personal issues of the play, the love of Imogen for Posthumus maintained through trials and the integration of natural simplicity with the civilized graces, find their proper integration in natural subjection to Cymbeline, as father and king.

To pass from *Pericles* and *Cymbeline* to *The Winter's Tale* is to leave the field of experiment for that of finished achievement. The play, a dramatization of Robert Greene's romance *Pandosto: The Triumph of Time* (1588), is less an ordinary 'comedy', even of the type of *Twelfth Night* or *A Midsummer Night's Dream*, than a construction approaching the *ballet* form, a strictly formal creation in which music plays an important though subsidiary part, and in which the main effects are achieved by the use of subtly interrelated poetic imagery. Its plot is perfectly adjusted to the new symbolic technique, and it is useful – if only to get away from the idea of realistic drama – to see its various stages as the successive movements, differing in feeling and tempo, which go to make up the unity of a quartet or a symphony. In accordance with this conception the first 'movement' would deal with the tragic break-up of existing unity through the passionate folly of one man. Leontes and Polixenes, respectively kings of Sicily and Bohemia (here clearly countries of the imagination), open the play as life-long friends; but from the moment of their first appearance their friendship contains seeds of division. Their 'affection', as we are told in the opening remarks of the courtier Camillo, 'cannot choose but branch now', and they have 'shook hands, as over a vast; and embraced, as it were, from the ends of opposed winds'. The threat of tragedy thus veiled in the apparent celebration of their unity soon takes shape in the passionate, jealous conviction of Leontes that Polixenes has replaced him in the affections of his wife Hermione.

The nature of this division is made clear in the course of Polixenes' account of the foundations upon which his friendship with Leontes had rested. 'We were', he exclaims,

> Two lads that thought there was no more behind
> But such a day to-morrow as to-day,
> And to be boy eternal . . .
> We were as twinn'd lambs that did frisk i' th' sun
> And bleat the one at th' other. What we chang'd
> Was innocence for innocence; we knew not
> The doctrine of ill-doing, nor dream'd
> That any did.

(I. ii)

The bond between the two kings, which dates from childhood, has rested on the youthful state of innocence; based on a sentimental ignoring of the reality of time, it assumed that it was possible to remain 'boy eternal'. The realities of human nature, however, make this impossible. Boyhood is necessarily a state of transition. Time corrupts those unprepared to oppose its action with a corresponding moral effort, and youthful innocence, left to itself, falls under the shadow of the 'doctrine of ill-doing'. The reality of a 'fallen' condition in man needs to be recognized in the process by which each individual human being passes from the state of original 'innocence' to that of 'experience'. Only through a conscious reaction to this reality can this idyllic state of childlike acceptance grow into an independent, conscious maturity.

In particular, and as a potent factor in separating the mature man from his childhood, time brings a capacity for sensual passion which may be good, if it leads to its natural fulfilment in the creative unity of the family, or evil and destructive, in the form of egoism and its consequences, jealousy overcoming all restraint of reason. In Leontes, it is the evil impulse which comes to the surface. His sexual passion thrusts reason aside, expressing itself in phrases as intense as they are broken and incoherent:

> It is a bawdy planet, that will strike
> Where 'tis predominant.
>
> (I. ii)
>
> No barricado for a belly ...
>
> (I. ii)
>
> I have drunk, and seen the spider.
>
> (II. i)

Moved by this spirit of unreason, he condemns his new-born child first to death, then to abandonment, and his wife to prison, without pausing to wait for the sentence of the divine oracle. That sentence, when it comes, proves Hermione to have been innocent: but not before she has died – or so Leontes believes – of grief, and before his son Mamillius has perished of grief, his new-born child been 'lost', and his friendship with Polixenes shattered beyond all apparent remedy. The first movement of destruction and disintegration is complete with Leontes' broken reaction to these successive blows: 'Apollo's angry; and the heavens themselves Do strike at my injustice' (III. ii. 144–5).

The 'second movement', although very short, contains the turning-point which is, in all these plays, an essential feature of the symbolic structure. It opens (III. ii) in a storm which carries on the idea of the divine displeasure and is treated, poetically, in a manner that recalls *Pericles*. As in the earlier play, the tempest serves as a background to the idea of birth; when the peasant who has witnessed the hurricane describes the drowning of a ship's crew in the angry seas, his father replies by showing in his arms a newly found child – the child of Leontes – adding, in words that echo a similarly crucial utterance in *Pericles*, 'thou mettest with things dying, I with things newborn'. The significance of the discovery is abundantly clear. The child, born of Leontes' imperfect passion, has no part in his sin; born in tempest and looking forward to future calm, she connects the tragic past with the restored harmony of the future and becomes the instrument of reconciliation.

Before this reconciliation can begin to take shape in the 'third movement', we have to pass over sixteen years. Leontes' daughter then reappears as Perdita (like Marina before her, symbolically named) and meets Florizel, the disguised son of Polixenes, at the rustic sheep-shearing organized by her supposed 'father', the shepherd who discovered her as a baby in the storm. Early in the scene the conflict between 'innocence' and 'experience' emerges when Perdita, in her role as 'queen' of the feast, rejects the flowers – 'carnations' and 'streaked gillyvors' – which the season offers her in the name of what she sees as 'nature', unsophisticated simplicity. To this rejection Polixenes, present in disguise, replies as the representative of an older generation, with a plea for 'experience', harmonizing growth:

> over that art
> Which you say adds to nature, is an art
> That nature makes. You see, sweet maid, we marry
> A gentler scion to the wildest stock,
> And make conceive a bark of baser kind
> By bud of nobler race. This is an art
> Which does mend nature – change it rather; but
> The art itself is nature.
>
> (IV. iv)

We are here at the heart of a debate, familiar in Renaissance literature, on the relationship between *nature* and *nurture*, natural simplicity and human, civilizing *improvement*, initial *nature* and completing *grace*. To Perdita's view of 'art' as a deformation of 'nature', Polixenes opposes another, of 'art' as completing 'nature', based on it indeed but as its crown and perfection. According to this view, it is the *nature* of man to be *artful*, and *human nature* expresses itself in *human art*. The conception is capable of expression in social terms, and Polixenes makes this explicit by discussing the process of grafting in terms of *marriage*: the union of the 'wildest stock' (in other words, 'nature', what Shakespeare sometimes calls 'blood', unregenerate humanity) to a 'scion', the product of civilized urbanity, of 'nature' in its completely human, fulfilled sense, which is 'grace'. Man, unlike the rest of the creation, is in a very important sense what he makes himself, at least as much as what he is before the making ('artful') process begins. The 'bark of *baser kind*' is made to conceive by a 'bud of *nobler* race': the idea of birth following on marriage thus acquires a new, wider meaning, becomes a completion, itself natural, of 'nature', an assumption by normal humanity of the crowning qualities, at once social, civilizing, and spiritual, of 'grace'.

The force of Polixenes' argument is marred, or at least conditioned, by the element of jealous, old man's possessiveness which will bear fruit in his actions before the end of the scene. In her reply Perdita speaks from her own youth and simplicity, with their promise, their right rejection of what in human relationships is corrupt, cynical, unnatural, and – as we might add – their necessary incompleteness. Promise and incompleteness, blended to correspond to the present stage of the action, are both confirmed when, in the process of offering her pastoral flowers to Florizel, she celebrates the return of life after the long winter of discontent:

> Now, my fair'st friend,
> I would I had some flow'rs o' th' spring that might
> Become your time of day – and yours, and yours,
> That wear upon your virgin branches yet
> Your maidenheads growing. O Proserpina,
> For the flowers now that, frighted, thou let'st fall
> From Dis's wagon! daffodils,
> That come before the swallow dares, and take
> The winds of March with beauty; violets, dim
> But sweeter than the lids of Juno's eyes
> Or Cytherea's breath; pale primroses,
> That die unmarried ere they can behold
> Bright Phoebus in his strength – a malady
> Most incident to maids; bold oxlips, and
> The crown-imperial.

> (IV. iv)

Beautiful as the speech is and for all its conclusiveness as a sign that the spring of reconciliation has dawned, the love it expresses still lacks the necessary maturity which only experience can provide. The emphasis laid, in the imagery, upon Spring, that is upon birth, inexperience, virginity, is balanced by an implicit sense of death, which the vitality indicated by the reference to the 'royal' flowers – 'bold oxlips' and 'the crown imperial' – can only partly counter. The flowers to which Perdita refers are 'pale' and 'dim'; they 'die un-married', in unfulfilled promise, having failed to 'behold Phoebus in his strength'.

Florizel's reply in turn expresses a similar desire to live outside time, to hold up the course of mutability in a way that is ultimately impossible:

> What you do
> Still betters what is done. When you speak, sweet,
> I'd have you do it ever. When you sing,
> I'd have you buy and sell so; so give alms;
> Pray so, and for the ord'ring your affairs,
> To sing them too. When you do dance, I wish you
> A wave o' th' sea, that you might ever do
> Nothing but that, move still, still so,
> And own no other function. Each your doing,
> So singular in each particular,
> Crowns what you are doing in the present deeds,
> That all your acts are queens.
>
> (IV. iv)

The most striking quality of the speech is its sensation of balance, of a continual relationship between motion and stillness. Every action of Perdita's – so Florizel asserts – involves *all* her perfections, is a complete expression of her natural queenliness: 'All your acts are queens'. And this, in turn, connects her with the central image of the speech – that of the wave, which is always in movement and yet ever the same. This intuition, which is one between the mutability of life – for change is the law of life, and life is made by changing – and the infinite value of the human experience which is conditioned by change but which is finally incommensurate with it, is one which will eventually be taken up into the complete conception: but not yet, for the pattern has still to be completed. That is why, at this moment of idyllic celebration, Polixenes enters to cast across it the shadow of aged, impotent anger, taking away his son, threatening Perdita with torture, and falling into something very like Leontes' sin.

Enough has been said to show that this great pastoral scene plays a far more important part in the structure of *The Winter's Tale* than would appear if we regard it as no more than a splendid piece of decorative make-believe. In pastoral Bohemia, as in primitive Britain, there exists a powerful contrast between Court sophistication and the simple life. Perdita is especially forthright on this subject. When Polixenes, with his sneering description of her as 'worthy enough a herdsman', accuses her of enticing Florizel to debase himself and threatens her with torture, her reply is a frank acceptance of the implied challenge:

> I was not much afeard; for once or twice
> I was about to speak and tell him plainly
> The selfsame sun that shines upon his court
> Hides not his visage from our cottage, but
> Looks on alike.
>
> (IV. iv)

Once again, however, Shakespeare's aim is not contrast but integration. The good life is not to be fully attained in pastoral abstraction, although many of its elements may be present in this idyllic form; nor is court life, if by that we mean a social existence subject to natural loyalties and based on the recognition of the deepest ties, necessarily corrupt or debased. The virtues of the one need to be infused into the grace of the other. That is why, when all the characters of the play converge upon Leontes' court, a subsidiary place is found for the Shepherd and Clown who, by the very fact of their having discovered and reared Perdita, have their own claim to participation in the complete pattern. Before this, their last appearance before Leontes' palace, it is true that they have been unmercifully scarified by Autolycus (who represents something very like the forces of wayward human anarchy, and whom Shakespeare has thrown in with an inconsequential but profoundly human gesture, lest his conception should seem too perfectly, abstractly balanced) but the fact remains that they *do* arrive, and that the Clown's gently ironic comment on social pretensions – 'so we wept – and there was the first gentleman-like tears that ever we shed' – throws, from its particular angle of simplicity, a light of its own upon the entire situation.

The final resolution is the work of the fourth and last 'movement'. We return, after a gap of sixteen years, to Leontes, whose courtiers have been urging him to marry again. The bond of wedlock, and its fulfilment in the shape of heirs, is repeatedly stressed in *The Winter's Tale*. The sanctity of Hermione has been from the first closely bound up with reverence for her motherhood; this connection was most intimately expressed in the comments on her pregnancy made by her two attendant ladies to the young Mamillius:

> LADY. The Queen your mother rounds apace ...

> SECOND LADY.　　　　She is spread of late
> Into a *goodly* bulk. *Good time* encounter her!
> (II. i)

The adjectives underline the presence in Hermione of a beneficent and creative fertility. Now, in the arguments addressed to Leontes by his courtiers, the fulfilment of the marriage-tie is associated with the royal craving for an heir. Leontes' own attitude is a delicate blend of apparently contrary emotions. Bound by a 'saint-like sorrow' which the memory of his queen's virtue keeps alive in him, he none the less shares the universal desire for an heir as fulfilment, as manifestation of the natural fertility of which his sin has deprived him. The child he so intensely desires can only be born of Hermione, whom he believes to be dead: can only, therefore, be the daughter whom he condemned to die.

At last, however, Leontes has repented enough. The final expiation of his past error coincides with the concentration of the whole action at his court. Florizel and Perdita, fleeing before the displeasure of Polixenes, seek refuge at another and wiser court, and all is ready for the final reconciliation. Leontes, in the presence of all the chief actors in the fable, is placed by the faithful Paulina before the life-like 'statue' of Hermione, which gradually comes to life by a process which corresponds to the definitive birth of a new life out of the long winter of penance and suffering. The statue seems to live, it breathes, is warm. It tortures Leontes with the poignancy of a sorrow that he now desires to hold, to make eternal. Deluded, as he still believes, into thinking that the image has the appearance of life, he exclaims:

> Make me to think so twenty years together!
> No settled senses of the world can match
> The pleasure of that madness.
> (v. iii)

Finally, as though in answer to his prayer, the 'statue' comes to life. It is not an accident that this slow awakening is conceived in 'religious' terms. Paulina, just before Hermione 'descends', says to Leontes:

> It is required
> You do awake your *faith*:

'faith', perhaps, not so much in any set of doctrines or beliefs, as in the presence of life 'graciously' renewed. Her final call makes it clear that what we are witnessing is a kind of 'resurrection':

> 'Tis time; descend; be stone no more; approach;
> Strike all that look upon with marvel. Come,
> I'll fill your grave up. Stir; nay, come away.
> Bequeath to death your numbness, for from him
> Dear life redeems you.

'Redeems you': although this is not said, and is not meant to be understood, in a Christian context, the Christian reverberations of the word are there, and are powerful as indications of a life renewed, restored to the full measure of its human possibilities. It is *not* a resurrection, of course, in the sense that it reverses or undoes the past. Hermione, who has never died, is restored to Leontes with the added signs of age and grief upon her; he has passed through an equal period of sterility and death, and there is no reason to suppose that his restored marriage will not be subject to the normal human destiny in time. His son, too, died in the now distant past, and no 'miracle' will bring him back to life. Men have to face, to recognize – in time – the *cost* of their perverse choices, and this Leontes has done. He cannot now escape, but he can build on the recognition of his fault a new and humanly fruitful life with his 'redeemed' wife.

What follows is no more than the natural consequence of this 'restoration'. Florizel and Perdita kneel, like Cordelia and Marina before them, to receive the blessing which Leontes is at last ready to give his daughter, also found again; whilst Polixenes, entering upon the scene of joy and reconciliation, completes it by consenting to her marriage with Florizel. With the marrying of Paulina to the faithful Camillo the pattern of reconciliation is at last complete. The natural love of the children, reinforcing the penitence of their parents – their recognition of the jealous, life-denying sins of maturity – has become an instrument of restoration, and the 'winter' represented by Leontes' years of resentful, aging self-punishment has passed through 'spring' into the 'summer' of gracious consummation and fulfilment.

Criticism of *The Tempest* has long been influenced by the notion of Shakespeare's 'Last Play'. Critics have tended to look for, and find to their satisfaction, a final statement, the summing-up of a lifetime's experience. The assumptions on which these conclusions are based are, perhaps, less than proven. *Henry VIII* is likely to be his work, either wholly or in collaboration with John Fletcher;[8] and there are reasons to believe that he may have had a hand in *The Two Noble Kinsmen*.[9] Given these possibilities, it seems rash to argue that the Epilogue to *The Tempest* represents a consciously final gesture of farewell on Shakespeare's part to his audience and his art.

Such finality as the play has may concern the author's mature reflection on the nature and limitation of the dramatic illusion. It should not be forgotten that the action opens in a storm at sea. As in other works by Shakespeare – *Twelfth Night* comes to mind[10] – the sea is associated with the larger forces of life, which men neither bring into being nor initiate, but which they can aspire, within limits, to shape to ends of their own. The storm has been a creation of Prospero's magic 'art', but the coincidence with the voyage to Tunis of his former enemies is the work of 'bountiful Fortune', presenting him with an occasion which he can either turn to his creative ends or for ever relinquish:

> by my prescience
> I find my zenith doth depend upon
> A most auspicious star, whose influence
> If now I court not, but omit, my fortunes
> Will ever after droop.
>
> (I. ii)

The relation to the dramatist's art seems clear. The materials of his art, including the 'characters' whose stage lives he moulds, are in an important sense *given*, cast up upon the shore of his predisposed awareness, to be used as his imagination dictates. Coming together at a time when he is disposed to receive them, they present themselves for his action upon them to become material for a play: material which he must be ready to seize and shape to his ends before it is carried away on the tides of life and escapes his controlling action.

The island, on this view, is the 'stage' on which the dramatic pattern is to be worked out. Like other locations of this kind in Shakespeare – one thinks of the Forest of Arden in *As You Like It*[11] – its presentation on a bare stage allows for it to be seen under as many different aspects as there are eyes to behold it. To the benevolent Utopian eyes of Gonzalo (II. i. 139–64), the island presents itself as the setting for an Arcadian anarchy founded on the spontaneous following of natural instinct: a community untainted by competition or the shadow of ambition. To the courtly cynics Antonio and Sebastian, on the other hand, the unreality of Gonzalo's dream is apparent. The 'ideal' society, as he conceives it, is founded on a benevolent amorality which leaves place for every kind of weed – 'nettle-seed', 'docks', and 'mallows' – to take possession of the soil. The fact that men like Antonio and Sebastian exist proves that some cultivation of the human terrain is necessary. The state of 'primitive' nature is one which men must outgrow to find their true, their distinctively human potentiality:[12] the problem is whether this development is to be towards 'good', in the shape of some acceptable moral and human standard, or towards the anarchy of unlimited personal self-assertion.

At this point it is well to remember that when Prospero came to the island he found it inhabited: inhabited, very notably, by Caliban. Half man and half beast, Caliban represents the best comment on Gonzalo's theorizings.[13] His is the *real* state of nature, and in his relation to his master – who at the close recognizes that 'this thing of darkness' (v. i. 275) is, even in an intimate sense, 'his' – the connection between 'nature' and the civil, moral state is expressly considered. Finding him on the island, Prospero tried to incorporate Caliban into the new order of moral realities. Caliban at once admits this, and turns the admission into a formidable indictment of the process which began by flattering him and finally became his tyrant. From his denunciation we learn, among other things, that Caliban's poetry was given him, at least in part, by Prospero. The imaginative appreciation was his own, but the gift of expression came to him from his new master: indeed, it is not clear that the native gift can be separated from, or is conceivable in the absence of, the means to give it expression. This is the old question, to which Shakespeare in one form or another insistently returns: *art* as the completion of *nature*, *art* as the distinctive expression of *human* nature.[14]

There is no suggestion that his possession of 'magic' power affords Prospero any simple answer to these problems. Caliban complains that he has been made a prisoner, who was formerly 'his own king' (I. ii. 342). Given his point of view, he is clearly in the right; but, equally, the very fact of Prospero's arrival introduced on the island a fresh reality, from which there could be no retreat, only a going forward – difficult, but indispensable – into a new balance. Prospero's retort shows the problem in all its complexity:

> I have us'd thee
> (*Filth as thou art*) with human care, and lodg'd thee
> In mine own cell, till thou didst seek to violate
> The honour of my child.
>
> (I. ii)

Caliban, who is indispensable to Prospero, whose animal nature is a true part of the human reality, is obstinately recalcitrant to all considerations of moral discipline or social restraint; and so, when he was given a measure of 'liberty', he used it to attack his master's dearest possession in the person of Miranda.

By the time we have reached the central turning-point of this action two plots – one contrived by Antonio and Sebastian against the sleeping Alonso and a second planned, as a kind of grotesque parody upon it, by Stephano, Trinculo, and Caliban against Prospero himself – have been launched, and the original seclusion of the island effectively shattered. That is how it has to be: no man is an island to himself, nor can aspire to live in isolated suspension from the pressures of real, time-conditioned existence. But Prospero – who is, let us remember again, the playwright aspiring to control his action – proposes to draw its threads to a harmonizing conclusion. To this end, he puts into the mouth of Ariel – disconcertingly disguised as a harpy – a speech addressed to the newcomers and intended to mark a turning-point in his contrivance.

> You are three men of sin, whom Destiny
> That hath to instrument this lower world
> And what is in't, the never-surfeited sea
> Hath caus'd to belch up you, and on this island

Where man doth not inhabit – you 'mongst men
Being most unfit to live . . .
                    But remember –
For that's my business to you – that you three
From Milan did supplant good Prospero;
Expos'd unto the sea, which hath requit it,
Him and his innocent child; for which foul deed
The pow'rs, delaying, not forgetting, have
Incens'd the seas and shores, yea, all the creatures,
Against your peace. Thee of thy son, Alonso,
They have bereft; and do pronounce by me
Ling'ring perdition (worse than any death
Can be at once) shall step by step attend
You and your ways; whose wraths to guard you from –
Which here, in this most desolate isle, else falls
Upon your heads – is nothing but heart's sorrow
And a clear life ensuing.

                                        (III. iii)

'I and my fellows', says Ariel, 'are ministers of Fate'. The implication
is that the events we have witnessed have a dimension which can be
called 'providential', a meaning in relation to some conception of
justice objectively conceived and valid. 'Destiny', says Ariel, 'hath to
instrument this lower world'. There *is* – he seems to affirm – a plan,
a purpose: *something* is indeed working itself out to a 'purposeful'
conclusion. 'Delaying, not forgetting', this Destiny watches – like
some more omniscient playwright – over the whole action to bring
the characters concerned in it to *judgement*. For this end, the various
actors – objects of a favourable imaginative conjunction – have been
brought together on this 'most desolate isle . . . where man doth not
inhabit'. Unless their sojourn there has shown them the need for
'heart's sorrow' and a 'clear life' to follow, their doom is certain. For
it is in the nature of uncontrolled self-affirmation, as the great
tragedies have consistently shown it, to lead to self-destruction; and
Prospero's contrived action, with its insistence upon ideas of repentance and amendment, seems to be conceived as nothing less than a
counterpoise to this process of ruin.

The last stages of the action can be seen as bringing this con-
ception to its conclusion in the process of questioning its final validity.
With Ferdinand and Miranda united under the eye of Prospero,
Alonso and his companions enter, spellbound, to be restored to the

full use of their daylight reason. To the sound of music, Prospero's characters are restored to what his 'action' conceives as the true sense of their lives:

> Their understanding
> Begins to *swell*, and *the approaching tide*
> Will shortly fill *the reasonable shore*
> That now lies foul and muddy.
>
> (v. i)

The entry into a new, or restored life is symbolized by a typically Shakespearean coincidence of blessing and forgiveness: the gesture by which fathers and children, separated by time and the action of passion, are reconciled. Ferdinand kneels for his father's blessing and is joined to Miranda. In her father's words, and in her wondering comment as she enters on her new life, the intuition of a reconciled, redeemed state is given clear expression:

> ALONSO.   Now all the blessings
>   Of a glad father compass thee about! ...
> MIRANDA.   O, wonder!
>   How many goodly creatures are there here!
>   How beauteous mankind is! O brave new world
>   That has such people in't!
>
> (v. i)

Although it is true that Prospero qualifies Miranda's enthusiasm with his gently ironic comment – 'Tis new to thee' – the sense of this is apparent. This is the world of *wonder* with which Shakespearean comedy is so consistently suffused:[15] the sense of life as at each moment infinitely new in its offered possibilities, surprising and evocative beyond the greatest human expectations. To live is to be capable of wonder, to respond to each moment of experience as new, unpredictable, and transforming. Ferdinand, on his side, recognizes that his bride has been given him by the design of 'immortal providence' and that he has received from Prospero nothing less than a second, a redeemed and enhanced life. As the children are finally joined, the two fathers are also brought together, Alonso craving pardon for past sin and Prospero granting forgiveness, both under the blessing of a divine grace.

This, however, germane as it is to the complete effect, cannot be the last word. We have to remember that we have been considering what we have agreed to call Prospero's 'play'; and this does not coincide at every point with Shakespeare's. As though to underline the element of illusion in Prospero's contriving, and almost immediately after Ariel's speech of judgement, he brings into being an explicitly dramatic entertainment – an action, as it were, within an action – summoning into being a set of vaguely 'classical' deities to celebrate the betrothal of Ferdinand and Miranda in appropriate terms of life, gracious fertility, and harvest fulfilment. It is not, by the standards to which Shakespeare has accustomed us, a very impressive 'play', and the elaborate, somewhat painstaking verse in which it is conveyed stands out, as it was surely intended to do, from the ease and fluency of what surrounds it. The point, however, lies principally in what follows. As soon as the 'masque' has ended, and after (to what the stage direction calls 'a strange, hollow, and confused noise') the actors have 'heavily vanished', the *real* world (as the play conceives it) returns to possess Prospero's thoughts with an unmistakable, almost a despairing urgency:

> I had forgot that foul conspiracy
> Of the beast Caliban and his confederates
> Against my life.
>
> (IV. i)

The recall to actuality moves Prospero to a deep uneasiness, which is not lost upon those around him. Ferdinand refers to 'some passion' that moves him 'strongly', and Miranda comments that

> Never till this day
> Saw I him touched with anger so distemper'd.
>
> (IV. i)

This is the Prospero who, far from being a benevolent magician with semi-divine attributes, has expressed himself repeatedly as an impatient, even testy old man grappling with the problem represented by Caliban, exercising over Ariel an uneasy control that borders on tyranny, and moved to lecture incautious youth on the need to keep its natural passions under strict, even harsh constraint. What follows are the words on the 'insubstantial pageant' which everyone remembers, but which not everyone has read in their context. We are to keep in mind that the 'spirits' which have melted 'into thin air' are Prospero's 'actors', and that 'this insubstantial pageant faded' is — whatever else it may turn out to be — in the first instance the spectacle he has just brought into being. Beyond this, the words reflect the anxious mood of an aging man burdened with the weight of his responsibility, conscious of the limitations of his magic in the face of the mysterious and always ungraspable 'reality' that so insistently breaks into, and dissolves, the imaginative harmonies it has brought so painstakingly into being. The last words of the speech are loaded with a sense of emotional burden:

> Sir, I am vex'd;
> Bear with my *weakness*; my *old brain* is troubled;
> Be not disturb'd with my *infirmity*.
> If you be pleas'd, retire into my cell
> And there repose; a turn or two I'll walk
> To still *my beating mind*.

(IV. i)

What, we may well ask, is happening at this point? It is of course impossible to be sure, easy to project into these words elements of our own creation: but the answer may perhaps be something like this: Shakespeare, in the person of his creation, Prospero, is asking himself, and asking us to consider with him, certain questions concerning the nature and the limitation of the dramatic illusion, with particular reference to the drama of fulfilment and reconciliation which is being enacted on the stage. As he reflects on these matters, still through the person of Prospero, he makes his character consider the action which he has brought into being — both the 'masque' within the play and the entire action to which it belongs — and, as a result, raise certain questions. They are questions, we may think, with which Shakespeare's dramatic life has, in one form or another, been persistently engaged. What part does the creative imagination play in the life of men? To what extent do its creations correspond to what we call, perhaps begging a large question, 'reality'? And is this 'reality' something that we bring into being by the strength of our imaginative commitment, or something that can be said — but, again, in what sense? — to be really, 'objectively' (as we so inadequately say) *there*? Shakespeare, in other words, is — if there is any truth in this argument — looking back on his lifetime dedicated to the writing of plays and confronting himself, asking himself what this effort of a lifetime may finally *mean*. Man, he may be saying, is distinguished from the rest of creation by the ability, and the need, to give a shape to his sense of his existence, to project it into formal patterns. In so doing he gives expression to the human need to feel that the patterns so created answer to something *real* in the nature of things, that life *has* a shape, a form, which we may be unable to perceive in any adequate or lasting way but which we are compelled to think of as *real*, as corresponding in some way to the nature of things.

It ought to be insisted, finally, that these considerations are advanced as questions, not offered as answers. Perhaps what the play finally 'says' – if the inadequate and even misleading word may be forgiven – is that man is a creature who has the faculty, and the *need*, to ask questions, and that the answers he finds are, of their very nature, such as to lead to further questions. At the end of the play Prospero, having set aside his 'magic', is about to return to Milan, not so much – it seems – to exercise benevolent rule there or to indulge in intellectual speculation, as to consider the prospect of his own human end: 'Every third thought shall be my grave'. Even now, his reconciling mood does not seem to extend very far towards the brother who remains very much what he has always been, and whom he addresses for the last time in terms of no noticeable benevolence:

> you, most wicked sir, whom to call brother
> Would even *infect my mouth*.
>
> (v. i)

In all this, and in the final Epilogue, in which Prospero, stepping forward on the now empty stage to address his final word to the spectators, seems to be recognizing that the dramatic illusion is the product of a marriage between the author's creative imagination and that of the audience, the implication seems to be that a play has *no* single meaning of the kind that can be abstracted from the action and proposed for approval or dissent in terms of its final and exclusive validity. It may be that in Ariel's great speech invoking 'Destiny' something was said that differs, by its firmness of assertion and gravity of emphasis, from anything else in the dramatist's work. It *may* be that Shakespeare is raising the question of the reality, the 'truth', of that conception of a destinal order to which so much in his earlier work seems to point, but which he is invariably careful *not* to affirm as 'real' outside the order of dramatic fiction. If this is so, the question raised is *not* followed, in the play, by a definite answer. It may be that Shakespeare finally refused to contemplate the kind of play which such an affirmation, taken to be literally 'true', might logically have implied; that he chose to remain true to a vision which has indeed its 'wonders', but wonders humanly made and sharing in the limitation of all that is human. For, in the words spoken by Theseus at the end of *A Midsummer Night's Dream* in relation to another and very 'human' entertainment: 'The best in this kind are but shadows; and the worst are no worse, if imagination amend them' (v. i. 209–10).

NOTES

1. The play, though published in quarto form in 1609, was omitted from the 1623 Folio and only incorporated into the Shakespeare canon in the Third Folio of 1664. Widely different explanations of this anomaly have been proposed.

2. The argument against divided authorship in both *Pericles* and *Cymbeline* was forcibly stated by G. Wilson Knight in *The Crown of Life* (1947) and elsewhere. Philip Edwards' article, *An Approach to the Problem of Pericles* (*Shakespeare Survey* 5, 1952) points more cautiously in the same direction.

3. An interesting comparison can be made with similar scenes of 'low life' in *Measure for Measure*.

4. We are reminded of Cordelia's affirmation of the 'bond' in her reply to her father in the opening scene of *King Lear* (i. i. 92–3).

5. For the tone of this compare Cleopatra's imagined evocation of the dead Antony:

> For his bounty,
> There was no winter in't; an autumn 'twas
> That grew the more by reaping.
>
> (v. ii)

6. Once again there is a parallel here with Lear's reconciliation to Cordelia. See *King Lear*, iv. vii. 22. For the part played by music in the same scene see l. 25 and Cordelia's reference to 'the untuned and jarring senses' (l. 16) which are now to be healed.

7. For the linguistic effect here compare Sonnet XCIV, l. 7: 'They are the lords and owners of their faces'.

8. G. Wilson Knight, in *The Crown of Life*, has argued in favour of undivided Shakespearean authorship for the play, to which he attributes great importance in his interpretation of the Shakespearean pattern.

9. Paul Bertram, in his book on Shakespeare and *The Two Noble Kinsmen*, has argued in favour of Shakespeare's sole authorship of the play. Most

critics, however, are unwilling to ascribe more than a limited number of scenes to him: and some would deny any participation by him in the play.

10. I am thinking especially of I. ii, with its account of the shipwreck which brings Viola to the shore of Illyria, and more specifically of the Captain's description of his last sight of her supposedly drowned brother (ll. 11–17).

11. See especially the dialogue between Rosalind and Orlando on different perceptions of time in the Forest, III. ii. 286–316.

12. Compare in *The Winter's Tale* Polixenes' speech on the innocence of boyhood friendship. See p. 366 above.

13. In the conception of Caliban there are evidently echoes of contemporary controversies, fuelled by European exploration of the New World, concerning the status and nature of the 'noble savage'.

14. See Polixenes' speech on the 'grafting' process in *The Winter's Tale* (p. 368 above).

15. Compare the words of Sebastian in *Twelfth Night*:

> This is the air; that is the glorious sun;
> This pearl she gave me. I do feel't and see't;
> And though 'tis wonder that enwraps me thus,
> Yet 'tis not madness.

(IV. iii)

CHANGING INTERPRETATIONS
OF SHAKESPEARE
KENNETH MUIR

Something has already been said about the characteristics of the
Elizabethan stage and of its audiences. The public theatres, whether
derived from inn-yards, from bear-baiting arenas, or from cockpits,
were open to the sky. The stage itself was a platform, an 'unworthy
scaffold', with no curtain or scenery; and atmosphere had to be conveyed by the words. The chief need of the actor was the ability to
speak verse well; the best actors preserved a nice balance between
naturalness and formality, both in speech and gesture, and the fact
that women's parts were taken by boys tended to have the same effect.
The audience was a cross-section of London – Puritans only excepted
– and whatever its limitations it possessed the supreme merit of regarding poetry as a natural means of expression, even when it was
far removed from the language of ordinary speech, and even when it
was delivered by actors in such a way as to emphasize, rather than
to conceal, the rhetorical devices employed by the poet. Robert
Bridges accused those 'wretched beings', the groundlings, of preventing Shakespeare from being a great artist. In fact we owe them a debt
of gratitude for demanding of Shakespeare poetry rather than realism,
and for preventing him from writing the academic plays which were
the pride of those poets whose work was 'never clapper-clawed by
the palms of the vulgar'.

During the reigns of James I and Charles I, the influence of the
private theatres and of the elaborate court masques made itself felt.
Scenery and artificial lighting gradually superseded the bare boards of
the Elizabethans. The admission fee to the private theatres excluded
the poorer classes, and as Puritanism tightened its hold on the mind
of the middle classes they also kept away from the theatre – particularly as the morality of the newer drama of Fletcher, Ford, and
Massinger was often dubious. As a result, plays were written to appeal
mainly to the Court and its hangers on. It is significant that soon

after Shakespeare's death, *Macbeth* was vandalized by the introduction of an operatic Hecate.

At the Restoration two theatres – and between 1682 and 1695 only one – were sufficient to satisfy the public demand. A generation earlier a smaller population had required no less than six. The new audience consisted of scum and dregs – the fashionable courtier and the unrespectable. Shakespeare's plays were then less popular than those of Beaumont and Fletcher, and they were frequently altered to suit the taste of the times. Actresses, now appearing for the first time, had to be provided for. At the end of *King Lear* Cordelia was made to live happily ever after as Edgar's wife, Miranda was given a sister, and Lady Macduff had her part enlarged. The plays were also hacked about so as to make them conform, more or less, to the neo-classical rules.

Yet the period from 1660 to 1890 was an age of great acting, and Betterton, Garrick, Kemble, Siddons, Kean, Macready, and Irving all appeared in Shakespearean roles in adapted versions of his plays. The decay of drama during the eighteenth century has been put down to the size of the theatres, which were now so huge that subtlety was no longer possible. It may rather be ascribed to the influx of the middle classes, who suffered from the delusion that sentimental comedy was more moral than the comedy of manners. Except for Sheridan and Goldsmith, there were no good dramatists between the death of Congreve and the advent of Shaw and Wilde. Shakespeare's plays were performed with elaborate scenery, and with savage cuts to make room for it. Those who really appreciated Shakespeare usually stayed away from the theatre, and we have the comic spectacle of Thomas Hardy in the front row of the gallery with his eyes glued not to the stage but to a text of the play.

The reform of Shakespearean performances began with the discovery of Gordon Craig's that unrealistic scenery with electric lighting need not impede the movement of the play, and with the discovery by William Poel that the plays could be performed on a bare stage, and that they became more dramatic if so staged. Granville-Barker's productions just before the First World War prepared the way for the Old Vic tradition of simple scenery and uncut texts. By this time, we may suppose, the spread of secondary and university education had created a public which wanted to see Shakespeare decently performed. Plays neglected for centuries were re-vived, and at Stratford and the Old Vic all the plays of the canon were performed. Acting today may not be as great as it was in the eighteenth century, but there is no doubt that the best modern directors understand the conventions of the Elizabethan stage and that we now have the chance of judging Shakespeare's competence as a dramatist. This was a good deal better than even Bradley suspected.

It would be idle to pretend that the modern playgoer is an ideal spectator of a Shakespeare play. Having studied them at school, he is likely to see the plays through the distorting mirror of the critics. he has lost the pleasures of ignorance and surprise and, as poetry is often alien to him, he will seldom catch the exact meaning of the more difficult speeches, whether the actors declaim them so as to convey mood rather than meaning, or speak the lines as though they were prose. Both methods, lacking the necessary blend of formality and naturalness, kill the poetry; and both methods are avoided by the best directors (Hall, Brook, Barton) and by the best actors and actresses (Gielgud, Ashcroft, Evans).

The best critics of the present century have given us a better understanding of Shakespeare than those of any previous age. His real greatness was hardly suspected in his own lifetime.[1] The first reference to his work is to be found in *A Groatsworth of Wit* (1592) – by Greene or Chettle – where he is attacked as an upstart crow beautified with the feathers of the University Wits. A few years later Meres compared him with Ovid, Plautus and Seneca; but the value of this tribute may be judged by the fact that he is classed with three dons, Leg and Edes as the best writers of tragedy, and Gager as 'the best for comedy amongst us'. But, during his lifetime, there were many tributes to the sweetness of his versification. The foolish Gullio, an undergraduate in *The Return from Parnassus*, was satirized for rating Shakespeare above Spenser and Chaucer. 'I'll worship sweet Mr Shakespeare,' he cries, 'and to honour him will lay his *Venus and Adonis* under my pillow.' Gullio obviously enjoyed the poem for its eroticism. So Gabriel Harvey, a Cambridge don, tells us that 'the younger sort' delighted in *Venus and Adonis*, although he admits that *Lucrece* and *Hamlet* 'have it in them to please the wiser sort'. Shakespeare had 'small Latin and less Greek' – which does not mean little Latin and no Greek – and the very fact that he was the most popular dramatist of his time made the academic critics suspicious. Even his fellow-dramatists lamented his lack of learning. Beaumont, writing to Jonson and probably echoing his correspondent's view, said that Shakespeare's best lines would be used by future critics to show

> How far sometimes a mortal man may go
> By the dim light of Nature.

Jonson himself complained of Shakespeare's bombast and lack of art; and when the players praised Shakespeare because 'he never blotted out line', Jonson retorted, 'Would he had blotted a thousand!' By 1630 Jonson, who was a learned man and a careful craftsman, had become irritated by the idolatrous admiration which was already being accorded to Shakespeare:

> I loved the man, and do honour his memory
> (on this side Idolatry) as much as any.

Yet Jonson himself was partly responsible for this idolatry. The elegy he contributed to the First Folio (1623) is perhaps the most magnificent tribute ever paid by one poet to another, for it not only ranks Shakespeare above Chaucer and Spenser, but above all the Greek and Roman dramatists. Not only was he the 'soul of the age', but 'for all time'; not only 'the wonder of our age', but also the 'star of poets'. Most remarkable, in view of Jonson's remarks elsewhere, is his praise of Shakespeare as an artist:

> Yet must I not give Nature all: Thy Art,
> My Gentle Shakespeare, must enjoy a part.
> For though the poet's matter Nature be,
> His art doth give the fashion. And that he,
> Who casts to write a living line, must sweat,
> (Such as thine are) and strike a second heat
> Upon the Muse's anvil: turn the same,
> (And himself with it) that he thinks to frame;
> Or for the laurel he may gain a scorn,
> For a good poet's made, as well as born.
> And such wert thou. Look how the father's face
> Lives in his issue, even so, the race
> Of Shakespeare's mind and manners brightly shines
> In his well turned and true filed lines:
> In each of which he seems to shake a lance,
> As brandish'd at the eyes of Ignorance.

The difference between the attitude displayed in this poem and Jonson's other recorded views on Shakespeare may partly be explained by the fact that it was a public commendation, whereas his other remarks were spoken in casual conversation or written as a counterblast to what he regarded as excessive praise. Perhaps he had not realized, until he read the plays collected for the First Folio, just how good they were.

Through the whole of the seventeenth century Jonson's art and learning were contrasted with Shakespeare's natural gifts, as in Milton's verses in the Second Folio and in his tribute in L'Allegro to Shakespeare's 'Native woodnotes wild' and Jonson's 'learned sock'. Although the plays were popular at the Court of Charles I, there was no written criticism of importance until after the Restoration; and then the plays were adapted by Davenant, Dryden, Shadwell and Tate to conform with the new taste. Even so altered they were less popular than those of Beaumont and Fletcher.[2] The critics generally blamed the barbarism of the Elizabethan age for the faults they professed to find in Shakespeare's plays, and they thought they knew better than their grandfathers how a play ought to be written. Dryden himself, though he sometimes expressed such fashionable views, was able to rise above them because of his wholehearted admiration for Shakespeare's poetic genius and for his ability in creating characters. He may seem to be mistaken in his conviction that the wit, language, conversation and taste of his own age were superior to those of the age of Elizabeth (*The Dramatic Poetry of the Last Age*, 1672). It is odd that the author of heroic plays should complain of Shakespeare's bombast, even though it was natural for one who paid due respect to the 'rules' to criticize Shakespeare's plots. Yet, when he speaks not for his age but from his heart, Dryden's admiration is not lacking in warmth:

He was the man who of all modern, and perhaps ancient, poets, had the largest and most comprehensive soul. All the images of nature were still present to him, and he drew them, not laboriously, but luckily; when he describes anything, you more than see it, you feel it too. Those who accuse him to have wanted learning give him the greater commendation: he was naturally learned; he needed not the spectacles of books to read nature; he looked inwards, and found her there. I cannot say he is everywhere alike; were he so, I should do him injury to compare him with the greatest of mankind. He is many times flat, insipid; his comic wit degenerating into clenches, his serious swelling into bombast. But he is always great, when some great occasion is presented to him.

(*Of Dramatic Poesy*, 1668)

Thomas Rymer had learning, common sense, and a coarse vein of wit, but he seems to have been entirely without aesthetic perception. His *Short View of Tragedy* (1692) contains a famous denunciation of *Othello* as 'a bloody farce, without salt or savour'. Iago is badly drawn because soldiers are 'open-hearted, frank, plain-dealing', and plays should deal with the normal rather than with the exceptional. Desdemona's marriage with Othello is incredible. The language of the play is often gross and inflated. Finally Rymer pokes fun at the moral of the play:

First, this may be a caution to all maidens of quality how, without their parents' consent, they run away with blackamoors ... Secondly, this may be a warning to all good wives, that they look well to their linen. Thirdly, this may be a lesson to husbands, that before their jealousy be tragical, the proof may be mathematical.

Rymer's criticism was more hostile than that of his contemporaries, but even Dryden showed respect for his views; Rowe admitted the justice of his criticisms, though suggesting that he ought also to have pointed out the beauties as well as the faults; Dennis lamented Shakespeare's neglect of poetic justice and his ignorance of the Classics, though he admitted that Rymer might by the same method have revealed faults *even in Waller*; and Pope said that Rymer was 'on the whole, one of the best critics we ever had'.

The weighing of faults and beauties was the favourite exercise of eighteenth-century critics.[3] We find it in the prefaces of the editors – Rowe, Pope, Theobald and Johnson. Pope's preface is largely in the tradition of the previous century. Shakespeare 'is not so much an imitator, as an instrument of Nature; and 'tis not so just to say that he speaks from her, as that she speaks through him'. He argues that Shakespeare's faults were largely due to the bad taste of his audience and to the fact that he was an actor; that there is undeniable evidence that Shakespeare corrected his work; and that the editors of the First Folio introduced many blunders and illiteracies for which the poet could not have been responsible. One of Pope's remarks has been offered as evidence of his breadth of outlook: 'To judge therefore of

Shakespeare by Aristotle's rules, is like trying a man by the laws of one country, who acted under those of another.'

Theobald, the first editor with an adequate knowledge of Elizabethan literature (1734), not only made many brilliant emendations but also restored the original text in many places, freeing it from Pope's unfortunate elegancies. He was the first to show that Shakespeare's anachronisms were due neither to ignorance nor to textual corruption, but to the 'too powerful blaze of his imagination which, when once raised, made all acquired knowledge vanish and disappear before it'.

Johnson's great preface (1765) is in some ways the culmination of the Shakespearean criticism of the previous hundred years. He tends to summarize faults and beauties, as so many of his predecessors had done. His list of faults covers the usual complaints: Shakespeare seems to write without any moral purpose, his plots are loosely constructed, his endings are huddled, he has many anachronisms, his jests are often bawdy, his tragedy is more forced than his comedy, his set speeches are often frigid or bombastic, and he indulges in quibbles: 'A quibble was to him the fatal Cleopatra for which he lost the world, and was content to lose it.'[4] But on two points Johnson takes an independent line. He defends Shakespeare's mingling of tragedy and comedy and his neglect of the three unities. His praise of Shakespeare as a 'faithful mirror of manners and of life', as a writer of comic dialogue, as a depicter of character, and so on, is magnificently phrased. In the course of his notes Johnson inserts some terse comments on the plays; and in his remarks on Falstaff and Polonius we can see the beginnings of that analysis of character which formed the staple of Romantic criticism.

In the last thirty years of the eighteenth century the reaction against the neo-classical attitude to Shakespeare was in full swing.[5] He was generally commended for ignoring the unities, and Mrs Montague and others defended him from the strictures of Voltaire. More significant, in view of the criticism of the next century, was the new interest in characterization displayed by Thomas Whatley (1770–85), who analysed and contrasted the characters of Richard III and Macbeth; by William Richardson (1774–89), who dealt with many of Shakespeare's chief characters from the point of view of the ruling passion; and by Maurice Morgann in his brilliant essay on Falstaff (1777). Although Morgann sought to prove that the fat knight was not a coward, he was fully aware that he was a character in a play. The essay contains some profound remarks on Shakespeare's method of characterization, especially the setting up of conflicting impressions in order to create the illusion of life.[6] If these three critics started a bad tradition in their analysis of character, the interest in character originated in the theatre: as early as 1735 there had been essays on Polonius and Hamlet, criticizing the common method of playing them.

One book published in 1794 had no immediate influence; but in recent years Walter Whiter's *Specimen of a Commentary* has acquired some importance as the first book in which Shakespeare's imagery was systematically studied.[7] Its chief merit is in its demonstration that the imagery is often connected by unconscious puns or other unconscious links. Whiter was even the first to point out iterative imagery and image clusters, such as the famous one of flatterers, dogs and melting sweets which was later to be rediscovered by Kellett and Spurgeon.[8] Apart from a few remarks by Coleridge, Dowden and Bradley, and an eccentric essay by Elwin (*Shakespeare Restored*, 1853), nothing else of importance was written about Shakespeare's imagery until the present day.

The Romantic critics all had something to say about Shakespeare. De Quincey has an eloquent explanation of the effectiveness of the knocking at the gate in *Macbeth*; Lamb, irritated by excessive praise of Garrick as an interpreter of Shakespeare, proclaimed that the tragedies could never be performed satisfactorily – we have to remember that he had seen only adaptations – and his accounts of the acting of Bensley as Malvolio and Iago are brilliant critical *aperçus*, although Lamb's Malvolio was neither Bensley's nor Shakespeare's,[9] and Keats in his letters has a number of remarks which go far to justify his belief that he understood Shakespeare to his depths.

Coleridge's Shakespearian criticism,[10] apart from a brilliant chapter in the *Biographia Literaria*, exists only in the form of lecture notes and in the record of his table talk. His greatest contribution is his continual insistence that every work of art must be judged by its own organic laws. If this sometimes led him to explain away Shakespeare's defects or to ascribe them to another hand, it also led him to recognize qualities which earlier critics had missed. He has brilliant notes on individual passages and profound comments on the poetry; but he specializes in analysis of character, as certain eighteenth-century critics had done before him, and it is this side of his work which sets the tone for most nineteenth-century criticism. The account of Hamlet's character given by him is a good sketch of his own, as he half realized – 'I have a smack of Hamlet myself, if I may say so.' But the over-reflective intellectualism he diagnosed formed the basis of many later Hamlets. Here, and in several other places, Coleridge was romanticizing Shakespeare, reading into the plays his own prepossessions; and although he himself understood the plays as poetic dramas, his method of abstracting the characters could be used by later critics who were without such understanding. It may also be said that he did not keep his admiration 'this side idolatry', and he lost sight of the fact that the plays were written to be performed.

Hazlitt, the best of all dramatic critics, was less in danger of forgetting that Shakespeare was a playwright; and despite the title of his book, *Characters of Shakespeare's Plays*, he was less concerned with characterization than Coleridge had been. Occasionally he allows his political views to cloud his judgement, as in his remarks on *Henry V* and *Coriolanus*; he is too often content with a sort of running commentary on the plays under discussion; and he owes a great deal to Coleridge. He has many true remarks, but of the kind which an ordinary intelligent reader might have made. Yet Hazlitt gives us a fuller and more satisfactory account of Shakespeare's plays than any previous critic.

Towards the end of the eighteenth century attempts had been made to determine the order of Shakespeare's plays by means of records and topical allusions, and by the middle of the next century the chronology had been settled with the help of versification tests. Critics both on the Continent (e.g. Brandes) and in England were thus enabled to discuss Shakespeare's development. Dowden's *Shakespeare: His Mind and Art* (1875) maintained its popularity well into the twentieth century. If its division of Shakespeare's career into such periods as 'In the Depths' and 'On the Heights' displayed a romantic idea of the relation of the poet to his work, its description of the characteristics of the Final Period, although sentimental in its expression, is probably nearer to the truth than the boredom diagnosed by Lytton Strachey (1906). Another Victorian book which had a long vogue was Moulton's 'scientific' study of *Shakespeare as a Dramatic Artist* (1885), in which he attempted to build up a theory of drama from Shakespeare's practice; but his formulations were too rigid and logical and too little concerned with poetic texture. Both in this book and in *The Moral System of Shakespeare* Moulton projected into the poet's work his own moral prepossessions. Although Shakespeare inherited a belief in the didactic function of drama, his moral ideas are never separable from the poetry, and they did not always coincide with those of the nineteenth century. Swinburne was a prolific writer on Shakespeare, but his inflated style is now unpalatable. The best Victorian criticism of Shakespeare is to be found in Pater's essays on *Measure for Measure* and the English Histories. His influence can be traced in Yeats' *Ideas of Good and Evil*, which in turn influenced Masefield's criticism.

The culmination of nineteenth-century criticism was Bradley's *Shakespearean Tragedy* (1904), and it is still an impressive book. He attempted to analyse each play as though he were an actor studying all the parts, not as a director to whom the characters are creations subordinated to a poetic conception. He was aware that the psychological point of view is not the same as the tragic, but he concentrated on the characters and has little to say about other things after his opening chapter. He ignored the conditions and conventions of the Elizabethan stage and complained of 'faults' which were no more than legitimate conventions of poetic drama. Yet he appreciated the poetry and emphasized that a Shakespearian tragedy was a dramatic poem. He wrote of the characters almost as though they were real people rather than as poetic creations, and he thought it necessary to explain away any inconsistencies in them. In spite of these limitations, and in spite of attempts by later critics to stress Othello's self-deception, the immaturity or wickedness of Hamlet, the damnation of Macbeth, and the corruption of Falstaff,[11] Bradley's conception of the characters is still, after three-quarters of a century, an orthodoxy to be questioned.

Robert Bridges, reacting against Bradley, but showing less understanding of the nature of drama, protested in *The Influence of the Audience on Shakespeare's Dramas* (1906) that Shakespeare's characters were not consistent, and that he continually sacrificed psychological truth to theatrical situations: Macbeth and Othello, for example, were far too sensitive to be murderers. About the same time Stoll began his long series of books which were designed to prove that Shakespeare deliberately chose to have the maximum contrast between the hero and his actions, that the inconsistency of the characters, obvious in the study, would not be noticed in performance, and that poetic drama dispenses with psychological truth. Stoll's books, of which the best is *Art and Artifice in Shakespeare* (1933), have the merit of showing that the poetic dramatist is unnaturalistic in his methods, and of calling attention to the function of conventions. Schücking analyses Shakespeare's technique from a similar point of view (*Character Problems in Shakespeare's Plays*, 1919, 1922), and stresses the primitive elements in the plays, as when villains proclaim their villainy. But many of his examples of primitive technique can be explained in other ways, and he seems not to realize that primitive techniques can be used by a great poet in a sophisticated way. Muriel C. Bradbrook (*Elizabethan Stage Conditions*, 1932; *Themes and Conventions of (Elizabethan Tragedy*, 1935, and many later books) demonstrates the creative use of conventions by the great Elizabethans; and S. L. Bethell (*Shakespeare and the Popular Dramatic Tradition*, 1944), covering some of the same ground, defended Shakespeare's conventions and anachronisms, and argued that his audience possessed multi-consciousness, enabling them to react to a scene in several different ways at the same time. J. I. M. Stewart, in his witty reply to Stoll and Schücking (*Character and Motive in Shakespeare*, 1949) argued that the apparent inconsistencies in Shakespeare's characters are a means of making them convincing, and that apparently primitive conventions may be reanimated by a great artist so as to reflect a reality which is confirmed by the discoveries of depth psychology.[12]

These books show the impact of increasing knowledge of the theatre of Shakespeare and his contemporaries; so too do Alfred Harbage's *Shakespeare and the Rival Traditions* (1952) and Bernard Beckerman's *Shakespeare at the Globe* (1962).

The resemblance between the early plays of Shakespeare and those of the University Wits had led to the disintegration of the canon by J. M. Robertson and others, and the handing over to other dramatists of those scenes and plays the critics disliked; and, later on, it led to its reintegration at the hands of Sir Edmund Chambers and in the brilliant essay by Lascelles Abercrombie.[13]

As early as 1901 Thorndike had written on *The Influence of Beaumont and Fletcher* on the plays of Shakespeare's last period, although the influence was at least reciprocal, and may have been the other way round. W. W. Lawrence examined *Shakespeare's Problem Comedies* (1931) in the light of Elizabethan preconceptions. Willard Farnham stressed *The Medieval Heritage of Elizabethan Tragedy* (1936). O. J. Campbell examined the relation of *Shakespeare's Satire* (1943) to contemporary trends. Schücking and Fredson Bowers wrote on the connection between *Hamlet* and the revenge plays of Kyd and Marston. Hardin Craig in *The Enchanted Glass* (1935) and Theodore Spencer in *Shakespeare and the Nature of Man* (1942) examined the poet's ideological heritage. Tillyard in *The Elizabethan World Picture* (1943) and *Shakespeare's History Plays* (1944) argued that Shakespeare expressed the orthodox views of his time; but how far Shakespeare really swallowed Tudor propaganda is a matter of opinion, as one can see from diverse interpretations of *Henry V*.[14] Lily B. Campbell argued that *Shakespeare's Histories* (1947) had a contemporary political moral and in *Shakespeare's Tragic Heroes* (1930) suggested that contemporary theories of psychology could throw light on the plays, although we may suspect that the poet's intuitive understanding of man was more use to him than his reading of Timothy Bright's *Treatise of Melancholy*. Noble provided the best accounts of *Shakespeare's Use of Song* (1923) until F. W. Sternfeld's *Music in Shakespearean Tragedy* (1963), and of *Shakespeare's Knowledge of the Bible* (1935). Geoffrey Bullough collected the *Narrative and Dramatic Sources of Shakespeare* (1957–75) with a valuable commentary on Shakespeare's use of them. Sister Miriam Joseph provided a comprehensive study of his use of rhetoric (*Shakespeare's Use of the Arts of Language*, 1947) and Brian Vickers wrote on *The Artistry of Shakespeare's Prose* (1968). T. W. Baldwin's comprehensive book on grammar-school education in the sixteenth century (*Shakspere's Small Latine and Lesse Greeke*, 1944) showed how the curriculum influenced Shakespeare. *William Shakespeare: A Documentary*

Life by S. Schoenbaum (1975) superseded all previous lives of Shakespeare by keeping close to the known facts, and by his sane commentary on them.[15]

It is, of course, impossible to divorce scholarship and criticism, and many of the books mentioned in the previous paragraph themselves contain criticism. Sir Edmund Chambers, who compiled nearly all the known facts about *The Elizabethan Stage* (1923) and about *Shakespeare* (1930), was also the author of a critical survey of his work; and John Dover Wilson wrote critical books on *Hamlet*, Falstaff and the comedies.[16] As a result of the work of scholars, critics have become more aware of the 'Elizabethan' Shakespeare. Like Bradbrook, they consider Shakespeare as a member of an acting company, while realizing that a great poet never belongs wholly to his own age. Even those who hesitate to credit Shakespeare with originality admit that he had a wide range of views to choose from; and, although most Elizabethan dramatists sacrificed character to situation, Shakespeare, starting with a plot, took great pains to create characters who would make the situation credible.

Modern critics have come to put more stress on Shakespeare the conscious artist, and we hear less now of the uneducated genius. What is extraordinary, as Hardin Craig showed, is the masterly ease with which Shakespeare utilizes what knowledge he has, or, as Eliot remarked, he acquired 'more essential history from Plutarch than most men could from the whole British Museum'. The man depicted by Baldwin, who learnt his craft by a study of Latin commentaries on Terence,[17] or the man who combined eight sources in *King Lear*, or five sources in a single speech in *Richard II*, was not the barbarian of genius depicted by some eighteenth-century critics. Virgil K. Whitaker's *Shakespeare's Use of Learning* (1953) and Madeleine Doran's *Endeavors of Art* (1954) are two valuable books on this subject; and they may be complemented by Una Ellis-Fermor's *Shakespeare the Dramatist* (1961), Norman Rabkin's *Shakespeare and the Common Understanding* (1967) and two books on the way in which his plays are constructed on scenes rather than on five-act structure – Emrys Jones' *Scenic Form in Shakespeare* (1971) and Mark Rose's *Shakespearian Design* (1972).

G. K. Hunter remarked[18] that T. S. Eliot 'virtually invented the twentieth-century Shakespeare in a collection of asides'. Hunter was arguing that Eliot was trying to turn Shakespeare into a symbolist poet. It is arguable that Eliot's greatness as a poet made his admirers respect even his least happy pronouncements. In his early criticism he was disastrously influenced by the disintegrators, by his odd belief that Elizabethan dramatists aimed at realism, and by his assumption that remarks made by characters (e.g. 'As flies to wanton boys are we to the gods') constitute Shakespeare's philosophy of life. In his later essays, influenced by his experience in the theatre and by the work of G. Wilson Knight, he spoke of the meaning below the level of plot and character and wrote eloquently of the plays of Shakespeare's final period. There is in fact no one twentieth-century Shakespeare and perhaps Knight, Empsom and Spurgeon had a more positive effect than Eliot on the Shakespeare of the second half of the century.

Knight's first important book, *The Wheel of Fire* (1930), was followed by *The Imperial Theme* (1931) and many others, including the impressive book on the plays of the final period, *The Crown of Life* (1947). Knight regarded his work as a continuation of Bradley's, but he is concerned primarily with the analysis of poetic and stage symbolism and with the subordination of character to the poetic meaning of the play. He considers the themes 'spatially' rather than temporally, although as an actor and director he was fully aware of the temporal sequence of events. His interpretations, although often controversial – e.g. on Hamlet, Isabella and *Henry VIII* – are perhaps the most original and influential of the last fifty years.

Many critics have been influenced by his work, notably L. C. Knights in *How Many Children had Lady Macbeth?* (1933), a pamphlet which was intended as a counterblast to Bradley. Indeed, when F. R. Leavis in his retrospect to *Scrutiny* summed up the achievement of that journal, he thought that the 'relegation' of Bradley was its most notable success. Leavis blamed Bradley for his 'failure to keep closely enough in touch with responses to particular arrangements of words' and he illustrated how one ought to read a page of Shakespeare. Yet when one examines his essay on *Othello* or Knights' early essay on Hamlet, one discovers that their real complaint was that Bradley had sentimentalized these two tragic heroes, whom they regarded as evil. Knights' *Some Shakespearean Themes* (1959) and *An Approach to Hamlet* (1960) show the *Scrutiny* method at its best; but neither critic, nor Derek Traversi, treats Shakespeare as a writer of stage plays.[19]

Harley Granville-Barker, himself an actor, dramatist and director, in his series of *Prefaces to Shakespeare* gave sound advice on how to produce the plays, how to act in them, and how to speak the lines. His work acts as a necessary corrective to those critics who regard the theatre with suspicion, if not with abhorrence.

William Empson's *Seven Types of Ambiguity* (1930) was avowedly influenced by an analysis by Robert Graves and Laura Riding of one of Shakespeare's sonnets. However much we may differ from Empson in the interpretation of some passages, there is no doubt that in this book, in *Some Versions of Pastoral* (1955) and in *The Structure of Complex Words* (1951) he has increased our understanding of the complexity of Shakespeare's style. His method links up with Whiter's demonstration of the way in which Shakespeare's images are often linked by conscious or unconscious quibbles. Molly M. Mahood's *Shakespeare's Word-Play* (1957) is the standard work on this topic and the Empsonian method carried to extremes is to be found in Stephen Booth's brilliant but wayward edition of the *Sonnets* (1977).

Caroline Spurgeon in *Shakespeare's Imagery and What it Tells us* (1935) tried by a systematic tabulation of the images to deduce Shakespeare's personality and beliefs and, with much greater success, the iterative image in each of the mature plays, and its use in interpreting them. In the following year W. H. Clemen's *Shakespeares Bilder*, translated and revised as *The Development of Shakespeare's Imagery* (1951), wisely stressed its dramatic function. E. A. Armstrong in *Shakespeare's Imagination* (1946) examined a number of image-clusters which recurred in play after play. R. B. Heilman, believing that Spurgeon's concentration on a single iterative image was misleading, produced two full-length studies of *King Lear* (*This Great Stage*, 1948) and *Othello* (*Magic in the Web*, 1956). Among later books may be mentioned Maurice Charney's *Shakespeare's Roman Plays* (1961). Most editors now think it necessary to discuss the imagery of the plays with which they are dealing.[20]

The increasing professionalism of Shakespeare criticism has led to hundreds of works on individual plays. All the major tragedies have been the subject of dozens of books and countless articles. On *Hamlet*, for example, there have been excellent books by Peter Alexander (*Hamlet: Father and Son*, 1955), Nigel Alexander (*Poison, Play, and Duel*, 1971), Ernest Jones (*Hamlet and Oedipus*, 1949), Bertram L.

Joseph (*Conscience and the King*, 1953), Harry Levin (*The Question of Hamlet*, 1959), Eleanor A. Prosser (*Hamlet and Revenge*, 1967) and Morris Weitz (*Hamlet and the Philosophy of Literary Criticism*, 1964). This list of books omits some seminal criticism of Hamlet by Harold Jenkins, Fredson Bowers, G. K. Hunter, and C. S. Lewis, merely because they were embodied in short articles. On *King Lear* there have been at least seven notable books: John F. Danby's *Shakespeare's Doctrine of Nature* (1949), William R. Elton's *King Lear and the Gods* (1966), Maynard Mack's *King Lear in Our Time* (1965), *Some Facets of King Lear*, edited by Rosalie L. Colie and F. T. Flahiff (1974), S. L. Goldberg's *An Essay on King Lear* (1974), John Reibetanz's *The Lear World* (1977), and Marvin Rosenberg's *The Masks of King Lear* (1972). Rosenberg studies the way the play has been performed against a background of interpretation, and he has written similar books on *Othello* and *Macbeth*. A book on Iago by Stanley E. Hyman (1970) discusses what he calls the illusion of his motivation, the plausible but contradictory explanations of the villain's conduct – and this has implications for the whole field of Shakespearean characterization. There are four books on *Measure for Measure*, the best being by Mary M. Lascelles (1953), three on *Troilus and Cressida*, two on *The Winter's Tale* by S. L. Bethell (1947) and Fitzroy Pyle (1969), two on *Love's Labour's Lost*, and one on *All's Well that Ends Well*, the least popular of the comedies, under the title *The Unfortunate Comedy* (1969).[21]

Despite this concentration on single plays, there have been plenty of wider studies of Shakespeare's various genres. Seven books on the comedies may be mentioned. H. B. Charlton's *Shakespearean Comedy* (1938) was primarily concerned with genre and characterization. He was out of sympathy with the problem plays and oddly spent more space on the early comedies than on *Twelfth Night*. John Russell Brown in *Shakespeare and his Comedies* (1957) suggested that they were written 'for the avowed purpose of expressing Shakespeare's attitude to life and his moral judgements upon it'; but C. L. Barber in *Shakespeare's Festive Comedy* (1959) argued that many of the comedies were celebratory rather than didactic. John Dover Wilson's *Shakespeare's Happy Comedies* (1962) is a relaxed and pleasant book, but belonging to an older tradition. Bertrand Evans in *Shakespeare's Comedies* (1960) stressed the way in which the characters, but not the audience, were kept in the dark about the situation. Alexander Leggatt, *Shakespeare's Comedies of Love* (1974), avoids theorizing, but succeeds very well in describing the unique qualities of the plays with which he deals. Lastly, Leo Salingar's *Shakespeare and the Traditions of Comedy* (1974) relates the comedies to the background of comic writing in classical, medieval and renaissance times. (This book is to be followed by a second volume dealing more directly with the comedies themselves.)

E. M. W. Tillyard's book *Shakespeare's History Plays* (1944), in which it was assumed that the poet subscribed to the orthodox Tudor view of a divinely sanctioned political order, has been questioned and modified by a number of later critics, e.g. D. A. Traversi's *Shakespeare from Richard II to Henry V* (1957), M. M. Reese's *The Cease of Majesty* (1961) and Robert Ornstein's *A Kingdom for a Stage* (1972). Of the scores of books dealing with some or all of the tragedies, there is space to mention only a few: Nicholas Brooke's *Shakespeare's Early Tragedies* (1968) and a work dealing with the last group, W. E. Farnham's *Shakespeare's Tragic Frontier* (1950), D. A. Traversi's *Shakespeare: The Roman Plays* (1963), Virgil K. Whitaker's *The Mirror up to Nature* (1965), Reuben A. Brower's *Hero and Saint* (1970) and John Holloway's *The Story of the Night* (1961) which takes issue with those critics who concentrate on the moral themes embodied in the tragedies, and proceeds to argue, less successfully, that the secret of the tragic heroes is that they are scapegoats.

Criticism of the plays of the last period has been designed to counteract Lytton Strachey's essay (1904), which was itself intended as a counterblast to Victorian sentimentality. By the time Hallett Smith wrote *Shakespeare's Romances* (1972) and Howard Felperin his *Shakespearean Romance* (1972), Strachey had been discounted; although neither critic went all the way with Knight nor agreed with the mythological interpretation of Northrop Frye in *A Natural Perspective* (1965).[22]

Most of those who have written on the Sonnets have been too much concerned with biographical implications. There have, however, been some admirable works of criticism: J. W. Lever's *The Elizabethan Love Sonnet* (1956), Edward Hubler's *The Sense of Shakespeare's Sonnets* (1952), J. B. Leishman's *Themes and Variations in Shakespeare's Sonnets* (1961), Stephen Booth's *An Essay on Shakes-*

peare's Sonnets (1969) and Giorgio Melchiori's *Shakespeare's Dramatic Meditations* (1975).[23]

There are a number of excellent books which do not belong to any of the categories mentioned. A. C. Sprague's discussion of the plays in the theatre – *Shakespeare and the Actors* (1944), *Shakespearian Players and Performances* (1953) – Anne Righter's *Shakespeare and the Idea of the Play* (1962), Brian Vickers' *The Artistry of Shakespeare's Prose* (1968), Philip Edwards' *Shakespeare and the Confines of Art* (1968), A. P. Rossiter's brilliant lectures, *Angel with Horns* (1961), and two books by Rosalie Colie, *Paradoxia Epidemica* (1966) and *Shakespeare's Living Art* (1974).

This survey has had to be confined mainly to criticism in English, although there has been good criticism in German,[24] French[25] and Russian.[26] Modern critics have two advantages over the great critics of the past: they have a greater knowledge of the conditions of Shakespeare's age, and modern editions of the plays are marginally closer to what Shakespeare wrote than those available to Johnson or Bradley.[27] But the proliferation of criticism makes it more and more difficult to say anything which is both new and true. Although modern movements in the theatre – the political theatre of Brecht, the Theatre of Cruelty, the Theatre of the Absurd – and new ideas (existentialism, psychoanalysis, Marxism) have led to re-interpretation of the plays, some of them already seem to be old-fashioned. Meanwhile Eliot's criteria remain valid:[28]

> The ideal Shakespeare critic should be a scholar, with knowledge not of Shakespeare in isolation but of Shakespeare in relation to the Elizabethan Theatre ... and of that Theatre in relation to the social, political, economic and religious conditions of its time. He should also be a poet; and he should be a 'man of the theatre'. And he should also have a philosophic mind.

NOTES

1. The early criticisms of Shakespeare are given by E. K. Chambers in his *William Shakespeare*. The six volumes of *Shakespeare: The Critical Heritage*, ed. Brian Vickers (1974–81) contain extracts of criticism until the end of the eighteenth century.

2. See *Beaumont and Fletcher on the Restoration Stage* by A. C. Sprague (1926) and *The Commonwealth and Restoration Stage* by Leslie Hotson (1928).

3. See *Shakespeare in the Eighteenth Century* by D. Nichol Smith (1928) and the Vickers volumes mentioned above.

4. See *Shakespeare's Wordplay* by M. Mahood (1965) and 'The Uncomic Pun' by Kenneth Muir in *The Singularity of Shakespeare* (1977).

5. See *The Genesis of Shakespeare Idolatry* by R. W. Babcock (1931).

6. See *Shakespearian Criticism* by Maurice Morgann, ed. Daniel A. Fineman (1972).

7. See Walter Whiter's *A Specimen of a Commentary* ed. Alan Over and Mary Bell (1967).

8. See *Suggestions* by E. E. Kellett (1923) and *Shakespeare's Imagery* by C. F. E. Spurgeon (1935).

9. Other accounts of Bensley's performance conflict with Lamb's.

10. See Coleridge's *Shakespearean Criticism*, ed. T. M. Raysor (1930, 1960).

11. T. S. Eliot's remarks on *Othello* are in his essay 'Shakespeare and the Stoicism of Seneca' (1927); F. R. Leavis's in 'Diabolic Intellect and the Noble Hero' (Reprinted in *The Common Pursuit*; L. C. Knights' 'Prince Hamlet' and *How Many Children had Lady Macbeth?* are reprinted in *Explorations* (1946).

12. The most interesting Freudian interpretations of *Hamlet* are *Hamlet and Oedipus* by Ernest Jones (1949) and *Dark Legend* by Frederic Wertham (1947).

13. 'A Plea for the Liberty of Interpreting'.

14. e.g. E. M. W. Tillyard, D. A. Traversi, M. M. Reese, John Dover Wilson and George Hibbard.

15. A compact edition followed in 1977 with some additional facts.

16. *What Happens in Hamlet* (1935), *The Fortunes of Falstaff* (1944).

17. T. W. Baldwin, *Shakspere's Five-Act Structure* (1947).

18. G. K. Hunter, *Dramatic Identities and Cultural Tradition* (1978), 299.

19. 'How should we read Shakespeare?' asks Knights and he answers: 'We start with so many lines of verse on a printed page which we read as we should read any other poem'.

20. See Kenneth Muir, *Shakespeare the Professional* (1973), 54–69.

21. By Joseph R. Price. W. H. Clemen has written a full-length study of *Richard III* and there are two books on *Timon of Athens*. It may be mentioned that there are Casebooks on half of Shakespeare's plays and three volumes of articles reprinted from *Shakespeare Survey* – Aspects of *Othello*, of *Macbeth* and of *Hamlet*.

22. Eliot's two lectures on the plays of Shakespeare's final period remain unpublished.

23. Kenneth Muir, *Shakespeare's Sonnets* (1979) gives a brief account of their critical history.

24. From Schlegel and Goethe to Landauer, Clemen and Robert Weimann, whose *Shakespeare and the popular tradition in the theater* (1978) is a revision of a book published earlier in German.

25. See Henri Fluchère's article in *Shakespeare Survey*, II, 'Shakespeare in France, 1900–1948'.

26. Tolstoy was one of a number of hostile critics, but since 1918 there have been many more sympathetic works, not all of them Marxist. They include

Stanislavsky Produces 'Othello' and G. Kozintsev's *Shakespeare: Time and Conscience* (1966).

27. e.g. Peter Alexander's edition of the complete works and many editions of individual plays, including the new Arden and the forthcoming New Oxford and New Cambridge. All these, and the New Penguin, benefit from a long line of textual critics in the present century from A. W. Pollard and W. W. Greg to Fredson Bowers, Charlton Hinman and Alice Walker.

28. Preface to Fluchère's *Shakespeare* (1953).

BEN JONSON, DRAMATIST

L. C. KNIGHTS

Fully to enjoy what Ben Jonson has to offer we need, in the first place, to understand an individual tone and accent that can only be defined in terms of the union of opposites. The manner is remarkably individual, yet informed with a strong sense of tradition: its appeal is to a common wisdom. A marked classical bent is combined with an Englishness that can digest erudition. A mode of expression that is grave, weighty, and sententious moves easily into high-spirited buoyancy. The voice of an insistent moralist is also that of a successful popular entertainer and the author of some of the best farces in the language.

It is unfortunate that in his critical writings Jonson has given a clue to only one side of himself; for between his own time and ours (when there has been something like a Jonson revival) the plays have been largely seen, not directly, but through what he himself said about the art of writing and the function of drama. Read the *Discoveries*,[1] together with the various Prologues and critical matter interspersed in the plays, and you are aware of a mind trained on the Classics, scornful of the sprawling productions of the London stage (and, it must be added, out of sympathy with plays that followed a different kind of dramatic logic from his own), and prepared to claim for his own comedies not only superiority but a place quite apart from the sort of thing that audiences were accustomed to applaud. The explicit appeal is always to 'scholars that can judge', not to the 'nut-crackers that only come for sight'. And the scholars, it is assumed, will applaud the author, not only for observing the unities 'of time, place, persons', but for strictly pursuing a didactic aim:

I would fain hear one of these autumn-judgements define once, *Quid sit comoedia?* if he cannot, let him content himself with Cicero's definition – till he have strength to propose to himself a better – who would have a comedy to be *imitatio vitae, speculum consuetudinis, imago veritatis;*[a] a thing through-out pleasant, and ridiculous, and accommodated to the correction of manners.

(*Every Man out of His Humour*, III. i)

'The office of a comic poet', he says, again appealing to the Ancients, is 'to imitate justice and instruct to life, as well as purity of language, or stir up gentle affections' (Dedication of *Volpone*, 'To the most noble and most equal sisters, the two famous Universities'). As for the 'purity of language', which Jonson stresses together with 'doc-trine' (so that solecisms and racked metaphors, in the Dedication just quoted, are dismissed in the same scornful sentence as brothelry and blasphemy), that too is the reward of following the classical precepts concerning Art, Imitation, and Exercise.

To this perfection of Nature in our Poet, we require Exercise of those parts, and frequent. If his wit will not arrive suddenly at the dignity of the Ancients, let him not yet fall out with it or be over hastily angry: offer to turn it away from study, in a humour; but come to it again on better cogi-tation; try another time with labour. If then it succeed not, cast not away the quills yet: nor scratch the wainscot, beat not the poor desk, but bring all to the forge and file, again; turn it anew. There is no Statute Law of the Kingdom bids you be a Poet against your will; or the first Quarter. If it come in a year or two, it is well. The common Rhymers pour forth verses, such as they are, *ex tempore*, but there never comes from them one sense worth the life of a day. A Rhymer, and a *Poet*, are two things. It is said of the incomparable Virgil that he brought forth his verses like a bear, and after formed them with licking.

(*Discoveries*, 130)

Now, it is certainly true that Jonson was a very learned man, that his plays were nourished by his familiarity with the Latin authors, and that he believed passionately in the moral function of the poet. It may also be assumed that when a creative writer theorizes in language as vigorous and telling as Jonson's, the critical theory is a rationalization of something intrinsic and fundamental to his art. Jonson's classical bent, his concern for the unities, and so on, is an expression of his own vigorous and simplifying vision of life, of his feeling that saying something effectively is largely a matter of not saying too much. His didactic insistence is neither the sermonizing of a pedant nor the camouflage of a popular writer conscious of Puritan

---

a 'the imitation of life, the mirror of manners, the image of truth;'

hostility to the stage; it expresses his sense of comedy as essentially a serious art. Jonson, in short, appealed to the Ancients not only because he felt for them the respect of any classically trained mind – a discriminating respect, it must be added[2] – but because they conferred authority on deeply congenial modes.

Yet that is only half the story. The best of Jonson's plays are living drama because the learning and 'classical' elements are assimilated by a sensibility in direct contact with its own age. The judgement, the operative standards, are those of a man who has read and thought, but the material, however transmuted, is supplied by direct observation. 'I believe', said Coleridge, 'there is not one whim or affectation in common life noted in any memoir of that age which may not be found drawn and framed in some corner or other of Ben Jonson's dramas.'[3] And not only whims and affectations: the tricks of shysters and crooks, mountebanks, lawyers, news-vendors, and monopoly-hunters are transferred to the stage with all the relish of one who sees for himself what is under his nose. Jonson's major themes, as we shall see, were taken from those that were of fundamental importance for his age. All we are concerned with here is his feeling for the surface of contemporary life, operative not only in the crowded canvas of *Bartholomew Fair* but in the smallest details. ' 'Slight, I bring you,' says Face of the lawyer's clerk,

> No cheating Clim o' the Cloughs, or Claribels,
> That looks as big as five-and-fifty, and flush;*
> And spit out secrets like hot custard –
> Nor any melancholic under-scribe,
> Shall tell the Vicar; but a special gentle,
> That is the heir to forty marks a year,
> Consorts with the small poets of the time,
> Is the sole hope of his old grandmother;
> That knows the law, and writes you six fair hands ...
>
> (The Alchemist, 1)

The special quality of texture of a portrait such as this derives from the artist's easy familiarity with popular ballad literature, popular sports and pastimes, and popular manners. Not only is Dapper

---

* Clim o' the Clough, the hero of a popular ballad; Claribel, perhaps from *The Faerie Queene*, IV. ix. The second line refers to the strongest possible hand in the game of Primero.

observed, he is inseparable from the context of common English life
that frames him. It was a sure instinct that led Jonson, in revising
Every Man in His Humour, to transfer his scene from Florence to
London and to make the characters unmistakably English.[4] English,
too, we may feel, is the spontaneous comic verve that breaks through
and blends with 'the correction of manners', that is indeed, in the best
plays, inseparable from the serious purpose that it serves. Jonson is not
only a master of quick-moving intrigue, he is a master of farce. And
what this means is that his comedy has the impact of something
directly presented to the senses. There is, as he was proud to proclaim,
no mere clowning ('no eggs are broken, Nor quaking custards with
fierce teeth affrighted'), but the comic vision is embodied in forms
that, for all their exaggeration and distortion, are substantially *there*.
And they are there, in the first place, because of Jonson's grasp of the
comic potentialities latent in everyday speech, of the gaucheries,
stupidities, and delusions that betray themselves in an ineptitude of
tone, and that readily lend themselves to a comic heightening:[5]

MATTHEW. Why, I pray you, sir, make use of my study, it's at your service.
STEPHEN. I thank you, sir, I shall be bold, I warrant you; have you a stool
there to be melancholy upon?
                                        (*Every Man in His Humour*, III. i)

ANANIAS.   They are profane,
Lewd, superstitious, and idolatrous breeches . . .
Thou look'st like antichrist, in that lewed hat.
                                           The Alchemist, IV. iv)

Jonson's views on style bear much the same relation to his actual use
of English as a dramatic medium as do his views on the nature and
function of drama to his actual achievement in his best plays: they
emphasize an element that is organic to his art, but one that draws its
life from a conjunction with other elements about which he did not
find it necessary to theorize. His expressed predilections were for
what are commonly called the classical virtues. 'The chief virtue of a
style', he says, following Quintilian, 'is perspicuity, and nothing so
vicious in it as to need an interpreter.' And he demands not only the
clear but the pregnant phrase. 'A strict and succinct style is that where
you can take away nothing without loss, and that loss to be manifest'
(*Discoveries*, 119). Now, clarity and directness are certainly features of

his verse, which has nothing of the Shakespearian complexity and subtlety ('metaphors far fetched', he said, 'hinder to be understood'); and in some of his best passages the unambiguous weighty style is a perfect expression of the moral seriousness behind it:

> There be two,
> Know more than honest counsels; whose close breasts
> Were they ripped up to light, it would be found
> A poor and idle sin, to which their trunks
> Had not been made fit organs. These can lie,
> Flatter, and swear, forswear, deprave, inform,
> Smile, and betray; make guilty men; then beg
> The forfeit lives to get their livings; cut
> Men's throats with whisperings ...
>
> (Sejanus, I. i)

Yet the phrases we have used so far, which apply well enough to the extract just quoted, do not even hint at the superb liveliness of a passage – at least equally characteristic – such as the following:

> I fear I shall begin to grow in love
> With my dear self, and my most prosperous parts,
> They do so spring and burgeon; I can feel
> A whimsy in my blood: I know not how,
> Success hath made me wanton. I could skip
> Out of my skin now, like a subtle snake,
> I am so limber. O! your parasite
> Is a most precious thing, dropt from above,
> Not bred 'mongst clods and clodpoles, here on earth.
> I muse, the mystery was not made a science,
> It is so liberally profest! Almost
> All the wise world is little else, in nature,
> But parasites or sub-parasites. And yet
> I mean not those that have your bare town-art,
> To know who's fit to feed them; have no house,
> No family, no care, and therefore mould
> Tales for men's ears, to bait that sense; ...
>
>   ... nor those,
> With their court dog-tricks, that can fawn and fleer,
> Make their revenue out of legs and faces,
> Echo my lord, and lick away a moth:
> But your fine elegant rascal, that can rise
> And stoop, almost together, like an arrow;
> Shoot through the air as nimbly as a star;
> Turn short as doth a swallow; and be here
> And there, and here, and yonder, all at once;

Present to any humour, all occasion;
And change a visor swifter than a thought!
This is the creature had the art born with him;
Toils not to learn it, but doth practise it
Out of most excellent nature: and such sparks
Are the true parasites, others but their zanis.

(*Volpone*, III. i)

The rhythmical animation, the colloquial language, the emphatic yet unforced alliteration, produce an impression of easy vigour in which, by purely linguistic means, the Parasite mimes (one might say dances) the role he describes. And the miming simultaneously 'places' what it so vividly communicates – places it in a language of colloquial contempt that owes nothing to classical precept or example but everything, surely, to popular habits of speech. Consider, for example, the effect of those 'court dog-tricks', or the grotesque transformation achieved as the obsequious movement of an arm becomes the momentary flicker of a *tongue* ('lick away a moth'), or the witty compression by which the parasite's progress – rising by stooping – is defined. This belongs to the same side of Jonson's genius as the opening quarrel scene in *The Alchemist*. What Coleridge called Jonson's 'sterling English diction' – with all the attitudes and habits of observation that this implies – is the basis of his poetry. Sometimes, as in the two *Odes* to himself, it blends easily with the idiom of one who can speak without affectation of warming himself by Pindar's fire; more often it assimilates to itself and transmutes matter derived from the Classics, so that lines from Catullus or Horace appear recreated in a poetry that is wholly English and contemporary.[6] Jonson, in short, is neither the classicist whose learning puts a barrier between himself and the experience of his age, nor the purely native product in whom a certain provinciality is the price of forthright vigour; he is a man who, having seen and learnt from other civilizations, is thoroughly at home in his own time and place. The result of this blend is an uncommon poise and strength.

With the possible exception of *Every Man in His Humour*, Jonson's earliest surviving plays may be left to the student of Elizabethan drama. The persistent reader of *Every Man out of His Humour*, *Cynthia's Revels*, and *The Poetaster* will from time to time find his reward – such, for example, as the noble lines in which Crites tells how:

> these vain joys· in which their wills consume
> Such powers of wit and soul as are of force
> To raise their beings to eternity,
> May be converted on works fitting men.
> And, for the practice of a forced look,
> An antic gesture, or a fustian phrase,
> Study the native frame of a true heart,
> And inward comeliness of bounty, knowledge,
> And spirit that may conform them actually
> To God's high figures, which they have in power;*
>
> (*Cynthia's Revels*, v. ii)

or the description of Virgil's poetry:

> so ramm'd with life
> It can but gather strength of life with being –†
>
> (*The Poetaster*, v. i)

but they are not plays that one looks forward with any relish to re-reading.[7]

Every Man in His Humour, in its revised form, has sufficient vigour to carry one's interest forward, but in the other plays named the exhibition of tedious follies becomes itself tedious. Opportunity is found for the different 'humours' to exhibit themselves or, derisively, each other; but the dismissal is too easy to engage much interest, and at times one feels that the whole display is simply part of what Herford and Simpson call Jonson's 'stupendous glorification of himself'. Such success as they have is largely a success of isolated satirical passages:

> Here stalks me by a proud and spangled sir,
> That looks three handfuls higher than his foretop;
> Savours himself alone ...
>
> (*Cynthia's Revels*, III. iv)

but the author's pervasive scorn for bad writers and nincompoops is no substitute for that 'unity of inspiration, radiating into plot and characters alike' (T. S. Eliot) that sustains the greater plays.

---

* i.e. in potentiality, which must be actualized in true being.

† Tempting as it is, it does not seem possible to assume that the Virgil of this play was intended to represent Shakespeare. See Herford and Simpson, I, 432–7, and IX, 534–5.

It is in *Sejanus* (1603), written for Shakespeare's company in their public theatre, that Jonson finds a major unifying theme, and enlists his powers in the cause of profoundly serious standards. The theme is pre-eminently *the* Jonsonian theme and, with variations, is to form the staple of his greater plays. It is, quite simply, inordinate desire – for power, for money, or for the enjoyment of the senses. 'Expect things greater than thy largest hopes to overtake thee' – the words that Sejanus addresses to the corrupt physician Eudemus might also be addressed to Sejanus himself, to the suitors in *Volpone*, to Sir Epicure Mammon in *The Alchemist*, or to FitzDottrel in *The Devil is an Ass*. They express what it is that links together all the main figures in the Jonson gallery.

If we ask how it was that Jonson's genius found release in this way, the answer is, I think, ready to hand. The issues with which he chose to deal were among the most deeply ingrained preoccupations of his age. It is important, even in a short space, not to over-simplify. The great redirection of human energies known as the Renaissance is no longer seen, as it was a century ago, simply as a movement of liberation, a necessary and glorious stage in the great march of Progress. When we think of the sixteenth century we think not only of 'the Development of the Individual'. 'the Revival of Antiquity', 'the Discovery of the World and of Man',★ but of the thrust of capitalist enterprise, the rise of economic individualism, the development of an a-moral 'realism' in political thought and action. We are aware, above all, of a great reorientation of attitude that prepared the way not only for the scientific achievements of the seventeenth century and the rationalism of the Enlightenment, but for the materialism of industrial civilization, the spiritual bewilderment of the nineteenth century, and the urgent anxieties of our own time. Now that we no longer believe in an almost automatic Progress of Humanity, we are perhaps in danger of reading back into the Renaissance, as a whole, a sinister significance that belongs in reality only to some of its multifarious aspects. The reality, of course, was complex and demands a complex assessment. But even when we recognize the great achievements of the age, we have to recognize also that it was (as most ages

★ The titles of the second, third, and fourth parts of Jacob Burckhardt's great work, *The Civilization of the Renaissance in Italy*, first published in 1860.

are) double-faced. The positive side lay in the more unfettered development of energies that could be made to serve – and have served – the cause of human living. The negative side was an inflation of the will at the expense of the spirit, the acceptance, *as an ideal*, of the desire to assert oneself, to use and dominate. And it was an ideal that could easily be invested with a certain spurious glamour.

> Lay out our golden wedges to the view,
> That their reflections may amaze the Persians.

> Is it not passing brave to be a king,
> And ride in triumph through Persepolis?

> And with our sun-bright armour, as we march,
> We'll chase the stars from heaven, and dim their eyes
> That stand and muse at our admired arms.

These quotations from Marlowe's *Tamburlaine* may serve to represent the element of fantasy that accompanied the attitudes of the new age to riches, pomp, and power.

It is precisely this aspect of the Renaissance and post-Renaissance world that, in his greater plays, Jonson takes for theme and, we may say, de-glamourizes. It may be suspected that in dealing critically with exaggerated claims that the individual may make on the world, an excessive assertion of the self, he himself was deeply engaged. ('Arrogance', as Herford and Simpson remark, 'was an emotion which Jonson profoundly understood.') But whatever self-searchings may at times have given resonance to his verse, it was the public world – and a major aspect of it – that called out his powers as a dramatist. His art – it has become a commonplace – is an art of exaggeration and caricature; but it draws directly and potently on the actual, now isolating and magnifying some impulse that 'in reality' would express itself in more complex and more devious ways, now crowding the stage with instances of greed or folly that had easily recognizable counterparts in the England of James I, as indeed they have today. And it is an art that is profoundly realist. Nourished by the Christian and classical traditions, and having much in common with a homely popular wisdom, it is entirely free from self-deceiving fantasy about the nature of either luxury or power.

> Ay, but an anger, a just anger, as this is,
> Puts life in man. Who can endure to see

The fury of men's gullets and their groins?
What fires, what cooks, what kitchens might be spared?
What stews, ponds, parks, coops, garners, magazines?
What velvets, tissues, scarfs, embroideries,
And laces they might lack? They covet things
Superfluous still; when it were much more honour
They could want necessary: what need hath nature
Of silver dishes or gold chamber-pots?
Of perfumed napkins, or a numerous family*
To see her eat? poor and wise, she requires
Meat only: hunger is not ambitious:
Say that you were the emperor of pleasures,
The great dictator of fashions for all Europe,
And had the pomp of all the courts and kingdoms,
Laid forth unto the show, to make yourself
Gazed and admired at; you must go to bed,
And take your natural rest: then all this vanisheth.
Your bravery was but shown; 'twas not possest;
While it did boast itself, it was then perishing.

(*The Staple of News*, III. iv)

This, from a comparatively late play (1626), may fairly be said to
represent the standard against which excessive desire is measured. It is
a standard that, expressed as it is here in great poetry, commands assent.[8] And, in an age that was tending to blur the distinctions between
the superfluous and the necessary, it was to the service of this standard
that Jonson brought his resources of scorn and mimicry and contemptuous caricature.

In *Sejanus* Jonson did more than find his theme, he contrived a
dramatic structure and established a mode within which he could say
what he had to say with the greatest effect. The major embodiment
of the theme – in this play the lust for power – is flanked by other
figures who share the same, or closely related, drives. Behind these,
again, we are aware of a world in which these drives are taken for
granted. Thus, in the two Senate scenes (III. i and v. x), grotesque
ballets of hypocrisy, we watch the construction of a world of falsehood that lends to the exaggerated and simplified figures of Sejanus,
Tiberius, and Macro an effect almost of versimilitude. At the same
time it is largely by means of this pervasive exaggeration and dis-

* In the Latin sense: a large household or a number of servants.

tortion that judgement is precipitated. The characters are inflated to a point where the final catastrophe appears as the inevitable outcome of the pressures working within them and expressed in the words they speak.*

In *Volpone* (1606) and *The Alchemist* (1610) the high-spirited comedy is there for all to see – the gulling of the suitors or the parody of the sales-talk of all nostrum-sellers in *Volpone*, the agility with which Subtle and Face 'play' their various dupes, who would ruin all if they met. But it is comedy that serves a completely serious purpose. There are no characters, such as Arruntius and Silius in *Sejánus*, who consistently express the author's own outlook. Jonson's peculiar triumph is, whilst apparently engaged in nothing more than building up a vigorous comic action, to enforce a variety of recognitions that blend into a deadly serious 'criticism of life'. At times the vicious characters themselves, without apparent incongruity, are made to indicate the reality that condemns them. More commonly the method is less apparent: a grotesquely expressed impulse is brought into direct relation with those aspects of the everyday world from which it has been isolated and magnified, and all alike share in the derisive placing implicit in the caricature. An example may make this clear.

In *The Alchemist*, where belief in alchemy and fortune-telling is substituted for the legacy-hunting of *Volpone* as a symbol of the desire for easy money, the high peak of caricature is the figure of Sir Epicure Mammon. We first see him at the opening of Act II, escorted by the sceptical Surly, on the day when he expects Subtle, the sham alchemist, to have discovered the secret of the transmutation of metals:

> Come on, sir. Now you set your foot on shore
> In *Novo Orbe*; here's the rich Peru:
> And there within, sir, are the golden mines,
> Great Solomon's Ophir! he was sailing to't,
> Three years, but we have reached it in ten months.
> This is the day wherein, to all my friends,
> I will pronounce the happy word, BE RICH;
> THIS DAY YOU SHALL BE SPECTATISSIMI.

---

* Sejanus' soliloquy beginning: 'Swell, swell, my joys; and faint not to declare/Yourselves as ample as your causes are...' (v. i) has something of the same effect as Mosca's soliloquy quoted on page 408 above.

Here is the familiar comic inflation; but it shades at once into something that is not only fantastic caricature.

> You shall no more deal with the hollow dye,
> Or the frail card ... No more
> Shall thirst of satin, or the covetous hunger
> Of velvet entrails for a rude-spun cloak,
> To be displayed at Madam Augusta's, make
> The sons of Sword and Hazard fall before
> The golden calf, and on their knees, whole nights,
> Commit idolatry with wine and trumpets:
> Or go a feasting after drum and ensign.
> No more of this. You shall start up young viceroys,
> And have your punks and punketees, my Surly.
> And unto thee I speak it first, BE RICH.

In these lines, by means of a succession of negatives, Mammon's gorgeous expectations are seen as kin to a shabbier actuality, which at the same time is revealed as sharing the patent self-delusion of the alchemist's dupe. The swelling expansiveness (ballasted by a few unobtrusive comments spoken by the author *through* his characters: 'the *hollow* dye' [leaded dice], 'the *frail* card', and, more explicitly, 'idolatry') reaches its deflating climax when Mammon reveals his idea of vice-regal pomp. Mammon, however, is now launched and the comic impossibilities multiply:

> This night I'll change
> All that is metal in my house to gold ...
>
> I will have all my beds blown up, not stuft:
> Down is too hard ...

But what gives the scene (like the wooing of Doll Common in IV. i) its distinctive note is that the audience can never *completely* disown Sir Epicure – or not for long at a time.

> In eight and twenty days,
> I'll make an old man of fourscore, a child,
> Restore his years, renew him, like an eagle,
> To the fifth age; make him get sons and daughters,
> Young giants; as our philosophers have done,
> The ancient patriarchs, afore the flood,
> But taking, once a week, on a knife's point,
> The quantity of a grain of mustard of it;
> Become stout Marses, and beget young Cupids.

This, though it shares with the speech last quoted an effect of comic exaggeration, is at least a little closer to the sons of Sword and Hazard, who, in turn, belong to our world. The whole play is built on a similar plan. Ananias is a comic freak, but his hypocrisy is real: 'casting [coining] of dollars is concluded lawful'. Kastril, the angry boy, is a recognizable social type:

> . . . a gentleman newly warm in his land, sir,
> Scarce cold in his one and twenty, that does govern
> His sister here; and is a man himself
> Of some three thousand a year, and is come up
> To learn to quarrel, and to live by his wits,
> And will go down again, and die in the country.

The day-dreams of Abel Drugger, the tobacco seller, and of Dapper, the lawyer's clerk, though as baseless as Mammon's, are taken from life. It is without any sense of incongruity that we see these figures led a dance, together with the gorgeous and impossible Sir Epicure Mammon.

Of Jonson's other plays little can be said here. *Epicoene, or The Silent Woman* (1609) and, I think, *Bartholomew Fair* (1614) belong to the category of stage entertainments: in them the fun is divorced from any rich significance – though many would disagree with this verdict[9]. *Catiline his Conspiracy* (1611) belongs with *Sejanus*, but although not so dull as it is supposed to be, it has not the spontaneous life of the earlier play. Only *The Devil is an Ass* (1616) belongs to the great Jonsonian species of serious comedy, of which *Volpone* and *The Alchemist* are the supreme examples. This play, although based on the fiction of a minor devil on holiday from hell who has had a bad time in the London world of business and fashion

> – You talk of a university! why, hell is
> A grammar school to this –

is a direct satire on contemporary economic abuses. The bogus schemes by which Meercraft raises money from a varied collection of greedy dupes reflect the motives and methods of many of the 'projectors'[a] who, in Jacobean England, were ready to take advantage of the new opportunities open to enterprise. As in the earlier comedies, there is a constant interplay between the world of caricature (in which FitzDottrell, the principal dupe, expects gold mountains from schemes of a comically impossible ingenuity) and sober reality, so that the criticism implied in the caricature is reflected back on the actual. But although *The Devil is an Ass* is so close to the contemporary scene that, according to Unwin, 'a study of its leading characters would be by far the best introduction to the economic history of the period',[10] Jonson's incisive handling of greed and folly raises it well above the level of a mere documentary. In *The Staple of News* (1626) satire directed against the newly established news industry ('a weekly cheat to draw money') is combined with a renewed attack on the power of money. But, instead of the vigorous comic invention of the earlier plays, there is a more mechanical use of a direct 'morality' convention (the Lady Pecunia [Money] appears in person, together with her train – Mortgage, Wax, etc.), and the play only lives in flashes of topical satire and a few fine passages. It was followed by *The New Inn* (1629), *The Magnetic Lady* (1632) and (perhaps, for the evidence is doubtful) the fragment of a pastoral, *The Sad Shepherd*. But, although the latter has been much admired, it is impossible to pretend that these later plays inspire any very lively interest. The Jonsonian world is completed by *The Staple of News*. At its centre stand the assured masterpieces – *Sejanus*, *Volpone*, and *The Alchemist*.

Jonson's world, though complete in itself, is not a large one. You cannot live in it for long at a time. In a sense its very completeness is against it. Nothing breaks through from the hidden world of longing or suffering; the prevailing mode is never disturbed by unexpected sympathies or glimpses of paradox. There is little in the plays that you can dwell on, as you find yourself dwelling on a play – or a few lines – of Shakespeare's, or a poem – or a few lines – of Blake's, so that new aspects of human nature (your own nature

a *Projector*, originally 'one who forms a project, who plans or designs some enterprise or undertaking' (*N.E.D.*), early in its career acquired the invidious sense of a speculator. 'But what is a projector?' – 'Why, one, sir, that projects Ways to enrich men, or to make them great, By suits, by marriages, by undertakings' (*The Devil is an Ass*, I. iii). In Jonson's time projects were usually associated with the unpopular monopolies. Gifford has an interesting note at the beginning of Act II of this play.

among others) and new possibilities of being are continually revealed. Exclusion was the condition of Jonson's achievement. But the best of his plays have qualities common to all great literature. They define with precision a permanent aspect of human nature. For what they isolate for sardonic inspection is a form of folly which, however grotesque in its dramatic representation, in Sejanus, Mammon, or Meercraft, is not confined to fools; it is simply the folly of inordinate desire. And although this, deeply considered, is a theme for tragedy, there is also a rightness in the particular form of Jonsonian comedy, in which simplified figures seem to blow themselves up until they burst, and schemes contrived with a remarkable and persistent ingenuity topple like a house of cards. 'Expect things greater than thy largest hopes to overtake thee.' The answer – Jonson's answer – comes when Volpone moralizes on the senile and still rapacious Corbaccio, who

> with these thoughts so battens, as if fate
> Would be as easily cheated on as he,
> And all turns air!

NOTES

1. Scholars have shown that *Timber, or Discoveries Made upon Men and Matter* was not an original critical work but Jonson's commonplace-book. The valuable edition by M. Castelain gives extracts from the classical and Renaissance writers on whom Jonson drew. See also the commentary on *Timber* in Herford and Simpson, *The Works of Ben Jonson*, Vol. XI, and J. E. Spingarn's *Critical Essays of the Seventeenth Century*, I, 221–2. It is of great interest to see how Jonson Englished, transformed, and added to the passages that appealed to him. A handy edition of *Discoveries* is that by G. B. Harrison in the Bodley Head Quartos.

2. See *Discoveries*, 21: '*Non minium credendum antiquitati* (That antiquity should not be believed in too much). I know nothing can conduce more to letters than to examine the writings of the Ancients, and not to rest in their sole authority, or take all upon trust from them ... For to all the observations of the Ancients we have our own experience which, if we will use and apply, we have better means to pronounce. It is true they open'd the gates, and made the way that went before us; but as guides, not commanders.' This is in the spirit of Dryden's remark, 'It is not enough that Aristotle has said so, for Aristotle drew his models of tragedy from Sophocles and Euripides: and, if he had seen ours, might have changed his mind.' (Saintsbury, *Loci Critici*, 158, Dryden, *Works*, ed. Walter Scott and George Saintsbury, Vol. XV, 390.)

3. *Coleridge on the Seventeenth Century*, ed. R. F. Brinkley, 639. Coleridge goes on to suggest a comparison with Hogarth.

4. 'Ben Jonson knew too little of Italy for effective realism, even had this been his aim. The transfer to London liberated his vast fund of local knowledge. The London of the Folio is crowded with precise localities which have only vague general equivalents in the Florence of the Quarto. It acquires a distinct physiognomy and atmosphere, as Florence never does. We hear of Fleet Street, Coleman Street, Thames Street, Houndsditch, Shoreditch, Whitechapel; of local features, like the Artillery Garden, and Islington ponds, of suburbs, like Hogsden and Finsbury. Similarly, well-known personages are introduced.' – Herford and Simpson, *Ben Jonson, the Man and His Work*, I, 359. The whole of this comparison between the Quarto and the Folio texts (358–70), which emphasizes the 'tendency towards a vernacular realism' in the latter, is important.

5. Dickens often uses similar methods, as when Tom Pinch, walking with Augustus Moddle ('I love another, she is another's, everything seems to be somebody else's'), remarks on the danger of the London streets, ' "I wonder" , said Tom, "that in these crowded streets, the foot-passengers are not oftener run over." Mr Moddle, with a dark look, replied: "The drivers won't do it" ' (*Martin Chuzzlewit*). On Dickens' relation to the Jonsonian tradition, see R. C. Churchill, 'Dickens, Drama and Tradition', in *Scrutiny*, X (1942).

6. For examples, see F. R. Leavis, *Revaluation: Tradition and Development in English Poetry*, 17–19, and L. C. Knights, *Drama and Society in the Age of Jonson*, 192–4.

7. For the connection with other 'humour' plays and with non-dramatic satire, see Part II, 71–90, above; and for a fuller account, including the 'war of the theatres', see Herford and Simpson, Vol. I, *Life of Jonson*, ch. II, and the separate introductions to the plays in the same volume.

8. A prose version of this passage occurs in *Discoveries*, 101; that it derives from Seneca, as Castelain points out in his edition (xxii and 68–71), does not of course affect what is said about it in the text. Jonson makes great poetry of his borrowing.

9. In 'Farce and Fashion in *The Silent Woman*' (*Essays and Studies by Members of the English Association*, 20, 1967) L. G. Salingar documents the dense topicality of *Epicoene*. Edward B. Partridge, in his Introduction to the Yale edition of the play, shows how criticism of society is mediated by the forms of speech assigned to the different characters. ('Speech is central to this play about society because to Jonson it is central to human life itself.') See also Partridge's *The Broken Compass*, ch. vii; and, on the linguistic skill of *Epicoene* and on 'the authentic geniality' of *Bartholomew Fair*, Jonas A. Barish, *Ben Jonson and the Language of Prose Comedy*, chs iv and v.

10. G. Unwin, 'Commerce and Coinage', in *Shakespeare's England*, I, 339–40. Unwin also says of this play, 'No one who knows the records of the time will charge Ben Jonson with wild exaggeration. He seems rather to err in the direction of pedantic realism.'

CHAPMAN AS TRANSLATOR AND
TRAGIC PLAYWRIGHT
PETER URE

Between 1594 and 1616 Chapman (c. 1559–1634) worked very hard. He translated the *Iliad* and the *Odyssey*, wrote six tragedies and about the same number of comedies, and composed enough original verse to fill nearly four hundred pages in the latest edition. This chapter is confined to the translation of Homer and the tragedies, and therefore deals with only about half of his work. There is good reason for this limitation. Most readers are not likely to appreciate his poems unless they have first been attracted by other things in Chapman. The comedies tell us less about Chapman's individual quality than the tragedies, which form a group easily distinguishable from other plays of the time. Chapman considered the translation of Homer to be his greatest work, and the ways in which he modified his original are themselves valuable clues to his artistic purposes. Knowledge of Chapman's mind and art acquired in the study of the tragedies and the Homer will not need to be *radically* revised in the light of the poems and the comedies.

The final, revised version of the Homer, into B. R. Haydon's copy of which Keats looked, appeared in 1616 as *The Whole Works of Homer Prince of Poets in his Iliads and Odysseys*.* It is a thick, unhandsome volume sprinkled with marginal notes and equipped with a slender but pugnacious commentary. Ben Jonson wrote some vigorous marginalia in his copy, making fun of the translator for his contumely towards other scholars, but he praised Chapman's later version of Hesiod, and may well have given general approval to the Homer. Pope, Coleridge, and Matthew Arnold all had praise, mingled with blame, for it. The modern reader, unlike Arnold, who

---

* Chapman also translated the *Hero and Leander* of Musaeus (1616), Hesiod's *Works and Days* (1618), the *Batrachomyomachia* and *Homeric Hymns* (? 1624) and Juvenal's Fifth Satire (1629).

censured Chapman for his Elizabethan fantasticality but was perhaps chiefly familiar with the *Iliads*, may be advised to begin with the *Odysseys*, which is written in a kindlier metre than the 'fourteener' of the other epic.

Chapman did play havoc with his original. His knowledge of Greek, exceptional for his time, was still not expert enough to release him from dependence on the great continental Hellenists. Chapman borrows freely from their Latin notes and renderings, and in his own commentary accuses them of bad scholarship. In the process Homer sometimes gets distorted. Transferring the Homeric measure into rhymed fourteeners (in the *Iliads*) or rhymed decasyllabics (in the *Odysseys*) also encouraged deflections. Chapman's love of antitheses, of rhetorical figures, his avoidance of the stock repetitive phrase, his brash anachronisms and colloquialisms, the touches here and there of 'English Senecan' rant are all Elizabethan, not Homeric.[1] Here, from the eleventh book of the *Iliads*, is an example of Chapman's handling of the epic simile, as full of light as Spenser's description of Prince Arthur:

> And as amidst the sky
> We sometimes see an ominous star blaze clear and dreadfully,
> Then run his golden head in clouds, and straight appear again;
> So Hector otherwise did grace the vant-guard, shining plain,
> Then in the rear-guard hid himself, and labour'd everywhere
> To order and encourage all; his armour was so clear,
> And he applied each place so fast, that, like a lightning thrown
> Out of the shield of Jupiter, in every eye he shone.
> And as upon a rich man's crop of barley or of wheat,
> Opposed for swiftness at their work, a sort of reapers sweat,
> Bear down the furrows speedily, and thick their handfuls fall:
> So at the joining of the hosts ran slaughter through them all.

A contrast to this is Anticlea's reply to her son Ulysses in Hell, in language involved, stately, and pathetic:

> 'O son', she answer'd, 'of the race of men
> The most unhappy, our most equal Queen
> Will mock no solid arms with empty shade,
> Nor suffer empty shades again t'invade
> Flesh, bones, and nerves; nor will defraud the fire
> Of his last dues, that, soon as spirits expire
> And leave the white bone, are his native right,
> When, like a dream, the soul assumes her flight.

The light then of the living with most haste,
O son, contend to. This thy little taste
Of this state is enough; and all this life
Will make a tale fit to be told thy wife.'

(*Odysseys*, IX)

Chapman's contempt for his critics – 'Asses at Thistles, bleeding as ye eat,' as he called them – sprang from his reverence for the poetic office. Like Drayton, he became the more melancholy and bitter the more he found reason to scourge the bad taste of his contemporaries and appeal from their neglect. The pugnacity so evident in the dedications and commentary to the Homer proceeded from his belief that he alone had been born to interpret aright the Prince of Poets. In some admirable lines in *The Tears of Peace* (1609) he tells how the spiritual form of Homer appeared to him in the green fields of Hitchin, his sacred bosom full of fire; perhaps no English poet enjoyed a like visitation until Blake dined with Isaiah. Such intercourse gave Chapman confidence in his right to clarify and enlarge his author's meaning with insights that no one before him had possessed. For Chapman, Homer is the witness to his faith in poetry, the first great composer of a visionary iconography: 'blind He all things saw':

> He, at Jove's table set, fills out to us
> Cups that repair Age sad and ruinous;
> And gives it built of an eternal stand,
> With his all-sinewy Odyssaean hand . . .
> He doth in men the Gods' affects[a] inflame,
> His fuel Virtue, blown by Praise and Fame.

As this passage shows, Chapman believed that the study of Homer persuaded men to virtue, and this belief helped to introduce into his translation some modifications of the original more radical than any I have yet mentioned. Chapman did not hold, as did some Renaissance scholars, that all Homer was one continued allegory, whose sugared least detail coated a moral pill. But he consistently saw Homer's personages as exemplifications of moral doctrine, as giant forms of justice and fortitude and their opposite vices. Unfortunately for Chapman, Homer had not articulated so clearly the moral roles of his heroes. The noblest of them can cry like children or play am-

a feelings.

biguous and sorry parts, unaware that, like Thomas Mann's Joseph, they are participating in a wonderful God-story. Chapman therefore felt impelled to make more plain what he thought Homer's grand design to be:

the first word of his Iliads, is μῆνιν, *wrath*: the first word of his Odysseys, ἄνδρα, *Man*: contracting in either word his each work's proposition. In one, *Predominant Perturbation*; in the other, *over-ruling Wisdom*: in one, the Body's fervour and fashion of outward Fortitude . . . in the other, the Mind's constant and unconquered Empire.

Thus Chapman's Homer acquires what has been called its 'ethical bias'. By interpolating, adjusting, sharpening, he brings out of Homer's golden haze what he conceives to be the central sun of his moral meaning. Achilles and Hector are transmogrified into warriors more perfect than Homer allowed. Agamemnon is seen as a man thrown from his true course by domineering passions. Their speeches are illuminated with the aphorisms which the Renaissance inherited from the classical moralists, and of which Homer was innocent. Odysseus becomes 'a moral hero of the Renaissance', as wise as Cato and as pious as Aeneas.[2] Such modifications do not necessarily make the version in its totality untrue to Homer's spirit, although they may outrage anyone seeking Homer's letter. They tell us something important about Chapman's ethical bias in his treatment of human character and his attitude towards poetry.

The bias can be detected in Chapman's tendency to read into human life and history the doctrines of the classical moralists, primarily of Epictetus, secondarily of Plutarch and Seneca. These Stoic writers taught that the hero must master his inward passions, and that the search for sensual gratifications outside himself will lay open the principles of his being defenceless before the storms of war, tyranny, and Fortune. This doctrine had enjoyed a revival in the neo-Stoic movement of the sixteenth century. Many trained themselves, and Chapman amongst them, to perceive Virtue, Justice, and Manhood, not as attributes fastened upon a man by popular suffrage and capable of being stolen from him by ill-luck or enemies, but as aspects of an inward unity, the 'god dwelling in the human body', which Marcus Aurelius honoured. That unity attained, man was fortified within and without. Ignorant of it, he was the helpless prey of his own passions, and became, in his relations with other men, either a persecutor or a victim. These ideas can be traced in systems so far apart in other respects as Giordano Bruno's and Calvin's. The vocabulary of contemporary arts and sciences is flooded with Stoic meanings.

Chapman was much attracted by the doctrine, but he could not escape from the antinomies that the neo-Stoic revival called forth in a milieu so generally busy with intellectual endeavour. If Chapman warmed himself at Stoicism's central fire, he was attracted by other lights as well. Some, like the political theory associated with Machiavelli's name, he did his best to extinguish. But with others, like the great Renaissance attempt to synthesize Christian teaching with Platonic, he attempted to illuminate his own work.

His attitude to poetry, his dominant interest in the business of rendering his vision of life and character in poetic terms, is also implied in his treatment of Homer. We need not be surprised that a poet like Chapman, who is profoundly influenced by a doctrine that seems to us chilly and rigoristic, should also believe that a 'holy fire and hidden heat' burns in the bosom of all true poets from Homer onwards, and should therefore continually strive after large and luminous effects and imaginative portrayals of truth. It has been pointed out that the Stoics, in spite of the passionless objectivity of their doctrines, really aimed at just such an imaginative portrayal of their relations with truth.[3] And Chapman, like other Renaissance artists, was conscious of a prevailing desire to reconcile Minerva, the spirit of a wise inner discipline, with Apollo, the heaven-aspiring genius of poetry.* Chapman would have seen no cogency in Blake's argument that the man who is occupied with mental and moral discipline becomes wrapped in a cold and spectral Selfhood that closes his eyes to God above and within; he is therefore free to embrace and exemplify the Platonic and Ficinian doctrine of poetic inspiration, that 'celestial fire':

> where high Poesy's native habit shines,
> From whose reflections flow eternal lines:
> Philosophy retir'd to darkest caves
> She can discover, and the proud world's braves
> Answer . . .

---

* Raphael's 'School of Athens' in the Vatican, as Professor Wittkower has pointed out, is one of the leading Renaissance attempts to symbolize this reconciliation.

Pope commented dryly that Chapman must have been 'an enthusiast in poetry', but for Chapman the term (which he does not himself use) would probably have had no colouring of fanatical extravagance. The mind of the heroic enthusiast, wrote Giordano Bruno, himself echoing St Augustine, 'aspires high by plunging into its own depths', for to reach the God within man is one road to God himself. Chapman would have pleaded guilty to such 'misconceit of being inspired', sustained by the example of his Homer, and the belief that there is a correlation between the truth which a poet perceives and the divine authority which bestows upon him the gift of revealing it, in all its force and beauty, to men.

Of the five tragedies written by Chapman between 1603 and 1611, four are drawn from recent French history: *The Tragedy of Bussy d'Ambois*, the double-play of *The Conspiracy and Tragedy of Charles Duke of Byron*, and *The Revenge of Bussy d'Ambois*. The fifth, *Caesar and Pompey*, is Chapman's only Roman play.★

All Chapman's tragedies may be described as dramatic studies of the interaction between a great man and his society. There are four main elements at work in this interaction: in the hero, his moral nature (his goodness or badness), and his outward role, as soldier, rebel, or servant to the king; ranged opposite to him in society are two kinds of men, the mouthpieces of Chapman's ideas on social order, or the hypostases of various kinds of social corruption. The plays are built up from the innumerable conflicts and harmonies which arise amongst these elements. This schematization suggests that Chapman's plays, like Marlowe's, tend, if we are thinking of them in terms of the contribution made by characterization to the total play, to be grouped round a single great figure. In the plays that bear their names, it is Bussy and Byron and, in *The Revenge of Bussy*, Clermont d'Ambois who hold our interest, while the other personages, ambitious prince, ideal king, political schemer, are more important for what they represent in relation to the protagonist than for what they are themselves.

Two of Chapman's heroes, Bussy and Byron, are great men flawed by their inability to control their inward passions and resist

★ Chapman's other tragedy is *The Tragedy of Chabot Admiral of France* (? *c.* 1612–25, probably revised by James Shirley); the so-called *Charlemagne* (? 1603–4), a manuscript play, has been attributed to Chapman by Schoell, but the attribution remains doubtful.

the outward temptations to which this inner disorder exposes them. The others, Clermont d'Ambois, Chabot, and Cato in *Caesar and Pompey*, are meant to be, so far as the exigencies of the plot in each case permit, 'exemplars of calm', men capable of achieving the εὐθυμία, inward peace, of Stoic teaching. Pompey oscillates between discipline and disorder, and finally comes to rest in Stoic fortitude. Chapman's subject in the tragedies is still, as in the Homer, μῆνιν, the wrath, and ἄνδρα, the man.

The Tragedy of Bussy is a good example of the method. When the play begins, France is no longer at war, and the soldier Bussy, poor and neglected, is therefore outside society, his natural habitat of court and camp. This society, represented by Monsieur, now reaches out to grasp Bussy and use him for its secret end, a design upon the crown. Bussy accepts the patronage, but on his own terms. He knows that to be a great man in the opinion of a corrupt society is to spend his life:

> In sights and visitations, that will make
> His eyes as hollow as his mistress' heart.

For himself, he will try to rise in court simply 'by virtue': he is 'a smooth plain ground [that] will never nourish any *politic* seed'. So he behaves rudely to the women of the court as a sign of his refusal to compromise with their corrupt world of political chambering and sexual hypocrisy. Society immediately begins to react to this strange nonconformist. The king is enthralled by Bussy's noble bearing and philosophical speeches; but the king's favourite, the Guise, senses a rival and Monsieur himself finally realizes that he has chosen the wrong man. When the news comes that Bussy is carrying on an intrigue with Tamyra, the wife of the Count Montsurry, the noble politicians see their chance to destroy him. For Bussy's love has taken his nature by storm and muddied the currents of his inward peace; and he is finally overthrown by the conjunction of the enemy passions, which have undermined the virtue within, with the outward machinations of his rivals. We grasp the full measure of his fall from philosophical grace when, in Act IV, in a vain attempt to escape from the jaws of the trap, he adopts the 'policy' which he had formerly repudiated. But he is an amateur at the game of politic murder, and is easily out-manoeuvred by experts like Monsieur and the Guise.

His end, none the less, asserts his greatness. As he dies, involved in horror and splendour, we realize how much Chapman's conception of him owes to the ancient idea of the classical hero, that Virtue which the Renaissance moralists allegorized from the myth of Hercules, he who moves continually towards the blazing pyre where mortality will be purged away and godhead assumed.

Byron, too, like Bussy, is related to a classical archetype. In portraying him, Chapman took some suggestions from Plutarch's orations on Alexander the Great.[4] But Byron, although he loudly lays claim to the giant robe of the hero, is flawed by corruptions foreign to Plutarch's Alexander. Choleric, ambitious, haunted by fantastic images of his own splendour, he has never attained inward peace, and therefore certain conspirators find him easier to be played on than a pipe. Their flattery stokes up the fuel in his own heart and turns him finally into a 'rotten exhalation', a meteor destroying itself as it burns up the waste stuff of the kingdom. Chapman makes it clear that Byron's inner corruption contributes as much to his fall as any outward agent, and we are continually enabled to measure its extent by comparing it with King Henry's 'over-ruling Wisdom'. Yet the ancient virtues visit Byron from time to time in glimpses that almost restore his manhood; he never becomes a mere dwarfish thief of honour, and can still be described in terms of virtue or its declination. This allows his death to seem sufficiently tragic as he, too, ascends the funeral pyre of Hercules and prepares to cast off the gross body.

Having written of the exemplars of wrath, Chapman turns to the exemplars of calm. Of these, Chabot is the most consistent, Cato the nearest to a literal interpretation of the Roman ideal of virtue, and the vacillating Pompey the most humanly plausible. They are all Odyssean figures. But Clermont, in *The Revenge of Bussy*, is Chapman's completest study of the Senecal man. He is calm where Bussy and Byron rage, self-contained where they are ambitious for external goods; and although placed like them in a corrupt society, he is able to judge it more fairly because he is more detached from it than they. Clermont is the most successful issue of previous attempts by other dramatists, including George Buchanan, William Alexander, Marston, Daniel, and Fulke Greville, to dramatize the Stoic Wise Man within a context of political equivocation.

But *The Revenge of Bussy* raises acutely a problem that haunts every investigation into Chapman's merits as a dramatist. How far did Chapman succeed in reconciling his obligations as a writer for the popular public playhouse with his interests in political morality and the relations between greatness and goodness? For such interests are not suitable for our stage unless they are broken down in the crucible of a true dramatic imagination. We have seen that Chapman was able to put things into Homer which are not really there, without making Homer fundamentally the less Homeric. His own explanation of this success is the best: he felt his bosom filled with Homer's fire. But in the drama this sustaining warmth is absent. *The Revenge*, for example, is classifiable as a revenge play in the tradition initiated by Kyd's *The Spanish Tragedy*. In reality, it is four acts of moralizing followed by a fifth in which the dramatist reluctantly sets in motion the traditional machinery of revenge and whining ghost, and – the sharpest incongruity of all – burdens the non-attached Clermont with the Revenger's bloody duty. These are contradictions to which all Clermont's moralizations on his task will not reconcile us.

Is a similar judgement on Chapman's other tragedies unavoidable? Was his imagination not of the kind that makes a successful playwright? It is fair to try to define more precisely some of the elements that go to compose the plays, and leave the final answer to the individual reader's experience.

Chapman did not despise the drama. 'Scenical representation', he wrote, 'is so far from giving just cause of any least diminution, that the personal and exact life it gives to any history, or other such delineation of human actions, adds to them lustre, spirit, and apprehension.' It may well have been the search for a more personal and exact life that caused Chapman to examine so exigently the nature of his protagonists and analyse the virtues and corruptions of their societies. It is not likely that Chapman saw this search as having a purely artistic objective; for the more lustrous and spirited the representation, the more efficiently, in Chapman's theory as well as Sidney's, it would inspire in the beholders that delight which would lead them to 'steal to see the form of goodness ere themselves be aware'.

But however inseparably the motives of artist and moralist combine in Chapman, it remains a fact that he is not content, as Marlowe is in *Tamburlaine*, merely to persuade us that a magnificent existence *is*, and leave us puzzling how, if at all, it fits into the scheme of things. Nor is he willing, as even Jonson sometimes is, to clap an intrusive moral over something profoundly disturbing to Panglossian complacency. Chapman likes to explain as fully as possible what has happened. Thus he provides in several discourses a number of explanations of why Bussy falls and what kind of man he is. Why was he created so hollow within, so vulnerable to Fortune? Are parts of him 'empty' of soul, the vital principle of virtue? Or is he indeed 'full-mann'd', and yet placed by Nature in a world which can only blunt and spoil her splendid instrument? And, restlessly, the characters in the play whom Chapman burdens with these speculations turn to Nature herself and accuse her of a random incompetence in her working. Byron's behaviour is explored in the same way, and the underground issues which are raised by his relationship with king and conspirator debated on the open stage. To the contemporary audience, who remembered the fall of Essex and the execution of the historical Byron at the beginning of the century, and who probably shared Chapman's interest in the behaviour of great men in a changing society, such questions must have seemed sufficiently to the point.

From material of this kind in the plays one can extract a body of opinion and label it Chapman's 'theory of man' or 'political beliefs'.[5] But that will not really tell us what place such things have in a play. It may even lead us – as it has led some critics – to beg the question by assuming that Chapman wanted the drama to be a vehicle for debate and speculation, and did not care whether these helped to bestow upon it a more 'personal and exact life' or not.

It is true that Chapman's questionings shape his dramatic devices. His characters cease to be men in action and become philosophers; they can assume the role of chorus or pause to examine their motives with a queer objectivity. Byron has speeches put into his mouth which transform him from a conspirator into a Chronos or a Muse of History; Cato's relation to Pompey is too bleakly modelled on that of the Epictetan sage to his disciple. These incongruities show that Chapman does not perfectly fuse his underlying moral theme with his men-in-action. In this he differs not only from Shakespeare and Jonson, but even from their inferiors like Heywood (*A Woman Killed with Kindness*) or Middleton (*The Changeling*). His tragedy is often more akin to the old moral play: there are moments in it when the human lineaments dissolve and the blank face of the hypostasis looks through, when the allegorical abstraction blots out the spirit of art. Thus, there is a curious split running up the character of King Henry in the Byron plays, who is sometimes the Ideal King, a mere abstraction from a handbook for princes, and sometimes simply Henry, raging at the malfeasance of a traitor in a way correspondent with the actualities of history and 'the fury and the mire of human veins'. Such fissures disturb us more in the drama than they do in a vast artefact like *The Faerie Queene*. The shift from mask to face and back again induces a shudder in the action, a momentary lack of focus while the audience adjusts itself from the homily to the warmer contemplation of men-in-action.

Here it is appropriate to bring into court what is generally taken to be Chapman's rueful comment on his own deficiencies, in the dedication to his second volume of Homer translations (1598):

> But woe is me, what zeal or power soever
> My free soul hath, my body will be never
> Able t'attend: never shall I enjoy
> Th'end of my hapless birth, never employ
> That smother'd fervour that in loathed embers
> Lies swept from light, and no clear hour remembers.
> O had your perfect eye organs to pierce
> Into that chaos whence this stifled verse
> By violence breaks, where glow-worm-like doth shine,
> In night of sorrow, this hid soul of mine,
> And how her genuine forms struggle for birth,
> Under the claws of this foul panther Earth...!

This is not really an unexpectedly humble admission that his verse is bad in the sense usually suggested. The 'loathed embers' are the clogging envelope of mortality, not of poetic incompetence, and the whole passage is one of many statements in Chapman's work about the Platonic dualism of soul and body which is an important aspect of his world-view. In Chapman's thought, the large-souled man, whether a Bussy or a poet, is always hampered by this dualism, although some, like Homer, can escape from it. In refusing to himself a Homeric status which he probably would not have granted to any of his contemporaries, Chapman is merely submitting to the burden of the dualism.

Moreover, the passage suggests that some of our discontentments with Chapman's dramatic characters may be resolved if we view the characters not as vitally incomplete, 'left headless for a perfect man' because of some deficiency in their creator's imagination, but as analogues to the artist's struggle as it is here described. Bussy and Byron, Clermont and Pompey, are studies of men striving to achieve their perfect images by hacking from them the 'excess of Humours, perturbations and Affects'. In *The Tears of Peace*, borrowing his similitude from Plotinus, Chapman compares such a struggle to the work of the sculptor who gradually cuts a human figure from an alabaster block. We are reminded that Michelangelo's 'Slaves' and 'Prisoners' are not to be thought of as 'left headless' by their maker once they are conceived as symbols of the birthpangs of giant forms, 'hid souls' writhing with violence in the stifled night of marble. If the analogy holds, it might be said that Chapman's unfinished men are wiser images of life than the pantomimic integrity with which, in the seventh book of *Paradise Lost*, the creatures burst perfectly formed from the ground, their 'smallest Lineaments exact'.

It is characteristic of Chapman to liken the artist-moralist's task to the sculptor's, for he has, in M. Schoell's phrase: '*l'imagination puissamment concrète*'. His dramatic verse is often exquisitely made to express his moralized conceptions of what a man's life may be: either a mist of passion ('wrath'), or a struggle to master it, to hack out the genuine forms of the soul, or a condition of Stoic concord. Its faults are that passion may sometimes slip into incoherence and concord into prosifying. In the speech of the wrathful Montsurry to Tamyra, as he compels her by torture to write a letter to her lover that will lure him into a trap, it is worth observing the vigour and fertility of the language, the complex cross-references to mythology, and the way in which the visual images emerge broken and struggling from the battle with Chapman's unsure syntax:

> Come, Siren, sing, and dash against my rocks
> Thy ruffian*^a* galley, rigg'd with quench for lust!
> Sing, and put all the nets into thy voice
> With which thou drew'st into thy strumpet's lap
> The spawn of Venus, and in which ye danced;
> That in thy lap's stead, I may dig his tomb,

And quit his manhood with a woman's sleight,
Who never is deceived in her deceit.
Sing (that is, write), and then take from mine eyes
The mists that hide the most inscrutable pander
That ever lapped up an adulterous vomit;
That I may see the devil, and survive
To be a devil, and then learn to wive:
That I may hang him, and then cut him down,
Then cut him up, and with my soul's beams search
The cranks[b] and caverns of his brain, and study
The errant[c] wilderness of a woman's face,
Where men cannot get out, for all the comets
That have been lighted at it: though they know
That adders lie a-sunning in their smiles,
That basilisks drink their poison from their eyes,
Yet still they wander there, and are not stay'd[d]
Till they be fetter'd, nor secure before
All cares devour them, nor in human consort
Till they embrace within their wife's two breasts
All Pelion and Cythaeron with their beasts.
Why write you not?[e]

In this speech[6] Montsurry's sexualized disgust ('quit his manhood' in l. 7 is charged with irony and means 'reward him for his sexual virility') and frenzied desire for violence modulate into a series of confused images which half-invite visualization: the very abrupt transition from the crannies of the brain to the woman's face, perhaps with the suggestion that the face will be found imaged in the lover's dissected brain, and the conception of that face both as a wilderness full of poisonous monsters lit by comets blazing with rotten material and a trap in which men are caught and lost. The playing with paradox in the final lines is found elsewhere as Chapman's means of expressing his view of man's dilemma, 'created sick', as Fulke Greville wrote, 'commanded to be sound', and one way in which he presents the giant form struggling for release from the imprisoning marble of the body:

a possibly here prostitute's 'bully', or protector, b crannies, c modern 'arrant', d both 'stopped' and 'comforted', e mythological references in this passage include a mingling of the story of Venus and Mars (the guilty pair trapped in nets by Vulcan) with Odysseus and the Sirens (Bussy or his pander as a vessel full-fraught (rigg'd) with means to quench Tamyra's lust, but wrecked on Montsurry's rocks) (II. 1–5); and the breasts seen as the mountains Pelion (home of the centaurs, images of lust) and Cythaeron (where Pentheus was torn to pieces by frenzied women).

> ... wretched world,
> Consisting most of parts that fly each other;
> A firmness breeding all inconstancy,
> A bond of all disjunction; like a man
> Long buried is a man that long hath lived;
> Touch him, he falls to ashes.
>
> (*The Tragedy of Byron*)

In Auden's words, Chapman finds poetic means to express his consciousness of man's 'condition of estrangement from the truth', of the 'ungarnished offended gap between what [men] so questionably are and what [they] are commanded without any question to become' (*The Sea and the Mirror*).

One of Chapman's favoured critical terms, as we have seen, is *lustre*, applied in Renaissance theory, as by Puttenham,[7] to *enargia*, or 'a goodly outward show set upon the matter with words'. For Chapman, its concomitant *energia*, a forcefulness of figurative language that will work inwardly upon the mind, is equally important. Montsurry's speech is both lustrous, set about with verbal ornament, and forceful in the sense of using its figures to reveal to the reader what is *in* the mind of the dramatic character. Chapman strives both to burnish his language outwardly and to give it inward significance. This, after all, is only the linguistic aspect of his philosophy of man, his search for the hero whose inward qualities are not betrayed or diminished by a false outward blaze but who can yet serve, like Cato, as a luminary to other men because he is 'full-mann'd', inwardly solid with virtue and 'soul'. Chapman contrives to present this awareness in such images as the comparison of the worthless man to the hollow colossus, outwardly splendid but within choked with rubbish or ballasted with lead. When he turns not to represent passion but to reflect upon the human situation, he often chooses the form of a visual image, an iconograph or emblem, which is as clear and lustrous as *enargia* requires, but at the same time has a correspondent inward meaning which operates with forceful *energia*. Such a passage as the comparison of religion to a tree growing and withering in the hearts of kings (*Tragedy of Byron*, III. i) has also the calm and elegiac note which distinguishes objective meditation upon truth from the dramatization of the wrathful man. I quote the concluding lines of an elaborate 'mute' emblem:

> The tree that grew from heaven
> Is overrun with moss; the cheerful music
> That heretofore hath sounded out of it
> Begins to cease, and as she casts her leaves,
> By small degrees the kingdoms of the earth
> Decline and wither; and look whensoever
> That the pure sap in her is dried-up quite,
> The lamp of all authority goes out,
> And all the blaze of princes is extinct.

Chapman is entitled to be judged in the light of his own poetic theory. In the heart of this lies a moralized conception of how poetry works and what it does. For Chapman, also, *le mot juste* is, as Professor Bullough has remarked of the Cambridge Platonist Henry More, an intelligible not an aesthetic quantity.

Like Jonson, Chapman thought of himself as living in an age whose very corruption required new discoveries of truth and fitness. Like Blake, he sought intellectual vision; and his reverence for Homer, who appeared to him:

> With eyes turn'd upward, and was outward blind,
> But inward past and future things he saw,

reminds us of More turning inwards to seek knowledge of truth, and of the visionary logic of the blind Milton: 'So much the rather thou, celestial light, Shine inward'. On one of Chapman's portraits his motto is inscribed: CONSCIVM EVASI DIEM: 'I fled the garish day'. Its corollary is to be found in the line from Ovid that Spenser wrote into *The Shepherd's Calendar*, and which all the poets who belong to Chapman's tradition would have understood: 'Est deus in nobis; agitante calescimus illo', 'There is a God within us, and by his force are we inspired'.

NOTES

1. For an account of these features, see P. B. Bartlett, 'Chapman's Revision of his *Iliads*', in *E.L.H., A Journal of English Literary History* II (1935); 'Stylistic Devices in Chapman's *Iliads*', in *Publications of the Modern Language Association of America* LVII (1942); H. C. Fay, 'Chapman's Sources for his Translation of Homer', 'Poetry, Pedantry and Life in Chapman's *Iliads*', in *Review of English Studies* (1951 and 1953).

2. For these modifications of Homer, see D. Smalley, 'The Ethical Bias of

Chapman's Homer', in *Studies in Philology*, XXXVI (1939), and P. B. Bartlett, 'The Heroes of Chapman's Homer', in *Review of English Studies*, XVII (1941).

3. See M. W. Croll, 'Attic Prose in the Seventeenth Century', in *Studies in Philology*, XVIII (1921), 112–13.

4. See Franck L. Schoell, *Etudes sur l'Humanisme continental en Angleterre* (Paris, 1926), 85. This book has been the starting-point for most later investigations into Chapman's intellectual background. For some further studies of the plays, see Una Ellis-Fermor, *The Jacobean Drama* (1936, 1974), R. H. Perkinson, 'Nature and the Tragic Hero in Chapman's Bussy Plays', in *Modern Language Quarterly*, III (1943); Michael Higgins, 'Chapman's Senecal Man', in *Review of English Studies*, XXI (1945); Peter Ure, 'The Main Outline of Chapman's Byron', in *Studies in Philology*, XLVII (1950). The present writer has offered a further and somewhat modified account of the tragedies in *Jacobean Theatre*, ed. J. R. Brown and B. Harris (1960), 226–47.

5. See, for example, Janet Spens, 'Chapman's Ethical Thought', in *Essays and Studies ... of the English Association*, XI (1925); Wyndham Lewis, *The Lion and the Fox* (1927); two essays in *The Parrott Presentation Volume* (1935), by Hardin Craig, on 'Ethics in the Jacobean Drama: the Case of Chapman', and C. W. Kennedy on 'Political Theory in the Plays of George Chapman'; R. W. Battenhouse, 'Chapman and the Nature of Man', in *E.L.H., A Journal of English Literary History*, XI (1945), and 'Chapman's Religion' in *Marlowe's Tamburlaine* (1941).

6. Some of the difficulties in this speech are discussed by James Smith, 'George Chapman', in *Scrutiny*, IV (1935). A general study of Chapman's figures is in E. Holmes, *Aspects of Elizabethan Imagery* (1929), 72–101.

7. Puttenham's *Art of English Poesy* (1589), III, iii (Gregory Smith ed. *Elizabethan Critical Essays*, II, 148), is a convenient statement about *enargia* and *energia*.

TOURNEUR AND
THE TRAGEDY OF REVENGE
L. G. SALINGAR

In Fulke Greville's *Life of Sidney* (c. 1610–12) there is a striking comment on Renaissance tragedy. Ancient tragedy, according to Greville, had been ultimately rebellious; it had sought 'to exemplify the disastrous miseries of man's life, . . . and so out of that melancholic vision, stir horror, or murmur against Divine Providence'. Modern tragedy, on the contrary, was dominated by moral law; it sought 'to point out God's revenging aspect upon every particular sin, to the despair, or confusion of mortality'. Both parts of this latter statement are significant. In emphasizing the moral consciousness of tragedy and the notion of rigorous divine punishment, Greville was completely in agreement with the majority of Elizabethan critics; Puttenham, for instance, some forty years earlier, had declared that the object of tragedy was to show 'the mutability of fortune, and the just punishment of God in revenge of a vicious and evil life'.[1] But Greville's statement also hints unconventionally at possible contradictions in interpreting the moral law (a hint expanded in his poetry). And whichever dramatists Greville may have had in mind, his reference to 'the despair, or confusion of mortality' might well be taken as the keynote of many of his contemporaries – particularly of Marston, Tourneur, and Webster in their outstanding group of revenge plays.

The best work of these three playwrights (1599–1614) coincides with the maturity of Shakespeare, whom they frequently echo. It is philosophical melodrama of the school of *Hamlet*; and, like most drama of the time, it draws heavily from Seneca, by way of Kyd and his *Spanish Tragedy* (c. 1589) – both Seneca the moral sage and Seneca the fabricator of ghastly revenges. The theme of revenge (the 'wild justice' of Bacon's essay) was popular in Elizabethan tragedy because it touched important questions of the day: the social problems of personal honour and the survival of feudal lawlessness; the political problem of tyranny and resistance; and the supreme question of providence, with its provocative contrasts between human vengeance and divine. *The Spanish Tragedy* and its successors present both kinds of vengeance with intricate irony and profuse, spectacular bloodshed. Horatio's formula at the end of *Hamlet* is applicable to them all:

> so shall you hear
> Of carnal, bloody, and unnatural acts,
> Of accidental judgements, casual slaughters,
> And, in this upshot, purposes mistook,
> Fall'n on the inventors' heads.

The horror is increased by ghost scenes, scenes of madness, and macabre contrasts between death and revelry. And, since the text 'Vengeance is mine, I will repay, saith the Lord' was both promise and prohibition, the avenger must commonly die in his triumph, like Kyd's Hieronimo and Vindice in Tourneur's *Revenger's Tragedy*. To this extent, the revenge plays are consistent demonstrations of the pattern of moral law, all the more impressive, on the assumptions of popular moralists, for their ability to 'strike astonishment to our thoughts, and amazement to our senses'.[2]

On the other hand, the pattern of moral law is broken, from Hieronimo onwards, by the 'monstrous resolution' of the avengers and the excitement of the leading characters:

> Thus therefore will I rest me in unrest,
> Dissembling quiet in unquietness.
> (*Spanish Tragedy*, III. xiii)

This unrest, this 'despair, or confusion', in Greville's phrase, can be traced, for example, through the role of Vindice, as unholy glee in his revenge alternates with dismay at the treachery it entails towards his mother and sister; or, again, through the incessant agitation of Marston and Webster. And the accent of their tragedies, especially Webster's, falls on defiance, not resignation:

> Though in our miseries, Fortune have a part,
> Yet, in our noble sufferings, she hath none –
> Contempt of pain, that we may call our own.

This restless individualism is partly due to Seneca, whose doctrines had been intertwined with those of the Reformation;[3] in more general terms, the source of the dramatists' 'despair, or confusion' is a conflict between religious pessimism and the Renaissance glorification of the natural man.

Most of these plays are set in Italy. Italy was appropriate to an exotic love story, like Marston's *Antonio and Mellida* (1599). But it was also the land of poisoning Cardinals – as in the lurid melodrama of the Borgias, *The Devil's Charter* (1607), by Barnabe Barnes, and again in Webster; the land of duelling and vendetta; and the land of the 'atheist' Machiavelli, ancestor of the villains who flaunt their 'policy' and manipulate the intrigue with the aid of needy subordinates. Above all, Italy stood for the two extremes of 'civility' and corruption. Ascham and others had repeated the proverb, 'the Englishman Italianate is the devil incarnate'; and the baleful fascination had been described again by Nashe in *The Unfortunate Traveller* (1594):

> *Italy*, the Paradise of the earth, and the Epicure's heaven, how doth it form our young master? ... From thence he brings the art of atheism, the art of epicurising, the art of whoring, the art of Sodomitry. The only probable good thing they have to keep us from utterly condemning it, is, that it maketh a man an excellent courtier ... which is, by interpretation, a fine close lecher, a glorious hypocrite.

The Italian revenge plays, accordingly, dwell on lust and moral corruption in place of the political themes of Shakespeare, Jonson, and Chapman. And the contrast Kyd makes between machiavellian and stoic now becomes a general contrast between the glitter of Italianate grandees – 'these wretched eminent things', as Webster calls them – and the discontented poverty of the gentlemen-scholars whom the dramatists advance as spokesmen. The portrayal of wealth and patronage by Marston, Tourneur, and Webster indicates the decay of the Tudor aristocracy, and the disenchantment of Elizabethan men of letters. The Italian setting is used for social complaint and for a generalized satire, which includes minor comic figures from the court or the underworld resembling those in *Hamlet* and the comedy of 'humours'.

This general and embittered satire was the main contribution of these three playwrights to a form of drama which had originated with Kyd as tragedy (or melodrama) illustrating the moral law. In one sense, however, this was a logical development. Popular religious drama, with its vigorous, often brutal irony, and the tradition of the

Dance of Death, had prepared the way for it. Similarly, the editor of Seneca's *Ten Tragedies* in English had claimed for his author that he 'beateth down sin' more weightily, and shows 'the guerdon of filthy lust, cloaked dissimulation and odious treachery' more 'bitingly' than any other pagan writer (1581). And, in the 1590s, poetic satire (Marston's chosen medium before he turned to the stage) resembled tragedy in dealing out savage punishment. In the 'biting' couplets of *Virgidemiae* (1598–9), Hall set out to 'unmask' and to lash the vices of the day; Marston's *Scourge of Villainy* came out in the same months, with similar pretensions –

> In serious jest, and jesting seriousness,
> I strive to scourge polluting beastliness –

and the menace of divine vengeance is never far away:

> O for a humour, look who yon doth go,
> The meagre lecher, lewd *Luxorio,*[a]
> 'Tis he that hath the sole monopoly
> By patent, of the suburb lechery . . .
> His eyes, his tongue, his soul, his all is lust,
> Which vengeance and confusion follow must.

So, too, in his Induction to Marston's *Malcontent*, Webster claims for stage satire that 'such vices as stand not accountable to law, should be cured as men heal tetters, by casting ink upon them'.

Thus the revenge plays combine mockery with their tragic image of retribution. Their satire incorporates the harsh levelling tendencies of the Dance of Death, together with more speculative criticism of society, drawn from Montaigne or the Stoics. There is more deliberate horror in this group of plays, but also more flexibility of mind and more intensity of feeling than in any previous English drama apart from Shakespeare.

But the tone of these plays, with one exception, is not only more subjective but more incoherent than that of the older popular drama. Marston begins his poetic satire more in sorrow than in anger:

> Thou nursing Mother of fair wisdom's lore,
> Ingenuous Melancholy, I implore
> Thy grave assistance;

a *Luxury* meant 'incontinence'. (Courtiers' patents of monopoly were highly unpopular just before 1600.)

and the plays are similarly afflicted by that feeling of personal indignity that Hamlet had considered reason for suicide:

> The insolence of office, and the spurns
> That patient merit of the unworthy takes.

So much so, that in Marston and Webster, with all their accomplishment, this tense self-consciousness finally breaks down the dramatic structure altogether.

In Tourneur's *Revenger's Tragedy*, on the other hand, though the strain is more violent, popular tradition makes for more solidity; and this play can be matched for concentrated power with any dramatic writing save the handful of the greatest.

John Marston (1576–1634) was one of those experimenting minds with force and gifts enough to arrest attention, but without the depth or else the self-knowledge necessary for the creation of a finished work of art. He could stimulate others but his own work is a tangle of unmastered emotions and undigested ideas. Some scruple or afterthought seems to intervene again and again between the personality of the dramatist and the action on the stage, so that the real centre of interest rests with neither but in some indefinite limbo that separates the two. His writing belongs to a period of nine years (1598–1607) following his Oxford studies and enrolment at the Middle Temple – a period which opened with erotic verses, succeeded at once by moral satire, and which included, in addition to some ten plays of his own, a stormy friendship with Ben Jonson and collaboration with him and Chapman in the lively comedy of *Eastward Ho!* He was ordained shortly afterwards (1609), and disappears from literature. It seems a reasonable inference that he found in the Church the source of moral authority vainly sought for in his plays.[4]

Marston's lack of balance is evident in his turgid diction and forced syntax, and in revealing adjectives like *strenuous* and *conscious*, which aroused Jonson's ridicule. Yet even his bad writing can be impressive; there is a baffled energy, an agonized search for the raw material of existence, beneath his fumbling and his posing. And he is capable of sudden touches of delicate beauty – 'The pale Andromeda bedew'd with tears' – as well as flashes of violent wit, like Antonio's outburst after reading aloud a counsel of patience from Seneca:

> Thou wrapt in furs, breaking thy limbs 'fore fires,
> Forbid'st the frozen Zone to shudder.

It was precisely from his frustration that Marston brought something new to the stage.

In *Antonio's Revenge* (1600) he twists Kyd's plot of intrigue and vengeance into a medium for his intimate moral excitement. Here, Marston is obsessed with an unmanageable vision of 'what men were, and are' and 'what men must be'. Revenge imposes a conflict between stoicism and passion.[5] The two stoics of this tragedy are charged with the repugnant task of avenging their predecessors in *Antonio and Mellida*. 'Man will break out, despite Philosophy', and the deed of blood is accomplished. But Marston's stoicism labours under the burden of a superhuman morality. Without Hieronimo's excuse of a vain recourse to law, Marston's Antonio is even more deeply infected by Senecan ruthlessness. Yet the poet cannot resist imparting a tone of ethical loftiness to his avenger's mouthings, so that he becomes at times a kind of pre-Nietzschean superman, beyond good and evil; as in the church scene (III. iii), before his father's hearse, where he stabs the murderer's innocent son with a kiss, a tag from Seneca, and the exulting cry:

> Methinks I pace upon the front of Jove,
> And kick corruption with a scornful heel,
> Gripping this flesh, disdain mortality.

As if in recoil, the Stoics acknowledge the moral law when their revenge is completed, not by dying, like Hieronimo, but through purgation:

> We know the world, and did we know no more,
> We would not live to know: but since constraint
> Of holy bands[a] forceth us keep this lodge
> Of dirt's corruption, till dread power calls
> Our souls' appearance, we will live enclos'd
> In holy verge of some religious order,
> Most constant votaries.   (v. vi)

But the gesture towards suicide here disturbs the religious theme of resignation; and equally, in the play as a whole, revulsion from life

---

a i.e. against suicide (cp. Hamlet's wish that 'the Everlasting had not fix'd His canon 'gainst self-slaughter').

itself ('this lodge Of dirt's corruption') is stronger than any feeling roused directly by the revenge theme. Characteristically, Antonio chooses for his disguise (IV. i) the role of a fool, insensible to passion.

In Marston's most effective play, the tragi-comedy of *The Malcontent* (1604),[6] this revulsion turns to satire; and with Altofront, the banished Duke of Genoa, returning for revenge under the alias of Malevole, the disguise of fool is exchanged for that of philosopher-buffoon, which enables him to retaliate directly against the world in general:

> this disguise doth yet afford me that
> Which kings do seldom hear, or great men use,
> *Free speech.*

A tangible opportunity arises, meanwhile, from the corruption of the usurper's court: the new Duke's favourite is the accepted lover of his Duchess. From the promiscuity of the Duchess and the favourite's ambition, there follow a series of ironic reversals which lead finally to Malevole's triumph and the repentance of his chief adversaries; and the swirling roundabout of passion, which had made the previous play absurd, now begins to approximate to the serio-comic gyrations of a satire of humours. One innovation is the prose of comic rhapsody which Marston concocts for the favourite's alternating speeches of gloating and frenzy (I. v-vii); and at one point he touches an irony of a sharper kind. While the Duke and his attendants prepare to kill the Duchess's lover in her bedchamber, two ladies cross the stage, deep in conversation with Maquerelle, the court bawd (II. iv). They are discussing a posset; and the burlesque of Maquerelle's professional advice, with its echo of the poetry of death and decay, gives a resonant undertone to the violence of the main intrigue:

... eat me of this posset, quicken your blood, and preserve your beauty, do you know Doctor Plaster-face? by this curd, he is the most exquisite in forging of veins, spright'ning of eyes, dyeing of hair, sleeking of skins, surphleing[a] of breasts, blanching and bleaching of teeth, that ever made an old lady gracious by torchlight; by this curd, la! ...

Men say, let them say what they will: ... if they lose youth and beauty, they gain wisdom and discretion: but when our beauty fades, good night with us, there cannot be an uglier thing to see than an old woman, from which, oh pruning, pinching, and painting, deliver all sweet beauties.

a washing with cosmetics.

This blending of disjointed chatter with the strain of comic rhapsody is at once grotesque and pathetic.

But Marston cannot submerge himself consistently in his play. The ironic speeches are over-written, especially those of the Malcontent himself, with his 'dreams, dreams, visions, fantasies, Chimaeras, imaginations, tricks, conceits'. Sometimes he is both irrelevant and obscene; at other moments, self-pitying:

> Only the Malcontent, that 'gainst his fate
> Repines and quarrels, alas, he's goodman tell-clock.

Like the invocation to melancholy at the beginning of his verse satire, this breaks down the dramatist's pretence to objectivity – a pretence already severely strained by the knowingness and vindictiveness in his treatment of sex. In his last two tragedies he rushes again from one extreme to another. *Sophonisba*, *Wonder of Women* and *The Insatiate Countess* show that Marston, to the end of his poetic career, was unable to bridge the gap between rhetorical idealism and rhetorical disgust.

There is no certainty about the authorship of that sombre master-piece, *The Revenger's Tragedy* (1606–7). Very little is known of the supposed author, Cyril Tourneur (c. 1570/80–1626), except that he was probably of gentle origin, that he saw military and diplomatic service abroad under the patronage of the Cecils and the Veres, and that he died in poverty. The one surviving play undoubtedly his, *The Atheist's Tragedy* (1611), though interesting and unusual, is so much inferior and unlike that many scholars would deny them a common author. And, since the disputed masterpiece is a tissue of resemblances to the work of many others – to Marston and Shakespeare, to Middleton, Jonson, Chettle, and Dekker – any unknown, impressionable genius of the time may have written it. But its imagery and moral tone are consistent with an obscure verse allegory on religion, *The Transformed Metamorphosis*, published by Tourneur in 1600; and to give the play to any other candidate (to Middleton, for instance) would raise problems of artistic continuity even more difficult than those involved in attributing it to the writer of *The Atheist's Tragedy*. With Tourneur, then, rests the benefit of the doubt.[7]

Whoever the author of *The Revenger's Tragedy*, the play is unique in its unremitting sardonic fury and compression of language. Few actions on the Jacobean stage are swept forward so impetuously; and nowhere, outside Shakespeare and Jonson, is the essence of the drama – the symbolization of evil – so firmly embedded in its imagery, in the sensory impact, the movement, the inner tension of its words. T. S. Eliot has pointed out the 'closeness of the emotional pattern' in *The Revenger's Tragedy*; and the plot, as M. C. Bradbrook has shown, is a network of ironic illustrations of villainy hoisted on its own petard, and of divine vengeance contrasted with human. The people of the play belong to this pattern completely; they have no humanity outside it, but are solely 'characters' in the Jacobean literary sense, abstract qualities of good or evil rhetorically heightened and endowed here with a burning intensity of passion. From the opening tirade, moreover, from Vindice's first harsh contradictions as, holding a skull in his hand, he watches the torch-lit procession of his enemies across the stage, it is evil that predominates:

> Duke! royal lecher! go, grey-haired adultery!
> And thou his son, as impious as he:
> And thou his bastard, true begot in evil:
> And thou his duchess, that will do with devil:
> Four excellent characters!★

'Swimming', 'swelling', 'hurrying', 'steeped' in evil, the court and their victims are carried headlong to destruction.

Evil tramples on goodness with the twofold irresistible forces of lust and of money. Human justice, as depicted, for example, by the Duke's son Lussurioso, is irretrievably corrupt:

> for offences,
> Gilt o'er with mercy, show like fairest women,
> Good only for their beauties, which washed off,
> No sin is uglier.†

(I. ii)

★ *Excellent* here means 'excelling, egregious' (compare the punning sense of *royal* in the first line); and *characters* has the sense indicated above (cp. Webster (?) in Overbury's *Characters*, 1615: 'To square out a character by our English level, it is a picture . . . quaintly drawn in various colours, all of them heightened by one shadowing'. According to the *O.E.D.* the word was not used in the senses of 'moral constitution' and 'personality in a play' until 1647 and 1749 respectively).

† cp. *Hamlet*, III. i. ('The harlot's cheek . . .'), *Lear*, IV, vi ('Plate sin with gold . . .'), and Marston's *Maquerelle*. For Lussurioso, an Italianized Morality name, cp. p. 440 above, and Middleton, *The Phoenix*.

For Vindice, divine justice carries a similar grim irony:

> Why does not earth start up,
> And strike the sins that tread upon't? O,
> Were't not for gold and women, there would be no damnation.
> Hell would look like a lord's great kitchen without fire in't*
> But 'twas decreed, before the world began,
> That they should be the hooks to catch at man.
>
> (II. i)

The hypnotism of evil, of predestined damnation, is felt with a kind of dulled anguish throughout the play – 'It is our blood to err, though hell gape wide'; and the effect of this is redoubled by the many references to time. Tourneur sets the 'vicious minute' of seduction against Vindice's premeditated moment of revenge (I. i); against the long months the old Duke requires for penitence, or the lifetime of his bastard, Spurio –

> Half-damned in the conception by the justice
> Of that unbribed everlasting law; –

or, finally, against 'the doom irrevocable' of judgement and execution: 'The hour beckons us. The headsman waits'. But purity, meanwhile, is remote or helpless: Vindice's sister, Castiza, is soured by poverty (II. i); his father, oppressed by the court, has died 'Of discontent, the noble man's consumption'; the mistress whose skull he carries has been poisoned by the Duke. And Vindice himself is sucked into the whirlpool of evil, forsaking his 'honesty' ('For to be honest is not to be i' the world') when he embarks on his revenge under the disguise of a pander to Lussurioso. From one aspect, the play is a nightmare of the Calvinist sense of sin.

Yet it is misleading to dwell on this exclusively;[8] the play has little, for example, of the spectral quality associated with nightmare. Narrowly intensified though it is, Tourneur's satire on evil, inseparable from his revenge theme, is remarkably concrete, exuberant, and alert. It belongs to the age, not to one mind alone; and there is a masterful, impersonal irony in the sequence of moral perversion and of punishment that runs through the play. In one part of his mind, however, in his raging horror of poverty and decay, Tourneur resents the laws

---

* *Hell ... in't*: alluding to the decay of 'hospitality'.

of his world. Conflict between these two attitudes precludes the detachment of genuine tragedy; but it contributes directly to the physical vigour of his satire.

Tourneur's images suggest continually that the court society he depicts has grossly perverted the natural, accepted standards of living. His spokesmen are depressed minor gentry; he identifies Nature and neglected innocence with the old-fashioned manor. A number of metaphors emphasize this point of view (vengeance is 'murder's quit-rent', for example); while to the court world of bribery and prosti-tution, with its shifting false appearances – the cosmetics, the torch-light, the jewels, the masks and revelling repeatedly pictured in the action and the poetry – Tourneur opposes his abiding reality, the skull. Such a contrast is essentially traditional. Much of the treatment is contemporary; from *The Malcontent* and the disciplined irony of Jonson's *Volpone* (1606), for example, comes Tourneur's general plan of a society of vicious humours which draws to itself a disguised avenger-satirist who hastens its inner tendency to dissolution. But his central metaphors of disguise or transformation also reach back, through Jonson, to popular tradition. And his satiric tirades gain vigour and assurance from the custom of the Morality plays dealing with social abuses, where the Deadly Sins disguise themselves from the other actors, but address the audience directly in mocking terms of frankness. What Tourneur himself contributes is a uniquely strict attention to his images, both as emblems and realities, and to his words, both as sounds and as clusters of meaning.

In Tourneur, the enraged melancholy of Marston is controlled and directed by a quicker social perception and a stricter economy of language. Vindice's first soliloquy is typical, with its moral loathing and its physical loathing of old age, gripped in extraordinary satiric concentration:

> O that marrowless age
> Should stuff the hollow bones with damned desires!
> And, 'stead of heat, kindle infernal fires
> Within the spendthrift veins of a dry duke,
> A parched and juiceless luxur. O God, one
> That has scarce blood enough to live upon;
> And he to riot it, like a son and heir!
> O, the thought of that
> Turns my abusèd heart-strings into fret ...

And, while Tourneur's imagery is unusually thick with seriously meant punning, as in Vindice's descant a moment later on the eye-sockets of the skull:

> When two heaven-pointed diamonds were set
> In those unsightly rings,

it is also capable of unusual realistic exactness. Nearness to colloquial prose is as much part of his strength as close-knit symbolism, and his verse, unlike Marston's, is seldom thrown out of stride by the pauses and diversions in its metrical onrush:

> Who'd sit at home in a neglected room,
> Dealing her short-lived beauty to the pictures,
> That are as useless as old men, when those
> Poorer in face and fortune than herself
> Walk with an hundred acres on their backs,
> Fair meadows cut into green foreparts?

This speech (II. i) has none of the romantic overtones of, for instance, Shakespeare's lines:

> The chariest maid is prodigal enough
> If she unveil her beauty to the moon.

In its place, however, Tourneur's shabby-genteel lifelessness is fully justified; 'pictures' is exactly right.

But Tourneur's greatest power appears in those tirades, or sinister extravaganzas, where his measured irony is united with images of fantastic distortion. These are mostly descriptions of revelling,[9] like the soliloquy of Spurio (a figure reminiscent of Edmund in *Lear*), where he pictures the 'whispering and withdrawing hour' of his bastardizing:

> Faith, if the truth were known, I was begot
> After some gluttonous dinner; some stirring dish
> Was my first father, when deep healths went round,
> And ladies' cheeks were painted red with wine.

> (I. ii)

This Breughel-like irony appears again in Antonio's account (I. iv) of the 'revelling night' when his wife had been raped:

> When torchlight made an artificial noon
> About the court, some courtiers in the mask,

Putting on better faces than their own,
Being full of fraud and flattery ...

It reaches its height in the dance of words of the temptation scene
(II. i), where Vindice in disguise, having won over his mother
Gratiana –

I would raise my state upon her breast;
And call her eyes my tenants –

now attempts with her aid to corrupt his sister for Lussurioso:

VINDICE. How blessed are you! you have happiness alone;
Others must fall to thousands, you to one,
Sufficient in himself to make your forehead
Dazzle the world with jewels, and petitionary people
Start at your presence ...*
O, think upon the pleasures of the palace!
Secured ease and state! the stirring meats,
Ready to move out of the dishes, that e'en now
Quicken when they are eaten!
Banquets abroad by torchlight! music! sports!
Bareheaded vassals, that had ne'er the fortune
To keep on their own hats, but let horns† wear 'em!
Nine coaches waiting – hurry, hurry, hurry –
CASTIZA. Ay, to the devil,
VINDICE. Ay, to the devil: [*Aside.*] To the duke, by my faith.
GRATIANA. Ay, to the duke: daughter, you'd scorn to think o'
the devil, an*a* you were there once ...

Fittingly, then, the final revenge, against Lussurioso, is executed
under cover of a masque (v. iii). But poetic justice has already been
dealt out in the scene of the 'unsunned lodge, Wherein 'tis night at
noon' (III. iv), and where the old Duke, also employing Vindice as his
pander, is lured into kissing the poison-smeared skull of Vindice's
mistress.

Before the Duke appears in this scene, Vindice utters his famous
soliloquy to the skull. His speech seems to echo two passages from
Middleton. One comes from *The Phoenix* (II. ii; 1604):

---

* *Dazzle ... presence*: cp. the jewels described in the temptation scene in *Volpone*
(III. iii); also *The Malcontent* (I. v) on the 'petitionary vassals' following a court
favourite.

† Refers to the stock Elizabethan jokes about cuckoldry.

a if.

> Why should this fellow be a lord by birth,
> Being by blood a knave, one that would sell
> His lordship if he like her ladyship?

The other, from *Your Five Gallants* (III. ii; *c.* 1605), where a highway-man, having robbed his companion, finds on him the very string of pearls he had stolen previously for his mistress:

> Does my boy pick and I steal to enrich myself, to keep her, to main-tain him? why, this is right the sequence of the world. A lord maintains her, she maintains a knight, he maintains a whore, she maintains a captain ...

For Vindice, however, this 'sequence of the world' concentrates the whole drama; while the skull, much as for Hamlet, becomes the final result, the unconscious goal, of all the transactions in a distorted society. 'Yon fellow' is at once his imagined highwayman, the ap-proaching Duke, and the Duke's youngest stepson (who has been executed for rape in the previous scene); and the skull now suggests 'all the betrayed women' of the play, in a tirade of astonishing com-pression and force:[10]

> Does the silkworm expend her yellow labours
> For thee? for thee does she undo herself?
> Are lordships sold to maintain ladyships
> For the poor benefit of a bewitching minute?
> Why does yon fellow falsify highways
> And put his life between the judge's lips,
> To refine such a thing, keeps horse and men
> To beat their valours for her?
> Surely we are all mad people, and they
> Whom we think are, are not; we mistake those;
> 'Tis we are mad in sense, they but in clothes.
>
> (III. v)

The silkworm here calls up both the physical qualities of gold, silk, and paleness, and a social contrast between the fine lady and the poor, sallow spinner or the 'careful sisters'* of the streets – a contrast made explicit in the next speech, but already telescoped here into the one

---

* cp. II. ii: 'And careful sisters spin that thread i' the night/That does maintain them and their bawds i' the day'. A tract of *c.* 1607, opposing commercial excess, lists, among Nature's bounties, 'from the poor silkworm, the costly apparel, of silks and velvets'; and adds: 'Are not these infinite blessings, sufficient for men to content them-selves with all, but they must needs go further?' (*Reason's Academy* – Sir John Davies, *Works*, ed. Grosart, ii, 196–7).

word 'undo'. From the third line onwards, the dissolution of social values (fiercely driven home by the alliteration) is identified with the contrasts of time and eternity current throughout the play; and the highwaymen (or courtiers) who 'beat their valours' provide an ironic climax, both in the arrested crescendo of the rhythm and in the vigorous image of self-destroying exertion. 'Beats' suggests 'baiting' (in the two senses of 'worrying' and 'feeding'), also the lowering ('abating') of 'values', as well as the whipping of horses;* once again, contradictory effects of social activity are fused into a single image by means of a pun.

A triumph like this involves tense equilibrium between seeing human actions as personal, individual, and seeing them allegorically, as incidents of an eternal design. But the tension could hardly be sustained. Especially in the sub-plot of temptation, the writing is sometimes forced and casuistic, or else (IV. iv) it relaxes into preaching (like Dekker's *Honest Whore*). In tempting his mother and sister, Vindice has been forced into an artificial dilemma, whereby the dramatist tries to fuse the religious suggestion of pollution on entry into 'the world' with the social dilemma underlying his whole play, his uncompromising alternative of poverty or corruption. This triumph, then, is largely emotional. In *The Atheist's Tragedy*,[11] Tourneur tries to solve his dilemma by reasoning; villainy appears as the product of a false philosophy of Nature, and the hero, withholding from revenge on religious scruples, is amply rewarded in worldly goods. This gives a new turn to the revenge theme; but the second play is slack and feeble by comparison with the first. *The Revenger's Tragedy* is the last, as well as the most brilliant, attempt to present the emotional conflicts of Renaissance society within the framework of moral allegory.

With the best known of these three dramatists, John Webster (*c.* 1578/9–?1632/3), the allegory has worn to shreds. Webster, is, in a sense, more modern – more sceptical and more romantic – than either of his predecessors. His paraphernalia of revenge and torture are neither purely sensational nor emblems of poetic justice, but are presented with an effort at naturalism, and with the aim of exciting nervous horror and foreboding; and his people declaim or philosophize

* *beat* and *bait* had the same sound; also to *beat* money meant to coin it (*N.E.D.*).

with an acrid tang of personality. He composed deliberately, re-shaping the phrases of Montaigne, or Sidney's *Arcadia*, or Donne into the fantastic similitudes of a fashionable 'character'-writer; he studied his theatrical associates with care;[12] and the tragedies which have made his fame, *The White Devil* (1611–12) and *The Duchess of Malfi* (1613–14), which happen to be the first of his own plays extant, are the fruits of ten years or more of dramatic apprenticeship. Webster is sophisticated; but his sophistication belongs to decadence. The poet's solemnity and his groping for a new basis for tragedy only serve to expose his inner bewilderment and his lack of any deep sense of communion with his public.

Webster sees Jacobean 'greatness' as hopelessly corrupt – so much is implied in his elegy for Prince Henry (*A Monumental Column*, 1612), as well as in the two Italian plays. And with it, all human values are tarnished. In a parable inserted in the elegy, Pleasure is said to have come to earth from heaven, only to be recalled on account of the prodigality of the times. She leaves behind a robe, which is donned in masquerade by Sorrow:

> And since this cursed mask, which to our cost
> Lasts day and night, we have entirely lost
> Pleasure, who from heaven wills us be advis'd
> That our false Pleasure is but Care disguis'd.

The loss of Pleasure and the masquerade of Care form the crux of the tragedies, to Webster's 'despair, or confusion'. At the same time, the revenge theme is both secondary and ambiguous, since Webster's avenging Dukes and Cardinals are at once the upholders of public convention and deep-dyed machiavellians. The main interest centres on two groups of victims trapped by fate, the lovers in each play and the two scholars driven into evil by poverty, Flamineo in *The White Devil* and Bosola in *The Duchess of Malfi*.

The emotions in these two plays are chaotic. The favourite source of Webster's imagery is not the charnel-house meditations for which he is noted, but the agonies of the torture-chamber – battering, choking, flaying, beheading; toothache, insomnia, fever; the stinging of bees; pressing to death with weights. And every sensation is in-flamed, every emotion becomes an orgy. The men in *The White Devil* speak in 'thunder'; the women are all 'furies'; 'earthquakes' bounce into the dialogue with the alacrity of hailstones. Storming, defying, bewailing, spartanizing; the set teeth, the bold front and the intolerable pang: these are almost the whole of Webster's tragical repertory. He is highly ingenious in the rendering of sensations:

> I'll make Italian cut-works in their guts
> If ever I return.
>
> (*W.D.*, I. i)

> I am confident, had I bin damn'd in hell,
> And should have heard of this, it would have put me
> Into a cold sweat.
>
> (*D.M.*, I. iv)

But his dialogue swings between maxims too sententious for the occasion and outbursts bordering on hysteria; while antithesis between pleasure and pain forms, in effect, the whole substance of his philosophy:

> Pleasure of life, what is't? only the good hours
> Of an ague.
>
> (*D.M.*, V. iv)

The virtuous wife in the earlier play and the tyrannous brother in the later are seized with exactly the same language of sadistic frenzy; the ruffian Lodovico and the gentle Duchess are made to die with exactly the same parade of Senecan bravado (*W.D.*, V. vi; *D.M.*, IV. ii). The only alternative is Webster's nostalgia for unattainable innocence, as in Cornelia's exquisite dirge ('Call for the robin-red-breast and the wren'; *W.D.*, V. iv), or in his many references in both plays to birds and to childhood.

This attitude vitiates what is relatively new (or Shakespearean) in his plays, their intimate flashes of personality. There is no parallel in Marston or Tourneur, for example, to Webster's romantic treatment of the criminal love between Duke Brachiano and his white devil, Vittoria. But while every sensation here is extremely vivid, the total effect is blurred. In the quarrel scene (IV. ii), for instance, the moral awakening of the lovers is swamped in their anguish for lost Pleasure:

> BRACHIANO. Your beauty! O, ten thousand curses on't!
> How long have I beheld the devil in crystal!
> Thou hast led me, like an heathen sacrifice,
> With music and with fatal yokes of flowers,
> To my eternal ruin. Woman to man
> Is either a God or a wolf . . .

> VITTORIA. Fare you well, sir; let me hear no more of you.
> I had a limb corrupted to an ulcer,
> But I have cut it off: and now I'll go
> Weeping to heaven on crutches . . .
> O that I could toss myself
> Into a grave as quickly . . . [*She throws herself upon a bed.*]

The quarrel as such leads to reconciliation, and thence to the lovers' doom; but their declamations lead nowhere. As usual in Webster, seeming changes of mind merely give a colouring of dramatic irony, while the characters continue as before; this theatrical sleight-of-hand links his methods of construction with those of Fletcher.

Unlike Vittoria, the Duchess of Malfi is almost blameless. A young widow, she remarries beneath her, secretly, and against her brothers' wishes; but these blemishes on her conduct, stressed in Webster's narrative source,[13] are almost unfelt in his portrayal of her gracious charm, shining out beside her brothers' blackness. Yet she, too, is pursued by guilt, by a premonition of disaster, even in her wooing:

> You do tremble:
> Make not your heart so dead a piece of flesh,
> To fear more than to love me. Sir, be confident:
> What is't distracts you? This is flesh and blood, sir;
> 'Tis not the figure cut in alabaster
> Kneels at my husband's tomb.
>
> (I. i)

This lends a kind of allegorical fitness to her long-drawn-out torments (Act IV), which bring her 'by degrees to mortification', but which otherwise deserve Shaw's gibe at Webster as 'Tussaud laureate'. Webster's finest sustained writing conveys with terrible immediacy her exhaustion and yearning to escape from consciousness:

> I'll tell thee a miracle –
> I am not mad yet, to my cause of sorrow.
> Th' heaven o'er my head seems made of molten brass,
> The earth of flaming sulphur, yet I am not mad:
> I am acquainted with sad misery
> As the tann'd galley-slave is with his Oar;
> Necessity makes me suffer constantly,
> And custom makes it easy. – Who do I look like now?
>
> (IV. ii)

Like the quarrel scene, however, this poignant declamation has no further effect on the moral scheme of the play. It marks the limit of Webster's insight; and the closing question (which invites the maid's comparison with 'reverend monuments') indicates his habitual falling back on showmanship. The remainder of the action consists of tedious moralizing, posturing, and blood-and-thunder.

But Webster's determination to manoeuvre his characters into a trap is most evident with the two scholar-villains, Flamineo and Bosola, who combine this role with that of malcontent satirist. Evidently Webster felt uneasy with this unlifelike stage convention,★ which belongs to the impersonal mode of 'humour' comedy; his satirists are more introspective and more mannered than their predecessors in Marston and Tourneur, but also more disjointed – Flamineo's temptation scene, for instance, is a hollow echo of Vindice's, and Bosola's disquisition on women's painting is gratuitous and nasty. Their strongest satiric note is the horror of economic 'necessity': Flamineo, with his bragging defiance on behalf of

> the beggary of courtiers,
> The discontent of churchmen, want of soldiers,
> And all the creatures that hang manacled,
> Worse than strappadoed, on the lowest felly
> Of Fortune's wheel,

which is varied, through 'all the weary minutes' of his life, with his anxiety about renewed poverty and neglect; or Bosola demanding 'Who would rely on these miserable dependancies, in expectation to be advanced tomorrow? what creature ever fed worse than hoping Tantalus?' Yet each is made to forfeit his hard-gained experience, as well as his conscience, in order to return to that very situation; their parts are manipulated so as to ring the changes on cynicism and remorse. And their sense of futility is extended to other characters as well. Later, in *The Devil's Law Case* (*c.* 1617) and *Appius and Virginia* (*c.* 1624), Webster returns again to themes of 'impossible desire' and situations where 'pity would destroy pity'. Haunted by his predecessors' conception of moral law, he can neither accept nor amend it; in a world he sees as corrupt through and through, he can only exploit his own discomfort.

Behind *The Revenger's Tragedy* are traditional ideas and attitudes of

★ See Flamineo's speech: 'It may appear to some ridiculous/Thus to talk knave and madman ...' (*W.D.*, IV. ii).

mind which were shared by the public as a whole in their life outside the theatre; with all its violent personal feeling, the drama does no more than give these public traditions flesh and blood. Webster's agitation and Webster's subtlety show the emergence of a new kind of tragedy, more romantic and more narrowly theatrical. But the kernel of Elizabethan popular tradition has crumbled away, and only the husk remains.

NOTES

1. Greville, *Life of Sidney* (ed. Nowell Smith, 1907), 221; Puttenham, *Art of English Poesy*, 1. chs xii–xv. See also Part II, p. 101, above.

2. F. T. Bowers, *Elizabethan Revenge Tragedy*, 259 (quoting J. Reynolds, *The Triumph of God's Revenge Against Murder*, 1621); on public opinion about revenge, see also Lily B. Campbell, in *Modern Philology*, XXVIII (1931).

3. See L. Zanta, *La Renaissance du Stoicisme au xvi⁰ siècle* and M. H. Higgins, 'The Development of the "Senecal Man"', in *Review of English Studies*, XXIII (1947).

4. T. Spencer, in *The Criterion*, XIII (1934); see P. J. Finkelpearl, *Marston*. On Marston's poetic style, see T. S. Eliot, *Selected Essays* (1934 edn), 221ff., and J. Peter in *Complaint and Satire*; on Marston as a man of the theatre, see the contributions of W. R. Gair, L. Lecoq and J. Jacquot in *Dramaturgie et Société*, ed. Jacquot.

5. See M. H. Higgins on 'The Stoic Hero in Marston', in *Modern Language Review*, XXXIX (1944); G. K. Hunter, 'English Folly and Italian Vice: the Moral Landscape of John Marston', in *Jacobean Theatre*, ed. J. R. Brown and B. Harris.

6. See B. Harris, ed., *The Malcontent*; Finkelpearl, *Marston*; B. Gibbons, *Jacobean City Comedy* (2nd edn), ch. v.

7. *The Revenger's Tragedy* (published anonymously in 1607) was first ascribed to Tourneur by a printer in 1656. For discussion of the arguments in favour of Middleton or an anonymous author, see P. B. Murray, *A Study of Cyril Tourneur* (1964); R. A. Foakes, ed., *The Revenger's Tragedy* (1966); S. Schoenbaum, *Internal Evidence and Elizabethan Dramatic Authorship* (1966); and the recent comments by M. Heinemann in *Puritanism and Theatre* (1980), 284–9; on *The Transformed Metamorphosis*, see Peter, *Complaint and Satire*, 303–308; Murray, *Tourneur*, ch. ii.

8. See T. S. Eliot, *Selected Essays*.

9. cp. Sir John Harington's letter describing the court festivities for the King of Denmark in 1606: 'I think the Dane hath strangely wrought on our good English nobles; for those, whom I could never get to taste good liquor, now follow the fashion, and wallow in beastly delights. The ladies abandon their sobriety, and are seen to roll about in intoxication'. There follows an uproarious account of the mask before the two kings in July, at which Faith, Hope, and Charity were not merely drunk but 'sick and spewing'; and

Harington contrasts this disorder with the court of Elizabeth. 'I ne'er did see such lack of good order, discretion, and sobriety, as I have now done. . . . The gunpowder fright is got out of all our heads, and we are going on, hereabouts, as if the devil was contriving every man should blow himself up, by wild riot, excess, and devastation of time and temperance. The great ladies do go well-masked, and, indeed, it be the only show of their modesty, to conceal their countenance; but alack, they meet with such countenance to uphold their strange doings, that I marvel not at aught that happens' (*Nugae Antiquae*, ed. Park, i, 348–53; cp. Chambers, *Elizabethan Stage*, i. 172).

10. For detailed analyses of this speech, see M. C. Bradbrook, *Themes and Conventions of Elizabethan Tragedy* (2nd edn), 164–5, and L. G. Salingar, '*R.T.* and the Morality Tradition', in *Scrutiny*, VI (1938). Tourneur's imagery is also analysed by U. M. Ellis-Fermor in *Modern Language Review*, XXX, 1935; by L. Lockert in *The Parrott Presentation Volume* (ed. Hardin Craig), 103ff.; and by I-S. Ewbank (Ekeblad), in *Modern Language Review*, LIV (1959). For a critical examination of the dramatic use of imagery by Tourneur, Webster and Middleton, see C. Ricks in *English Drama to 1710* (*Sphere History of Literature in the English Language* Vol. 3), ed. Ricks, 306–53.

11. See H. Jenkins in *Review of English Studies*, XVII (1941), a suggestive study of Tourneur's work as a whole; M. H. Higgins, on 'Calvinistic Thought in *A. T.*', in *Review of English Studies*, XIX (1943); I. Ribner, ed., *A.T.*; Murray, *Tourneur*, ch. iii. For the religious restraint on vengeance in *A.T.*, cp. Chapman, *Revenge of Bussy D'Ambois* (*c.* 1610), and see the following studies: P. Simpson, 'The Theme of Revenge in Elizabethan Tragedy', in *Proceedings of the British Academy*, XXI (1935); F. T. Bowers, *Elizabethan Revenge Tragedy*, 139ff.; H. H. Adams, in *Journal of English and Germanic Philology*, XLVIII (1949); T. M. Tomlinson, 'The Morality of Revenge: Tourneur's Critics', in *Essays in Criticism*, X (1960).

12. See *The White Devil* (to the Reader); see R. W. Dent, *Webster's Borrowing*. On Webster's life and background, see new material in M. C. Bradbrook, *Webster*. On his plays, see Bradbrook, *Themes and Conventions* (2nd edn), 179–205, 265; I-S. Ewbank (Ekeblad), 'The "Impure" Art of John Webster', *Review of English Studies*, NS IX (1958); G. K. and S. K. Hunter, eds, *Webster* (Penguin Critical Anthology); Lever, *Tragedy of State*; Ricks (n. 10 above).

13. Webster's source was Wm. Painter, *The Palace of Pleasure*, 1566 (ed. J. Jacobs, 1890, III). See G. Boklund's two studies of Webster's treatment of his narrative sources.

MIDDLETON'S TRAGEDIES

JOHN D. JUMP

The author of *Women Beware Women* (*c.* 1621) and *The Changeling* (1622) was sixteen years younger than Shakespeare, and wrote his two memorable tragedies some years after Shakespeare's death. The plays themselves leave us in no doubt whatsoever that he knew, and had learned from, Shakespeare's works. Nevertheless, they cannot be dismissed as merely derivative. Thomas Middleton (1580–1627) is, more completely and exclusively than any of his contemporaries, a realist. His tragedies carry conviction not as allegories or symbolist poems or expanded metaphors but as presentations of human character, holding our attention by their profundity and truth. At the same time, they are not naturalistic plays of the modern kind. Middleton is a poetic dramatist, and takes full advantage of the peculiar opportunities available to him as such. In particular, his blank verse is an instrument such as T. S. Eliot tried to shape for himself in *The Cocktail Party*; 'a form of versification and an idiom which would serve all my purposes, without recourse to prose, and be capable of unbroken transition between the most intense speech and the most relaxed dialogue' (*Poetry and Drama*). The value of such an instrument to the dramatist can be amply illustrated from Middleton's tragedies.

When he began *Women Beware Women*, he had been writing dramatic blank verse for about twenty years. His best plays had been comedies of intrigue presenting that contemporary class war in which needy and amorous gallants cuckolded, and were fleeced by, greedy and ambitious tradesmen; in writing these, he had, between 1602 and 1613, served his apprenticeship to realism. He had also written, or participated in, several romantic comedies and a single rambling and incoherent tragedy, *Hengist, King of Kent; or, The Mayor of Queenborough* (*c.* 1616–20).[1] These various works consist very largely of prose; but they had also given Middleton much practice in writing verse. As a result, his mature verse is easy, supple, and compact, capable of adjusting itself as readily and as unobtrusively to the most pedestrian as to the most imaginative of meanings.

Above all, it is dramatic. When, in *Women Beware Women* (III. i), Bianca is invited by the Duke to a banquet, the first impulse of her anxious husband Leantio is to conceal her. Her indignant protest against this, her scornful diagnosis of his behaviour, and after he has desperately and pleadingly explained it, her mocking laughter, vicious taunts, and off-hand departure are all conveyed in verse which makes no pretence of being decorative but is flexible, forceful, and concise.

> BIANCA. Would you keep me closer yet?
>   Have you the conscience? you're best e'en choke me up, sir:
>   You make me fearful of your health and wits,
>   You cleave to such wild courses; what's the matter?
> LEANTIO. Why, are you so insensible of your danger
>   To ask that now? the Duke himself has sent for you
>   To lady Livia's to a banquet, forsooth.
> BIANCA. Now I beshrew you heartily, has he so!
>   And you the man would never yet vouchsafe
>   To tell me on't till now? you show your loyalty
>   And honesty at once; and so farewell, sir.
> LEANTIO. Bianca, whither now?
> BIANCA. Why, to the Duke, sir;
>   You say he sent for me.

Even more forceful and concise, thanks to a homely but unexpected and ludicrously applied image which both expresses and implicitly criticizes her attitude, is Bianca's contemptuous retort, earlier in the same scene, to the rather sententious speech of Leantio's mother in defence of her home:

> Troth, you speak wondrous well for your old house here;
> 'Twill shortly fall down at your feet to thank you,
> Or stoop, when you go to bed, like a good child,
> To ask your blessing.

In general, however, Middleton makes surprisingly little use in this play of the more obviously poetical resources of language. Many of the most telling speeches are brief, plain, almost prosaic statements, such as Hippolito's summing-up in the final scene:

Lust and forgetfulness has been amongst us,
And we are brought to nothing.

This summing-up refers to both of the plots which compose
Women Beware Women, the plot of Bianca's abandoning her husband
Leantio for her seducer the Duke of Florence, and the plot of Isabella's
marrying the mentally retarded Ward in order to cover up her affair
with Hippolito. Employing mainly verse dialogue such as has just
been illustrated, Middleton is able to present the main characters in
both plots with a degree of naturalism that was unusual on the early
seventeenth-century stage; at the same time, the swift unfolding of
events which was always permissible on that stage gave him the
chance, which he took, of presenting characters who undergo significant development within the five-act limits.

The play opens with the arrival of Bianca and Leantio at his
mother's house. Bianca is silent; but Leantio, in his excited volubility,
reveals himself almost as if in a dramatic monologue. He, a bourgeois
who might almost have come from the world of Middleton's
comedies, has eloped with the daughter of a wealthy Venetian family.
In his speeches, he discloses in turn his ardent possessiveness, his
habitual anxiety, his self-congratulation on his marriage as a step con-
ducive to prudent and orderly living, and his uneasiness at having
stolen his bride. But his pride in his possession makes it impossible for
him to repent this theft. His mother suggests that Bianca may chafe
at the meanness of her new life. While asking his mother not to make
her discontented by such talk, Leantio denies this; and Bianca, speaking for the first time, insists that she will be content with a quiet
life shared with him. Soliloquizing, he determines to keep her safely
hidden, with his mother's help, from his fellow-Florentines. There is
a bumptious, callow eagerness about his speeches in this scene; a naïve,
febrile pride in his acquisition; and a rather priggish self-satisfaction.

When, in I. iii, he has to leave home on business for a few days, he
is torn between his desire for Bianca and the industry and thrift which
are habitual with him and in any case obligatory. Bianca's charms fail
to detain him, however; and she consoles herself after his departure
by watching a procession. One member of this, the Duke of Florence,
observes her at the window. For her part, she has already heard of
him from her mother-in-law; informed of his age, she has replied
that fifty-five is

no great age in man; he's then at best
For wisdom and for judgement.

The seduction takes place in II. ii. The Duke's procuress is Livia, a
wealthy court lady who in II. i has already performed a similar service
for her brother Hippolito. By this time we know her well as a hearty,
affectionate, lax creature, with a sardonic view, often wittily expressed, of the injustice to women of the marital relationship. In II. ii
she displays her cunning even more elaborately than in Hippolito's
service. She invites Leantio's mother to her house, cajoles her into the
admission that she has her son's wife living with her, and invites
Bianca to join them. Her courtly speech of welcome to Bianca is a
striking instance of Middleton's practised use of an unobtrusive
metrical form to control tempo, pause, emphasis, and, above all, the
complex and varying tone of natural speech which these subserve; at
the end of it, Livia presents to Bianca her friend Guardiano,

A gentleman that ladies' rights stands for,
That's his profession.

He proceeds to show Bianca the 'rooms and pictures' while the older
ladies settle down to a game of chess.

This situation – Leantio's mother engaged in a game of chess while
Bianca is led unawares to her seducer – gives scope for that play of
dramatic irony, innuendo, and *double entendre* which Middleton so
often introduces to give concentration and depth to his tragic scenes
and which makes this particular episode verge on grim comedy.

LIVIA. Alas, poor widow, I shall be too hard for thee!
MOTHER. You're cunning at the game, I'll be sworn, madam.
LIVIA. It will be found so, ere I give you over.   [*Aside.*]
    She that can place her man well –
MOTHER. As you do, madam.
LIVIA. As I shall, wench, can never lose her game:
    Nay, nay, the black king's mine.
MOTHER. Cry you mercy, madam!
LIVIA. And this my queen.
MOTHER. I see't now.

In the theatre for which the play was written, the latter part of
Bianca's tour of the house was enacted on the upper or balcony stage
while the game of chess continued below, both pairs of characters involved being simultaneously visible to the audience. In these circum-

stances, there can have been no mistaking the chess-players' sidelong allusions – deliberate on Livia's part, unconscious on her opponent's – to what is afoot elsewhere in the building.

Confronted by the Duke, Bianca is surprised and indignant. But the most significant thing in her speeches is her eventual appeal to him not to make her act against the dictates of her conscience. Evidently she fears the forces in herself which infidelity would release; she wishes to continue in the retirement and restraint which Leantio represents. The Duke, however, woos imperially, promises lavishly, and prevails; and when Bianca rejoins the chess-players the change in her has already begun. To be sure, she is horrified and indignant at her betrayal; but she can also state ominously to Guardiano:

> I'm made bold now,
> I thank thy treachery; sin and I'm acquainted,
> No couple greater.

In the following scene (III. i), passages from which have already been quoted, she is a very different person. She is discontented and demanding; off-hand when Leantio returns home smugly congratulating himself on the affectionate welcome which awaits him; and ruthlessly scornful when his mother, who knows nothing of her seduction, falls in with her desire to accept the Duke's invitation. Her behaviour at the banquet (III. ii) fully confirms the inferences which are to be drawn from all this; she is no longer capable even of the single remorseful aside of the previous scene; she can now contradict her own earlier utterances by declaring that in marriage women strive mostly for 'th' upper hand'; knowing that Leantio is compelled to stand by, 'a grudging man', while the Duke courts her, she makes a 'Bitter scoff' about willing cuckolds; and in the same spirit she pronounces, obviously with oblique reference to her own early married life, that the Ward might make a tolerable husband for Isabella if he were to be absent from home for long stretches. The greedy vanity which events have disclosed is now predominant in her and cannot be sated by any lesser person than the Duke himself; Leantio is callously dismissed.

Nor is he any longer the innocent he had been. During the earlier part of this scene, his embittered tone as he comments upon his own hollow merriment gives indirect outlet to his abject misery. After

Bianca's departure, however, he expresses his grief directly in soliloquy with a greater depth and maturity of feeling than he has hitherto manifested. He concludes that 'some close bawd' is responsible for what has happened, and at once, by a stroke of dynamic irony typical of Middleton, becomes aware of Livia who finds herself attracted to him and has for some time been trying to catch his attention. Her erotic advances meet with no response until he decides independently that for his own well-being he must hate Bianca. He then becomes Livia's lover. To judge by his behaviour in IV. i, however, his principal motive in this is to demonstrate to his wife that he too can find acceptance, and indeed generous maintenance, elsewhere. Their dialogue in this scene shows that there is now little to choose between them.

The sub-plot performs a similar function to that of the sub-plot in *King Lear*; it echoes the main plot, extending and varying the exemplification there given of the central theme of 'lust and forgetfulness'. In both actions, the wife of a young and simple husband has a more experienced man as her lover; but in the sub-plot the husband is a lustful and brutish simpleton whom Isabella marries only in order to cloak her affair with Hippolito. For Livia, playing the same role as in the main plot, has already brought these two together by falsely convincing Isabella that she is not Hippolito's niece. These central characters are presented with touches of shrewd psychology; but the importance of the sub-plot, which is, not surprisingly, the less fully worked out and realized of the two, is derived mainly from its participation in the whole design of the play.

In the last act, Middleton falls back on to one of the conventional tragic endings of his time: the treacherous revels. No doubt custom made this acceptable to the Jacobean audience; but to most modern readers this bout of amateur theatricals which results in the deaths of the Duke, Bianca, Livia, Guardiano, Hippolito, and Isabella seems both incredible and silly. (Leantio has already been killed by Hippolito, acting, ironically enough, as the defender of his sister's honour.) The vengeful performers commit murder and suicide with blade, arrow, and poison gas; blundering domestics present an envenomed goblet to the wrong spectator; and the plotter who gives the signal for opening the trap-door falls himself on to the spikes below. This ridiculous holocaust, manifestly the work of a dramatist who had lost

interest in his characters as soon as their emotional development –
or deterioration – was complete, makes it impossible to praise *Women
Beware Women* as an entire work of art. But a play containing scenes
such as those of Bianca's seduction, the banquet, and Leantio's visit to
his wife's lodging at court, and involving personages such as Leantio,
Livia, and, above all, Bianca herself, has clearly an enduring importance.

The Changeling is known to have been written by Middleton in
collaboration with William Rowley (*c.* 1585–1626). But that part of
it for which Middleton must have been mainly responsible – the
scenes composing the main plot – is usually, and justly, held to be his
masterpiece.

For this work, his characteristic verse has developed a special tone.
This is anticipated here and there in *Women Beware Women*; thus, to
the sentence

> Lust and forgetfulness has been amongst us,
> And we are brought to nothing

the falling rhythm superimposed upon the almost inaudible metrical
beat gives a hushed, brooding intensity which suggests many passages
in the later play. The full emergence of this tone seems to be connected with Middleton's extraordinary reliance in *The Changeling*
upon the soliloquy or aside. He had made copious use of this in his
earlier plays, very often as a handy mechanism for quickly taking up
the slack of an intrigue; but in *The Changeling* it becomes the natural
and inevitable vehicle for some of his most important perceptions,
and as such provides many of the chief occasions for the exploitation
of the verse tone which is characteristic of the play. Thus, early in
II. i the evil and repulsive De Flores, that 'ominous ill-fac'd fellow',
soliloquizes on his need to obtrude himself on Beatrice-Joanna in
order to enjoy the sight of her even at the cost of her reviling him:

> Yonder's she;
> Whatever ails me, now a-late especially,
> I can as well be hanged as refrain seeing her;
> Some twenty times a-day, nay, not so little,
> Do I force errands, frame ways and excuses,
> To come into her sight; and I've small reason for't,
> And less encouragement, for she baits me still
> Every time worse than other; does profess herself

The cruellest enemy to my face in town;
At no hand can abide the sight of me,
As if danger or ill luck hung in my looks.

In this speech, the language is plain, the imagery subdued, the metrical pattern unemphatic. True, the alliteration in 'force errands, frame ways' underlines De Flores' determined pursuit of Beatrice. But in the main the passage consists of a series of almost prosaic utterances which, varying in speed and separated by pregnant pauses, admirably reflect the movements of a brooding mind which scornfully contemplates its own thraldom and tortures itself by dwelling upon insults received.

This attitude of isolated, self-regarding brooding is typical of the central characters in *The Changeling*; it is, indeed, entirely appropriate that they should slip off so frequently into soliloquy and aside. In some scenes, the asides constitute a regular accompaniment to the unfolding dialogue, the result being that the speakers seem simultaneously to communicate with each other and to cry out from their respective solitudes. Thus, the soliloquy from which an extract has just been quoted is followed by a passage in which De Flores and Beatrice speak almost entirely in asides, he enduring her mounting anger without reply, she addressing him with impatient disgust and voicing aside the disturbance which she feels in his presence. When, in II. ii, Beatrice is about to overcome her instinctive detestation of De Flores so far as to employ him to murder her unwelcome fiancé, their dialogue is again inaugurated by a passage consisting almost entirely of asides; in these, she concludes that it is expedient to mask her loathing, and he hugs himself with glee at her gentler and eventually almost familiar way of addressing him. In both passages, the asides, often ironically juxtaposed with the speeches uttered aloud, keep vividly present the inner natures of the two unscrupulous egoists, she innocent, he experienced, who are heading for conflict.

In III. iv the conflict is fought out. Beatrice proposes to pay De Flores well for the murder and then to marry Alsemero, with whom she has fallen desperately in love. 'Honest' De Flores, however, has his own idea of the form his reward should take. He has already hinted ominously, in II. ii, that the crime will bind them to each other: 'Why, are not both our lives upon the cast?' Joining her after committing the murder, he declares aside that his 'thoughts are at a banquet' and congratulates himself on 'the sweet recompense' which he will now be able to demand as the price of his continued silence. He tells her of the murder, forcing her to face what he has done, and accepts from her as a gift the ring which she had once sent to the dead man. Something in his manner of accepting it – he is resenting her assumption that she can pay him off with it – makes her ask whether she has unwittingly offended him: ''Twere misery in me to give you cause, sir.' His reply is menacingly ambiguous:

> I know so much, it were so; misery
> In her most sharp condition.

When she offers him gold, he rejects it as 'salary', asking

> . . . is anything
> Valued too precious for my recompense?

Beatrice fails to understand; 'I'm in a labyrinth', she complains aside. Desperately, she begs him to fly. He refuses to do so alone:

> Why, are not you as guilty? in, I'm sure,
> As deep as I; and we should stick together

With the same curt familiarity, he eventually speaks out.

> DE FLORES. Come, kiss me with a zeal now.
> BEATRICE. Heaven, I doubt him!   [Aside.]
> DE FLORES. I will not stand so long to beg 'em shortly.
> BEATRICE. Take heed, De Flores, of forgetfulness,
>   'Twill soon betray us.
> DE FLORES. Take you heed first;
>   Faith, you're grown much forgetful, you're to blame in't.

Beatrice dares not, and will not, understand him; so he becomes brutally explicit. She protests in a tone of startled innocence, making appeal, ironically enough, to her 'honour' and her 'modesty':

> BEATRICE. Why, 'tis impossible thou canst be so wicked,
>   Or shelter such a cunning cruelty,
>   To make his death the murderer of my honour!
>   Thy language is so bold and vicious,
>   I cannot see which way I can forgive it
>   With any modesty.
> DE FLORES. Push!*ᵃ* you forget yourself;
>   A woman dipp'd in blood, and talk of modesty!

ᵃ pish.

He is harshly contemptuous, both at this point and subsequently when she tries to reassert the superiority in social rank which would protect her from him:

> DE FLORES. Push! fly not to your birth, but settle you
> In what the act has made you; you're no more now.
> You must forget your parentage to me;
> You are the deed's creature; by that name
> You lost your first condition, and I challenge[a] you,
> As peace and innocency has turn'd you out,
> And made you one with me.
> BEATRICE. With thee, foul villain!
> DE FLORES. Yes, my fair murderess.

Her pride broken, Beatrice kneels and pleads. But he is not to be swayed:

> Can you weep Fate from its determin'd purpose?
> So soon may you weep me;

and the scene closes with his raising her, embracing her, and tenderly assuring her that she will 'love' him 'anon'. Throughout this scene, the dialogue has the quiet, brooding intensity, achieved by the counterpointing of intimate, urgent, but almost prosaic utterances against a barely audible metrical pattern, which has already been described.

Beatrice's history, summarized in De Flores' assurance to her that she will 'love' him 'anon', is the history of her learning to use, to accept, and to need De Flores. Despite her hostile treatment of him, there are suggestions, even in the first two acts, that she is not only revolted but also fascinated by him, however little she may care to admit it to herself. The incident of the gloves, which concludes I. i, carries such a suggestion; later, as has been seen, she admits – and she repeats the admission – that she finds his presence disturbing; and he, soliloquizing towards the end of II. ii, cynically and grossly reminds us that 'Some women are odd feeders'. After she has become his mistress, she grows completely dependent upon him. In V. i, when it seems likely that her plot for concealing her unchastity from Alsemero, whom she has just married, will miscarry, it is De Flores who thinks of starting a fire, raising the alarm so that Beatrice can join

a claim.

her husband in the confusion, and murdering Diaphanta the untrust-worthy waiting-woman in circumstances which will make it appear that she perished in the flames. Beatrice is delighted by his resource-fulness and exclaims:

> I'm forc'd to love thee now,
> 'Cause thou provid'st so carefully for my honour.

But De Flores will have no truck with 'honour'; he reduces their motives to a selfish desire for secure sensual enjoyment:

> 'Slid,*a* it concerns the safety of us both,
> Our pleasure and continuance.

Soliloquizing a little later, Beatrice says that she loves him for his 'care' and 'service'; when he raises the alarm, she cries, 'Here's a man worth loving!'; and, to her father's commendation of De Flores as 'good on all occasions', she retorts, in one of the many hauntingly ironical lines in the play, 'A wondrous necessary man, my lord.' In-deed, he is now more necessary to her than any other man; she has learned to 'love' him; her degradation is complete.

So complete is it that in v. iii she tries to dispel her husband's doubts as to her fidelity by confessing to her original fiancé's murder as proof of her devotion to himself. The immediate result of this grotesque miscalculation is that Alsemero repudiates her as a mur-deress; the remoter consequence is that De Flores, charged with murder, discloses her infidelity. Stabbed by De Flores, who then commits suicide, she utters her own epitaph in the most memorable words in the whole play. She addresses her father:

> O, come not near me, sir, I shall defile you!
> I am that of your blood was*b* taken from you
> For your better health; look no more upon't,
> But cast it to the ground regardlessly,
> Let the common sewer take it from distinction:
> Beneath the stars, upon yon meteor,
> > [*Pointing to* DE FLORES.]
>
> Ever hung my fate, 'mongst things corruptible;★
> I ne'er could pluck it from him; my loathing

---

a an oath, *b* which was.

★ It was believed that all above the moon was eternal, all below it subject to decay. The stars were therefore unchanging; but meteors, which were held to occur below the moon, were 'corruptible'.

Was prophet to the rest, but ne'er believ'd:
Mine honour fell with him, and now my life.

The grave intensity of this requires no further comment now; nor does the melancholy falling rhythm which regulates its quiet phrases. More unusual in Middleton's work is the striking image of 'the common sewer': filth should be consigned to the sewer; and Beatrice, reviewing her failure to resist her degradation, welcomes the loss of her separate identity which the image implies. De Flores, however, remains an egoist to the last. Despite his having been haunted by his crime, he dies impenitent, revelling in the thought that he has had Beatrice to himself:

> I thank life for nothing
> But that pleasure; it was so sweet to me,
> That I have drunk up all, left none behind
> For any man to pledge me.

The sub-plot of *The Changeling* has found few admirers. Swinburne condemns it outright; Mr T. S. Eliot and Miss U. M. Ellis-Fermor express their disapproval quietly but unequivocally. But Professor William Empson and, following him, Miss M. C. Bradbrook defend it as performing a function similar to that of the sub-plot in *Henry IV* Part 1. They claim that what happens in it implies a criticism, without which the work would be incomplete, of the characters and events of the main plot. Miss Bradbrook points out that the title itself links the plots; it refers both to Antonio, who is disguised as a 'changeling' or half-wit, and to Beatrice, who is in fact a 'changeling' or inconstant woman. Moreover, in a series of speeches at the end of v. iii the reference of the title is extended to several other characters in the two parts of the play. All of these are changed, either in appearance or more radically, by passion.

But the plots are not linked only by the title. In each, a 'disguised' lover suddenly reveals himself to the heroine. But, whereas in iii. iv Beatrice succumbs to De Flores, Isabella the asylum-keeper's wife virtuously repels the sham idiot Antonio in iii. iii. When the servant Lollio enters and, believing that she means to take Antonio as her lover, tries to blackmail her as De Flores in the following scene blackmails Beatrice, Isabella's response is to threaten to get Antonio to cut his throat. Her level-headedness is contrasted with the insane passion of Beatrice for Alsemero and of De Flores for Beatrice.

In all of her scenes she is encircled by madmen, representing the bestial element in man. As Professor Empson says, 'the effect of the vulgar asylum scenes is to surround the characters with a herd of lunatics, howling outside in the night, one step into whose company is irretrievable' (*Some Versions of Pastoral*). Beatrice takes this step; but Isabella does not.

Clearly, the dramatists knew what they were doing when they planned to insert this sub-plot. But does the execution of it – probably Rowley's – come up to requirements? One obstacle in the way of its appreciation today is that readers are unlikely to think lunacy a laughing matter. But even if, by a flight of the historical imagination, this obstacle is overcome, it may still be felt that there is much merely tedious fooling to be endured. When, in I. ii, the jealous husband Alibius says, 'I am old, Lollio', and Lollio retorts, 'No, sir, 'tis I am old Lollio', one can respond only with a wondering pity for the author who thought such backchat worth ink and paper. Is it perhaps some sense of the inadequacy of these scenes for their purpose which leads Professor Empson, in the passage just quoted, to step up his account with the gratuitous emotive phrase 'in the night'?

There is no need, however, to take the intention for the deed when we turn to the tragedy of Beatrice herself or to the first four acts of *Women Beware Women*. These are among the age's greatest achievements in drama, differing sharply from the tragedies of Webster and Tourneur and Shakespeare himself in that they are dependent hardly at all upon patterns of poetic imagery for their effect. True, Miss Bradbrook argues that each of Middleton's tragedies is given a distinct tone by the use of certain dominating images. In *The Changeling*, De Flores' desires are linked in this way with the appetite for food and drink; and the effect he has upon the good people of the play is repeatedly compared with that of poison. In *Women Beware Women*, images of food and drink occur much more often; and their effect is reinforced and complicated by images of plague and disease, treasure and jewels, and, in the last two acts, light and darkness. Nevertheless, as Miss Bradbrook admits, it is not necessary to grasp the schemes of imagery in order to appreciate these plays. Relatively few of the images are fully realized; their contribution to the total effect is merely to confirm in some slight degree that view of each play's action which is more potently suggested by Middleton's significant, often ironical, juxtapositions of characters, speeches, and events and his lucid, flexible, highly dramatic but always unobtrusive verse.

NOTE

1. For a higher estimate of the merits of this play, see R. C. Bald's edition of it (New York 1938), xliii–liv, and Schoenbaum's *Middleton's Tragedies* (New York, 1955), 69–101.

ELIZABETHAN AND JACOBEAN COMEDY

D. J. ENRIGHT

This synoptic essay aims at a tentative definition of typical Eliza-bethan–Jacobean comedy – the so-called 'realistic comedy', that is – together with a sketch of the later course of comedy through the transitional work of the Jacobean and Caroline writers up to the ap-parently assured, 'upper-class' and distinctly limited achievement of the Restoration theatre.

It seems indisputable that Ben Jonson stands at both the heart and the peak of Jacobean comedy, and that his *Volpone* (1605) is the greatest comedy in English. The comedies of Shakespeare belong to a different *genre* – romantic comedy, a form which can be used safely only by the kind of genius powerful enough to survive its rarefied atmosphere and to achieve a balance between humour, romance and wisdom. A study of the three comedies, Shakespeare's *The Merchant of Venice*, Jonson's *Volpone*, and Massinger's *A New Way to Pay Old Debts*, suggests an illuminating approach to the subject. All three are concerned with problems arising from money, but it is *Volpone* that stands out as a complete and solid statement, while neither of the others quite succeeds in coping with the questions which it poses. At the end of *A New Way to Pay Old Debts* we are left with the 're-generated' Wellborn, who has recovered his possessions from Sir Giles Overreach and hopes to recover his reputation, in the conven-tional manner, on the battlefield – a slight and dubious figure in comparison with the ruined and insane Overreach.

Somewhat similarly, at the end of *The Merchant of Venice* we have to believe that the giant Shylock has been demolished by a legalistic quibble (albeit something which, since he insisted on the letter of the law, he should have guarded against), while the unimpressive Bassanio and the melancholic Antonio, both beneficiaries of mere luck, remain to enjoy the fruits of Belmont. In both these cases we cannot rid ourselves of the impression that, poetically speaking, the villain is the real hero. Overreach and Shylock are powerful creations – what is missing is the key to their characters; poetry and plot pull in opposite directions. The figure of Volpone, on the other hand, is a finished creation, all the questions which his behaviour raises are answered in the play itself: he is constructed and then demolished, demolished by his own cleverness, there being nobody else on stage clever enough to do it, while the other two linger on in some uncertain limbo of the imagination. In Massinger's case this is due, one must suppose, to a failure in talent; in Shakespeare's, to the conventions of romantic comedy.

These remarks are no denigration of Shakespeare's comedies; of their kind, they are obviously the finest we possess. But it needs to be suggested that a more serious kind of comedy exists, even though Jonson is the only English genius of first rank who worked in it. Romantic comedy, in Shakespeare's hands, took on Shakespearean stature; nonetheless, for all their inimitable beauties, his comedies raise issues which they do not finally resolve. That we tend to forget this is perhaps due to the fact that Shakespeare did resolve those issues elsewhere – in the tragedies and, to some extent, the tragi-comedies.

Our beginning must be with John Lyly (1554–1606), whose work points to the nature of the drama's later development and bifurcation. Lyly wrote for a refined, aristocratic audience; his plays were performed by companies of boy actors in 'private theatres' – the price of admission was higher, the audience more comfortably seated, and its behaviour presumably more restrained – as distinguished from the 'public', popular theatres in which Marlowe's tragedies were given. Good examples of Lyly's work are *Campaspe* (1584) and *Endimion* (1588), written for the greater part in the style which (after the same author's novel, *Euphues*) we call 'euphuistic' – a mixture of laboured elegance, unnatural history, classical allusion, contrived antithesis and occasional flashes of genuine wit. Campaspe's soliloquy in IV. iv is characteristic:

> Foolish wench, what hast thou done? That, alas, which cannot be undone, and therefore I fear me undone ... The love of kings is like the blowing of winds, which whistle sometimes gently among the leaves, and straightways turn the trees up by the roots; or fire which warmeth afar off, and burneth near hand; or the sea ...

Endimion treats primarily of the legend of the young man who falls in love with the moon, and the treatment is uncomic, rather learned, with a philosophical air about it. But the sub-plot character Sir Tophas is a comic caricature who leads straight to the less complex of Jonson's 'humorous' characters. Sir Tophas's 'humour' is bellicosity:

> There cometh no soft syllable within my lips; custom hath made my words bloody and my heart barbarous. That pelting [*paltry*] word love, how waterish it is in my mouth; it carrieth no sound. Hate, horror, death are speeches that nourish my spirits.

Sir Tophas has a long family history: before him went Herod and Cain, the 'roarers' of the Miracle plays, and behind him come Jonson's Bobadill and Shakespeare's Pistol. But Sir Tophas is learned as well – 'I am all Mars and Ars' – and the Latin tags that fall from him remind us of Tim and his tutor in Middleton's *A Chaste Maid in Cheapside* and of Holofernes in Shakespeare's *Love's Labour's Lost*, just as the fairies who dance round Endimion call to mind another Shakespearian comedy. Moreover, the scene in which the ladies, pretending to be in love with the old knight, provoke him into further eccentricity points forward to a common situation in Jacobean and Restoration comedy. Sir Tophas finally conceives a passion for the old hag Dipsas – his 'humour' has not been corrected, it is merely ousted by a different one, exactly as happens in Fletcher's *The Humorous Lieutenant*.

Lyly's work contains all these various elements because they were ready to hand; he was not the man to give comedy its later direction and force. His work resembles something looked at through an unfocused telescope: it is vaguely allegorical, vaguely philosophical, vaguely satirical, vaguely romantic. It is true that he seems a popular writer when compared with Restoration dramatists, yet like them he wrote for the Court. The difference between them is the difference between the Court of Elizabeth and that of Charles II, and reminds us that the distinction between polite culture and popular culture was a matter of 'degree' in Lyly's time but an abyss when Congreve wrote. It is in comparison with Jonson that we see how much Lyly forfeited when he devoted himself to what was specifically 'of the Court'.

If the romantic elements in the comedy of Lyly (and of Robert

Greene) were developed by Shakespeare, the realistic and satirical elements reached their apotheosis in the work of Ben Jonson. Jonson is the subject of a separate essay, and here we are concerned with him only incidentally, as the figure against whom all 'realistic comedy' has to be measured. But a word in explanation of the 'theory of humours' may not be out of place. A human being is a blend of different elements or 'humours', and the 'humorous' character is the outcome of a preponderance of one particular 'humour'. Such characters must be given 'pills to purge, And make them fit for fair societies'. The theory of humours does not of course explain Jonson's greatness, but it can be seen that, in the hands of a poetic genius who has inherited moral feelings which are at once a national tradition and a fiercely personal concern, the comedy of humours can readily develop into what would be better called the 'comedy of morals', were it not that the latter term is apt to be confused with moralizing. The secret of Jonson's superiority lies in the fact that whatever explicit moralizing he indulges in is superfluous; there is no need to 'draw' a moral, because the moral is there all the time, at the heart of the play, in the poetry. The moral quality of Jonson's dramatic verse is finer and more potent by far than his occasional polemics; the latter, whatever their usefulness at the time, have served to obscure his reputation and to foster the supposition that there are only two kinds of comedy – romantic comedy, written by Shakespeare, and manners comedy, written by such wits as Congreve, Sheridan, Wilde and Shaw.

There is no need to speak here of Thomas Dekker (c. 1572–1632), whose hearty, patriotic piece, *The Shoemaker's Holiday* (1600), is well known. Nor of Thomas Heywood (c. 1574–1641), who, as T. S. Eliot remarks, 'would in any age have been a successful dramatist'. We are conscious of a stronger personality in the work of John Marston (1576–1634), a rough-tongued satirist whose ostensible moral purpose is often belied by an insistent undercurrent of obscene innuendo. The plot of *The Dutch Courtesan* (1605) is more heavily sordid than is usual among plays of its sort; after the lumpish and reiterated satire of *The Fawn* (1606) we hardly feel in accord with the hero's cheerful summing-up: 'Never grieve nor wonder – all things sweetly fit'; and despite the happy and equitable ending of *The Malcontent* (1604) – an extremely interesting play, though doubtfully in the category of comedy – we are inclined to echo Malevole's earlier exclamation: 'O world most vile!' George Chapman (*c.* 1559–1634) is more important as a tragedian, and we need only name *A Humorous Day's Mirth* (probably performed in 1597, a year before Jonson's first 'humours' play) and *All Fools* (1599). *Eastward Ho!* (1605), in which he collaborated with Marston and Jonson, is a lively morality on the theme of social pretension and the good and bad apprentices: a combination of Dekker's *The Shoemaker's Holiday* with Massinger's *The City Madam*.

Of Jonson's followers in comedy, Thomas Middleton (1580–1627) and Philip Massinger (1583–1640) are the most important. Middleton's *A Trick to Catch the Old One* (1608) and *A Chaste Maid in Cheapside* (*c.* 1613) are excellent farces. The plot of the latter – Allwit, the contented cuckold, lives merrily on the wages of his wife's sin – reminds us that the change which is so striking in Restoration comedy is by no means a change of plot material. It is a question of range: Middleton's play, unsubtle as it is, has a wider emotional reach. If his characters are 'humours', then in the Jonsonian manner their eccentricities open outwards into a more spacious, healthier world. The 'humours' of Restoration comedy are inbred: in effect they amount to an ever-narrowing concentration upon an intellectualized sexuality which seeks novelty from metaphors of the hunt, of gaming, even of collecting china. The world of Jonson and Middleton seems small and limited at first glance; on examination it broadens out, its implications expanding like the rings on a pond. But the Restoration world, for all its sophistication and 'civilization', has an emotional range hardly greater than that of an animal in a cage – an animal, despite its apologists and despite Wycherley's few outbursts, that seems to have chosen its cage. Indeed, whenever this comedy seems about to contend with some deeper feeling, the dramatist's control breaks under the strain – and we are left, for instance, with the hysteria of Manly in Wycherley's *The Plain Dealer* (1676).

If we compare Volpone with Horner, a character from Wycherley's *The Country Wife* (1675) – both are 'foxes feigning death' – we can estimate the loss in range and depth between the Elizabethan-Jacobean and the Restoration. In brief, it is the difference between a system of religious morality which was the heritage of a nation and a system of manners which was the privilege of a social elite. In his *Restoration Comedy*, Bonamy Dobrée maintained a radically dissimilar conception of what this difference implies, and his point of view is so concisely expressed that readers may like to have it quoted: 'the comedy of humours was only more profound in that it appealed to some supposedly absolute standard of morality, while the comedy of manners took for its norm that of the *honnête homme*'. It may be felt that Dobrée's 'only' is a rather large one, and that his description of the standard of morality as 'supposedly absolute' bears little meaning in social and poetic contexts. Compared with Jonson's 'conscience, which I must always study before fame', this *honnête homme* is an exotic, the thin reflection of a small and not very important social class. It is true that the comedy of manners often has the advantage in ready vivacity and smoothness, and is more agile in the manipulation of personalities. But grace is gained at the expense of depth, a generally competent prose at the expense of a frequently rich poetry. In the best of Jonson we find a complexity of attitude; in the best of Congreve a complexity of situation. (Today there is a sense of 'costume' about Restoration comedies which *Volpone* and *The Alchemist*, despite their remoteness in setting from the late twentieth century, do not convey.) We are on our way from the simple Revenge plot of *Hamlet* – vehicle of an experience whose analysis has baffled critics of every generation – to the 'well-made', ingeniously plotted play of modern times.

Sophisticated 'polite' comedy had existed before, in the work of Lyly, but the theatre of the Restoration was the first emergence of a consciously minority drama – and in considering the significance of this we must remember that it was partly through drama that English culture had hitherto remained comparatively unified and truly national. It marks, that is to say, the first great stage in that differentiation of entertainment which manifests itself today in increasingly watertight compartments, compartments that are also increasingly taken for granted.

Some change was bound to happen, of course, as medieval conceptions of social unity, anonymity, and identity of purpose gradually declined and were superseded by the individualistic impetus towards separation, freedom and betterment. This process (which it would be worse than vain to deplore) had begun long before the time of

Shakespeare and Jonson, but it was in their day that the struggle between 'Medieval' and 'Renaissance' came to a head – it was then that it showed itself as something intensely personal and urgent, and a theme for art. A little later the theorist stepped in, and the drama exchanged the examination of behaviour as its subject for the observation of behaviour.

Middleton and Massinger already represent an earlier stage in this process. What strikes one about them is their quality of diluted Jonson – in Massinger's case this is partly a question of plagiarism – but, if only in dilution, something of Jonson's vitality is there. We feel it in some of Allwit's speeches; for instance, 'The founder's come to town' (*A Chaste Maid in Cheapside*, II. ii), where there is something of the splendid Jonsonian immediacy of realization in the cuckold's contemplation of his happy lot. What is most notably missing is the undercurrent of criticism, the self-deflation, which accompanies the corresponding soliloquies of Volpone.

The notes that shrill out in Restoration comedy had long been sounding, though in concert with others, in early Jacobean drama. Bianca in Middleton's tragedy, *Women Beware Women*, says:

> Too fond is as unseemly as too churlish:
> I would not have a husband of that proneness
> To kiss me before company for a world . . .
>
> (III. i)

It is a sentiment that we encounter over and over again in the Restoration – for example, Etherege's *She Would if She Could* (1668): 'What an odious thing it is to be thought to love a wife in good company'. But with Middleton there is something of the medieval conception of 'decorous' behaviour, moderation and modesty behind it (that Bianca is busy betraying her husband simply adds a piquant irony to the situation). When we reach Etherege and Congreve this attitude has lost its traditional connotations and can be related only to 'the fashion'. It is not immoderate and unseemly behaviour that the people of Restoration comedy strive to avoid – far from it – it is merely the ridicule of their peers. What was a feeling at the same time religious, moral and social has now become (on the stage, at any rate) purely social, a question of 'face'.

Another stock theme of Jacobean comedy is the clash between

social classes, particularly between the citizen (often a shopkeeper) and the courtier; but the social issue is not yet divorced from the moral. Middleton and Massinger (who is concerned with merchants rather than shopkeepers) satirize both parties without any very strong prejudice – apart from what remains of their feeling for 'degree'; this, for instance, comes from the former's *The Family of Love* (1608):

Of all men I love not these gallants; they'll prate much but do little: they are people most uncertain; they use great words, but little sense; great beards, but little wit; great breeches, but no money.

A weightier example is provided by Massinger's comedy, *The City Madam* (1632), when Mr Plenty, 'a rough-hewn gentleman, and newly come to a great estate', reminds Sir Maurice Lacy, a young aristocrat seeking to mend his fortunes by marrying a rich merchant's daughter, that

> my clothes are paid for
> As soon as put on; a sin your man of title
> Is seldom guilty of ...

Sir Maurice retorts:

> thy great-grandfather was a butcher,
> And his son a grazier; thy sire, constable
> Of the hundred, and thou the first of your dunghill
> Created gentleman.

(I. ii)

The tendency of the play as a whole is summed up by Lord Lacy in these words:

> A fit decorum must be kept, the court
> Distinguished from the city.

(III. ii)

Significantly, Dryden was to remark that the conversation of such vulgar creatures as Cob and Tib – characters in Jonson's *Every Man In His Humour* – 'can be no jest to them [i.e. gentlemen] on the theatre, when they would avoid it in the street'.

Before leaving Middleton, further mention must be made of his effective farce, *A Trick to Catch the Old One*. The plot revolves round Witgood's recovery of his wealth from his usurer uncle, Lucre, through the pretence of courting a rich country widow – actually a disguised courtesan – and there can be little doubt that it was here Massinger found the idea for his much superior play, *A New Way to Pay Old Debts* (*c.* 1625). A brief comparison of the two brings out that superiority in both intention and achievement: Massinger's play is probably the only other comedy to approach Jonson's work at all closely in respect of power and conviction. In *A Trick to Catch the Old One*, the villainy is diluted and spread over the two rival usurers, Lucre and Hoard; in *A New Way to Pay Old Debts* it is concentrated in the figure of Sir Giles Overreach. Extra seriousness derives from the fact that the 'decoy' in Massinger's play actually is a rich and virtuous widow, while Wellborn is a character with uncomfortable social implications where Witgood is merely a coarse and frivolous stage property. Middleton's play, then, is an elementary piece of theatre, less interesting than either *A Chaste Maid in Cheapside* or *The Roaring Girl* (1611, with Dekker), whereas in Massinger's play there is a good deal of the disconcerting penetration into situations which are more than topical that characterizes the higher (if sometimes less comic) comedy. The play shocks more than it amuses, and it transmits its shock mainly through the presence of 'Cormorant Overreach', a character (obviously created with an eye on Volpone: 'This Sir Giles feeds high, keeps many servants ... Rich in his habit, vast in his expenses') who grows too powerful for Massinger to control in the way that Jonson controls Volpone.

The curses of the families he has ruined, Sir Giles tells us, make him as wretched

<blockquote>
as rocks are
When foamy billows split themselves against
Their flinty ribs; or as the moon is moved,
When wolves, with hunger pined, howl at her brightness.
I am of a solid temper, and like these
Steer on a constant course ...
</blockquote>

(IV. i)

The weakness of *A New Way to Pay Old Debts* lies in its author's failure, having gone so far, to present any positive standards strong enough to counteract the poetic effect of Sir Giles. Wellborn, Lady Allworth, and even the noble Lord Lovell are not big enough to do this. From a consideration of the plot of *Volpone* it might be supposed that the situation there is even more desperate, for the villain's victims are sordid wretches, Celia and Bonario are ludicrous in their protestations of outraged virtue ('I would I could forget I were a creature'), and the magistrates of Venice are feeble if not shabby figures. Does Volpone, despite his formal condemnation by the court, get away with the honours, then? The answer is that he condemns himself; the play's positive standards are in the poetry itself, and they are, in fact, most sharply invoked and energetically exercised in the 'wicked' speeches of Volpone himself. Jonson's attitude operates through the imagery and rhythms in which his villains or his reprobates (among them Sir Epicure Mammon, more than a simple figure of fun) express themselves, and he therefore needs no mouthpiece of virtue on the stage.

Massinger has to depend to a greater extent on specifically 'good' characters, and they let him down. It is a commonplace that virtuous characters generally prove tedious in the theatre: Jonson's technique would seem the only one that allows of great moralistic comedy. In this respect Massinger reminds us that we are nearing an age of prose when dramatists relied increasingly on character manipulation and plotting. It is not surprising, then, to detect weaknesses in his poetry; most noticeable is his habit of tangled speeches, crowded with awkward parentheses, suggesting an intermediate stage between poetry and prose in which neither mode is happy. Similarly, the unnecessary explanatory remarks which he interjects – a kind of programme notes – suggest the disintegration of the Elizabethan theatre public, the breakdown of stage conventions, and the approach of 'realism' in the modern sense.

Yet Massinger is a considerable writer. The speeches of Luke in *The City Madam* have traces of Volponian magnificence which are not merely borrowings (see especially 'When you appear, Like Juno, in full majesty', III. ii, and the opening soliloquy in the following scene). Sir John Frugal, moreover, is one of the last pleasantly positive characters to appear in English comedy; he compares well with Wycherley's attempt to do something similar with Manly in *The Plain Dealer*.

Decadence is more prominent in the comedies of John Fletcher (1579–1625), which are of an unmemorable, neutral type, deficient in both the vigour of the Jacobeans and the surface precision and polish of the Restoration. What soon strikes us in *Wit Without*

Money (*c.* 1614) and *The Humorous Lieutenant* (1618) is that the erst-while 'humours' have degenerated into whimsies. Valentine, in the former play, interests Fletcher only as a social oddity; the 'birds of prey' in *Volpone* interest Jonson as exemplars of moral miasma. The verse has a smoothness and superficial elegance in striking contrast to the physical energy of Jonson, the erratic profundity of Massinger and the vulgar strength of Middleton and Marston, and we note a softening and even inconsequence of metaphor which reflects a slackening in moral excitement since the greater writers. Fletcher is Elizabethan in one sense; the romantic verse of his love scenes is thick with the conventional imagery of the Elizabethan lyric. We may cite IV. iii of *The Elder Brother* (left unfinished), with its Cupids, velvet leaves, wanton springs and perfumed flowers – the kind of Elizabethanism that would appeal to a more 'refined' writer.

The clash between citizen and courtier has become the plot *par excellence* in the comedy of Richard Brome (an 'apprentice' of Jonson's, he died in 1652), of whom we should notice *The New Academy* (*c.* 1628) and *The Sparagus Garden* (1635), and also the cheerful piece, *A Jovial Crew, or The Merry Beggars* (1641). The comic possibilities have grown somewhat stereotyped: the citizen is un-couth, well-to-do and ambitious to be polite, while the courtier or gallant is polite (apart from being foul-mouthed), lecherous and ambitious to be well-to-do. The former's money and wife are there-fore to be attempted by the latter. But Brome maintains a precarious balance between them, deferring to 'degree' rather than to fashion. Even so, the differentiation of taste and purpose between the classes is growing plainer.

While Brome and Shirley might be classed as precursors of the Restoration playwrights, that description would do less than justice to the latter writer. James Shirley (1596–1666) is interesting in his own right. Though he shows no original genius, his style is neat, fluent, rather colourless, yet simple rather than insipid. The emotional pressure is never very high, and the metaphorical tension so slack that presumably he wrote in verse only because it was the tradition. Yet this makes for a fresher atmosphere than we find in much of Beaumont and Fletcher. Shirley is concerned with a polite society which has not yet grown altogether complacent about the rest of the world; *Love in a Maze* (1631) and *Hyde Park* (1632) deal with fashionable problems, but the terms are often still Jacobean. In the former play Sir Gervase Simple is described as 'a knight with lordships, but no manors!' [a pun on *manners*], one who

> has crept
> Into a knighthood, which he paid for heartily;
> And, in his best clothes, is suspected for
> A gentleman.
>
> (I. i)

But *The Lady of Pleasure* (1635) is more deserving of attention. Shirley's moderation of outlook can be gauged if we compare the play with Wycherley's *The Country Wife*, which bears a certain similarity in plot. The 'Lady of Pleasure' is Lady Bornwell, who has forced her husband up to town so that she can lead a life *à la mode*. Memories of older ways of living still trouble the social scene; they persist behind her account of a lady's 'morning work':

> LADY BORNWELL. We rise, make fine,
>   Sit for our picture, and 'tis time to dine.
> LITTLEWORTH. Praying's forgot.
> KICKSHAW. 'Tis out of fashion.
>
> (I. i)

There are feelings still in the air which the Restoration 'purified' away: satire against luxury, some genuine appreciation of the country life, a lament for the decay of hospitality ('We do feed like princes, and feast nothing else but princes', II. i). And Bornwell's exit in IV. ii, which takes us back through Jonson right to the Morality, would have seemed naïve, banal or hypocritical to a Restoration audience:

> He is good
> That dares the tempter, yet corrects his blood.

In the end, however, *The Lady of Pleasure* is Restoration. We cannot but feel that Lady Bornwell's final repentance, her willingness to return to the country and submit herself to her husband's will, is largely the result of fear and injured vanity.

Of developments in drama under Charles I, it is only necessary here to mention the French *précieuse* influences, manifested in long and formal debates on the subject of Platonic Love, which – in the plays of Suckling, say – represent a further stage in the depopularization of the theatre. By 1642, when the theatres were officially closed, dramatists had chosen their audience: the court, and not the nation. The Puritan persecution of playwrights and players would naturally confirm them in their choice; they must have seen themselves as more than ever 'the king's men'. And when the court with its changed fashions was restored under Charles II, the fashions of comedy had changed too, for there was no solid weight of belief and opinion to keep it steady.

THE DECLINE OF TRAGEDY

L. G. SALINGAR

The creative period of Elizabethan and Jacobean tragedy had come
to an end when Shakespeare left the theatre in 1613. His successors as
principal writers for the King's Men, the predominant actors' company, were Francis Beaumont (1584/5–1616) and John Fletcher
(1579–1625), who together set their stamp on playwriting for the rest
of the century. The romantic tragedies and tragi-comedies of Beaumont and Fletcher and, after them, of Massinger, Ford, Shirley,
Davenant, and the courtly amateurs under Charles I, developed consistently into the Heroic Drama of the age of Dryden. They mark at
once a decisive change in the social outlook of the theatre and a
striking artistic decadence. In tragic even more than in comic writing
what the late Jacobean and Caroline stages offered was no longer a
representative national art but a diversion for a single class – the court
aristocracy. Middleton's work apart, it was theatrical in the most
limiting senses, emotionally shallow, arbitrary, and confined.

This new phase might be dated from 1609, at a time when division
of feeling between 'court' and 'country' was already apparent; for in
1609 the King's Men began to concentrate on their newly acquired
'private' playhouse, the Blackfriars, where their takings were probably twice as high as at their 'public', unroofed theatre, the Globe.
Henceforth there grew up two kinds of stage public in place of one –
the fashionable patrons of London's three 'private' houses, and the
rowdy populace, with less and less of a middle-class leavening, who
attended the 'public' theatres for old favourites like Marlowe. The
Blackfriars audience was supplied by a kind of syndicate headed by
Beaumont and Fletcher. The younger son of a judge and the younger
son of a worldly Elizabethan bishop, these two writers themselves
were typical members of the new and self-conscious Stuart aristocracy gravitating to London and the Jacobean court.

They worked together from about 1608 to 1613, when Beaumont

married an heiress, and at least fifty-four plays are connected with their names.[1] Two of these are now attributed solely to Beaumont, the better poet; seven, including the most notable, to their partnership; fifteen solely to Fletcher, who prolonged his success until 1625; and the remainder to Fletcher with some indistinct collaborators, principally Massinger, from 1613 onwards. This group of 'Beaumont and Fletcher' plays captured the lead in fashionable taste after Shakespeare's retirement, as stage records indicate: thus, in the years 1616–42, the King's Men alone gave 43 productions of 'Beaumont and Fletcher' at court, or more than a third of their 113 identified court performances, as against sixteen of Shakespeare and only seven of Jonson. And their general repertory for the same years, with 170 plays known on their active list, contained forty-seven of 'Beaumont and Fletcher' beside only sixteen of Shakespeare (less than half his output) and only nine of Jonson. The 1647 Folio of Beaumont and Fletcher, with its chorus of courtly tributes, contains a preface by Shirley, which reveals the nature of their success; theirs, he says, was 'the wit that made the Blackfriars an academy ... usually of more advantage to the hopeful young heir than a costly, dangerous foreign travel, with the assistance of a governing monsieur or signor to boot'. And 'the young spirits of the time', he adds, 'whose birth and quality made them impatient of the sourer ways of education, have from the attentive hearing these pieces, got ground in point of wit and carriage of the most severely-employed students, while these recreations were digested into rules, and the very pleasure did edify'. 'Birth and quality', 'wit and carriage', the promise of exclusive initiation by way of ready-made entertainment – Shirley's advertisement corresponds exactly to the spirit of the plays.

Very little remains in the tragedies of Beaumont and Fletcher and their followers of the national consciousness that Shakespeare had brought to tragedy from his history plays; on the contrary, their heroes and heroines are dwellers in a charmed circle, touchily defensive towards their privileges, but free from any responsibility outwards. The ethical motifs of the revenge plays – the main basis of the older tragedy – have lost their association with the problem of divine justice and shrunk to melodramatic clichés; while the grim, varied humour of the older tragedy is reduced to a low comedy of parvenus and poltroons, monotonously devised to set off the nobility of the main actors. And, as Shirley implies, the main actors themselves have lost contact with 'the sourer ways' of Elizabethan humanism. There is no Faustus, or Hamlet, or Bussy D'Ambois in the later tragedies; the humanist gravity and the note of excited speculation have gone, and with them the tension and the stoic grandeur of the individual profoundly at odds with his universe. Instead, the later heroes conform to a single type. Whether they storm and languish, like Philaster, or 'hold it as commendable to be wealthy in pleasure As others do in rotten sheep and pasture', like the rake in Fletcher's comedy, they are all of them Cavalier gallants idealized, and their adventures move invariably on the plane of love and honour.

With *Philaster* (*c.* 1609) and *A King and No King* (1611), Beaumont and Fletcher introduced a new kind of tragi-comedy, which came to characterize a whole generation. Among many others, there followed such plays as Massinger's *Bondman* (1623), Ford's *Lover's Melancholy* (1628), and *Love and Honour*, by Davenant (1634).[2] The action of these plays commonly passes from a mysterious quarrel or disappearance, through episodes of concealed identity and mistaken purpose, to the moment of discovery that brings about the triumphant dénouement; in other words, they derive from romances like *The Arcadia* (or from recent French or Spanish variants), which lent themselves readily to mannered pastoral scenes (as in Fletcher's *Faithful Shepherdess*; 1608–9), and to high-flown language of courtly compliment. Some tragi-comedies rely on vigorous adventure, like Fletcher's *Island Princess* (*c.* 1621) or Middleton and Rowley's *Spanish Gipsy* (*c.* 1623). Others, with their scenes of religious conversion, renunciation or martyrdom, are coloured by the mood of the Counter-Reformation, like Fletcher and Massinger's *Knight of Malta* (*c.* 1619) and Massinger's *Renegado* (1624) and *The Maid of Honour* (*c.* 1625?). And after 1633, plays intended for the patronage of the Queen, such as Cartwright's *Royal Slave* (1636),[3] preoccupied themselves with the niceties of Platonic love. But the whole series of tragi-comedies from *Philaster* onwards is made up of the chivalric adventures and the love-dilemmas of *The Arcadia*, transposed into terms of Stuart gallantry; and the whole series adopts a tone of flattery towards its public, whether the playwright is nominally exalting, or reproving, or merely providing a day-dream. Moreover, the formal tragedies of Beaumont and Fletcher and their followers are barely to be distinguished from these tragi-comedies; the same romantic style pervades all of their writing.

A theatrical code of honour, exalted and exclusive, contains the whole substance of tragedy or tragi-comedy for Beaumont and Fletcher; and it marks a fundamental difference, despite surface resemblances, from such a play as *Cymbeline*, written about the same time and for the same theatre as *Philaster*. Ostensibly, the code is a rigid one. Yet the dramatists feel it to be insecure, and strain to exalt it for that very reason. The early Stuart aristocracy was divided and disoriented, while 'honour' was a doubtful quantity at the venal court of James I.[4] Hence the dramatists waver or bluster in their treatment of essential themes. Roman plays like Fletcher's *Bonduca* (*c.* 1613) or Fletcher and Massinger's *False One* (*c.* 1620), with their tough, disgruntled officers – a common stage type – imply some uneasy criticism of James's pacific foreign policy and of the atmosphere at court. And a deeper uncertainty pervades Beaumont and Fletcher's treatment of sexual love, shifting from idealization to a boisterous guffaw within the limits of a single play. Where tragic lust is the proposed theme, as in *Cupid's Revenge* (*c.* 1608) or *Thierry and Theodoret* (*c.* 1617), the result is grotesque melodrama; while the more imposing tragi-comedy of *A King and No King*, where the hero is smitten with a supposedly incestuous passion, is only saved from the same effect by the artifice of a concealed identity. Again, Beaumont and Fletcher's *Maid's Tragedy* (*c.* 1610) and Fletcher's *Valentinian* (1610/14) – the two best of their formal tragedies – both present a direct clash between matrimonial honour and loyalty to the throne. Occasionally the playwrights acknowledge their uncertainty, as when Amintor, the wronged husband in *The Maid's Tragedy*, exclaims:

> What a wild beast is uncollected man!
> The thing, that we call honour, bears us all
> Headlong to sin, and yet itself is nothing.
>
> (IV. ii)

But, in general, they bluff their way out of their problems. In *The Maid's Tragedy*, for example, the Ophelia-like second heroine is used to distract attention from the main problem, and in *Valentinian* the avenging husband is so coarsened at the end that his original motives

are forgotten. In both tragedies, the moral issue is first debated, then
burked.

Tragedies and tragi-comedies, then, have the same theatrical purpose – to save the appearances of a social code by the artifice of their
plots. Facility in contriving surprise and suspense takes the place, for
Beaumont and Fletcher, of moral insight or intellectual honesty.

Their heroic characters are always inflated. Honour is immovable,
passion irresistible; alternately shipwrecked and rescued by Fate, their
sentiments are supereminently lofty, arbitrary, and chaotic. The
common tenor of heroic feeling is that of some amazing force surmounting gigantic obstacles; like Philaster in his 'manly rage':

> Set hills on hills betwixt me and the man
> That utters this, and I will scale them all,
> And from the utmost top fall on his neck,
> Like thunder from a cloud;
>
> (II. i)

or, again, like Evadne, in *The Maid's Tragedy*, avenging herself on her
royal seducer:

> ... 'tis so many sins
> An age cannot repent 'em; and so great,
> The gods want mercy for. Yet I must through 'em.
>
> (v. ii)

And the mysterious extravagance of such sentiments is part of their
heroic aura – as when the princely lovers in *Philaster* (IV. iii) prepare
to carry out their suicide pact before the eyes of an astonished rustic.
But it is also characteristic of Beaumont and Fletcher – and increasingly of their successors – that these exalted tones are blended with
pathos, particularly erotic pathos. The same extravagant impulse
drives the forsaken virgin in *The Maid's Tragedy* and the conquering
but love-lorn Arbaces; the one seeks 'Some yet-unpractised way to
grieve and die', the other, in despair, will pull on himself 'a heap
Of strange yet uninvented sin':

> Secret scorching flames
> That far transcend earthly material fires
> Are crept into me, and there is nò cure:
> Is it not strange, Mardonìus, there's no cure?
>
> (*A King and No King*, III. iii)

Moreover, the dramatists have already invited romantic sympathy for Arbaces, precisely on the score of an unstable temperament – his 'sudden extremities' (I. i) – which earlier writers would have treated as a fantastic 'humour'.

For Beaumont and Fletcher, then, heroic self-assertion is finally indistinguishable from self-surrender. An 'empty title' of honour is sufficient either to rouse or to quell a supreme resolution, so that Amintor is checked, in his righteous fury, simply by the 'sacred name' of the King, while in *Valentinian* the dishonoured wife and the dishonoured general both turn to death with automatic abandon. Even the determination to avenge one's honour becomes in the last resort a submission to instinct at once reckless and pathetic. Thus the champion of honour in *The Maid's Tragedy* exclaims:

> I hope my cause is just; I know my blood
> Tells me it is; and I will credit it.
>
> (III. ii)

Coleridge remarks of Beaumont and Fletcher's women that honour for them is 'a sort of talisman, or strange something, that might be lost without the least fault on the part of the owner';[5] and the playwrights can only elevate their heroes' emotions as they do by relieving them of any moral responsibility.

This arbitrary motivation brought about the collapse of Elizabethan stage rhetoric. The collapse can be illustrated by comparing a speech (probably Beaumont's) from *The Maid's Tragedy* (II. i) with another by Heywood from *A Woman Killed With Kindness* (IV. v; 1603). Both passages convey the anguish of an injured husband by means of rhetorical exclamation; but the force of Heywood's writing springs from its very reserve, its bourgeois caution, which makes for tension between the speaker's feelings and his desire for moral balance.

> A general silence hath surprised the house,
> And this is the last door. Astonishment,
> Fear, and amazement play against my heart,
> Even as a madman beats upon a drum.
> Oh, keep my eyes, you Heavens, before I enter,
> From any sight that may transfix my soul;
> Or, if there be so black a spectacle,
> Oh, strike my eyes quite blind; or, if not so,

> Lend me such patience to digest my grief
> That I may keep this white and virgin hand
> From any violent outrage of red murder!
> And with that prayer I enter.

There is a continuous sense of moral values here. But in the speech of Amintor – when, on his wedding night, Evadne has insisted that she will be his wife in name alone – there is no such impression of moral continuity. The writer is not even concerned with personal feeling, so much as with carriage and reputation:

> I know too much. Would I had doubted still!
> Was ever such a marriage night as this!
> Ye powers above, if you did ever mean
> Man should be used thus, you have thought a way
> How he should bear himself, and save his honour.
> Instruct me in it; for to my dull eyes
> There is no mean, no moderate course to run:
> I must live scorn'd, or be a murderer.
> Is there a third? Why is this night so calm?
> Why does not heaven speak in thunder to us,
> And drown her voice?

What is most striking here is the way the speaker surrenders to his confusion. And his horror matches lamely with the conversational, theorizing ring of the language. The empty, sweeping gestures of the verse, the straining and blurring of emotions, are the characteristics of stage decadence.

Nevertheless, this psychology of extremes succeeded with its public. In his preface to the Beaumont and Fletcher Folio, for example, Shirley selects for special praise their handling of 'manly rage' and hapless love, the two stock emotions of the Cavalier theatre. Each of these passions is seemingly all-possessive but both are 'raised to that excellent pitch ... that you shall not choose but consent and go along with them, finding yourself at last grown insensibly the very same person you read'.

Fletcher's second associate, Philip Massinger (1583–1639), had much finer potentialities. He is a serious and skilful playwright, judicious and eloquent. He is easily strongest, with Jonson's examples behind him, as the moral satirist of *A New Way to Pay Old Debts* (c. 1625) and *The City Madam* (1632). But his tragedies and tragi-comedies, the bulk of his work, are at best coldly impressive, at their worst simply dull. They suffer from the influence of Beaumont and Fletcher in their wilful romanticism and their over-contrived plots. And Massinger's fatal defect is what T. S. Eliot calls his lack of mental courage, his 'impoverishment of feeling'.

The son of a gentleman serving the Herbert family, Massinger was a supporter of William Herbert, Earl of Pembroke, the chief of the peers opposed to Buckingham's administration. His plays contain on-slaughts on Buckingham's foreign policy, conceived as the product of a mercenary and effeminate society;[6] they hark back to the Tudor world of the great noble household, orderly and independent, with an honoured place for the humanist as a moral adviser. Unlike Fletcher, therefore, he will not identify himself with his audience; his constant aim is to instruct, to drive home a lesson in morality. But his morality is academic. His verse rhetoric has developed away from emotion, towards the marshalling of argument; and his borrowings from classical literature, as from Shakespeare, are an expression of his taste, not his imagination. He is a Stoic, but with none of Chapman's intensity or daring; virtue for him is chiefly the heroism of the defeated, as with Camiola at the climax of The Maid of Honour, 'dead to the world', or the 'passive fortitude' of the exiled king throughout Believe As You List (1631).

Massinger can never really decide between his conservative ethics and the romantic values of Fletcher. Consequently the feelings and even the action of his plays fall apart. In his favourite tragedy, The Roman Actor (1626), he abandons the main plot for a long digression about the dignity of the stage. The Duke of Milan (c. 1621) presents an unstable hero in the manner of A King and No King, and in the same manner shifts its moral ground by a theatrical trick. The Bond-man claps together an Arcadian love story and a politically pointed history; perhaps it was intended to find unity in the theme of slavery to the passions, but no such unity is achieved. And a similar disunity mars the two domestic tragedies, The Fatal Dowry (c. 1619) and The Unnatural Combat (c. 1626). In all these plays Massinger fails because he shies away from his main problem, the actual human significance of 'honour'.

The Fatal Dowry (written with Nathan Field) makes a favourable example. Here Charalois, the man of honour, is zealous for his principles, otherwise modest and reserved. The first action shows his self-sacrifice for the memory of his noble father; the second, and main, action concerns his marriage, his wife's betrayal, and his subsequent revenge. After carefully building up sympathy for Charalois, the play ends with a catastrophe which is both an effective *coup de théâtre* and a neat restatement of the doctrine that revenge must be left to heaven. In a sense this moral reversal at the end has been prepared for by the solemn atmosphere of three separate trial scenes; but it makes a debating point, not a dramatic resolution, because the hero's direct emotions, dramatically the crux of the matter, have been dismissed in the body of the play with a few trite phrases. As a whole, the play reveals Fletcher's code of honour warping what is left of the old revenge conventions[7] – though it is still virile by comparison with the sentimental revised version by Rowe, *The Fair Penitent* (1703).

The emotional hollowness of *The Fatal Dowry* and its forensic atmosphere are equally significant. Massinger's people can only convey emotion in the style of Beaumont and Fletcher, by superlatives of quantity; or else they plead a case about themselves, justifying or condemning. The wife's confession in *The Fatal Dowry* is typical in its moral tone and its incongruously leisured, deliberate construction:

> O my fate!
> That never would consent that I should see
> How worthy you were both of love and duty,
> Before I lost you; and my misery made
> The glass in which I now behold your virtue!
> While I was good, I was a part of you,
> And of two, by the virtuous harmony
> Of our fair minds, made one; but since I wandered
> In the forbidden labyrinth of lust,
> What was inseparable is by me divided. —
> With justice, therefore, you may cut me off,
> And from your memory wash the remembrance
> That e'er I was; like to some vicious purpose
> Which, in your better judgement, you repent of,
> And study to forget.
>
> (IV. iv)

The colourless imagery here, beside the elaborate, even sinuous conduct of the periods, shows how Massinger has distorted the verse rhetoric of the stage. He has reduced it to an etiquette of external declamation, anticipating a Caroline refinement perhaps, but losing the sap of the Elizabethans. He is elegant without exactness and ponderous without weight.

In Massinger the characters are always self-conscious, but conscious of themselves as public voices, reputations. Conversely, the characters of John Ford (1586–1639?) reflect the taste of their period for aristocratic privacy.[8] The old stage setting of public bustle has receded; the distinctive note of the speeches is subdued, introspective. Ford is the most delicate stage poet of his time; but, on the other hand, the pathos of frustration is his only subject. His three main tragedies – following *The Lover's Melancholy* in the years 1628–32 – bear the eloquent titles of *'Tis Pity She's a Whore*, *The Broken Heart*, and *Love's Sacrifice*; while his soberest work, *Perkin Warbeck* (c. 1633), nominally historical, becomes a study of passive constancy and fortitude, in a mood recalling Massinger. Ford's indifference to public values, however, marks a further degree in the social conversion of tragedy. Above all, it marks the dissolution of tragedy as an art, since the poet has no objective standard of judgement remaining to check his liquefying emotions.

Although he follows Burton's psychology, and although he stresses the conflict between desires of the heart and 'the laws of conscience and of civil use', Ford is no modernist pleading for release of inhibitions, as several critics have suggested.[9] Pathos is his aim, not moral revolt. The theme of incest in *'Tis Pity*, for example, is not analysed psychologically but is presented as a supreme case of star-cross'd love, essentially the same in kind as that of Romeo and Juliet. And the same pathos is invoked, in *The Broken Heart*, for the virtuous Penthea, who wastes away under a yoke that she regards as legalized adultery because it breaks her pre-contract with her lover, Orgilus; or, again, for Fernando and Bianca in *Love's Sacrifice*, withholding from technical adultery but expiring as the martyrs of Platonic restraint. Clearly, Ford intends to make these restraints on love come more and more from within. Nevertheless, his object here as a dramatist, recalling Webster in *The Duchess of Malfi*, is simply to exploit the pathos of a noble suffering. With Fernando, with Penthea, with the miraculous composure of Calantha also in *The Broken Heart*, and again in *Perkin*

Warbeck, a melancholy resignation forms the core of the drama: 'They are the silent griefs which cut the heart-strings'. It is a variant of the older stoicism, but a stoicism now entirely self-pitying and theatrical. The air is warm with the altar-smoke and tears of amorous devotion, with the steam of transfixed and bleeding hearts. Apart from their resignation, moreover, Ford's lovers can only flounder despairingly. Hence the emotional restraint which ties the knot of his tragedies passes directly into a yearning for release through death.

Sometimes this prevailing mood rises to the anguish of *'Tis Pity*:

> Brother, dear brother, know what I have been,
> And know that now there's but a dining-time
> 'Twixt us and our confusion;

more generally, it keeps to the listless, nostalgic cadence of *The Broken Heart*:

> Death waits to waft me to the Stygian banks,
> And free me from this chaos of my bondage;

in either case, it remains the mood of a man who has turned his back on life. Yet there is also a complacent, a sophisticated air about Ford, most noticeable in the scenes of mannered perversity – evidently to the taste of the day[10] – like those where Giovanni murders his sister and then astounds the banqueters with her heart 'upon his dagger', or where Orgilus courteously bleeds Ithocles to death. And Ford's obsessive monotony is all the more striking because his major work is full of borrowings and echoes from Shakespeare's generation; he even keeps the plot machinery of the old revenge plays. Since he had published his first poems as early as 1606 and was writing for the stage by 1621 – originally, as a partner of Dekker and of Webster – he can be regarded, in stage history, as a belated Jacobean. In the disintegration of tragedy, he is the successor to Webster – but a Webster whose sombre power has been filtered off through Beaumont and Fletcher's romanticism.

Ford is also the first, and by far the best, of the Caroline tragic playwrights. His relaxed pathos, his punctilio, his sentimental ardours represent the courtly ideal of Davenant, Shirley, and the amateurs of the 1630s. But the dramatic style of his younger rivals sinks to incredible levels of dreariness. They are wooden and precious in their approach to tragedy or tragi-comedy; above all, they are bored. And even in the more congenial form of the masque, Milton's *Comus* (1634), the one living work of the period, stands apart from the courtly theatre and reverts for its poetry to Shakespeare, not to any writer for the Caroline stage.

With Beaumont and Fletcher, then, the theatre had ceased to attract the best poets or demand the best from the intelligence of its public. Not only a puritan like Milton but a courtly poet like George Herbert seems to belong to a different world. Tragedy suffered more than the other forms of drama from the resulting mental debility.

NOTES

1. See U. M. Ellis-Fermor, *Jacobean Drama* (1947 edn), 308ff., 328ff., on the authorship of the 'Beaumont and Fletcher' plays, but see also C. Leech, *The John Fletcher Plays*. For their stage history, see G. E. Bentley, *Jacobean and Caroline Stage*; and 'Shakespeare and the Blackfriars Theatre', in *Shakespeare Survey*, I, ed. A. Nicoll (1948).

2. See J. W. Tupper's edition of *Love and Honour* (Boston, 1909); cp. L. B. Wallis, *Fletcher, Beaumont and Company*.

3. In W. Cartwright, *Plays and Poems* (ed. G. Blakemore Evans, University of Wisconsin, 1951).

4. cp. C. H. Firth, *The House of Lords during the Civil War* (1910), chs i–ii. See above, pp. 30–31, 36–7.

5. S. T. Coleridge, *Select Poetry and Prose* (ed. S. Potter), 409; cp. 393ff.

6. See S. R. Gardiner, *The Political Element in Massinger* (*Transactions of the New Shakespeare Society*, 1875–6) and *History of England, 1603–42*, VII, 200–204, 327–41; also B. T. Spencer's edition of *The Bondman* (Princeton, 1932). On Pembroke, see Clarendon's *History* (1826 edn), I, 100–102; cp. M. Heinemann, *Puritanism and Theatre* (which shows that there was more political opposition in the drama of Massinger's time than the present article suggests).

7. cp. F. T. Bowers, *Elizabethan Revenge Tragedy*, ch. vi.

8. cp. D. Mathew, *The Age of Charles I*, ch. x. See C. Leech, *Ford and the Drama of his Time*. For fresh assessments of *Perkin Warbeck*, see P. Ure's edn and A. Barton in *English Drama*, ed. M. Axton and R. Williams, 69–93.

9. e.g. G. F. Sensabaugh, *The Tragic Muse of John Ford*. The view taken here follows P. Ure's articles on *Love's Sacrifice* (1950) and on *The Broken Heart* (1951: both reprinted in his *Elizabethan and Jacobean Drama*).

10. See *'Tis Pity*, v. vi, *The Broken Heart*, IV. iv, *Love's Sacrifice*, v. iii; and cp. Sir William Davenant, *The Cruel Brother* (v. i; 1627: *Dramatic Works*, ed. J. Maidment and W. H. Logan, I); James Shirley, *The Traitor* (v. i; 1631).

Among recent studies of this period, s. Schoenbaum challenges the concept of 'decadence' in *Dramaturgie et Société*, ed. J. Jacquot, 829–45, and M. Neill illustrates the sophistication of theatrical taste in 'The Caroline Audience', in *Studies in English Literature*, XVIII (1978); cp. Bradbrook, *Themes and Conventions* (2nd edn), 256–60, 266.

PART IV

APPENDIX

COMPILED BY BRIAN VICKERS

To avoid unnecessary duplication books which are referred to frequently in the Author bibliographies are grouped together in Section VII ('General Studies and Collected Essays'), and numbered in sequence. References to them later are by their number and the author's surname.

C.H.E.L.	Cambridge History of English Literature
E.E.T.S.	Early English Text Society
E.L.H.	ELH. A Journal of English Literary History
E.L.	Everyman's Library edition
E & S	Essays and Studies
J.W.C.I.	Journal of the Warburg and Courtauld Institutes
M.S.	Mermaid Series edition
N.M.	New Mermaid edition
P.B.A.	Proceedings of the British Academy
P.M.L.A.	Publications of the Modern Language Association of America
R.E.S.	Review of English Studies
R.P.	Revels Plays edition
R.R.D.S.	Regent's Renaissance Drama Series edition
R.Q.	Renaissance Quarterly
Sh. Q.	Shakespeare Quarterly
Sh. S.	Shakespeare Survey
T.R.H.S.	Transactions of the Royal Historical Society
W.C.	World's Classics edition
W.T.W.	Writers and their Work (British Council bio-bibliographical pamphlets)
ed., edn	edited, edition
facs.	facsimile
pub.	published
repr.	reprinted
rev.	revised
tr.	translated
b.	born
d.	died
c.	circa
?	probably

FOR FURTHER READING AND REFERENCE

The Social Setting

I. HISTORY AND POLITICS (see also II, IV)

Allen, J. W. *History of Political Thought in the 16th Century* (London, 1928); *English Political Thought, 1603-60* (London, 1938)

Appleby, A. B. *Famine in Tudor and Stuart England* (Stanford, Ca., 1978)

Ashley, M. *England in the 17th Century* (Pelican, 1952)

Ashton, R. *The City and the Court, 1603-1643* (Cambridge, 1979)

Aylmer, G. E. *The King's Servants* (London, 1961)

Baker, H. *The Race of Time. Three Lectures on Renaissance Historiography* (Toronto, 1967)

Baumer, F. L. *The Early Tudor Theory of Kingship* (New Haven, 1940)

Beckingsale, B. W. *Elizabeth I* (London, 1963)

Bindoff, S. T., *Tudor England* (Pelican, 1950)

Bindoff, S. T. et al. (eds) *Elizabethan Government and Society: essays presented to Sir John Neale* (London, 1961); especially J. Hurstfield. 'The Succession Struggle in Late Elizabethan England' and W. T. MacCaffrey, 'Place and Patronage in Elizabethan Politics'

Black, J. B. *The Reign of Elizabeth* (Oxford, 1936)

Bourcier, E. (ed.) *The Diary of Sir Simonds D'Ewes 1622-1624* (Paris, 1974)

Bridenbaugh, C. *Vexed and Troubled Englishmen 1590-1642. The Beginnings of the American People* (Oxford, 1968)

Camden, William. *The History of the Most Renowned and Victorious Princess Elizabeth, Late Queen of England*, sel. ed. W. T. MacCaffrey (Chicago, 1970)

Carter, C. H. (ed.) *From the Renaissance to the Counter-Reformation: Essays in Honour of Garret Mattingly* (New York, 1965)

Cheyney, E. P. *A History of England, 1588-1603* (2 vols, London, 1926)

Cruickshank, C. G. *Elizabeth's Army* (2nd edn Oxford, 1966)

Davies, G. *The Early Stuarts* (Oxford, 1937)

Dewar, M. *Sir Thomas Smith: a Tudor Intellectual in Office* (London, 1964)

Dunkel, W. *William Lambarde, Elizabethan Jurist 1536-1601* (New Brunswick, N. J., 1965)

Elliott, J. H. *Europe Divided, 1559-1598* (London, 1968)

Elton, G. R. *England Under the Tudors* (London, 1955; rev. 1962); *The Tudor Constitution* (Cambridge, 1960)

Esler, A. *The Aspiring Mind of the Elizabethan Younger Generation* (Durham, N. C., 1966)

Evans, J. X. (ed.) *The Works of Sir Roger Williams* (Oxford, 1972): military treatises

Ferguson, A. B. *Clio Unbound. Perception of the Social and Cultural Past in Renaissance England* (Durham, N. C., 1979)

Fox, L., (ed.) *English Historical Scholarship in the 16th and 17th Centuries* (London, 1956)

Fussner, F. S. *The Historical Revolution: English Historical Writing and Thought, 1580–1640* (London, 1962); *Tudor History and the Historians* (New York, 1970)

Gardiner, S. R. *A History of England, 1603–42*: I–IV (London, 1883–4)

Greenleaf, W. H. *Order, Empiricism and Politics: Two Traditions of English Political Thought, 1500–1700* (London, 1964)

Hale, D. G. *The Body Politic: A Political Metaphor in Renaissance English Literature* (The Hague, 1971)

Harrison, G. B. *Elizabethan Journals, 1591–1603* (3 vols, London, 1928–33); *A Jacobean Journal* (London, 1940); *The Life and Death of Robert Devereux Earl of Essex* (London, 1937)

Hexter, J. H. *Reappraisals in History* (London, 1961)

Hill, C. *The Century of Revolution 1603–1714* (2nd edn, London, 1980)

Holdsworth, W. S. *History of English Law*: IV–V (London, 1924); see also Vol. I in 7th edn, rev. S. B. Chrimes (London, 1956)

Hurstfield, J. *Elizabeth I and the Unity of England* (London, 1960)

Jones, W. J. *The Elizabethan Court of Chancery* (Oxford, 1967)

Kantorowicz, E. H. *The King's Two Bodies* (Princeton, N. J., 1957)

Lamont, W. and Oldfield, S. (eds) *Politics, Religion and Literature in the Seventeenth Century* (London, 1975; E.L.)

Levine, M. (ed.) *Tudor England, 1485–1603. A Bibliographical Handbook* (Cambridge, 1968)

Levy, F. J. *Tudor Historical Thought* (San Marino, Ca., 1967)

MacCaffrey, W. *The Shaping of the Elizabethan Regime* (Princeton, 1968)

McConica, J. K., *English Humanists and Reformation Politics* (Oxford, 1965)

McIlwain, C. H. (ed.) *The Political Works of James I* (Cambridge, Mass., 1918)

Mares, F. H. (ed.) *The Memoirs of Robert Carey* (Oxford, 1972)

Mathew, D. *James I* (London, 1967)

Mattingly, G. *Renaissance Diplomacy* (London, 1955; Peregrine, 1965); *The Defeat of the Spanish Armada* (London, 1959)

Morris, C. *Political Thought in England: Tyndale to Hooker* (London, 1953)

Neale, J. E. *Queen Elizabeth* (London, 1934; Pelican, 1960); 'The Elizabethan Political Scene', in P.B.A. XXIV (1948) and in *Catherine de Medici* (below); *The Elizabethan House of Commons* (London, 1949, Peregrine, 1963); *Elizabeth I and her Parliaments* (2 vols, London, 1953–7); *Essays in Elizabethan History* (London, 1949); *The Age of Catherine de Medici and other Essays* (London, 1963)

Notestein, W. 'The Winning of the Initiative by the House of Commons', in P.B.A. XI (1924); repr. 1968

Pearson, A. F. S. *Church and State: Political Aspects of Sixteenth-century Puritanism* (Cambridge, 1928)

Pennington, D., and Thomas, K. (eds) *Puritans and Revolutionaries, Essays in 17th-Century History Presented to Christopher Hill* (Oxford, 1979)

Praz, M. 'Machiavelli and the Elizabethans', in P.B.A. XIII (1928), and in *The Flaming Heart* (New York, 1958)

Raab, F. *The English Face of Machiavelli* (London, 1964); but see S. Anglo, 'The Reception of Machiavelli in Tudor England: a Reassessment' in *Il Politico* (University of Pavia), XXXI (1966)

Read, C. *Mr Secretary Walsingham and the Policy of Queen Elizabeth* (3 vols, Oxford, 1925); *The Tudors: Personalities and Practical Politics in 16th Century England* (New York, 1936); *Mr Secretary Cecil and Queen Elizabeth* (London, 1955); *Lord Burghley and Queen Elizabeth* (London, 1960)

Read, C. (ed.) *Bibliography of British History: Tudor period, 1485–1603* (2nd edn, Oxford, 1959)

Rice, G. P. (ed.) *The Public Speaking of Queen Elizabeth: Selections from her Official Addresses* (New York, 1951)

Rowse, A. L. *The Expansion of Elizabethan England* (London, 1955)

Russell, C. *The Crisis of Parliaments. English History, 1509–1660* (London, 1971)

Smith, A. G. R. *The Government of Elizabethan England* (London, 1967); (ed.) *The Reign of James VI and I* (London, 1973)

Smith, L. B. 'English Treason Trials and Confessions in the 16th Century', *Journal of the History of Ideas*, XV (1954)

Talbert, E. W. *The Problem of Order. Elizabethan Political Commonplaces* (Chapel Hill, N. C., 1962)

Trevelyan, G. M. *England Under the Stuarts* (London, 1904)

Walcott, R., *The Tudor-Stuart Period of English History (1485–1714): a Review of Changing Interpretations* (New York, 1964)

Wernham, W. B. (ed.) *New Cambridge Modern History*, Vol. III: *The Counter-Reformation and Price Revolution, 1559–1610* (Cambridge, 1968)

Williams, P. *The Tudor Regime* (Oxford, 1979)

Williamson, J. B. *The Myth of the Conqueror: Prince Henry Stuart, a Study in 17th Century Personation* (New York, 1978)

Willson, D. H. *The Privy Councillors in the House of Commons 1604–29* (Minneapolis, 1940); *King James VI and I* (London, 1956)

Wilson, C. *England's Apprenticeship, 1603–1673* (London, 1965)

Zagorin, P. *The Court and the Country. The Beginning of the English Revolution* (London, 1969)

Zeefeld, W. G. *Foundations of Tudor Policy* (Cambridge, Mass., 1948)

II. THE SOCIAL AND ECONOMIC BACKGROUND

Bacon, F. *Essays* (1597–1625; W.C. and E.L.); *Letters and Life*, 7 vols, in *Works* ed. Spedding (London 1857–1874; New York, 1968)

Bamford, F. (ed.) *A Royalist's Notebook, 1622–52* (London, 1936)

Birch, T. (ed.) *The Court and Times of James* (2 vols, London, 1848)

Breton, N. *A Mad World My Masters and Other Prose Works* ed. U. Kentish-Wright (2 vols, London, 1929)

Byrne, M. St C. (ed.) *The Elizabethan Home* (London, 1949)

Cavendish, G. *Life of Wolsey* (1557; E.E.T.S., 1959); ed. R. Sylvester (London, 1962)

Chamberlain, John *Letters*, ed. N. E. McClure (2 vols, Philadelphia, 1939); ed. E. Thomson (London, 1966)

Dekker, T. *The Gull's Hornbook* (1609; Temple Classics)

Donno, E. S. (ed.) *An Elizabethan in 1582: The Diary of Richard Madox, Fellow of All Souls* (London, 1976)

Dunham, W. H., and Pargellis, S. (eds) *Complaint and Reform in England, 1463–1714* (New York, 1938, 1968)

Furnivall, F. J. (ed.) *Robert Laneham's Letter ... the Entertainment at Kenilworth* (1575; London, 1907)

Hakluyt, R. *Voyages* (1582; E.L. 8 vols); selections ed. J. Beeching (Penguin, 1972)

Harington, Sir John *A New Discourse of a Stale Subject. The Metamorphosis of Ajax*, ed. E. S. Donno (London, 1962); *Nugae Antiquae* (personal notes and letters; 2 vols, ed. T. Park, 1804)

Harrison, W. *Elizabethan England* (i.e. Harrison's *Description*, 1577–87); ed. L. Withington and F. J. Furnivall (London, 1876); ed. G. Edelen (Ithaca, N.Y., 1968)

Hazlitt, W. C. (ed.) *Inedited Tracts. Illustrating the Manners ... of Englishmen; 1579–1618* (Roxburghe Library, 1868; New York, 1963)

Herbert of Cherbury *Autobiography*, ed. J. M. Shuttleworth (London, 1976)

Judges, A. V. (ed.) *The Elizabethan Underworld* (London, 1930; 1965)

Kinney, A. F. (ed.) *Elizabethan Backgrounds* (Hamden, Conn., 1975)

Lambarde, W. *Eirenarcha* (1602); *Archeion: or, a Discourse upon the High Courts of Justice in England,* ed. C. H. McIlwain and P. L. Ward (Cambridge, Mass., 1957)

Lamond, E. (ed.) *A Discourse of the Common Weal* (1549; Cambridge, 1893)

Naunton, Sir R. *Fragmenta Regalia* (1641) ed. E. Arber (London, 1930); on Elizabeth's courtiers

Nichols, J. *The Progresses of Queen Elizabeth* (3 vols, London, 1823; New York, 1966); *The Progresses of King James I* (4 vols, London, 1828; New York, 1966)

Percy, H. (Earl of Northumberland) *Advice to His Son* (1609; ed. G. B. Harrison, London, 1930)

Quinn, D. B. and A. M. (eds) *Virginia Voyages from Hakluyt* (London, 1973)

Quinn, D. B. (ed.) *The Last Voyage of Thomas Cavendish, 1591–1592* (Chicago, 1975)

Smith, Sir Thomas *De Republica Anglorum* (in English, 1583); ed. L. Alston (Cambridge, 1906); see Talbert, no. 39 in section VII below

Smyth, J. *The Berkeley Manuscripts* (*c.* 1618); ed. Sir John Maclean (3 vols, London, 1883)

Sorlien, R. P. (ed.) *The Diary of John Manningham of the Middle Temple, 1602–03* (Hanover, N. H., 1977)

Stow, J. *A Survey of London*, ed. C. L. Kingsford (2 vols, Oxford, 1908); ed. H. B. Wheatley (E.L.)

Stubbes, P. *Anatomy of Abuses* (1583); ed. F. J. Furnivall (London, 1877)

Tawney, R. H., and Power, E. (eds) *Tudor Economic Documents* (3 vols, London, 1924)

Ungerer, G. (ed.) *A Spaniard in Elizabethan England: The Correspondence of Antonio Pérez's Exile* (2 vols, London, 1976)

Wilson, J. Dover (ed.) *Life in Shakespeare's England* (1911; Pelican, 1944)

Wilson, T. (the elder) *A Discourse upon Usury* (1572); ed., with Introduction, by R. H. Tawney (London, 1925)

Wilson, T. (the younger) *The State of England, A.D. 1600*; ed. F. J. Fisher, *Camden Miscellany* XVI (1936)

Wright, L. B. (ed.) *The Elizabethans' America* (London, 1965)

Akrigg, G. P. V. *Jacobean Pageant; or, The Court of King James I* (Cambridge, Mass., 1962)

Anglo, S. *Spectacle, Pageantry, and Early Tudor Policy* (Oxford, 1969)

Ashton, R. (ed.) *James I By His Contemporaries* (London, 1969)

Aydelotte, F. *Elizabethan Rogues and Vagabonds* (Oxford, 1913)

Byrne, M. St C. *Elizabethan Life in Town and Country* (rev. edn, London, 1961)

Camden, C. *The Elizabethan Woman: a Panorama of English Womanhood 1540–1640* (London, 1952)

Campbell, M. *The English Yeoman* (*under Elizabeth and the Early Stuarts*) (New York, 1942)

Clapham, J. H. *A Concise Economic History of Britain* (Cambridge, 1949)

Clark, G. N. *The Wealth of England, 1496–1760* (London, 1946)

Clark, P., and Slack, P., (eds) *Crisis and Order in English Towns 1500–1700: Essays in Urban History* (London, 1972)

Coleman, D. C., and John, A. H. (eds) *Trade, Government and Economy in Pre-Industrial England: Essays Presented to F. J. Fisher* (London, 1976)

Cross, C. *The Puritan Earl: the Life of Henry Hastings* (London, 1960)

Dodd, A. H. *Life in Elizabethan England* (London, 1961)

Dunlop, I. *Palaces and Progresses of Elizabeth I* (London, 1962)

Fisher, F. J. 'The Development of London as a Centre of Conspicuous Consumption in the 16th and 17th Centuries', in T.R.H.S. XXX (1948); 'Commercial Trends . . . in 16th Century England' and 'London's Export Trade in the Early 17th century' in *Essays in Economic History*, ed. E. M. Carus-Wilson (London, 1954)

Fisher, F. J. (ed.) *Essays in the Economic and Social History of Tudor and Stuart England in Honour of R. H. Tawney* (Cambridge, 1961)

Fox, E. 'The Diary of an Elizabethan Gentlewoman', in T.R.H.S. II (1908)

Gleason, J. H. *The Justices of the Peace in England 1558–1640* (Oxford, 1969)

Heckscher, E. *Mercantilism*, rev. E. F. Söderlund (2 vols, London, 1956)

Hexter, J. *Reappraisals in History* (London, 1961): chs iv, 'The Education of the Aristocracy in the Renaissance'; v, 'The Myth of the Middle Class in Tudor England'; vi, 'Storm Over the Gentry'.

Hill, J. W. *Tudor and Stuart Lincoln* (Cambridge, 1956)

Hoskins, W. G. 'The Leicestershire Farmer in the 16th Century', in *Essays in Leicestershire History* (Liverpool, 1951); 'An Elizabethan provincial town: Leicester', in *Studies in Social History*, ed. J. H. Plumb (London, 1955)

Hurstfield. J. *The Queen's Wards: Wardship and Marriage under Elizabeth I* (London, 1958)

Jordan, W. K. *Philanthropy in England 1480–1660: a Study of the Changing Pattern of English Social Aspirations* (London, 1959)

Kamen, H., *The Iron Century: Social Change in Europe 1550–1660* (London, 1971)

Kerridge, E. *Agrarian Problems in the Sixteenth Century and After* (London, 1969)

Knights, L. C. *Drama and Society in the Age of Jonson* (London, 1937)

Laslett, P. *The World We Have Lost* (London, 1965)

Lee, S. (ed.) *Shakespeare's England* (2 vols, Oxford, 1916)

Lipson, E. *Economic History of England*: II–III (London, 1943 edn)

MacCaffrey, W. T. *Exeter, 1540–1650: the Growth of an English Country Town* (Cambridge, Mass., 1958)

Mathew, D. *The Jacobean Age* (London, 1938); *The Age of Charles I* (London, 1951)

Mohl, R. *The Three Estates in Medieval and Renaissance England* (New York, 1933)

Nef, J. U. *Industry and Government in France and England, 1540–1640* (Philadelphia, 1940)

Nicoll, A. (ed.) *Shakespeare Survey*, XVII (1964): 'Shakespeare in his Own Age'.

Notestein, W. *English Folk* (London, 1938); *The English People on the Eve of Colonization, 1603–1630* (London, 1954)

Parks, G. B. *Richard Hakluyt and the English Voyages* (rev. edn, New York, 1961)

Pearson, L. E. *Elizabethans at Home* (Stanford, 1957, 1967)

Pendry, E. D. *Elizabethan Prisons and Prison Scenes* (Salzburg, 1974)

Plucknett, T. F. *A Concise History of the Common Law* (5th edn, London, 1956)

Powell, C. *English Domestic Relations, 1487–1653* (New York, 1917)

Prest, W. R. *The Inns of Court under Elizabeth I and the Early Stuarts 1590–1640* (London, 1972)

Prestwich, M. *Cranfield: Politics and Profits under the Early Stuarts* (Oxford, 1966)

Quinn, D. B. (ed.) *The Hakluyt Handbook* (2 vols, London, 1974)

Ramsey, P. *Tudor Economic Problems* (London, 1963); *The Price Revolution in Sixteenth-Century England* (London, 1971)

Reynolds, G. *Elizabethan and Jacobean Costume, 1558–1625* (London, 1951)

Richardson, W. C. *A History of the Inns of Court: with Special Reference to the Period of the Renaissance* (Louisiana, 1979)

Robertson, H. M. *The Rise of Economic Individualism* (Cambridge, 1933)

Rowse, A. L. *The England of Elizabeth; the Structure of Society* (London, 1951)

Salgādo, G. *The Elizabethan Underworld* (London, 1975)

Samuelsson, K. *Religion and Economic Action*, tr. E. G. French and D. C. Coleman (London, 1961): a critique of Tawney and Weber.

Sargent, R. M. *At the Court of Queen Elizabeth: the Life and Lyrics of Sir Edward Dyer* (London, 1935; Oxford, 1968)

Simpson, A. *The Wealth of the Gentry, 1540–1660. East Anglian Studies* (Cambridge, 1961)

Stone, L. *The Crisis of the Aristocracy 1558–1641* (Oxford, 1965); (abridged edn, London, 1967); *The Causes of the English Revolution 1529–1642* (London, 1972); *The Family: Sex and Marriage in England, 1500–1800* (New York, 1977)

Stone, L. (ed.) *Social Change and Revolution in England, 1540–1640* (London, 1965): review of the controversy over the status of the gentry, with important essays by Hexter, Trevor-Roper, Stone, Tawney, Hill, and others.

Strachan, M. *The Life and Adventures of Thomas Coryate* (Oxford, 1962)

Strong, R. C. 'The Popular Celebration of the Accession Day of Queen Elizabeth I', in J.W.C.I. XXI (1958); *The Renaissance Garden in England* (London, 1979)

Supple, B. E., *Commercial Crisis and Change in England, 1600–1642* (Cambridge, 1959)

Tawney, R. H. *The Agrarian Problem in the 16th Century* (London, 1912; New York, 1967); *Religion and the Rise of Capitalism* (London, 1937 edn); but see Samuelsson, above; *Social History and Literature* (Cambridge, 1950); 'The Rise of the Gentry, 1558–1640' and 'Postscript', in *Essays in Economic History*, ed. E. M. Carus-Wilson (London, 1954); *Business and Politics under James I: Lionel Cranfield as Merchant and Minister* (Cambridge, 1958)

Thirsk, J. (ed.) *The Agrarian History of England and Wales, IV, 1500–1640* (Cambridge, 1967)

Traill, H. D. and Mann, J. S. (eds) *Social England*, Illustrated edn, II–III (London, 1902)

Trevelyan, G. M. *English Social History* (London, 1940); Illustrated edn, II (London, 1950; Pelican, 1967)

Unwin, G. *Industrial Organisation in the 16th and 17th Centuries* (London, 1904); *Studies in Economic History* (London, 1927); *The Gilds and Companies of London* (London, 1938 edn); *Collected Papers*, ed. R. H. Tawney (London, 1958)

Waldman, M. *Elizabeth and Leicester* (London, 1950)

Williams, P. *Life in Tudor England* (London, 1964)

Wilson, E. C. *England's Eliza* (Cambridge, Mass., 1939; 1966)

Wilson, F. P. *The Plague in Shakespeare's London* (Oxford, 1927, 1963)

Yates, F. A. 'Queen Elizabeth as Astraea', in J.W.C.I. X (1947); 'Elizabethan

Chivalry', in J.W.C.I., XX (1947); *Astraea: The Imperial Theme in the Six-teenth Century* (London, 1975)

Zagorin, P. *The Court and the Country* (London, 1969): Puritanism and the Civil War.

The Cultural Setting

III. EDUCATION: INTELLECTUAL AND SOCIAL IDEALS

Ascham, R. *The Schoolmaster* (1570; ed. Wright, Cambridge, 1904)

Bacon, F. *Essays* (1597–1625; W.C. and E.L.); *The Advancement of Learning* (1605; W.C. and E.L.)

Campbell, L. B. (ed.) *The Mirror for Magistrates* (1559–1610; Cambridge, 1938); *Additions* (Cambridge, 1946); repr. (New York, 1960)

Castiglione, B. *The Book of the Courtier* (1528; tr. Sir Thomas Hoby, 1561; E.L.), tr. C. S. Singleton (New York, 1959); tr. G. Bull (Penguin, 1967)

Cornwallis, Sir W. *Essayes* (1600–1601; ed. D. C. Allen, Baltimore, 1946)

Cressy, D. (ed.) *Education in Tudor and Stuart England* (London, 1975)

Daniel, S. *Musophilus: Containing a General Defence of all Learning*, ed. R. Himelick (West Lafayette, Ind., 1965); also in *Poems* ed. Sprague.

Elyot, Sir T. *The Governor* (1531; E.L.); ed. H. S. Croft (2 vols, London, 1880)

Erasmus, D. *Colloquies*, tr. C. R. Thompson (Chicago, 1965)

More, Sir T. *Utopia* (1516; tr. R. Robynson, 1551; E.L.); ed. E. Surtz and J. Hexter (New Haven, 1964); tr. P. Turner (Penguin, 1965)

North, Sir T. *Lives of the Noble Grecians and Romans ... by Plutarch* (tr. 1579); selection, ed. R. H. Carr (Oxford, 1906); selection, *Shakespeare's Plutarch*, ed. T. J. B. Spencer (Penguin, 1967)

Peacham, H. *The Complete Gentleman* (1622); ed. G. S. Gordon (Oxford, 1906); ed., with other works, by V. B. Heltzel (Ithaca, N.Y., 1962)

Pepper, R. D. (ed.) *Four Tudor Books on Education* (Gainesville, Fla., 1966): T. Elyot, *The Education or Bringing up of Children*; F. Clement, *The Petie Schole with an English Orthographie*; D. Fenner, *The Arts of Logicke and Rethorike*; W. Kempe, *The Education of Children in Learning*.

Watson, F. (ed.) *Vives: On Education* (Cambridge, 1913)

Wright, L. B. (ed.) *Advice to a Son: Precepts of Lord Burghley, Sir Walter Raleigh, and Francis Osborne* (Ithaca, N. Y., 1962)

Baldwin, T. W. *Shakespere's 'Small Latine & Lesse Greeke'* (2 vols, Urbana, Illinois, 1944)

Bolgar, R. R. *The Classical Heritage and its Beneficiaries* (Cambridge, 1954)

Caspari, F. *Humanism and the Social Order in Tudor England* (Chicago, 1954)

Charlton, K. *Education in Renaissance England* (London, 1965)

Costello, W. T. *The Scholastic Curriculum at Early Seventeenth-Century Cambridge* (Cambridge, Mass., 1958)

Craig, H. *The Enchanted Glass: The Elizabethan Mind in Literature* (New York, 1936)

Curtis, M. *Oxford and Cambridge in Transition* (Oxford, 1959)

Einstein, L. *Tudor Ideals* (London, 1921)

Ferguson, A. B. *The Articulate Citizen and the English Renaissance* (Durham, N. C., 1965)

Garin, E. *Italian Humanism: Philosophy and Civic Life in the Renaissance*, tr. P. Munz (Oxford, 1965)

Hunter, G. K. *John Lyly. The Humanist as Courtier* (London, 1962)

Jayne, S. *Library Catalogues of the English Renaissance* (Berkeley, Ca., 1956)

Kelso, R. *Doctrine for a Lady of the Renaissance* (Urbana, Ill., 1929; 1956); *The Doctrine of the English Gentleman in the 16th Century* (Urbana, 1929)

Lievsay, J. *Stefano Guazzo and the English Renaissance 1575–1675* (Chapel Hill, N. C., 1961)

Mason, J. E. *Gentlefolk in the Making* (Philadelphia, 1935)

Philips, M. M. *The 'Adages' of Erasmus: A Study with Translations* (Cambridge, 1964), abridged as *Erasmus on his Times* (Cambridge, 1967)

Seigel, J. E. *Rhetoric and Philosophy in Renaissance Humanism* (Princeton, 1968)

Simon, J. *Education and Society in Tudor England* (Cambridge, 1966)

Webster, C. (ed.) *Samuel Hartlib and the Advancement of Learning* (Cambridge, 1970)

Wormald, F., and Wright, C. E. (eds) *The English Library before 1700* (London, 1958)

IV. RELIGION, PHILOSOPHY AND SCIENCE

Anglo, S. (ed.) *The Damned Art. Essays in the Literature of Witchcraft* (London, 1977)

Blench, J. W. *Preaching in England, 1450–1600* (Oxford, 1964)

Buckley, G. T. *Atheism in the English Renaissance* (Chicago, 1932; New York, 1965)

Butterworth, C. C. *The Literary Lineage of the King James Bible* (1941, 1971)

Chandos, J. (ed.) *In God's Name. Examples of Preaching in England from the Act of Supremacy to the Act of Uniformity, 1534–1662* (London, 1971)

Collinson, P. *The Elizabethan Puritan Movement* (London, 1967)

Coolidge, J. S. *The Pauline Renaissance in England. English Puritanism and the Bible* (Oxford, 1970)

Cremeans, C. D. *The Reception of Calvinist Thought in England* (Urbana, Ill., 1949)

Davies, H. *Worship and Theology in England. Vol. II: From Andrewes to Baxter and Fox, 1603–1690* (Princeton, 1975)

Dickens, A. G. *The English Reformation* (London, 1964)

Emerson, E. *English Puritanism from John Hooper to John Milton* (Durham, N. C., 1968)

Firth, K. R. *The Apocalyptic Tradition in Reformation Britain, 1530–1645* (Oxford, 1979)

Frere, W. H., and Douglas, C. E. (eds) *Puritan Manifestos* (London, 1954)

George, C. H. and K. *The Protestant Mind of the English Reformation, 1570–1640* (Princeton, 1961)

Greenslade, S. L. 'English Versions of the Bible 1525–1611' in *The Cambridge History of the Bible* (Cambridge, 1963)

Haller, W. *The Rise of Puritanism, 1570–1642* (New York, 1938); *Foxe's 'Book of Martyrs' and the Elect Nation* (London, 1963)

Haugaard, W. P. *Elizabeth and the English Reformation: the Struggle for a Stable Settlement of Religion* (Cambridge, 1968)

Hill, C. *Society and Puritanism in Pre-revolutionary England* (London, 1964)

Holden, W. P. *Anti-puritan Satire, 1572–1642* (New Haven, 1954)

Hughes, P. *The Reformation in England* (5th edn, rev., London, 1963)

Hurstfield, J. (ed.) *The Reformation Crisis* (London, 1965)

Jordan, W. K. *The Development of Religious Toleration in England ... to the Death of Queen Elizabeth* (Cambridge, Mass., 1932); *1603–1640* (Cambridge, Mass., 1936; both repr. 1965)

Kitch, M. J. (ed.) *Capitalism and the Reformation* (London, 1967)

Kittredge, G. L. *Witchcraft in Old and New England* (Cambridge, Mass., 1929; New York, 1956)

Knappen, M. M. (ed.) *Two Elizabethan Puritan Diaries* (Chicago, 1933); *Tudor Puritanism* (Chicago, 1939)

Knowles, D. *The Religious Orders in England, III, The Tudor Age* (Cambridge, 1959)

Low, A., *Augustine Baker* (New York, 1970): English mysticism

Macfarlane, A. *Witchcraft in Tudor and Stuart England* (London, 1970)

McGee, J. S. *The Godly Man in Stuart England: Anglicans, Puritans, and the Two Tables, 1620–1670* (New Haven, 1976)

MacGregor, G. *A Literary History of the Bible: From the Middle Ages to the Present Day* (Abingdon, 1968)

Maclure, M. *The Paul's Cross Sermons, 1534–1642* (Toronto, 1958)

Merrill, T. F. (ed.) *William Perkins 1558–1602, English Puritanist. His Pioneer Works on Casuistry* (Nieuwkoop, 1966)

Milward, P. *Religious Controversies of the Elizabethan Age. A Survey of Printed Sources* (Ilkley, 1977)

Morgan, I. *The Godly Preachers of the Elizabethan Church* (London, 1965)

Mosse, G. L. *The Holy Pretence: A Study in Christianity and Reason of State from William Perkins to John Winthrop* (Oxford, 1957): Machiavelli; Puritan casuistry

New, J. F. *Anglican and Puritan: The Basis of Their Opposition, 1558–1640* (Stanford, Ca., 1966)

Partridge, A. C. *English Biblical Translation* (London, 1973)

Pearson, A. F. S. *Thomas Cartwright and Elizabethan Puritanism* (Cambridge, 1925)

Pettit, N., *The Heart Prepared: Grace and Conversion in Puritan Spiritual Life* (New Haven, 1966)

Philips, J. *The Reformation of Images: Destruction of Art in England 1535–1660* (Berkeley, Ca., 1973)

Porter, H. C. (ed.), *Puritanism in Tudor England* (London, 1970)

Roberts, J. R. (ed.) *A Critical Anthology of English Recusant Devotional Prose, 1558–1603* (Pittsburgh, 1966)

Rosen, B. (ed.) *Witchcraft* (London, 1969)

Sasek, L. A. *The Literary Temper of the English Puritans* (Baton Rouge, La., 1961)

Seaver, P. S. *The Puritan Lectureships: The Politics of Religious Dissent, 1560–1662* (Stanford, Ca., 1970)

Seymour-Smith, M. (ed.) *The English Sermon, Vol. I: 1550–1650* (Cheadle, 1976)

Southern, A. C. *Elizabethan Recusant Prose 1559–1582* (London, 1950)

Southwell, R. S. J. *Two Letters, and Short Rules of a Good Life* ed. N. P. Brown (Charlottesville, Va., 1973)

Thomas, K. *Religion and the Decline of Magic. Studies in Popular Beliefs in Sixteenth- and Seventeenth-Century England* (London, 1971; rev. edn Penguin, 1973)

Thompson, C. R. *The English Church in the 16th Century* (Ithaca, N.Y., 1958)

Trevor-Roper, H. R. *Religion, the Reformation and Social Change* (London, 1967)

Trinterud, L. J. (ed.) *Elizabethan Puritanism* (New York, 1971)

Walker, D. P. *The decline of Hell. Seventeenth-Century Discussions of Eternal Torment* (London, 1964)

Walzer, M. *The revolution of the Saints. A Study in the Origins of Radical Politics* (London, 1966): Calvinism, Puritanism and Politics

White, H. C. *Tudor Books of Saints and Martyrs* (Madison, Wis., 1963)

Williamson, G. A. (ed.) *Foxe's Book of Martyrs* (abridged edn; London, 1965)

Allen, D. C. *The Legend of Noah, Renaissance Rationalism in Art, Science, and Letters* (Urbana, Ill., 1949, 1963); *Doubt's Boundless Sea, Skepticism and Faith in the Renaissance* (Baltimore, 1964)

Burckhardt, J. *The Civilization of the Renaissance in Italy* (1860; Engl. tr., Phaidon ed.)

Bush, D. *The Renaissance and English Humanism* (Toronto, 1939)

Carré, M. H. *Phases of Thought in England* (Oxford, 1949)

Cassirer, E. *The Individual and the Cosmos in Renaissance Philosophy* tr. M. Domandi (Oxford, 1963)

Cassirer, E. *et al.* (eds) *The Renaissance Philosophy of Man* (Chicago, 1948, 1963)

Coffin, C. M. *Donne and the New Philosophy* (New York, 1937)

Craig, H. *The Enchanted Glass: the Elizabethan Mind in Literature* (New York, 1936)

Davies, S. (ed.) *Renaissance Views of Man* (Manchester, 1978)

Ellrodt, R. *Neoplatonism in the Poetry of Edmund Spenser* (Geneva, 1960)

Ferguson, W. K. et al. *The Renaissance: Six Essays* (New York, 1953; rev. 1962)

Garin, E. *Italian Humanism: Philosophy and Civic Life in the Renaissance*, tr. P. Munz (Oxford, 1965)

Gilbert, N. W. *Renaissance Concepts of Method* (New York, 1960)

Harris, V. *All Coherence Gone* (Chicago, 1949)

Haydn, H. *The Counter-Renaissance* (New York, 1950)

Hoopes, R. *Right Reason in the English Renaissance* (Cambridge, Mass., 1962)

Huizinga, J. *The Waning of the Middle Ages* (London, 1924; Pelican, 1955); *Men and Ideas* (London, 1960)

Kristeller, P. *Renaissance Thought: The Classic, Scholastic, and Humanist Strains* (New York, 1961); *Renaissance Thought II: Papers on Humanism and the Arts* (New York, 1965); *Eight Philosophers of the Italian Renaissance* (Stanford, 1964; London, 1965); *Renaissance Thought and Its Sources* (New York, 1979)

Levi, A. *French Moralists: The Theory of the Passions 1585 to 1649* (Oxford, 1964)

Lewis, C. S. *The Discarded Image: an Introduction to Medieval and Renaissance Literature* (Cambridge, 1964)

Lovejoy, A. O. *The Great Chain of Being* (Cambridge, Mass., 1936)

Ong, W. *Ramus: Method and the Decay of Dialogue* (Cambridge, Mass., 1958)

Popkin, R. H. *The History of Scepticism from Erasmus to Descartes* (Assen, rev. edn 1964); *The History of Scepticism from Erasmus to Spinoza* (Berkeley, Ca., 1980)

Randall, J. H. *The Career of Philosophy from the Middle Ages to the Enlightenment* (New York, 1962)

Rice, E. F. *The Renaissance Idea of Wisdom* (Cambridge, Mass., 1958)

Rivers, I. *Classical and Christian Ideas in English Renaissance Poetry* (London, 1979)

Røstvig, M.-S. *The Happy Man: Studies in the Metamorphoses of a Classical Ideal 1600–1700* (Oslo, 1954; rev. edn 1962)

Spencer, T. *Shakespeare and the Nature of Man* (Cambridge, 1943)

Tillyard. E. M. W. *The Elizabethan World Picture* (London, 1943; Peregrine, 1963)

Trinkaus, C., *In Our Image and Likeness: Humanity and Divinity in Italian Humanist Thought* (2 vols, London, 1970)

Van Leeuwen, H. G. *The Problem of Certainty in English Thought, 1630–90* (The Hague, 1963)

West, R. H. *The Invisible World* (Athens, Ga., 1939; New York, 1969): Elizabethan concepts of the supernatural, especially in drama.

Wiley, M. L. *The Subtle Knot: Creative Scepticism in 17th Century England* (London, 1952); *Creative Sceptics* (London, 1966)

FOR FURTHER READING AND REFERENCE

Willey, B. *The Seventeenth-Century Background* (London, 1938; Penguin, 1962); *The English Moralists* (London, 1964)

Winny, J. *The Frame of Order* (London, 1957)

Yates, F. *Giordano Bruno and the Hermetic Tradition* (London, 1964)

Allen, D. C. *The Star-crossed Renaissance* (Duke, N. C., 1941; London, 1966)

Babb, L. *The Elizabethan Malady* (Michigan, 1952): melancholy and psychology

Burtt, E. A. *The Metaphysical Foundations of Modern Physical Science* (rev. edn London, 1932)

Butterfield, H. *The Origins of Modern Science* (London, 1951)

Capp, B. *English Almanacs, 1500–1800. Astrology and the Popular Press* (Ithaca, N. Y., 1979)

Copeman, W. S. *Doctors and Disease in Tudor Times* (London, 1960)

Debus, A. G. *The English Paracelsians* (London, 1965); *The Chemical Philosophy: Paracelsian Science and Medicine in the Sixteenth and Seventeenth Centuries* (2 vols, New York, 1977); *Man and Nature in the Renaissance* (Cambridge, 1978)

Derry, T. K., and Williams, T. I. *A Short History of Technology* (Oxford, 1960)

Gille, B. *Engineers of the Renaissance* (Cambridge, Mass., 1966)

Harvey, W. *The Circulation of the Blood* (1628) and other works, tr. and ed. K. J. Franklin (E.L.)

Heninger, S. K. *A Handbook of Renaissance Meteorology* (Durham, N. C., 1960); *Touches of Sweet Harmony: Pythagorean Cosmology and Renaissance Poetics* (San Marino, Ca., 1974); *The Cosmographical Glass: Renaissance Diagrams of the Universe* (San Marino, Ca., 1977)

Hill, C. *The Intellectual Origins of the English Revolution* (Oxford, 1965); but see H. R. Trevor-Roper in *History and Theory*, V (1966)

Jenkins, R. *Links in the History of Engineering and Technology from Tudor Times* (Cambridge, 1936)

Johnson, F. R. *Astronomical Thought in Renaissance England* (Baltimore, 1937; New York, 1968)

Kargon, R. H. *Atomism in England from Harriot to Newton* (Oxford, 1966)

Kocher, P. H. *Science and Religion in Elizabethan England* (San Marino, Ca., 1953)

Koyré, A. *From the Closed World to the Infinite Universe* (Baltimore, 1968)

Maclean, I. *The Renaissance Notion of Woman. A Study in the fortunes of scholasticism and medical science in European intellectual life* (Cambridge, 1980)

Nicolson, M. *The Breaking of the Circle: Studies on the Effect of the 'New Science' on 17th Century Poetry* (Evanston, Ill., 1950); *Science and the Imagination* (Ithaca. N. Y., 1956)

Shirley, J. W. (ed.) *Thomas Harriot: Renaissance Scientist* (Oxford, 1974)

Shumaker, W. and Heilbron, J. L. (eds) *John Dee on Astronomy: Propaedeumata Aphoristica (1558 and 1568), Latin and English* (Berkeley, Ca., 1978)

Webster, C. *The Great Instauration: Science, Medicine and Reform 1626–1660* (London, 1975)

Webster, C. (ed.) *The Intellectual Revolution of the Seventeenth Century* (London, 1974)

Wightman, W. P. *Science and the Renaissance: the Emergence of the Sciences in the 16th Century* (2 vols, London, 1962)

V. MUSIC AND THE VISUAL ARTS

Abraham, G., and Hughes, A. (eds) *The New Oxford History of Music. IV. The Age of Humanism, 1540–1630* (London, 1968)

Boyd, M. G. *Elizabethan Music and Musical Criticism* (Philadelphia, 1940, rev. 1962)

Brown, D. *Thomas Weelkes* (London, 1969); *Wilbye* (London, 1974)

Brown, H. M. *Music in the Renaissance* (Englewood Cliffs, N. J., 1976)

Carpenter, N. C. *Music in the Medieval and Renaissance Universities* (Norman, Okla., 1958)

Chappell, W. *Old English Popular Music*, ed. H. Woolridge (2 vols, London, 1893; New York, 1961)

Cunningham, J. P. *Dancing in the Inns of Court* (London, 1965)

Dent, E. *Foundations of English Opera* (Cambridge, 1928)

Doe, P. *Tallis* (London, 1968, 1976)

Fellowes, E. H. *William Byrd* (London, 1936, 1948); *Orlando Gibbons* (London, 1951)

Finney, G. L. *Musical Backgrounds for English Literature: 1580–1650* (New Brunswick, N. J., 1962)

Gibbon, J. M. *Melody and the Lyric Form, Chaucer to the Cavaliers* (London, 1930)

Greenberg, N., *et al.* (eds) *An Elizabethan Song Book* (London, 1954)

Hollander, J. *The Untuning of the Sky: Ideas of Music in English Poetry, 1500–1700* (Princeton, 1961)

Ingram, R. W. 'Words and Music', in (27), Section VII below.

Jacquot, J. (ed.) *Musique et Poésie au XVI e Siècle* (Paris, 1964)

Kerman, J. *The Elizabethan Madrigal* (New York, 1962)

Lang, P. H. *Music in Western Civilization* (London, 1942)

Ledger, P. (ed.) *The Oxford Book of English Madrigals* (London, 1978)

Le Huray, P. *Music and the Reformation in England* (London, 1967; Cambridge, 1978)

Long, J. H. (ed.) *Music in English Renaissance Drama* (Lexington, Ky., 1968)

Mackerness, E. D. *A Social History of English Music* (London, 1964)

Mellers, W. *Music and Society* (London, 1946); *Harmonious Meeting; a Study of the Relationship Between English Music, Poetry, and Theatre, c. 1600–1900* (London, 1965)

Morley, Thomas *A Plaine and Easie Introduction to Practicall Musicke*, ed. A. Harman (London, 1952)

Neighbour, O. *The Music of William Byrd. Vol. III.: Consort and Keyboard Music* (Berkeley, Ca., 1978)

Obortello, A., *Madrigali italiani in Inghilterra* (Milan, 1949)

Osborn, J. M. *The Autobiography of Thomas Whythorne* (London, 1961)

Pattison, B. *Music and Poetry of the English Renaissance* (London, 1948; rev. edn 1970)

Poulton, D., *John Dowland. His Life and Works* (Berkeley, Ca., 1972)

Reese, G. *Music in the Renaissance* (New York, 1954)

Sabol, A. (ed.) *Four Hundred Songs and Dances from the Stuart Masque* (rev. edn, Providence, R. I., 1978)

Scholes, P. *The Puritans and the Music* (London, 1934)

Simpson, C. M. *The British Broadside Ballad and its Music* (New Brunswick, N. J., 1966), and see the review by Ward, J., which contains additional material: 'A Propos of the Broadside Ballad and its Music', in *Journal of the American Musicological Society*, xx (1967)

Spink, I. *English Song, Dowland to Purcell* (London, 1974)

Stevens, D. W. *Thomas Tomkins* (London, 1957); *Tudor Church Music* (London, 1961)

Stevens, J. 'The Elizabethan Madrigal', in E & S, XI (1958)

Strunk, O., (ed.) *Source Readings in Music History* (London, 1952)

Walker, E. *A History of Music in England*, 3rd edn, rev. J. A. Westrup (Oxford, 1952)

Warlock, P. *The English Ayre* (London, 1926)

Woodfill, W. L. *Musicians in English Society from Elizabeth to Charles I* (Princeton, 1953)

Auerbach, E. *Tudor Artists* (London, 1954); *Nicholas Hilliard* (London, 1961)

Bush, D. *Mythology and the Renaissance Tradition in English Poetry* (Minneapolis, 1932; rev. New York, 1963)

Buxton, J. *Elizabethan Taste* (London, 1963)

Chew, S. C. *The Virtues Reconciled, An Iconographic Study* (Toronto, 1947); *The Pilgrimage of Life* (New Haven, 1962)

Dictionary of English Portraiture (4 vols, London, 1979–), Vol. I, *The Middle Ages to the Early Georgians. Historical Figures Born Before 1700*, ed. A. Davies (London, 1979)

Freeman, R. *English Emblem Books* (London, 1948, 1968)

Girouard, M. *Robert Smythson and the Architecture of the Elizabethan Era* (London, 1966).

Henkel, A. and Schöne, A. *Emblemata: Handbuch zur Sinnbildkunst des XVI. und XVII. Jahrhunderts* (Stuttgart, 1967); Supplement (Stuttgart, 1976): but see review in *Renaissance Quarterly*, XXIII (1970)

Hind, A. M. *Engraving in England in the 16th and 17th Centuries* (3 vols, Cambridge, 1952)

Höltgen, K. J. *Francis Quarles, 1592–1644. Meditativer, Dichter, Emblematiker, Royalist* (Tübingen, 1979)

Klibansky, R., Panofsky, E. and Saxl, F. *Saturn and Melancholy* (London, 1964)

Lees-Milne, J. *Tudor Renaissance* (Art and Architecture; London, 1951)

Panofsky, E. *Studies in Iconology: Humanistic Themes in the Art of the Renaissance* (New York, 1936; rev. 1962); *Meaning in the Visual Arts* (New York, 1955); *Renaissance and Renascence in Western Art* (Stockholm, 1960; London, 1970)

Pevsner, N. (ed.) *The Buildings of England* (Penguin)

Praz, M. *Studies in Seventeenth-Century Imagery* (2 vols, London, 1939–47; rev. edn Rome, 1964); Supplement (Rome, 1974)

Seznec, J. *The Survival of the Pagan Gods; The Mythological Tradition and Its Place in Renaissance Humanism and Art* tr. B. Sessions (New York, 1953)

Strong, R. *The Portraits of Queen Elizabeth* (London, 1963); *The English Icon: Elizabethan and Jacobean Portraiture* (London, 1969); *The Cult of Elizabeth; Elizabethan Portraiture and Pageantry* (London, 1977)

Summerson, J. *Architecture in Britain, 1530–1830* (Harmondsworth, 1953); *Inigo Jones* (Penguin, 1966)

Tervarent, G. de *Attributs et symboles dans l'art profane 1450–1600. Dictionnaire d'un langage perdu* (Geneva, 1958–1964)

Tipping, H. A. (ed.) *English Homes, Period III, Late Tudor and Early Stuart, 1588–1649* (2 vols, London, 1922–7)

Waterhouse, E. K. *Painting in Britain, 1530–1790* (Harmondsworth, 1953)

Whinney, M. *Sculpture in Britain, 1530–1830* (Harmondsworth, 1964)

Wind, E. *Pagan Mysteries in the Renaissance* (2nd, rev. edn Penguin, 1967)

Winter, C. *Elizabethan Miniatures* (Harmondsworth, 1943)

The Literature

VI. BIBLIOGRAPHIES AND REFERENCE

General

Chapman, R. W. *et al. Annals of English Literature 1475–1960. The Principal Publications of Each Year Together With An Alphabetical Index of Authors With Their Works* (2nd edn, rev., Oxford, 1961)

Harbage, A. *Annals of English Drama 975–1700* (London, 1940); 2nd edn, rev. S. Schoenbaum (London, 1964); Supplement (Evanston, Ill., 1966); Second Supplement (Evanston, Ill., 1970)

Cambridge Bibliography of English Literature ed. F. W. Bateson (4 vols, Cambridge, 1940); Supplement ed. G. G. Watson (1957)

New Cambridge Bibliography of English Literature ed. G. G. Watson (5 vols, Cambridge, 1969–77); *Volume I: 600–1660* (1974)

The Year's Work in English Studies (pub. by the English Association, London, 1919–)

Annual Bibliography of English Language and Literature (Modern Humanities Research Association, Cambridge, 1920–)

P.M.L.A.: Annual Bibliography (New York, 1956–)

Renaissance

Beal, P. *Index of English Literary Manuscripts, Vol. 1: 1450–1625* (London, 1980)

Greg, W. W. *A Bibliography of the English Printed Drama to the Restoration* (4 vols, London, 1939–59)

Halkett, J. and Laing, J. *A Dictionary of Anonymous and Pseudonymous Publications in the English Language: 1475–1640*, rev. edn J. Horden (London, 1980)

Heninger, S. K., Jr. *English Prose, Prose Fiction, and Criticism to 1660: a Guide to Information Sources* (Detroit, 1976)

Jones, W. R. (ed.) *The Present State of Scholarship in Sixteenth-Century Literature* (Columbia, Mo., 1978)

Mish, C. G. *English Prose Fiction, 1600–1700* (3 vols, Charlottesville, Va., 1952, rev. 1967)

Pollard, A. W. and Redgrave, G. R. *A Short-Title Catalogue of Books Printed in England ... 1475–1640* (London, 1926); rev. edn W. A. Jackson, F. S. Ferguson, K. F. Pantzer (3 vols, London, 1976–)

Shaaber, M. A. *Check-List of Works of British Authors Printed Abroad, in Languages Other than English, to 1641* (New York, 1975)

Tilley, M. P. *A Dictionary of Proverbs in England in the 16th and 17th Centuries* (Ann Arbor, Mich., 1950)

Studies in Philology (North Carolina): Annual Bibliography of Renaissance Studies (1922–69)

Renaissance Quarterly, formerly *Renaissance News* (Renaissance Society of America: New York, 1947–); since 1975 amalgamated with *Studies in the Renaissance*

Bibliothèque de l'Humanisme et de la Renaissance: Annual Bibliography of Renaissance Studies (Geneva, 1966–80; Chicago, 1981–)

Studies in English Literature, 1500–1900 (Houston: Rice University, 1961–) quarterly review of Renaissance studies

English Literary Renaissance (Amherst, Mass., 1971–): regular bibliographical surveys of individual authors

Further bibliographies of this period can be found in the next section, in the works of Brooke (52), Bush (38), Lewis (17), de Sola Pinto (13), and Wilson ed. Hunter (54)

VII. GENERAL STUDIES AND COLLECTED ESSAYS

(In this section items are numbered in sequence; in sections below they are referred to by the author's surname and the number.)

1. *Cambridge History of English Literature*, III–VI (1908)
2. Lee, S. *The French Renaissance in England* (New York, 1910)
3. Scott, J. G. *Les sonnets élisabéthains* (Paris, 1929)
4. Empson, W. *Seven Types of Ambiguity* (London, 1930, rev. 1947; Peregrine, 1962)

5. Pearson, L. E. *Elizabethan Love Conventions* (Berkeley, 1933; London, 1966): Petrarchism and the Sonnet

6. Bradbrook, M. C. *Themes and Conventions of Elizabethan Tragedy* (Cambridge, 1935; rev. edn Cambridge, 1980)

7. Harbage, A. *Cavalier Drama* (New York, 1936; 1964)

8. Knights, L. C. *Drama and Society in the Age of Jonson* (London, 1937; Peregrine, 1962)

9. John, L. C. *The Elizabethan Sonnet Sequences: Studies in Conventional Conceits* (New York, 1938; 1964)

10. Wilson, F. P. *Elizabethan and Jacobean* (Oxford, 1945)

11. McManaway, J. G. (ed.) *Joseph Quincy Adams Memorial Studies* (Washington, D.C., 1948)

12. Mahood, M. M. *Poetry and Humanism* (London, 1950)

13. de Sola Pinto, V. *The English Renaissance, 1510–1688* (London, 1938; rev. 1951)

14. Eliot, T. S. *Selected Essays* (London, 3rd enlarged edn 1951)

15. Danby, J. F. *Poets on Fortune's Hill* (London, 1952); repr. as *Elizabethan and Jacobean Poets* (London, 1964)

16. Smith, H. *Elizabethan Poetry* (Cambridge, Mass., 1952)

17. Lewis, C. S. *English Literature in the Sixteenth Century Excluding Drama* (Oxford, 1954)

18. Bradbrook, M. C. *The Growth and Structure of Elizabethan Comedy* (London, 1955; Peregrine, 1963; rev. edn Cambridge, 1973)

19. Evans, M. *English Poetry in the 16th Century* (London, 1955, 1967)

20. Sells, A. L. *The Italian Influence in English Poetry from Chaucer to Southwell* (London, 1955)

21. Lever, J. W. *The Elizabethan Love-Sonnet* (London, 1956)

22. Peter, J. *Complaint and Satire in Early English Literature* (Oxford, 1956)

23. Bowers, F. *Elizabethan Revenge Tragedy* (Princeton, 1940; rev. 1959)

24. Campbell, L. B. *Divine Poetry and Drama in 16th-Century England* (Cambridge, 1959)

25. Kernan, A. *The Cankered Muse: Satire of the English Renaissance* (New Haven, 1959)

26. Brown, J. R., and Harris, B. (eds) *Stratford-upon-Avon Studies* Vol. 1: *Jacobean Theatre* (London, 1960)

27. Brown, J. R., and Harris, B. (eds) Vol. 2: *Elizabethan Poetry* (London, 1960)

28. Brown, J. R., and Harris, B. (eds) Vol. 3: *Early Shakespeare* (London, 1961)

29. Brown, J. R., and Harris, B. (eds) Vol. 5: *Hamlet* (London, 1963)

30. Brown, J. R., and Harris, B. (eds) Vol. 8: *Later Shakespeare* (London, 1966)

31. Brown, J. R., and Harris, B. (eds) Vol. 9: *Elizabethan Theatre* (London, 1966)

32. Ornstein, R. *The Moral Vision of Jacobean Tragedy* (Madison, Wis., 1960)

33. Wilson, F. P. *17th Century Prose* (Cambridge, 1960)

34. Bluestone, M., and Rabkin, N. (eds) *Shakespeare's Contemporaries* (Englewood Cliffs, N. J., 1961; 1970)

35. Clemen, W. *English Tragedy before Shakespeare: The Development of Dramatic Speech* tr. T. S. Dorsch (London, 1961)

36. Ellis-Fermor, U. *The Jacobean Drama* (London, 1936; rev. 1965)

37. Kaufmann, R. J. (ed.) *Elizabethan Drama. Modern Essays in Criticism* (Galaxy Books; New York, 1961)

38. Bush, D. *English Literature in the Earlier 17th Century* (Oxford, 1945; rev. edn 1962)

39. Talbert, E. W. *The Problem of Order. Elizabethan Political Commonplaces* (Chapel Hill, N. C., 1962)

40. Waith, E. M. *The Herculean Hero in Marlowe, Chapman, Shakespeare and and Dryden* (London, 1962)

41. Wright, L. B., and La Mar, V. (eds) *Life and Letters in Tudor and Stuart England* (Ithaca, N. Y., 1962)

42. Hosley, R. (ed.) *Essays on Shakespeare and Elizabethan Drama. In Honour of Hardin Craig* (London, 1963)

43. Alexander, P. (ed.) *Studies in Shakespeare* (London, 1964)

44. Mehl, D. *The Elizabethan Dumb Show* (London, 1965)

45. Muir, E. *Essays on Literature and Society* (London, 1949, 1965)

46. Purves, A. C. (ed.) *Theodore Spencer: Selected Essays* (New Brunswick, N. J., 1966)

47. Alpers, P. J. (ed.) *Elizabethan Poetry. Modern Essays in Criticism* (London, 1967)

48. Peterson, D. L. *The English Lyric from Wyatt to Donne* (Princeton, 1967)

49. Prosser, E. *Hamlet and Revenge* (London, 1967)

50. Winters, Y. *Forms of Discovery. Critical and Historical Essays on the Forms of the Short Poem in English* (Chicago, 1967) ch. i: 'Aspects of the Short Poem in the English Renaissance'.

51. Bentley, G. E. (ed.) *The 17th Century Stage* (London, 1968)

52. Brooke, T. 'The Renaissance, 1485–1660', in *A Literary History of England*, ed. A. C. Baugh (New York, 1948); with revised bibliographies (London, 1968)

53. Gibbons, B. *Jacobean City Comedy* (London, 1968; rev. edn 1980)

54. Wilson, F. P., *The English Drama 1485–1585* ed. G. K. Hunter (Oxford, 1969)

55. Muir, K. and Schoenbaum, S. (eds) *A New Companion to Shakespeare Studies* (Cambridge, 1970)

56. Wilson, F. P. *Shakespearian and other Studies*, ed. H. Gardner (Oxford, 1969)

57. Lewis, C. S. *Studies in Medieval and Renaissance Literature*, ed. W. Hooper (Cambridge, 1966, 1979)

58. Lewis, C. S. *Selected Literary Essays*, ed. W. Hooper (Cambridge, 1969)

59. Grundy, J. *The Spenserian Poets* (London, 1969)

60. Donaldson, I. *The World Turned Upside Down: Comedy from Jonson to Fielding* (Oxford, 1970)

61. Kermode, J. F. *Shakespeare, Spenser, Donne: Renaissance Essays* (London, 1971)
62. Lever, J. W. *The Tragedy of State* (London, 1971)
63. Kirsch, A. C. *Jacobean Dramatic Perspectives* (Charlottesville, Va., 1972)
64. Ure, P. *Elizabethan and Jacobean Drama*, ed. J. C. Maxwell (Liverpool, 1974)
65. Gordon, D. J. *The Renaissance Imagination*, ed. S. Orgel (London, 1975)
66. Keach, W. *Elizabethan Erotic Narratives: Irony and Pathos in the Ovidian Poetry of Shakespeare, Marlowe, and their Contemporaries* (New Brunswick, N. J., 1977)
67. Axton, M., and Williams, R. (eds) *English Drama: Forms and Development, Essays in Honour of M. C. Bradbrook* (Cambridge, 1977)
68. Hunter, G. K. *Dramatic Identities and Cultural Tradition. Studies in Shakespeare and his Contemporaries* (Liverpool, 1978)
69. Brooke, N. *Horrid Laughter in Jacobean Tragedy* (London, 1979)
70. Ribner, I. *Jacobean Tragedy: The Quest for Moral Order* (London, 1962, 1979)
71. Carey, J. (ed.) *English Renaissance Studies. Presented to Dame Helen Gardner* (Oxford, 1980)

VIII. ELIZABETHAN ENGLISH

Atkins, J. W. H. 'The Language from Chaucer to Shakespeare', in C. H. E. L., III (Cambridge, 1909)
Baugh, A. C. *A History of the English Language* (New York, 1935)
Bolton, W. F. *A Short History of Literary English* (London, 1967)
Bradley, H. 'Shakespeare's English', in *Shakespeare's England* (Oxford, 1916)
Dobson, E. J. *English Pronunciation, 1500–1700* (2 vols, Oxford, 1957)
Evans, M. 'Elizabethan Spoken English', in *Cambridge Journal*, IV (1951)
Hulme, H. *Explorations in Shakespeare's Language* (London, 1962)
Jones, R. F. *The Triumph of the English Language* (London, 1953)
Kökeritz, H. *Shakespeare's Pronunciation* (New Haven, 1953)
Quirk, R. 'Shakespeare's Language', in (55)
Strang, B. M. H. *A History of English* (London, 1970)
Willcock, G. D. 'Shakespeare and Elizabethan English', Sh S., VII, 1954
Wilson, F. P. 'Shakespeare and the Diction of Common Life', in P.B.A., XXVII, (1941); repr. in *Shakespeare Criticism 1935–1960* ed. A. Ridler (W.C.)
Wyld, H. C. *A History of Modern Colloquial English* (Oxford, 1936; rev. 1953)

IX. CRITICISM, RHETORIC AND LITERARY THEORY

Fraunce, A. *The Arcadian Rhetorike* (1588) ed. E. Seaton (Oxford, 1950)
Gilbert, A. H. (ed.) *Literary Criticism: Plato to Dryden* (Detroit, 1962)
Hardison, O. B. (ed.) *English Literary Criticism: The Renaissance* (New York, 1963)

Hoskins, J. *Directions for Speech and Style* (c. 1599) ed. H. H. Hudson (Princeton, 1935)

Jones, E. D. (ed.) *English Critical Essays: 16th–18th centuries* (London, 1922; w.c.)

Kinney, A. F. (ed.) *Markets of Bawdrie: the Dramatic Criticism of Stephen Gosson* (Salzburg, 1974)

Peacham, H. *The Garden of Rhetoric* (1593), ed. W. G. Crane (Gainesville, Fla., 1954); facs. edn (Menston, Yorks., 1968)

Puttenham, G. *The Arte of English Poesy* (1589) ed. G. Willcock and A. Walker (Cambridge, 1936, 1970); facs. edn (Menston, Yorks., 1968)

Rainolds, J. *Oratio in Laudem Artis Poeticae* (c. 1572) ed. and tr. W. Ringler and W. Allen (Princeton, 1942); but for the ascription of this treatise to Henry Dethick see J. W. Binns in *The Library* xxx (1975)

Smith, G. G. (ed.) *Elizabethan Critical Essays* (2 vols, Oxford, 1904)

Spingarn, J. E. (ed.) *Seventeenth Century Critical Essays I* (Oxford, 1909)

Tayler, E. W. (ed.) *Literary Criticism of 17th Century England* (New York, 1967)

Wilson, T. *The Art of Rhetoric* (1553) ed. G. H. Mair (Oxford, 1909)

Allen, D. C. *Mysteriously Meant: The Rediscovery of Pagan Symbolism and Allegorical Interpretation in the Renaissance* (Baltimore, Md., 1970)

Atkins, J. W. H. *English Literary Criticism: The Renascence* (London, 1947)

Attridge, D. *Well-weighed Syllables; Elizabethan Verse in Classical Metres* (Cambridge, 1974)

Bolgar, R. R. *The Classical Heritage* (Cambridge, 1954)

Bradbrook, M. C. *Shakespeare and Elizabethan Poetry* (London, 1951; Peregrine, 1965)

Braden, G. *The Classics and English Renaissance Poetry. Three Case Studies* (New Haven, 1978); incl. Golding's Ovid, *Hero and Leander*.

Colie, R. *Paradoxia Epidemica: The Renaissance Tradition of Paradox* (Princeton, 1966); *The Resources of Kind: Genre-Theory in the Renaissance* (Berkeley, Ca., 1973)

Conley, C. H. *The first English Translators of the Classics* (New Haven, 1927)

Craig, H. *The Enchanted Glass* (New York, 1936; Oxford, 1960)

Curtius, E. R. *European Literature and the Latin Middle Ages*, tr. W. Trask (New York, 1953)

Doran, M. *Endeavors of Art: A Study of Form in Elizabethan Drama* (Madison, Wis., 1954)

Fletcher, A. *Allegory: The Theory of a Symbolic Mode* (Ithaca, N. Y., 1964)

Hardison, O. B. *The Enduring Monument, A Study of the Idea of Praise in Renaissance Literary Theory and Practice* (Chapel Hill, N. C., 1962)

Hathaway, B. *The Age of Criticism: The Late Renaissance in Italy* (New York, 1962)

Herrick, M. T. *Comic Theory in the 16th Century* (Urbana, Ill., 1950)

Hollander, J. *Vision and Resonance. Two Senses of Poetic Form* (New York, 1975)

Hough, G. *A Preface to 'The Faerie Queene'* (London, 1962)

Howell, W. S. *Logic and Rhetoric in England, 1500–1700* (Princeton, 1956)

Ing, C. *Elizabethan Lyrics: A Study of ... Metres and their Relation to Poetic Effect* (London, 1951, 1968)

Javitch, D. G. *Poetry and Courtliness in Renaissance England* (Princeton, N. J., 1978)

Joseph, Sister Miriam *Shakespeare's Use of the Arts of Language* (New York, 1947, 1963)

Kennedy, G. A. *Classical Rhetoric and its Christian and Secular Tradition from Ancient to Modern Times* (Chapel Hill, N. C., 1980)

Klein, D. *The Elizabethan Dramatists as Critics* (New York, 1963)

Lanham, R. A. *A Handlist of Rhetorical Terms. A Guide for Students of English Literature* (Berkeley, Ca., 1968)

Lewis, C. S. *The Allegory of Love* (Oxford, 1936; New York, 1958)

Matthiessen, F. O. *Translation: An Elizabethan Art* (Cambridge, Mass., 1931)

Rubel, V. L. *Poetic Diction in the English Renaissance. From Skelton through Spenser* (New York, 1941)

Smith, W. D. *Tudor Figures of Rhetoric* (Whitewater, Wis., 1972)

Sonnino, L. A. *A Handbook to 16th Century Rhetoric* (London, 1968)

Spingarn, J. E. *History of Literary Criticism in the Renaissance* (New York, 1899)

Starnes, De Witt, T., and Talbert, E. W. *Classical Myth and Legend in Renaissance Dictionaries* (Chapel Hill, N. C., 1955)

Stroup, T. B. *Microcosmos, The Shape of the Elizabethan Play* (Lexington, 1965)

Sweeting, E. J. *Early Tudor Criticism* (Oxford, 1940)

Thompson, J. *The Founding of English Metre* (London, 1961)

Tuve, R. *Elizabethan and Metaphysical Imagery* (Chicago, 1947)

Vickers, B. W. *Classical Rhetoric in English Poetry* (London, 1970)

Wallerstein, R. *Studies in 17th Century Poetic* (Madison, Wis., 1950)

Weinberg, B. *A History of Literary Criticism in the Italian Renaissance* (2 vols, Chicago, 1961)

White, H. O. *Plagiarism and Imitation during the English Renaissance* (Cambridge, Mass., 1935; London, 1967)

Wimsatt, W. C. and Brooks, C. *Literary Criticism. A Short History* (New York, 1957)

X. DRAMA (see also VII, IX, XI, XIII)

Adams, H. A. *English Domestic or Homiletic Tragedy, 1575–1642* (New York, 1943)

Adams, J. C. *The Globe Playhouse* (Cambridge, Mass., 1943)

Anglo, S. *Spectacle, Pageantry, and Early Tudor Policy* (Oxford, 1969)

Armstrong, W. A. *The Elizabethan Private Theatres* (London, 1958)

Axton, M. *The Queen's Two Bodies: Drama and the Elizabethan Succession* (London, 1977)

Baker, H. *Induction to Tragedy* (Louisiana, 1939)

Barber, C. L. *The Idea of Honour in the English Drama, 1591–1700* (Stockholm, 1957)

Baskervill, C. R. *The Elizabethan Jig and Related Song Drama* (Chicago, 1928; New York, 1965)

Bentley, G. E. *The Jacobean and Caroline Stage* (7 vols, Oxford, 1941–68); 'Shakespeare and the Blackfriars Theatre', in Sh.S., I (1948); *The Profession of Dramatist in Shakespeare's Time* (Princeton, 1971)

Bergeron, D. M. *English Civic Pageantry 1558–1642* (London, 1971)

Berry, H. (ed.) *The First Public Playhouse: The Theatre in Shoreditch, 1576–1598* (Montreal, 1979)

Bevington, D. M. *From 'Mankind' to Marlowe* (Cambridge, Mass., 1962); *Tudor Drama and Politics* (Cambridge, Mass., 1968)

Bluestone, M. *From Story to Stage: The Dramatic Adaptation of Prose Fiction in the Period of Shakespeare and His Contemporaries* (The Hague, 1974)

Boas, F. S. *University Drama in the Tudor Age* (London, 1914; New York, 1978)

Bradbrook, M. C. *Elizabethan Stage Conditions* (Cambridge, 1932, 1968); *The Rise of the Common Player* (London, 1962); *English Dramatic Form* (London, 1965); *The Living Monument. Shakespeare and the Theatre of his Time* (Cambridge, 1976)

Campbell, L. B. *Scenes and Machines on the English Stage during the Renaissance* (Cambridge, 1923; New York, 1960)

Campbell, O. J. *Comicall Satyre and Shakespeare's 'Troilus and Cressida'* (San Marino, Ca., 1938)

Chambers, E. K. *The Medieval Stage* (2 vols, Oxford, 1903); *The Elizabethan Stage* (4 vols, Oxford, 1923; rev. 1945)

Champion, L. S. *Tragic Patterns in Jacobean and Caroline Drama* (Knoxville, Tenn., 1977)

Craik, T. W. *The Tudor Interlude* (Leicester, 1958)

Dessen, A. C. *Elizabethan Drama and the Viewer's Eye* (Chapel Hill, N. C., 1977)

The Elizabethan Theatre (Hamden, Conn., 1970–); Vols I–III, ed. D. Galloway; Vols IV–, ed. G. R. Hibbard

Ellis-Fermor, U. *The Frontiers of Drama*, rev. edn with bibliography by H. Brooks (London, 1964)

Empson, W. *Some Versions of Pastoral* (London, 1935; Peregrine, 1966)

Farnham, W. *The Medieval Heritage of Elizabethan Tragedy* (Berkeley, Ca., 1936; rev. 1956)

Foakes, R. A. 'Elizabethan Acting', in E & S, VII (1954)

Fordyce, R. *Caroline Drama: A Bibliographic History of Criticism* (London, 1978)

Frost, D. L. *The School of Shakespeare* (Cambridge, 1968)

Gardiner, H. C. *Mysteries' End* (New Haven, 1946)

Gildersleeve, V. C. *Government Regulation of the Elizabethan Drama* (New York, 1908)

Glatzer, P. *The Complaint of the Poet: The Parnassus Plays* (Salzburg, 1977)

Greenfield, T. N. *The Induction in Elizabethan Drama* (Eugene, Or., 1970)

Greg, W. W. *Pastoral Poetry and Pastoral Drama* (London, 1906); *Dramatic Documents from the Elizabethan Playhouses* (2 vols, Oxford, 1931)

Harbage, A. *Cavalier Drama* (New York, 1936, 1964); *Shakespeare's Audience* (New York, 1941); *Shakespeare and the Rival Traditions* (New York, 1952)

Henslowe, P. *Diary*, ed. W. W. Greg (2 vols, London, 1904); ed. R. A. Foakes and R. T. Rickert (Cambridge, 1961); facs. ed. R. A. Foakes (London, 1976)

Herrick, M. T. *Tragicomedy* (Urbana, Ill., 1926); *Italian Comedy in the Renaissance* (Urbana, Ill., 1960)

Hillebrand, H. N. *The Child Actors* (Urbana, Ill., 1926)

Hodges, C. W. *The Globe Restored* (London, 1953)

Hosley, R. Articles in Sh.S., x (1957); XII (1959; repr. in 1951); XIII (1960); Sh. Q., VIII (1957); XIV (1963); XV (1964); and in (55)

Hotson, L. *Shakespeare's Motley* (London, 1952)

Hunter, G. K. 'Seneca and the Elizabethans' in Sh.S., XX (1967) and in (68)

Ingram, W. *A London Life in the Brazen Age: Francis Langley 1548–1602* (Cambridge, Mass., 1978)

Isaacs, J. *Production and Stage Management at the Blackfriars Theatre* (London, 1933)

Jacquot, J. (ed.) *Fêtes de la Renaissance* (2 vols, Paris, 1956); *Le Lieu Théâtral à la Renaissance* (Paris, 1964); *Dramaturge et Société ... aux 16ᵉ et 17ᵉ siècles* (Paris, 1968)

Joseph, B. L. *Elizabethan Acting* (rev. edn London, 1964)

Kernodle, G. *From Art to Theater: Form and Convention in the Renaissance* (Chicago, 1944)

Leech, C. and Craik, T. W. (eds) *The Revels History of Drama in English, 1576–1613* (London, 1975)

Lefkowitz, M. *William Lawes* (London, 1960); 'The Longleat Papers of Bulstrode Whitelocke' (on masque production), in *Journal of the American Musicological Society* 18 (1965)

Leggatt, A. *Citizen Comedy in the Age of Shakespeare* (Toronto, 1973)

Lenman, T. *Sebastian Westcott, the Children of Paul's and 'The Marriage of Wit and Science'* (Toronto, 1975)

Levin, R. *The Multiple Plot in English Renaissance Drama* (Chicago, 1971); *New Readings vs Old Plays. Recent Trends in the Reinterpretation of English Renaissance Drama* (Chicago, 1979)

Logan, T. P., and Smith, D. S. (eds) *The Predecessors of Shakespeare* (Lincoln, Neb., 1973): bibliographies of modern studies of Marlowe, Greene, Kyd, Nashe, Lyly, Peele, Lodge *et al.*; *The Popular School* (Lincoln, Neb., 1975): bibliographies of Dekker, Middleton, Webster, Heywood, Munday, Drayton *et al.*; *The New Intellectuals* (Lincoln, Neb., 1977): bibliographies of Jonson, Chapman, Marston, Tourneur *et al.*; *The Later Jacobean & Caroline Dramatists* (Lincoln, Neb., 1978): bibliographies of Beaumont and Fletcher, Massinger, Ford, Shirley, Brome, Davenant *et al.*

Long, J. H. (ed.) *Music in English Renaissance Drama* (Lexington, Ky., 1969)

Lynch, K. M. *The Social Mode of Restoration Comedy* (New York, 1926)

Murray, J. T. *English Dramatic Companies, 1558–1642* (2 vols, London, 1910; New York, 1963)

Nagler, A. M. *A Source Book in Theatrical History* (New York, 1952); *Shakespeare's Stage* (New Haven, 1958)

Nicoll, A. *Stuart Masques and the Renaissance Stage* (London, 1938)

Orgel, S. *The Illusion of Power; Political Theatre in the English Renaissance* (Berkeley, Ca., 1975)

Orgel, S., and Strong, R. *Inigo Jones; the Theatre of the Stuart Court* (2 vols, London, 1973)

Orr, D. *Italian Renaissance Drama in England Before 1625: the Influence of 'Erudita' Tragedy, Comedy, and Pastoral on Elizabethan and Jacobean Drama* (Chapel Hill, N. C., 1970)

Palme, P. *Triumph of Peace: A Study of the Whitehall Banqueting House* (Stockholm, 1956)

Prouty, C. T. (ed.) *Studies in the Elizabethan Theatre* (Hamden, Conn., 1963)

Radcliffe-Umstead, D. *The Birth of Modern Comedy in Renaissance Italy* (Chicago, 1969)

Read, R. B. *Bedlam on the Jacobean Stage* (New York, 1952, 1970)

Renaissance Drama, ed. S. Schoenbaum (Northwestern U. P., Ill., annually); new series (1968–) Vol. 1, on masques

Reynolds, G. F. *The Staging of Elizabethan Plays At the Red Bull Theater, 1605–25* (Colorado, 1940; New York, 1966)

Rhodes, E. L. *Henslowe's Rose; The Stage and Staging* (Lexington, Ky., 1976)

Ribner, I. *The English History Play in the Age of Shakespeare* (London, 1957; rev. 1965)

Ricks, C. (ed.) *Sphere History of Literature in the English Language, Vol. 3. English Drama to 1700* (London, 1971)

Ristine, F. H. *English Tragicomedy: its Origin and History* (New York, 1910, 1963)

Schelling, F. E. *Elizabethan Drama* (2 vols, New York, 1908)

Schoenbaum, S. *Internal Evidence and Elizabethan Dramatic Authorship* (London, 1966)

Seltzer, D. 'The Actors and Staging', in (55)

Shakespeare Survey, I (1948), II (1949), XII (1959)

Shapiro, M. *Children of the Revels: the Boy Companies of Shakespeare's Time and their Plays* (New York, 1977)

Sibley, G. M. *The Lost Plays and Masques 1500–1642* (Ithaca, N. Y., 1933; New York, 1971)

Sisson, C. J. *Lost Plays of Shakespeare's Age* (Cambridge, 1936; London, 1970); *The Boar's Head Theatre: an Inn-Yard Theatre of the Elizabethan Age*, ed. S. Wells (London, 1972)

Smith, I. *Shakespeare's Blackfriars Playhouse: Its History and its Design* (New York, 1964)

Southern, R. *The Staging of Plays before Shakespeare* (London, 1973)

Spencer, T. *Death and Elizabethan Tragedy* (1936; New York, 1960)

Thompson, E. N. S. *The Controversy Between the Puritans and the Stage* (New York, 1903, 1972)

Tomlinson, T. B. *A Study of Elizabethan and Jacobean Tragedy* (Cambridge, 1964)

Waith, E. M. *Ideas of Greatness: Heroic Drama in England* (London, 1971)

Welsford, E. *The Court Masque* (Cambridge, 1927)

Wickham, G. *Early English Stages, 1300–1660. Vol I: 1300–1576* (rev. edn London, 1980)

Wilson, J. D. 'The Puritan Attack on the Stage', in C.H.E.L., VI

Withington, R. *English Pageantry* (2 vols, London, 1918–20)

XI. POPULAR CULTURE, PROSE FICTION

Armin, R. *A Nest of Ninnies* (the Fool tradition; 1608; ed. J. P. Collier, Shakespeare Society, 1842)

Clark, A. (ed.) *Shirburn Ballads, 1585–1616* (London, 1907)

Furnivall, F. J. (ed.) *Robert Laneham's Letter . . . the Entertainment at Kenilworth* (1575; London, 1907)

Halliwell, J. O. (ed.) *Tarlton's Jests* (Shakespeare Society, 1844)

Hazlitt, W. C. (ed.) *Shakespeare Jestbooks* (3 vols, London, 1864)

Henderson, P. (ed.) *Shorter Novels: Elizabethan* (Deloney, Greene, Nashe; E. L., 1929)

Johnson, Richard *The Most Pleasant History of Tom a Lincolne*, ed. R. S. M. Hirsch (Columbia, S. C., 1978)

Judges, A. V. (ed.) *The Elizabethan Underworld* (pamphlets; London, 1930; 1965)

Lawlis, M. (ed.) *Elizabethan Prose Fiction* (New York, 1967)

Mish, C. C. (ed.) *The Anchor Anthology of Short Fiction of the Seventeenth Century* (New York, 1963)

Munday, A. *The English Roman Life*, ed. P. J. Ayres (Oxford, 1980)

Rollins, H. E. (ed.) *Old English Ballads, 1553–1625* (Cambridge, 1920); *A Pepysian Garland, 1595–1639* (ballads; Cambridge, 1922)

Salgādo, G. (ed.) *Coney-Catchers and Bawdy Baskets* (Penguin, 1972)

Spencer, T. J. B. (ed.) *Elizabethan Love Stories* (Penguin, 1968)

Stillinger, J. (ed.) *Anthony Munday's 'Zelauto'* (Carbondale, Ill., 1963)

Stubbes, P. *Anatomy of Abuses* (1583); ed. F. J. Furnivall (London, 1877)

Thoms, W. J. (ed.) *Early English Prose Romances* (3 vols, London, 1828; rev. 1907)

Winny, J. (ed.) *The Descent of Euphues* (Cambridge, 1957)

Zall, P. M. (ed.) *A Hundred Merry Tales and other English Jestbooks of the 15th and 16th Centuries* (Lincoln, Nebr., 1963)

Baker, E. A. *A History of the English Novel*: II (London, 1929)

Baskervill, C. R. *The Elizabethan Jig and Related Song Drama* (Chicago, 1929; New York, 1965)

Bradbrook, M. C. *The Rise of the Common Player* (London, 1962)

Brand, J. *Popular Antiquities of Great Britain* (ed. Ellis, London, 1853)

Chambers, E. K. *The Medieval Stage* I, Bk II (folk drama; Oxford, 1903); *The English Folk-Play* (Oxford, 1933)

Chandler, F. W. *The Literature of Roguery* (2 vols, Boston, 1907)

Davis, W. R. *Idea and Act in Elizabethan Fiction* (Princeton, N. J., 1969)

Ernle, R. E. *The Light Reading of Our Ancestors* (London, 1927)

Farnham, W. 'The Mediaeval Comic Spirit in the English Renaissance' in (11), Section VII above

Firth, C. H. 'Ballad History of the Later Tudors', in T.R.H.S., III (1909); 'Ballad History of James I', T.R.H.S., V (1911); 'Ballads and Broadsides', in *Shakespeare's England* II (Oxford, 1916).

Harner, J. L. *English Renaissance Prose Fiction, 1500–1660: an Annotated Bibliography of Criticism* (London, 1978)

Herford, C. H. *Literary Relations of England and Germany in the 16th Century* (London, 1886)

Hodgart, M. J. C. *The Ballads* (London, 1950)

Jusserand, J. J. *The English Novel in the Time of Shakespeare* (London, 1890)

Nelson, W. *Fact or Fiction. The Dilemma of the Renaissance Storyteller* (Cambridge, Mass., 1973)

O'Connor, J. J. *Amadis de Gaule and its Influence on Elizabethan Literature* (New Brunswick, N. J., 1970)

O'Dell, S. *A Chronological List of Prose Fiction in English 1475–1640* (Cambridge, Mass., 1954)

Patchell, M. *The Palmerin Romances in Elizabethan Prose Fiction* (New York, 1947)

Pettet, E. C. *Shakespeare and the Romance Tradition* (London, 1949)

Pruvost, R. *Matteo Bandello and Elizabethan Fiction* (Paris, 1937)

Randall, D. B. *The Golden Tapestry: a Critical Survey of Non-chivalric Spanish Fiction in English Translation (1543–1657)* (Durham, N. C., 1963)

Rollins, H. E. 'The Black-letter Broadside Ballads', in P.M.L.A., XXXIV (1919)

Routh, H. V. 'Social Literature in Tudor Times', in C.H.E.L., III, and 'London and the Development of Popular Literature', in C.H.E.L., IV

Schlauch, M. *Antecedents of the English Novel, 1400–1600* (London, 1963)

Simpson, C. M. *The British Broadside Ballad* (New Brunswick, N. J., 1966)

Sisson, C. J. *Lost Plays of Shakespeare's Age* (Cambridge, 1936)

Tiddy, R. J. E. *The Mummer's Play* (Oxford, 1923)

White, H. C. *Social Criticism in Popular Religious Literature of the 16th Century* (New York, 1944)

Wilson, F. P. Survey of Jestbooks in *Huntington Library Quarterly*, II (1938) and in (56)

Wright, L. B. *Middle-class Culture in Elizabethan England* (chs xi–xv; Chapel Hill, N. C., 1935)

XII. AUTHORS, BOOKS, PATRONS AND PUBLIC

Adamson, J. W. 'Literacy in England in the 15th and 16th Centuries', in *The Library* (1930)

Bennett, H. S. *English Books and Readers Vol. II, 1558 to 1605* (Cambridge, 1965); *Vol. III, 1603 to 1640* (Cambridge, 1970)

Blagden, C. *The Stationer's Company: a History, 1403–1959* (London, 1960)

Bradbrook, M. C. *The Rise of the Common Player* (London, 1962)

Cipolla, C. M. *Literacy and Development in the West* (Pelican, 1969)

Clair, C. *A History of Printing in Britain* (London, 1965)

Cressy, D. *Literacy and the Social Order. Reading and Writing in Tudor and Stuart England* (Cambridge, 1980)

Eisenstein, E. *The Printing Press as an Agent of Change* (2 vols, Cambridge, 1978)

Greg, W. W. *Some Aspects and Problems of London Publishing between 1550 and 1650* (Oxford, 1953); and *Collected Papers* ed. J. C. Maxwell (Oxford, 1966)

Hunter, G. K. *John Lyly. The Humanist as Courtier* (London, 1962)

Irwin, R. *The Heritage of the English Library* (New York, 1964); ch. xi, 'Evidences of literacy'

Miller, E. H. *The Professional Writer in Elizabethan England* (Cambridge, Mass., 1959)

Rosenberg, E. *Leicester, Patron of Letters* (New York, 1955)

Rostenberg, L. *Literary, Political, Scientific, Religious and Legal Publishing, Printing and Bookselling in England, 1551–1700* (New York, 1965)

Saunders, J. W. *The Profession of English Letters* (London, 1964)

Sheavyn, P. *The Literary Profession in Elizabethan England* (1909); rev. J. W. Saunders (Manchester, 1967)

Williams, F. B. *Index of Dedications and Commendatory Verses in English Books before 1641* (London, 1962)

Wilson, F. P. 'Authors and Patrons in Tudor and Stuart Times', in (11), Section VII above

Wilson, J. D. (ed.) *Life in Shakespeare's England* (ch. vi, 'Books and Authors'; Pelican, 1944)

AUTHORS AND WORKS

Anthologies and Minor Works

I. POETRY

Alexander, N. (ed.) *Elizabethan Narrative Verse* (London, 1967)

Allott, R. (comp.) *England's Parnassus* (1600), ed. C. Crawford (Oxford, 1913)

Ault, N. (ed.) *Elizabethan Lyrics* (London, 1949); *Seventeenth-Century Lyrics* (London, 1950)

Carroll, D. A. (ed.) *Everard Guilpin: Skialetheia or A Shadowe of Truth, in Certaine Epigrams and Satyres* (Chapel Hill, N. C., 1974)

Chambers, E. K. (ed.) *The Oxford Book of 16th Century Verse* (Oxford, 1932; rev. 1961)

Donno, E. S. (ed.) *Elizabethan Minor Epics* (London, 1963)

Donow, H. S. *A Concordance to the Sonnet Sequences of Daniel, Drayton, Shakespeare, Sidney, and Spenser* (Carbondale, Ill., 1969)

England's Helicon (1600; 1614) ed. H. Macdonald (London, 1949, 1962)

Evans, M. (ed.) *Elizabethan Sonnets* (London, 1977; E.L.)

Fellowes, E. H. (ed.) *English Madrigal Verse 1588–1632* (Oxford, 1920); rev. and enlarged by F. W. Sternfeld and D. Greer (Oxford, 1967)

Gransden, K. W. (ed.) *Tudor Verse Satire* (London, 1970)

Grierson, H. J. C., and Bullough, G. (eds) *The Oxford Book of 17th Century Verse* (Oxford, 1934)

Grundy, J. *The Poems of Henry Constable* (London, 1960)

Hebel, J. W., and Hudson, H. H. (eds) *Poetry of the English Renaissance, 1509–1660* (with detailed notes; New York, 1932)

Hiller, G. G. (ed.) *Poems of the Elizabethan Age* (London, 1977)

Hunter, W. B. Jr. (ed.) *The English Spenserians* (Salt Lake City, Utah, 1971)

Lucie-Smith, E. (ed.) *The Penguin Book of Elizabethan Verse* (Penguin, 1965)

Macdonald, R. H. (ed.) *William Drummond of Hawthornden: Poems and Prose* (Edinburgh, 1976)

McNulty, R. *Ludovico Ariosto's Orlando Furioso* (Oxford, 1972): Sir John Harington's translation (1591)

Miller, P. W. (ed.) *Seven Minor Epics of the English Renaissance, 1596–1624*, facs. edn (Gainesville, Fla., 1967)

Pollard-Brown, N., and McDonald, J. H. (ed.) *The Poems of Robert Southwell, S.J.* (Oxford, 1967)

Robertson, J. (ed.) *Poems by Nicholas Breton Not Hitherto Reprinted* (Liverpool, 1952)

Rollins, H. E. (ed.) *Tottel's Miscellany* (1557–1587) (2 vols, Cambridge, Mass., 1928–9); *The Paradise of Dainty Devices* (1576–1606) (—, 1927); *A Gorgious Gallery of Gallant Inventions* (1578) (—, 1926); *A Handefull of Pleasant Delites* (1584) (—, 1924); *Brittons Bowre of Delights* (1591, 1597) (—, 1933); *The Phoenix Nest* (1593) (—, 1931); *The Arbor of amorous Devices* (1597) (—, 1937); *Englands Helicon* (1600, 1614) (2 vols, —, 1935); *A Poetical Rapsody* (1602–21), (2 vols, —, 1931–2)

II. PROSE

Aldington, R. (ed.) *A Book of 'Characters'* (London, 1924)

Harris, D. J. (ed.) *Elizabethan Prose* (London, 1968)

Harris, V., and Husain, I. (eds) *English Prose 1600–1660* (New York, 1965)

Hebel, J. W. (ed.) *Prose of the English Renaissance* (with notes; New York, 1952)

Lievsay, J. L. (ed.) *Daniell Tuvill, 'Essays Politic and Moral' and 'Essays Moral and Theological'* (Charlottesville, Va., 1971)

Mahl, M. R. (ed.) *17th Century English Prose* (New York, 1968)

Morley, H. (ed.) *Character Writings of the 17th Century* (London, 1891)

Muir, K. (ed.) *The Pelican Book of English Prose I: Elizabethan and Jacobean* (Pelican, 1956)

Novarr, D. (ed.) *17th Century English Prose* (New York, 1967)

Roberts, M. (ed.) *Elizabethan Prose* (London, 1933)

Stanwood, P. G., and O'Connor. D. (eds) *John Cosin: A collection of private devotions* (Oxford, 1967)

Ure, P. (ed.) *The Pelican Book of English Prose II: 17th Century* (Pelican, 1956)

Vickers, B. W. (ed.) *Seventeenth Century Prose* (London, 1969)

Wilson, J. D. (ed.) *Life in Shakespeare's England: a Book of Elizabethan Prose* (Cambridge, 1911)

III. DRAMA

Adams, J. Q. (ed.) *Chief Pre-Shakespearean Dramas* (Cambridge, Mass., 1924)

Armstrong, W. A. (ed.) *Elizabethan History Plays* (London, 1965, w.c.); cont.: Bale *King John*; Anon. *Edward III*; Anon. *Woodstock*; Ford *Perkin Warbeck*; Davenport *King John and Matilda*

Bond, R. W. (ed.) *Early plays from the Italian* (Oxford, 1911)

Brooke, C. F. T. (ed.) *The Shakespeare Apocrypha* (Oxford, 1908)

Craik, T. W. (ed.) *Minor Elizabethan Tragedies* (London, 1974; E.L.)

Cunliffe, J. W. (ed.) *Early English Tragedies* (Oxford, 1912)

Dodsley, R. (ed.) *A Select Collection of Old Plays* (ed. W. C. Hazlitt, 15 vols, London, 1874–6; New York, 1964)

Eliot, T. S. (ed.) *Seneca's Tragedies* (Eng. trans., 1581; 'Tudor Translations', 2 vols, London, 1927)

Evans, H. A. (ed.) *English Masques* (London, 1897)

Everitt, E. B., and Armstrong, R. L. (eds) *Six Early Plays Related to the Shakespeare Canon* (Copenhagen, 1965)

Gomme, A. H. (ed.) *Jacobean Tragedies* (London, 1969)

Harrier, R. C. (ed.) *An Anthology of Jacobean Drama* (2 vols, New York, 1963)

Horne, H. H. (ed.) *Nero and Other Plays* (M.S., 1888)

Lawrence, R. G. (ed.) *Early 17th Century Drama* (London, 1963; E.L.); *Jacobean and Caroline Comedies* (London, 1973; E.L.); *Jacobean and Caroline Tragedies* (London, 1975; E.L.)

Lefkowitz, M. (ed.) *Trois Masques à la Cour de Charles Ier d'Angleterre* (Paris, 1970): by Shirley, Davenant, I. Jones, W. Lawes

McIlwraith, A. K. (ed.) *Five Elizabethan Comedies* (London, 1934, w.c.); *Five Stuart Tragedies* (London, 1953, w.c.)

Salgādo, G. (ed.) *Three Jacobean Tragedies* (Penguin, 1965; rev. 1969); *Four Jacobean city comedies* (Penguin, 1975)

Spencer, T. J. B., and Wells, S. (eds) *A Book of Masques, in Honour of Allardyce Nicoll* (Cambridge, 1967); 14 masques, 1604–53

Sturgess, K. (ed.) *Three Elizabethan Domestic Tragedies* (Penguin, 1969)

Thorndike, A. (ed.) *Minor Elizabethan Drama* (2 vols, E.L., 1910)

Wine, M. L. (ed.) *The Tragedy of Master Arden of Faversham* (London, 1973; R.P.)

Note: The chief anonymous plays of the period can be found in the above collections and in the *Malone Society Reprints*: bibliography in Chambers, *Elizabethan Stage IV*, or in Harbage and Schoenbaum, *Annals of English Drama*. Two notable editions of anonymous plays are *Woodstock; A Moral History*, ed. A. P. Rossiter (London, 1946), and *The Three Parnassus Plays*, ed. J. B. Leishman (London, 1949).

Authors

ASCHAM, ROGER (1515–68): Humanist; b. Yorkshire (?); St John's College, Cambridge; prominent Greek scholar; *Toxophilus*, on archery and education, pub. 1545; tutor to Princess Elizabeth, 1548; secretary to English ambassador to Charles V, 1550–53; private tutor and secretary to Queen Elizabeth, 1558; said to have lived and died in poverty owing to addiction to dicing and cock-fighting; chief work on education, *The Schoolmaster*, pub. 1570.

Whole Works, ed. J. A. Giles (4 vols, London, 1864–5)
English Works, ed. W. A. Wright (Cambridge, 1904)
The Schoolmaster, ed. J. E. B. Mayor (London, 1863; New York, 1968); ed. R. J. Schoeck (Ontario, 1966); ed. L. V. Ryan (Ithaca, N. Y., 1968)
See F. Caspari, *Humanism and the Social Order in Tudor England* (Chicago, 1954)
   L. V. Ryan, *Roger Ascham* (Stanford, Ca., 1963)

BEAUMONT, FRANCIS (1584–1616): Dramatist; son of Sir Francis Beaumont of Grace-dieu, Leicestershire; Oxford, 1597; Inner Temple, 1600; friend of Drayton and Jonson; collaborated with Fletcher from *c.* 1608 to 1613; first play, *The Woman Hater*, pub. 1607.

The Works of Francis Beaumont and John Fletcher ed. A. Glover and A. R. Waller (10 vols, Cambridge, 1905–12); ed. F. Bowers (Cambridge, 1966–)
Select Plays (M.S., 2 vols; and E.L.)
A King and No King, ed. R. K. Turner (London, 1964; R.R.D.S.)
Beggars Bush (with Massinger) ed. J. H. Dorenkamp (The Hague, 1967)
The Knight of the Burning Pestle, ed. A. S. Murch (New York, 1908); ed. J. Doebler (London, 1967; R.R.D.S.); ed. A. Gurr (Edinburgh, 1968); ed. M. Hattaway (London, 1969; N.M.)
The Maid's Tragedy, ed. H. B. Norland (London, 1968; R.R.D.S.); ed. A. Gurr (Edinburgh, 1969)
Philaster, ed. A. Gurr (London, 1969; R.P.); ed. D. J. Ashe (London, 1975; R.R.D.S.)
Rollo, Duke of Normandy, ed. J. D. Jump (Liverpool, 1948)
The Woman's Prize, ed. G. B. Ferguson (The Hague, 1966)
See W. W. Appleton, *Beaumont and Fletcher* (London, 1956)
   D. L. Frost, *The School of Shakespeare* (Cambridge, 1968)
   A. Harbage, *Shakespeare and the Rival Traditions* (New York, 1952)
   C. Leech, *The John Fletcher Plays* (London, 1962)

K. Lynch, *The Social Mode of Restoration Comedy* (New York, 1926)

B. Maxwell, *Studies in Beaumont, Fletcher, and Massinger* (Chapel Hill, N. C., 1939)

N. C. Pearse, *John Fletcher's Chastity Plays: Mirrors of Modesty* (Lewisburg, Pa., 1973)

A. H. Thorndike, *The Influence of Beaumont and Fletcher on Shakespeare* (Worcester, Mass., 1901)

E. M. Waith, *The Pattern of Tragicomedy in Beaumont and Fletcher* (New Haven, 1952)

L. B. Wallis, *Fletcher, Beaumont and Company* (New York, 1947)

Essays by Bradbrook (6), Harbage (7), Danby (15), Bradbrook (18), Edwards (26), Ornstein (32), Wilson (54), Ellis-Fermor (36), Kirsch (63)

BROME, RICHARD (d. 1652): Dramatist; nothing known of birth or earlier life; served Jonson in some capacity (possibly secretary); wrote for King's Company.

Works of Richard Brome (3 vols, London, 1873)

The Antipodes and *A Mad Couple Well Matched* in *Six Caroline Plays* ed. A. S. Knowland (London, 1966; w.c.)

The Antipodes, ed. A. Haaker (London, 1967; R.R.D.S.)

A Jovial Crew, ed. A. Haaker (London, 1968; R.R.D.S.)

See C. E. Andrews, *Richard Brome* (New Haven, 1913; Hamden, Conn., 1972)

    J. L. Davis, *The Sons of Ben* (Detroit, 1967)

    I. Donaldson, *The World Upside Down: Comedy from Jonson to Fielding* (Oxford, 1970)

    A. L. Harbage, *Cavalier Drama* (New York, 1936, 1964)

    R. J. Kaufman, *Richard Brome, Caroline Playwright* (New York, 1961)

BURTON, ROBERT (1577–1640): Psychologist; b. Leicestershire; Nuneaton and Sutton Coldfield schools; Christ Church, Oxford; vicar of St Thomas's, Oxford; rector of Segrave, Leicestershire.

The Anatomy of Melancholy ed. A. H. Bullen (3 vols, London, 1893); ed. F. Dell and P. Jordan-Smith (New York, 1927); ed. H. Jackson (3 vols, London, 1932; E.L.)

See L. Babb, *Sanity in Bedlam* (East Lansing, 1959)

    R. A. Fox, *The Tangled Chain: The Structure of Disorder in the 'Anatomy of Melancholy'* (Berkeley, Ca., 1976)

    B. G. Lyons, *Voices of Melancholy* (London, 1971)

    W. R. Mueller, *The Anatomy of Robert Burton's England* (Berkeley, Ca., 1952)

    J. M. Murry, *Countries of the Mind* (London, 1922)

    J. Simon, *Robert Burton et L'Anatomie de la Mélancolie* (Paris, 1964)

    J. Webber, *The Eloquent 'I'. Style and Self in Seventeenth-Century Prose* (London, 1968)

Essays by Wilson (33), Bush (38), Colie (Section IX above)

CAMPION, THOMAS (1567–1620): Poet and musician; son of John Campion, one of the cursitors of Chancery Court; Peterhouse, Cambridge; law student; degree in medicine; found patron in Sir Thomas Monson; wrote masques 1607–13; renowned among contemporaries as musician as well as poet.

Works ed. P. Vivian (Oxford, 1909, 1966); ed. W. R. Davis (New York, 1967; London, 1969)

Observations in the Art of English Poesie, in G. G. Smith (Section IX above); ed. J. Hart, w. sel. poems (Cheadle, 1976)

See H. C. Colles, *Voice and Verse* (London, 1928)

> M. T. Eldridge, *Thomas Campion; his Poetry, and Music, 1567–1620* (New York, 1971)
>
> C. Ing, *Elizabethan Lyrics* (London, 1951, 1968)
>
> M. M. Kastendieck, *Thomas Campion, England's Musical Poet* (New York, 1938, 1963)
>
> E. Lowbury, T. Salter, and A. Young, *Thomas Campion; Poet, Composer, Physician* (London, 1970)
>
> W. Mellers, *Music and Society* (London, 1946)
>
> B. Pattison, *Music and Poetry of the English Renaissance* (London, 1948)
>
> P. Warlock, *The English Ayre* (London, 1926)

CHAPMAN, GEORGE (*c.* 1559–1634): Poet and dramatist; b. Hertfordshire; claimed to be self-taught but perhaps studied at Oxford; travelled abroad; served in Netherlands wars (?); first poem, *The Shadow of Night*, 1594; writing for stage from *c.* 1595–1603; patrons – Essex, then Prince Henry 1604–12, then Somerset; friends and/or collaborators – Marlowe, Harriot the astronomer, Inigo Jones, Marston, and Jonson; imprisoned with Marston and Jonson for offending the Scots in *Eastward Ho!*, 1605; translated the *Iliad* and *Odyssey*, 1598–1616; much of his life spent in poverty.

Works ed. R. H. Shepherd (London, 1875–92)

Tragedies (London, 1910) and *Comedies* (London, 1914) ed. T. M. Parrott

The Plays of George Chapman: The Comedies, ed. A. Holaday and M. Kiernan (Urbana, Ill., 1970–)

Best Plays by George Chapman (M.S.)

All Fools, ed. F. Manley (London, 1968; R.R.D.S.)

Bussy d'Ambois ed. J. Jacquot (Paris, n.d. [1960]); ed. R. J. Lordi (London, 1964; R.R.D.S.); ed. N. Brooke (London, 1964; R.P.); ed. M. Evans (London, 1965; N.M.)

Eastward Ho! (Chapman, Jonson, and Marston), ed. C. G. Petter (London, 1973; N.M.); ed. R. W. Van Fossen (Manchester, 1979; R.P.)

The Gentleman Usher, ed. J. H. Smith (London, 1970; R.R.D.S.)

The Revenge of Bussy d'Ambois ed. R. J. Lordi (Salzburg, 1977)

The Widow's Tears ed. E. M. Smeak (London, 1967; R.R.D.S.); ed. A. Yamada (London, 1975; R.P.)

Chapman's Homer ed. Allardyce Nicholl (2 vols, London, 1957). Contains *Iliad* (Vol I), *Odyssey* and the *Lesser Homerica* (Vol. 2). For his translations from Musaeus, Hesiod, and Juvenal consult *Hymns and Epigrams of Homer* ed. R. Hooper (London, 1888) and see Schoell below.

Poems ed. P. B. Bartlett (New York, 1941). For *Hero and Leander*, poem completed by Chapman, see Marlowe's *Poems* ed. L. C. Martin.

See T. Bogard, *The Tragic Satire of John Webster*, Part One (Berkeley and Los Angeles, 1955)

> M. C. Bradbrook, *George Chapman* (London, 1977; W.T.W.)
>
> D. Bush, *Mythology and the Renaissance Tradition* (rev. New York, 1963)
>
> D. J. Gordon, 'Chapman's *Hero and Leander*', in (65)

J. Jacquot, *George Chapman, sa vie, sa poésie, son théâtre, sa pensée* (Paris, 1951)
C. S. Lewis, 'Hero and Leander', in P.B.A., XXXVIII (1952), and in (47)
G. de F. Lord, *Homeric Renaissance: the 'Odyssey' of G. Chapman* (New Haven, 1956)
M. MacLure, *George Chapman, a Critical Study* (London, 1966)
E. Rees, *The Tragedies of George Chapman* (Cambridge, Mass., 1954)
F. L. Schoell, *Études sur l'humanisme continental en Angleterre* (Paris, 1926)
R. B. Waddington, *The Mind's Empire. Myth and Form in George Chapman's Narrative Poems* (London, 1974)
J. W. Weiler, *George Chapman – the Effect of Stoicism upon his Tragedies* (New York, 1949)
L. R. Zocca, *Elizabethan Narrative Poetry* (New Brunswick, N. J., 1950)
Essays by Bradbrook (18), Ure (26), Ornstein (32), Ellis-Fermor (16), Battenhouse (37), Bush (38), Waith (40), E. Muir (45), Lever (62), Ribner (70)

DANIEL, SAMUEL (1562–1619): Poet; b. near Taunton; son of music-master and brother of John Daniel, a great song composer; Magdalen Hall, Oxford; travelled in France and Italy; tutor in various noble families; patrons included Sidney's sister and Fulke Greville; translating 1585; first poems (sonnets), 1591; held minor court offices; wrote four court entertainments, 1603–14; managed the Queen's Revels Children and helped to found a Children's Company at Bristol, 1615; d. in retirement in Somerset.

Complete Works, ed. A. B. Grosart (5 vols, London, 1885–96; New York, 1963)
Civil Wars ed. L. Michel (New Haven, 1958)
'Delia' sonnets in Sidney Lee, *Elizabethan Sonnets* (London, 1904)
Poems and a Defence of Ryme ed. A. C. Sprague (Cambridge, Mass., 1930; London, 1950)
A Vision of the Twelve Goddesses (masque) ed. H. A. Evans in *English Masques* (Glasgow, 1897)
Musophilus ed. R. Himelick (West Lafayette, Ind., 1965)
Cleopatra ed. M. Lederer (Louvain, 1908)
Philotas ed. L. Michel (London, 1949)
A defence of Rhyme, in G. G. Smith (Section IX above)
See Joan Rees, *Samuel Daniel* (Liverpool, 1964)
    C. Schaar, *An Elizabethan Sonnet Problem* (Lund, 1960): Daniel and Shakespeare
    C. Seronsy, *Samuel Daniel* (New York, 1967)
    P. Spriet, *Samuel Daniel, 1563–1619: Sa vie – Son œuvre* (Paris, 1968)
Essays by Scott (3), John (9), Lewis (17), Lever (21), Bush (38), Spencer (46)

DAVIES, SIR JOHN (1569–1626): Poet; b. Tilsbury, Wiltshire; Winchester and Oxford; entered Middle Temple and formed literary friendships *c.* 1588; disbarred for assault on a fellow-member of the Middle Temple, 1598–1601; prominent administrator in Ireland under James I; appointed Lord Chief Justice of England but died of apoplexy before taking office.

Works ed. A. B. Grosart (2 vols, London, 1876)
Orchestra, ed. E. M. W. Tillyard (London, 1945)
Poems in *Silver Poets of the 16th Century* G. Bullett (E.L.); ed. C. Howard (New York, 1941); ed. R. Krueger and P. Nemser (Oxford, 1975)

See E. M. W. Tillyard, *The Elizabethan World Picture* (London, 1943) and *Five Poems*
(London, 1948)
J. L. Sanderson, *Sir John Davies* (Boston, Mass., 1975)
Essays by Spencer (46), Eliot (47)

DEKKER, THOMAS (*c.* 1572–*c.* 1632): Dramatist and pamphleteer; Londoner;
writing continually from 1598; frequent stage collaborations; took part against
Jonson in 'War of the Theatres', 1599–1601; in prison for debt, 1613–19.

Plays ed. F. Bowers (Cambridge, 1953–1961); *Introduction, Notes and Commentaries,*
ed. C. Hoy (4 vols, Cambridge, 1980–)
The non-dramatic works ed. A. B. Grosart (5 vols, London, 1884–6; New York,
1963)
Plague Pamphlets ed. F. P. Wilson (Oxford, 1925)
Selected Writings ed. E. D. Pendry (London, 1967)
The Gull's Hornbook ed. R. B. McKerrow (London, 1904, 1907)
A Knight's Conjuring, ed. L. M. Robbins (The Hague, 1974)
Lust's Dominion, ed. J. L. Brereton (Louvain, 1931)
The Roaring Girl (with Middleton), ed. A. Gomme (London, 1976; N.M.)
The Shoemaker's Holiday ed. J. B. Steane (Cambridge, 1965); ed. P. C. Davies
(Edinburgh, 1968); ed. D. J. Palmer (London, 1975; N.M.); ed. R. L. Smallwood
and S. Wells (Manchester, 1979 R.P.)
See J. H. Conover, *Thomas Dekker: An Analysis of Dramatic Structure* (The Hague,
1968)
K. L. Gregg, *Thomas Dekker, a Study in Economic and Social Backgrounds* (Seattle,
1924)
M. L. Hunt, *Thomas Dekker: A Study* (New York, 1911)
M. T. Jones-Davies, *Un peintre de la vie londonienne: Thomas Dekker* (2 vols,
Paris, 1958)
A. V. Judges, *Elizabethan Underworld* (London, 1930; 1965)
G. R. Price, *Thomas Dekker* (New York, 1969)
Essays by Knights (8), Bradbrook (18), Brown (26), Ellis-Fermor (34 and 36),
Gibbons (53)

DELONEY, THOMAS (d. 1600): Ballad-writer and novelist; Norwich silkweaver; writing ballads in London, 1586 (?); aroused official displeasure in
1596 by reference to the Queen in a ballad; turned to novel writing; d. in
poverty.

Works ed. F. O. Mann (Oxford, 1912; 1967)
Novels ed. M. E. Lawlis (Bloomington, Ind. 1961)
Jack of Newbury and *Thomas of Reading* in *Shorter Novels, Elizabethan and Jacobean*
(E.L.)
The Garland of Goodwill (ballads), reprinted J. H. Dixon (London, 1842)
See A. Chevalley, *Thomas Deloney: le roman des métiers au temps de Shakespeare*
(Paris, 1926)
R. G. Howarth, *Two Elizabethan Writers of Fiction: Thomas Nashe and Thomas
Deloney* (Cape Town, 1950)
M. E. Lawlis, *Apology for the Middle Class: The Dramatic Novels of Thomas
Deloney* (Bloomington, Ind. 1960)
M. Schlauch, *Antecedents of the English Novel, 1400–1600* (London, 1963)

DRAYTON, MICHAEL (1563–1631): Poet; b. Hartshill, Warwickshire; son of prosperous trades-people; page in house of Sir Henry Goodere; lasting friendship with Anne Goodere ('Idea' in his sonnets); poems of many kinds, 1591–1630; writing plays for Henslowe, 1597–1602; found patron in Sir Walter Aston; made many literary friendships.

> *Works* ed. J. W. Hebel (4 vols, Oxford, 1931–5); 5th vol. ed. K. Tillotson and B. H. Newdigate (Oxford, 1941; all rev. 1961)
> *Three Plays*, ed. K. Sturgess (Penguin, 1970)
> *Poems* (selected) ed. J. Buxton (2 vols, London, 1953)
> See J. A. Berthelot, *Michael Drayton* (New York, 1967)
>> P. G. Buchloh, *Michael Drayton, Barde und Historiker, Politiker und Prophet* (Neumünster, 1964)
>> D. Bush, *Mythology and the Renaissance Tradition* (rev. New York, 1963)
>> O. Elton, *Michael Drayton, A Critical Study* (London, 1905)
>> R. F. Hardin, *Michael Drayton and the Passing of Elizabethan England* (Lawrence, Ka., 1973)
>> C. Maddison, *Apollo and the Nine: a History of the Ode* (London, 1960)
>> N. C. de Nagy, *Michael Drayton's 'England's heroical epistles'; a study in themes and compositional devices* (Bern, 1968)
>> B. H. Newdigate, *Michael Drayton and his circle* (Oxford, 1941; corr., 1961)
>> L. R. Zocca, *Elizabethan Narrative Poetry* (New Brunswick, N. J., 1950)
> Essays by Scott (3), John (9), Smith (16), Lever (21), Grundy (59)

FLETCHER, JOHN (1579–1625): Dramatist; b. Rye, Sussex; son of clergyman (later Bishop of London) and member of prominent literary family; began writing for stage *c.* 1607, first with Beaumont, then in collaboration with Massinger and others; died of plague.

> Works and Criticism – See under Beaumont

FORD, JOHN (1586–*c.* 1640?): Dramatist; member of landed Devonshire family (?); Oxford; Middle Temple, 1602; early poems, 1606; writing for stage from 1613.

> *Works* ed. W. Gifford (2 vols, 1827); rev. A. Dyce (3 vols, London, 1869, 1895)
> *Dramatic Works*. Vol. I ed. W. Bang (Louvain, 1908). Vol. II ed. H. de Vocht (Louvain, 1927); Selected plays in M.S. and E.L.
> *The Broken Heart* ed. B. Morris (London, 1965; N.M.); ed. D. K. Anderson (London, 1968; R.R.D.S.)
> *'Tis Pity She's A Whore*, ed. N. W. Bawcutt (London, 1966; R.R.D.S.); ed. B. Morris (London, 1968; N.M.); ed. D. Roper (London, 1975)
> *Perkin Warbeck* ed. M. C. Struble (Seattle, 1926); ed. D. K. Anderson (London, 1965; R.R.D.S.); ed. P. Ure (London, 1968; R.P.) and in *Elizabethan History Plays* ed. W. A. Armstrong (W.C.)
> *Three Plays*, ed. K. Sturgess (Penguin, 1970)
> See D. K. Anderson, *John Ford* (New York, 1972)
>> R. Davril, *Le Drame de John Ford* (Paris, 1954)
>> D. M. Farr, *John Ford and the Caroline Theatre* (London, 1979)
>> R. Huebert, *John Ford, Baroque English Dramatist* (Montreal, 1977)

AUTHORS AND WORKS

C. Leech, *John Ford and the Drama of his Time* (London, 1957)
H. J. Oliver, *The Problem of John Ford* (Melbourne, 1955)
M. J. Sargeaunt, *John Ford* (Oxford, 1935)
G. F. Sensabaugh, *The Tragic Muse of John Ford* (London, 1944)
M. Stavig, *John Ford and the Traditional Moral Order* (Madison, Wis., 1968)
Essays by Bradbrook (6), Eliot (14), Ornstein (32), Ellis-Fermor (36), Kaufmann (37), Kirsch (63), Ure (64), Barton (67)

GASCOIGNE, GEORGE (1542?–77): Poet; b. Bedfordshire; son of Sir John Gascoigne; Cambridge; entered Gray's Inn; M.P. for Bedford; went to Holland to escape creditors, 1573, and did military service there; one of the first of Elizabethan gentry to turn to literature as an aid in making a career – poems, plays, novel-writing, moral pamphlets.

Works ed. J. W. Cunliffe (2 vols, Cambridge, 1907–1910)
A Hundreth Sundrie Flowers ed. C. T. Prouty (Colombia, Missouri, 1942); ed. B. M. Ward and R. L. Miller (Port Washington, N. Y., 1975)
The steele glas and *The complaints of Phylomene*, ed. W. L. Wallace (Salzburg, 1975)
Notes of Instruction in English Verse, in G. G. Smith (Section IX above)
Life by C. T. Prouty (New York, 1942, 1966)
See R. C. Johnson, *George Gascoigne* (New York, 1972)
   J. Thompson, *The Founding of English Metre* (London, 1961)
Essays by Peterson (48), Winters (50)

GREENE, ROBERT (c. 1558–92): Dramatist and novelist; b. Norwich; Cambridge; travelled and began writing for press before taking M.A.; became leader of Bohemian literary group, London; reputation for dissipation, mainly owing to his own sensational confessions in autobiographical pamphlets.

Bibliography by T. Hayashi (Metuchen, N. J., 1971)
Complete Works ed. A. B. Grosart (15 vols, London, 1881–6; New York, 1964)
Plays ed. T. H. Dickinson (M.S.)
Plays and Poems ed. J. C. Collins (2 vols, Oxford, 1905)
A looking glasse for London and England, ed. T. Hayashi (Metuchen, N. J., 1970)
Ciceronis Amor: Tullies love ed. C. H. Larson (Salzburg, 1974)
Friar Bacon and Friar Bungay ed. D. Seltzer (London, 1964; R.R.D.S.); ed. J. A. Lavin (London, 1969; N.M.)
James IV, ed. J. A. Lavin (London, 1967; N.M.) ed. N. Sanders (London, 1970; R.P.); ed. C. H. Stein (Salzburg, 1977)
Pamphlets ed. G. B. Harrison (Bodley Head Quartos); in A. V. Judges (ed.) *The Elizabethan Underworld* (London, 1930; 1965); G. Salgãdo (ed.) *Coney-Catchers and Bawdy Baskets* (Penguin, 1972)
Planetomachia, ed. D. F. Bratchell (Letchworth, 1979)
Two novels in *Shorter Elizabethan Novels* (E.L.)
Pandosto in *The Descent of Euphues* ed. J. Winny (Cambridge, 1957)
See F. Ferrara, *L'opera narrativa di Robert Greene* (Venezia, 1957)
   T. Hayashi, *A textual study of Robert Greene's 'Orlando Furioso', with an Elizabethan text* (Muncie, Ind., 1973)
   E. H. Miller, *The Professional Writer in Elizabethan England* (Cambridge, Mass., 1959)

R. Pruvost, *Robert Greene et ses romans* (Paris, 1938)

M. Schlauch, *Antecedents of the English Novel 1400–1600* (London, 1963)

S. L. Wolff, *The Greek Romances in Elizabethan Prose Fiction* (New York, 1912, 1961)

Essays by Bradbrook (19), Sanders (28), Clemen (35), Muir (42)

GREVILLE, FULKE (1554–1628); Poet; b. Beauchamp Court, Warwickshire; Shrewsbury and Cambridge; joined school friend Sidney at court, 1577; held many official positions; great patron of letters; d. from wound inflicted by discharged servant.

Works ed. A. B. Grosart (4 vols, London, 1870)

Life of Sidney ed. N. C. Smith (Oxford, 1907)

Poems and Dramas ed. G. Bullough (2 vols, London, 1939, 1969)

Selected Poems ed. T. Gunn (London, 1968); *Selected Writings* ed. J. Rees (London, 1973)

The Remains; being poems of monarchy and religion ed. G. A. Wilkes (London, 1965)

See M. W. Croll, *Works of Fulke Greville* (Philadelphia, 1904)

    R. A. Rebholz, *The Life of Fulke Greville, first Lord Brooke* (Oxford, 1971)

    J. Rees, *Fulke Greville, Lord Brooke, 1554–1628; a Critical Biography* (London, 1971)

    R. Waswo, *The Fatal Mirror; Themes and Techniques in the Poetry of Fulke Greville* (Charlottesville, Va., 1972)

Essays by Scott (3), John (9), Ellis-Fermor (36), Peterson (48), Winters (50), I. Morris (Sh.S. XIV, 1968)

HALL, JOSEPH (1574–1656): Poet; b. Ashby-de-la-Zouche; Emmanuel, Cambridge, 1589; Puritan leanings; verse satires, 1597; also Utopian prose satire and 'character' writings; much religious prose; Bishop of Exeter, 1627; defended episcopacy against Milton, 1641.

Works ed. P. Wynter (10 vols, Oxford, 1863)

Poems ed. A. Davenport (Liverpool, 1949)

The Discovery of a New World ed. H. Brown (Cambridge, Mass., 1937)

Heaven upon earth and *Characters of Vertues and Vices* ed. R. Kirk (New Brunswick, N. J., 1948)

Character Writings of the 17th Century ed. H. Morley (London, 1891)

See B. Boyce, *The Theophrastan Character in England to 1642* (Cambridge, Mass., 1947: London, 1967)

    D. Bush, *English Literature in the Early 17th Century* (Oxford, 1945; 1962)

    F. L. Huntley, *Bishop Joseph Hall, 1574–1656. A Bibliographical and Critical Study* (Cambridge, 1979)

    T. F. Kinloch, *The Life and Works of Joseph Hall, 1574–1656* (London, 1951)

    L. D. Tourney, *Joseph Hall* (Boston, Mass., 1979)

HARVEY, GABRIEL (1545?–1631): Teacher of rhetoric and classical literature; born at Saffron Walden, eldest son of prosperous ropemaker; Christ's College, Cambridge; in 1570 became Fellow of Pembroke Hall, where he met Spenser, who became a lifelong friend and with whom he discussed the practicability of strict Latin verse-models (Harvey is represented in *The Shepherds Calendar* as Hobbinol); led a quarrelsome life at Cambridge, frequently suing for office and being passed over; moved to Trinity Hall in 1578, in which year

he presented celebratory verses to Queen Elizabeth on her visit to Audley
End; with his *Foure Letters* of 1592 entered into a violent controversy with
Greene; Nashe came to the defence of Greene with a series of brilliantly
abusive pamphlets from *Strange News* (1593) to *Have with you to Saffron Walden*
(1596); in 1599 it was ordered that 'all Nashes bookes and Dr Harvey's bookes
be taken wheresoever they may be found' and that they should not be reprinted; later life spent quietly at Saffron Walden.

Works ed. A. B. Grosart (3 vols, London, 1884–5)
Foure Letters, and Certaine Sonnets: Especially Touching Robert Greene ed. G. B.
    Harrison (London, 1922; Edinburgh, 1967)
Ciceronianus ed. H. S. Wilson, tr. C. A. Forbes (Lincoln, Nebraska, 1954)
The Letter Book of Gabriel Harvey ed. E. J. Scott (Camden Society, London, 1884)
Marginalia ed. G. C. Moore Smith (Stratford-on-Avon, 1913)
Excerpts from his literary criticism in G. G. Smith (Section IX above)
See P. A. Duhamel, 'The Ciceronianism of Gabriel Harvey', *Studies in Philology*,
    XLIX (1952)
    H. Haydn, *The Counter-Renaissance* (New York, 1950)
    G. C. Moore Smith, introduction to edn of *Pedantius* (Louvain, 1905)
    W. Schrickx, *Shakespeare's Early Contemporaries: The Background of the Harvey-
        Nashe Polemic and 'Love's Labour's Lost'* (Antwerp, 1956)
    V. F. Stern, *Gabriel Harvey. His Life, Marginalia and Library* (Oxford, 1979)
    H. S. Wilson, 'The Humanism of Gabriel Harvey', in (11)

HEYWOOD, THOMAS (*c.* 1570–1641): Dramatist; b. Lincolnshire (?); Cambridge (?); earliest play, *The Four Prentices of London* (pub. 1615), may have
been written as early as 1592; from 1596 writing and acting for Admiral's
Company; produced much non-dramatic work in verse and prose (e.g. *An
Apology for Actors, c.* 1608); claimed for himself in 1633 'two hundred and
twenty (plays) in which I have had either an entire hand, or at the least a
main finger'.

Dramatic Works ed. R. H. Shepherd (6 vols, London, 1874)
Best Plays ed. A. W. Verity (M.S.)
A woman killed with kindness ed. R. W. Van Fossen (London, 1961; R.P.)
An Apology for Actors (Shakespeare Society, 1841); ed. R. H. Perkinson (New
    York, 1941)
The Fair Maid of the West, ed. R. K. Turner (London; 1968; R.R.D.S.)
Love's mistress, or The Queen's masque ed. R. C. Shady (Salzburg, 1977)
The rape of Lucrece ed. A. Holaday (Urbana, Ill., 1950)
See F. S. Boas, *Thomas Heywood* (London, 1950)
    A. M. Clark, *Thomas Heywood* (Oxford, 1931)
    M. Grivelet, *Thomas Heywood et le drame domestique élizabéthain* (Paris, 1957)
Essays by Eliot (14), Bradbrook (18), Brown (42), Grivelet (Sh.S., XIV, 1961)

HOOKER, RICHARD (1553?–1600): Theologian; b. Heavitree, Exeter; Corpus
Christi College, Oxford; became Fellow of College; Master of the Temple,
1585; held various livings; leading Anglican controversialist.

Bibliography 1593–1724 by W. S. Hill (Cleveland, Ohio, 1970)

Works, ed. W. S. Hill, *et al.* (8 vols, Cambridge, Mass., 1977–)

Laws of Ecclesiastical Polity, ed. J. Keble, rev. R. W. Church and F. Paget (3 vols, Oxford, 1888); abridged ed. A. S. McGrade and B. W. Vickers (London, 1976)
Books I–IV ed. R. Bayne (2 vols, E.L.): Book VIII, ed. R. A. Houk (New York, 1931)

See J. W. Allen, *Political Thought in the 16th Century* (London, 1928)
M. H. Carré, *Phrases of Thought in England*, ch. vi (Oxford, 1949)
A. P. d'Entrèves, *The medieval contribution to political thought: Thomas Aquinas, Marsilius of Padua, Richard Hooker* (London, 1939)
W. S. Hill (ed.) *Studies in Richard Hooker* (Cleveland, Ohio, 1972)
J. S. Marshall, *Hooker and the Anglican Tradition* (London, 1963)
C. Morris, *Political Thought in England: Tyndale to Hooker* (London, 1953)
C. J. Sisson, *The Judicious Marriage of Mr Hooker and the Birth of the 'Laws of Ecclesiastical Polity'* (Cambridge, 1940)
I. Walton, *Lives*, ed. G. Saintsbury (W.C.)

Essays by Talbert (39)

JONSON, BENJAMIN (1572–1637): Dramatist; b. Westminster; son of minister; Westminster School; bricklayer till enlisted; writing for Henslowe by 1597; leading figure in 'War of the Theatres'; regarded as leader among London poets and wits; wrote masques for court which were regarded with great favour by James, 1605–31; from 1616 granted pension as 'King's poet'; succeeded Middleton as city chronologer.

Bibliography 1947–72 by D. H. Brock and J. M. Welsh (Metuchen, N. J., 1974)

The Works of Ben Jonson ed. C. H. Herford, P. and E. Simpson (11 vols, Oxford, 1925–52; 1965–70)

Best Plays of Ben Jonson ed. B. Nicholson (M.S.)

Complete Plays of Ben Jonson ed. F. E. Schelling (E.L.)

Five Plays ed. Herford and Simpson (London, 1953, W.C.)

Three Comedies ed. M. Jamieson (Penguin, 1966)

Complete Masques, ed. S. Orgel (Yale, 1969); *Selected Masques*, ed. S. Orgel (Yale, 1970)

Every Man in his Humour ed. A. Sale (London, 1949); ed. M. Seymour-Smith (London, 1966, N.M.); ed. G. B. Jackson (Yale, 1969); ed. J. W. Lever (London, 1972; R.R.D.S.)

Sejanus ed. J. Barish (Yale, 1965); ed. W. F. Bolton (London, 1966, N.M.)

Volpone ed. D. Cook (London, 1962); ed. A. Kernan (Yale, 1962); ed. J. B. Bamborough (London, 1963); ed. P. Brockbank (London, 1968; N.M.); ed. J. Halio (Edinburgh, 1968); ed. J. W. Creaser (London, 1978)

Epicoene ed. D. Beaurline (London, 1967; R.R.D.S.); ed. E. B. Partridge (Yale, 1971)

The Alchemist ed. F. H. Mares (London, 1967; R.P.); ed. J. B. Steane (Cambridge, 1967); ed. D. Brown (London, 1966; N.M.); ed. S. Musgrove (Edinburgh, 1968); ed. A Sale (London, 1969); ed. A Kernan (Yale, 1974)

Bartholomew Fair ed. E. A. Horsman (London, 1960; R.P.); ed. M. Hussey (London, 1964; N.M.); ed. E. M. Waith (Yale, 1963); ed. E. Partridge (London, 1964; R.R.D.S.); ed. D. Duncan (Edinburgh, 1972); ed. G. B. Hibbard (London, 1977; N.M.)

Catiline ed. W. F. Bolton and J. F. Gardner (London, 1973; R.R.D.S.)

The Devil is an Ass ed. M. Hussey (London, 1967)

The Staple of News ed. D. R. Kifer (London, 1976; R.R.D.S.)

Timber, or Discoveries ed. G. B. Harrison (London, 1923, Edinburgh, 1966); in Herford and Simpson, VIII (text) and XI (notes); excerpts in collections by Spingarn and Tayler (Section IX above); *Ben Jonson's Literary Criticism*, ed. J. D. Redwine (Lincoln, Neb., 1970)

Poems ed. B. H. Newdigate (Oxford, 1936); ed. G. B. Johnston (London, 1954); ed. W. B. Hunter (New York, 1963); ed. I. Donaldson (London, 1975); ed. G. Parfitt (Penguin, 1975)

See *The Man and his Work*, in Hereford and Simpson, 1–11

J. B. Bamborough, *Ben Jonson* (London, 1970)

J. A. Barish, *Ben Jonson and the Language of Prose Comedy* (Cambridge, Mass., 1960)

J. A. Barish (ed.) *Twentieth Century Views: Ben Jonson* (New Jersey, 1963)

L. Beaurline, *Ben Jonson and Elizabethan Comedy: Essays in Dramatic Rhetoric* (San Marino, Ca., 1978)

G. E. Bentley, *Shakespeare and Jonson. Their Reputations in the 17th Century Compared* (2 vols, Cambridge, 1945); but see D. L. Frost in Sh.Q., nXVI (1965)

W. Blisset, J. Patrick, and R. Van Fossen (eds) *A Celebration of Ben Jonson* (Toronto, 1973)

O. J. Campbell, *Comicall Satyre and Shakespeare's 'Troilus and Cressida'* (San Marino, Ca., 1938)

L. Champion, *Ben Jonson's 'Dotages': A Reconsideration of the Late Plays* (Lexington, Ky., 1967)

M. Chan, *Music in the Theatre of Ben Jonson* (Oxford, 1980)

J. L. Davis, *The Sons of Ben. Jonsonian Comedy in Caroline England* (Detroit, 1967)

A. C. Dessen, *Jonson's Moral Comedy* (Evanston, Ill., 1971)

D. Duncan, *Ben Jonson and the Lucianic Tradition* (Cambridge, 1979)

J. J. Enck, *Jonson and the Comic Truth* (Madison, Wis., 1957)

W. T. Furniss, 'Ben Jonson's Masques' in *Three Studies in the Renaissance* (New Haven, 1958)

A. H. Gilbert, *The Symbolic Persons in the Masques of Ben Jonson* (Durham, N. C., 1948)

D. J. Gordon, Essays on Jonson's Masques in J.W.C.I., VI (1943) and XII (1949), repr. in (65), Section VII above

G. J. Jackson, *Vision and Judgment in Ben Jonson's Drama* (New Haven, 1968)

A. Kernan (ed.) *Two Renaissance Mythmakers. Christopher Marlowe and Ben Jonson* (London, 1977)

R. E. Knoll, *Ben Jonson's Plays* (Lincoln, Neb., 1964)

D. McPherson, *Ben Jonson's Library and Marginalia; an Annotated Catalogue*, Studies in Philology v 71. Texts and Studies (Chapel Hill, N. C., 1974)

J. C. Meagher, *Method and Meaning in Jonson's Masques* (Notre Dame, Ind., 1966)

A. Nicoll, *Stuart Masques and the Renaissance Stage* (London, 1957)

S. Orgel, *The Jonsonian Masque* (Cambridge, Mass., 1965)

E. B. Partridge, *The Broken Compass* (London, 1958)

D. B. J. Randall, *Jonson's Gypsies Unmasked* (Durham, N. C., 1974)

A. H. Sackton, *Rhetoric as a Dramatic Language in Ben Jonson* (New York, 1948, 1968)

C. G. Thayer, *Ben Jonson: Studies in the Plays* (Norman, Ok., 1963)

W. Trimpi, *Ben Jonson's Poems; a Study of the Plain Style* (Stanford, Ca., 1962)

C. F. Wheeler, *Classical Mythology in the Plays, Masques, and Poems of Ben Jonson*

(Princeton, 1938; Port Washington, N.Y., 1970)
Essays by Harbage (7), Knights (8), Eliot (14), Bradbrook (18), Hill (26), Armstrong (26), Partridge (31), Ornstein (32), Ellis-Fermor (36), Gibbons (53), Salingar (67)

KYD, THOMAS (1558–94): Dramatist; b. London, son of a scrivener; Merchant Taylors' School; worked as a scrivener before writing plays and translations (?); connected with Marlowe.

    Works, ed. F. S. Boas (Oxford, 1901, rev. 1955)
    The Spanish Tragedy ed. P. Edwards (London, 1959; R.P.); ed. B. L. Joseph (London, 1964; N.M.) ed. A. S. Cairncross (London, 1967; R.R.D.S.); ed. T. W. Ross (Edinburgh, 1968); ed. J. R. Mulryne (London, 1970; N.M.)
    See H. Baker, *Induction to Tragedy* (Baton Rouge, Louisiana, 1939)
        F. T. Bowers, *Elizabethan Revenge Tragedy* (Princeton, 1940; rev. 1959)
        F. Carrère, *Le Théâtre de Thomas Kyd* (Toulouse, 1951)
        P. Edwards, *Thomas Kyd and Early Elizabethan Tragedy* (London, 1966)
        A. Freeman, *Thomas Kyd: Facts and Problems* (Oxford, 1967)
        H. Hawkins, *Likenesses of Truth in Elizabethan and Restoration Drama* (Oxford, 1972)
        P. B. Murray, *Thomas Kyd* (New York, 1970)
    Essays by Barish (31), Clemen (35), Empson (37), Harbage (42), Johnson (42), Mehl (44), Prosser (49)

LODGE, THOMAS (*c.* 1558–1625): Novelist and poet; son of a Lord Mayor of London; Merchant Taylors' School; Trinity, Oxford, 1573; Lincoln's Inn, 1578; began writing 1579 with defence of plays; with Cavendish's expedition to South America, 1591–3; wrote poems, novels, pamphlets, and plays; took medical degree at Avignon, 1600, and became a Catholic, but returned to London to practise.

    Complete Works ed. E. Gosse (4 vols, Hunterian Club, 1875–83; New York, 1963)
    A Margarite of America ed. G. B. Harrison (Oxford, 1927)
    Rosalynde ed. W. W. Greg (London, 1907); facs. ed. L. M. Robbins (London, 1972)
    The Wounds of Civil War, ed. J. W. Houpert (London, 1970; R.R.D.S.)
    See D. Bush, *Mythology and the Renaissance Tradition in English Poetry* (Minneapolis, 1932; rev. New York, 1963)
        N.B. Paradise, *Thomas Lodge: The History of an Elizabethan* (New Haven, 1931; London, 1970)
        W. D. Rae, *Thomas Lodge* (New York, 1967)
        M. Ryan, Jr, *Thomas Lodge, Gentleman* (Hamden, Conn., 1959)
        C. J. Sisson, *Lodge and Other Elizabethans* (Cambridge, Mass., 1933; New York, 1966)
        E. A. Tenney, *Thomas Lodge* (Ithaca, N. Y. 1935)
    Essays by Scott (3), John (9), Keach (66)

LYLY, JOHN (*c.* 1554–1606): Dramatist and novelist; b. Canterbury; Oxford; patron – Earl of Oxford; struggled for place at court; famous for his novel

Euphues, 1578; writing plays for children's acting companies of Chapel Royal *c.* 1584; wrote pamphlet supporting cause of bishops in Martin Marprelate controversy; M.P. for Hindon, Aylesbury, and Appleby, 1589–1601.

Works ed. R. W. Bond (3 vols, Oxford, 1902; 1967)
Euphues ed. M. W. Croll and H. Clemons (London, 1916; New York, 1964)
Galathea and *Midas* ed. A. Lancashire (London, 1970; R.R.D.S.)
Mother Bombie ed. K. M. Lea (London, 1948); ed. A. H. Andreadis (Salzburg, 1975)
J. Winny (ed.) *The Descent of Euphues* (Cambridge, 1957)
See J. A. Barish, 'The Prose of John Lyly', in E.L.H., XXIII (1956)
    J. W. Houppert, *John Lyly* (Boston, Mass., 1975)
    G. K. Hunter, *John Lyly* (London, 1962); *Lyly and Peele* (London, 1968; W.T.W.)
    V. M. Jeffery, *John Lyly and the Italian Renaissance* (Paris, 1929; New York, 1969)
    P. Saccio, *The Court Comedies of John Lyly* (Princeton, N. J., 1969)
Essays by Parks (11), Lewis (17), Bradbrook (18), Powell (31), Knight (34 and 37)

MARLOWE, CHRISTOPHER (1564–93): Dramatist and poet; son of prosperous Canterbury shoemaker; King's School, Canterbury, and Cambridge; government agent; writing for theatre *c.* 1586; murdered in tavern brawl.

Works and Life ed. R. H. Case *et al.* (6 vols, London, 1930–33; New York, 1961)
Works ed. C. F. Tucker Brooke (London, 1910); also M.S.
Complete Works ed. F. T. Bowers (2 vols, Cambridge, 1973)
Plays ed. L. Kirschbaum (New York, 1962); ed. I. Ribner (New York. 1964); ed. J. B. Steane (Penguin, 1969); ed. R. Gill (London, 1971)
Complete Plays and Poems, ed. E. D. Pendry and J. C. Maxwell (London, 1976; E.L.)
Tamburlaine I and II ed. J. D. Jump (London, 1967; R.R.D.S); ed. J. W. Harper (London, 1971; N.M.); ed. I. Ribner (New York, 1974)
Doctor Faustus 1604–16; Parallel Texts ed. W. W. Greg (Oxford, 1950)
Doctor Faustus; A Conjectural Reconstruction ed. W. W. Greg (Oxford, 1950)
Dr. Faustus ed. J. D. Jump (London, 1962; R.P.); ed. R. Gill (London, 1965; N.M.); ed. I. Ribner (New York, 1966); ed. K. Walker (Edinburgh, 1973)
Dido and *Massacre at Paris* ed. H. J. Oliver (London, 1968; R.P.)
Edward II ed. W. M. Merchant (London, 1967; N.M.); ed. R. Gill (Oxford, 1967); ed. I Ribner (New York, 1970)
The Jew of Malta ed. R. W. Van Fossen (London, 1965; R.R.D.S.); ed. T. W. Craik (London, 1966: N.M.); ed. N. W. Bawcutt (Manchester, 1978)
Poems ed. M. MacLure (London, 1968; R.P.); ed. S. Orgel (Penguin, 1971)
See S. Ando, *A Descriptive Syntax of Christopher Marlowe's Language* (Tokyo, 1976)
    E. B. Asibong, *Comic Sensibility in the Plays of Christopher Marlowe* (Ilfracombe, 1979)
    J. Bakeless, *The Tragicall History of Christopher Marlowe* (2 vols, Cambridge, Mass., 1942; Westport, Conn., 1970)
    R. W. Battenhouse, *Marlowe's Tamburlaine: a Study in Renaissance Moral Philosophy* (1941; rev. edn Nashville, Tenn., 1964)
    J. P. Brockbank, *Marlowe: Dr Faustus* (London, 1963)
    D. Bush, *Mythology and the Renaissance Tradition in English Poetry* (Minneapolis, 1932; rev. New York, 1963)

L. M. Chan and S. A. Pedersen, *Marlowe Criticism: a Bibliography* (London, 1978)

D. Cole, *Suffering and Evil in the Plays of Christopher Marlowe* (Princeton, 1962)

J. P. Cutts, *The Left Hand of God: A Critical Interpretation of the Plays of Christopher Marlowe* (Haddonfield, N. J., 1973)

F. B. Fieler, *Tamburlaine, Part I, and its Audience* (Gainesville, Fla., 1961)

K. Friedenreich. *Christopher Marlowe. An Annotated Bibliography of Criticism since 1950* (London, 1979)

G. K. Hunter, 'The Theology of Marlowe's *The Jew of Malta*', in J.W.C.I., XXVII (1964) and in (68)

W. Keach, *Elizabethan Erotic Narratives* (New Brunswick, N. J., 1977)

A. Kernan (ed.) *Two Renaissance Mythmakers. Christopher Marlowe and Ben Jonson* (London, 1977)

R. E. Knoll, *Christopher Marlowe* (New York, 1969)

P. H. Kocher, *Christopher Marlowe: A Study of His Thought, Learning and Character* (London, 1946)

C. Leech, (ed.) *Twentieth Century Views: Marlowe* (Englewood Cliffs, N. J., 1964)

H. Levin, *The Overreacher* (Cambridge, Mass., 1952; London, 1954)

M. MacLure (ed.) *Marlowe: the Critical Heritage, 1588–1896* (London, 1979)

B. Morris (ed.) *Christopher Marlowe* (London, 1968)

W. Sanders, *The Dramatist and the Received Idea* (Cambridge, 1968)

J. B. Steane, *Marlowe* (Cambridge, 1964; rev. edn 1970)

Tulane Drama Review, Marlowe Centenary Issue (VIII; Summer, 1964)

J. Weill, *Christopher Marlowe. Merlin's Prophet* (Cambridge, 1977)

F. P. Wilson, *Marlowe and the Early Shakespeare* (Oxford, 1953)

L. R. Zocca, *Elizabethan Narrative Poetry* (New Brunswick, N. J., 1950)

Essays by Bradbrook (6), Eliot (14), Brooke (31), Duthie (34), Clemen (35), Ribner (37), Mahood (37), Waith (40), Lewis (47)

MARSTON, JOHN (1576–1634): Dramatist; b. Oxfordshire; son of lawyer; Brasenose, Oxford, 1591; Middle Temple, 1594; first writing, 1598; engaged with Dekker in 'War of the Theatres' against Jonson (1599–1601), with whom he later became friendly; wrote plays for boys' companies; ordained, 1609.

The Plays of John Marston ed. H. H. Wood (3 vols, Edinburgh, 1934–9)

The Poems of John Marston ed. A. Davenport (Liverpool, 1961)

The Malcontent ed. M. L. Wine (London, 1965; R.R.D.S.); ed. B. Harris (London, 1967, N.M.); ed. G. K. Hunter (London, 1975; R.P.)

Antonio and Melida ed. G. K. Hunter (London, 1966; R.R.D.S.); ed. W. R. Gair (Manchester, 1978; R.P.)

Antonio's Revenge ed. G. K. Hunter (London, 1966; R.R.D.S.)

The Dutch Courtesan ed. M. L. Wine (London, 1965; R.R.D.S.); ed. P. Davison (Edinburgh, 1968)

The Fawn ed. G. A. Smith (London, 1965; R.R.D.S.); ed. D. A. Blostein (Manchester, 1978; R.P.)

The Scourge of Villainie ed. G. B. Harrison (London, 1925; Edinburgh, 1966)

See J. Axelrad, *Un Malcontent Élizabéthain: John Marston* (Paris, 1956)

O. J. Campbell, *Comicall Satyre …* (San Marino, Ca., 1938)

A. Caputi, *John Marston, Satirist* (Ithaca, N. Y., 1961)

P. J. Finkelpearl, *John Marston of the Middle Temple. An Elizabethan Dramatist in his Social Setting* (London, 1969)

R. A. Foakes, *Marston and Tourneur* (London, 1978; w.t.w.)

R. W. Ingram, *John Marston* (Boston, 1978)

M. Scott, *John Marston's Plays. Theme, Structure and Performance* (London, 1978)

Essays by Eliot (14), Bradbrook (18), Peter (22), Kernan (25), Hunter (26), Ornstein (32), Spencer (34 and 46), Ellis-Fermor (36), Schoenbaum (37), Mehl (44), Prosser (49), Gibbons (53), Ure (64), Hunter (68)

MASSINGER, PHILIP (1583–1640): Dramatist; b. Salisbury; son of officer in household of the Herbert family, who became his patrons; Oxford, 1602; began writing for stage *c.* 1613, collaborating with Fletcher and others.

The Plays ed. W. Gifford (London, 1809, 1813); ed. F. Cunningham (London, 1868)

Ten Plays ed. A. Symons (M.S.)

The Plays and Poems, ed. P. Edwards and C. Gibson (5 vols, Oxford, 1976)

Selected Plays, ed. C. Gibson (Cambridge, 1978)

The Poems ed. D. S. Lawless (Muncie, Ind., 1968)

The City-Madam ed. T. W. Craik (London, 1964; N.M.); ed. C. Hoy (London, 1964; R.R.D.S)

The Fatal Dowry (with N. Field) ed. T. A. Dunn (Edinburgh, 1969)

A New Way to Pay Old Debts ed. T. W. Craik (London, 1964; N.M.)

The Roman Actor ed. W. L. Sandidge (Princeton, N. J., 1929)

The Unnatural Combat ed. R. S. Telfer (Princeton, N. J., 1932)

See A. H. Cruickshank, *Philip Massinger* (Oxford, 1920)

T. A. Dunn, *Philip Massinger* (Edinburgh, 1957)

Essays by Knights (8), Harbage (9), Eliot (14), Edwards (42)

MIDDLETON, THOMAS (1580–1627): Dramatist; b. London; aristocratic background; Oxford, 1598; writing pamphlets, 1597; plays, 1602 onwards; and pageants, 1613; collaborated with William Rowley and other dramatists; in disfavour with the government for his anti-Spanish play, *A Game at Chess* (1624); city chronologer, 1620–26.

Works ed. A. H. Bullen (8 vols, London, 1885–6)

Ten plays ed. H. Ellis (M.S.; 2 vols, 1887–90)

Selected Plays ed. D. L. Frost (Cambridge, 1978)

Three Plays ed. K. Muir (London, 1975; E.L.)

The Changeling ed. N. W. Bawcutt (London, 1958, 1961 [corr.]; R.P.); ed. P. Thomson (London, 1964; N.M.); ed. G. Williams (London, 1967; R.R.D.S.); ed. M. W. Black (Philadelphia, 1966)

A Fair Quarrel (with Rowley), ed. R. V. Holdsworth (London, 1974; N.M.); ed. G. R. Price (London, 1977; R.R.D.S.)

A Game at Chess ed. R. C. Bald (Cambridge, 1929); ed. J. W. Harper (London, 1966; N.M.)

Michaelmas Term ed. R. Levin (London, 1967; R.R.D.S.); ed. G. R. Price (The Hague, 1976)

A Mad World, My Masters ed. S. Henning (London, 1965; R.R.D.S.)

A Chaste Maid in Cheapside ed. A. Brissenden (London, 1968; R.R.D.S.); ed. R. B. Parker (London, 1969; R.P.); ed. C. Barber (Edinburgh, 1969)

The Roaring Girl (with Dekker), ed. A. Gomme (London, 1976; N.M.)

The Second Maiden's Tragedy ed. A. Lancashire (Manchester, 1978; R.P.)

A Trick to Catch the Old One ed. G. J. Watson (London, 1968; N.M.); ed. C. Barber (Edinburgh, 1968); ed. G. R. Price (The Hague, 1976)

Women Beware Women ed. R. Gill (London, 1968; N.M.); ed. C. Barber (Edinburgh, 1969); ed. J. R. Mulryne (London, 1975; R.P.)

See also: 'Drama: Anthologies' (above) under Gomme, Lawrence, Salgādo

See R. H. Barker, *Thomas Middleton* (New York, 1958)

> A. Covatta, *Thomas Middleton's City Comedies* (Lewisburg, Pa., 1973)
>
> D. M. Farr, *Thomas Middleton and the Drama of Realism* (Edinburgh, 1973)
>
> M. Heinemann, *Puritanism and Theatre. Thomas Middleton and Opposition Drama under the Early Stuarts* (Cambridge, 1980)
>
> D. M. Holmes, *The Art of Thomas Middleton* (Oxford, 1970)
>
> D. J. Lake, *The Canon of Thomas Middleton's Plays* (Cambridge, 1975)
>
> J. R. Mulryne, *Thomas Middleton* (London, 1979; W.T.W.)
>
> S. Schoenbaum, *Middleton's Tragedies* (New York, 1955)

Essays by Bradbrook (6), Knights (8), Eliot (14), Bradbrook (18), Parker (26), Ornstein (32), Ellis-Fermor (36), Mehl (44), Gibbons (53)

NASHE, THOMAS (*c.* 1567–1601): Pamphleteer; b. Lowestoft; son of minister; Cambridge; in London *c.* 1588 as one of University Wits writing for stage and press; wrote pamphlets against authors of Marprelate tracts and against Gabriel Harvey.

Works ed. R. B. McKerrow (5 vols, Oxford, 1904–10); rev. edn by F. P. Wilson and W. W. Greg (Oxford, 1958)

Selected Works ed. S. Wells (London, 1964); ed. J. B. Steane (Penguin, 1972)

The Unfortunate Traveller ed. H. F. B. Brett-Smith (Oxford, 1927) and in *Shorter Elizabethan Novels* (E.L.)

Nashe-Harvey pamphlets in G. G. Smith (Section IX above)

See O. J. Campbell, *Comicall Satyre* (San Marino, Ca., 1938)

> G. R. Hibbard, *Thomas Nashe* (London, 1962)
>
> R. G. Howarth, under Deloney
>
> E. H. Miller, *The Professional Writer in Elizabethan England* (Cambridge, Mass., 1959)
>
> W. Schrickx, *Shakespeare's Early Contemporaries: the Background of the Harvey-Nashe Polemic and 'Love's Labour's Lost'* (Antwerp, 1956)

Essays by Lewis (17), Bradbrook (18), Kernan (25)

PEELE, GEORGE (*c.* 1557–96): Dramatist; son of London citizen and salter; Christ's Hospital and Oxford; successful player as well as playwright; reputation for dissipation; wrote pageants in later years.

Life and Works general ed. C. T. Prouty (3 vols, New Haven, 1952–1970)

Works ed. A. H. Bullen (2 vols, London, 1888)

Selected Poems ed. S. Purcell (South Hinksey, 1972)

The Old Wives Tale ed. P. Binnie (Manchester, 1980; R.P.)

See L. R. Ashley, *Authorship and Evidence: a Study of Attribution and the Renaissance Drama, Illustrated by the Case of G. Peele* (Geneva, 1968); *George Peele* (New York, 1970)

> D. H. Horne, *George Peele* (New Haven, 1953)

G. K. Hunter, *Lyly and Peele* (London, 1968; w.t.w.)
Essays by Bradbrook (18), Jenkins (34), Clemen (35), Prosser (49)

RALEGH, SIR WALTER (*c.* 1552–1618): Poet, philosopher, soldier, explorer; son of Devonshire gentleman; Oxford; associate of leading scholars and scientists; expedition to Virginia, 1584; Guiana, 1595, etc.; one of Elizabeth's most prominent courtiers, 1579–86; imprisoned in Tower for alleged complicity in plots against James I, 1603; released, 1616, for expedition to Orinoco; arrested and executed after failure of expedition. Most of his poems were written in 1579–1603; his *History of the World* was written during his imprisonment in the Tower.

> *Life* by D. B. Quinn (London, 1947); by W. M. Wallace (Princeton, 1959)
> *Works* ed. Oldys and Birch (8 vols, Oxford, 1829; New York, 1962)
> *History of the World*, selections ed. C. A. Patrides (London, 1971)
> *Poems* ed. A. M. C. Latham (London, 1951); *Selections* ed. Latham, (London, 1965)
> *Selected Prose* ed. G. E. Hadow (Oxford, 1917)
> *The Discovery of Guiana* (Hakluyt Society, III, 1848; and in *Hakluyt's Voyages*, E.L.)
> See M. C. Bradbrook, *The School of Night* (Cambridge, 1936)
> P. Edwards, *Sir Walter Raleigh* (London, 1953)
> Sir C. Firth, 'Raleigh's History', in *Essays Historical and Literary* (Oxford, 1938; 1968)
> S. J. Greenblatt, *Sir Walter Ralegh; the Renaissance Man and his Roles* (New Haven, 1973)
> H. Haydn, *The Counter-Renaissance* (New York, 1950)
> Christopher Hill, 'Raleigh – Science, History and Politics', in *Intellectual Origins of the English Revolution* (Oxford, 1965)
> R. Lacey, *Sir Walter Ralegh* (London, 1973)
> P. Lefranc, *Sir Walter Ralegh, Écrivain; L'Oeuvre et les Idées* (Paris, 1968)
> W. Oakeshott, *The Queen and the Poet* (London, 1960)
> J. Racin, *Sir Walter Ralegh as Historian* (Salzburg, 1974)
> A. L. Rowse, *Ralegh and the Throckmortons* (London, 1962)
> E. Strathmann, *Sir Walter Ralegh: A Study in Elizabethan Skepticism* (New York, 1951)

SACKVILLE, THOMAS (1536–1608); Poet, aristocratic background and Inner Temple; collaborated with Thomas Norton in *Gorboduc* (1561) and contributed (1563) to *The Mirror for Magistrates*; then devoted himself to public career – Earl of Dorset; Lord Treasurer of the Privy Council; Chancellor of Oxford University.

> *Works* ed. R. Sackville-West (London, 1859)
> *Gorboduc* (with T, Norton): ed. J. W. Cunliffe, *Early English Classical Tragedies* (Oxford, 1912), in *Five Elizabethan Tragedies*, ed. A. K. McIlwraith (London, 1959, w.c.); ed. I. B. Cauthen Jr. (London, 1970; R.R.D.S.)
> *The complaint of Henry, Duke of Buckingham*, ed. M. Hearsey (New Haven, 1936)
> *The Mirror for Magistrates* ed. L. B. Campbell (Cambridge, 1938, 1946; New York, 1960)
> See P. Bacquet, *Un contemporain d'Elisabeth I: T. Sackville, L'homme et l'œuvre* (Geneva, 1966)

H. Baker, *Induction to Tragedy* (Baton Rouge, Louisiana, 1939)

N. Berlin, *Thomas Sackville* (New York, 1974)

W. Farnham, *The Medieval Heritage of Elizabethan Tragedy* (Berkeley, 1936)

Essay by Clemen (35)

SHAKESPEARE, WILLIAM (1564–1616): Dramatist; b. Stratford-on-Avon; son of prominent yeoman–citizen; probably educated at Stratford Grammar School; married, 1582; in London, *c.* 1584–92, acting, and writing plays and poems; leading sharer in Earl of Leicester's company (later, 1594, Lord Chamberlain's men, acting in their own Globe Theatre, 1599–1613, and also in the fashionable Blackfriars from 1608; renamed the King's men, 1603, the most successful company of the day, both at court and with the general public); friend of the Earl of Southampton; granted coat-of-arms, 1596; bought New Place, 1597, and other property later; retired to Stratford, 1611.

Note. *Due to the vast amount of Shakespeare criticism this section of the Bibliography is necessarily more selective than others. General studies which include Shakespeare and which are listed elsewhere are not repeated here. Although most of the items in the Bibliography are relevant to the full understanding of Shakespeare, especially relevant material will be found in Sections VII–X above.*

Biography

G. E. Bentley, *Shakespeare: A Biographical Handbook* (New Haven, 1961)

E. K. Chambers, *William Shakespeare: A Study of Facts and Problems* (2 vols, Oxford, 1930; abr. by C. Williams, 1933)

M. Eccles, *Shakespeare in Warwickshire* (Madison, Wis., 1961)

E. L. Fripp, *Shakespeare Man and Artist* (2 vols, Oxford, 1938, 1964)

H. N. Gibson, *The Shakespeare Claimants* (London, 1962)

B. R. Lewis (ed.) *The Shakespeare Documents* (2 vols, Stanford, 1940)

J. G. McManaway, 'Recent Studies in Shakespeare's Chronology', in Sh.S., III (1950)

S. Schoenbaum, *Shakespeare's Lives* (Oxford, 1970); *William Shakespeare: A Documentary Life* (Oxford, 1975; compact edn Oxford, 1977)

C. J. Sisson, 'The Mythical Sorrows of Shakespeare', in (43)

Editions: Facsimiles

Quarto Facsimiles ed. W. W. Greg and C. Hinman (Oxford, 1939–)

First Folio Facsimile ed. H. Kökeritz (New Haven, 1954)

C. Hinman ed. *The Norton Facsimile. The First Folio of Shakespeare* (New York, 1968)

The Poems in Facsimile (New Haven, 1964)

One-Volume Texts

Tudor Shakespeare ed. P. Alexander (London, 1951)

Complete Works ed. C. J. Sisson (London, 1953)

The Complete Pelican Shakespeare ed. A. Harbage (London, 1969)

The Riverside Shakespeare ed. G. B. Evans (Boston, Mass., 1974)

Complete Works ed. D. Bevington (Glenview, Ill., 1980)

Attributed Plays

The Shakespeare Apocrypha ed. T. Brooke (London, 1908)
Six Early Plays Related to the Shakespeare Canon ed. E. B. Everitt and R. L. Armstrong (Copenhagen, 1965)

Separate Plays

Arden ed. W. J. Craig and R. H. Case (London, 1899–1924); *New Arden*, rev. edn U. M. Ellis-Fermor *et al.* (1951–)
New Shakespeare ed. J. D. Wilson *et al.* (Cambridge, 1921–68)
New Variorum ed. H. H. Furness *et al.* (Philadelphia, 1871–)
Penguin ed. G. B. Harrison (1937–59)
Signet ed. S. Barnet *et al.* (New York, 1960–)
New Penguin ed. T. J. B. Spencer *et al.* (London, 1967–)

General Reference

Annual Bibliographies can be found in the periodicals listed above (Section VI), also in Sh.S. and Sh.Q.
E. A. Abbott, *A Shakespearean Grammar* (London, 1870 edn)
J. Bartlett, *Complete Concordance to Shakespeare* (London, 1894)
D. Bevington, *Shakespeare* (Goldentree Bibliography: Arlington Heights, Ill., 1978)
O. J. Campbell and E. G. Quinn (eds), *A Shakespeare Encyclopedia* (London, 1966)
W. Ebisch and L. L. Schücking, *A Shakespeare Bibliography* (Oxford, 1931; Supplement, 1936)
H. Granville-Barker and G. B. Harrison (eds) *A Companion to Shakespeare Studies* (Cambridge, 1934)
F. E. Halliday, *A Shakespeare Companion* (London, 1952; Penguin, 1964)
K. Holzknecht, *The Backgrounds of Shakespeare's Plays* (New York, 1950)
T. H. Howard-Hill, *Oxford Shakespeare Concordances* (37 vols, Oxford, 1969–73)
J. G. McManaway and J. A. Roberts, *A Selective Bibliography of Shakespeare* (Charlottesville, Va., 1975)
K. Muir and S. Schoenbaum (eds), *A New Companion to Shakespeare Studies* (Cambridge, 1970)
C. T. Onions, *A Shakespeare Glossary* (Oxford, 1911)
E. Partridge, *Shakespeare's Bawdy* (London, 1955)
A. Schmidt, *Shakespeare-Lexicon* (2 vols, rev. G. Sarrazin, Berlin, 1972; New York, 1968)
G. R. Smith, *A Classified Shakespeare Bibliography 1936–1958* (Pennsylvania, 1963)
M. Spevack, *A Complete and Systematic Concordance to the Works of Shakespeare* (8 vols, Hildesheim and New York, 1968–75); *The Harvard Concordance to Shakespeare* (Cambridge, Mass., 1973)
S. Wells (ed.) *Shakespeare: Select Bibliographical Guides* (London, 1973)

Textual Studies

F. Bowers, *On Editing Shakespeare* (Philadelphia, 1955; rev. edn Charlottesville, Va., 1966); *Textual and Literary Criticism* (Cambridge, 1959); *Bibliography and Textual Criticism* (Oxford, 1964), but see J. K. Walton in Sh.S., XIX (1966)

F. Bowers (ed.) *Studies in Bibliography* (1948–; University of Virginia), an annual periodical with many studies of Shakespeare's text.

G. I. Duthie, *The 'Bad' Quarto of 'Hamlet'* (Cambridge, 1941); old-spelling edition of *King Lear* (Oxford, 1949); *Elizabethan Shorthand and the First Quarto of 'King Lear'* (Oxford, 1950)

W. W. Greg, *The Editorial Problem in Shakespeare* (rev. edn, Oxford, 1954); *The Shakespeare First Folio* (Oxford, 1955)

C. Hinman, *The Printing and Proof-Reading of the First Folio of Shakespeare* (2 vols, Oxford, 1963)

E. A. J. Honigmann, *The Stability of Shakespeare's Text* (London, 1965)

T. H. Howard-Hill, *Shakespearian Bibliography and Textual Criticism. A Bibliography* (Oxford, 1971); *Ralph Crane and some Shakespeare First Folio Comedies* (Charlottesville, Va., 1972)

L. Kirschbaum, *Shakespeare and the Stationers* (Columbus, Ohio, 1955)

D. F. McKenzie, 'Shakespearian Punctuation – A New Beginning', in R.E.S., X (1959); 'Printers of the mind', *Studies in Bibliography*. XX (1969)

R. B. McKerrow, *Introduction to Bibliography for Literary Students* (Oxford, 1928); *Prolegomena for the Oxford Shakespeare* (Oxford, 1939)

A. W. Pollard, *Shakespeare's Fight with the Pirates* (Cambridge, 1920; rev. 1937); *Shakespeare's Hand in the Play of 'Sir Thomas More'* (Cambridge, 1923)

C. J. Sisson, *New Readings in Shakespeare* (2 vols, Cambridge, 1956)

E. M. Thompson, *Shakespeare's Handwriting* (London, 1912)

A. Walker, *Textual Problems of the First Folio* (Cambridge, 1953)

F. P. Wilson, *Shakespeare and the New Bibliography*, ed. H. Gardner (London, 1970)

J. D. Wilson, *The Manuscripts of Shakespeare's 'Hamlet'* (2 vols, Cambridge, 1934)

Source Materials

T. W. Baldwin, *Shakespere's 'Small Latine and Lesse Greeke'* (2 vols, Urbana, Illinois, 1944)

M. W. Black, 'The Sources of Shakespeare's *Richard II*' in (11)

E. A. Block, 'On the Sources of *King Lear*', in Sh.Q., X (1959)

M. C. Bradbrook, 'The Sources of *Macbeth*' in Sh.S., IV (1951); 'What Shakespeare did to Chaucer's *Troilus and Criseyde*', in Sh.Q., IX (1958)

G. Bullough (ed.), *Narrative and Dramatic Sources of Shakespeare* (8 vols, London, 1957–75)

R. R. Cawley, 'Shakespeare's use of the voyages in *The Tempest*', in P.M.L.A., XLI (1926)

H. Craig, 'Motivation in Shakespeare's Choice of Materials', in Sh.S., IV (1951)

S. Guttman, *The Foreign Sources of Shakespeare's Works* (New York, 1947): bibliography up to 1940; list of translations available to Shakespeare.

J. E. Hankins, *Shakespeare's Derived Imagery* (Lawrence, Kansas, 1953)

A. Hart, *Shakespeare and the Homilies* (London, 1934; New York, 1970)

E. A. Honigmann, 'Shakespeare's Lost Source Plays', *Modern Language Review*, XLIX (1954)

G. K. Hunter, 'Shakespeare's Reading', in (55)

M. Lascelles, *Shakespeare's 'Measure for Measure'* (London, 1953)

R. A. Law, 'Belleforest, Shakespeare and Kyd', in (11)

K. Muir, *Shakespeare's Sources* (London, 1957–; rev. 1977)

R. Noble, *Shakespeare's Biblical Knowledge* (London, 1935)

R. K. Presson, *Shakespeare's 'Troilus and Cressida' and the Legends of Troy* (Madison, Wis., 1953)

C. T. Prouty, *The Sources of 'Much Ado about Nothing'* (New Haven, 1951)

J. Satin (ed.), *Shakespeare and his Sources* (Boston, 1966)

T. J. B. Spencer (ed.) *Shakespeare's Plutarch* (Penguin, 1964); *Elizabethan Love Stories* (Penguin, 1968)

E. E. Stoll, 'Source and Motive in *Macbeth* and *Othello*', in *From Shakespeare to Joyce* (New York, 1944)

A. Thompson, *Shakespeare's Chaucer: A Study in Literary Origins* (Liverpool, 1978)

J. A. K. Thomson, *Shakespeare and the Classics* (London, 1952)

J. W. Velz, *Shakespeare and the Classical Tradition: A Critical Guide to Commentary, 1660–1960* (Minneapolis, 1968)

V. K. Whitaker, *Shakespeare's Use of Learning* (San Marino, Ca., 1953)

F. P. Wilson, 'Shakespeare's Reading', in *Sh.S.*, III (1950) and in (56)

Influence of the Theatre and Dramatic Tradition (see Section x above)

H. Baker, *Induction to Tragedy* (Baton Rouge, La., 1939)

B. Beckerman, *Shakespeare at the Globe, 1599–1609* (New York, 1962)

G. E. Bentley, *Shakespeare and His Theatre* (Lincoln, Neb., 1964, 1976)

S. L. Bethell, *Shakespeare and the Popular Dramatic Tradition* (London, 1948)

D. Bevington, *From 'Mankind' to Marlowe* (Cambridge, Mass., 1962); 'Shakespeare the Elizabethan Dramatist', in (55)

M. C. Bradbrook, 'Shakespeare's Primitive Art', P.B.A., LI (1965); *Shakespeare the Craftsman* (London, 1969)

R. W. David, 'Shakespeare and the Players', in (43)

W. Farnham, *The Medieval Heritage of Elizabethan Tragedy* (Cambridge, 1936; rev. Oxford, 1957)

A. Gurr, *The Shakespearean Stage, 1574–1642* (Cambridge, 1970; rev. 1981)

A. Harbage, *Shakespeare and the Rival Traditions* (New York, 1952); *Theatre for Shakespeare* (Toronto, 1956)

C. W. Hodges, *The Globe Restored* (London, 1953; rev. 1968); *Shakespeare's Second Globe* (London, 1973)

G. K. Hunter, 'Shakespeare and Lyly' in *John Lyly* (London, 1962)

T. J. King, *Shakespearean Staging, 1599–1642* (Cambridge, Mass., 1971)

D. Mehl, *The Elizabethan Dumb Show* (London, 1965)

K. Muir, *Shakespeare as Collaborator* (London, 1960)

I. Ribner, *The English History Play in the Age of Shakespeare* (London, 1957; rev. 1965)

A. Righter, *Shakespeare and the Idea of the Play* (London, 1962; Penguin, 1967)

N. Sanders, 'The Comedy of Greene and Shakespeare', in (28)

W. D. Smith, *Shakespeare's Playhouse Practice: a Handbook* (Hanover, N.H., 1975)

T. Spencer, *Death and Elizabethan Tragedy* (Cambridge, Mass., 1936)

B. Spivack, *Shakespeare and the Allegory of Evil* (New York, 1958)

E. W. Talbert, *Elizabethan Drama and Shakespeare's Early Plays* (Chapel Hill, N.C., 1964)

P. Ure, 'Shakespeare and the Drama of his Time' in (55)

A. S. Venezky, *Pageantry on the Shakespearean Stage* (Boston, 1951)

G. Wickham, *Shakespeare's Dramatic Heritage* (London, 1969)

F. P. Wilson, *Marlowe and the Early Shakespeare* (Oxford, 1953)

Language, Style and Structure

E. A. Armstrong, *Shakespeare's Imagination* (London, 1946, rev. edn 1963)

M. L. Arnold, *Soliloquies of Shakespeare* (New York, 1911)

M. A. Bayfield, *A Study of Shakespeare's Versification* (Cambridge, 1920)

T. W. Baldwin, *Shakespeare's Five-Act Structure* (Urbana, Ill., 1947); but see H. L. Snuggs, *Shakespeare and Five Acts* (New York, 1960)

F. Berry, *The Shakespeare Inset: Word and Picture* (London, 1965)

G. L. Brook, *The Language of Shakespeare* (London, 1976)

W. Clemen, *The Development of Shakespeare's Imagery* (London, 1951; rev. edn 1977); *Shakespeare's Dramatic Art* (London, 1972)

N. Coghill, *Shakespeare's Professional Skills* (Cambridge, 1964)

E. A. Colman, *The Dramatic Use of Bawdy in Shakespeare* (London, 1974)

R. W. David, *The Janus of Poets* (Cambridge, 1935)

M. Doran, *Shakespeare's Dramatic Language* (Madison, Wis., 1976)

P. Edwards *et al.* (eds), *Shakespeare's Styles. Essays in honour of Kenneth Muir* (Cambridge, 1980)

W. Empson, *The Structure of Complex Words* (London, 1951)

W. T. Jewkes, *Act Division in Elizabethan and Jacobean Plays* (Hamden, Conn., 1959)

E. Jones, *Scenic Form in Shakespeare* (Oxford, 1971)

P. Jorgensen, *Redeeming Shakespeare's Words* (Berkeley, Ca., 1962)

Sister M. Joseph, *Shakespeare's Use of the Arts of Language* (New York, 1947, 1966)

F. C. Kolbe, *Shakespeare's Way* (London, 1930)

P. V. Kreider, *Repetition in Shakespeare's Plays* (Princeton, 1941)

M. M. Mahood, *Shakespeare's Wordplay* (London, 1957)

R. G. Moulton, *Shakespeare as a Dramatic Artist* (rev., London, 1893; New York, 1966)

F. W. Ness, *The Use of Rhyme in Shakespeare's Plays* (New Haven, Conn., 1941)

H. T. Price, *Construction in Shakespeare* (Ann Arbor, Mi., 1951)

G. H. W. Rylands, *Words and Poetry* (1928)

Shakespeare Survey, VII (1954) and XXIII (1970)

F. A. Shirley, *Shakespeare's Use of Off-Stage Sounds* (Lincoln, Neb., 1963)

D. L. Sipe, *Shakespeare's Metrics* (New Haven, Conn., 1968)

C. F. Spurgeon, *Shakespeare's Imagery And What It Tells Us* (Cambridge, 1935); but see L. Hornstein, 'Analysis of Imagery: A Critique of Literary Method', in P.M.L.A., LVII (1942)

B. W. Vickers, *The Artistry of Shakespeare's Prose* (London, 1968, 1980); 'Shakespeare's Use of Rhetoric', in (55)

G. D. Willcock, *Shakespeare as a Critic of Language* (London, 1934); 'Language and Poetry in Shakespeare's Early Plays', in P.B.A., XL (1954)

A. Yoder, *Animal Analogy in Shakespeare's Character-Portrayal* (New York, 1947)

The Poems and Sonnets

Sonnets, ed. H. E. Rollins (New Variorum; 2 vols, Philadelphia, 1944); ed. T. G. Tucker (Cambridge, 1924); ed. C. L. Barber (New York, 1962); ed. M. Seymour-Smith (London, 1963); ed. W. G. Ingram and R. T. H. Redpath (London, 1964); ed. J. D. Wilson (New Cambridge ed., 1966); ed. S. Booth (New Haven, 1977)

Narrative Poems ed. H. E. Rollins (New Variorum; Philadelphia, 1938); ed. F. T. Prince (New Arden, London, 1960); ed. J. C. Maxwell (New Cambridge, 1966); T. W. Baldwin, *On the Literary Genetics of Shakespeare's Poems and Sonnets* (Urbana, Ill., 1950)

S. Booth, *An Essay on Shakespeare's Sonnets* (New Haven, 1969)

M. C. Bradbrook, *Shakespeare and Elizabethan Poetry* (London, 1951)

L. Hotson, *Shakespeare's Sonnets Dated* (London, 1949); but see F. W. Bateson, 'Elementary, my dear Hotson!' in *Essays in Criticism*, I (1951)

E. Hubler, *The Sense of Shakespeare's Sonnets* (Princeton, 1952)

E. Hubler *et al.*, *The Riddle of Shakespeare's Sonnets* (London, 1962), especially essays by N. Frye, R. P. Blackmur.

R. Jakobson and L. G. Jones, *Shakespeare's Verbal Art in 'Th' Expence of Spirit'* (The Hague, 1970)

W. Keach, on *Venus and Adonis* in (66), Section VII above

L. C. Knights, 'Shakespeare's Sonnets', in *Explorations* (London, 1946)

M. Krieger, *A Window to Criticism: Shakespeare's Sonnets and Modern Poetics* (Princeton, 1964)

H. Landry, *Interpretations in Shakespeare's Sonnets* (Berkeley, Ca., 1963); ed. *New Essays on Shakespeare's Sonnets* (New York, 1976)

J. B. Leishman, *Themes and Variations in Shakespeare's Sonnets* (London, 1961)

J. W. Lever, '20th Century Studies in Shakespeare's Poems', in Sh.S., XV (1962); 'Shakespeare's Narrative Poems', in (55)

W. H. Matchett, '*The Phoenix and the Turtle*' (The Hague, 1965)

G. Melchiori, *Shakespeare's Dramatic Meditations: An Experiment in Criticism* (Oxford, 1976)

R. P. Miller, on *Venus and Adonis* in E.L.H., XIX (1952) and XXVI (1959)

K. Muir, *Shakespeare's Sonnets* (London, 1979)

R. Noble, *Shakespeare's Use of Song* (London, 1923)

M. Nowottny, 'Formal Elements in Shakespeare's Sonnets: Sonnets I–VI', in *Essays in Criticism*, II (1952)

R. D. Putney, '*Venus and Adonis*: Amour with Humour', in *Philological Quarterly*, XX (1941)

P. J. Seng, *The Vocal Songs in the Plays of Shakespeare. A Critical History* (Cambridge, Mass., 1967)

B. H. Smith (ed.) *Discussions of Shakespeare's Sonnets* (Boston, 1964)

Essays on the *Sonnets* in Scott (3), Empson (4), Pearson (5), John (9), Smith (16), Lewis (17), Lever (21), Alpers (47: Knights, Barber, Watkins), Winters (50)

The Comedies

C. L. Barber, *Shakespeare's Festive Comedy* (Princeton, 1959; New York, 1963)

J. W. Bennett, '*Measure for Measure*' as Royal Entertainment (New York, 1966)

R. Berry, *Shakespeare's Comedies: Explorations in Form* (Princeton, 1972)

S. L. Bethell, *The Winter's Tale* (London, 1949)

B. O. Bonazza, *Shakespeare's Early Comedies: a structural analysis* (The Hague, 1966)

M. C. Bradbrook, *Shakespeare and Elizabethan Poetry* (London, 1951; Peregrine, 1965)

M. Bradbury and D. J. Palmer (eds) *Stratford-upon-Avon Studies 14: Shakespearean Comedy* (London, 1972)

J. R. Brown, *Shakespeare and his Comedies* (London, 1957); 'The Interpretation of Shakespeare's Comedies: 1900–1953', Sh.S., VIII (1955)

O. J. Campbell, *Shakespeare's Satire* (London, 1943); *Comicall Satyre and Shakespeare's 'Troilus and Cressida'* (San Marino, Ca., 1938)

L. S. Champion, *The Evolution of Shakespeare's Comedy* (Cambridge, Mass., 1970)

N. Coghill, 'Six Points of Stage-Craft in *The Winter's Tale*', in Sh.S., XI (1958)

P. Edwards, 'Shakespeare's Romances: 1900–1957', in Sh.S., XI (1958)

PART FOUR

B. Evans, *Shakespeare's Comedies* (Oxford, 1962)

H. Felperin, *Shakespearean Romance* (Princeton, N.J., 1973)

R. A. Foakes, *Shakespeare: The Dark Comedies to the Last Plays: From Satire to Celebration* (London, 1971)

N. Frye, *A Natural Perspective: the Development of Shakespearean Comedy and Romance* (London, 1965)

C. Gesner, *Shakespeare and the Greek Romance* (Lexington, Ky., 1970)

R. H. Goldsmith, *Wise Fools in Shakespeare* (Michigan, 1955)

W. Green, *Shakespeare's 'Merry Wives of Windsor'* (Princeton, 1962)

L. Hotson, *Shakespeare's Motley* (London, 1952); *The First Night of 'Twelfth Night'* (London, 1954)

R. G. Hunter, *Shakespeare and the Comedy of Forgiveness* (New York, 1965)

D. G. James, *The Dream of Prospero* (Oxford, 1968)

R. Kimbrough, *Shakespeare's 'Troilus and Cressida' and Its Setting* (London, 1964)

G. W. Knight, *The Crown of Life* (London, 1947)

L. C. Knights, 'Appearance and Reality in *Troilus and Cressida*', in *Some Shakespearean Themes* (London, 1959)

B. Knox, '*The Tempest* and the Ancient Comic Tradition', in *English Stage Comedy*, ed. W. K. Wimsatt (New York, 1955)

M. M. Lascelles, *Shakespeare's 'Measure for Measure'* (London, 1953)

W. W. Lawrence, *Shakespeare's Problem Comedies* (London, 1931; Penguin, 1969)

F. R. Leavis, 'The Criticism of Shakespeare's Late Plays: A Caveat', and '*Measure for Measure*', both in *The Common Pursuit* (London, 1952; Peregrine, 1962)

C. Leech, '*Twelfth Night' and Shakespearian Comedy* (Toronto, 1965)

A. Leggatt, *Shakespeare's Comedy of Love* (London, 1974)

L. Lerner (ed.) *Shakespeare's Comedies* (Penguin, 1967)

T. McFarland, *Shakespeare's Pastoral Comedy* (Chapel Hill, N. C., 1972)

R. Miles, *The Problem of Measure for Measure: A Historical Investigation* (London, 1976)

M. Mincoff, '*Measure for Measure*: A Question of Approach', in *Shakespeare Studies*, II (1968)

B. A. Mowat, *The Dramaturgy of Shakespeare's Romances* (Athens, Ga., 1976)

K. Muir, *Shakespeare's Comic Sequence* (Liverpool, 1979)

A. D. Nuttall, *Two Concepts of Allegory: 'The Tempest'* (London, 1967)

P. A. Olson, '*Midsummer Night's Dream* and the Meaning of Court Marriage', in E.L.H., XXIV (1957)

D. J. Palmer, (ed.) *Shakespeare: the late Comedies* (Penguin, 1971)

D. L. Peterson, *Time, Tide, and Tempest: A Study of Shakespeare's Romances* (San Marino, Ca., 1973)

E. C. Pettet, *Shakespeare and the Romance Tradition* (London, 1949, 1970)

P. G. Phialas, *Shakespeare's Romantic Comedies* (Chapel Hill, N. C., 1966)

E. M. Pope, 'The Renaissance Background of *Measure for Measure*', Sh.S., II (1949)

F. Pyle, *The Winter's Tale. A Commentary on the Structure* (London, 1969)

A. Righter, *Shakespeare and the Idea of the Play* (London, 1962; Penguin, 1967) '*Love's Labour's Lost*', in Sh.Q., IV (1953)

A. P. Rossiter, *Angel with Horns* (London, 1961), chs iv–viii

L. G. Salingar, 'The Design of *Twelfth Night*', in Sh.Q., IX (1958); *Shakespeare and the Traditions of Comedy* (Cambridge, 1974)

E. Schanzer, *Shakespeare's Problem Plays* (London, 1963)

H. Smith, 'Shakespeare's Romances', *Huntington Library Quarterly*, XXVI (1964)

J. Smith, *Shakespearian and other Essays* (Cambridge, 1974)

C. Still, *Shakespeare's Mystery Play* (London, 1926)

E. M. W. Tillyard, *Shakespeare's Last Plays* (London, 1938); *Shakespeare's Problem Plays* (London, 1950)

D. P. Young, *Something of Great Constancy: 'Midsummer Night's Dream'* (New Haven, 1960); *The Heart's Forest: A Study of Shakespeare's Pastoral Plays* (New Haven, 1972)

The Histories

P. Alexander, *Shakespeare's 'Henry VI' and 'Richard III'* (Cambridge, 1929)

W. A. Armstrong (ed.) *Shakespeare's Histories: An Anthology of Modern Criticism* (Penguin, 1972)

C. L. Barber, *Shakespeare's Festive Comedy* (Princeton, 1959): on Falstaff

S. L. Bethell, 'The Comic Element in Shakespeare's Histories', in *Anglia*, LXXI (1952)

J. P. Brockbank, 'The Frame of Disorder: *Henry VI*', in (28)

L. B. Campbell, *Shakespeare's 'Histories'; Mirrors of Elizabethan Policy* (San Marino, Ca., 1947)

W. Clemen, *A Commentary on Shakespeare's 'Richard III'* (London, 1968)

H. Jenkins, 'Shakespeare's History Plays: 1900–1951', in Sh.S., VI (1953)

E. Jones, *The Origins of Shakespeare* (Oxford, 1977)

W. Kaiser, *Praisers of Folly* (London, 1964): on Falstaff

E. Kantorowicz, *The King's Two Bodies: A Study in Medieval Political Theology* (Princeton, 1957): on *Richard II*

H. A. Kelly, *Divine Providence in the England of Shakespeare's Histories* (Cambridge, Mass., 1970)

L. C. Knights, 'Shakespeare's Politics', in P.B.A., XLIII (1958), and in *Further Explorations* (London, 1965)

M. Manheim, *The Weak King Dilemma in the Shakespearean History Plays* (Syracuse, N. Y., 1973)

R. Ornstein, *A Kingdom for a Stage: The Achievement of Shakespeare's History Plays* (Cambridge, Mass., 1972)

J. Palmer, *Political Characters of Shakespeare* (London, 1945)

R. B. Pierce, *Shakespeare's History Plays: The Family and the State* (Columbus, Ohio, 1971)

M. E. Prior, *The Drama of Power: Studies in Shakespeare's History Plays* (Evanston, Ill., 1973)

M. M. Reese, *The Cease of Majesty* (London, 1961)

A. P. Rossiter, chs i–iii in *Angel with Horns* (London, 1961)

E. W. Talbert, *The Problem of Order* (Chapel Hill, N. C., 1962); *Elizabethan Drama and Shakespeare's Early Plays* (Durham, N. C., 1964)

E. Tillyard, *Shakespeare's History Plays* (London, 1944; Penguin, 1962)

J. Wilders, *The Lost Garden. A View of Shakespeare's English and Roman History Plays* (London, 1978)

F. P. Wilson, *Marlowe and the Early Shakespeare* (London, 1953)

J. D. Wilson, *The Fortunes of Falstaff* (Cambridge, 1943)

The Roman Plays

J. Adelman, *The Common Liar: An Essay on 'Antony and Cleopatra'* (New Haven, 1973)

A. Bonjour, *The Structure of 'Julius Caesar'* (Liverpool, 1958)

A. C. Bradley, 'Shakespeare's *Antony and Cleopatra*' in *Oxford Lectures on Poetry* (London, 1909); '*Coriolanus*' in (43)

P. A. Cantor, *Shakespeare's Rome. Republic and Empire* (Ithaca, N. Y., 1976)

M. Charney, *Shakespeare's Roman Plays: The Function of Imagery in Drama* (Cambridge, Mass., 1961); ed. *Discussions of Shakespeare's Roman Plays* (Boston, 1964)

U. Ellis-Fermor, '*Coriolanus*', in *Shakespeare the Dramatist* (London, 1961)

A. W. MacCallum, *Shakespeare's Roman Plays and their Background* (London, 1910, 1967)

J. E. Phillips, Jr., *The State in Shakespeare's Greek and Roman Plays* (New York, 1940, 1967)

J. L. Simmons, *Shakespeare's Pagan World: The Roman Tragedies* (Hassocks, 1973)

T. J. B. Spencer, 'Shakespeare and the Elizabethan Romans', in Sh.S., X (1957)

B. W. Vickers, *Shakespeare: Coriolanus* (London, 1976, 1982)

The Tragedies

N. Alexander, *Poison, Play, and Duel. A Study in Hamlet* (London, 1971)

P. Alexander, *Hamlet: Father and Son* (Oxford, 1955)

A. C. Bradley, *Shakespearean Tragedy* (London, 1904)

N. Brooke, *Shakespeare: King Lear* (London, 1963); *Shakespeare's Early Tragedies* (London, 1968)

R. Brower, *Hero and Saint: Shakespeare and the Graeco-Roman Tradition* (Oxford, 1971)

J. R. Brown, *Shakespeare: Macbeth* (London, 1963)

L. B. Campbell, *Shakespeare's Tragic Heroes: Slaves of Passion* (Cambridge, 1930; London, 1961)

S. Cavell, 'The Avoidance of Love: a Reading of *King Lear*', in *Must We Mean What We Say?* (New York, 1969)

J. V. Cunningham, *Woe or Wonder: the Emotional Effect of Shakespearian Tragedy* (Denver, Colorado, 1951)

W. C. Curry, *Shakespeare's Philosophical Patterns* (Baton Rouge, La., 1937)

J. F. Danby, *Shakespeare's Doctrine of Nature* (London, 1949)

J. W. Draper, *The 'Hamlet' of Shakespeare's Audience* (Durham, N. C., 1938)

T. S. Eliot, '*Hamlet*' and other essays in (14)

G. R. Elliott, *Scourge and Minister* (Durham, N. C., 1951): on *Hamlet*

W. R. Elton, '*King Lear*' and the Gods (San Marino, Ca., 1966)

W. Farnham, *Shakespeare's Tragic Frontier* (Berkeley, 1950)

N. Frye, *Fools of Time: Studies in Shakespearian Tragedy* (Toronto, 1967)

S. L. Goldberg, *An Essay on 'King Lear'* (Cambridge, 1974)

R. B. Heilman, *This Great Stage* (Baton Rouge, La., 1948): on *King Lear; Magic in the Web* (Lexington, Ky., 1956): on *Othello*

T. R. Henn, *The Harvest of Tragedy* (London, 1956)

E. A. J. Honigmann, 'The Politics in *Hamlet* and the World of the Play', in (29)

D. G. James, *The Dream of Learning* (Oxford, 1951): on *Hamlet* and *Lear*

P. Jorgensen, *Lear's Self-discovery* (Berkeley, Ca., 1967)

H. D. F. Kitto, *Form and Meaning in Drama* (London, 1956): on *Hamlet*

G. W. Knight, *The Wheel of Fire* (rev. London, 1949); *The Imperial Theme* (rev. London, 1951)

F. R. Leavis, 'Diabolic Intellect and the Noble Moor' in *The Common Pursuit* (London, 1952, Peregrine, 1962): on *Othello*; but see J. Holloway, *The Story of the Night* (London, 1961), Appendix 1

C. Leech, *Shakespeare's Tragedies, and Other Studies in 17th Century Drama* (London, 1950)

H. Levin, *The Question of Hamlet* (London, 1959)

C. S. Lewis, '*Hamlet*; the Prince or the Poem?' in (43)

M. D. Long, *The Unnatural Scene: A Study in Shakespearean Tragedy* (London, 1976)

M. Mack, 'The Jacobean Shakespeare', in (26); '*King Lear*' in Our Time (Berkeley, 1965)

M. Mack, Jr., *Killing the King. Three Studies in Shakespeare's Tragic Structure* (New Haven, 1973)

I. Morris, *Shakespeare's God. The Role of Religion in the Tragedies* (London, 1972)

E. Muir, '*King Lear*', in (45)

K. Muir, 'Shakespeare and the Tragic Pattern', P.B.A., XLIV (1958)

R. Nevo, *Tragic Form in Shakespeare* (Princeton, 1972)

H. N. Paul, *The Royal Play of 'Macbeth'* (New York, 1950)

M. N. Proser, *The Heroic Image in Five Shakespearian Tragedies* (Princeton, 1965)

E. Prosser, *Hamlet and Revenge* (London, 1967)

J. Reibetanz, *The 'Lear' World* (London, 1977)

W. Rosen, *Shakespeare and the Craft of Tragedy* (Cambridge, Mass., 1960)

W. Sanders and H. Jacobson, *Shakespeare's Magnanimity. Four Tragic Heroes, Their Friends and Families* (London, 1978)

C. J. Sisson, *Shakespeare's Tragic Justice* (London, 1962)

T. Spencer, *Shakespeare and the Nature of Man* (Cambridge, 1943)

B. Spivack, *Shakespeare and the Allegory of Evil* (New York, 1958): on *Othello*

F. W. Sternfeld, *Music in Shakespearean Tragedy* (London, 1963)

R. Walker, *The Time is Out of Joint* (London, 1948): on *Hamlet*; *The Time is Free* (London, 1949): on *Macbeth*

M. Weitz, '*Hamlet*' and the Philosophy of Literary Criticism (London, 1964)

V. K. Whitaker, *The Mirror up to Nature: The Technique of Shakespeare's Tragedies* (San Marino, Ca., 1965)

J. D. Wilson, *What Happens in 'Hamlet'* (Cambridge, 1951)

The history of Shakespeare criticism

E. L. Avery, C. B. Hogan, A. H. Scouten, G. W. Stone, Jr and W. Van Lennep, *The London Stage 1660–1800: A Calendar of Plays, Entertainments and Afterpieces* (11 vols, Carbondale, Ill., 1960–68)

R. W. Babcock, *The Genesis of Shakespeare Idolatry, 1766–1799* (Chapel Hill, N. C., 1931; New York, 1978)

M. M. Badawi, *Coleridge: Critic of Shakespeare* (Cambridge, 1973)

D. Bartholomeusz, *Macbeth and the Players* (Cambridge, 1969)

G. E. Bentley, *Shakespeare and Jonson, Their Reputations in the 17th Century Compared* (2 vols, Cambridge, 1945); but see D. L. Frost in Sh.Q., XVI (1965)

R. Cohn, *Modern Shakespeare Offshoots* (Princeton, N. J., 1976)

S. T. Coleridge, *Shakespearean Criticism* ed. T. M. Raysor (2 vols, Cambridge,

Mass., 1930; E.L.); *Coleridge on Shakespeare: The Text of the Lectures of 1811–12*, ed. R. A. Foakes (London, 1971)

P. S. Conklin, *A History of Hamlet Criticism, 1661–1947* (New York, 1947, 1957)

R. W. David, *Shakespeare in the Theatre* (Cambridge, 1979)

J. W. Donohue, Jr, *Dramatic Character in the English Romantic Age* (Princeton, N. J., 1970): *Macbeth* and *Richard III*, Garrick to Kemble

G. B. Evans (ed.), *Shakespeare: Aspects of Influence* (Cambridge, Mass., 1975)

B. Everett, 'The Figure in Professor Knights's Carpet', and 'The New *King Lear*', in *Critical Quarterly*, II (1960); 'Reflections on the Sentimentalist's *Othello*', in *Critical Quarterly*, III (1961)

D. A. Fineman (ed.), *Maurice Morgann: Shakespearian Criticism* (Oxford, 1972)

W. Hazlitt, *Characters of Shakespeare's Plays* (London, 1957; E.L.)

S. Johnson, *Johnson on Shakespeare*, ed. W. Raleigh (London, 1908); ed. W. K. Wimsatt (New York, 1960; Penguin, 1969); ed. A. Sherbo, 2 vols, in the Yale *Works of Dr Johnson* (New Haven, 1968)

F. Kermode (ed.), *Four Centuries of Shakespearian Criticism* (New York, 1965)

L. C. Knights, 'How Many Children Had Lady Macbeth?', in *Explorations* (London, 1946; Peregrine, 1964)

O. Le Winter (ed.), *Shakespeare in Europe* (New York, 1963)

L. Marder, *His Exits and His Entrances: Shakespeare's Reputation* (Philadelphia, 1963)

J. Munro *et al.* (eds), *A Shakespeare Allusion Book* (2 vols, Oxford, 1932)

G. C. Odell, *Shakespeare from Betterton to Irving* (2 vols, London, 1920; New York, 1966)

A. Ralli, *A History of Shakespearian Criticism* (2 vols, London, 1932)

J. Ripley, *Julius Caesar on Stage in England and America, 1599–1973* (Cambridge, 1980)

M. Rosenberg, *The Masks of Othello* (Berkeley, 1961): three centuries of acting and criticism; *The Masks of King Lear* (Berkeley, 1972); *The Masks of Macbeth* (Berkeley, 1978)

H. M. Schueller (ed.), *The Persistence of Shakespeare Idolatry* (Detroit, 1964)

D. N. Smith, *Shakespeare in the 18th Century* (Oxford, 1928)

D. N. Smith (ed.), *18th Century Essays on Shakespeare* (Glasgow, 1903; Oxford, 1963); *Shakespeare Criticism 1623 to 1840* (London, 1916, W.C.)

C. Spencer (ed.), *Five Restoration Adaptations of Shakespeare* (Urbana, Ill., 1965)

H. Spencer, *Shakespeare Improved* (Cambridge, Mass., 1927)

A. C. Sprague, *Shakespeare and the Actors: The Stage Business in His Plays (1660–1905)* (Cambridge, Mass., 1944; New York, 1963); *Shakespearian Players and Performances* (Cambridge, Mass., 1953)

B. W. Vickers (ed.), *Shakespeare: The Critical Heritage 1623–1801* (6 vols, London, 1974–81)

Modern criticism: general studies and collections

P. Alexander, *Shakespeare's Life and Art* (London, 1939)

J. Arthos, *The Art of Shakespeare* (London, 1964)

D. Bevington and J. L. Halio (eds), *Shakespeare. Pattern of Excelling Nature* (Cranbury, N. J., 1978)

E. A. Bloom (ed.), *Shakespeare 1564–1964* (Providence, R. I., 1964)

J. L. Calderwood, *Shakespearean Metadrama* (Minneapolis, 1971)

P. Cruttwell, *The Shakespearean Moment* (London, 1954)

W. C. Curry, *Shakespeare's Philosophical Patterns* (Baton Rouge, La., 1937)

AUTHORS AND WORKS

E. Dowden, *Shakespeare's Mind and Art* (London, 1878)

G. I. Duthie, *Shakespeare* (London, 1961)

W. Edens *et al.* (eds), *Teaching Shakespeare* (Princeton, N. J., 1977)

P. Edwards, *Shakespeare and the Confines of Art* (London, 1968)

U. Ellis-Fermor, *The Frontiers of Drama* (rev. London, 1964); *Shakespeare the Dramatist* (London, 1961)

R. M. Frye, *Shakespeare and Christian Doctrine* (Princeton, 1963)

H. Granville-Barker, *Prefaces to Shakespeare* (London, 1927–1948, 1958)

A. C. Hamilton, *The Early Shakespeare* (San Marino, Ca., 1967)

A. Harbage, *Shakespeare's Audience* (New York, 1941, 1961); *As They Liked It: A Study of Shakespeare's Moral Artistry* (New York, 1947); *Conceptions of Shakespeare* (Cambridge, Mass., 1966); *Shakespeare Without Words* (London, 1973)

P. Hartnoll (ed.), *Shakespeare in Music* (London, 1964)

R. G. Hunter, *Shakespeare and the Mystery of God's Judgements* (Athens, Ga., 1976)

P. Jorgensen, *Shakespeare's Military World* (Berkeley, Ca., 1956)

G. W. Keeton, *Shakespeare's Legal and Political Background* (London, 1967)

L. Kirschbaum, *Character and Characterization in Shakespeare* (Detroit, 1962)

L. C. Knights, *'Hamlet' and other Shakespearean Essays* (Cambridge, 1980)

C. Leech and J. M. R. Margeson (eds), *Shakespeare 1971: Proceedings of the World Shakespeare Congress, Vancouver* (Toronto, 1973)

H. Levin, *Shakespeare and the Revolution of the Times* (New York, 1976)

J. H. Long, *Shakespeare's Use of Music . . . in 7 comedies; Shakespeare's Use of Music: The Final Comedies; The Histories and Tragedies* (Gainesville, Fla., 1955, 1961, 1972)

J. G. McManaway (ed.), *Shakespeare 400* (New York, 1964)

W. M. Merchant, *Shakespeare and the Artist* (London, 1959)

K. Muir, *Last Periods of Shakespeare, Racine, Ibsen* (Detroit, 1961)

E. W. Naylor, *Shakespeare and Music* (London, 1896; rev. 1931)

A. Ridler (ed.), *Shakespeare Criticism, 1919–1935* (London, 1936; w.c.); *Shakespeare Criticism, 1935–1960* (London, 1961)

A. P. Rossiter, *Angel with Horns* (London, 1961)

W. Sanders, *The Dramatist and the Received Idea* (Cambridge, 1968)

L. L. Schücking, *Character-Problems in Shakespeare* (London, 1922)

A. Sewell, *Character and Society in Shakespeare* (Oxford, 1951)

J. I. M. Stewart, *Character and Motive in Shakespeare* (London, 1949)

E. E. Stoll, *Art and Artifice in Shakespeare* (London, 1933); *Shakespeare and Other Masters* (Cambridge, Mass., 1940); *Shakespeare Studies* (New York, rev. 1942)

J. Sutherland and J. Hurstfield (eds), *Shakespeare's World* (London, 1964)

D. A. Traversi, *Approach to Shakespeare* (London, 1938; rev. 1957)

M. Van Doren, *Shakespeare* (New York, 1939)

W. B. C. Watkins, *Shakespeare and Spenser* (Princeton, 1950)

C. B. Watson, *Shakespeare and the Renaissance Concept of Honor* (Princeton, 1961)

Note: There are already too many collections of modern Shakespeare criticism to list here individually. Amongst the publishers of these series are: Prentice-Hall (*Twentieth Century Views*), Macmillan (*Casebooks*), Penguin, Oxford University Press New York (*Galaxy Books*), Thomas Crowell (*Casebooks*), Chicago University Press.

SHIRLEY, JAMES (1596–1666): Dramatist; b. London; Merchant Taylors' School and Oxford; took Orders and obtained living in Hertfordshire; after conversion to Catholicism, became schoolmaster; wrote for theatre, *c.* 1625–

1642; followed patron, Earl of Newcastle, to Civil War for a time; died from terror and exposure in Great Fire of London.

Works ed. W. Gifford and A. Dyce (6 vols, London, 1833)

Best Plays ed. E. Gosse (London, 1888; M.S.)

The Wedding and *The Lady of Pleasure* in *Six Caroline Plays* ed. A. S. Knowland (London, 1962; W.C.)

The Cardinal, ed. C. R. Forker (Bloomington, Ind., 1964); ed. R. G. Lawrence (Section XIII above)

The Traitor, ed. J. S. Carter (London, 1965; R.R.D.S.)

The Gentleman of Venice ed. W. F. Engel (Salzburg, 1976)

Poems ed. R. L. Amstrong (New York, 1941)

See G. Bas, *James Shirley, 1596–1666; dramaturge caroléen* (Lille, 1973)

 K. M. Lynch, *The Social Mode of Restoration Comedy* (New York, 1926)

 A. H. Nason, *James Shirley, dramatist* (New York, 1915)

Essays by Bradbrook (6), Harbage (7)

SIDNEY, SIR PHILIP (1554–86): Poet and novelist; b. Penshurst; aristocratic background (nephew of Earl of Leicester); Shrewsbury and Oxford, 1567; entrusted with many diplomatic missions by Elizabeth; banished from court, 1580, for outspoken opposition to Elizabeth's marriage with the Duke of Anjou; did most of his writing 1580–83 (at Wilton House, the home of his sister, then Countess of Pembroke); reconciled with the Queen and knighted, 1583; went to Holland as Governor of Flushing during Spanish war with Netherlands; died of wounds during relief of Zutphen.

Bibliography of criticism, 1941–70 by M. A. Washington (Columbia, Mo., 1972)

Life by Fulke Greville, ed. M. W. Wallace (Cambridge, 1915); by M. Wilson (London, 1931); by John Buxton, *Sir Philip Sidney and the English Renaissance* (London, 1954); by J. M. Osborn, *Young Philip Sidney, 1572–77* (New Haven, 1972)

Works, ed. A. Feuillerat (4 vols, Cambridge, 1912–26; '*Old*' *Arcadia* [original version] in Vol. IV; '*New*' or revised version in Vol. I)

The Countess of Pembroke's Arcadia. (*The Old Arcadia*), ed. J. Robertson (Oxford, 1973)

Miscellaneous Prose, ed. K. Duncan-Jones and J. A. Van Dorsten (Oxford, 1973)

Selected Prose and Poetry, ed. R. Kimbrough (New York, 1969)

Poems, ed. W. A. Ringler, Jr (Oxford, 1962)

Selected Poems, ed. K. Duncan-Jones (Oxford, 1973)

Concordance to the Poems of Sir Philip Sidney, ed. H. S. Donow (Ithaca, N. Y., 1975)

Astrophil and Stella, ed. M. Putzel (New York, 1967)

Psalms, ed. J. C. A. Rathmell (New York, 1963)

Apology for Poetry, ed. G. K. Shepherd (London, 1965); ed. J. A. van Dorsten (London, 1966); ed. F. G. Robinson (Indianapolis, 1970); also in collections of criticism by G. G. Smith, A. Gilbert and E. D. Jones (Section IX, above)

See A. K. Amos, Jr, *Time, Space and Value: The Narrative Structure of the 'New Arcadia'* (Lewisburg, Pa., 1976)

 F. Caspari, *Humanism and the Social Order in Tudor England* (Chicago, 1954)

 D. Connell, *Sir Philip Sidney: The Maker's Mind* (Oxford, 1977)

 S. M. Cooper, *The Sonnets of Astrophel and Stella. A Stylistic Study* (The Hague, 1968)

 R. Delasanta, *The Epic Voice* (The Hague, 1967)

C. Freer, *Music for a King* (Baltimore, 1972): on the psalms

M. S. Goldman, *Sir Philip Sidney and the Arcadia* (Urbana, Ill., 1934)

A. C. Hamilton, *Sir Philip Sidney: A Study of his Life and Works* (Cambridge, 1977)

R. Howell, *Sir Philip Sidney. The Shepherd Knight* (London, 1968)

D. Kalstone, *Sidney's Poetry: Contexts and Interpretations* (Cambridge, Mass., 1965)

R. Kimbrough, *Sir Philip Sidney* (New York, 1971)

R. C. McCoy, *Sir Philip Sidney: Rebellion in Arcadia* (New Brunswick, N. J., 1979)

R. L. Montgomery, *Symmetry and Sense: The Poetry of Sir Philip Sidney* (Austin, Texas, 1961)

K. O. Myrick, *Sir Philip Sidney as a Literary Craftsman* (Cambridge, Mass., 1935)

J. G. Nichols, *The poetry of Sir Philip Sidney* (Liverpool, 1974)

S. A. Pears (ed.), *The correspondence of Sir P. Sidney and H. Languet* (London, 1845)

N. L. Rudenstine, *Sidney's Poetic Development* (Cambridge, Mass., 1967)

Sidney's Arcadia: W. R. Davis, *A Map of Arcadia: Sidney's Romance in Its Tradition* and R. A. Lanham, *The Old 'Arcadia'* (London, 1965)

J. Thompson, *The Founding of English Metre* (London, 1961)

A. D. Weiner, *Sir Philip Sidney and the Poetics of Protestantism* (Minneapolis, Ma., 1978)

S. L. Wolff, *The Greek Romances in Elizabethan Fiction* (New York, 1912; 1961)

R. B. Young, *English Petrarke*, in *Three Studies in the Renaissance* (New Haven, 1958)

R. W. Zandvoort, *Sidney's 'Arcadia': a Comparison Between the Two Versions* (Amsterdam, 1929; 1966)

Essays by Scott (3), Empson (4), John (9), Danby (15), Smith (16), Lewis (17), Lever (21), Robertson (27), Talbert (39), Spencer (46), Winters (50)

SPENSER, EDMUND (1552–99): Poet; b. London; Merchant Taylors' school; took M.A. Cambridge 1576, where met Gabriel Harvey, their correspondence about poetry being issued in *Three Letters* (1580); published *Shepherd's Calender* in 1579, five editions by 1597; employed by Leicester 1579 as secretary to the Lord Deputy of Ireland 1580, remaining in Ireland as public official until 1598; visited London to publish *Faerie Queene* (Books I–III: 1590; Books IV–VI: 1596); granted life pension by the Queen, 1591; minor poems published 1591 (*Complaints*, including *Mother Hubberds Tale*, a satiric attack on Lord Burghley, which may have led to the volume being suppressed), 1595 (*Amoretti* and *Epithalamion*, recording his courtship and marriage; *Colin Clouts Come Home Againe*, a pastoral about himself and Ralegh, including satire against the Court); advocated harsher government policies against the rebels in prose work *A View of the Present State of Ireland* (1598); Sheriff-designate of Cork, 1598, but forced to flee Ireland by Tyrone's rebellion; delivered official despatches to the Privy Council, Christmas 1598; died in Westminster the month following.

A. C. Judson, *The Life of Edmund Spenser* (London, 1946)

Works, Variorum Edition, ed. E. Greenlaw, C. G. Osgood, F. M. Padelford, *et al.* (10 vols, Baltimore, 1932–58; 1966)

Poetical Works, eds J. C. Smith and E. De Selincourt, 3 vols, (Oxford, 1909–10; one vol. edn 1912)

Faerie Queene, ed. W. J. Hales (2 vols, 1910; E.L.); ed. A. C. Hamilton (London, 1977); Book I ed. P. C. Bayley (London, 1966); Book II ed. P. C. Bayley (London, 1965); Books I and II eds R. Kellogg and O. Steele (New York, 1965), *Selected Poetry* ed. H. Maclean (New York, 1968)

Mutabilitie Cantos, ed. S. P. Zitner (London, 1968)

A View of the Present State of Ireland, ed. W. L. Renwick (Oxford, 1970)

See P. J. Alpers, *The Poetry of the Faerie Queene* (Princeton, N. J., 1967); ed., *Edmund Spenser* (Penguin Critical Anthology, 1969)

J. Aptekar, *Icons of Justice: Iconography and Thematic Imagery in the 'Faerie Queene' V* (New York, 1969)

J. W. Bennett, *The Evolution of the 'Faerie Queene'* (Chicago, 1942)

H. Berger, *The Allegorical Temper. Vision and Reality in Book II of Spenser's 'Faerie Queene'* (New Haven, 1957; Hamden, Conn., 1967); (ed.) *Spenser: a Collection of Critical Essays* (Englewood Cliffs, N. J., 1968)

D. Brooks-Davies, *Spenser's Faerie Queene. A Critical Commentary on Books I and II* (Manchester, 1977)

F. I. Carpenter, *A Reference Guide to Edmund Spenser* (Chicago, 1923)

D. Cheney, *Spenser's Image of Nature: Wild Man and Shepherd in the 'Faerie Queene'* (New Haven, 1966)

Critical Essays on Spenser from ELH (Baltimore, Md., 1970)

R. M. Cummings (ed.) *Edmund Spenser: The Critical Heritage* (London, 1971)

T. K. Dunseath, *Spenser's Allegory of Justice in the 'Faerie Queene' V* (Princeton, 1968)

R. M. Durling, *The Figure of the Poet in Renaissance Epic* (Cambridge, Mass., 1965)

R. Ellrodt, *Neoplatonism in the Poetry of Spenser* (Geneva, 1960)

M. Evans, *Spenser's Anatomy of Heroism: A Commentary on 'The Faerie Queene'* (Cambridge, 1970)

A. Fletcher, *The Prophetic Moment: an Essay on Spenser* (Chicago, 1971)

A. D. S. Fowler, *Spenser and the Numbers of Time* (London, 1964); but see review by W. Nelson in R.Q., XVIII (1965)

R. Freeman, *The Faerie Queene: A Companion for Readers* (London, 1970)

A. C. Hamilton, *The Structure of Allegory in 'Faerie Queene'* (Oxford, 1961); (ed.), *Essential Articles on Edmund Spenser* (Hamden, Conn., 1972)

A. K. Hieatt, *Short Time's Endless Monument: the symbolism of the Numbers in Spenser's 'Epithalamion'* (New York, 1960)

R. A. Horton, *The Unity of the 'Faerie Queene'* (Athens, Ga., 1978)

G. Hough, *A Preface to 'The Faerie Queene'* (London, 1962)

H. S. V. Jones, *A Spenser Handbook* (New York, 1930)

C. S. Lewis, *The Allegory of Love* (Oxford, 1936); *Spenser's Images of Life*, ed. A. Fowler (Cambridge, 1967)

I. G. MacCaffrey, *Spenser's Allegory: The Anatomy of Imagination* (Princeton, N. J., 1976)

W. McNeir and F. Provost (eds), *Edmund Spenser: An Annotated Bibliography 1936–1972* (Pittsburgh, Pa., 1976)

W. R. Mueller, and D. C. Allen (eds), *'That Soueraine Light': Essays in Honor of Edmund Spenser, 1552–1952* (Baltimore, 1952)

W. Nelson, *The Poetry of Edmund Spenser* (New York, 1963)

J. Nohrnberg, *The Analogy of the Faerie Queene* (Princeton, N. J., 1977)

M. O'Connell, *Mirror and Veil: The Historical Dimension of Spenser's 'Faerie Queene'* (Chapel Hill, N. C., 1977)

W. L. Renwick, *Edmund Spenser* (London, 1925)

T. P. Roche, *The Kindly Flame: a study of the Third and Fourth Books of Spenser's 'Faerie Queene'* (Princeton, N. J., 1964)

R. Sale, *Reading Spenser: An Introduction to the Faerie Queene* (New York, 1968)

H. Tonkin, *Spenser's Courteous Pastoral: Book Six of the 'Faerie Queene'* (Oxford, 1972)

R. Tuve, *Allegorical Imagery: some mediaeval books and their posterity* ed. T. P. Roche (Princeton, N. J., 1966)

E. Welsford, *Spenser's 'Fowre Hymnes' and 'Epithalamion': a Study of Spenser's Doctrine of Love* (Oxford, 1967)

A. Williams, *Flower on a Lowly Stalk: the 'Faerie Queene' VI* (East Lansing, 1967)

K. Williams, *Spenser's 'Faerie Queene': the World of Glass* (London, 1966)

TOURNEUR, CYRIL (*c.* 1570/80–1626): Dramatist; career obscure; first poem, 1600; other writings, 1605–13; appears to have been befriended by the Vere family, and the Cecils; employed in Netherlands, 1613; served as Sir Edward Cecil's secretary in unsuccessful Cadiz Expedition, 1625; disembarked among sick in Ireland and died there.

Works, ed. Allardyce Nicoll (London, 1930, 1963)
Webster and Tourneur (chief tragedies) ed. J. A. Symonds (M.S.)
The Atheist's Tragedy, ed. I. Ribner (London, 1964; R.P.); ed. B. Morris and R. Gill (London, 1976; N.M.)
The Revenger's Tragedy, ed. R. A. Foakes (London, 1966; R.P.); ed. L. J. Ross (London, 1967; R.R.D.S.); ed. B. Gibbons (London, 1967, N.M.)
For other editions see 'Drama: Anthologies' (Section XIII above) under Gomme, Lawrence, Salgādo
See P. B. Murray, *A Study of Cyril Tourneur* (London, 1964)
    S. Schoenbaum, *Middleton's Tragedies* (New York, 1955)
    S. Schuman, *Cyril Tourneur* (Boston, 1977)
Essays by Bradbrook (6), Eliot (14), Peter (22), Bowers (23), Ornstein (32), Lisca (34), Ellis-Fermor (36), Salingar (37), Nicoll (42), Prosser (49)

WEBSTER, JOHN (*c.* 1578–1632/4): Dramatist; son of wealthy coach-maker in West-Smithfield, near the Fortune and Red Bull theatres; married in haste *c.* March, 1606; worked as cartwright; freeman of Merchant Taylor's Company, 1615; wrote for Henslowe *c.* 1602; collaborated with several contemporary playwrights, particularly Dekker, but gradually abandoned collaboration for independent work; helped to prepare Lord Mayor's pageant, 1624.

Works, ed. F. L. Lucas (4 vols, London, 1927; 2 of the vols, repr. and rev. 1958);
Select Plays (E.L.). See also under Tourneur
Three Plays, ed. D. C. Gunby (Penguin, 1972)
The Duchess of Malfi, ed. J. R. Brown (London, 1964; R.P.); ed. E. Brennan (London, 1964; N.M.); ed. C. Hart (Edinburgh, 1972)

The Devil's Lawcase, ed. F. A. Shirley (London, 1972; R.R.D.S.)

The White Devil, ed. J. R. Brown (London, 1960; rev. 1966; R.P.); ed. E. Brennan (London, 1966; N.M.); ed. C. Hart (Edinburgh, 1970); ed. J. R. Mulryne (London, 1970; R.R.D.S.)

See also 'Drama: Anthologies' (Section XIII, above) under Gomme, Lawrence, Salgādo

Characters in *The Overburian Characters*, ed. W. D. Paylor (Oxford, 1936)

See T. Bogard, *The Tragical Satire of John Webster* (Berkeley and Los Angeles, 1955)

    G. Boklund, *The Sources of 'The White Devil'* (Uppsala, 1957); '*The Duchess of Malfi': Sources, Themes, Characters* (Cambridge, Mass., 1962)

    M. C. Bradbrook, *John Webster, Citizen and Dramatist* (London, 1980)

    A. Dallby, *The Anatomy of Evil, a Study of John Webster's 'The White Devil'* (Lund, 1974)

    R. W. Dent, *John Webster's Borrowing* (Berkeley, Ca., 1960)

    G. K. and S. K. Hunter (eds), *John Webster: a Critical Anthology* (Penguin, 1969)

    C. Leech, *John Webster* (London, 1951)

    D. D. Moore, *Webster and his Critics 1617–1964* (Baton Rouge, La., 1966)

    B. Morris (ed.), *John Webster* (London, 1970)

    P. B. Murray, *A Study of John Webster* (The Hague, 1969)

Essays by Bradbrook (6), Bowers (23), Mulryne (26), Ellis-Fermor (36), Ornstein (32), Ewbank (37), Mehl (44)

NOTES ON CONTRIBUTORS

CHARLES BARBER Reader in English Language and Literature, and Chairman of the School of English, University of Leeds, till retirement in 1980. Author of *The Story of Language* (1964), *Early Modern English* (1976); editor of three plays by Thomas Middleton (Fountainwell Drama Texts).

D. J. ENRIGHT Writer, formerly university teacher. Publications include *Shakespeare and the Students* (1970) and *Collected Poems* (1981); editor of *A Choice of Milton's Verse* (1975), *Rasselas* (1976) and *The Oxford Book of Contemporary Verse 1945–1980*.

ANDREW GURR Professor of English, Reading University; author of *The Shakespearean Stage, 1574–1642* (1970), *Hamlet and the Distracted Globe* (1978), *Writers in Exile* (1981); editor of *Philaster*, *Richard II* and *The Tempest*.

JOHN D. JUMP Died 1976. Was Professor of English Literature in the University of Manchester. Author of *Matthew Arnold* (1955) and *Byron* (1972); general editor of *The Critical Idiom* series.

L. C. KNIGHTS King Edward VII Professor Emeritus of English Literature, the University of Cambridge. Author of *Drama and Society in the Age of Jonson* (1937) and *Some Shakespearean Themes* (1960). Selections from other work have recently appeared as '*Hamlet' and Other Shakespearean Essays* (1979) and *Selected Essays in Criticism* (1981). He is a Foreign Honorary Member of the American Academy of Arts and Sciences.

J. C. MAXWELL Died 1976. Reader in English Literature at Oxford University, Professor of English, Newcastle University, and Fellow of Balliol College, Oxford. Collaborated with John Dover Wilson on the *Cambridge New Shakespeare* and was one of the editors of *Notes and Queries*. Edited Wordsworth's *The Prelude* (1971).

D. F. MCKENZIE Professor of English Language and Literature, Victoria University, Wellington, New Zealand. Author of *The Cambridge University Press, 1696–1712*, 2 vols. (1966) and *Stationers' Company Apprentices, 1605–1800*, 3 vols. (1961–78).

WILFRED MELLERS Professor of Music, University of York, until retirement in 1981. Author of *François Couper and the French Classical Tradition* (1950), *Music in a New Found Land: Themes and Developments in American Music* (1964) and *Bach and the Dance of God* (1981). Has composed about fifty published works.

KENNETH MUIR Formerly King Alfred Professor, University of Liverpool. Author of *Shakespeare's Tragic Sequence* (1972), *Shakespeare's Comic Sequence* (1979), *Shakespeare's Sonnets* (1979).

J. C. A. RATHMELL Fellow of Christ's College, and Lecturer in English at the University of Cambridge. Author of *Literature, Patronage and Politics in the Age of Jonson* (to be published shortly), and editor of *The Psalms of Sir Philip Sidney and the Countess of Pembroke* (1963).

W. W. ROBSON Masson Professor of English Literature, University of Edinburgh. Author of *Critical Essays* (1966) and *Modern English Literature* (4th impr. 1979).

LEO SALINGAR Fellow of Trinity College and Lecturer in English, the University of Cambridge; author of *Shakespeare and the Traditions of Comedy* (1974) and articles on Elizabethan and Jacobean drama.

DEREK TRAVERSI Professor Emeritus, Swarthmore College, Pennsylvania, U.S.A. Successively British Council Representative in Uruguay, Chile, Iran, Spain and Italy (1948–70). Author of *An Approach to Shakespeare* (1938, 1956, 1968), *T. S. Eliot: the Longer Poems* (1976), and *The Literary Imagination: Studies in Dante, Chaucer and Shakespeare* (in press).

PETER URE Died 1969. Was Joseph Cowen Professor of English Literature at Newcastle University. Author of three books about Yeats; editor of a Pelican book of seventeenth century prose, *Richard II* and John Ford's *Perkin Warbeck*.

BRIAN VICKERS Professor of English and Renaissance Literature at the ETH Zurich. Author of *Towards Greek Tragedy* (1973), *The Artistry of Shakespeare's Prose* (1968, 1979), *Francis Bacon and Renaissance Prose* (1968); editor of *Shakespeare: The Critical Heritage, 1601–1800*, 6 vols. (1970–81).

IAN WATT Professor of English and Director of the Humanities Centre, Stanford University, California. Author of *The Rise of the Novel* (1957), *Conrad in the Nineteenth Century* (1980); currently writing the second volume of the Conrad book, and a study entitled *The Myths of Modern Individualism: Faust, Don Quixote, Don Juan, Robinson Crusoe*.

INDEX

Where the names of authors appear in brackets, this implies comparison with influence on, or influence by, the main author concerned.